Warrior Pursuits

THE JOHNS HOPKINS UNIVERSITY
STUDIES IN HISTORICAL AND POLITICAL SCIENCE
128TH SERIES (2010)

1. Eliza Earle Ferguson, *Gender and Justice: Violence, Intimacy, and Community in Fin-de-Siècle Paris*

2. Lisa T. Sarasohn, *The Natural Philosophy of Margaret Cavendish: Reason and Fancy during the Scientific Revolution*

3. Brian Sandberg, *Warrior Pursuits: Noble Culture and Civil Conflict in Early Modern France*

Warrior Pursuits

Noble Culture and Civil Conflict
in Early Modern France

BRIAN SANDBERG

Johns Hopkins University Press
Baltimore

This book has been brought to publication with the generous assistance of Northern Illinois University.

Johns Hopkins Paperback edition, 2017
9 8 7 6 5 4 3 2 1

Johns Hopkins University Press
2715 North Charles Street
Baltimore, Maryland 21218-4363
www.press.jhu.edu

The Library of Congress has cataloged the hardcover edition of this book as follows:
Sandberg, Brian, 1968–
Warrior pursuits : noble culture and civil conflict in early modern France / Brian Sandberg.
    p. cm. — (The Johns Hopkins University studies in historical and political science)
Includes bibliographical references and index.
ISBN-13: 978-0-8018-9729-0 (hardcover : alk. paper)
ISBN-10: 0-8018-9729-7 (hardcover : alk. paper)
1. Nobility—France, Southern—History—17th century. 2. Elite (Social sciences)—France, Southern—History—17th century. 3. Soldiers—France, Southern—History—17th century. 4. Militarism—France, Southern—History—17th century. 5. Violence—France, Southern—History—17th century. 6. Social conflict—France, Southern—History—17th century. 7. Political culture—France, Southern—History—17th century. 8. France, Southern—Social conditions—17th century. 9. France, Southern—Politics and government—17th century. 10. France—History—Bourbons, 1589–1789. I. Title.
  HT653.F7S26 2010
  305.5'22094409032—dc22   2010001216

A catalog record for this book is available from the British Library.

ISBN-13: 978-1-4214-2398-2
ISBN-10: 1-4214-2398-7

Frontispiece: The surrender of the Huguenot city of Montauban to a royal army led by Louis XIII and Cardinal Richelieu, 21 August 1629. *Réddition de la ville de Montauban,* anonymous painting, ca. 1640, MV 612, Château de Versailles, Versailles, France. Photo: Jean Popovitch, Réunion des Musées Nationaux / Art Resource, NY.

Special discounts are available for bulk purchases of this book. For more information, please contact Special Sales at 410-516-6936 or specialsales@press.jhu.edu.

For my parents,
Barbara and Bernie Sandberg

Contents

Acknowledgments   *xi*

Introduction   *xv*

Note on Citations and Translations   *xxviii*

Prologue   3

PART I   THE PROFESSION OF ARMS

1 The Great Quantity of Nobility That Is Found Here:
Southern France and Its Warrior Elite   11

2 The Grandeur and Magnificence of His Household:
Noble Households and Kinship   33

3 He Had No Trouble Helping Himself to Money:
Crédit and Noble Finances   53

PART II   THE BONDS OF NOBILITY

4 With the Assistance of My Particular Friends:
Clientage and Friendship   79

5 The Dignity and Authority of Their Charges:
Officeholding and Political Culture   115

6 Actions the Most Perilous Being the Most Honorable:
Honor and Courage   151

PART III   THE CULTURE OF REVOLT

7 The Call to Arms from All Quarters:
Rituals of Arming 189

8 A Great Multitude of Soldiers:
Personal Armies   223

9 The Zeal of This Nobility:
Violent Performances   253

Conclusion   285

List of Abbreviations   293
Notes   295
Bibliography   343
Index   383

Early seventeenth-century France and its principal roads. Map by Melchior Tavernier, *Carte géographique des postes qui traversent la France* (1632), BNF, Cartes et Plans, Ge D 13432. Photo courtesy Bibliothèque Nationale de France.

Acknowledgments

This book is the result of a long intellectual journey, a transatlantic existence, and a prolonged writing process. The project began as a dissertation at the University of Illinois at Urbana-Champaign, where my mentor, John A. Lynn, provided invaluable guidance, support, and inspiration during my research and writing. Geoffrey Parker and Paul W. Schroeder guided my development as a historian and served on my dissertation committee. Professors Caroline Hibbard, John Rule, Paul Bernard, Donald Queller, Megan McLaughlin, John F. Guilmartin, Mark Grimsley, Allan Millett, and Carl Estabrook at the University of Illinois and the Ohio State University were vital in the shaping of my project and my historical thinking. William Beik, Mack Holt, Barbara B. Diefendorf, Denis Crouzet, Sharon Kettering, Arlette Jouanna, Michael Wolfe, Kathryn Reyerson, Orest Ranum, Mark Greengrass, Douglas Baxter, Laurence Fontaine, David Buisseret, and Raymond A. Mentzer all provided valuable guidance on archival sources and interpretations.

A Graduate College On-Campus Dissertation Research Grant, a Graduate College Dissertation Travel Support Grant, and a Humanities Student Research Fund Grant from the University of Illinois at Urbana-Champaign provided funding for my preliminary research. A Graduate College Dissertation Travel Grant and University Fellowship from the University of Illinois then made possible my extended research in Paris and Languedoc. A National Endowment for the Humanities Fellowship with the Medici Archive Project, a Jean Monnet Fellowship from European University Institute, and a Pforzheimer Fellowship with the Harry Ransom Humanities Research Center allowed me to refine my manuscript and exploit additional French sources.

Colleagues in France offered wonderful advice about conducting historical research in French archives and living in the country. Archivists and librarians at the Bibliothèque Nationale de France, the Archives Nationales, the Archives de la Ministère des Affaires Étrangères, and the Bibliothèque de la Société de l'Histoire du Protestantisme Française provided support and materials in Paris. I received a friendly reception and much assistance from the personnel at the Archives Départementales de l'Hérault, de l'Haute-Garonne, de Lozère, du Tarn, de l'Aude, de l'Ardeche, and du Gard. I also appreciated the aid given me at the Archives Municipales de Montpellier, Toulouse, and Béziers. Jean-Pierre Capelle, Stéphane Durand, Jean-Pierre Dormois, Danielle Bertrand-Fabre, and Philippe Hupé all provided practical assistance for an American living in Paris, Montpellier, and Toulouse.

The long process of writing and revising the manuscript unfolded in the markedly different environments of Champaign, Paris, Fiesole, Florence, and Chicago. Henry Tom of the Johns Hopkins University Press provided excellent editorial guidance and support throughout the development of the book. An anonymous reader provided extremely helpful comments and criticisms that improved the manuscript. My colleagues Jim Schmidt, Sean Farrell, and Aaron Fogleman at Northern Illinois University assisted in reading sections of the text. I greatly appreciate the comments and suggestions from session participants and audiences at numerous historical conferences, including French Historical Studies, Western Society for French History, Renaissance Society of America, and Sixteenth Century Society and Conference. Workshops at the European University Institute and the Early Europe Group at the University of Illinois at Urbana-Champaign provided additional feedback. Peter Dreyer did an excellent job of copyediting the manuscript, tightening the prose and clarifying details.

Several sections of this book incorporate research previously published in different forms as "'The Magazine of All Their Pillaging': Armies as Sites of Second-Hand Exchanges during the French Wars of Religion," in *Alternative Exchanges: Second-Hand Circulations from the Sixteenth Century to the Present,* ed. Laurence Fontaine (New York: Berghahn Books, 2008), 76–96; "'Se couvrant toujours . . . du nom du roi.' Perceptions nobiliaires de la révolte dans le sud-ouest de la France, 1610–1635," *Histoire, Économie et Société* 17 (1998): 423–440; and "'The Furious Persecutions That God's Churches Suffer in This Region': Religious Violence and Coercion in Early Seventeenth-Century France," *Proceedings of the Western Society for French History* 29 (2003): 42–52.

I would like to thank several professors at the University of Texas at Austin who shaped my historical consciousness, interests, and approaches. I am deeply indebted to John Lamphear and Nancy Barker for their guidance on independent research projects and their confidence in my historical work. David Bowman, Brian P. Levack, Michael B. Stoph, George B. Forgie, Bruce J. Hunt, Terry Jordan, G. Howard Miller, Dan Aynesworth, and Clarence G. Lasby displayed their devotion to undergraduate teaching and widened my understanding of history and European culture.

For comradeship, exchange, support, and friendship on both sides of the Atlantic, thanks go to Chris Bains, Yv-Anne Vieuville, Luca and Vanessa Secci, Leila Stasi, Megan Metters, Paolo Cassandro, Pinar Artiran, Leo Rossano, Yuki Kamiya, Alessio Assonitis, Sheila Barker, Greg Horwitch, Paolo and Ana Mezza, Alberto Gioannini, Suze Hewitt, Cécile Tainturier, Nicolas Le Roux, Xavier Le Person, Yann Lignereux, Laetitia Marc, Paul Cheney, Alan Potofsky, Paul Cohen, Linda Clemmons, Scott McKinlay, Mike Hughes, Roy McCullough, Mike Pedrotty, David Coleman, Rick Lundell, John Stapleton, Jamel Ostwald, Tom Arnold, Cliff Rogers, Larry Marvin, Pradeep Barua, Nick Proctor, Susan Book, Zuska Paulikova, and Karolina Terry. I shall always have fond memories of living in the student communities at the Cité Universitaire Internationale in Paris and at Pavillon 7 of the Résidence Universitaire de la Colombière in Montpellier.

A special thanks to Laura Kramer for all her patience and understanding while I labored to complete this manuscript, which benefited greatly from her careful critiques. Blake Sandberg offered creative inspiration, artistic advice, and brotherly support. Finally, I would like to thank my parents, Barbara and Bernie Sandberg, for their constant support and encouragement through the midwestern winters, budget French travels, expensive phone calls, transatlantic book shipments, and skipped holidays that this project entailed. This book is dedicated to them.

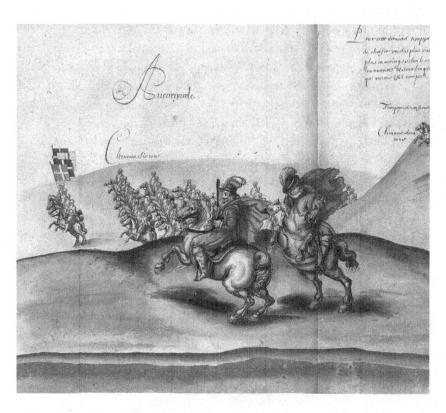

Warrior noble officers leading the rear guard of an army. Drawing in Benedit de Vassallieu, "Discours sur la conduite et l'emploi de l'artillerie," BNF, Mss. fr. 388, detail of f° 112v–113. Photo courtesy Bibliothèque Nationale de France.

Introduction

I n these quarters . . . we speak of nothing but the assemblies of soldiers and of the ordinary passage of those of Languedoc in small groups." So a French nobleman described the outbreak of civil conflict in southern France in 1614, which was marked by mobilization of troops "against the wishes of monsieur de Montmorency," the provincial governor of Languedoc.[1] Bands of soldiers continually raided the southern French countryside in the early seventeenth century, pillaging villages and threatening châteaux. Armies routinely marched across Languedoc and the neighboring province of Guyenne, occupying or besieging the towns and cities that stood in their path. Each year, residents of these provinces complained of the "troubles," "movements," and "disorders" that disrupted economies, ravaged communities, and ruined entire regions. Provincial nobles were the crucial orchestrators of all of this violence, actively financing, organizing, and directing civil warfare.

This book is about noble culture and civil conflict during this turbulent period of French history, analyzing in detail how provincial nobles engaged in revolt and civil warfare between 1598 and 1635. It aims to produce a cultural history of civil conflict by probing the intersections of noble culture, state development, and civil violence in early seventeenth-century French society. The southern French provinces of Guyenne and Languedoc suffered almost continual religious strife and civil conflict in this period, providing an excellent case for investigating the dynamics of early modern civil violence.

An official from Languedoc who lived through these conflicts later reflected on the causes of the violence that had devastated his province in the early seventeenth century. "All these evils," he explained, "came from the ignorance of bishops . . . , the licentiousness and impiety of civil wars, the ambition of the great, and the temerity of the small."[2] This remark nicely captures one of the prominent understandings of the calamities of civil warfare during the French Wars of Religion (1562–1629). Profound religious divisions between Catholics and Calvinists in French society continued to fuel civil warfare after the 1598 Edict of Nantes, leading many to blame impiety or heresy for their woes. Calvinists represented a small religious minority within the kingdom as a whole, but they were concentrated in the religiously mixed provinces of Guyenne and Languedoc, producing constant religious tensions between the opposing confessional communities. The kingdom also suffered from serious political instability in the early seventeenth century, prompting fears of sedition and revolt either by "the great" or "the small"—the powerful nobles or the common people. The assassination of King Henri IV in 1610 and the installation of a regency government for his young son, Louis XIII, only worsened the political tensions, noble rivalries, and "licentiousness" in areas that were far from the royal court. Contemporaries describe the "emotions" and "passions" that produced incessant "revolt" and "rebellion" in southern France throughout the early seventeenth century.

The central argument of this book is that southern French nobles engaged in *warrior pursuits*—social and cultural practices of violence designed to raise personal military forces and to engage in civil warfare in order to advance various political and religious goals. Whatever the proximate causes of each distinct civil conflict, warrior nobles significantly influenced the conduct and outcomes of civil warfare. A chronicler in Languedoc explained the continuation of fighting in southern France in 1616, despite a general peace agreement that was intended to halt the widespread civil warfare throughout the kingdom, by saying: "Our nobles, unable to wage war at large, waged it in detail."[3]

Warfare was a way of life for these military elites. Arlette Jouanna employs the phrase "warrior utopia" to interpret French nobles' idealized perception of warfare as a space of honor, bravery, and valor. The famous Gascon military commander Blaise de Monluc serves as a model for the expression of such warrior ideals and utopian values.[4] Although modern perceptions of warfare often depict armed conflict and combat as dystopian horrors, early modern French warrior nobles articulated a positive, even utopian, vision of violence. French nobles, and the artists and authors they commissioned, constructed multiple spaces for demonstrating their nobility through martial displays. They believed that their engagement in civil warfare—both practices and experiences—constituted an expression of warrior manliness, nobility, and dignity. Warrior nobles' violent discourses, gestures, and activities all aimed at fulfilling this bellicose vision.

The violent practices of warrior nobles raise a number of questions about the complex interrelationships between noble culture, state development, and civil violence: Why did southern France experience such extensive civil conflict and religious violence in this period? Who were the military elites of Languedoc and Guyenne and what were their motivations for participating in civil warfare? How did these warrior nobles organize military forces and direct armed violence in successive civil wars? What role did civil violence play in early modern French political culture? And, finally, how did the operations of civil violence shape warrior noble culture and broader French society?

This study approaches these interconnected historical issues through a cultural exploration of violence in early modern France, interpreting early seventeenth-century noble culture and civil conflict through three interrelated analytic concepts: *the profession of arms, the bonds of nobility,* and *the culture of revolt.* These three concepts effectively describe crucial dimensions of southern French culture and society between 1598 and 1635. New conceptions of the profession of arms and the bonds of nobility developed as patterns of noble association, royal administration, and military organization shifted in this period. These conceptions became linked to a distinct culture of revolt that was defined by the forms of political culture, religious reform, and confessional violence under the legal regime of the 1598 Edict of Nantes. The organization of the book will develop around these analytic concepts, allowing each part of the book to consider the intertwined relationships between noble culture, state development, and civil violence from a different perspective.

THE PROFESSION OF ARMS

The provincial warrior nobles of southern France embraced the *métier des armes,* or profession of arms, eagerly engaging in civil warfare. Early seventeenth-century French notions of this profession differed from later conceptions of military service with formalized systems of ranks and promotions. Nonetheless, warrior nobles already associated the profession of arms with vocation, career, and office during the reigns of Henri IV and Louis XIII. Antoine de Laval considered it to be one of five noble professions suitable for young nobles to pursue, and he exhorted them to employ dispassionate reason in practicing the military arts.[5] Jean de Billon's influential 1615 military treatise advocated serious study of new military principles and addressed itself to France's young warrior nobles, "la jeunesse françoise suivant les armes."[6] François de Bonne duc de Lesdiguières stressed the gravity of practicing warfare, arguing that "the profession of war is in my opinion the most elevated and difficult of all human activities, seeing that it treats and decides the affairs of kings, states, kingdoms, possessions, honor, and the lives of kings and their subjects."[7] Numerous French treatises on nobility, influenced by Baldessare Castiglione's *The Book of the Courtier* (*Il Libro del cortegiano*, 1528), provided advice on ideal noble bearing and proper social behavior that communicated and promoted the profession of arms as the natural sphere of noble activity.[8]

Sharp confessional divisions cut across both early seventeenth-century Guyenne and neighboring Languedoc, prompting Catholic and Calvinist warrior nobles alike to defend confessional agendas and engage in religious violence. The profession of arms thus defined them as a distinct military elite within the broader provincial nobility. Their warrior identities were articulated by their seigneurial possessions, local connections, and regional affiliations. Contemporaries describe jealousies and rivalries between the prominent families of the vast province of Guyenne, expanding on the bellicose reputation of Gascon nobles and reflecting the prevalence of political associations and armed assemblies during civil conflicts.

In the early seventeenth century, provincial warrior nobles oriented their ideals and conceptions of family around the profession of arms. Both Catholic and Calvinist families were influenced by new ideals of piety and discipline, and patriarchs organized their households for civil warfare. Complex and multiple notions of kinship defined their families and their extended relations. The need to justify violence and defend political allegiances reinforced concerns about lineage, which could be addressed by celebrating warrior ancestors and producing martial genealogies. In praising the Montmorency family in 1612, Antoine Arnauld asserted that "the nobility and the generosity of blood are not recognized as much by public histories, titles, or the paintings of ancestors, as by the noble and magnanimous actions of successors."[9] Warrior nobles often sought marriage alliances with other families within the provincial military elite, reinforcing their political affiliations and military connections. Anne de Lévis duc de Ventadour pledged to his father-in-law, Henri I de Montmorency duc de Montmorency, for example, that he was "obliged by birth and alliance" to be attentive to "the affairs of the family."[10]

Considerable wealth was needed to pursue the profession of arms and wage civil warfare, but French provincial nobles could draw on extensive financial resources. To mobilize troops, they relied on a complex combination of capital, esteem, and influence, associated with the contemporary concept of *crédit*,[11] which could be obtained through loans, investments, military entrepreneurship, and political action. Gaining military and political experience proved vital to establishing and maintaining a noble's reputation for creditworthiness. Henri I de

Montmorency recommended an officer to Marie de Médicis, for example, by citing "the *crédit* that his name and his office . . . have earned him in this government."[12] Warrior nobles in Guyenne and Languedoc struggled to protect their patrimonies and to defend their privileges during the costly and destructive civil wars of the early seventeenth century.

THE BONDS OF NOBILITY

Bonds of nobility formed as warrior nobles' personal relationships became centered around civil violence. Civil warfare affected their cultural and social practices through multiple interpersonal connections. Nobles bonded through shared experiences in civil conflict, but civil war also severed bonds and created divisions within noble culture. Theories of the cultural practices of everyday life suggest ways of interpreting warrior noble culture as loosely organized, with permeable boundaries and space for individualized "manners of doing" and "modes of operation."[13] French military elites engaged in violence using overlapping bonds of nobility—clientage, office, and honor—to construct their armed forces and to conduct religious politics.

Clientage bonds and conceptions of friendship configured warrior nobles' modes of association as they participated in warfare. The king and his ministers promoted an idyllic vision of friendship that would ideally bind all French subjects "to live from now on in good union, friendship, and concord under the benefits of his edicts and decrees."[14] Such pronouncements accompanied each early seventeenth-century peace agreement, intended especially for an audience of military elites who valued friendship highly. French nobles displayed affection and sociability through broad friendship networks, often described by scholars as *réseaux d'amitié*.[15] Affective language, extravagant promises, and polite gestures were seen as testimonials to the depth of noble friendship. Each outbreak of civil conflict forced warrior nobles to choose between various personal and political connections, cutting some friendship ties and reinforcing others. Warrior noble *amitié*, friendship, gradually became transformed into a martial relationship in which *amis,* friends, functioned as military clients and political supporters in clienteles. Prestige, military, administrative, seigneurial, and urban relations were all vital in forming clienteles and engaging in civil warfare. A devoted comrade or close advisor could be described as an "intimate friend," signaling a more restrictive relationship within a clientele.[16] Patrons had to manage complex interpersonal relationships among noble clients to maintain their clienteles during civil wars.

Officeholding linked warrior nobles, who often acquired multiple offices through a combination of royal appointments, purchases, and favors. Patrons distributed abundant favors through their powers of appointment, obtaining offices and commands for their followers, as when François de Bonne duc de Lesdiguières succeeded in gaining appointments as fortress governors for two of his clients in 1604.[17] Clients who received offices as favors from their patrons were called *créatures*, having been "created" by their patrons.[18] Official bonds ideally reinforced royal authority by creating ties of mutual dependency and loyalty between noble officeholders, allowing them to implement the king's will throughout the kingdom. Provincial military elites were certainly eager to perform royal service, but civil conflicts influenced their exercise of office, as they confronted challenges to their authority, crafted political affiliations, pursued confessional agendas, and mobilized troops in often chaotic situations. A contemporary pamphlet complained of "the confusion that the number of officers seems to bring" to the implementation of royal orders, explaining that "the malice of men, the diversity of religions, and the licentiousness of wars have created many diverse offices."[19]

The warrior nobles of Languedoc and Guyenne grappled with the difficulties of navigating the overlapping jurisdictions and fragmented authorities of officeholders in those vast provinces. Public and private service blurred significantly as official bonds and military service became personal. Henri II de Montmorency duc de Montmorency proclaimed that he had "reserved the power to name those who will command the said troops in each diocese," specifying that all of the troops in his government of Languedoc were to obey the newly appointed officers as they would the provincial governor himself.[20] Warrior nobles' officeholding practices merged with their military activities, shaping the entire political culture of southern France.

The bonds of honor that were forged in civil warfare influenced warrior nobles' social behavior and political activity. French noble culture enunciated powerful ideals of honor and courage through court festivities, civic ceremonies, martial displays, and celebratory publications. These elaborate and multifaceted performances valorized the sanctity, quality, reputation, and precedence of warriors. Their honor culture also developed its own specific principles, closely associating conceptions of honor with political and religious affiliations in civil conflict. After the death of the *connétable* Henri I de Montmorency in 1614, his son Henri II de Montmorency rewarded the members of the household and renewed the bonds of honor between his family and his father's noble clients: "the nobles who had honored the *connétable* came from all corners of Languedoc to

offer him their services with the same affection that they had rendered to his father." The young duc de Montmorency "esteemed the generosity of these offers
much more than everything that he was capable of giving," reinforcing the
bonds of honor with great "courtesy."[21] In Languedoc and Guyenne, warrior
honor involved direct military participation in civil warfare through repeated
demonstrations of courage and armed prowess before an audience of noble peers.
These noblemen gained honor by performing *faits d'armes*, feats of arms, or by
exercising military command. These actions served as *preuves d'honneur*, proofs
of honor, that could enhance a noble's status and elicit admiration from their
peers. Warrior nobles involved in civil conflicts had to act constantly to preserve
their personal and family honor from challenges and attacks.

THE CULTURE OF REVOLT

A *culture of revolt* defined warrior nobles' participation in organized civil warfare
in early seventeenth-century France through a set of shared assumptions and
practices concerning civil conflict. I am using "revolt" here in a particular way
to describe the justifications for violence and the waging of civil warfare during
a transitional period in the history of the concepts of revolt and rebellion. The
earlier Huguenot and Catholic League notions of tyrannicide had been largely
dispelled, but later seventeenth-century articulations of a "right to resist" had
not yet been fully formulated. Observers of violence in France often used corporeal metaphors to describe the condition of the kingdom, as in a pamphlet that
deplored that, "the illness of this state . . . is such and the corruption of its
humors so malignant, that it no longer senses its pain."[22] Such descriptions of
the ill body of the state called for the application of medicine by the king or his
nobles. The king wielded a brand of revolt, designating disorderly opponents
as criminals guilty of lèse-majesté, but nobles could appropriate the king's
authority to label their own rivals as "quarrelsome," "seditious," "criminals,"
and "rebels."

Early seventeenth-century warrior nobles championed violence as the natural
sphere of noble activity, engaging personally in civil warfare. Civil conflicts, then,
represented spaces where "beautiful warrior acts" could be performed and "heroic virtues" expressed before an audience of noble peers.[23] A pamphlet celebrating the bellicose deeds of Henri de Lorraine duc de Mayenne offers a description
of precisely such a space: "the warrior luster awakes many people, who leave their
books and pens to grasp a sword."[24] Arlette Jouanna's important study *Le Devoir
de révolte* analyzes the language of *partis, factions, cabales,* and *unions* in political

pamphlets and manifestos, finding that nobles had a duty to revolt in the name of preserving the kingdom's ancient constitution and its political system of mixed monarchy.[25] Manuscript correspondence and reports from Languedoc and Guyenne reveal other regional political, religious, and military concerns that propelled civil warfare in southern France, however, challenging the notion that nobles felt a constitutional duty to revolt. Warrior nobles asserted personal interests, promoted confessional agendas, and pursued political programs through their engagement in civil warfare.

Rituals of arming reveal complex motivations for civil violence in early seventeenth-century France. The act of *prise d'armes*, or taking up arms, came to define warrior nobles and their participation in military activities. The southern French nobles Pons de Lauzières marquis de Thémines and the seigneur de Castelnau de Roquefeuil took up arms during a dispute in 1604, when they were "found in arms, accompanied by a good number of their friends, creating such disorder that the entire region is rumbling."[26] A highly developed vocabulary associated taking up arms with adopting political and religious positions by depicting nobles as raising arms, *lever des armes*, or bearing arms, *porter les armes*. This rich language reflects the ways in which warrior nobles instigated and justified violence, allowing a detailed exploration of what Jouanna calls the "rituals of revolt."[27] In early seventeenth-century France, revolt was both a label used by the monarchy against its opponents and a way of understanding civil conflict for nobles who engaged in civil violence.[28] A distinct culture of revolt influenced warrior nobles' practices of taking up arms and mobilizing their clienteles.

The warrior nobles of Languedoc and Guyenne were the key organizers of civil warfare in southern France. The royal state lacked a monopoly on violence, relying instead on provincial nobles to respond to disorder during the early decades of the seventeenth century. Powerful regional nobles formed their own field armies by recruiting locally. Armand de Gontaut baron de Biron, an important French army commander and military thinker during the French Wars of Religion, recommended "raising companies at the place where one thinks that there will be a conflict . . . [so that] those of the other party will not prevail in attracting soldiers to their side through payments or promises."[29] Although nobles organized warfare locally using seigneurial and clientage connections, their military forces were far from "feudal" in nature. The personal armies led by southern French warrior nobles can be described as "aggregate-contract armies," consisting of ad hoc and temporary assemblies of various hastily raised units, which also exhibited some features of the emerging "state-commission" army style.[30] South-

ern French warrior nobles personally maintained these armies through improvised logistical services and adapted institutions of war finance.

Warrior nobles engaged zealously in civil warfare through violent gestures
and performances. Despite occasional royal interventions, provincial elites normally directed violence in southern France through performances of command.
When a royal army had been "greatly weakened in all of the small sieges," Louis
XIII and his advisors summoned forces from Haut Languedoc and commissioned "diverse persons to raise regiments" to strengthen the army and besiege
Montpellier in 1622.[31] Provincial warrior nobles in Languedoc and Guyenne experienced command as a chaotic continuum of arming, maneuvering, and combat during civil conflicts. Noblemen such as Anne de Lévis duc de Ventadour and
Joachim de Beaumont baron de Brison directed their personal military forces to
wage a dynamic form of warfare involving simultaneous raids, sieges, and battles.
Warrior nobles and their entourages formed violent communities during military campaigns. Religious activism and confessional politics shaped the military
elites' understandings of faith, heresy, and the meaning of violence, with zealous
Catholic and Calvinist nobles engaging in performances of religious violence
based on their interpretations of God's will.

INTERPRETING WARRIOR PURSUITS

The violent practices of warrior nobles can be discerned in diverse manuscripts
and rare printed sources conserved in the Bibliothèque Nationale de France, the
Archives Nationales, various Archives Départementales, and other archival collections in France. Reports and letters from military officers in the provinces of
Languedoc and Guyenne to royal ministers and court nobles provide the most
detailed accounts of religious politics and civil conflict in southern France. Instructions, *ordonnances*, correspondence, and minutes written by the king
and his ministers allow us to gauge royal responses to those conflicts. Military
and financial records detail warrior nobles' roles in directing civil warfare and
war finance. Personal correspondence and family papers provide rare but intimate glimpses into noble households and cultural practices. Printed polemical
pamphlets demonstrate the religious and political causes that motivated nobles'
involvement in civil conflicts and advertised their prominence in French society. Published treatises on nobility, military arts, history, and piety provide information on contemporary understandings of military techniques and social
activities that guided noble participation in civil conflicts. This extensive body
of documentation provides important new evidence on warrior nobles' armed

activities and violent practices, but understanding their warrior pursuits requires reexamining some common assumptions about culture, state, and violence.

Several overlapping historical and theoretical debates animate this investigation of noble culture and civil violence in early seventeenth-century France. One dispute concerns whether or not French noble culture acted as a modernizing force, progressively spreading manners and civility throughout European societies.[32] Another debate questions precisely how nobles participated in early modern politics and what roles they played in state development processes.[33] Finally, a discussion has arisen about the reasons for the pervasiveness of dueling and personal violence among early modern nobles.[34] Each part of this book combines approaches from cultural history, state development theory, and military history in an attempt to analyze early modern warrior noble culture and civil conflict from a different perspective. The interrelated concepts of the profession of arms, the bonds of nobility, and the culture of revolt effectively contribute to major historiographical and theoretical debates in three areas: noble culture, royal government, and civil violence.

First, the experiences of the warrior nobles of Languedoc and Guyenne that emerge from this analysis force a reconsideration of the dynamics of noble culture. The pervasiveness and intensity of their warrior pursuits challenge Norbert Elias's model of a progressive domestication and pacification of nobles through a "civilizing process" that communicated etiquette and manners throughout European societies, providing a basis for modern cultural norms and behavior.[35] Far from becoming domesticated, early seventeenth-century warrior nobles avidly participated in a violent noble culture defined by civil and religious conflict. The persistent physical aggression and personal violence that characterized French noble culture intersected with broader forms of organized violence and armed conflict in the early seventeenth century, representing much more than feuding among squabbling noble families.[36] The violent gestures and martial behavior of early seventeenth-century warrior nobles seriously question Elias's modernizing narrative of progressive civility and disarmament.[37] Nobles who were active in Languedoc and Guyenne in the early seventeenth century are especially interesting because these two provinces had the most significant mixed-confessional populations and the most sustained civil conflicts in the period. A revival of interest in the historical roles that elites have played in societies allows this reconsideration of French warrior nobles to contribute to the growing field of European nobility studies.[38] Recent social and cultural history research demonstrates the resiliency and dynamism of the French nobility, despite earlier historians' portrayals of early modern nobles as backward "feudal" elites or as opponents of bureaucratic states.

Second, understanding warrior pursuits alters existing conceptions of how the relationships between nobles and the royal state operated, forcing a revision of models of state development in the early modern period. Ministerial governments led by Maximilien de Béthune duc de Sully and Armand-Jean du Plessis cardinal de Richelieu have long been seen as consciously formulating centralizing policies of state-building, and the early seventeenth century has been seen as the "crucial phase" of the construction of French "absolutism."[39] Analyzing French nobles' relationships with the monarchy through theories of practice suggests various ways in which warrior nobles simultaneously furthered their own political and religious aims through royal service.[40] Ruses, improvisations, manipulations, and creative acts of disobedience could all be employed within the culture of revolt, and these "tactics of diversion" can be interpreted as inventions of everyday life.[41] The dynamic roles that provincial military elites played in civil conflicts question the centrality of the royal state, challenge the notion of conscious state-building, and demonstrate the limited nature of early modern central administration. Warrior nobles emerge in this analysis as significant historical actors within early modern French political culture and military institutions, rather than as mere obstacles to the development of a centralizing absolutist state. Henri IV and Louis XIII both relied heavily on provincial nobles to raise personal armies and finance warfare, since no standing royal army yet existed. This book's findings thus confirm many of the criticisms of absolutism as a distinct stage of state development, at least for the early decades of the seventeenth century.[42] Assertions of royal power in southern France during this period depended on close collaboration with regional military elites. Provincial nobles claiming to act in the name of the king were intimately involved in the changing practices of warfare and military administration that would gradually reshape the royal state and French society as a state-commission army coalesced in the mid-seventeenth century.

Third, cultural studies of violence are especially useful in examining the military elite's role in early modern civil conflict. My interpretations of warrior nobles' violent activities in Languedoc and Guyenne are informed by methodologies of performative violence, which examine "the processes through which violence is actualized—in the sense that it is both produced and consumed."[43] Performative models of violence interpret warfare as connected with more intimate forms of bodily injury, killing, and trauma through a series of performance

acts.[44] These models allow a more comprehensive approach to conflict that examines military, social, economic, judicial, cultural, and gender dimensions of
violence simultaneously. Investigating how southern French warrior nobles
enacted performances of violence suggests new meanings of civil warfare and
its role in early modern French society. The intensity and confusion of the civil
conflicts studied here question our assumptions about the nature of civil warfare. The bonds of nobility expose the complex association processes that military elites used to maneuver within French political culture during civil conflicts. The viciousness and routinization of near-continuous civil and religious
warfare in southern France in this period inserted violence into the ordinary.[45]
Pervasive raiding and siege warfare marked the everyday lives of the residents of
Languedoc and Guyenne through routines of killing and destruction. The warrior nobles who organized and directed civil warfare experienced a brutality and
intimacy of violence that blurred the boundaries between agents and victims of
violence. The culture of revolt in early modern southern France produced
forms of targeted violence and localized coercion that resemble the "logic of violence" that Stathis N. Kalyvas has discerned for more modern civil conflicts.[46]

These new interpretations of nobility, state, and violence effectively bridge
the divide between the sixteenth-century French Wars of Religion and the seventeenth-century Rise of Absolutism historiographies, suggesting a reconceptual-
ization of noble culture and violence in the broader narrative of early modern
French history. Examining the culture of revolt exposes transitions in nobles'
conceptions of violence and their practices of civil warfare in the early decades
of the seventeenth century. Important political, military, and religious transformations were affecting French nobles precisely in this period. The Edict of Nantes
of 1598 had instituted a new set of legal and institutional frameworks concerning
confessional divisions within the kingdom.[47] Counter-Reformation missionaries
and new Catholic devotional practices were spreading throughout southern
France by the 1590s.[48] Sweeping changes in early modern military technologies,
techniques, and organizations were affecting contemporary European states and
societies in the late sixteenth and early seventeenth centuries. Warrior nobles
performed their rituals of arming and employed personal violence against a
backdrop of a gradual evolution in army styles from aggregate-contract armies
to state-commission armies.[49] Finally, even though royal administrators were
asserting new governmental principles that were shaping French political culture and officeholding, nobles' practices of warfare challenge the dominant absolutist narrative of a centralizing and expanding French state in this period.[50]
The ways in which southern French nobles responded to these historical devel-

opments reveal changing dimensions of noble culture and shifting practices of warfare. The culture of revolt prevailed in Languedoc and Guyenne as long as these particular forms of warrior noble culture, army style, and religious conflict continued to dominate southern French society.

✝

The three parts of this book construct a comprehensive history of violence in early seventeenth-century France in order to expose the martial activities of southern French warrior nobles. Examining the intersections of the profession of arms, the bonds of nobility, and the culture of revolt reveals a complex and nuanced series of warrior pursuits—complementing and extending recent scholarship on noble culture, state development, and civil violence by providing new interpretations of noble violence and novel reflections on early modern French noble culture. This interpretive approach demonstrates the potential advantages of conducting historical research that combines military history and cultural history.

Note on Citations and Translations

Early seventeenth-century texts present numerous difficulties and inconsistencies, due to poor orthography and a lack of systematization of spelling, even for proper names. I have used the accepted modern French forms for all personal names, even in quotations, for ease of cross-referencing: Henri IV, Marie de Médicis, and Jean Calvin. Contemporaries used a variety of spellings, and many individuals, even royal family members, spelled their names differently at different times, for example, Henri II de Montmorency's name was often spelled Montmorancy, Monmorancy, or Mommorency. I therefore refer to the seigneur de Châtillon, not seigneur de Chastillon, and to the duc d'Épernon, not d'Espernon. Noble titles are left untranslated, such as duc de Montmorency, marquis de Portes, comte de Rieux, baron d'Aubais, and seigneur de Chevrilles. Likewise, the corresponding estates are left untranslated: duché, comté, baronnie, and seigneurie. I initially refer to nobles using their first names and principal titles without commas, as in Henri de Lorraine duc de Mayenne.

All translations are mine unless otherwise noted, and they aim at readability. In untranslated French text, the spelling has been left as in the original as much as possible, except that the Latin practices of using *v* for *u* and *j* for *i* have been adjusted. Early seventeenth-century documents often use extensive abbreviations, such as "V. M^{té}" for *vôtre majesté*, but these have been expanded in translated texts. Citations of rare printed pamphlets include their archival locations, unless available in digitized collections.

The generic names of seventeenth-century government institutions are italicized on first use, but not thereafter. To avoid confusion with the English Parliament, which was a quite different kind of consultative body, *parlement* is not translated. The états particulier de Languedoc are listed as the estates of Languedoc.

Translating offices frequently leads to more confusion than clarification. For example, *maréchal* can be translated as "marshal," but then several types of marshal must be distinguished: *maréchal de France, maréchal de camp*, and *maréchal-de-logis*. I have only done so when sensible and helpful translations can be made. Many offices are already accepted in English without translations, so *intendants, sénéchals, baillis* are left untranslated, but I have translated *gouverneur* as "governor." The reader may assume that all references to governors are to provincial governors unless specifically indicated as a "regional governor," or *gouverneur du pays*. I use "town or fortress governor" to refer to a *gouverneur particulier*, and "lieutenant general" for a *lieutenant-général*. Standard regimental ranks are translated, as in "captain" for *capitaine*. As with government institutions, names of offices are italicized only when they are defined in the text.

Descriptions of military formations and bodies are simplified, for example, *hommes de guerre* is translated as "soldiers." When the numbers of troops are counted by *cheval* and *pied*, I have sometimes translated as "horse" and "foot," sometimes as "cavalry" and "infantry," for the sake of clarity. Military formations and types of units are italicized when defined, but not elsewhere.

Place-names are also modernized, using accepted French designations when possible. So the Cévennes mountains are indicated—not the older spellings of Cevenes, Sevenes, or Sevennes. The old Gardon river is the Gard, and the Tar is the Tarn. Town names are regularized: Villeneuve-de-Berg not Villeneuve or Villeneuve de Berc, and Vallons-pont-d'Arc, not Vallons. Town designations specifying their region are used, so St-Felix-Lauraguais, not simply St-Felix. Modern spellings for towns are also used, so Alès instead of Alais, and Nîmes for Nismes. I have avoided anglicizing French names, so I have used Haut Languedoc, not Upper Languedoc. Using modern French spellings for all geographical features should help readers find obscure towns, châteaux, and regions.

The terms for frequently cited types of documents, such as *controlle des troupes, état, état des troupes, lettres patentes, mandement, mémoire, ordonnance*, and *quittance* are not translated or italicized. The only exception to this are well-known documents that have an accepted English translation, such as the Edict of Nantes, peace of Montpellier, and peace of Alès.

French currency was based on the *livre tournois* (French pound), a money of account that amounted to twenty *sous*, and each sou was worth twelve *deniers* (penny). The gold *écu* was more valuable, worth at least several *livres tournois*, but it fluctuated. In the text, where French currency terms are not italicized, *livre tournois* is frequently abbreviated to *livre*.

A 1632 ordonnance fixing exchange rates offers a gauge for the monetary value of the *livre tournois* in comparison with other major European currencies:

1 Spanish *pistolle*	=	8 *livres tournois*, 10 *sous*
1 Italian *pistolle*	=	8 *livres tournois*, 4 *sous*
1 gold *écu*	=	4 *livres tournois*, 10 *sous*
1 double *ducat*	=	9 *livres tournois*, 10 *sous*
1 *saquin*	=	4 *livres tournois*, 12 *sous*
1 quarter *écu*	=	17 *sous*
1 *teston*	=	16.5 *sous*

But, since the ordonnance was issued during a civil war by Gaston d'Orléans, the "rebel" brother of Louis XIII, the values may not reflect "real" currency exchange rates. Gaston had received monetary contributions from various European states, and he may have been trying to inflate the value of his money to pay for his army in Languedoc. This possibility is suggested by the indication that the ordonnance was to be published and distributed, and that inhabitants of Languedoc were to accept the currencies at these rates with "no difficulty" (ordonnance de Gaston d'Orléans, Archives Départementales de l'Hérault, A 53, f° 119).

Warrior Pursuits

An early seventeenth-century warrior noble grasping his sword. Engraving by Jacques
Callot, *La Noblesse. Le Cavalier en tenue de campagne,* BNF, Estampes, Réserve Ed 25,
boîte 13. Photo courtesy Bibliothèque Nationale de France.

Prologue

enri II de Montmorency fumed when he heard of the surrender of the garrison at the château de Privas in February 1621. The duc de Montmorency had personally established this garrison overlooking the southern French town less than a year earlier, intending to calm the religious violence between Calvinists and Catholics in the surrounding region of Vivarais. As governor of the sprawling province of Languedoc, which included Vivarais, Montmorency had personally led troops to Privas and had placed one of his closest subordinates in charge of this new garrison.[1] The soldiers stationed in the château only temporarily defused conflict, since spiritual renewal movements and confessional politics continued to fuel tensions throughout southern France. The predominantly Calvinist residents of Privas resented the installation of the château garrison, which was probably composed primarily of Catholic soldiers. Local Huguenot, or French Calvinist, troops soon seized control of the town and surrounded the isolated château.

The surrender of the garrison force represented not only the resumption of the civil warfare and religious violence that had already plagued southern France for decades, but also a blow to the twenty-five-year-old duc de Montmorency's personal prestige and authority. For three successive generations, the influential Montmorency family had held the government of Languedoc, but here their dominance was being challenged. The young duc was "so stung that he dreamed only of ways of promptly making amends for this affront."[2] Montmorency, who may have been motivated by his Catholicism as much as his anger, responded quickly by using his personal wealth and connections to begin raising troops and organizing a small army. In early March, the duc sought the financial assistance of the estates of Languedoc and, while some in the assembly thought that it was not advisable to raise troops until they received direct orders from the king, Montmorency was too impatient to wait for a response.[3]

As the duc de Montmorency was preparing his troops to march in Languedoc, Jean-Louis de Nogaret de La Valette duc d'Épernon was deciding how to respond to the growing civil war in the neighboring province of Guyenne. The duc d'Épernon was a powerful Catholic noble "of great condition and of great credit," who was eager to prove his loyalty and worth to the young king Louis XIII. The sixty-seven-year-old duc d'Épernon had served several French kings and had been a favorite companion of Henri III, but during the previous two years Épernon had sided with Marie de Médicis, the king's mother, in two disastrous civil conflicts that would become known as the Wars of Mother and Son.[4] The duc had been pardoned as part of a negotiated settlement, but his position and influence had been greatly diminished by his participation in these failed campaigns. Épernon had begun to reconstruct his relationship with the king by hosting Louis XIII and the royal court at his château de Cadaillac late in 1620. Now, in early 1621, he hoped to restore his position through royal service in civil warfare when he received orders to raise troops to counter Huguenot mobilizations in the Béarn region.[5] The duc used his own extensive credit to raise troops, since the king sent "neither money nor men" to assist him.[6] Épernon's service in Béarn, and later in blockading the Huguenot city of La Rochelle, did not ultimately provide him with glory, but would successfully demonstrate to the king his loyalty and usefulness.[7]

Gaspard III de Coligny seigneur de Châtillon faced perplexing choices in early 1621. The seigneur de Châtillon was governor of Montpellier and Aigues-mortes for the king, but also acted as commander of all Huguenot troops of Bas Languedoc established by a Calvinist assembly in La Rochelle, which was then organizing for the "legitimate and necessary defense of the Reformed churches in France."[8] Châtillon, like many other Huguenot nobles in southern France, sought to protect and support his coreligionists in his region through military force, but also contemplated negotiations to maintain Protestant interests and preserve Calvinism. As civil conflict widened in early 1621, Châtillon raised several thousand soldiers around his government of Montpellier and the staunchly Calvinist city of Nîmes.[9] These Huguenot troops skirmished against the Catholic forces in Bas Languedoc, while Châtillon pursued negotiations with his adversaries in an attempt to secure key Calvinist communities in the region.[10] Huguenots in Languedoc increasingly worried about Châtillon's talks with

Catholics and his growing rivalry with Henri II de Rohan duc de Rohan, the popular Huguenot commander in nearby Haut Languedoc and Haut Guyenne. By the end of the year, Châtillon would negotiate a personal settlement with Louis XIII and switch allegiances, abandoning his former Calvinist allies.[11]

Each of these nobles confronted civil warfare differently in 1621, providing fascinating insight into noble culture and violence in early seventeenth-century France. Thousands of French nobles served as officers, cavalrymen, and volunteers in Catholic and Calvinist military forces during the 1621–1622 civil war, participating in civil violence to advance various interests and agendas. Much of the fighting occurred in the regions of southern France with the highest concentration of Huguenots and the most heavily mixed-confessional populations, the provinces of Guyenne and Languedoc. Huguenots controlled a number of predominately Calvinist cities and towns as *places de sûreté*, or security towns, that had been established by successive religious peaces of the late sixteenth century, including the 1598 Edict of Nantes.[12] During civil conflicts, Catholics and Calvinists both attempted to seize communities that were held by the opposing confession or that had mixed-confessional populations, making Nérac, Négrepelisse, Montauban, Sommières, and Montpellier all targets for siege warfare. Nobles across southern France responded to outbreaks of civil conflict by rapidly raising military forces through their clients and local contacts. The provincial nobles of Languedoc and Guyenne participated eagerly in a series of civil conflicts in southern France during the early seventeenth century, but their motives, allegiances, and interests seem just as inscrutable as those of the duc de Montmorency, the duc d'Épernon, or the seigneur de Châtillon. These elites consistently portrayed their martial acts in civil warfare as honorable and heroic, despite the brutal violence they often inflicted on their enemies and on ordinary civilians.

Enigmatic figures such as the duc de Montmorency are fascinating in part because they conjure up images of the romanticized southern French noblemen in Alexandre Dumas's *The Three Musketeers* and Edmond Rostand's *Cyrano de Bergerac*. Romantic novelists, playwrights, and artists of the nineteenth century drew heavily on early modern noble culture, especially celebrating French nobles' expressions of masculinity and honor in combat and dueling.[13] Film adaptations of *The Three Musketeers*, *Cyrano de Bergerac*, *La Reine Margot*, and other swashbuckling epics continue to diffuse images of sixteenth- and seventeenth-century nobles, who are often depicted as aggressive, factional, extravagant, and frivolous. The dramatic flamboyance of these literary and cinematic depictions often mischaracterizes early modern culture and obscures the crucial significance of nobles in early modern French society. The historical nobles of southern France examined here represented important historical actors, exerting enormous influence on the provincial society, the political culture, and the royal state as they engaged in violence.

A NOBILITY IN ARMS

The subjects of this study are the warrior nobles of the provinces of Languedoc and Guyenne, but who exactly constituted this nobility in arms? French nobles had long distinguished themselves from other members of society by carrying swords as symbols of their nobility and as personal weapons. During the religious wars, French nobles usually carried a *rapier*, a primarily civilian sword popular for dueling, as their principal weapon of distinction.[14] The early seventeenth-century jurist Charles Loyseau points out that "all nobles except those of the long robe have the right to bear the sword as the insignia and mark of nobility."[15] Loyseau's discussion of the *épée*, or sword, explains why many historians have focused precisely on the sword in defining the gradations within the French nobility, portraying the *noblesse d'épée* as a distinct social group in competition with the judicial nobility, or *noblesse de robe*.[16] Varying titles, ranks, dignities, and offices produced much more nuanced contours of the French nobility, dissolving any clear distinctions between the *noblesse d'épée* and *noblesse de robe*, however. During the chaos of the religious conflicts of the late sixteenth and early seventeenth centuries, noblemen who had never fought became embroiled in civil warfare. Low-ranking nobles gained promotion, and some non-noble families were ennobled, through their military service. All elite families sought to live nobly, adopting martial symbols of distinction besides the rapier, including spurs, collars of knightly orders, crosses of military orders, and sculpted armor. The widespread civil violence along the roads and across the countryside caused nobles of all ranks, and many non-nobles, to carry swords when traveling. Entire noble lineages disappeared and new ones emerged as noble families suffered wartime casualties and intermarried with families of different ranks.[17] Even as Loyseau wrote about the distinctions within the nobility in the early seventeenth century, the category of a *noblesse d'épée* made little sense to his contemporaries.

What truly set warrior nobles apart from other French nobles during the religious wars was not carrying a sword, but being *en armes*. From an early age, warrior nobles immersed themselves in a culture of arms that celebrated martial themes and the use of military weapons, not just the civilian rapier.[18]

A contemporary dictionary explains that a man was armed when he was "equipped with arms for war, that is with all pieces, as when one says armed from head to foot."[19] These correlations of nobles with the use of armor and military weapons reinforced the long-standing cultural linkages between nobility and mounted warfare, since an elite armored cavalryman was still referred to as a *gendarme, homme d'armes,* or *homme bien armé.* Many warrior nobles served as gendarmes in the *compagnies d'ordonnance,* heavy cavalry companies financed by the king, which provided the focal point for military reform projects.[20] Powerful nobles surrounded by entourages of gendarmes could be portrayed as great warriors, as when a pamphlet hailed the duc d'Épernon as "one of the most honorable warriors and protectors of the crown."[21] Noble military officers could be described as *personnes de qualité, personnes de commandement* and *de condition,* or simply as *gentilhommes,* gentlemen.[22] The large numbers of young nobles who flocked to join armies during civil wars—bringing their own weapons, armor, and horses—were often referred to as *nobles volontaires* or *la noblesse.* A contemporary siege narrative therefore describes a nobleman who was "eighteen to twenty years old" as leading a charge at the siege of Montpellier, "accompanied by five or six volunteers about the same age."[23]

All of these nobles can usefully be described as warrior nobles, members of a distinct military elite within the broader French nobility who defined their social roles through their personal use of arms and their military activity. This *noblesse guerrière,* or warrior nobility, represented a relatively small military elite with disproportionate power in the context of sustained civil warfare in late sixteenth- and early seventeenth-century France.[24] Thousands of nobles who were members of this military elite engaged in civil conflict through particular forms of officeholding, social distinction, political association, and confessional activism. Their political power and social positions became dependent on their bellicose practices and their engagement in civil conflict. Warrior nobles repeatedly offered to raise troops for their patrons, their allies, and their king. Alfonse d'Ornano's promise that "whatever happens, I will always be ready to mount my horse," exemplifies nobles' expressions of their willingness to serve in armed conflict.[25] Warrior nobles can thus be seen as members of a specific culture who distinguished themselves from other members of French society through their embrace of civil violence.

✝

Orienting their everyday lives around violence, southern French nobles profoundly shaped early modern French politics and society through their warrior pursuits. Powerful *grands,* or great nobles, such as the duc d'Épernon and the duc de Montmorency clearly exercised sweeping power in the provinces of Guyenne and Languedoc through their military and administrative offices. Lower-ranking warrior nobles also influenced southern French society significantly through their conduct of civil warfare. All of these provincial nobles had to negotiate the particular contexts of civil conflict in southern France during this confusing period of ongoing religious reform, serious confessional violence, shifting political affiliations, and constant civil warfare. The body of this book will explore how the violent practices of this military elite affected noble culture, royal administration, and civil violence in the early seventeenth century. Provincial nobles who waged civil warfare could readily agree with their contemporary Nicolas Faret, author of an influential treatise on noble conduct and courtly behavior, that the nature of French nobility was "naturally warrior."[26]

PART ONE

The Profession of Arms

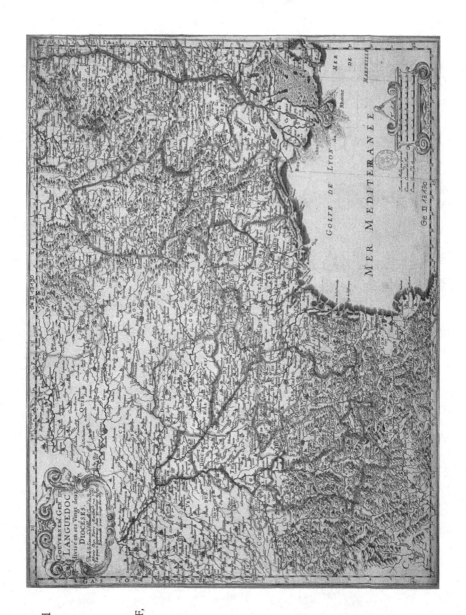

The province of Languedoc showing its administrative and religious divisions in the seventeenth century. Map by Nicolas Sanson d'Abbeville, *Gouvernement général du Languedoc, divisé en ses vingt deux diocèses* (Paris, 1667). BNF, Cartes et Plans, GE D 13130. Photo courtesy Bibliothèque Nationale de France.

CHAPTER ONE

The Great Quantity of Nobility
That Is Found Here

Southern France and Its Warrior Elite

N obles in each sénéchaussée across France assembled in the summer and autumn of 1614 to select deputies, usually one from each estate, to attend the meeting of the Estates General that Marie de Médicis had called to deal with the problems of civil conflict in the kingdom. The deputies from the province of Languedoc who made the journey north to Paris for the opening of the Estates General in October were overwhelmingly warrior nobles. Many of the clergy elected as deputies of the first estate, such as Louis de Nogaret de La Valette, were from warrior families. The representatives of the second estate were almost exclusively warrior nobles like François de La Jugie comte de Rieux and Antoine-Hercule de Budos marquis de Portes. Even some of the deputies for the third estate were military elites, such as Louis de Gondin, who was consul of Uzès in 1614 and would go on to command a Huguenot infantry regiment as a mestre de camp in the 1620s. The meeting of the Estates General that these deputies attended must have seemed rancorous and frustrating to these provincial nobles accustomed to the productive, if limited, meetings of the provincial estates of Languedoc. The Languedoc nobles engaged in preparing a *cahier de doléance* to list their concerns and grievances, then argued over the order in which they would sign the document. When the meeting of the Estates General closed in February 1615, very little had been accomplished.[1]

When the warrior noble deputies headed home to report back to their fellow Languedoc nobles, they returned to a province already concerned with other regional affairs. The provincial governor, Henri I de Montmorency, had recently

died and had been replaced by his son Henri II, who had assembled the provincial
estates in the town of Pézenas, even while the Estates General was still meeting
in Paris. In December 1614, an elaborate funeral ceremony for the deceased
governor had been held, attended by many prominent regional nobles. The provincial elites who assembled in Pézenas debated precedence issues and deliberated on the problems the province faced. Disorders within the province and
disturbances along the Spanish border particularly worried the nobles.[2]

The meetings of the Estates General and the estates of Languedoc in 1614
reveal the contours of the Languedoc elites and suggest the importance of the
warrior nobles in the provincial life of southern France. This chapter introduces
the powerful military elites in Languedoc and the neighboring province of Guyenne and explores the divided regions of southern France in which they lived.
In the early seventeenth century, these two provinces had profound confessional
divisions and a long history of religious conflict.

THE NOBILITY OF THIS REGION STOOD IN ARMS

On the eve of the French Revolution, in 1784, the estates of Languedoc sponsored an effort to catalogue the nobility of the province and assess the prominent
families of the region. This project involved searching for nobles and calling on
noble families to submit documentation establishing their nobility and service
for inclusion in a publication to be known as *Le Roi d'armes du Languedoc*.[3] The
French Revolution intervened and apparently halted the project permanently,
and we are still left with as imperfect a knowledge of the identities of the provincial nobles as early modern French people had.

A nobleman narrating civil warfare in Vivarais in the early seventeenth century captured contemporary understandings of provincial warrior nobles, relating that "the nobility of this region stood in arms." This description of Vivarais
nobles standing in arms encapsulated the image of a noble gentleman prepared
for battle, wearing armor and bearing military arms, not the civilian rapier. This
passage indicates both the extent of regional violence and the active participation
of the local warrior nobles in civil warfare through their armament.[4] The provincial nobles who engaged in warrior pursuits in southern France were members
of a provincial military elite that was defined by the exercise of arms, divided
into different ranks, and delimited by vague boundaries.

Exercise of Arms

Warrior nobles had a special relationship to violence in French society that revolved around the exercise of the profession of arms. "Since every man has to choose a profession . . . ," Nicolas Faret reasons in a contemporary treatise on nobility, "it seems to me that there is none more honorable or more essential to a gentleman than that of arms."[5] The use of weapons did not represent a profession in the modern sense of a specialized occupational career, yet the notion of a profession of arms implies the depth of nobles' identification with weapons.[6] Warrior nobles trained in the use of weapons from a very young age, and Faret's observation that this profession was essential to nobles suggests an appreciation of the pervasiveness of military activity in early modern French noble culture. The readiness of warrior nobles to take up arms reveals both a strong familiarity with weapons and "an acceptance of warmaking as a legitimate and familiar activity," as Kristen B. Neuschel argues.[7] Jonathan Dewald rightly insists on "the centrality of warfare as one of the myths that defined the early modern nobility."[8] Early modern French understandings of profession as *métier*, which envisioned functions as related to instruments, might suggest approaching the profession of arms concept in a narrower, practical manner.[9] Considering the concept of the profession of arms as a *métier* that involved actually using weapons allows us to distinguish warrior nobles as a more restricted social group: only the nobles who exercised the *métier des armes* by engaging in warrior pursuits can be considered warrior nobles.

During the French Wars of Religion, warrior nobles in southern France were heavily armed and immersed in a culture of arms. These provincial elites normally lived in fortified châteaux or old medieval towers on their estates, complete with defensible walls and domestic armories. The dangers of civil warfare and banditry prompted nobles to arm themselves when traveling across the southern French countryside. The nobles of Guyenne and Languedoc were also very active in the urban culture of the cities and towns in their regions, and they regularly entered them with large armed entourages. Many noble families had their own *hôtels particuliers*, or urban residences, whose defensible structures provided them with protective strongholds within civic centers. Nobles who acted as town governors usually commanded a community's old medieval walls, gates, principal towers, and garrison troops. The bastioned fortifications and citadels surrounding some strategic urban centers normally had a noble governor, who controlled a garrison and its armory. Warrior nobles clearly dealt with weaponry, fortifications, and military administration in their daily lives during the civil wars of the late sixteenth and early seventeenth centuries.

French warrior noble culture was powerfully shaped by the prospect of violence and the actual experience of combat. Warrior nobles regularly engaged in military training and preparation, including weapons training, horsemanship exercises, and mock battles. Other popular noble activities—although not specifically military in nature—such as horse-riding, hunting, jousting, and dueling prepared noble skills that were useful in combat. Physical violence was arguably *normal* for French warrior nobles, an activity specific to their social group, fully within social expectations for their behavior.

The officeholding warrior nobles who were the key organizers of warfare emerged as the predominant provincial elites in southern France as the concepts of military commander and *officier* became increasingly linked in the late sixteenth and early seventeenth centuries.[10] Although the profession of arms distinguished warrior nobles from other social groups, they were not isolated from the rest of French society. Warrior nobles were not members of a strictly ordered officer class, but were part of a broader noble and officeholding elite that interacted with other social groups in southern France. Warrior nobles' political, cultural, and social roles were mixed with various military duties and obligations. A modern observer might categorize the various activities of a captain in that context as those of a politician, a commander, a spy, a negotiator, an administrator, a judge, an entrepreneur, a tax collector, and a banker. The profession of arms defined the social group of the warrior nobles, but still allowed for a wide range of social interactions.

Defining warrior nobility through nobles' engagement in the profession of arms necessarily privileges a masculine perspective on French elites. The organization and practice of early seventeenth-century warfare were overwhelmingly masculine activities, but women were also involved in civil conflict as camp followers, refugees, victims, and occasionally combatants.[11] Southern French noblewomen participated in civil conflict through information gathering, religious politics, war financing, military patronage, and civic defense. Noblewomen also managed their households when their fathers or husbands were away from their residences, potentially assuming control of garrisons and armories, especially at family châteaux. Although noblewomen will be considered at points, this study nonetheless adopts a primarily masculine perspective appropriate for the analysis of this predominantly masculine dimension of French society. This approach is informed by a historicized theory of masculinities in which "the object of knowledge is not a reified 'masculinity' . . . , rather, *men's places and practices in gender relations.*"[12] While the present work does not constitute a study of masculinity per se, this method allows for a consideration of gendered aspects of honor, political culture, and violence in warrior noble culture.[13]

Different Species of Nobility

The French nobility of the early modern period was composed of a series of elites with different statuses, diverse characteristics, and distinct privileges. Individuals attained nobility through birth or ennoblement, and nobles strove simultaneously to assert their precedence over other nobles and to set themselves off from non-nobles. The bewildering complexity of nobles' ranks and precedence claims led the author of an important seventeenth-century treatise on nobility to attempt to identify all the "different species of nobility."[14] The early seventeenth-century jurist Charles Loyseau uses similar language to differentiate nobles using three "degrees of nobility" and numerous subdivisions, delimiting the hierarchies of titles ranging from common seigneurs to the ducs and princes at the apex of the French nobility.[15] Numerous other distinctions within the nobility granted certain nobles membership in military orders, access to various assemblies, and claims to precedence. Nobles' seigneurial rights gave them particular legal prerogatives to exercise, and royal service brought honorific designations—such as *chevalier, écuyer,* and *gendarme.* The early seventeenth-century concept of nobility represented a dignity involving a complex mixture of distinctions based on birth, merit, virtue, title, wealth, and status that were highly elaborated in legal texts and treatises on nobility.

Although warrior nobles constituted a distinct social group, they did not constitute a single social class. A wide variety of warrior nobles participated in civil warfare in early seventeenth-century southern France, and they were divided into various hierarchical strata. The *grands* who lived in the region and who held high military commands represented the apex of the provincial military elites. Below these powerful nobles were a number of prominent regional nobles who held significant military commands and major provincial administrative offices. Other warrior nobles held offices in military units active in the region. Many additional nobles who experienced combat as members of compagnies d'ordonnances, as noble volunteers, or as bodyguards should be considered part of the warrior nobility. Such provincial nobles had close contact with the officeholding nobles and could be promoted to military offices through their military service.

All of these noble practitioners of the profession of arms were engaged in directing religious violence and civil warfare in early seventeenth-century France.

Members of other social groups were also involved in waging and supporting warfare, but warrior nobles were the principal organizers of warfare during civil conflicts, employing their military offices, clientage networks, and wealth to mobilize armies and wage warfare. Early seventeenth-century French military systems relied on local and regional nobles to mobilize rapidly to deal with border threats and civil conflicts, especially when religious conflicts broke out in the confessionally divided regions of southern France. These noble commanders and captains acted as military entrepreneurs, equipping their troops with arms, ammunitions, clothing, and supplies largely at their own expense when they raised troops. Armies could only assemble in their encampments with the funding and organization supplied by warrior nobles using a complicated system of informal war finance. Whenever food and supplies were lacking, warrior nobles coerced local populations to provide needed items or allowed their soldiers to plunder civilians' homes in the war zones. These warrior elites regularly commanded military units and entire armies, selecting targets for an often widespread application of massive violence through raiding warfare and sieges.

Early modern French nobles had to negotiate the complex subgroupings and hierarchies of the "different species of nobility" in their daily lives. Perhaps nowhere could the variations among French nobles be seen more clearly than in political and religious ceremonies. Each ceremony held during a meeting, assembly, or procession had the potential to create precedence disputes over distinctions of order and rank. When such disputes could not be resolved through negotiation, nobles were often quick to challenge their rivals to duels. Significant precedence quarrels could lead to long-standing grudges, or even localized civil warfare between nobles. Precedence disputes, then, allow us to glimpse differentiations and contestations among the nobility, but only within a small group of nobles assembled in one place at a specific moment.

Too Long to Enumerate

An account of the civil conflict in Languedoc in 1629 recorded that the duc de Montmorency was "followed by all these seigneurs and nobles, whose names would be too long to enumerate."[16] Surely most of these nobles would be considered warrior nobles, but their names are unrecorded and their warrior identities are lost among the seemingly innumerable provincial nobles. The overall size of the extensive provincial nobility in Languedoc and Guyenne during the early seventeenth century is still difficult to assess. The best estimates suggest that in the late sixteenth and early seventeenth centuries, the entire French nobility numbered 41,000 to 50,000 families, perhaps 100,000 to 150,000 persons in all, or slightly over 1 percent of the estimated total population of approximately eighteen million.[17] Thousands of those nobles owned seigneuries in Guyenne and Languedoc, the two largest provinces in early modern France, and limited statistical data have been compiled about these elites. The more restrictive number of warrior nobles active in these southern French provinces is impossible to gauge, although some estimates suggest that half or more of French noblemen participated in military activities in the early modern period.[18]

Whatever the overall dimensions of the nobility in Languedoc and Guyenne, clearly the warrior nobles constituted a small, yet extraordinarily powerful, provincial elite. A few contemporary documents provide lists of provincial noble families in southern France, but any assessment of prominent nobles in this period offers only a momentary glimpse at a dynamic elite. Noble families were always being created, divided, recreated, and destroyed by the ennoblements, marriages, and deaths of noble family members. Major noble families from other provinces could gain prominence in Languedoc and Guyenne by acquiring lands and offices there. Frequent exchanges or sales of seigneuries, châteaux, hôtels, and offices among nobles ensured that early seventeenth-century noble families in southwestern France remained highly mobile and unstable. There are also suggestions that the number of nobles was growing slightly in this period amidst a general population expansion. Emmanuel Le Roy Ladurie, the foremost specialist on the history of Languedoc, describes a "population explosion" in the sixteenth century, followed by a stagnation of agricultural productivity in the early seventeenth century.[19]

In Languedoc, the *recherches de noblesse* of the second half of the seventeenth century give us some sketchy notions of the number of nobles and noble families in that province. These official administrative inquests required nobles to demonstrate their noble status by producing a series of documents known as *preuves*—normally including royal acts, court records, wills, and property transactions—that might be accepted as proof their nobility.[20] There were some less systematic *enquêtes* into the nobility of some regions of France in the early sixteenth century, but the earliest comprehensive *recherche* in Languedoc was conducted by the intendant Claude Bazin de Bezons and his commission between 1668 and 1671, as part of a royal *maintenue de noblesse* throughout the kingdom.[21] Nicolas Lamoignon de Basville, intendant of Languedoc during the second half of Louis XIV's reign, directed another *recherche*, which was completed in 1698. His assessment counted 4,486 noble families in Languedoc at that time, however, Lamoingnon de Basville judged that only 116 noble families could be considered "ancient."[22] The *recherches* are unreliable demographic sources, since the process of confirming or denying noble status was inherently political. Some nobles seem to have felt that confirmation of their noble status was unnecessary. Powerful noble families in Languedoc such as the Lévis-Mirepoix, Lévis-Ventadour, and Crussol are simply not present in Bazin de Bezons's *recherche*.[23] These investigations nonetheless provide the best estimates of the noble population of Languedoc in the late seventeenth century.

The *recherches* have extremely limited value for evaluating the number of nobles in the early seventeenth century or earlier periods. Nobles could easily produce forged or altered documents in their *preuves*, fabricating genealogies and past family histories to enhance the reputation of their lineages. The *recherches* cannot take into account demographic shifts affecting the noble population. Numerous early seventeenth-century noble lineages were extinguished in the civil conflicts and the epidemics in that period. Other noble families disappeared through marriage, merging of cadet lineages, exile, or moving to other regions of France. Some Calvinist nobles took flight after the Edict of Alès in 1629. At the same time, nobles from other regions of France migrated to southern France. So, since the size of the nobility can only be assessed at certain points during the early modern period, the *recherches* can only provide vague guidelines and limited information on noble families in Languedoc and Guyenne.

Contemporaries' knowledge of the overall dimensions of the provincial nobility was probably very impressionistic. Early seventeenth-century nobles knew the other noble families in their localities intimately, but had only vague notions of the scale of the entire provincial nobility. The political disputes and civil violence in Languedoc and Guyenne during the late sixteenth and early seventeenth centuries created an environment in which noble families could quickly rise or fall—destroyed by the shifting alliances and political reversals. Ennoblement and promotion offered the possibility of social mobility and enhancement of status in early seventeenth-century France. Ennoblement appears to have been exceedingly rare in this period, since only ten nobles are listed in the registers of the chambre de comptes de Montpellier as having been ennobled during the period 1562–1629. Of these, six were ennobled between 1610 and 1627.[24] However, there were other ways of becoming noble in early modern France, and some new provincial nobles may have emerged in this period. Power and status also shifted in the provinces of Languedoc and Guyenne as nobles from other regions took up offices and bought seigneuries in southern France. Many nobles in southern France felt that the quality of nobility itself was threatened by civil war. One noble family's genealogy remarked that "many nobles and ancient families find themselves unable to demonstrate and prove with titles the long continuation of their ancestors and predecessors; these faults are rather common and are practiced at all times and in every province."[25] The dimensions of the early seventeenth-century warrior nobility in Languedoc and Guyenne remain elusive.

THE PRINCIPAL SEIGNEURS OF GUYENNE AND GASCOGNE

The immense province of Guyenne sprawled across southwestern France from the Atlantic Ocean eastward up the Garonne river and its tributaries toward the Pyrenees and Languedoc.[26] Legacies of English rule in Aquitaine, the Hundred Years' War, and the rise of the Albret-Navarre dynasty had left a jumbled mix of overlapping administrative, judicial, and seigneurial jurisdictions in early seventeenth-century Guyenne. All of the regions of the province had nebulous identifications, flexible boundaries, administrative variations, and local customs that the nobles of Guyenne had to negotiate.[27] Henri IV's ascension to the throne of France had altered Guyenne's relationships with the extensive Albret-Navarre territories in the region. Then, in 1607, Henri reattached to the kingdom of France all of the seigneuries that had been held by the Valois kings. Thus, numerous seigneuries and comtés, as well as the duchés d'Alençon, d'Albret, and de Vendôme, became part of an expanded province of Guyenne.[28]

Depictions of Gascon nobles as jealous and quarrelsome solidified during the religious wars. An English assessment of the French kingdom in the 1580s recorded that Guyenne provided "everything that man needs. But the inconvenience is that it is impossible to live there because of the civil wars that have ruined everything, putting the noble families in perpetual quarrels."[29] When rumors reached the province in 1615 that Louis XIII would grant Antoine-Arnaud de Pardaillan seigneur de Gondrin a position as lieutenant general in Guyenne, Antoine de Roquelaure marquis de Roquelaure and other prominent regional nobles grumbled. Paul Phélypeaux seigneur de Pontchartrain, secrétaire d'État for Marie de Médicis at the time, reported that this move had created "great discontentment among several principal seigneurs in Guyenne and Gascogne, who are so jealous of each other that they could not, in any way, put up with someone doing something for [just] one of them."[30] A year later, an anonymous report would depict the "great jealousies among the leaders" of Huguenots in Guyenne.[31] These descriptions highlight the rivalries and precedence disputes that epitomized Gascon noble culture in the late sixteenth and early seventeenth centuries. Yet, much of the jealousy and violence that contemporaries often described as Gascon character traits stemmed from the sharp religious divisions among the nobles of Guyenne that exacerbated noble rivalries and political disputes in the early seventeenth century. This section identifies prominent Guyenne nobles who were involved in civil conflict in this period, placing them into the context of the complex religious divisions and disputes in the region.[32]

Bordeaux and Its Hinterland

At the mouth of the Garonne, the port city of Bordeaux, already famous for its wine trade, was the political and population center of Guyenne with about 35,000 to 40,000 inhabitants in the early seventeenth century.[33] Bordeaux was a predominantly Catholic city, with a Jesuit college and an active Catholic devotional movement.[34] As the seat of a parlement, the provincial government, and an archbishopric, it was a key location for competitions between groups surrounding the great noble families who were active in Bordeaux affairs during this period.[35] Henri II de Bourbon prince de Condé was governor of Guyenne from 1610 to 1616, and the Mayenne branch of the Lorraine dynasty briefly became influential in the region with its possession of the government of Guyenne from 1616 until 1621. The Escoubleau de Sourdis family rose to prominence here by holding the archbishopric of Bordeaux. The Nogaret de La Valette family, headed by the duc d'Épernon, had long played a role in Bordeaux politics. The duc built his château de Cadillac near Bordeaux, and in the 1620s, the family became even more powerful in the region by obtaining the post of governor of Guyenne.[36]

Beyond Bordeaux stretched the famous Médoc, Graves, Sauternes, and Entredeux-Mers wine-producing regions, where many prominent nobles owned estates around the mouth of the Garonne river. Catholic warrior nobles here included the Esparbès de Lussan and Lausignan families. Further inland, members of the Jaubert de Barrault family acted as sénéchal de Bazadais in the early seventeenth century, raising troops for Catholic armies in the 1620s.[37] The Calvinist Favas family lived in this region and Jean de Favas was governor of Casteljaloux, a Huguenot place de sûreté.[38]

Gascogne and Armagnac

South of the Bordelais and Bazadais lay the broad region of Gascogne.[39] Alexandre Dumas's The Three Musketeers has made fictionalized seventeenth-century Gascon nobles famous throughout the world. The numerous warrior nobles who really lived in Gascogne during the early seventeenth century led less romantic

lives than Dumas suggests, but his portrayal does capture the importance of violence in Gascon nobles' lives. The association between Gascogne and violence is
an old one. As Ian Roy notes, "Gascony enjoyed the reputation of being fertile only
in soldiers, its poor upland soil breeding a hardy race, whose sons were forced to
seek their fortunes beyond their ancestral walls."[40] Blaise de Monluc played on
this reputation in his late sixteenth-century *Commentaires,* enumerating the qualities of great warriors before triumphantly asserting that "I believe we Gascons
are better provided of them than any other people of France, or perhaps of Europe, and many good and great captains have gone out of it within these fifty
years."[41] An English report on France from the 1580s reveals similar attitudes on
the bellicose nature of Gascons: "The inhabitants of Guyenne are almost always
devoted to arms more than any other province of France. There are very good
infantry and arquebusiers, but because of the confusion of civil war, very poorly
disciplined."[42] A 1615 pamphlet evoked the bellicose character of Gascon nobles,
calling them "good soldiers."[43]

Numerous warrior nobles living in the Gascogne region indeed joined in the
fighting throughout southern France in the 1610s and 1620s. Bernard de Bay-
lens, an influential Catholic noble, acted as sénéchal de Landes and governor of
the small town of Dax in the early seventeenth century. Nearby Mont-de-Marsan,
which had been an important Calvinist garrison town in the late sixteenth century, was governed by the baron de Castelnau, a member of the Castille family
in the early seventeenth century. Antoine III de Gramont comte de Gramont had
a château near Bidache and held the government of Bayonne, a town already
famous for its ham in the seventeenth century.[44]

The communities situated on the slight hills and along the small rivers in the
Armagnac region were marked by the legacies of religious divisions and conflict.
The Albret lineage held vast estates in this region, and Jeanne d'Albret queen of
Navarre had actively promoted Calvinist reform in the region during the mid-
sixteenth century. The strength of Calvinism in the region could still be seen in
the early seventeenth century through the participation of the Ségur de Pardaillan and Astaracs families in the Huguenot cause. Catholics also had powerful
protectors in Armagnac, such as Antoine-Arnaud de Pardaillan seigneur de Gondrin, who was lieutenant general in Guyenne. Haut Armagnac, the region surrounding the town of Auch, was increasingly a center of Counter-Reformation
activity in the early seventeenth century. A new archbishop, Léonard de Trappes,
entered Auch in 1600 and energetically promoted Catholic renewal.[45] Antoine de
Roquelaure, lieutenant general in Guyenne in the 1610s, actively promoted the
Counter-Reformation.

The sparsely populated, and almost solidly Catholic, valleys of Bigorre were governed by Antoine de Campeils seigneur de Luc, who had become sénéchal de Bigorre in 1596. The inhabitants of Comminges were also predominantly Catholic, and noble families such as the Lansac had provided significant support for the Catholic League.[46] The small town of Muret, famous for Simon de Montfort's victory over the Albigensians there in 1206, had been viewed by Catholics in the religiously divided neighboring region of Haut Languedoc as a potential refuge since the beginning of the French Wars of Religion.[47]

Agenais, Condomois, and Périgord

François d'Esparbès de Lussan marquis d'Aubeterre governed the Agenais and Condomois region, which straddled the Garonne river north of Armagnac. Condom, a town situated on the Baïse river, and much of its neighboring region had heavily Catholic populations. However, mixed-confession villages and some Calvinist-dominated communities were scattered across the Condomois countryside. Nérac had been a key Calvinist center from the early days of the French Reformation due to its situation on the landholdings of the Albrets and Navarres. In the early seventeenth century, the town still had a significant Huguenot population, a *chambre mi-partie,* and a largely Calvinist hinterland.[48] The Huguenot Caumont–La Force family was active in Nérac during the civil wars of the early seventeenth century.

Agen, a small city on the banks of the Garonne river, had been contested by Calvinists and Catholics during the early religious wars, before becoming an important center of Catholic League activity in Guyenne in the 1580s and 1590s. The Monlucs and other Catholic noble families owned hôtels in the center of this community, which had a population of around 6,500.[49] The city increasingly became a center of Counter-Reformation Catholicism under the leadership of a dynamic bishop who regularly visited his parishes and lay Catholic nobles such as the Esparbès de Lussan, Villars, and Gélas.[50] The region surrounding Agen was disputed by Calvinists and Catholics, and several communities in Agenais were split almost evenly between the two confessions.[51] The powerful Huguenot Caumont family held numerous seigneuries in Agenais and protected Protestant worship on their lands and in the towns of Clairac and Tonneins.[52]

Northeast of the Agenais, the Dordogne river valley provided the main commercial artery for the Périgord, as well as a communication line between Calvinist communities like Castillon and Sainte-Foy, Bergerac, and Sarlat. Bergerac continued to serve as a place de sûreté in the early seventeenth century, its well-fortified walls providing a refuge for Périgord Huguenots with the protection of the Caumont family, who held the adjacent seigneurie of La Force.[53] These Calvinist towns were ringed by nearby Catholic communities, and southern Périgord was sharply divided. A small Calvinist minority attempted to maintain its privileges in predominantly Catholic Libourne, presumably with the assistance of governor La Bellue.[54] The nearby hilltop town of Fronsac was known as one of the best fortified towns of all Guyenne. The Catholic Orléans family was one of the prominent families in the region, and the duc de Fronsac would die fighting Huguenots at the siege of Montpellier.[55]

Northern Périgord was more solidly Catholic, and the city of Périgueux, with a population of around 8,000, provided an important devotional center for nearby villagers.[56] The Catholic Bourdeilles and Aydie families were two of the most powerful families in this area, and Henri de Bourdeilles acted as sénéchal de Périgord in the early seventeenth century.[57] Despite the Catholic strength in northern Périgord, a few Calvinist communities such as Mussidan and Montignac were scattered along the river valleys.[58]

Haute Guyenne

The nobles living on the plateaus of Haute Guyenne dealt with a seriously divided confessional landscape. In Haut Quercy, the village of Rocamadour represented a major pilgrimage site for devout Catholics, who emulated the great medieval king Louis IX's visit to Rocamadour's *vierge noire*, a statue of the Virgin Mary venerated by Catholics for its miraculous powers.[59] The Lauzières were one of the most powerful Catholic families in Haut Quercy, and Pons de Lauzières marquis de Thémines was sénéchal de Quercy.[60] The small town of Figeac, governed by members of the Béthune family, was an important Calvinist center in the same region.[61] The religiously mixed town of Cahors nestled in a sharp bend in the Lot river, providing an urban center for the many nobles living in Haut Quercy.

Calvinist reform had swept through Montauban, Quercy's largest city, following the conversion of the city's bishop in 1556.[62] Montauban had quickly become one of the most important Huguenot strongholds in the entire kingdom, and had been considered a place de sûreté in successive religious peaces since 1570. Calvinists probably composed over 90 percent of the city's estimated population of 17,000 by the early seventeenth century.[63] The Huguenot leadership of Montauban had fortified the city with an extensive system of bastions.[64] Following the Edict of Nantes, the tiny Catholic minority managed to restore a limited religious practice in the city.[65] A Calvinist *collège* and academy were founded around 1600, making Montauban one of the key centers of Reformed learning in southern France.[66] In the countryside around Montauban, some small towns adhered to Catholicism, but much of Bas Quercy was dominated by Calvinism.

Confessional tensions troubled the easternmost stretches of Guyenne, known as Rouergue. The Catholic Noailles family held seigneuries near Villefranche-de-Rouergue, and François de Noailles was sénéchal in Rouergue in the early seventeenth century.[67] In central Rouergue, Rodez remained solidly Catholic, with an active bishop who controlled half of the town as a seigneurie.[68] Rodez had supported the Catholic League in the late sixteenth century and served as the focal point for a Catholic devotional movement in the region in the early seventeenth century.[69] Huguenot nobles dominated much of rugged southern Rouergue, however, including the small town of Vabre.[70] Nearby Saint-Affrique was a confessionally mixed town, controlled at least part of the time by Calvinists, who expelled their Catholic neighbors at least once.[71] Millau, the largest town in southeastern Rouergue, was a vital Calvinist center, which had hosted a major Huguenot political assembly in 1573.[72]

ALL OF THE NOBILITY AND CAPTAINS OF LANGUEDOC

A 1621 pamphlet celebrating the capture of a small town near Nîmes by the duc de Montmorency and "all the nobility and captains of Languedoc" left these provincial elites unnamed.[73] But early modern residents of Languedoc clearly recognized certain warrior noble families as prominent and preeminent in their regions. The process of distinguishing these principal families among the warrior nobility was obviously highly subjective, but appraisals of noble status probably did reflect somewhat noble families' abilities to position themselves and to exercise their power relationships. Nobles assessed family status comparatively and relatively, not only on the basis of reputation and longevity, but on actions and changing contexts. Contemporaries' evaluations of noble families reveal their assumptions about status and power, and also allow us to consider more carefully the provincial elites.

A contemporary manuscript entitled, "Rolle des principales & plus ancieñes maizons du Languedoc dont j'ay peu avoir memoire," gives us an excellent glimpse into the warrior nobility of the province of Languedoc.[74] This document provides a contemporary author's judgments regarding the principal noble families of the province in the form of a list of noble seigneuries and families with brief descriptions providing details of the family's titles, offices, possessions, and history. The contemporary list thus allows an examination of the distribution of prominent noble families within the province of Languedoc.

Haut Languedoc and Foix

Across the Garonne river from Guyenne, the fertile plains and hills of Haut Languedoc extended throughout the western part of Languedoc. Grain and wine grown on the estates around Toulouse was transported down the Garonne river and sold in Bordeaux. Pastel cultivation produced one of Haut Languedoc's most valuable commodities, although a contemporary Toulousain writer claimed that the disruptions of the civil wars had greatly diminished the pastel trade.[75] Most of the prominent noble families of Haut Languedoc lived in the broad plains of the Ariège, Garonne, and Tarn rivers—clustered around the significant small cities, such as Albi and Castres, and the large city of Toulouse.

A number of powerful warrior nobles lived near Toulouse, a city known as *la ville rose* for its many buildings constructed with a combination of rose-colored brick, white mortar, and white stone. Toulouse was the largest city in Languedoc in the early seventeenth century with a population of about 40,000, making it one of the largest cities in all of France in the early modern period.[76] Under the guidance of its *capitouls*, or magistrates, Toulouse had developed a reputation as a cosmopolitan city with a vibrant urban culture, prestigious university, and respected parlement. The literary and theatrical activities of Toulousains attracted the prince de Condé, the duc de Montmorency, the duc de Ventadour, and their followers for extended stays.[77] Rose-colored hôtels served as residences for the noble families, presidents and judges of parlement, and other urban elites who lived in the city. These "magnificent buildings" were adorned with ornaments sculpted from marble brought down the Garonne from the Pyrennes mountains.[78]

Toulouse had a deserved reputation as a center of militant Catholicism, and the vast majority of prominent nobles in the Toulouse region seem to have been staunchly Catholic.[79] At the beginning of the French Wars of Religion, Huguenots had briefly taken control of the city in May 1562. Catholic Toulousains had retaliated, massacring Calvinists, burning their homes, and firmly reestablishing Catholic domination. A religious procession was inaugurated to rejoice at the "deliverance" of Toulouse from the Huguenots, and the relics of Saint-Sernin continued to be carried through the city streets in annual celebrations until the French Revolution.[80] Yet another wave of violence against Huguenots erupted in the city in 1572, as Toulousains enacted their own slaughter after hearing of the Saint Bartholomew's Day Massacre in Paris.[81] Toulouse later acted as a base for

Counter-Reformation Catholicism through its numerous lay confraternities and its support for the Catholic League from 1589. By the early seventeenth century, Toulouse was becoming a major center for the new Counter-Reformation religious orders in southern France, under the protection of the archbishop of Toulouse, François de Joyeuse. The influential Catholic Nogaret de La Valette family controlled the archbishopric of Toulouse in the 1610s and 1620s and established a significant presence in the city. The Catholic barons de Cornusson, from a different La Valette family, held the important post of sénéchal de Toulouse.

Another series of powerful Catholic families resided in the region around the Catholic stronghold of Albi, known as the Albigeois. Albi's towering fortress-like red brick cathedral Sainte-Cécile continued to remind inhabitants and travelers of the repression of the Albigensian heresy in the thirteenth century. The Elbène, Lescure, and Amboise d'Aubijoux families played active roles in the affairs of *la ville rouge*, as Albi was known.[82] Small Catholic towns were scattered through Albigeois, and Gaillac had become a center of militant Catholicism during the French Wars of Religion. Some Protestant nobles lived in the Albigeois region, and the small town of Rabastens was an important Huguenot base in western Albigeois. Lombers and Réalmont, with significant Calvinist populations, were contested during the civil wars, with the support of Huguenot nobles such as the vicomte de Panat and the marquis de Malauze.

In the adjacent diocese of Montauban, Calvinist and Catholic nobles competed for control of the towns in the Tarn and Garonne river valleys. Montauban, a Calvinist city, was located in the provincial government of Guyenne, but its diocese fell under the jurisdiction of the provincial government of Languedoc. The small Calvinist towns of Mas Grenier and Villemur in the diocese of Montauban amounted to Huguenot enclaves in a predominantly Catholic region based around the fortified towns of Castelsarrasin and Montech, where the bishop of Montauban sometimes sheltered when exiled from his city.[83]

The dioceses of Lavaur and Castres had deeper confessional divisions. Castres was a confessionally mixed town, in which probably about 10,000 people resided during the early seventeenth century.[84] The town had been politically controlled by Calvinists since 1574, and the site of a judicial *chambre mi-partie* since 1579, yet Catholics increasingly reestablished themselves there beginning around 1595.[85] The Calvinists in Castres were also divided among themselves, between moderate Huguenots and militant followers of the duc de Rohan.[86] Noble families such as the Bouffard-Madianes, Cardaillacs, and Toulouse-Lautrecs contended with the problems of religious violence and civil conflict in Castres and its mountainous hinterland.[87]

Further south, warrior nobles lived in the valleys and plains in the dioceses of Rieux, Saint-Papoul, and Carcassonne. The Bertiers, a family from Toulouse, were also prominent in the small town of Rieux, which was located on one of the tributaries of the Garonne river southwest of Toulouse. The Bertier family held the bishopric of Rieux for almost the entire seventeenth century.[88] The La Jugie family was prominent both in the diocese of Rieux, where the family held a comté, and in the diocese of Carcassonne—whose precedence rights François de La Jugie vociferously defended at the estates of Languedoc in 1614.[89] The famous medieval walls ringing the hilltop old town of Carcassonne enclosed a largely Catholic community, overlooking the hôtels of the Montmorencys, Lestangs, and other noble families in the new town below.[90] The Voisins, Lordat, and Roger families actively participated in the civil wars from their estates in the diocese of Carcassonne.[91]

Toward the Pyrenees mountains, the hilly dioceses of Limoux-et-Alet and Mirepoix were largely Catholic, but with Calvinist minorities. Various members of the Lévis family struggled to control the diocese of Mirepoix—the area where the Albigensians had made their last stand at the château de Montségur in 1244. One branch of the Lévis family, led by the marquis de Mirepoix, was firmly Catholic—with numerous estates in the region and support among other Catholic families, such as the La Barthe. The Lévis-Léran family, on the other hand, included militant Calvinists, who would lead Huguenot forces in the diocese.

Southwest of Haut Languedoc and nestled in the arms of the Pyrenees, Foix was a region sharply divided by religious belief. The Saint-Pol family was one of the preeminent families of the diocese of Foix. The Monlucs married into the ancient Foix family and took control of the famous medieval château de Foix, which overlooked the town and the Ariège river below.[92] Further down the Ariège, the small town of Pamiers was the seat of a bishopric controlled by the Esparbès de Lussan family in the early seventeenth century. Pamiers had a mixed population of Calvinists and Catholics, and control of the town changed hands several times through sieges and expulsions during the French Wars of Religion.[93] Not far from the village of Artigat, which has been so closely analyzed by Natalie Zemon Davis, Le Mas-d'Azil was a Calvinist stronghold that was actively supported by the Huguenot nobles in the region.[94]

Bas Languedoc

The warrior nobles of Bas Languedoc largely lived in châteaux and towns along the coastal plain running from the border with Spanish Rousillon to the mouth of the Rhône river. The nobles here enjoyed the warm, sunny climate of the

Mediterranean coast unlike the nobles living in cooler regions of Haut Languedoc and Foix. In coastal Languedoc, the wheat fields, vineyards, and olive trees of nobles' seigneuries spread out over the plains, and châteaux and towns perched on small hills.

The old Roman city of Narbonne lay along the Mediterranean coast near the Spanish border, with a channel linking it to the sea and providing the city with direct access to long-distance commerce, including the pastel trade.[95] Narbonne was the seat of a politically important archbishopric, since the archbishop of Narbonne presided over the meetings of the estates of Languedoc. The baron de Luc, a member of the Thézan family, had close connections with the Montmorencys and served as governor of Narbonne in the early seventeenth century. The Catholic Gléon, Narbonne, Puisserguier, and Pujot families all held substantial lands in the diocese of Narbonne.[96]

Just up the coast from Narbonne lay the small dioceses of Béziers, Agde, and Lodève. The hilltop town of Béziers offered sanctuary for Catholics amidst large numbers of Calvinists in the surrounding region. The Thézan family resided close to Béziers and held the baronnie de Poujol.[97] The Bonsis, a family of Florentine immigrants, held the bishopric of Béziers for three generations and were very influential in the town.[98] At a short distance northeast, the small town of Pézenas served as the principal residence for the Montmorency family in Languedoc. Near the coast on the mouth of the Hérault river, Agde provided a center for the Guerre and Avanson families who lived in that town's diocese. Lodève was the seat of a bishopric, but nearby Clermont-de-Lodève was a Huguenot place de sûreté. The Clermont and Faugères families lived near the small town of Lodève, which butted up against a low mountain range.

Montpellier, with perhaps 16,300 residents, was one of the few major cities of the kingdom with a heavily mixed population of Calvinists and Catholics.[99] Approximately 60 percent of the city's residents were Huguenots in the early seventeenth century.[100] The sharp religious split invited attempts by members of both confessions to establish firm control over the urban space, and the community experienced successive periods of Calvinist and Catholic domination during the religious wars.[101] Although Montpellier remained an important regional commercial center, its cloth industry and trade seem to have suffered from the disruptions of religious conflicts, especially during sieges in 1562, 1577, and 1622. The city was known for its medical faculty at the University of Montpellier and its white stone hôtels. Many Montpellier elite families had invested in rural landholdings during the sixteenth century, resulting in "a swelling of the ranks of a new, urban-based nobility."[102] Noble families such as the Montlaurs and Roquefeuils played a major role in the city's urban culture. The Catholic La Croix family lived in nearby Castries, but was also integrally involved in Montpellier life and politics. The Caïla de Saint-Bonnet family similarly involved themselves in Montpellier from their nearby landholdings, including Restinclières. Other warrior nobles resided around Lunel, a Huguenot place de sûreté, and Mauguio, which lay east of Montpellier along the Mediterranean coast.

The marshy Camargue region around the mouth of the Rhône was only sparsely populated, but members of the Coligny and Harambures families vied over control of the port of Aigues-Mortes, from which King Louis IX had launched his crusades. The small towns of Aigues-Vives and Marsillargues in the diocese of Nîmes had significant Huguenot populations in the early seventeenth century.[103] Beaucaire, overlooking the Rhône river upstream from the Camargue and across from the papal enclave at Avignon, remained under the influence of the Fain family. This key town safeguarded navigation on the Rhône, the major commercial artery for Mediterranean commerce along eastern Languedoc all the way to the city of Lyon.[104]

Nîmes retained its Roman influence, with its ancient amphitheater and temple, but had become markedly less Catholic as the Reformation spread in the mid-sixteenth century.[105] During the French Wars of Religion, Nîmes became a Huguenot bastion and by the beginning of the seventeenth-century, 83 percent of the overall population of about 13,700 were Calvinists.[106] Nîmes remained an important Reformed religious center throughout the early seventeenth century, with active educational institutions, publishing industries, and street preaching. The Calvinist consistory of Nîmes worked to maintain moral discipline within the community.[107] Huguenot nobles living in and around Nîmes, such as the Louet de Calvisson, Baschi, and Beaumont families, were often able to dominate local politics.

Further inland from Nîmes, the coastal plains give way to the foothills of the Cévennes mountains, which run along the northern parts of the dioceses of Nîmes and Uzès. In the Causse limestone plateau region north of Ganges, the Calvinist Assas family challenged the Catholic Montfaucons for local dominance. The Bérard, Roure, and Budos families were preeminent in the area around the small town Calvinist towns of Alès and Anduze, and a number of nobles lived in châteaux and small towns situated in the Gard River valley. The Catholic Crussols commanded respect due to their ducal rank and extensive landholding around their residence in the Catholic town of Uzès, and the La Garde de Chambonas, Pluviers, and La Fare families owned seigneuries in the surrounding diocese. The Albert family, which would become prominent through the elevation of the duc de Luynes in 1617, was influential around the strategic Rhône crossing at Pont-Saint-Esprit.

Gévaudan, Velay, and Vivarais

Few warrior nobles could be found in the sparsely populated highland plateaus, gorges, and mountains of the Gévaudan, which were better suited to sheepherding than wheat cultivation. Yet some nobles, including the Tournels and Montbretons, lived in and around Mende, Villefort, Meyrueis, and other small towns in Gévaudan. The Catholic Crusy de Marcillac family held the bishopric and seigneurie of Mende in the early seventeenth century.[108] Numerous Calvinist communities sheltered in the Cévennes mountains of the Gévaudan, but even these isolated towns became sites of religious struggles in the early seventeenth century. The Catholic Budos family became heavily involved in the politics of the Gévaudan region in the 1610s and 1620s, largely due to the ongoing religious problems.

East of Gévaudan, the Cévennes mountains merged with the Massif Central in the Velay region. Nobles in this isolated area must have felt somewhat out of touch with the rest of the province of Languedoc. Velay nobles periodically assembled in their own estates of Velay to discuss regional problems, often meeting in or near the remote town of Le Puy-en-Velay, the most important population center in the Velay region and an important religious and cultural center for Velay nobles.[109] The town and an adjacent monastery were perched on top of huge volcanic rocks jutting up along the upper Loire River. Le Puy-en-Velay lay on an important Catholic pilgrimage route and its cathedral housed one of the most famous *vierges noires*.[110] The town's population was predominantly Catholic, but the few Calvinist residents were very vocal, at least according to one Catholic resident.[111] The Hautefort family was one of the most prominent noble families active in Le Puy-en-Velay, but the Polignac family lived just north of Le Puy-en-Velay and also exercised significant influence on the town. Both families were Catholic.[112]

The nobles of Vivarais lived in the valleys and canyons winding through the Cévennes mountains and along the Rhône.[113] This sparsely populated mountainous region was deeply divided between adherents of Catholicism and Calvinism, and its nobles were also split between the two confessions. The La Tour Gouvernet, Chambaud, and Beaumont families had become Calvinist in the sixteenth century and were heavily involved in Protestant politics in and around the town of Privas, a key Huguenot place de sûreté and one of the most important towns in Vivarais despite its size of only some 2,500 residents.[114] Meanwhile, the Catholic Tournons held extensive lands in northern Vivarais, with an imposing château overlooking the Rhône.[115] The Lévis-Ventadour family had extensive influence throughout Vivarais due to its ducal ranking and its close connections to the Montmorencys, but they also controlled the towns of Annonay and La Voulte in the region. Other prominent Catholic nobles in Vivarais included the d'Ornano, Balazuc de Montréal, and La Baume de Suze families. Many of these nobles gathered periodically in meetings of the regional assembly, and Vivarais barons had a rotating membership in the estates of Languedoc.

✝

A great number of nobles exercised arms in the southern French provinces of Guyenne and Languedoc. The profession of arms defined this group as a powerful military elite, but one that was fragmented into varying "species" of nobility. The indistinct margins of the provincial warrior nobility suggest that this important military elite represented a significant proportion of the broader regional nobility. The warrior nobles of Guyenne seem to have been predominantly Catholic, but a significant minority of the military elite championed Calvinism. The province of Languedoc was even more sharply divided, with broad areas of local Calvinist majorities protected by Huguenot nobles, as well as strongly mixed confessional regions. This presentation of the provincial military elite and the cultural geography of southern France now allows us to explore how noble kinship shaped the profession of arms.

An early seventeenth-century noble family praying at their dinner table. Engraving by Abraham Bosse, *La Bénédiction de la table* (ca. 1635). BNF, Estampes, Réserve, Ed 30 (11)-Fol. Photo courtesy Bibliothèque Nationale de France.

CHAPTER TWO

The Grandeur and Magnificence of His Household

Noble Households and Kinship

W hen describing Henri II de Montmorency's youth and the negotiations for his marriage, Montmorency's secretary and biographer marveled at "the grandeur and magnificence of his household." Henri married Maria Felicia Orsini, daughter of a Roman noble, in a ceremony at the Louvre in July 1613. Less than a year later, the young duc de Montmorency received news of his father's death in the province of Languedoc and headed to his family's château near Pézenas to take up his father's provincial government.[1] On his arrival in Languedoc, Henri "rewarded all his [father's] servants," and began reorganizing his household as the new patriarch of the Montmorency family.[2] The Montmorencys unquestionably constituted one of the most powerful noble families in all of France, but what did it mean to be the head of this grand and magnificent family?

The profession of arms structured kinship and shaped the everyday lives of the family and staff members of warrior households. This chapter explores the ways in which the warrior nobles of Guyenne and Languedoc lived kinship and devised strategies to survive civil conflict in the early seventeenth century. Southern French nobles, I suggest, conceived of family simultaneously as kinship, household, lineage, and alliance. Armed noble families organized the warrior practices through which military elites participated in civil warfare.

KINDRED WARRIORS
A Thousand Gentlemen, My Relatives

The warrior nobles who dominated provincial life in southern France during the early modern period defined themselves largely through their familial relationships. Noble households provided sites of family interaction, but nobles also engaged broad kinship networks encompassing bonds with uncles, aunts, and cousins, as Kristen B. Neuschel has shown.[3] Repeated intermarriages and remarriages among noble lineages produced a proliferation of multiple cousin and half-cousin relationships. The pervasive use of the salutations *mon cousin* and *ma cousine* in noble correspondence reveals the importance of perceived closeness within broad conceptions of kinship. Nobles and members of the royal family also employed such greetings to establish proximity and kinship with the king, even when no blood relationship justified such language. Some of these extended kinship ties remained weak connections, but distant kinship relations could be activated during family crises. Nobles, both women and men, often corresponded with distant kin in their requests for pardon, leniency, or ransom during the religious wars. Numerous cousins and more distant relatives came to the aid of Charles de Valois comte d'Auvergne during his imprisonment, for example.[4] After the comte's release, Henri II de Montmorency thanked Marie de Médicis, pledging his loyalty and promising that "a thousand gentlemen, my relatives," would be ready to join him in an oath of fidelity.[5] Similarly, when François V de La Rochefoucauld arrived at the siege of La Rochelle with 1,500 noble followers, he famously exclaimed to Louis XIII: "Sire, there is not a single one of these who is not my relative."[6] How are we to interpret such extraordinary claims of kinship?

My understanding of early modern French warrior noble families has been influenced by anthropological studies of kinship, and in particular by Pierre Bourdieu's notion of kinship as a very complex set of relationships that can be read in multiple ways. By distinguishing between *official kinship* and *practical kinship*, Bourdieu shows how official kinship structures are opposed by strategic uses of kinship relations. Despite official genealogical connections, families actually construct themselves through *representational kinship* by creating collective self-representations and actively promoting the idea of the family through members' strategic uses of kinship. Bourdieu suggests that families attempt to manage kinship relations through a series of interrelated approaches, arguing that "marriage strategies are inseparable from inheritance strategies, fertility strategies, and even educational strategies, in other words from the whole set of

strategies for biological, cultural and social reproduction that every group implements in order to transmit the inherited powers and privileges, maintained or
enhanced, to the next generation."[7]

Bourdieu's approaches to kinship are useful in studying the warrior nobles of
southern France because of their ability to describe families and kinship practices flexibly. Early seventeenth-century nobles created and re-created their conceptions of family using multiple kinship strategies. Warrior noble patriarchs
used overlapping definitions of kinship and layered conceptions of family to
organize their households. Laurence Fontaine provides a model for applying
Bourdieu's method critically, using a diffuse notion of kinship that "intervenes"
in many aspects of life through an array of different relationships. Taking a
constructivist approach to kinship, Fontaine argues for "the great diversity of
social forms of kinship, which have been clearly illustrated in the case of the
nobility."[8]

Warrior nobles constructed kinship through a series of complex family strategies. Historians have sometimes criticized Bourdieu's concept of *habitus* as overly
structuring social relations, including within families, but his notion of family
strategies reveals ways in which families maneuvered within, around, and
against existing constraints.[9] During the French Wars of Religion, noble family
decision-making processes could so be hesitant, indecisive, and protracted that
they threaten to undermine the notion of coherent family strategies. As Paul-
André Rosental has suggested, family strategies were rarely composed through
"an efficient calculation by individuals exercising clear and coherent choices."[10]
Despite the often dominating position of patriarchs within households, noble families were complex social groupings with varying compositions and competing interests. Noblewomen and even children played significant roles in information-
gathering, communication, and decision-making. The formulation and enaction
of warrior noble family strategies involved discussion and deliberation among
a number of individuals within and beyond kinship networks. Warrior noble
households nonetheless crafted approaches to pressing concerns and responses
to crises, even if these solutions were often imperfect or ill-conceived.

Noble families attempted to formulate strategies in accordance with the ideals
and expectations of contemporary noble culture. During the sixteenth century,
humanist and religious reform movements had created new ideals of the noble
family. Humanists' concerns with "right living" and their use of family metaphors for authority influenced noble ideals.[11] Beginning in the late sixteenth
century, Neostoic philosophy increasingly guided nobles' perceptions of virtue,
self-discipline, and moral education.[12] Humanist principles and classical Greek

and Roman writings continued to inform early seventeenth-century authors' discussions of kinship and the household.[13] Olivier de Serres, a Languedoc noble, provided a model of noble seigneurial life in his *Théâtre de l'agriculture et mesnage des champs* (1600).[14] Some common Christian themes of patriarchal authority, moral obligation, family devotion, and natural law sustained Calvinist and Catholic families.[15] Both Huguenot and Catholic noble families were concerned with displaying their piety in the confessionally divided areas of southern France. At the same time, sharp differences between Catholic and Reformed notions of the family influenced nobles' kinship practices during the religious wars.[16]

Catholic reform conceptions of the family stressed obedience and submission to God's will, linking paternal authority to royal and divine rule. André Burguière argues that "the family was at the center of the strategy of religious reconquest of the Church," which employed moral education and new devotional models to link Catholic families with the domesticated Holy Family.[17] Catholic reflections on family ideals drew on religiously inspired and anti-Huguenot writing, such as Pierre de Ronsard's immensely popular poetry.[18] Catholic bishops and preachers encouraged Catholic families to participate fully in Catholic renewal through lay devotions and charity. François de Sales's *Introduction à la vie dévote* (1608) provided families with a guide to a devout life that emphasized the importance of Catholic lay devotions in serving and glorifying God.[19] Some devout Catholic noble families responded to such calls to divine service by placing family members in bishoprics and religious orders. Many Catholic warrior nobles in southern France provided extensive patronage for convents, monasteries, collèges, and missions that actively promoted Counter-Reformation initiatives and Catholic renewal.

Calvinist ideals of the family shaped Huguenot noble kinship patterns and family identities. Jean Calvin's Christ-centered theology deemphasized the Holy Family to concentrate on the solitary figure of Jesus crucified. Echoes of Calvinist preaching on Christ and the family can be seen in early seventeenth-century sources, such as a Languedoc Huguenot noble's will that praised Christ as "conqueror of death" and his savior.[20] Calvin's teachings stressed obedience to God's will and provided new modes of establishing discipline in the Godly Community. French communities with significant Calvinist populations created local consistories to maintain moral discipline and manage conflicts within Huguenot families. Calvinists regarded family devotion and worship as vital, and Huguenot families engaged in group Bible reading and psalm singing. "The household should be a second place of worship, and the family a little church, devotional writers repeated time and again," according to Philip Benedict.[21] Calvinist notions of family and fatherhood stressed parental duties and responsibilities. Although Jean Calvin had initially hesitated to recognize Huguenots who were executed for heresy as martyrs, by the late sixteenth century, Calvinists readily extolled "martyrs" who died in the "true faith."[22] Huguenot descriptions of the afflictions of God's children often went beyond descriptions of the martyrdom of individuals to express an ideal of the suffering Huguenot family.[23] For example, an early seventeenth-century account of religious conflict in Vivarais complained that Huguenots were being forced to go to Catholic mass, consoling "the families that God affirms against this persecution"[24]

Gender dynamics shaped nobles' attempts to attain confessional familial ideals and to forge family identities during the French Wars of Religion. Warfare represented a fundamental family activity for warrior nobles in this period, including the participation of noblewomen in various aspects of conflict—especially finance, information, and defense. Warrior noble families tended to celebrate masculine kinship during the civil wars as they engaged broad male kin networks in common military operations. Fathers and sons often participated in warfare together, and extensive logistical documents referring to noble officers as *père et fils* suggest how common it was for male family members to serve in the same military units. Alexandre de Lévis displayed filial devotion as he expressed his desire to join a new unit that his father was raising in 1621, taking leave of the Catholic army in which he was already serving.[25] Uncle-nephew relationships, which often involved pseudo-patriarchal authority, could also be strengthened through joint military service, as the close relationship between the marquis de Portes and Henri II de Montmorency shows. Common fraternal bonds united brothers, cousins, and more distant male relatives who participated in warfare together. Conceptions of warrior noble kinship gained coherence by having multiple male family members directly involved in warfare, often over successive generations. Participation in civil conflicts thus increasingly prompted early seventeenth-century warrior noble families to organize themselves around the practice of violence, producing a particular form of patriarchal household.

In the Interest of His Household

Noble conceptions of the family unit centered on the *maison*, or household, with the warrior noble patriarch as head of the family, organizing kinship relations and household personnel around him.[26] Patriarchy operated simultaneously by focusing attention on the person of the patriarch and by defining the complex gender relations that composed the *maison*.[27] Patriarchal power derived from the assumption that the father occupied a natural position of dominance over his family, and this belief was supported by contemporary literature discussing families and households. The patriarchal control of fathers in southern France drew on Roman legal traditions and familial practices surrounding the figure of the *pater familias*. In contrast with provinces in northern France, Languedoc and Guyenne were both influenced by written law that provided clear judicial backing for patriarchal authority. Wives and children were subordinated to the power of fathers, and all of the members of households were subject to the patriarchal control. As one historian explains, "the structure of the early modern European family was patriarchal and authoritarian, emphasizing stability and continuity."[28] Patriarchal domination could be incredibly powerful, and a warrior noble father would claim to exercise his power "in the interest of his household."[29]

Patriarchal authority operated through the marriage bond between husband and wife that lay at the core of the noble household. Medical, philosophical, legal, and religious discourses in early modern France argued that females were naturally weaker and disorderly. Husbands thus needed to vigilantly oversee and control their wives, who were expected to be obedient and accept patriarchal authority.[30] Social conventions prescribed proper behavior for both husbands and wives, whose comportments were closely observed by their birth families, effectively tempering patriarchal control. Partners in married couples were hardly equal, yet there is also evidence that some early modern noble couples established mutual affection, respect, and even collaboration.[31]

Married couples normally sought to have children as soon as possible both to produce heirs and to fulfill the expectations of the couple's parents and extended families. The birth of children extended the conjugal family and confirmed patriarchal status of the noble father. Although early modern conjugal families have sometimes been portrayed as cold and emotionless, noble parents often expressed happiness and pride in their children.[32] Both noblemen and women played roles in caring for children and shaping their early development. Practical guides to childcare and medical advice increasingly shaped noble childraising in the late sixteenth and early seventeenth centuries.[33] Patriarchal control was considered especially important for sons, and a mother's influence was regarded as particularly dangerous for male children. Given such attitudes among early seventeenth-century French nobles, the closeness of Louis XIII and Gaston de Bourbon to their mother, Marie de Médicis, is striking.[34] Noble fathers and mothers were expected to fulfill various parental responsibilities, especially in educating their children and providing them with moral guidance. Noble parents were concerned with upholding the religiosity and piety of their families, and the moral formation of children often amounted to a sort of religious socialization within the household.[35]

Parental guidance required the obedience and respect of their offspring, but noble children also played significant roles of their own within their fathers' households. Both Calvinist and Catholic confessions emphasized the Ten Commandments' obligation of children to honor their fathers and mothers. Children fulfilled patriarchal ideals of family reproduction, but also extended familial control over estates, offices, and institutions as children adopted administrative responsibilities. Male children in warrior noble families often took up governmental and military offices at a young age, enhancing their status within their fathers' households.

Patriarchs positioned themselves at the center of a complex series of relationships, which encompassed numerous persons beyond their immediate relatives. A noble household in the early seventeenth century normally included a broader group of nobles, including extended family members, clients, pages, and guests. Noble heads of households maintained personal secretaries, financial assistants, artisans, cooks, laborers, stablehands, valets, and servants to manage their properties and affairs.[36] Many of the personnel of the household also played a decidedly military role for noble families during the civil wars. Personal bodyguards protected warrior nobles and accompanied them on trips and during ceremonies. Armorers and smiths worked to fashion and repair arms and armor for the noble and his followers.

Patriarchal authority had to adapt to the spatial dimensions of warrior noble households, and particularly the domestic space of the *maison*, or house. Warrior noble families in early seventeenth-century Languedoc and Guyenne resided in fortified châteaux that were often partially remodeled medieval castles. The country *maison* revolved around the noble's relationship to violence during the civil wars, and a château would be stockpiled arms and munitions. Although French nobles are frequently depicted as a sedentary and static elite, early seventeenth-century warrior nobles households in Languedoc and Guyenne were actually highly mobile and dynamic. Instead of noble families being tied to one ancient manor in the countryside, warrior nobles frequently moved back and forth among their multiple châteaux and landholdings. Nobles frequently had complete furnishings for only one of their châteaux and took their furniture and decorations with them when they visited another. High-ranking nobles such as ducs, comtes, and marquises were especially likely to own multiple homes. The powerful Arpajons used the château d'Arpajon and the château de Séverac, and may have had more functioning châteaux among their many seigneuries. Even lower-ranking noble families could possess several châteaux, often scattered across several dioceses. The Assas family, for example, traveled between their château d'Assas in the diocese of Montpellier and château de Lavit in the diocese of Nîmes. The Gabriacs held the seigneuries of Beaufort and Gabriac in Rouergue, and in the early seventeenth century they inherited a second residence, the château d'Avèze in the diocese of Gard. Similarly, the Clermont family had several châteaux in Bas Languedoc in this period. Many nobles in southern France also owned hôtels in towns and cities located close to their landholdings. A few noble families had even purchased hôtels in Paris, although this would only become a regular practice for the prominent warrior nobility of Guyenne and Languedoc in the late seventeenth and eighteenth centuries.

Since warrior nobles were so mobile, the notion of household could also be attached to the patriarch's person and his immediate followers. A reduced mobile household—often composed primarily of male family members, clients, and servants—accompanied a warrior noble wherever he went. Antoine-Hercule de Budos marquis de Portes, who was patriarch of the Budos family in the early seventeenth century, provides an example of the flexibility of contemporary practices of organizing households. The Budos family resided in their châteaux at Portes and Theyrargues, near Saint-Ambroix in Languedoc, but Antoine-Hercule was rarely at either residence. The marquis de Portes frequently accompanied his nephew Henri II de Montmorency on trips, military campaigns, and processions. Portes periodically traveled to attend meetings of the estates of Languedoc and the estates of Gévaudan, and even ventured to Paris several times during his life. Almost every year, the marquis de Portes led troops on campaigns throughout Languedoc during the civil wars of the 1610s and 1620s.[37] Patriarchal authority had to grapple with great physical distances, since noble families were often effectively divided into multiple households when traveling or when family members needed to stay in different communities.

Contradictions and compromises arose in warrior noble households over the application of patriarchal authority. Some seventeenth-century philosophical writings identified varieties of "imperfect" families and contemplated the flaws of patriarchy.[38] A household without children represented one type of "imperfect" family. Married couples that remained childless failed to produce a patriarchal household, undermining the statuses of both husband and wife within broader kinship networks. Households headed by unmarried nobles were also considered problematic. Unmarried warrior noblemen who established their own *maisons* obtained independence from their parents, but their own patriarchal authority remained tenuous and their households' stability was precarious. Jean du Caïla de Saint-Bonnet de Toiras's spectacular military successes won him fame and a maréchal's baton, but he never married and died without children. The dangers of childbirth in the early modern period ensured that there were many motherless families in French society. Fathers thus sometimes headed single-parent families after the deaths of their wives, but many patriarchs eventually remarried in order to re-create a complete patriarchal household.

Theoretically, a patriarch's preferences determined his household's religious practices, but personal conscience and religious choice allowed another sort of "imperfect" family to develop, mixed-religious families. Documents occasionally reveal conflicts over religiosity within households, with wives or children opposing patriarchs' confessional identifications. To preserve his family's pious Catholic reputation, one noble from southern France successively altered his will to punish or reward members for their religious choices, disinheriting a daughter for abandoning her convent and his eldest son for becoming a Muslim. The son was reintegrated into the family after his father recognized him as a "good Christian," but he later disappointed his father by becoming a Calvinist.[39]

Especially troubling for nobles in the late sixteenth and early seventeenth-centuries was the anomalous situation of the fatherless household. Warrior nobles enthusiastically exercised the profession of arms, and the extensive civil violence in this period ensured that many noble patriarchs died violent deaths. Noble widows thus sometimes headed single-parent families, acting as the guardians of their young sons. The single-parent royal households of Catherine de Médicis and Marie de Médicis after the tragic deaths of their husbands provided models for noblewomen throughout the kingdom during the religious wars. Many noblewomen directed households at least temporarily during the long absences of their husbands from home because of administrative duties, military campaigns, or imprisonment.

The statuses of male children within patriarchal households produced contestation and challenges to patriarchal authority. Young men were expected to accept fatherly guidance and direction until they were declared adults. Noble fathers who lived long lives created problematic situations for adult sons eager to establish their independence and access their inheritances. The three adult sons of Jean-Louis de Nogaret de La Valette duc d'Épernon all experienced difficult relations with their father, who continued to act as patriarch well into his eighties. Aging fathers sometimes resigned military and administrative offices in order to permit their sons to assume their charges. Noble families with multiple seigneuries could assign secondary or newly acquired titles to sons during the father's lifetime. Épernon's second son Bernard, for example, held the title of marquis de La Valette until he was elevated as duc de La Valette in 1622. Only much later would he become duc d'Épernon upon his father's death. Sons sometimes took up causes in civil conflicts against the will of their fathers. For example, a Huguenot father sought pardon for his son, whose "youth and bad company had led him among the rebels, to the great displeasure of his father."[40] Some sons even faced off against their fathers from opposing camps during civil wars.

Families often provided the settings for disagreement and dispute among various family members and personnel within a household, but rivalries and conflicts between male children were particularly intense. The markedly different statuses accorded the *aîné* (eldest son and principal heir) and *cadets* (younger sons) created intense jealousies among sons. Different legal standings and potentialities for inheritance divided elder and younger brothers.[41] The dramatic quarrels and conflicts between Louis XIII and Gaston de Bourbon within the royal family suggest how similar filial hostility could erupt in powerful noble families. In cases of a patriarch's remarriage, the first wife's sons held higher status than those born of successive wives, often producing resentment.

Extramarital sexual relations provoked some of the most intense conflicts within noble households. Warrior noblemen had ample opportunity to engage in sexual relations while away from home, especially when traveling to court, carrying out administrative duties, or participating in military campaigns. Such sexual relations rarely upset patriarchal authority, but noblemen also sometimes engaged in extramarital sex with persons within their own households. The presence of mistresses and illegitimate children could create extreme tensions in a household. Henri IV's sexual activity with his mistress Gabrielle d'Estrées was widely known, and their illegitimate children were prominent at the early seventeenth-century court.[42] The participation of Estrées's sons César and Alexandre de Vendôme in the conflicts between Louis XIII and Marie de Médicis in the 1610s foregrounded the issue of the status of illegitimate children within French families. Illegitimate children were so prevalent in French society that a body of legislation and legal opinion directly discussed the process of legitimizing "bastard" children and the status of legitimized nobles.[43] Some married noblewomen engaged in sex with other partners, but ran tremendous risks in doing so, facing potential wife-beating or even murder. If adultery was tolerated at times, it was not considered socially or religiously acceptable. Nobles who engaged in scandalous extramarital affairs, or who were merely rumored to do so, could be threatened with ridicule by their peers. Rumors, religious discipline, and legal sanctions increasingly limited transgressions of sexual norms in the late sixteenth and early seventeenth centuries.

Noble households could ultimately disintegrate, as kinship relations ruptured. Tensions could lead to the separation of husbands and wives, sometimes accomplished by wives entering convents. A couple's failure to produce an heir could lead to a separation, as was the case with Henri de Lévis and Marie-Liesse de Luxembourg, or to the annulment of their marriage. Estranged children might spend years separated from their parents. Such disruptions of elite households nonetheless reveal how crucial the concepts of kinship and *maison* were for warrior noble families.

ANCIENT ALLIES
These Great Men among Your Ancestors

An early seventeenth-century warrior noble family represented a household and simultaneously a lineage. Warrior nobles conceived of their families through a temporal conception of kinship, regarding their families as continuous linear progressions of male blood. The idea of lineage was expressed through the familiar image of a tree branching from a common noble root. The author of one noble family's genealogy claimed that he was motivated by his desire "to know these great men among your ancestors who have so gloriously established honor for their descendents."[44] Lineage stressed patriarchy as it constructed kinship across generations through inheritance and legacy. Nobles' lineage conceptions would initially seem to leave little room for consideration of kinship relations, but lineages actually proved to be a highly flexible methods of conceiving of a multigenerational family in the early modern period.

An ideology of *race* pervaded early modern French noble culture, setting the concept of lineage into discourses on blood and ancestry. Arlette Jouanna's research demonstrates that nobles were thought to inherit qualities, transmitted through their blood, which established coherent family characteristics and behavior across generations. Even vast temporal distance between members of a lineage became crunched by this notion of *race*.[45] Physical similarities between nobles and their ancestors were established through portraits, and facial resemblance was considered especially important in exhibiting the continuity of lineages. Portrait galleries and collections of miniatures constituted only part of families' attempts to emphasize masculine kinship and to elaborate their lineages.

Warrior noble heads of households employed a variety of representational strategies to associate themselves with their lineages, but also to distinguish themselves and to proclaim their patriarchal authority. Patriarchs used unique coats of arms, often composed of elements of their parents' devices, as symbols of their households.[46] Manuscript and printed armorials and emblem books can be seen as nobles' attempts to forge lineages and display masculinity. The author of a seventeenth-century compilation of emblems highlighted the importance of the representation of lineage in establishing nobles' authority, noting that "politics can be learned through devices, as history is learned through medals."[47] Specially designed liveries worn by pages and other household servants proclaimed the magnificence of their masters. Young noblemen had to craft their own patriarchal authority when they separated from their father's oversight and formed their own households. The significance of this sort of identification can especially be seen when cadets established their households as distinct branches of a noble lineage.

Seventeenth-century warrior nobles viewed their lineages as full of moral lessons, and they approached their families' past through the ideal of exemplary history. Nobles created personal visions of the past by examining their own lineages. A noble's family history was useful and relevant as an example to emulate, or in certain cases to be avoided. For example, Henri II de Montmorency's biographer felt that the duc was inspired by his frequent reading of his grandfather's exploits. A noble was challenged by the past to live up to the examples of his predecessors.[48] The moral reputation and honor of a family was bound up, a seventeenth-century genealogist explained, in "the virtue of all these great men, your predecessors."[49]

Noble families coordinated officeholding through their lineage's control of offices and officeholding practices. Kin groups controlled, transmitted, bought, sold, and exchanged offices. Families commonly held offices for generations, passing the office down through the lineage. Although individual nobles acted as officers, families normally regarded offices as part of family domains that were to be used for the benefit of the entire kin group. Kinship interests, then, were vital in the exercise of office for the lineage.

The concept of lineage gave warrior noble families a way to establish a legacy of military service and prove the worth of the family. The language used in offers of service emphasized the remembering and recounting of past military activities, and much of this language focused on a numeric accounting of time spent performing services. Offers of royal service and appointments to offices referred to the length of a noble's own past service, the legacy of his family's service, and notable instances of exemplary actions. A summation of maréchal de Praslin's military record, for example, took care to enumerate his "forty-five years of great services rendered to France."[50] The accounting of services could be directly related to another form of accounting—the financial kind. A 1626 ledger book summarizes the services of the Ambres company to justify its payments and to make known the commander's request for "the reimbursement of the costs and expenses that he has already incurred." This sort of accounting represented a historical perspective of service that was central for lineages.[51]

Noble families celebrated their involvement with violence and guarded even the memories of their participation in civil warfare. Many families conserved letters, commissions, receipts, and other documents demonstrating their service in warfare. These documents were later used to request compensation or to prove families' noble status during the *recherches de la noblesse* under Louis XIV. The descendants of the sieur de Saint-Girauld, for example, brought forth his commissions as captain, signed by duc de Montmorency, as part of their proofs of nobility.[52] Nobles associated themselves with former kings and great commanders, claiming to have served them well. Nobles' recounting of their families' services was not done merely to contemplate esoteric interests or to discuss abstract ideas like merit, but to define their lineages. Political motives often shaped nobles' narratives of family military activities, since nobles used the idea of lineage as a justification for their present and future services. For example, warrior nobles often appealed to history to justify their appointments to new offices.[53] Nobles also attempted to establish the historical legacy of their families' services to support their requests for favors and rewards. One noble reminded the secrétaire d'État of his family's record of service by "beseeching the king to remember the signal services that [a family member] rendered and to leave some mark of this memory on our lineage."[54] This practice helps explain why noble families would construct increasingly elaborate genealogies and histories of their service throughout the seventeenth and eighteenth centuries.[55]

Genealogies were part of broader family strategies that nobles used in constructing their lineages. Warrior noble families seem to have begun to regard genealogy as a vital response to the conditions of civil warfare. According to one early seventeenth-century genealogy, "the unhappiness of civil wars, with their animosities and particular quarrels, has been so dangerous for some noble families of this kingdom that the only inheritance for gentlemen is the hereditary possession of their nobility, along with the total ruin of their *maisons*."[56] The systemization of genealogies and *recherches de noblesse* would come only later in the seventeenth century, but the conception of lineage was clearly already highly developed in the early decades of the century.

Lineages might appear to be strictly linear and biologically determined projections of kinship, but warrior noble families consciously crafted their ancestries. French noble patriarchs claimed patrilineal descent as an unbroken chain of honor, but when convenient or necessary, noble families would create new lineages by defining separate branches of the family based on cadets. For example, a younger noble son could become powerful enough to rival or surpass his older brother in power, reputation, or wealth. This situation often split a family into separate lineages, with the younger son becoming the patriarch of a new branch. Noble families also tried to guard the reputation of their lineage, ensuring that the family members were considered *de bonne maison*. When a family was tainted with scandal, a new lineage could be created to preserve the reputation of the family by casting out offending members into another lineage or by erasing the memory of the connection of the family to the old lineage. Alternatively, a family might adopt a new name, drawn from an allied lineage or a new seigneurie, effectively changing the family name and establishing a new lineage.[57] Nobles could also invent blood relations with ancestors, composing genealogies with falsified documents but risking violating laws against usurpation of nobility.

Noble families sometimes faced the effacement of their lineages during civil wars. The inability of a couple to produce male children created the prospect that a lineage might falter as its patrimony was absorbed into another lineage. Conflicts often arose among household members and distant kin over the definition of lineages, especially when families seemed fragile. Uncle-nephew relationships were often particularly complicated for warrior nobles. Michel Nassiet observes that "after the death of his father, the eldest son might see his relationship with his paternal uncle become . . . conflictual, if the partition of the patrimony was still pending or if the cadet contested it."[58] Many warrior nobles were killed during the civil wars, and numerous lineages disappeared each generation in the late sixteenth and early seventeenth centuries.[59] Correspondingly, as old warrior noble lineages were eliminated, new lineages were constantly emerging through ennoblement, promotion, inheritance, and marriage.

His Alliances with Many Great Families of the Kingdom

While struggling to establish the longevity and continuity of their lineages, warrior noble families entered into marriage alliances that forged symbolic and legal unions of families through the creation of kinship during a particular generation. Noble families that claimed ancient lineages simultaneously represented potentially ephemeral alliances that merged two or more families, and transferred money, land, titles, and offices between them.[60] Following a wedding, the extended relatives of a married couple strove to maintain the alliance and perpetuate the union that bonded together the two families. If death or disaster befell the newly formed couple, the allied families would obviously both be impacted. If, on the other hand, the new alliance prospered, the kin relations could stand to benefit from the marriage alliance.

Warrior noble families used diverse marriage strategies in their attempts to maintain or advance their status and patrimony. Noble patriarchs often attempted to arrange hypergamous marriages for their children with higher-ranking families, since such a match confirmed patriarchal authority and raised the household's status. Although many noble families could not hope to marry up into families of markedly higher status and wealth, they normally firmly resisted hypogamous alliances with families of sharply lower rank. Among the broader provincial nobility, marriage alliances between distinguished families and lesser noble families were always possible, as were marriages between new and old noble families. Entering into *mésalliance*, an extreme form of unequal marriage in which nobles wedded commoners, created scandal within noble culture and posed a dangerous threat to social stability, although such alliances did occur and cases of *mésalliance* among noble widows may have been common.[61] The vast majority of noble families seem to have concluded homogamous marriages with other families at a roughly similar social rank. Members of ducal families, for example, tended to arrange alliances with other prominent families among the *grands*, and they uniformly avoided *mésalliance*.[62]

Even when arranging homogamous marriages with families of similar rank, noble families employed a wide array of marriage strategies. Warrior noble patriarchs attempted to maintain their dominion over the family patrimony through marriage alliances that preserved their families' inheritance and strengthened their political relationships. Not surprisingly, then, many warrior noble families in Languedoc and Guyenne arranged alliances with families that were immersed in the same clientage and military networks. Confessional affiliation clearly guided warrior nobles' marriage strategies, as Catholic and Calvinist nobles married into the families with whom they participated in religious conflict. Anne de Lévis duc de Ventadour married Marguerite de Montmorency, solidifying his military connections with the duc de Montmorency. The Calvinist military commander Charles-René du Puy de Tournon marquis de Montbrun married into the powerful Huguenot La Force family.[63] Michel Nassiet's detailed study of

noble marriage strategies in the fifteenth and sixteenth centuries reveals a series of patterns of cyclical intermarriages and repeated alliances between the
same lineages.[64] First-cousin marriages seem to have been somewhat rare, but
many families sought alliances with more distant cousins.[65] Many nobles opted
to forge endogamous alliances by intermarriage within the wider branches of
their families, since alliances between cousins allowed for nobles to protect patrimonies from passing out of a lineage's hands. Noble families could select the
eldest daughter of a family lacking male children as bride for one of their sons,
hoping that their new daughter-in-law would later inherit the allied lineage's
properties and wealth.[66] Noble families often seem to have adopted differing
strategies for their successive children, privileging the eldest son and dealing
with younger sons and daughters in various ways. Although various strategies
of arranging marriages thus allowed families to construct kinship to fit their
immediate needs and concerns, determining families' marriage strategies ret-
roactively from the resulting matches risks misunderstanding the processes of
forging alliances and the operations of the marriage market.

The selection of spouses resulted not from simple rational choices, but from
complex processes of discussion and debate within noble households. The selection of suitable matches was often done under the supervision of noble patriarchs, who attempted to exert control over their family members' sexuality and
bodies through the selection of children's marriage partners. However, the relatively late age at which many nobles married and the ideals of marital love may
have given children increased voice in choosing their spouses, and the possibility of clandestine marriages undermined patriarchal control.[67] Mothers, aunts,
and sisters were often closely involved in selecting potential partners through
correspondence, *salons*, and gift exchanges.[68] Extended relatives entered into the
decision-making process by proposing matches and introducing suitors.

Families' marital strategies had to adapt to the desires of various brokers
who mediated in marriage negotiations. These negotiations were often protracted
affairs in the early seventeenth century, since they involved not only the two
families in question but other interested individuals and families. The resulting
matches were frequently the product of tortuous maneuvers and strategic contestations, rather than a mere conscious selection of marriage partners by two
noble patriarchs. Royal family members and ministers often played important
roles in marriage negotiations between the *grands* and other prominent noble
families. Marie de Médicis actively worked to arrange warrior noble marriages
in the 1610s, including that of the young Henri II de Montmorency to Maria
Felicia Orsini.[69] After the Orsini bride arrived in Languedoc, the groom's father,

Henri I de Montmorency, expressed his satisfaction with his new daughter-in-law and praised the queen mother's judgment in arranging the marriage, saying that "I feel infinitely obliged to Your Majesty for the honor that you have given my son in choosing for his wife such a wise and virtuous princess, whose presence brings me such joy."[70] After 1617, Louis XIII's personal approval became vital for concluding marriages among many of the *grands*, and even some prominent provincial noble families. In the provinces of Languedoc and Guyenne, noble patrons often brokered marriages between their noble clients' families. There are hints that prominent judges, lawyers, and notaries may have also played roles in facilitating marriages among provincial noble families, especially in negotiating the detailed status provisions and financial exchanges that were integral to weddings.

Written marriage contracts formalized the alliance and designated the amount of the *dot*, or dowry, that the bride's family would provide to the groom. The groom's family often guaranteed certain funds and belongings, called a *douaire*, for the use of the bride. The spectacular marriage of Henri II de Montmorency and Maria Felicia Orsini involved the exchange of a *dot* of 600,000 livres and a *douaire* of 300,000 livres and a château.[71] Most warrior noble marriage contracts stipulated exchanges of more modest, though still appreciable, sums. Gloriande de Thémines reportedly had a dowry of 42,000 écus (126,000 livres) when she married Louis d'Arpajon in 1622.[72] The financial aspects of dowries are examined in more detail below, but it is important at this point to recognize that dowries often represented relative appraisals of family status at the moment of a marriage alliance more than fixed monetary exchanges. When marriage alliances brought new seigneuries or titles into a family, the patriarch might add a new name or change the family name to demonstrate the alliance's significance or to show newly acquired status.[73] Name changing revealed the degree to which warrior nobles responded to momentary situations and conceived of their families as immediate temporal constructions. Marriage contracts thus established social status and confirmed precedence rankings within warrior noble culture.

Marriage ceremonies reinforced the creation of kinship through alliance. Clergy provided confessional sanction for marriage alliances and confirmed religious discipline in marriage ceremonies. The bonding of the couple was sustained by family members or friends who witnessed the ceremony.[74] Family members, close local allies, and coreligionists were present at marriage rites. These witnesses confirmed the new alliance and in theory gave their consent to the arrangements and took on responsibilities to support the couple. Marriage ceremonies thus reinforced confessional solidarity and produced alliances that confirmed religious boundaries. Catholic warrior nobles' weddings might assemble a number of officers who normally participated in religious conflict together. The ceremonies of Calvinist warrior nobles similarly replicated military networks.

Mixed-confession alliances presented particular problems for weddings in early seventeenth-century southern France. Philip Benedict provides notarial evidence on mixed-confession marriage patterns in Montpellier, noting that "mixed marriages in seventeenth-century France were generally preceded by the formal conversion of one party or the other, generally the woman, so that both halves of the future couple could qualify as members of the same church at the time of their marriage." Partners who converted prior to the marriage ceremonies sometimes reconverted later, leading some historians to argue that such conversions were "purely strategic."[75] However, there were many plausible motivations for ostensibly mixed-confession marriages, and we should not jettison religious motivations in examining family strategies. Not only could mixed-confession marriages reflect families' pragmatism, or perhaps even mutual toleration, but they may also suggest the interplay of confessional politics within families. Many of these alliances may have resulted from sincere conversions at the time of marriage or from families' hopes of bringing about "true" conversions of spouses' initially "strategic" ones.

Wedding ceremonies were often soon followed by births, since nobles intended for marriage alliances to reproduce and perpetuate their families. Families needed a male child to serve as principal heir according to the norms of primogeniture, and most families strove to have several male children, given the high infant mortality rates of the early modern period. Reproduction was considered vital to married noblewomen's honor and central to their status within their families. Childbirth was extremely dangerous in the early modern period, and many noblewomen died in labor. As we have already seen, marriage sometimes resulted in "imperfect" families that failed to reproduce due to impotency, infant mortality, or a parent's death. Noble households anticipated pregnancies and rejoiced at successful births as great events that extended conjugal families and fulfilled marriage alliances.

Baptism ceremonies, witnessed by extended family members, clients, and friends, provided vital contexts for the forging of kinship. Calvinists and Catholics invested godparenting with sacred significance in differing ways, but both regarded godparents' spiritual kinship and promised support as important. As Robert A. Schneider has shown, godparenting "was endowed with specifically

religious meanings," yet at the same time baptism provided "an occasion to declare formal friendships, create fictive kinships, and affirm social solidarities."[76]
Grandparents or noble patrons often served as godparents at noble baptisms.
Henri II de Montmorency, for example, seems to have participated in numerous
Catholic baptisms in southern France.[77] Huguenot nobles similarly acted as god-
fathers for Calvinist noble children. The Calvinist noble Claude de Calvière
baron de Saint-Côme served as godfather at the 1622 baptism of Charles de Baschi, son of the Huguenot commander Louis II de Baschi baron d'Aubais.[78] The
successful reproduction celebrated in baptism thus established spiritual kinship
between a child, his or her parents, and their extended relatives and fictive kin,
reaffirming the couple's status and securing the marriage alliance.

✝

Early seventeenth-century conceptions of kinship significantly influenced how
warrior nobles participated in civil conflicts. Prominent provincial nobles'
household organizations promoted patriarchal authority and announced their
families' grandeur. Multifaceted conceptions of kinship suggest some of the
ways in which noble families crafted their identities within noble culture. Their
understandings of lineage celebrated family memory and promoted political and
religious action in the name of cherished ancestors. Warrior nobles crafted marriage alliances that reflected military concerns as well as family strategies, so the
profession of arms greatly influenced warrior households and their kinship practices. As we shall see in the next chapter, warrior noble families adopted highly
complex strategies for mobilizing their wealth and maintaining their status,
which were shaped by their use of credit and their involvement in civil violence.

A warrior noble family's château, suggesting their seigneurial wealth. Drawing by Étienne Martellange, *Le Château de Polignac près de la ville du Puy,* BNF, Estampes, Dessins Martellange 142. Photo courtesy Bibliothèque Nationale de France.

CHAPTER THREE

He Had No Trouble Helping Himself to Money

Crédit *and Noble Finances*

W hen Jean-Louis de La Valette duc d'Épernon raised Catholic forces in southwestern France in 1617, "he had no difficulty helping himself to money from [the king's] receipts for the levy of his troops." He justified his use of royal tax money on grounds that he was acting to oppose Calvinist sedition in La Rochelle and to advance "the king's service." Nearly five thousand men soon assembled, funded "with these sums, although small, and something of his own," according to the duc's secretary.[1] Épernon could undoubtedly draw on immense financial resources in contributing "something of his own" to the mobilization of this Catholic army.

Warrior nobles exploited diverse sources of wealth and credit in order to engage in civil conflict. Members of the provincial military elite in southern France had extensive landholdings and seigneurial wealth. Although early modern French nobles are often depicted as purely landed elites, warrior nobles clearly amassed monetary wealth and invested in ways that can be considered capitalistic. Their significant financial investments in officeholding and status positions accumulated new types of wealth. The contemporary concept of *crédit*, a mixture of financial status and personal reputation, suggests how warrior nobles exploited complex financial instruments to accumulate experience, wealth, and influence. Provincial military elites also relied on their *crédit* to protect their patrimonies and to defend their privileges during destructive civil wars. *Crédit* underpinned the entire profession of arms.

NOBLE WEALTH

Warrior noble families constructed their households flexibly, but their practical kinship relations were limited and conditioned by their material possessions and assets. Comprehending how warrior noble families participated in provincial life requires some understanding of noble wealth. Unfortunately, assessing the wealth available to noble families in the sixteenth and seventeenth centuries is complicated by poor and incomplete documentation.[2] "Can [Gilles de] Gouberville be considered as a wealthy man? I would not presume to say," George Huppert observes frankly of one of the nobles he studied.[3] Even where substantial records of noble finances remain, one can never be sure of the veracity of noble families' financial claims. Nobles had many incentives for hiding income and misrepresenting their actual worth. Warrior nobles probably underestimated their income routinely in their pleas for financial assistance from the monarch and from provincial institutions. Many of the noblemen who claimed to have been impoverished by warfare and disasters during religious and civil wars may have exaggerated their losses to obtain compensation. Underreporting income enabled nobles to avoid paying a variety of fees and indirect taxes. The most reliable appraisals of noble families' finances and seigneurial revenues were probably those that were performed in conjunction with marriage contracts, wills, or estate settlements after death. Yet, these financial documents, often held in disorganized and uncatalogued notarial archives, might take a lifetime to examine at the provincial level.

While only a fragmentary and unsatisfactory sketch of warrior noble finances can be drawn here, an understanding of warrior nobles' economic resources and financial activities can be developed. Until recently, early modern French nobles were usually portrayed as idle, wasteful, and unresourceful because of their lavish spending. They were assumed to be ignorant of economic relations and disdainful of mercantile wealth. But early modern nobles actually seem to have fairly well appreciated the proto-capitalist market relations that were playing an increasing role in early modern European economies. Early seventeenth-century French warrior nobles undertook commercial investments and viewed their wealth through an expansive notion of patrimony that included the traditional emphasis on landed wealth, but that also incorporated income from *rentes*, offices, and other sources. We can gain a better understanding of nobles' economic power and resources by exploring the complex financial strategies that they used to manage their seigneurial, monetary, official, and status wealth.

Seigneurial Wealth

One of the main sources of income for noble families was their seigneurial wealth. Peasants who lived on seigneuries in early modern France usually rented land as sharecroppers by repaying their noble landlord with portions of their crops. Other tenants on seigneuries paid rents to the noble lord in monetary form. While seigneurial wealth is normally thought of as landed wealth, seigneurial income also included the economic benefits derived from numerous seigneurial rights and dues.[4] Nobles received seigneurial dues such as the *droit de corvée*, which involved peasants' labor obligations to maintain the lord's domain, roads, and other elements of the seigneurie. Peasants often had to pay to have their wheat ground at the lord's mill, and had limited access to the forests, ponds, and wildlife on his seigneurie. Nobles also profited from toll payments to transport goods through their seigneuries, and these could be especially lucrative along rivers. Many nobles in Languedoc and Guyenne maintained vineyards and profited from wine sales.

Seigneurial wealth in the seventeenth century was very flexible. Noble families derived immense wealth and regular payments from their estates, but only if they managed them carefully. William Weary has shown that to obtain their landed incomes, noble families frequently needed to demand payments of dues, engage in debt collection, and even make confiscations.[5]

Nobles could also potentially make huge profits off the rural land market by buying and selling seigneuries. Making investments in repairing châteaux could increase the value of a seigneurie. Some nobles invested in improving the land on their seigneuries by draining swamps and reallocating lands. Building projects, such as road improvements and bridge building, could further enhance the value of seigneuries.[6] When nobles needed to raise money quickly or felt that they could make profits on the land market, they sold seigneuries for anywhere between several thousand and several hundred thousand livres.[7]

The records of seigneurial rents and land purchases provide a glimpse into seigneurial wealth, and offer one of the few ways to gauge the relative wealth of nobles in early modern France.[8] In the provinces of Languedoc and Guyenne, we can only really guess at the wealth of a few powerful *grands* in this period. The duc d'Épernon probably received around 139,000 livres each year in landed income, out of a total income of perhaps 294,000 livres.[9] The Montmorency family controlled lands worth between 125,000 and 150,000 livres in the 1560s. The precise seigneurial fortunes of regional nobles below the exalted ranks of the *grands* are very difficult to assess.

Ecclesiastical benefices provided a substantial portion of the seigneurial wealth of noble families that controlled the landed wealth of the abbeys and bishoprics they held. Families that were in charge of abbeys in the early modern period often managed large assets. Bishops received a significant portion, and often as much as 30 to 40 percent, of the total revenues of their dioceses. In addition to the *dîme*, or tithe, that the Roman Catholic Church collected, taxes, offerings, and fees swelled a bishop's coffers. The archbishopric of Toulouse and the bishopric of Albi in Languedoc, as well as the bishoprics of Rodez and Cahors in Guyenne, received substantial incomes, which were above average when compared to other ecclesiastical benefices in France. The wealth of these benefices was in part due to the seizures of property of the Cathars during the suppression of the Albigensian heresy in the thirteenth century.[10] Families holding bishoprics struggled to maintain their income and to defend their ecclesiastical properties from Huguenot seizures during the sixteenth-century religious wars. Calvinists frequently occupied and redistributed Catholic church lands and properties in Languedoc and Guyenne.

Warrior noble families sought to expand their seigneurial wealth whenever possible. Inheritance could bring new seigneuries into families, dramatically changing their fortunes. Land transfers accompanied marriages, and seigneurial wealth often made up significant portions of brides' dowries. Some noble families were able to greatly increase their seigneurial wealth through successive marriage alliances, however, these methods only brought seigneurial wealth to families occasionally and unpredictably. Participation in civil warfare offered great opportunities for warrior nobles to gain seigneurial wealth, since army commanders routinely rewarded their loyal officers with lands and châteaux confiscated from their enemies.

Monetary Wealth

While studies of the French nobility still often associate noble wealth primarily with landed assets, early seventeenth-century warrior nobles were immersed in a monetary economy. Financial exchanges pervaded the social relations, office-holding practices, and market activities in which nobles routinely engaged.[11] Although nobles could inherit vast fortunes, sometimes little of their initial wealth was monetary, since previous generations often left massive debts to be paid off by their heirs. Nobles relied heavily on the monetary wealth that they amassed from diverse sources.

Marriages brought in vast new moneys through dowries paid by the bride's family to the groom. Noble patriarchs normally negotiated dowry amounts, which were agreed upon in marriage contracts that also specified the method of payment and provisions for the use of the dowry.[12] While dowries could sometimes amount to tens of thousands of livres, only a portion of a dowry was liquid, since the bulk of it would be reserved for the bride's protection. Dowries were often paid in successive installments from father to daughter, which could stretch over many years.[13] Noble families also had to save money for their own daughters' dowries. Adrien de Monluc must have received a huge dowry when he married into the powerful Foix-Carmain family in 1592, but Monluc later had to provide a considerable dowry of 100,000 livres for his daughter's marriage into the Escoubleau family in 1612.[14] Nobles also had to contend with a competitive marriage market, as average dowry amounts seem to have gradually increased during the late sixteenth and seventeenth centuries.[15]

Pensions provided many warrior nobles with direct monetary payments from the royal treasury. Royal pensions could be unreliable sources of income, however, since payments were often irregular, and they might be entirely suspended.[16] Warrior noble families often received significant indirect monetary income from the king and various royal institutions. The king paid for the personal bodyguards of many nobles, and especially for many of the *grands*. Royal and provincial institutions frequently paid for nobles' garrisons, or for a portion thereof. Royal family members and powerful patrons distributed monetary gifts to the nobles who served them. Warrior nobles often benefited from monetary payments and gifts to their clients and followers by other individuals and institutions.

Warrior noble families used complex investment and fiscal strategies to manage large monetary fortunes in the early modern period. Managing money involved negotiating the complex systems of accounting and varying coin values of sixteenth- and seventeenth-century money. Transactions normally relied on the "money of account" of the livre tournois to determine prices, then varying types of coins—each with a value relative to the money of account—would be used in payments.[17] Nobles used their money in capitalistic fashion by making investments, borrowing funds, lending money, and engaging in commerce. Although debates about the acceptability of noble investment in commercial activities raged in French pamphlet literature in the seventeenth century, many nobles did participate in mercantile enterprises. Some invested indirectly, using front men to handle transactions, but nobles did invest their monetary wealth in mining, artisanal crafts, and certain commercial enterprises.[18]

Sixteenth- and seventeenth-century French nobles also invested in *rentes*, or annuities, which were sold both by nobles and the monarch in two ways. The *rente foncière* that had emerged in the late medieval period provided nobles with a means to transfer land, houses, and other properties to another person in return for an annuity held in perpetuity. The *rente constituée* was a sixteenth-century development of *rente* practices in which only money was exchanged. Nobles using this form of *rente* would invest a sum of money with a noble, banking family, municipality, or royal family member in return for a perpetual annuity that provided them with a regular annual income. *Rentes constituées* issued by municipalities or the monarch were an early form of government bonds. For warrior nobles, *rentes* provided excellent opportunities to raise cash quickly through what essentially amounted to personal loans that could be easily negotiated. *Rentes* of both types were attractive to early modern French nobles because, as Raymond A. Mentzer explains, they provided "secure investment opportunities" at "competitive rates of return."[19] Nobles investing in *rentes* could negotiate lucrative contracts providing loan repayment rates of between 8 and 10 percent. By the sixteenth century, George Huppert suggests, "everyone who lived nobly was a possessor of *rentes*."[20] The Calvinist Lacger family in Languedoc, which invested more than a third of its resources in *rentes* during the seventeenth century, gives us some indication of how popular *rentes* were among nobles in southern France.[21]

In the late sixteenth and early seventeenth centuries, many nobles invested large sums in *rentes sur l'Hôtel de ville* in Paris, essentially government bonds, receiving interest payments in installments in return.[22] Noble families were thus creditors of the monarchy, providing substantial funds for the operation of government, with the assurance that they would receive regular income from the fixed interest payments provided by the *rentes*. Some French nobles also invested in other credit institutions located in more distant commercial centers, such as the Monte di Pietà di Firenze.[23] Warrior nobles also acted as bankers themselves, extending both short-term and long-term loans to tenants, clients, and other members of society, which were often arranged by notaries.

To fund their investments, warrior noble families raised extensive amounts of money through personal loans and sales of goods. Nobles used expensive jewelry as collateral for personal loans from banking elites, noble patrons, and clients. Jewelry, clothing, and arms could be sold off to acquire specie quickly. Additional monetary wealth could be raised through sales of lands, rights, contracts, and other assets. Warrior nobles collected additional monetary income through their participation in civil warfare since commanding troops allowed warrior nobles to benefit directly from the plundering and pillaging that accompanied sixteenth- and seventeenth-century warfare. Whenever towns and cities were taken by siege, victorious armies would pillage the inhabitants' goods, and officers would claim their share of the plunder. Noble officers and their troops also received monetary payments from communities eager to avoid the destructive tendencies of marauding soldiers. Some nobles acquired vast monetary wealth by seizing taxes from financial officials during civil conflicts. Following military campaigns, nobles also gained recompensation for their military services and their expenses incurred in financing war. For example, Louis XIII granted Marc-Antoine de Graves sieur de Longuet a pension of 1,200 livres in 1630 specifically in recognition of his military services.[24] Negotiated peaces that were intended to end civil conflicts often included vast pensions to nobles.[25]

If periods of civil conflict gave warrior nobles opportunities to enhance their monetary wealth, violence and social chaos could also play havoc with noble finances. Many noble families in southern France experienced interruptions of their monetary income because of the destructiveness of civil warfare and the breakdown of communications. The burdensome costs of raising and maintaining troops to participate in civil conflict forced many nobles to incur huge debts during and after civil wars. Regional economic disruption and broader changes in economic conditions due to civil conflict could radically upset noble family fortunes, as well as the general monetary economy.

Official Wealth

Warrior nobles invested heavily in royal officeholding, deriving official wealth through income, profit, and remuneration. Since at least the twelfth century, some royal offices had been sold, and increasing numbers of appointments were made this way throughout the late medieval period. By the early sixteenth century, many types of financial and judicial offices were being legally sold to eager investors on an official market, and over the course of that century, venality—the practice of buying and selling offices—became more generalized and regular. Despite the growing royal acceptance of venality, the redistribution of offices occurred largely in extralegal, unsanctioned, and informal ways.[26]

Jurists and some warrior nobles did continue to debate the merits of sales of judicial offices, but venality was a legally accepted aspect of military and administrative officeholding by the early 1600s. Disagreements and conflicts occurred over the types of regulations, numbers of offices to be sold, costs of purchasing offices, and methods of transferring offices, but the principle of venality was well established and nobles frequently exchanged royal offices on a fluctuating market.

To become an officer, one had to be nominated or commissioned, but most offices were either explicitly or implicitly hereditary. An office that had been declared hereditary was simply passed on to the legal heir at the death of the officeholder. For other offices, an officer could obtain a *survivance* to assure the transmission of his office to his heir. An officer could also resign in favor of another individual of his choice, using a *résignation*. Once families gained an office, they had to take on the costs of carrying out the office's functions, which could be extremely high. The royal budget rarely granted sufficient funds to any royal officers to meet the actual costs of administration. Furthermore, the royal court and noble culture promoted expectations that noble officers would maintain their official status through attention to their own appearance and that of their followers and servants. Maintaining appearances included dressing well, entertaining fellow nobles, granting gifts and favors, and lavish spending.

Investing in offices required the initial investment of immense sums in the purchase of office through the venal system.[27] The costs of investing in offices could be astronomical, especially for offices at royal court and in the military high command. Purchasing command as an infantry captain would cost thousands of livres. A mestre de camp of a prestigious infantry regiment might pay 69,000 livres for his command in the 1620s.[28] The seigneur de Châtillon purchased the government of the town of Aigues-Mortes for 30,000 écus (90,000 livres) in 1616.[29] A systematic study of the costs of military offices is complicated by insufficient documentation until the mid-seventeenth century.

While investing in purchasing offices could be quite expensive, officeholding provided nobles with secure, regular income. Once purchased, offices would only provide the officeholder with an income worth a fraction of the investment, but noble families relied heavily on the steady official incomes conferred by the regular pensions and *gages* attached to many offices. For example, Henri II de Montmorency received a regular pension of 10,000 livres for his position as admiral of France between 1616 and 1626.[30] As the provincial governor of Guyenne, the duc d'Épernon received 16,000 livres pension and 6,000 livres for *états et appointements* during a typical year. The king gave Épernon an annual pension of 10,000 livres for his position as colonel-général de l'infanterie français, as well as a salary of 20,000–30,000 livres and an additional grant of a percentage of the *gages*.[31] In contrast, the seigneur de Châtillon received a smaller pension of 3,000 livres for his post as admiral of Guyenne.[32] While the pensions and *gages* that most nobles received as officeholders were often relatively small, noble families could hold an office over numerous generations and then could sell it to recoup the investment at any time. During the early seventeenth century, the prices of many offices were soaring on a fluctuating office market, and nobles could hope to gain substantial profits for their offices when they sold them.[33]

Gifts and gratifications, which were given by individuals and institutions as compensation for services or favors performed by nobles, further bolstered their incomes. The king frequently granted gratifications to officeholders in addition to their regular pensions and *gages*, but the amount of these gratifications varied, unlike the set amounts of the regular pensions. The gratification given to the duc de Montmorency each year for his office of admiral of France usually exceeded the amount of his regular pension.[34] The estates of Languedoc voted to grant a series of gratifications at almost every meeting, usually providing the largest sums to the provincial governor and the lieutenant general. In a series of grants from the estates in January 1622, the duc de Ventadour received 10,000 livres, the comte de La Voulte got 4,000 livres, and the duc d'Uzès took in 5,000 livres. Meanwhile, various nobles, consuls, and clergy shared over 200,000 livres.[35] Gratifications could significantly augment the income of provincial nobles. Antoine-Hercule de Budos marquis de Portes received gratifications of 6,000 livres several times during the 1610s and 1620s.[36]

Having engaged enormous sums in purchasing and maintaining their offices, nobles expected to gain substantially from their investments. Personal and family financial gain through official duties was not only accepted, it was condoned and encouraged by noble culture. Military elites who gained financially through civil warfare were lauded by their peers, though their methods were frequently condemned by their enemies. The complicated question of whether or not most noble officers gained or lost money through their officeholding investments is difficult to answer fully. Clearly, military elites advanced large amounts of their personal fortunes to pay costs incurred in the fulfillment of their official duties. But noble officers received both official and unofficial remuneration from the monarch and other governmental bodies.

Officers could attempt to recoup their investments through repayments granted by judicial courts or by the monarchy for their personal expenditures made in the exercise of office. The chambre des comptes de Montpellier and the cour des aides de Montpellier both compensated nobles for their financial losses incurred in official duties in Languedoc. However, requests were frequently denied, for numerous reasons. Even if nobles' requests for remuneration were granted, they could be very late or in much reduced amounts. In the 1620s, the cour des aides was still considering cases that stretched back to the 1580s and 1590s.[37] Nobles often relied on their patrons to obtain compensation from the courts for them. For example, Montmorency intervened on the behalf of the sieur de Bertich-ières, who wanted to be recompensed for the government of Aigues-Mortes.[38] The king could grant royal pensions paid from the royal treasury to nobles as a form of recompense, but pensions rarely amounted to more than a supplemental income for noble officeholders in the early seventeenth century.

Of course, nobles knew that direct, state-controlled financial remuneration was insufficient and unreliable. They also expected to gain from their offices in other ways. Noble officeholders received compensation for their financial in-vestment in the form of status, influence, followers, and clients. These benefits could lead to further gains of additional offices, influence, and power. Since of-fices were viewed as investments, nobles also hoped to gain money through sales of offices. Most nobles seem to have sold off offices in order to invest in new ones. During the negotiations for sales of offices, noble patrons looked out for their clients. When Jean Zamet sold his regiment to Roger du Plessis marquis de Liancourt in 1622 for 22,000 écus, he arranged for Liancourt to give 1000 écus to Louis de Pontis, Zamet's lieutenant, in an agreement directly linked to the sale of the office.[39] Whatever the balance sheet of their financial costs and ben-efits, nobles unquestionably attempted to advance their financial interests through their exercise of office.

Status Wealth

Historians have long recognized the importance of lavish spending for early modern noble families, and French nobles spent vast sums on clothing, furnish-ings, art, and other luxuries. Although nobles' displays of wealth have been seen as frivolous extravagances, recent work stresses the importance of conspicuous consumption as a vital means of establishing and securing nobles' statuses and self-identities. Nobles defined themselves partially through their ability to live nobly, that is, to be able to afford a luxurious lifestyle and a standard of living befitting a French noble on the basis of peers' judgements. The extravagant dis-plays of wealth so popular with early modern nobles established status wealth, but also represented ways of furthering their political aims and developing eco-nomic investments.

The display of wealth to enhance status was perhaps most conspicuous in the person of the noble. Members of the military elite dressed in the finest clothing made of the highest-quality fabrics, including silk and velvet. Warrior nobles often wore colorful embroidered silk doublets over their billowing white shirts with delicate lace collars and trim. Flamboyant hats and bright plumes topped off the well-dressed warrior noble's costume. Huguenot nobles normally dressed in a somewhat more austere fashion than their Catholic counterparts, since Calvinist preaching stressed the sinfulness of extravagance. Where Catholic nobles frequently wore clothing of many bright colors, Huguenots tended to dress in more sober hues of black, gray, and brown. Despite these differences, all French nobles set themselves off from the rest of society by wearing swords, which served as distinguishing marks of their nobility. Warrior nobles carried expensive swords with ornate gilded guards, which were often encrusted with precious stones. When on campaign, warrior nobles may have dressed somewhat less ostentatiously, but they then donned ornate armor and helmets trimmed with precious metals to display their status.

Nobles surrounded themselves with large retinues of followers as shows of status wealth and of power. Nobles outfitted large households with huge numbers of servants and bodyguards, which required investing in clothing, armor, arms, equipment, supplies, and horses for their followers. Warrior nobles competed to have the largest and most impressive households in their regions. Household servants and bodyguards sometimes wore liveries, often consisting of identical doublets, designed to distinguish their noble patriarch and confirm his status. Elements of spending on households also amounted to economic investment. For example, nobles actively engaged in the buying and selling of expensive horses, often reaping huge profits from the horse trade.[40] All of this spending on households went well beyond mere conspicuous consumption, since bodyguards and noble retainers obviously provided nobles with protection and a means to intimidate others.

Expenditures on their properties also offered warrior nobles ways of enhancing their prestige and status. When nobles armed their bodyguards and followers, they drew on the market in arms and armor to invest in huge stockpiles of arms and ammunition to create armories in their châteaux. The size of these armories went well beyond the needs of nobles' households, amounting to magazines that could be used to raise troops if needed. Warrior nobles also invested large sums in fortifying châteaux and improving their defenses as a means of providing protection and of improving their status within their local areas. Many nobles remodeled their châteaux or built entirely new châteaux in the early seventeenth century to enhance their prestige and increase the market value of their seigneuries. Architectural treatises by Leon Battista Alberti, Jacques Androuet de Cerceau, Pierre Le Muet, and others were available in new editions and translations, providing French nobles ideas and advice about how to use their status wealth in building projects.[41] Nobles in Languedoc and Guyenne purchased urban space and built hôtels to display their importance within towns and cities. Warrior nobles' urban residences were defensible sites within urban areas, but the hôtels were also built to impress, with elaborate balconies and stairways built around open courtyards. Festivities, concerts, plays, and ceremonies could all be held in the hôtels to assert and show off the status wealth of their noble owners. These hôtels represented long-term investments that could later be sold when noble families needed to raise cash or when prices rose for land in cramped urban areas, which was increasingly sought after.

Early modern French nobles invested in lavish furnishings for their châteaux and hôtels as ways of displaying their status wealth. Nobles' homes were often adorned with ornate walls, often lined in fine wood paneling, and tiled floors. Expensive glass windows let abundant light into most rooms. Rooms were filled with hand-carved wooden armoires, chests, and chairs. Tables were adorned with velour tablecloths, and could be set with fine dishes and silverware. Each château included a library filled with expensive leather-bound books. Embroidered draperies and tapestries graced the windows and walls of noble homes.[42] One Languedoc noble family was able to afford a number of Flemish tapestries, as well as several tapestries from Bergamo and from the Ottoman Empire. Painted portraits and other paintings decorated the walls of most noble residences. An altar occupied a key place in a Catholic noble family's home, and religious art was prominent, including crosses, crucifixes, and images of the Virgin Mary. Calvinists viewed such religious art objects as idols and avoided having them in their homes. Huguenot nobles tended to have more sober, but still elaborate, decoration in their châteaux and hôtels.[43] The opulence and grandeur of nobles' belongings and furnishings thus served to showcase their status wealth to all visitors.

CRÉDIT AND INFLUENCE

Early modern French noble families' management of wealth is incomprehensible without an understanding of the multilayered concept of *crédit*. Jonathan Dewald argues that *crédit* "became a central metaphor of seventeenth-century public life," as nobles engaged in market capitalism, investment banking, and complex financial activities.[44] Recent research demonstrates that seventeenth-century French nobles were important creditors of monarchic institutions and public finance.[45] Tracing the circulation of wealth through early modern French noble families exposes extensive financial credit operations. Early seventeenth-century warrior nobles mobilized and employed wealth using numerous flexible credit mechanisms both within and beyond their households.

These financial transactions reveal new dimensions of noble families' power, as early modern French conceptions of *crédit* operated simultaneously in economic, social, and cultural fields. Social assessments of a warrior noble's financial credit and reputation were critical both for the maintenance of his patriarchal authority and for the functioning of his household. Masculinity and creditworthiness intersected in appraisals of the status and wealth of early modern nobles in France and throughout Europe.[46] Disputes over honor, debt repayment, and fiscal reputation merged, provoking conflicts and duels in the early seventeenth century. Early modern French nobles used a language of *crédit* to discuss their exchanges, obligations, and services—both financial and political.[47] This language acquired pervasive implications by the early seventeenth century: "*crédit* was derived from personal reputation, rank, title and family name, wealth, officeholding, clients, and patrons."[48] *Crédit* thus represented a social evaluation of personal and family influence and power in a variety of spheres.

Warrior noble families sought to extend their *crédit* by activating kinship and mobilizing their wealth. A recommendation by Henri II de Montmorency for a family member illustrates the reciprocal exchanges of service and favor involved in engaging political and social *crédit*. Montmorency writes directly to the queen regent to make his recommendation, already performing a valuable service. He then explains that his cousin asked to be given leave to go to the royal court himself, but Montmorency needs his help in Languedoc because of his "faithfulness" and "*crédit*." Thus Montmorency asks that the queen regent allow his cousin to continue to serve as mestre de camp of the regiment of Languedoc.[49] Montmorency's letter also reveals the evaluations of confidence, creditworthiness, and faithfulness implicit in everyday operations of personal and family *crédit*. In assessing nobles' political influence, Sharon Kettering distinguishes sharply between authority and *crédit*: "authority was the formal exercise of structured power. *Crédit* was influence outside the formal exercise of structured power which, nonetheless, determined its operation."[50] Early seventeenth-century nobles' discussions of influence and power suggest that authority and *crédit* overlapped significantly, however. In 1622, for example, the duc de Montmorency sought to establish "someone of *crédit* and authority to command" in the dioceses of Castres and Lavaur.[51] Noble officers acted as creditors for the monarch through direct loans to royal family members, purchases of *rentes sur l'Hôtel de Ville*, and indirect loans. The intersections between formal and informal power become clearer by examining warrior noble families' attempts to promote their influence and extend their *crédit* by defending their privileges, protecting their patrimonies, and gaining experience.

Gaining Experience

Warrior noble families strove to extend their *crédit* and expand their influence within French society. Historians have recently found that social mobility was much more possible in early modern France than many had previously thought. New noble families were created frequently through ennoblement and through marriage between nobles and commoners. Noble families could rise spectacularly in society by acquiring powerful offices, favors, or wealth. Royal favorites such as Henri III's *mignons* or Marie de Médicis's favorite, Concino Concini, provide the most striking examples of such meteoric ascension, but other noble families were also showered with royal favors. Given the possibilities of advancement, noble families had to be ready to take advantage of new opportunities. Replicating noble families involved not only sexual reproduction, but also preparing heirs to assume family-controlled offices and positions. Family strategies for status advancement thus envisioned children's education and training as a series of formative experiences that simultaneously improved the child and extended the family's *crédit*.

Warrior noble families promoted their young men, and especially the eldest sons, through early education. Following a period of initial instruction and moral formation within their own households provided by parents and tutors, many noble boys were sent away from home for education in other nobles' households or boarding schools to learn Latin and modern language skills. Tutorial education also emphasized classical culture and preparation for the exercise of power by focusing on subjects such as history, geography, geometry, and politics.[52] An inventory of the possessions of the Languedoc noble François de La Jugie comte de Rieux may provide some indication of noble reading interests. Rieux's library contained two of the fundamental military treatises used in the early seventeenth century—the *Commentaires* of Blaise de Monluc and the *Discours militaires* of François de La Noue. Political works, including Jean Bodin's *Les Six livres de la République* and Aristotle's *Politics*, could have provided a basic knowledge of politics and officeholding. The library also included histories like the *Chroniques de France* and the *Histoire de Grenade espagnol*.[53] The Rieux's library thus compared fairly well with those of some contemporary provincial governors, both in size and composition.[54]

Adolescent noblemen entered colleges or academies for rigorous instruction in mathematics, history, and philosophy, as well training in practical skills like horseriding, dancing, and fencing. Antoine de Pluvinel's method of instruction became very influential in early seventeenth-century French noble instruction, and later disseminated through publication of his *Instruction du roy en l'exercice de monter à cheval* (1625).[55] Calvinist noble families could select from a number of Huguenot academies founded in the southern French cities of Montauban, Orthez, Montpellier, Nîmes, and Orange. Alternatively, Huguenots could send their sons further away to academies in Calvinist-dominated territories such as Geneva, Sedan, the Netherlands, or the Palatinate.[56] Following Henri IV's official re-admittance of the Society of Jesus into France in 1603, Jesuit colleges proliferated there, attracting numerous members of Catholic noble families.[57] Young warrior nobles often served as pages, entering the household service of powerful noble families, and if possible the *grands*.[58] Some managed to find positions in the extensive households and bodyguards of royal family members, such as Marie de Médicis, Gaston de Bourbon, and Anne d'Autriche.[59]

European travel and service in foreign courts often complemented a young warrior nobleman's education. The concept of *le grand tour* as a formative experience for French noblemen was already developing by the late sixteenth century. An extended voyage to Italy, centered on a prolonged visit to Rome, became an integral part of French ideals of noble learning and cultivation. As Margaret M. McGowan shows, "sixteenth-century Frenchmen sought information on and stimulation from Rome; they wanted to possess its fragments and artefacts."[60] Henri II de Rohan duc de Rohan learned from Italy's governments, monuments, and fortifications during his 1600 tour.[61] Henri II de Bourbon prince de Condé traveled throughout Italy in 1622 on an extensive pilgrimage tour.[62] Although many southern French warrior nobles were probably never able to follow the example of these *grands*, a few *récits de voyage*, or travel journals, reveal that some nobles from Languedoc and Guyenne were recording their voyages to Italy.[63] These nobles' travels abroad also expanded their families' *crédit* by renewing and building connections at foreign courts. Henri de Schömberg explicitly recognized such processes in recommending his son for a visit to the Medici court in Florence, pointing out that "I was also in Florence for my exercises."[64]

Military experience and service in foreign armies increasingly formed a significant component of warrior nobles' military education in the late sixteenth
and early seventeenth centuries. Foreign experience could give young noblemen
a baptism by fire, expose them to foreign ideas on military practices, and intro-
duce them to new military methods. Southern French warrior nobles clearly had
ample opportunities to participate in military operations within France during
the late sixteenth and early seventeenth centuries, but foreign service offered
exposure to different tactical and technical developments, especially through
the formalized military education offered at foreign military academies.[65] Many
Huguenot nobles learned from their experiences of serving with the Dutch re-
publican armies, while French Catholics served in Spanish forces during the
Dutch Revolt—except during the Twelve Year Truce of 1609 to 1621, when there
were fewer military opportunities in the Netherlands.[66] Other French noble families sent their sons to Italian states or German principalities to gain military
experience. Some young French nobles embraced lingering crusading ideals to
serve on the Mediterranean galleys with the Knights of Saint John or the Caval-
ieri di Santo Stefano against their Ottoman and North African enemies. For
example, the young Henri de Nogaret de La Valette comte de Candalle served on
Florentine galleys in 1613, calling the experience "the best and most courageous
academy" that he could have chosen.[67]

One of the most valuable aspects of foreign service for French noblemen was
to provide them recommendations for, or direct access to, military offices within
France. For example, a letter of recommendation from a German prince for
captain Tournon indicates that "after a long stay in Germany," Tournon had
decided to return to France to offer his services to the king. The German prince
stresses that he writes the letter of recommendation because Tournon "particularly professed that he considered that a word of recommendation would facilitate his access to Your Majesty." Thus, he hopes that Louis XIII can give Tournon
"some place among the other servants."[68]

Military officeholding and wartime experience within France was much
more important for warrior nobles during the early seventeenth century, however, bringing vital experience of recruiting "native" troops, dealing with domestic political situations, campaigning with Francophone armies, and tasting
French civil warfare. Young provincial noblemen often learned warrior pursuits
through their service as officers in family-controlled military units, or as governors of fortresses and cities in southern France. Nobles had to learn French
political practices and military techniques through experience in civil conflict
within the kingdom.

Offices were crucial in providing training and education for the young men in noble families. Nobles had to develop basic knowledge and skills in a wide range of disciplines through officeholding experience. Officeholding gave warrior nobles a means of attaining military and administrative experience to supplement their education. Seventeenth-century nobles assumed that the exercise of office included self-promotion and advancement. The idea of career or vocation served to focus nobles' advancement aims and to channel ambition. Careers were not, as they have often been portrayed, exclusively based on occupations, though. A noble's career was not properly judicial or military or administrative, rather, nobility itself was a career. Warrior nobles used their experience and service to pursue higher status and power. Careers represented the expression of nobles' attempts to promote their personal and family interests.[69]

The civil warfare of the early seventeenth century presented an opportunity for nobles to gain more experience in leadership and to benefit from the fruits of victories. The outbreak of warfare almost always meant vast mobilization, with new military units and new officers. Many of these new offices would be temporary, since the offices were meant to fill out units designed to meet crises and then be disbanded. Nobles understood the system well and eagerly sought temporary military offices for family members. The vicomte de Mirepoix, for example, eagerly sought a command for his son during recruitment efforts in 1621.[70] Gaining experience would allow the young nobleman to begin to advance the family's position and extend its influence.

Protecting the Patrimony

Warrior noble families struggled to maintain their *crédit* by protecting their patrimonies. Disputes and conflicting claims over inheritances, transactions, and financial agreements often framed noble families' financial decision-making. Lengthy lawsuits could mire families' attempts to use their wealth actively, especially when family members argued over inheritance provisions.[71] Noble families developed various techniques for defending their status and preserving their patrimonies.

Noble families managed their monetary and status wealth by conserving and investing wisely, attempting to maintain their *crédit* and to keep their wealth concentrated. They regularly arranged contracts, transferred monies, and settled debts using the services of notaries who acted as "artisans of credit."[72] The fixed monetary income that nobles received from stipends, pensions, *rentes*, and rental properties often proved inadequate for their spending needs, producing cash shortages. Nobles raised money through the expedients of debt collection, land sales, and loans, while simultaneously curtailing excessive spending. Nobles struggled to combat the massive financial drain of conspicuous consumption that was so necessary to live nobly. Noble consumption often represented a valuable investment in political and social capital, but their perpetual expenditures on dining, drinking, gambling, ceremonies, and warfare could not be immediately recouped.

Noble families preserved their seigneurial wealth through successful marriage alliances and biological luck. Warrior nobles were extremely concerned with the birth and development of their children, especially the eldest son, because male children were so necessary to maintain seigneurial wealth. Noble families had to worry about daughters carrying seigneurial wealth away from the family with their dowries. This explains why noble families with many daughters tried to forge cousin marriages in order to preserve seigneurial holdings. Primogeniture played a role in preserving seigneurial wealth by ensuring that the bulk of a family's seigneurial holdings would be kept together as a unit and transmitted to the eldest son. Nobles also had to guard against alienating too many seigneuries when monetary demands were pressing.

Assuring the successful transfer of seigneurial wealth through inheritance was key to the maintenance of noble patrimony, so the last will and testament served as a vital vehicle for preserving wealth in early modern France. Most noble families in Languedoc and Guyenne probably approached inheritance in much the same way as the Lacger family, which stressed "masculine predominance and patrimonial impartibility." Noble families probably favored the eldest son as *héritier universal et général,* giving only small amounts to younger sons and daughters. According to Raymond A. Mentzer, "most elite families adopted the strategy of investing a disproportionately large share, one-half to two-thirds and occasionally more, of their resources in the oldest male of the succeeding generation."[73] Nobles also used wills to distribute wealth to valued causes, institutions, and followers. For example, noble wills in southern France frequently provided money to religious institutions and to local poor as charity. These grants often furthered familial goals by giving to monasteries where family members resided, or by promoting family charities.[74]

Early modern noble families struggled to maintain their official wealth by assuring successful transitions and controlling offices. When natural or violent death created vacancies in offices held by a noble, family members acted to protect their patrimony. The replacement of an officer represented not merely the transfer of an office, but an important aspect of officeholding and influence.

When nobles sold or exchanged their offices, the timing and method of handling office transfers were crucial for noble officeholders. Sometimes, they distributed some offices to male children, even if they were too young to exercise their charges. An older person, usually a family member, then acted for the minor until his majority, creating a regency model of officeholding on a smaller scale. As a boy, Henri II de Montmorency was appointed governor of the town of Narbonne, but since he was too young to exercise this charge, the lieutenant of his father's compagnie d'ordonnance commanded at Narbonne until Montmorency's majority.[75] Noble families depended on this practice to continue to exercise their influence and control of offices, even when circumstances created a lack of male office candidates of suitable age to exercise their office. Not all minorities were unplanned, though. In 1620 the duc de Châtillon received a commission for a garrison company, which he had specifically requested for his two-year-old son.[76] Clearly, families managed officeholding in order to protect their patrimonies and develop their official wealth.

Warrior nobles also arranged for replacements when they resigned from offices. When the sieur de Montgla wished to resign from his office of governor of the château de Termes on the Spanish frontier, he contacted the duc de Montmorency, promising "to treat with no one" without discussing the proposed replacement with the duc. Resigning offices and providing for replacements was a common practice. Possible reasons to resign from an office included incapacity, leaving an office to an heir, resigning in order to purchase another office, or exchanging offices with another noble (sometimes through the king). Nobles frequently resigned from their offices in order to let a younger family member gain experience. Indeed, nobles who lived long lives could monopolize a family's offices, creating a situation where younger family members could not grow into the offices that they saw as their due. For example, the duc d'Épernon's eighty-year-long career of service prevented his sons from gaining early independence and service, leading to periodic family conflicts. Officers could also retire from an office in order for a client to take up that office.

Given the importance of protecting noble families' investments in offices, the focus of most historians' treatments of venality in early seventeenth-century France has been on the *paulette*, a payment that allowed noble families to select the replacement when the officeholder died, thus practically guaranteeing that they could keep the office within the family. Criticisms of venality had been voiced by the parlement de Paris as early as the 1560s, and new objections to the *paulette* were raised at the meeting of the Estates General in 1614, leading to the suspension of the *paulette* from 1617 to 1620.[77] The tensions surrounding the *paulette* arose against the backdrop of a broad period of multiplication of the number of offices during the late sixteenth and seventeenth centuries.[78]

Noble families relied on *survivances*, inherited legacies, to transfer offices from generation to generation. The monarch had certain prerogatives concerning the transmission of offices, and the king could even seize offices in certain cases involving the forty-days' clause, death without survivance, rebellion, or other crimes. The principle of *survivances* was regularized for venal offices, but it generally applied for non-venal offices as well. The duc de Montmorency made sure that his nephew received an informal *survivance* of the office of lieutenant general, for example.[79] When illness or injuries incapacitated a noble, his offices could be temporarily conferred upon another. If an illness seemed very serious or terminal, offices could be transferred as a *survivance*. In 1619, François d'Estrades asked the secrétaire d'État to request that the king grant him "the estate of mestre de camp held by monsieur de Montesquieu, my brother, who is in such a state that the doctors count him lost." In the letter, Estrades claims that he is requesting his transfer only because his sick brother had begged him to ask the king for the office once he recognized the severity of his illness. Estrades buttresses his request with a reminder that "I hope [to receive], from the goodness of the king and from his justice, some recompense" for the losses he has already incurred.[80]

Protecting patrimonies also involved renewing the obligations of *crédit* and fulfilling familial duties when assuming inheritances. Nobles were expected to support family members in their efforts to aid their clients, and when a noble died, his successors were to carry on his projects and legacies. So, in a recommendation, the duc de Montmorency followed through on his father's attempts to have a garrison augmented for the sieur de Guillomont.[81] In another case, Henri II de Montmorency wrote a recommendation for a noble because of his "faithful affection" for the service of the king, but also because of the "testimonies that he has rendered in all occasions to present himself and to make known [how important] his merit was to the late king, and according to the particular inclination that the late monsieur the connétable [Montmorency's father] had for him."[82] These examples show how *crédit* was used to confirm patrimonial legacies and status wealth.

During civil conflicts of the late sixteenth and early seventeenth centuries, nobles' prospects of protecting their patrimonies became more difficult and complex. Noble families could lose substantial wealth or even their entire patrimonies through destruction and the death of family members in warfare. Participation in civil conflict could lead to disgrace if nobles backed the wrong side in a dispute, with the accompanying losses of official income. Nobles often claimed impoverishment because of their great expenditures in the king's service and due to the devastation of civil warfare. One noble recounted his great sufferings and debts, referring to himself tragically as the "poorest gentleman in France."[83] Such references to impoverishment can be considered aspects of a trope of the "poor noble," as they used discussions of poverty tactically in their attempts to gain pensions, offices, and favors.

Indeed, many nobles profited from their participation in civil and religious conflicts. According to the historian Robert Harding, "the wars opened the possibility of great wealth, but whether it materialized or not depended on personal ambitions and luck."[84] Warrior nobles, then, could potentially profit spectacularly from their participation in civil warfare, but they also ran great risks of losing everything.

Defending Privileges

Maintaining *crédit* required relentless efforts by noble families to defend their privileges from encroachments and erosions. As members of the second order, nobles held numerous corporate privileges distinct from members of other orders in French society.[85] Early modern theories of mixed monarchy and *res publica* allowed nobles privileges of consultation and participation in monarchical government.[86] Most warrior noble families were thus involved in government decision-making administration at some level, and some had the nominal right to attend meetings of the king's council as *conseillers du roi*. The profession of arms granted warrior noble families certain specific privileges related to the practice of warfare. Warrior nobles wore distinguishing clothing and symbols— including swords, armor, golden collars, and sashes—to announce their distinctive status. Each warrior noble family operated as a unique privilege set, defined in relation to other noble families and to other members of society through their familial prerogatives. This identification of families with specific series of privileges helps explain why warrior nobles never seem to have acted as a unified social class. Warrior nobles could rarely rally around common interests, since their privileges and rights were far from uniform.

Warrior nobles attempted to apply their extensive privileges on their landholdings through their seigneurial rights, which represented a wide range of economic and status prerogatives. Nobles tried to control activities such as hunting and gathering firewood, as well as the use of farmlands, forests, crops, mills, roads, and bridges on their seigneuries. A noble patriarch theoretically had near complete legal authority over his family and all the people who resided on his seigneurial properties, but exercising such power was extremely difficult during the French Wars of Religion. Seigneuries that were invested with titles—such as baronnies, comtés, and marquisats—included even more extensive privileges. Because these privileges were so important, warrior nobles were concerned to maintain their hold on higher-ranking seigneuries. Henri I de Montmorency duc de Montmorency asked the regency government to reserve the "ancient baron-nies" for the "great families of the kingdom."[87]

Most noble families had been granted exemptions from taxes, fees, and other payments, but these extensive privileges varied by region and by family. Noble families did not pay the famous *taille* tax, one of the most significant taxes in the kingdom. Many warrior noble families held privileges that functioned as im-munities from performing specific acts or duties. Although noble families were exempt from civil taxation, noble families nonetheless contributed money to the royal government in a variety of ways. Nobles on the rolls of the *ban et arrière ban*, or feudal levy, either served with a number of followers when the *ban* was summoned or paid a fee in commutation of their military service. Nobles often used their monetary wealth to act as creditors of the royal government through *rentes* and loans. Families holding bishoprics paid a *décime*, normally a tenth of the income of the benefice, at the king's request as a voluntary contribution. The *décime* was originally used specifically to finance crusades but gradually regular-ized into a means of royal fund-raising.[88] Noble families managed jurisdictional variations and negotiated with royal officials in order to reconfirm their privi-leges when contributing funds.

Lawsuits and legal procedures served to protect noble families' interests and prerogatives. Southern French noble families defended their legal privileges in sovereign courts, most notably, the parlement de Toulouse and parlement de Bordeaux.[89] Huguenot nobles in Languedoc and Guyenne had recourse to the *chambres de l'édit*, special chambers of parlements established by the Edict of Nantes to consider cases involving Calvinists, one of which was located in Cas-tres.[90] Nobles frequently sought financial reimbursements and legal opinions from other sovereign courts, such as the cour des aides de Montpellier and the chambre des comptes. The courts of sénéchaux and other regional jurisdictions managed disputes among noble families. Warrior nobles initiated lawsuits to recover outstanding debts and dues from their seigneurial tenants, but they also had to defend themselves from suits brought against them by persons claiming losses from religious violence and confiscations.[91] Engaging in all these legal activities required warrior nobles to coordinate frequently with judges, lawyers, and notaries in order to preserve their privileges.

Noble families were constantly concerned with precedence because it openly recognized and confirmed families' privileges. Officeholding granted nobles sweeping authority, but also required them to protect the extensive privileges that they held through their offices. The power and duties of an office often included numerous customary privileges and precedence concerns. Warrior nobles frequently participated in civic and religious processions, entries, assemblies, and other ceremonies. Historians have recognized the importance of social status in such events, stressing precedence competitions between guilds, law courts, religious institutions, and other corporations. The order and placement of individuals in ceremonies and processions signified rank, so any change in precedence reevaluated nobles' interrelationships, effectively altering a family's privileges. Warrior nobles continually negotiated precedence in everyday activities involving formal meetings and etiquette. Every gathering of nobles created a potential for disagreement and contestation over whose privileges superseded those of the other nobles. Breaches of established precedence frequently produced disputes, angry arguments, and even duels among nobles, precisely because their families' privileges and personal honor were at stake. Noble families seem to have been almost obsessively concerned with preserving their privileges and assessing their status in relation to other noble families. An intense competitiveness arose among warrior noble families over maintaining their privileges and upholding their rank in society.

✝

The provincial warrior nobles of Guyenne and Languedoc were capable of dominating regional politics and culture through their wealth and influence. Diverse forms of noble wealth allowed warrior nobles to manage their patrimonies and employ their wealth creatively to maintain their regional dominance. Provincial military elites' concerns over status, *crédit*, and wealth ultimately led to regional power struggles and armed rivalries between noble families. Warrior nobles relied on their family wealth and personal *crédit* to practice their warrior pursuits and to wage civil warfare in early seventeenth-century France. The following chapter examines how warrior nobles employed bonds of nobility to construct provincial power and authority beyond their households and relatives.

PART TWO

The Bonds of Nobility

A civic entry ceremony, showing warrior nobles riding together with their clients and friends. Engraving by Pierre Matthieu, *L'Entrée de tres-grand, tres-chrestien, tres-magnanime, et victorieux prince Henry IIII roy de France & de Navarre, en sa bonne ville de Lyon le IIII septembre l'an MDXVCV* (Lyon: Pierre Michel, 1595), BNF, Réserve, 4-LB35-642, planche avant la page 1, detail. Photo courtesy Bibliothèque Nationale de France.

CHAPTER FOUR

With the Assistance of My Particular Friends

Clientage and Friendship

In 1621, after seizing control of the small town of Montcrabeau in southern France "with the assistance of my particular friends," François d'Esparbès de Lussan marquis d'Aubeterre anticipated royal validation of his action.[1] Provincial nobles often referred to their armed noble followers as *amis*, or friends, during civil conflicts in Languedoc and Guyenne. Friendship in this context alluded to a masculine bond among nobles engaging together in the profession of arms. Powerful noble patrons cultivated such friendships, organizing clienteles that were geared toward performing military service and promoting political causes. Gatherings of a nobleman's friends reflected his military capabilities, political power, and social status.

Friendship could also be a much more personal relationship. Anne de Lévis duc de Ventadour described one of his clients as "a gentleman of great merit who is one of my intimate friends because he and his predecessors have rendered such good services to this house."[2] Language of intimacy, affection, and brotherhood infused warrior nobles' discussions of their friendships. Reflecting the emotional intensity of relations between some warrior noblemen in the early modern period, Louis de Pontis claimed that his early patron Louis Berton de Crillon "loved me with a father's tenderness."[3] Mature noble patrons cared for their younger clients, providing them with guidance, gifts, and favors. Bonds of friendship, or *amitié*, clearly influenced nobles' participation in civil warfare through their clienteles, however, competing representations of noble friendships—as fatherhood and as brotherhood—created tensions within French warrior noble culture.

What did noble friendship really mean in the context of pervasive civil war-fare? Although *amitié* could create strong affective relationships, friendship seems to have been strongly associated with clientage. Various clientage bonds forged warrior noble culture and shaped noble attitudes beyond their households and families. Warrior nobles' political, religious, military, and cultural practices operated through their interpersonal connections, ensuring that clienteles acted as key sites for the development of bonds of nobility. The immediacy and inse-curity of localized civil conflict prompted provincial nobles to seek stronger con-nections with other nobles in their regions. Warrior nobles needed to be able to count on the quick responses of their clienteles, since the civil warfare in this period was characterized by sharp religious divisions and localized confronta-tions. Civil violence fundamentally shaped the ways in which warrior nobles constructed clientage bonds in the early seventeenth-century Languedoc and Guyenne, defining a distinct period of clientele development in French history.

FORMING CLIENTELES

Southern French nobles maintained broad friendship and clientage networks during peacetime, associating with diverse groups of elites. Brief periods of rela-tive peace in the early seventeenth century allowed for open association with noble friends of diverse religious and political affiliations. Even in peacetime, warrior noble patrons cultivated elaborate clientage relationships with numer-ous noble clients, attracting followers through a dynamic process of clientele formation. Many nobles actively sought the patronage of higher-ranking nobles, often courting multiple patrons simultaneously. The outbreak of civil conflict demanded difficult, even gut-wrenching, choices for warrior nobles, who were inevitably caught in webs of connections, allegiances, loyalties, and promises. Civil warfare severely curtailed the ability to associate freely within provincial noble culture, forcing nobles to choose between their conflicting loyalties by reaf-firming certain clientage bonds and severing others. Military officers could still maintain affiliations with other patrons who supported the same cause during a civil war, particularly if the nobles served in the same field army. Warrior no-bles were frequently torn between their connections to several potential patrons who identified with different political or religious causes, so the formation of clienteles ironically hinged upon the breaking of ties between nobles even more than on the building of support. Clienteles coalesced through a process of re-nouncing allegiances, denying requests, and undermining relationships. Dur-ing periods of civil warfare, nobles refused to acknowledge certain loyalties and delayed fulfilling commitments, denying potential patrons their full backing. Thus, clientele formation during civil conflict involved the reaffirmation of certain bonds and the severance of other connections, producing clienteles with tighter coherence despite their fluid characteristics.

In choosing sides, warrior nobles took great risks, placing their offices, landholdings, honor, families, and lives in jeopardy. A dispute between Jacques-Nompar de Caumont duc de La Force and Antoine III de Gramont marquis de Gramont in Béarn in 1613 "put all of the nobility of this region in turmoil, for they are lined up on one side or the other."[4] Nobles might be ridiculed and challenged by their opponents for their choices of allegiances during civil wars. Ridicule and insult were serious injuries in noble culture, but many nobles paid a much higher price for their choices in civil conflict. Many lost fortunes and properties, and they invariably risked losing followers, angering associates, and alienating the king. Some nobles lost their own lives, and many more suffered the deaths of family members, friends, and followers.

The act of *prise d'armes*, or taking up arms, was the decisive moment of choosing sides in civil conflict.[5] Taking up arms gave clienteles their most coherent form, as warrior nobles assembled with their military companions. Nobles who raised new infantry regiments used established clientage bonds to select their subordinate officers, so many regimental officers served with the same patron each time he raised troops. The style and composition of a warrior noble's clientele was frequently modified and transformed during warfare. Noble clients who previously had held no military positions within a clientele took on new wartime roles. Most warrior clienteles utilized mixed forms of clientage consisting of various prestige, military, administrative, urban, or seigneurial relationships among the provincial warrior nobles.

Prestige Clientage

Warrior nobles with elevated rank and status became the foci for prestige clientage bonds. Prestige clientage bonds obviously characterized the *grands*, whose families' exalted rank attracted large numbers of clients, but family prestige also operated at all levels of the French nobility. Within many regions and communities, clienteles emerged that were based on the local prestige of a noble family and little else. Prestige clienteles relied on a noble's family status, regional reputation, and renown—frequently established over several generations—to attract followers.

Many *grands* had significant warrior noble clienteles in Guyenne and Languedoc based primarily on their prestige. Jean-Louis de Nogaret de La Valette duc d'Épernon, for example, had a large prestige clientele in Guyenne, well out of proportion to his political and military power in the 1610s. Épernon's prestige had originally stemmed from his status as an advisor and favorite during the reign of Henri III.[6] Even though his influence at court and his political power had diminished since 1588, his prestige and regional reputation remained quite strong. While his officeholding and military leadership contributed to the maintenance of his clientele, his regional prestige within Guyenne provided the core of his noble following.[7] His appointment to the office of provincial governor of Guyenne in 1622 merely allowed him to expand his clientele even further through administrative connections.[8]

Henri II de Montmorency's clientele was multifaceted, but had a strong prestige element. Montmorency had extensive administrative and military connections through his governorship of Languedoc, but the prestige of the Montmorency family extended well beyond Languedoc. His family's widespread landholdings, ancient status, presence at court, and near continuous military service during the religious wars assured the duc de Montmorency real notoriety. The governor's prestige was enhanced by his successful campaigns against Calvinists in Languedoc and later by his military leadership in Italy. Large numbers of Catholic nobles, attracted by his prestige, flocked to Montmorency's clientele to serve as his bodyguards or as volunteer nobles in his household and military retinue. The duc de Montmorency's prestige drew large numbers of provincial noble supporters during the 1632 civil war, despite the lack of a Huguenot enemy.[9]

Several great nobles attempted to establish new prestige clienteles in southern France during this period. The duc de Mayenne had just started to use his post as governor of Guyenne effectively to attract provincial noble clients when he was killed at the siege of Montauban in 1621.[10] The king's own brother, Gaston de Bourbon duc d'Orléans, attracted prestige clients in southern France, but his followers were decimated by participation in plots and civil warfare.[11] After his great victory at the battle of Castelnaudary in 1632, Henri de Schömberg comte de Nanteuil seemed poised to forge a significant prestige clientele in Languedoc, since he was already a maréchal de France and he enjoyed the favor of Louis XIII and Richelieu. The beheading of Henri II de Montmorency at Toulouse a month after Castelnaudary removed the most powerful noble in the province, and many of Montmorency's provincial followers had been killed or disgraced during the civil war. Schömberg was quickly named governor of the province, but his death later the same year prevented the establishment of a clientele as broad as Montmorency's had been. Charles de Schömberg immediately succeeded him as governor, but he lacked his father's experience and positions, and his clientele seems to have relied on administrative rather than prestige bonds.[12]

One of the few *grands* from outside Languedoc and Guyenne to successfully establish a strong prestige following in those provinces was Henri II de Rohan duc de Rohan. The Rohan family had one of the most elevated Calvinist lineages in the entire kingdom, attracting many Huguenot noble followers. Rohan's appointment as general in Languedoc by the Huguenot assembly at La Rochelle allowed him to extend his connections with the Calvinist nobility in the province. Huguenot nobles in the Cévennes and Bas Languedoc, in particular, were attracted to Rohan's great noble status and his example as a staunch Protestant fighter. French Calvinists associated Rohan and his brother, Soubise, with devout Reformed religiosity, personal dedication, and political protection because of their family's prestige and reputation.[13]

Prominent regional nobles also attracted clients based on their prestige within southern French noble culture. Pons de Lauzières marquis de Thémines established an extensive prestige clientele built around his family's growing prominence and reputation in Haute Guyenne and Haut Languedoc.[14] While aspects of Thémines's clientele were military and administrative, his family's prestige within the region was vital to the expansion of his clientele. Charles de Gontaut duc de Biron's fame as a military commander and maréchal de France had enabled him to extend his prestige clientage throughout much of Guyenne in the late sixteenth century. When Biron's involvement in a series of plots in 1601–1602 led to his arrest and execution, regional nobles worried about his powerful clientele's potential reaction.[15]

Religious conviction and status influenced the formation of regional nobles' prestige clienteles. The religious dimension of prestige was closely connected to a family's reputation for sincere conviction, overt piety, and confessional loyalty. Gaspard III de Coligny seigneur de Châtillon attracted many Calvinist clients because of his family's prestige—his grandfather was the great Huguenot military leader Gaspard II de Châtillon comte de Coligny, known as Admiral Coligny, who had been assassinated at the beginning of the Saint Bartholomew's Day Massacre in 1572. The seigneur de Châtillon's prestige was enhanced by his service in civil conflicts in Languedoc and his leadership of French Calvinists fighting against the Spanish in the Netherlands in the 1610s. Châtillon's *gentilshommes et domistiques* in 1621 and 1622 included an impressive array of Huguenot nobles from Languedoc.[16] Châtillon's submission to royal authority during the 1621–1622 civil war seriously hurt his prestige among the Calvinist nobility, though.

Military Clientage

Military clientage linked nobles with their subordinate officers, campaign entourages, and warrior noble comrades. In the early seventeenth century, military clienteles formed primarily because of noble participation in civil conflict. During military campaigns, relationships between military officers often came to dominate other links between patrons and clients. While all clientele genres incorporated military elements during civil wars, military clienteles developed primarily around nobles' existing military connections. Instead of giving their prestige or administrative clients new military positions, patrons of military clienteles used their ties to subordinate military officers and noble comrades from previous campaigns to extend military clientage. Some nobles with military clienteles in southern France operated without the local support provided by seigneuries and administrative offices. Warrior noble patrons with limited abilities to produce clienteles using other methods had to rely on their regimental offices and martial experience to build clienteles. Military clientage could be very advantageous to noble patrons, since it relied on widespread connections that were not dependent on one specific geographic area. Further, military clienteles had a very strong coercive potential because of their ability to mobilize organized military forces, commanded by noble officers with strong clientage bonds between them.

Command relationships bound a military patron's regimental and company officers to him. Nobles personally selected their subordinate officers, who confirmed their status as clients by accepting their patron's power to command them. Nobles often joined military clienteles because of the opportunities for new commands through military clientage. Military patrons frequently granted command of captured towns and fortifications to infantry captains who were their own clients, as when Hector de Gélas de Voisins marquis d'Ambres took control of the capitulated town of La Caune in 1628.[17] Such temporary positions could later become confirmed as official governorships. Henri de Rohan frequently gave independent commands to the nobles in his company of gendarmes. As Catholic troops approached Montpellier in 1622, the duc de Rohan left a group of gendarmes under the command of the maréchal de logis Laudes, who then led the cavalry in combat.[18] Many nobles served with the same regiment in campaign after campaign, despite intervening demobilizations. Deaths and defections during protracted civil conflicts nonetheless ensured that military clienteles remained fluid. Clients who became dissatisfied with a patron might renounce their loyalty and give up their military offices, often to take up offices under new patrons.

The blurring of the distinctions between a warrior nobles' clients and subordinates gave added power to regimental officers, and especially to mestres de camp. Patrons with military clienteles attracted military retinues composed of noble household members and volunteers. While these clients held no official subordinate positions, they performed ad hoc military roles as scouts, messengers, bodyguards, and cavalry. Members of a military retinue usually had close contact with their patron and often seem to have enjoyed favored status within the clientele. Serving together through shared hardships and experiences strengthened clientage bonds between nobles. Military campaigns allowed nobles to form tight connections and social relations, even if they were not in the same units. Combat experience created close ties between nobles who served under fire together, building camaraderie and trust between them. Patrons sometimes provided clothing, arms, or insignias to promote a feeling of unity among their military clients. Dining and drinking on campaign allowed these clients to share experiences. Members of military clienteles extolled the fighting and leadership abilities of their patron and members. Connections between military patrons and clients appear to have been among the strongest bonds created within noble culture, especially during extended periods of civil warfare.

The Calvinist Joachim de Beaumont baron de Beaumont-Brison constructed a significant military clientele in Vivarais in the 1620s. The baron fought in a series of conflicts over the predominantly Calvinist town of Privas between 1619 and 1621, gaining a reputation as *le brave Brison* for his role in defending Huguenot causes. Regional Calvinist nobles joined the baron de Beaumont as military clients, apparently regarding him as one of the most prominent Huguenot military leaders in Languedoc.[19] Joachim de Beaumont became a Huguenot maréchal de camp and governor for the Reformed churches in the region of Vivarais, allowing him to expand his military clientele and to quickly raise significant military forces within the region and the neighboring Cévennes mountains. The baron de Beaumont's extensive Calvinist military clientage allowed him to lead small Huguenot armies in successive civil wars until his death in 1628.[20]

Jean de Caïla de Saint-Bonnet marquis de Toiras used military clientage to advance his career and to build considerable influence with southern French warrior nobles. Caïla de Saint-Bonnet was a fairly unremarkable local noble until he gained prominence through his military service in the gardes françaises, a royal household regiment, in Languedoc in 1621 and 1622. When he was named maréchal de camp in 1625, the marquis de Toiras began to attract a substantial military clientele to accompany his victories in the 1620s. But his military campaigns often carried him far from Languedoc to fight around La Rochelle and in

Italy. His frequent absences from Languedoc inhibited his ability to build wide-spread regional connections there, so his clientele remained primarily military in nature.[21]

The military clientele of Gabriel de La Vallée des Fossées marquis d'Everly developed along a very different trajectory. La Vallée des Fossées, who was not a Languedoc native, formed a military clientele in Languedoc after he was named governor of the new citadel of Montpellier in September 1626. Lacking any local landholdings or connections, the marquis was forced to develop his clientele almost exclusively through military connections. La Vallée des Fossées success-fully defended Montpellier twice, against an attack by the duc de Rohan in Janu-ary 1628 and against the duc de Montmorency and Gaston d'Orléans in 1632.[22] These successes allowed La Vallée des Fossées to consolidate his military clien-tele and expand his support network within the city and surrounding region of Bas Languedoc. The marquis replaced Jacques du Caïla de Saint-Bonnet as sé-néchal of Montpellier after the latter was removed from his post for supporting Montmorency and Gaston d'Orléans during the 1632 civil war. This new post gave La Vallée des Fossées increased local power and an opportunity to develop urban and administrative dimensions of his clientele, but it remained predomi-nantly military.[23]

Administrative Clientage

Administrative clientage developed through warrior nobles' provincial offices and governmental connections. Each provincial administrative position required nobles to use both official and unofficial connections in the performance of their managerial duties. Since early seventeenth-century provincial government lacked rigid hierarchical organization, nobles could easily develop administra-tive clienteles as local conditions allowed within regions of southern France. Warrior nobles who were involved in provincial administration became focal points for the arbitration of local disputes and issues, and they received a steady flow of petitions and requests.

Governors of towns and châteaux built local administrative clienteles around their subordinate administrators and official contacts with area nobles. Posi-tions as governors of towns and châteaux gave warrior nobles connections to local administrative personnel involved in maintaining fortifications and garri-sons, as well as access to localized social networks, fortified bases, and political clout. René d'Hautefort established an administrative and urban clientele at Le Puy-en-Velay using his offices of governor of the town and sénéchal of the surrounding region of Velay. Hautefort had a reputation as a staunch Catholic who had previously acted as a Catholic League leader in Velay and an ally of the powerful duc de Joyeuse, and his administrative role as town governor complemented his existing prestige clientage within the region.[24] The Hautefort family patriarch seems to have groomed his eldest son, Claude, for leadership of his administrative clientele, granting Claude the family's vicomté of Cheylane and providing him with military experience. When residents of Le Puy-en-Velay refused to acknowledge René d'Hautefort's authority as governor of the town, his sons and clients took twelve inhabitants hostage as bargaining chips in negotiations. In the end, the town agreed to recognize René d'Hautefort as their governor, allowing him to enter the gates in July 1616 with an entourage including his sons and "several other gentlemen from Vivarais."[25]

Sénéchaux, baillis, and regional governors could use their regional executive power and judicial authority to build administrative clientage.[26] Alexandre de Lévis marquis de Mirepoix developed a broad following while serving as sénéchal in Carcassonne and in Béziers.[27] Adrien de Monluc comte de Carmaing, grandson of the famous Blaise de Monluc, served as sénéchal de Foix beginning in 1612.[28] The comte de Carmaing organized fortification repairs and garrisons using his administrative connections in the 1616.[29] Adrien de Montluc would later let his administrative clientele languish without his presence, when he moved to Paris and established himself as an urban noble.[30] François de Noailles comte d'Ayen administered the region of Rouergue as its governor, frequently acting as an arbitrator in disputes between warrior nobles.[31] Noailles provided advocacy for communities in the Rouergue, requesting that garrisons installed by other nobles be removed.[32] The comte d'Ayen sent one of his clients to oversee the razing of a château in Rouergue in 1612.[33]

Some nobles developed more extensive provincial administrative clienteles based on official authority to govern the immense provinces of Languedoc or Guyenne. Provincial governors such as the ducs de Montmorency, the duc de Mayenne, and the duc d'Épernon attracted numerous noble followers eager to aid in the implementation of their orders and directives. The administrative clientage of provincial governors frequently overlapped with prestige clienteles, since most major provincial offices were filled by powerful nobles from established families of *grands*. A number of lieutenant generals in Guyenne and Languedoc led their own extensive administrative clienteles during the early seventeenth century. Anne de Lévis duc de Ventadour long conducted everyday administrative duties in Languedoc, acting with full authority when the provincial governor was absent.[34] When Anne de Lévis died in 1622, Henri de Lévis baron de La

Voulte assumed his father's titles and administrative roles. Antoine de Roquelaure marquis de Roquelaure served as lieutenant general in Guyenne in the
1610s and early 1620s, gathering an extensive administrative clientele around
him. Roquelaure often negotiated to resolve disputes between warrior nobles in
southwestern France, giving him additional credibility and political clout.[35] An
indication of Roquelaure's arbitration skills is given by a serious quarrel that
developed in his absence from Guyenne in 1616 between his son-in-law, who
claimed to be authorized to act in his absence, and another powerful warrior
noble in the province, the seigneur de Gondrin.[36]

   Although provincial governors and lieutenants general easily attracted broad
administrative clienteles, nobles holding provincewide authority through unsanctioned or provisional office had to cultivate relationships to fully develop administrative clientage. Henri II de Rohan duc de Rohan was granted provincial
administrative authority by Huguenot assemblies at La Rochelle in the 1620s,
giving him the possibility of building up an administrative clientele in Languedoc.
The duc de Rohan lacked localized ties, however, and failed to develop many
clients in the provincial government, leaving him with a somewhat weak administrative clientage bonds.[37]

Urban Clientage

Some warrior nobles constructed urban clientage through their municipal offices and civic connections. Unlike nobles in northern France, many nobles in
Languedoc and Guyenne had urban dwellings and occupied key offices in the
municipal government. These elites with urban connections did not include
merely the newly ennobled families, but also many of the highest-ranking warrior noble families in southern France. The Montmorency family dominated the
small town of Pézenas, while the Monlucs held influence over the residents of
Agen. Other warrior nobles had an urban presence in major provincial cities such
as Bordeaux, Montauban, Toulouse, Castres, Montpellier, and Nîmes. Urban clientage depended on warrior nobles' residence or frequent presence in a town or
city. Many nobles in southern France maintained urban hôtels, usually constructed with heavy gateways opening into rectangular dwellings with central
courtyards, which could easily act as fortifications. Nobles could provide protection to urban clients by using their hôtels as places of refuge during civil conflicts within the town. Many patrons found clients and recruited troops in urban
settings. The large number of Huguenot infantry commanders from Nîmes reveals how tight-knit urban connections could be.[38]

Warrior nobles whose families had occupied consular office often had extensive urban clienteles. While consuls could certainly build municipal administrative clientage relationships, the temporary and provisional nature of consular authority tended to prevent the development of significant consular administration. Most consul posts had a duration of only one year, giving the *consulat*, or consular government, a rotating nature, and making it difficult for nobles to cultivate official administrative connections while serving as consuls. Since civic bureaucracy was fairly limited and consuls performed duties with few official subordinates, warrior nobles elected as consuls often exercised power through their urban clienteles instead of relying on administrative connections. Consular office was an important sign of prominence for a warrior noble with an urban clientele, giving his clients enhanced status during his term.

Local warrior noble families and other noble elites often vied for control of the *consulat* in annual elections. Warrior nobles frequently held consul posts in communities in Guyenne and Languedoc, and those who held, or ran for, consular office could be expected to have substantial urban clienteles. Claude de Calvière baron de Saint-Côme provides a interesting example of a noble who gradually constructed an urban clientele in Nîmes based on his proximity to the city. The baron's château de Saint-Côme was located just west of Nîmes and he developed seigneurial ties with other Protestant nobles in the countryside surrounding Nîmes. He used his authority as first consul of Nîmes in 1623 to appoint several of his urban clients as subordinate officers in his own regiment de Saint-Côme. Ysac Brun seigneur de Castanet was a captain in the regiment before being elected first consul of Nîmes himself in 1625. Claude de Calvière supported Nîmes's declaration of support for the duc de Rohan that year, raising a regiment of 1,000 infantry for the Huguenot cause in Languedoc. Calvière's urban clientage collapsed after he led a failed attempt on the village of Bellegarde, southeast of Nîmes, and died of wounds he received in the attack.[39]

During civil conflicts, the composition of the *consulat* was often vital in determining the fate of a community. Consuls not only ran civic government and administration, but made religious policies, determined loyalties, and controlled access to communal spaces during civil conflicts. Religious conflict produced increased competition over consul offices between urban clienteles in the late sixteenth and early seventeenth centuries. Many towns in Languedoc and Guyenne had a *mi-partie*, or mixed confessional, *consulat* in which consuls from both Catholic and Calvinist faiths led municipal government. Nobles of each confession tried to strengthen their urban clienteles and win control of the *consulat* by gaining more consul posts. Paul Arnauld seigneur de La Cassagne, first consul of Nîmes in 1629, had a company of chevaux-légers and a large urban following. When he was imprisoned by Catholic forces, La Cassagne remained confident in his position and "resisted the threats and promises of the court with much magnanimity." But the duc de Rohan feared that La Cassagne's urban clientele would allow him to act independently: "for, being the first consul of Nîmes and having credit there, he hoped, by this means, to make a powerful party there and to detach it from the reformed."[40] Urban clienteles participated in localized religious and political struggles throughout southern France, not just in Nîmes. Jean de La Croix baron de Castries became first consul in Montpellier as part of attempt to establish Catholic control over the town after the peace of Montpellier in 1622.[41] Catholic nobles like Castries acted to exploit Catholic military victories by expanding their urban clienteles. A royal decree of 1631 reinforced this tendency by imposing a requirement that the first consul must always be Catholic, weakening Huguenot warrior nobles' abilities to form effective urban clienteles.[42] In some communities, elections became tightly controlled by the town governors or by a group of nobles acting as an oligarchy within the town.

Many sénéchaux, baillis, and town governors also developed unofficial urban clienteles. The administrative demands of governing towns provided governors with social connections to consuls, militia commanders, and elite families within the towns. Henri de Fain baron de Péraut was governor of the town and château of Beaucaire and developed an urban clientele there.[43] Other governors were only able to maintain administrative or military clientage in an urban setting, because of a lack of local urban connections. Friction and mutual hostilities often divided governors of towns from other urban nobles, preventing them from producing effective urban clientage.

The clientele of Jean de La Valette baron de Cornusson provides an interesting example of a Catholic sénéchal's urban clientage bonds within the city of Toulouse. The La Valette family had regional influence and was based at a village just northeast of Toulouse. Jean de La Valette was sénéchal de Toulouse, an administrative position from which he could gain an impressive urban following. As sénéchal, La Valette was able to surround himself with prominent local nobles, including counselors to the sénéchal de Toulouse, who seem to have usually been significant nobles who contributed to the *ban et arrière-ban* tax. Because Toulouse was a large city with many powerful nobles and administrative bodies, including the parlement de Toulouse, the baron de Cornusson was forced to compete for local prominence.[44] The baron got an opportunity to expand his urban clientele when he was charged with raising a company of gendarmes and an infantry regiment for the 1621 siege of Montauban. He assembled local nobles to take up positions as captains in his regiment and they recruited in the city. La Valette's regiment served under the duc d'Angoulême in Haut Languedoc, then under the eyes of the king at Montauban. After the failure of that siege, Cornusson's regiment was demobilized, but his urban connections continued to develop.[45] La Valette commanded a gendarme company during much of the 1620s, and one of his subordinate officers in 1624 was from the du Pins family in Toulouse. In 1627, he raised a cavalry company of 120 men to serve with the duc de Ventadour, which was much larger than his gendarme company had been in 1621.[46] When Huguenots began to raise armies in Languedoc in 1629, Richelieu drew up a plan to oppose them. The list of nobles who could quickly raise troops within Languedoc included Cornusson.[47] Cornusson's Toulousain clients could evidently be counted on to support him.

Henri II de Bourbon prince de Condé also developed a significant urban clientele in Toulouse using his local connections in addition to his prestige to build a following. The prince de Condé frequently visited Toulouse during the civil wars of the 1620s, using the town as a base of operations. The baron de Cornusson had to learn to deal with Condé's intermittent presence in Toulouse and his growing influence. Condé attended a session of the parlement de Toulouse in January 1628 to ensure that his directives were implemented.[48] The prince worked closely with the premier président of the parlement de Toulouse during the 1628 campaign, a sign of his growing urban clientele. Condé's close ties to the Toulousain urban elites may have prompted him to issue a directive forbidding the lodging of troops in Toulouse in 1629, thus exempting the Toulouse nobles from paying for costly maintenance and lodging of soldiers.[49]

Urban clienteles were often difficult to manage, as the experience of the marquis d'Aubeterre at Agen suggests. In November 1615, François I d'Esparbès de Lussan marquis d'Aubeterre assembled the three orders of the town of Agen, where he was sénéchal, to secure the town and address the widening civil conflict in Guyenne. "In this assembly," Aubeterre reported, "the members asked me to station two companies of one hundred men each from my regiment in their town, for their safety as well as to repulse any raids and plots that might be launched against the service of the king."[50] The marquis seems to have deftly managed the assembly and his clients within the town, and he readily agreed to send his infantry into Agen.

Soon afterwards, however, Aubeterre's authority in Agen and his control over his clientele was threatened. The marquis heard that the consuls of Agen had met to discuss the situation "at the counsel and secret persuasion of one of this town's inhabitants, who is a creature of monsieur le prince [de Condé] and a factional man." During their secret deliberations, the consuls agreed to send a representative to plead for Louis XIII to send another two infantry companies, which would not be under Aubeterre's command. Aubeterre, incensed, wrote to the secrétaire d'État, asking him "to oppose entirely their intention and ruin their design." The marquis claimed that "besides the useless expense to the king, this would also give them a way to show contempt for my authority. . . . Thus, please make sure, monsieur, that they are sent back, for I secretly hope to ruin their cabal."[51] Aubeterre's clear concern was to maintain personal control of the military forces in and around Agen, and his anxiety is underscored by another letter he wrote the same day to request the authority to raise five new companies for his infantry regiment. By associating the leaders of Agen with a creature of the prince de Condé, Aubeterre was able to suggest to the court that the consuls were conspiring with a rebel, thus tainting them with suspicion. Within the context of Guyenne provincial politics, however, Aubeterre sought to manage the consuls and to avoid direct confrontation with his urban clients.

Seigneurial Clientage

Seigneurial clientage was based on a noble's *seigneurie*, or fief, and the relationships associated with it.[52] This form of clientage drew on a noble's own landholdings in an area and on his familial and seigneurial ties to other local elites. Many warrior noble families gradually acquired numerous seigneuries—often in several dioceses or even across provincial boundaries—through marriage, inheritance, purchase, and reward. As noble families accumulated multiple seigneuries, they gained new connections with tenants and neighbors, even if distance complicated the cultivation of clientage. Warrior nobles thus continued to use seigneurial relationships to construct their clienteles, allowing them to build local support for their religious and political agendas.

The notion of homage, long regarded as the basis of seigneurial relationships, was extremely ambiguous in the early seventeenth century. Homage had developed during the early medieval period as a ritual symbolizing and strengthening the vassalic relations of feudalism.[53] In the fifteenth and sixteenth centuries, homage was gradually deemphasized and almost abandoned, although nobles still discussed the duties of faithfulness and homage.[54] By the seventeenth century, nobles who owed seigneurial service to a lord sometimes still participated in ceremonies of homage when they inherited their estates, but many then regarded any feudal obligation as having been fulfilled. The Polignac family continued to rely on homage ceremonies to reinforce their lordship over their vassals in seventeenth-century Velay, asking their vassals to pledge to serve the vicomte in warfare against any enemy.[55] Other nobles completely disregarded seigneurial traditions of homage, allegiance, and service. Although homage ceremonies and other feudal aspects of seigneurial relations were increasingly ambiguous, seigneurial ties continued to have significance for many warrior nobles, but operating as a social bond rather than as a feudal obligations system. Shifting understandings of homage and obligations were not the only factors altering seigneurial relations, however.

In early modern France, seigneuries were defined jointly as properties and jurisdictions. Although seigneuries had originally been granted in the medieval period as temporary, provisional landholdings, by the seventeenth century they had long been considered properties. Seigneurial landholding practices had diversified, and nobles routinely bought and sold entire seigneuries.[56] When buying or selling whole seigneuries was impractical or undesirable, small parcels of farmland, woods, or vineyards might be exchanged. Nobles could also acquire seigneurial rights without buying the associated land. Co-seigneuries developed when a seigneurie was divided among heirs or when a partition was made to sell off portions of estates. Nobles who were co-seigneurs might regard each other as equals, but some co-seigneurs were subordinated to their counterparts.[57] Leases of seigneuries could also be constructed through purchase–buy back contracts that specified that the seller had the option of repurchase after a set time period.[58] Louis XIII frequently redistributed seigneuries during civil wars, granting warrior nobles in Languedoc and Guyenne seigneurial properties and rights from estates confiscated from nobles accused of revolt. Henri II de Montmorency, for example, was granted additional seigneurial rights as a reward for his military service in Languedoc.[59] Complex property relationships had largely replaced vassalic bonds, both disrupting and promoting seigneurial connections between nobles.

In addition to the proprietary status granted to a seigneur, each noble held extensive rights throughout his seigneurial jurisdiction. Seigneuries gave their noble lords authority over local administration and seigneurial justice. As a judge, the seigneur arbitrated in all disputes and legal matters on his seigneurie through his seigneurial court. Warrior nobles often had to assert their seigneurial rights to jurisdiction over cases against other judges and courts.[60] The noble played an administrative role within his jurisdiction, presiding over village assemblies and influencing local politics. Proprietary and jurisdictional conditions would vary widely from seigneurie to seigneurie, even within one noble's landholdings. These judicial and administrative roles gave nobles influence in arbitration cases and allowed them to extend clientage to nobles within their seigneurial jurisdictions.[61]

The management of seigneurial property depended on a highly complex system of rights, obligations, dues, and payments. Based at his château, a nobleman personally controlled his *domaine*, also known as a *réserve seigneuriale*, or *demesne*, which was a portion of the seigneurie reserved for his own direct needs. Warrior nobles were often intimately involved in the everyday management of their *domaines*, corresponding regularly with their seigneurial intendants and clients when they were away.[62] Beyond his *domaine*, the noble landholder indirectly controlled various aspects of his seigneurie through *bans*, or monopolies. The seigneur also acted as a landlord, exercising indirect control over all of the *censives*, portions of farmland on the seigneurie that were leased by tenant farmers.[63]

This distribution of leased land on seigneuries actually promoted the formation of seigneurial clienteles. While many tenants were peasants, some of a seigneur's tenants might be town elites or even noblemen, especially on larger estates. Local nobles became tenants of major nobles, renting farmlands to expand their agricultural incomes beyond what they received from their own estates. Nobles with large landholdings thus had the best potential for developing seigneurial clienteles. Warrior noble families such as the Roure possessed extensive landholdings in Guyenne and Languedoc, with numerous seigneuries scattered over widely separated areas—all providing potential seigneurial connections to local nobles.[64] Large landholders might also gain seigneurial clients by having nobles take charge of managing the agricultural operations at some of their seigneuries. While many of the seigneurial officials handling finances and administration on seigneuries were non-noble, powerful elites such as the ducs de Montmorency could give nobles charge of managing their seigneurial councils, châteaux, garrisons, and forests.[65]

Seigneurial clienteles tended to have the strongest familial character of any form of clientage, and they almost always incorporated numerous familial seigneurial connections. Warrior nobles frequently held a number of different seigneuries, several of which would be held by the head of the family, while others would be distributed to sons, brothers, uncles, or cousins. François d'Amboise, for example, granted his son one of his family's baronnies in 1635.[66] Relatives who acted as seigneurial clients could often hope to gain additional lands through later grants or at their patron's death. Immediate familial ties and marriage ties were thus reinforced through landholding and inheritance. Warrior nobles often gave some of their lands to their sons so that they could cultivate their own seigneurial client relationships.[67]

Religious reformations and confessional conflicts severely disrupted seigneurial relationships by breaking down seigneurial bonds and dividing families. During religious wars, some co-seigneurs—such as the co-seigneurs of the town of Mirabel—found themselves in opposing religious and political camps. Some Huguenot vassals refused to do homage to Catholic lords, while others, like Fulcrand II d'Assas, paid homage when they inherited their estates, but then considered all of their obligations fulfilled.[68] Many Catholic nobles refused to deal with "heretic" Calvinist nobles at all. Some families were split into separate branches by confessional choices and opposing loyalties during civil conflicts.

Seigneurial clienteles could effectively exercise coercive power both within seigneurial jurisdictions and in surrounding regions. Nobles in seigneurial clienteles could usually intimidate tenants and villages easily, demanding loyalty and extracting resources from the peasants. Seigneurial clienteles could strongly influence, if not control, political activity within seigneurial holdings, even if they were quite expansive. Although the duc de Ventadour was frequently absent from his lands while leading Catholic armies in the 1610s and 1620s, he attempted to manage the consular elections and local politics within his seigneurie of Vauvert.[69] Nobles could also compel or coerce their tenants to serve them militarily as an extension of the *guet et garde* seigneurial right. Peasants on seigneuries had long been required to pay for the upkeep of château fortifications and to serve as château guards in times of danger, in return for allowing the peasant communities on the seigneurie to have shelter behind the walls of the château. In the early seventeenth century, nobles often recruited their nonnoble seigneurial tenants as soldiers in their infantry regiments.

Warrior nobles throughout southern France thus employed varying strategies of clientele formation to build political and military support. Many noble patrons cultivated mixed prestige, military, administrative, urban, and seigneurial clientage bonds among the provincial military elite. These clientage relationships were complex and shifting, but warrior clienteles took sharper form as civil warfare forced patrons and clients to sever certain bonds and reinforce others.

MANAGING CLIENTELES

As warrior noble clienteles developed, clientage bonds established multiple power relationships among noble clients. Although clientage has often been described as operating fundamentally through reciprocal patron-client ties, diverse associations and allegiances developed between the French nobles affiliated with an early seventeenth-century clientele. Warrior noble clienteles were as contentious as they were fluid, since clients could maintain their loyalties to a patron, but simultaneously cultivate connections with other prominent elites. Noble clients could easily renounce their allegiances and abandon their client-age engagements, so patrons always had to remain attentive to prevent the disruption of their clienteles.

Warrior nobles had to act constantly to maintain their clientage bonds and to manage tensions within their clienteles. Members of the military elite regularly provided political support, advocacy, arbitration, connections, and favors to their noble clients. Many of these forms of political patronage and sociability coincide with the activities of early modern courtiers, ministerial elites, and judicial nobles that have already been studied by historians. This section focuses on several aspects of clientage with strong military dimensions that were particular to warrior noble clienteles. Military officers routinely supplied health care, food, and lodging for their noble clients during military campaigns. Warrior nobles expected that their patrons and associates would provide them with personal security and offer refuge to their families. Warrior clienteles also organized armed assistance for noble clients, exerting coercion on other nobles and on southern French communities during civil wars.

Care and Provision

Warrior nobles personally provided for the physical needs of their noble followers during civil conflicts—hosting dinners, arranging lodging, distributing money, and providing health care. Patrons' commitment to care for their clients was especially strong during military campaigns. Military elites often expressed this power relation in paternalist terms, with a patron acting like a father providing for his children. In providing for their followers, patrons hoped both to display their magnanimity and uphold their clients' status and rank. While Norbert Elias's influential model of the "civilizing process" has prompted examinations of noble dining and manners, few studies have examined the broader implications of provisioning in noble culture.[70]

Providing food for clients could be an enormous task for noble patrons, and was often handled though semi-official processes of military administration. Prominent nobles hosted magnificent banquets at their châteaux when hosting royal family members and grands, seeking simultaneously to impress their peers and their clients. The duc d'Épernon organized a lavish dinner for the prince de Condé in 1611, served on a "buffet with seventeen levels and with several basins and other dishes of pure gold."[71] Warrior nobles organized ample, if less ostentatious, meals for their clients and troops who accompanied them on military campaigns, arranging for bread, water, and meat on march routes and in siege encampments. Typically, subordinate officers and household members would arrange for municipal officials and army provisioners to provide food directly to clients or, alternatively, to advance payments for purchasing it.[72] An aide de camp who arranged for food for the followers of Just-Henri de Tournon comte de Tournon, a Catholic commander who was operating in Vivarais in 1627, prepared copious meals of bread, wine, mutton, and beef paid for by army logistical officials.[73] Huguenot nobles in the besieged city of Montauban dined together in a garden while visiting one of the defensive fortifications.[74] During civil conflicts, the provisioning of clienteles and military units were thus closely interrelated.

Providing for clienteles was expensive, since feeding and lodging noble followers not only involved arranging for their personal needs, but also feeding the valets, servants, and horses that accompanied nobles on campaign.[75] Noble officers received extra pay and extra rations in order to feed and care for their followers and households. Providing food for mounted bodyguards or for a compagnie d'ordonnance could take significant organization. The prescribed daily rations of a single gendarme during one campaign amounted to three pounds of white bread and three pounds "between white and gray," four jars of wine, and two pounds of mutton. Each gendarme's horses had to be provided with oats and fifty pounds of hay per day.[76] Not surprisingly, nobles were provided with better meals than common soldiers, who could only look forward to a basic ration of bread and wine. Nobles, in contrast, could expect larger servings and more meat in their diets.

Noble patrons continued to care for their followers at a distance when they were geographically separated during military campaigns. Like many other nobles, the duc de Rohan regularly sent out orders for Huguenot towns to provide for his clients' needs when they were operating in their localities. In 1628, for example, Rohan ordered the consuls of the town of Alès to pay Jean d'Artigues, maréchal de logis for Rohan's household, 260 livres and 10 sous for him to use to cover the expenses of "seven volunteer gentlemen in our suite" for a single day.[77] Patrons' abilities to extend food, lodging, and medical care to clients even beyond the reach of their households and military units indicates the significant organizational and financial capabilities of clienteles.

Providing for the needs of clients also entailed repaying followers for their expenses. Noble patrons attempted to provide monetary remuneration to the clients who had assisted them by advancing funds. Warrior noble clienteles routinely raised capital during civil conflicts through various credit mechanisms that re-circulated money through southern French society. Military patrons had to manage multiple loans within their clienteles to pay for the enormous costs of army mobilization, operations, and demobilization each campaigning season. Antoine Cardaillac de Lévis comte de Bioule claimed to have been "constrained to advance large sums" to several of his "friends" in order to raise and arm his chevaux-légers and some infantry companies in 1621.[78] Warrior noble families kept elaborate account books, receipts, and contracts relating to their loans and distributions of money.[79] Henri II de Montmorency made sure that royal fiscal officers and regional financial institutions would reimburse nobles in his entourage for specific losses that they incurred while serving with him.[80] Montmorency frequently ordered the repayment of the costs of supplies and rations paid for by his officers during military campaigns.[81] Such remuneration amounted to a deferred provision of clients' material needs, but significant delays could undermine trust and threaten client loyalties.

Caring for the health and well-being of clients was another key concern for nobles. Early modern armies had few formal medical services, and noble patrons thus played an important role in arranging medical care for their wounded and ill clients. Some nobles paid personal surgeons to accompany them and their clienteles on campaign. Noble patrons also had to make arrangements for the care of clients and soldiers who became too sick or incapacitated to accompany them. Local hospitals, religious houses, and individuals' homes might allow followers to recuperate, but frequently demanded money to pay for the care. The ordonnances of the duc de Rohan show that he regularly provided for sick and incapacitated followers. The municipal government of Alès was to pay for the care of Jacques Blachière de Lussan and his followers "during the time that he is obliged to remain there because of his illness." Blachière, a noble cavalryman in the chevaux-légers of the baron d'Alès, stayed in the town for sixteen days recovering from his illness and 36 livres were paid on his behalf.[82] The medical needs of clients such as Blachière often demanded the personal attention and care of noble patrons, and suggest the scope of nobles' responsibilities toward their followers.[83]

Warrior noble patrons not only provided for their clients, but also for their soldiers and other commoners who sought their assistance. This broad social role as provider helps explain the large baggage trains and campaign communities accompanying armies in the early seventeenth-century.[84] But noble patrons' responses to the needs of commoners remained impersonal and distant in contrast to the affection displayed in their attention to the needs of their noble clients. Subordinate officials and household members, whenever possible, handled the needs of these non-nobles, while relations with clients always carried some sense of personal obligation.

Protection and Security

Warrior patrons provided physical security and political protection for their clients, their families, and their properties during civil conflicts. Military elites understood protection as a normal, natural, and positive aspect of warrior noble culture rather than as an odious, unnatural, but necessary reliance on illegitimate power. Noble patrons often provided personal protection for their clients using influence, safe-conducts, and bodyguards to safeguard their followers. Louis de Pontis's patron personally helped him escape from imprisonment in the early seventeenth century.[85] Other noble patrons worked to free their clients who were captured and imprisoned during civil wars, negotiating for their release and often paying their ransoms.[86] Henri de Luxembourg comte de Saint-Pol was "greatly offended" when one of his subordinate officers was arrested while traveling in Guyenne in 1613 and held for the payment of a fine. The comte seems to have felt that his own honor was being challenged, so he sought to have his client released and to avoid making any payment.[87] Protection by patrons was vital during periods of civil warfare, assuring the survival of clients and providing an important rationale for clientele relations.

Protection entailed providing refuge at patrons' châteaux and hôtels, as well as in fortifications they governed. Huguenot nobles sheltered local Calvinists in their own residences and at the places de sûreté, or security towns, that they personally controlled.[88] Warrior nobles provided military protection to their clients, arming them with weapons and aiding them with the recruitment and organization of troops. Nobles worked to supply artillery and munitions to their clients for major defensive efforts. Clients expected their patrons to provide relief of their châteaux and governments when enemy armies threatened them with siege. Patrons often acted to protect their noble clients from harm by intimidating or confronting their local rivals and enemies.[89]

Warrior nobles were especially concerned to protect their clients when they switched allegiances or made separate peaces. The duc d'Épernon had to shield his clients several times when he was accused of the crime of lèse-majesté during the turbulent regency of Marie de Médicis and Wars of Mother and Son.[90]

Jacques-Nompar de Caumont marquis de La Force's Huguenot clients in Guyenne and Béarn were vulnerable when he abandoned the Calvinist cause and submitted to royal authority in 1622.[91] The duc de Rohan acted to protecting his Huguenot followers in Languedoc in successive religious peaces in the 1620s.[92]

The Huguenot commander Gaspard III de Coligny seigneur de Châtillon's decision to make a separate peace agreement with the monarchy and submit to Louis XIII in 1621 reveals how noble patrons acted to protect their clients. Many of Châtillon's clients, such as Louis II de Baschi baron d'Aubais, felt that their patron was betraying the Huguenot cause and refused to join in his submission. These nobles abandoned Châtillon's clientele, seeking other prominent Calvinist patrons—notably the duc de Rohan. Châtillon tried to protect his remaining noble followers, who were scattered across the province of Languedoc, often in isolated and vulnerable positions, by appealing to the king to help protect his clients who were now subject to Huguenot reprisals. Prominent provincial nobles, such as Jean de Narbonne de Faugères de Cailus baron de Rocquelz, needed protection because of his high profile. The regional nobles Claude d'Airbaudouze, Jean Duranc, and Jean de Rochemore all continued to support Châtillon in the midst of civil warfare, despite his submission to the king. Châtillon specified that Jacques de Cambres de Serignac was isolated at his home, presumably to indicate that he was especially susceptible to Calvinist retaliation.[93]

The seigneur de Châtillon also extended protection to a wide range of associates beyond his warrior noble clientele who depended on him to some degree for protection and patronage. When he joined the Catholic and royalist forces in 1621, he sought to protect his followers and dependents, especially in Aigues-Mortes and Montpellier, places he governed. Châtillon included all of "the consuls and inhabitants of the town of Aigues-Mortes and the officers of the garrison" in his protection. He further promised to protect his followers and the royal officers from towns like Beaucaire, Nîmes, Mende, and Montpellier who were refugees within the walls of Aigues-Mortes, and tried to protect a number of inhabitants of Montpellier who had fled when the duc de Rohan's Huguenot forces took control of the city. Châtillon's dependents in Montpellier included many prominent juridical elites in the chambre des comptes and cour des aides. Several lawyers, a treasurer, and a professor at the faculty of medicine also needed protection. Châtillon also extended his aid to a surgeon, two butchers, two ministers, and numerous townspeople indicated simply as "bourgeois."[94] Warrior patrons thus sometimes provided security to soldiers and other commoners beyond their noble clients.

Armed Coercion

Warrior noble clientage bonds operated through both outright and implied co-ercion as clienteles exerted power in southern French political culture. Military patrons established coercive power over their own noble clients, managing cli-entage partially as an extension of their authority to command armed forces. Noble clients accepted the power of patrons to command them and willingly acquiesced to a certain notion of military and social discipline while operating in clienteles. Patrons established a degree of precedence within their clienteles, selecting subordinates and commanding clients to perform tasks. Through such mild coercive techniques, patrons attempted to ensure that their clients followed their will. Should a noble fail to acquiesce to his patron's wishes, there was al-ways the coercive threat of retaliation by the patron and his entire clientele—through ostracism or armed retribution. Despite the fraternal discourses of *am-itié* and Christian brotherhood employed in warrior noble culture, vastly unequal power relationships among nobles meant that a clientele never fully represented a band of warrior brothers.

Noble patrons attracted impressive armed entourages of mounted noble cli-ents that could act coercively across southern France. The size and appearance of nobles' clienteles also announced distinctions in rank and importance. Nobles' entourages clearly varied widely by the rank and status of the noble. For example, François de La Madeleine marquis de Ragny, a maréchal de camp commanding troops in the Cévennes in 1623, would have been highly visible and imposing with his train of fifty horses. In contrast, Ragny's two aides-de-camp had only four horses each, and the captain of his bodyguard a mere three. These officers would have been hardly distinguishable from the gendarmes, who normally pos-sessed two steeds.[95] The sieur Alizon, guidon of the compagnie d'ordonnance of the duc de Ventadour, had a train of three valets, four horses, and one mule.[96] The proximity of the noble to his landholdings and governments seems to have influenced the coercive potential of his retinue. Noble retinues were expensive to maintain and provision, especially during long military campaigns. It was, therefore, easier for a noble to mobilize his clientele fully as a retinue when close to his landholdings.

Patrons used their military retinues and clienteles for local and regional intimi-dation and coercion through civic entries, urban ceremonies, hunts, and rural rides. The displays and processions that militant clienteles enacted in public spaces al-lowed them to assert power in relation to other individuals and communities in provincial society. Gatherings of clients at their patron's château or hôtel could assert coercive power by announcing the prominence of their noble patron and threatening neighbors. Warrior noble clienteles staged entry ceremonies through city gates each time a walled community accepted a new governor or garrison. Assemblies of clienteles in urban communities often resembled rallies, display-ing allegiances and political power openly in ways that threatened rival local nobles.[97] The thunderous noise created by large numbers of horses, armed no-bles, valets, fanfare, and music attracted attention whenever warrior nobles as-sembled. The colorful visual aspects of noble coats of arms, liveries, banners, and armor could seem menacing as easily as festive.[98] Clienteles were, after all, assemblies of warrior nobles bearing arms as weapons, signs, and threats.

The clienteles of southern French warrior nobles regularly applied coercion against rival nobles and confessional opponents through raiding warfare against nearby châteaux and communities. The coercive aspects of warrior noble clien-teles were magnified by their extensive military recruiting operations in south-ern France. Noble clients often recruited troops directly for their patron's infan-try regiments and cavalry companies. In a French society accustomed to living with armies and frequent episodes of civil warfare, every gathering of nobles was likely to be interpreted as a coercive move. The parlement de Toulouse fre-quently deliberated on *assemblées en armes*, condemning nobles for gathering with their armed clienteles.[99] Once assembled, clienteles displayed an armed coercive presence with a potential to act violently. Organized clienteles could immediately be ready to strike militarily, and they thus posed a threat to the entire region around them. Understandably, the parlement de Toulouse fre-quently denounced any assembly of nobles, whether or not they had taken any offensive action.[100]

Warrior patrons had to act to manage the coercive potential of their clientage bonds, avoiding tensions within their clienteles and preventing undesirable con-flicts with other clienteles. Relations between Henri II de Rohan duc de Rohan and Gabriel de Lévis-Léran baron de Léran provide insight on how clientage bonds could dissolve in violence. The baron de Léran, a Huguenot noble with landholdings and connections in the dioceses of Mirepoix and Foix, entered the military clientele of the duc de Rohan as a Huguenot commander in Foix, leading campaigns there in 1621 and 1622. The duc de Rohan later sent Huguenot troops under a noble named Brétigny to aid in the defense of the town of Le Mas-d'Azil in Foix in 1625, potentially supplanting Léran's authority in the region. The baron de Léran disputed Brétigny's authority, leading to a rift with Rohan. The strain on the duc de Rohan's clientele became even more apparent when Brétigny's brother and Léran's brother-in-law, who were both followers of Rohan, fought a duel at the town of Castres leaving Léran's kinsman dead. The incensed baron de Léran then severed his ties with Rohan and sought vengeance against him.[101]

Warrior noble patrons thus had to respond attentively to the urgent needs of their clients during civil conflicts, while remaining vigilant for signs of brewing tensions within their clienteles. Maintaining clientage bonds among armed noble clients represented an intricate art of negotiation and conflict resolution.

REFASHIONING CLIENTELES

Not only did maintaining clienteles demand noble patrons' constant attention, but warrior nobles sometimes transformed their clienteles completely and refashioned them around new clients as a result of external pressures, internal chaos, or expanded opportunities. Military threats could force patrons to regroup their clienteles, strengthening them by attracting different groups of clients. Whenever a noble patron's rivals altered their clienteles, he might need to respond by reshaping his own. The deaths or defections of key clients could throw a clientele into confusion.

Whatever a patron's intentions, the refashioning of clienteles involved agency on the part of all of the noble clients affiliated with the clientele. Warrior patrons could not simply recast their entourages through deliberate self-fashioning, since complex power relationships bound together the members of warrior noble clienteles. Repeated failures of a patron to advocate for his clientele might prompt his clients to lose confidence in him. Finally, newly acquired offices, family connections, or estates might offer possibilities to expand a clientele in new directions.

This section examines four specific cases of warrior noble clienteles in Guyenne and Languedoc led by Louis d'Arpajon marquis de Séverac et vicomte d'Arpajon, Louis I de Lescure baron de Lescure, Louis II de Baschi baron d'Aubais, and Guillaume de Balazuc de Montréal. Each of these noble patrons utilized multiple types of clientage bonds to form their clienteles. The analysis traces how each of these clienteles developed during the civil wars of the early seventeenth century, as some clientage relationships dissolved and new ones were established.

The Transforming Clientage of a Prestigious Noble

The case of Louis d'Arpajon marquis de Séverac et vicomte d'Arpajon demonstrates how a prestigious noble could progressively transform his clientage bonds with regional nobles. Louis d'Arpajon was born into a prominent family in

Rouergue. His father, Jean d'Arpajon, provided him with regional family prestige and extensive landholdings, including the seigneuries of Séverac-le-Château, Montal, Salvainhac, Caumont, and Montclar. The Arpajon family claimed to be descendants of the kings of Aragon, and while this did not place the family in the ranks of the *grands*, it did give them somewhat heightened status among the regional nobility. The Arpajon château de Sévérac in Rouergue also gave the family right to entry to the estates of Rouergue.[102] As Louis d'Arpajon began to form his own clientele in the 1610s, he seems to have utilized his prestige and his vast seigneurial holdings to attract clients during the civil conflict in Rouergue in 1615 and 1616.[103]

At this point—when the vicomte could have easily enmeshed himself within regional politics and society to expand his clientele in Rouergue—Louis d'Arpajon struck out to transform his clientele, reforming it not primarily around his seigneurial or prestige connections, but around new military connections that he cultivated while serving with nobles of regions beyond Rouergue. He served as a noble volunteer with the duc de Lesdiguières in 1617. Then, in 1621, Arpajon raised an infantry regiment at his own cost and fought with the Catholic forces at the sieges of Tonneins, Saint-Antonin, Félissant, and Montauban in Guyenne and Languedoc. Arpajon's service during the 1622 campaign gave him new opportunities to establish connections and reshape his clientele. He served as a maréchal de camp in the field army of César duc de Vendôme in 1622. Vendôme, half-brother of Louis XIII, was influential at the royal court and perhaps introduced Arpajon to new military connections. During the siege of Saint-Antonin in June 1622, Arpajon and the other commanders got to meet personally with the king, who came to oversee the conduct of the siege.[104]

Arpajon's military service in Languedoc seems to have prompted him to expand his connections to the province. His mother, Jaquette de Castlenau de Clermont-Lodève, was from an ancient Languedoc family that had been quite prominent in Languedoc noble society, holding high ecclesiastical and administrative offices.[105] The vicomte d'Arpajon also emphasized this redefinition of his clientele through his 1622 marriage to Gloriande de Lauzières de Thémines, whose family had extensive influence in Haut Languedoc and Haut Guyenne.[106]

Louis d'Arpajon forged a powerful military clientele in Haut Languedoc in the 1620s through his service in Catholic armies, which won him recognition and new clients. He served in the army of the duc de Montmorency in 1627, leading a cavalry attack at the battle of Souilles.[107] The premier président, or chief justice, of the parlement de Toulouse praised Arpajon in a letter to the cardinal de Richelieu, a sign of his growing presence in Languedoc.[108] When Arpajon participated in the fighting in Haut Languedoc and the Pyrenees in 1628, the needs of his military clientele and troops clashed with the desires of his other clients and allies. Arpajon imposed heavy contributions of 4,400 livres on the dioceses of Haut Languedoc in 1628. The estates of Languedoc repaid the dioceses the next year, but Arpajon's contributions policies seem to have been causing dissension between him and other nobles both in the provincial estates and throughout the region of Haut Languedoc.[109] Arpajon led troops against Huguenot forces in the region around Millau in 1628, attacking the town of Meyrueis. During these efforts, his brother, Alexandre d'Arpajon, raised "forty gentlemen of my friends" and four hundred infantry to aid him.[110]

Arpajon led troops to join François de Bassompierre for the investment of Montauban in the spring of 1629, assembling them in the diocese of Albi and ordering the diocese to pay for their supplies.[111] Town consuls and residents of the diocese complained to the estates of Languedoc that they were *vexes et travaillés* because of the "excess of evils they have done in the said diocese." The infantry were "composed of robbers and brigands who commit all sorts of acts of hostility against the good and faithful subjects of the king."[112] Arpajon then became embroiled in a dispute with the archbishop of Toulouse over taxes he imposed in the diocese of Toulouse to pay for his troops. The archbishop complained to the estates of Languedoc, claiming that the duc de Montmorency had revoked Arpajon's authority to levy taxes. Arpajon reportedly sent his own complaints directly to the king.[113] The peace of Alès on 28 June 1629 ended hostilities, and Montauban submitted to royal authority before the siege could advance.[114] Arpajon was by now a fixture in Languedoc warrior noble society, with numerous military and seigneurial clients from Languedoc along with his seigneurial clients from Rouergue.

The 1632 civil war forced Louis d'Arpajon, like so many other Languedoc nobles, to adapt his clientele once again. Arpajon was listed as an able leader in a March 1632 plan for the recruitment of royal troops to counter the forces of Gaston d'Orléans and the duc de Montmorency in Languedoc. How exactly he contributed to the maréchal de Schömberg's campaign against Montmorency that autumn is unclear, but after the defeat of Montmorency's army at Castelnaudary, Arpajon was rewarded handsomely with appointment as one of the three new lieutenant generals of Languedoc.[115] With this position, Arpajon was obliged to accept significant provincial responsibilities and develop new administrative clients. His clientele became a mixed one, centered firmly on the province of Languedoc, but with diverse elements remaining from his earlier emphases on his Rouergue prestige and his regimental military offices.

The Broadening Clientage of an Albigeois Noble

Louis I de Lescure baron de Lescure provides an interesting perspective of a regional Catholic noble's changing clientage practices in Haut Languedoc. The Lescure family's principal château and seigneurie was just east of the solidly Catholic town of Albi. Louis, a chevalier and a *gentilhomme ordinaire de la chambre du roi*, was a prominent noble in the diocese of Albi, holding a seat in the diocesan assembly. Louis de Lescure's successive marriages to four noblewomen gave him connections with prominent regional families such as the La Valettes and the Elbènes, but his remarriages meant that these ties were ephemeral and not particularly firm.[116] Louis de Lescure's clientage continued to rely on his seigneurial and urban connections in and around Albi.

During the civil conflicts of the early seventeenth century, the baron de Lescure served as an officer in Catholic armies in the Albigeois region. The provincial governor, the duc de Montmorency, reacted swiftly when Jean de Castelpers vicomte de Panat and his Huguenot troops seized the town of Lombers in early 1616, sending a commission on 26 March to the baron de Lescure to raise an army to retake Lombers. Montmorency gave Lescure power to select his subordinates and to raise whatever forces were necessary. Lescure's troops would be paid and supplied by the diocese of Albi, which would be reimbursed by the estates of Languedoc at a later date. Lescure responded by raising an infantry regiment of twelve companies, eighty gendarmes, and forty carabins to besiege Lombers.[117]

When the baron de Lescure needed additional cavalry support, he again turned to his noble clients around Albi. Lescure's recruitment practices show the importance of clientage bonds in military operations during the religious wars. Lescure empowered Hector-François de Corneillan vicomte de Corneillan to raise a company of 145 gendarmes, as well as giving him license to summon his client, the sieur du Trouchet, who raised a company of 90 carabins. Similarly, François de Boisson baron de Bournazel raised a company of 70 gendarmes directly for the baron de Lescure, while the baron d'Elbes formed his own company of 50 carabins under Bournazel's authority. The seigneur de Saint-Projet mobilized another 75 gendarmes for Lescure, and Baptiste de La Faramondie seigneur de Grèzes raised 40 carabins.[118] Once he had recruited and organized his forces, the baron de Lescure quickly advanced, besieging the towns of Lombers and Fauch, both under control of the Calvinist vicomte de Panat. Lescure and his clients successfully carried out the sieges and forced the capitulation of the towns.[119] As a good patron, Lescure provided for his noble clients and their soldiers during the siege. Several documents suggest the care with which Lescure provided for his wounded soldiers after the siege was completed.[120]

The conqueror of Lombers then became embroiled in the affairs of the town, which fundamentally reshaped his clientele. Montmorency named Lescure governor of the town and château de Lombers soon after its capture. When civil war broke out again in early 1619, Montmorency reconfirmed Lescure's authority at Lombers. Only in 1620 did Louis XIII finally confirm Lescure's appointment as "captain of the château de Lombers," but the baron's position as governor of Lescure had already become the key to his changing clientele.[121]

Lescure's position as a patron was severely challenged by the civil war of 1621–1622. Huguenots suddenly seized control of the town of Lombers, but Lescure's garrison in the château de Lombers was able to hold out and wait for assistance to mount a siege and retake the town.[122] The records of the siege of Lombers in 1621 allow a glimpse of Louis I de Lescure's troops and his clientele. Lescure's gendarmes that year were all nobles, with the possible exception of the trumpeter Antoine Verger. Jean de Roquefeuil sieur d'Arthès was from a seigneurie neighboring Lescure's own landholdings. Five of Lescure's gendarmes were probably younger nobles from minor families, since they are listed with a notation of *écuyer*.[123] The 1621 siege of Lombers again demonstrates how Lescure organized violence through his clientage relations. One of Lescure's clients, Gaspard de Seguy, took charge of writing to the consuls of Albi for munitions and aid in prosecuting the siege.[124]

The approach of Louis XIII's army in the autumn of 1621 for the siege of Montauban allowed Lescure to develop new connections to the *grands* who accompanied the army. Lescure seems to have raised five additional companies for the siege of Montauban that year.[125] Despite the failure of the royal siege of Montauban and the demobilization of most forces, Lescure's clientele continued to expand. During the 1622 campaign, Lescure operated in the Albigeois under the command of the duc de Vendôme, illegitimate brother of Louis XIII, whose army invested Lombers on 26 July 1622. Lescure was closely involved in the management of troops and supplies for the siege, as Vendôme's army quickly dug trenches and deployed six cannon, despite sorties made by the Calvinist defenders of the town. The Huguenot military commander in the Albigeois, Henri de Bourbon-Malauze marquis de Malauze, brought troops from Castres and attempted to relieve the siege on 29 July, but Vendôme's troops were prepared for them and after a brief skirmish Malauze withdrew. The failure to relieve the siege apparently convinced the Huguenot troops in Lombers to flee at night. On 30 July, Vendôme's troops entered Lombers without resistance and

pillaged the town. The walls and fortifications of the town were supposedly dismantled, but this seems unlikely, since Vendôme led his men almost immediately to invest the nearby town of Briatexte. Lescure's government was back in
his hands, but its physical integrity, human potential, and symbolic value had all
been seriously damaged.[126]

By the mid-1620s, Lescure's clientele had shifted considerably from one focused heavily on the town of Albi to a broader, more regional emphasis. Lescure's
town government at Lombers and his participation in numerous civil conflicts
across the diocese of Albi had led him to seek new clients. When civil warfare
broke out again in 1625, Lescure again found himself on the defensive. He raised
an infantry regiment in 1625 in the Albigeois and defended the town of Teillet,
located southeast of Albi, against the Huguenot troops under the command of
François de Lusignan marquis de Lusignan. Lusignan's regiment assaulted the
town, forcing Lescure's men to find shelter in the château until Lusignan was
recalled by the duc de Rohan for another siege. Only when the maréchal de
Thémines assembled his army in Haut Languedoc did Lescure get significant
support against the Huguenot troops in the region.[127]

Lescure refashioned his clientele again in the late 1620s as his clientele became
less dependent on his government of Lombers.[128] Lescure continued to exercise
considerable influence in the town of Albi itself in the late 1620s, but his clientele
had become much more diverse. The infantry companies of both Louis and his
son from his regiment de Lescure were garrisoned at Albi in 1628, maintaining
the baron's connections there.[129] In 1627, Montmorency gave Lescure new broad
powers to command all of the infantry and cavalry raised in the diocese of Albi and
to lead these troops to "all of the places and localities where the necessity of the
king's service requires."[130] In 1628, Lescure was again given broad powers, including instructions to guard the crossings on the river Tarn for the duc de Montmorency.[131] While the king's army conducted the siege of Privas in the Vivarais in
1629, Lescure worked to raise an infantry regiment in the diocese of Albi in preparation for an attack on the Huguenot-controlled town of Castres to the south. The
peace of Alès halted conflict before a siege could be launched, but Lescure's preparations show that his clientele maintained its broadened focus.[132]

The Shifting Clientage of a Calvinist Militant

Louis II de Baschi baron d'Aubais's clientele presents an interesting case of
mixed seigneurial, urban, and military clientage. Louis II inherited the seigneurie of Le Cailar and the baronnie d'Aubais, both located near the town of Nîmes

in Bas Languedoc. He and his brother Charles de Baschi seigneur de Saint-Estève effectively translated their kinship relations and seigneurial relations into regional prominence in the 1610s and 1620s.

A Calvinist noble, Aubais initially formed close seigneurial connections with nearby Huguenot nobles. In 1614, he married Anne de Rochemore, whose family was closely involved in urban politics and administration in both Montpellier and Nîmes.[133] The baron d'Aubais found an ally and friend in Claude de Calvière baron de Saint-Côme, who held a baronnie located just a few miles from Aubais. Calvière, a fellow Huguenot, was present at the baptism of Aubais's son Charles in August 1622. Aubais and Calvière fought together in Huguenot armies until the latter died in 1626 of wounds suffered in a siege.[134] Aubais's seigneurial followers included Jacques des Vignolles seigneur de Pradès et de La Croix, who served in Aubais's company of chevaux-légers.[135]

The baron d'Aubais enthusiastically supported Calvinist militant causes, throwing his support behind the Huguenot military leader Gaspard III de Coligny seigneur de Châtillon in Bas Languedoc in 1621. Aubais raised several cavalry units for Châtillon's Huguenot army and fought against the duc de Montmorency's Catholic army as a cavalry commander during the spring and summer. Châtillon ordered supplies for Aubais's companies of carabins and chevaux-légers during the campaign that year.[136] But when Châtillon submitted to royal authority, Aubais was not listed among his protected clients, having switched his allegiance to the duc de Rohan, under whom he would serve throughout the civil wars of the 1620s.[137]

Aubais soon became one of Rohan's closest subordinates in Languedoc, relying heavily on his military offices as mestre de camp and cavalry captain, as well as on his military clients, throughout the 1620s. Rohan increasingly gave Aubais independent commands and greater responsibilities. The latter participated in peace negotiations in 1625 and aided Rohan in his efforts to ratify the peace in 1626.[138] Aubais commanded Rohan's forces in Bas Languedoc when the duc led his main army into the Cévennes mountains in 1627.[139] These high-profile commands and his growing stature as a Huguenot military officer allowed Aubais to attract more Calvinist military clients. He even made his older brother, Charles de Baschi, into a military client. Charles recruited a cavalry company and served under his brother's orders. Aubais attracted sixty-five warrior noble clients to serve in his company of gendarmes.[140]

In the late 1620s, Aubais's clientele continued to grow, allowing the baron to seize Le Pouzin, attack Baix-sur-Baix, then lead the advance guard of Rohan's army in Vivarais in 1628.[141] When Huguenots in Haut Languedoc sent urgent requests for aid in mid-1628, Rohan entrusted Aubais with the relief force that successfully lifted the Catholic siege of Saint-Affrique. Rohan praised Aubais for aiding in the defense of the town, saying that he "did his duty well."[142] Rohan then sent Aubais to Castres to "accommodate the divisions" between two prominent Calvinist nobles with urban clienteles there. Aubais calmed the tensions somewhat and ensured Huguenot control of the town.[143]

Aubais again mobilized his clients and recruited troops in and around Nîmes for service in Rohan's armies in 1629, but Rohan grew increasingly frustrated with him and his other subordinates.[144] When the town of Alès was threatened by the approach of a royal army in 1629, Rohan offered Aubais command of the defense of the town. Rohan promised "to place around him all the best men that he had," and give him support, but Aubais refused the offer because, at least as Rohan saw it, Aubais "had made a resolution not to find himself in any besieged place."[145] Unlike Rohan, Aubais threw his support behind the efforts to reach a negotiated settlement with Louis XIII that resulted in the peace of Alès. After the end of the civil wars, Aubais maintained his reputation as a Calvinist militant and many of his seigneurial and military clients continued to serve in his military units.[146]

The Expanding Military Clientage of an Infantry Officer

Guillaume de Balazuc de Montréal's military career suggests how provincial nobles could expand their clientage through regimental offices and military commands during the early seventeenth-century civil wars. The Balazuc de Montréal family held the seigneuries of Montréal, Chazeaux, Lanas, and Sanillac, located southwest of the small town of Aubenas in Vivarais.[147] These extensive landholdings provided Montréal with a series of seigneurial connections, but his clientele was based primarily on his military offices and his considerable experience with warfare. Throughout the 1610s and 1620s, Montréal led an infantry regiment as a mestre de camp, his principal military office. Successive civil wars allowed him to summon his military clients and exercise enhanced authority. In 1617, Montréal and other Catholic nobles from Vivarais raised regiments to fight Huguenot forces in Gévaudan. Serving under Antoine-Hercule de Budos marquis de Portes in the adjacent region of Gévaudan allowed Guillaume to renew his family's long-standing affiliation to the Budos family, and to establish closer connections to the duc de Montmorency, Portes's nephew.[148] During the 1610s, Montréal's military clientele remained somewhat limited, but it was greatly reshaped by the eruption of serious civil warfare in Languedoc in 1621.

After raising troops, Montréal joined other Catholic forces gathering in Vivarais in 1621. This small army blockaded Villeneuve-de-Berg, and Montréal directed a series of attacks on its *faubourgs*, forcing the town to capitulate. He quickly reaped rewards for his conquest of Villeneuve-de-Berg.[149] The duc Montmorency arrived the day after Villeneuve-de-Berg surrendered to inspect the town, ordering public celebrations of the victory and holding a Catholic mass in the town for the first time in sixty-two years. Very soon afterwards, Montréal was made governor of Villeneuve-de-Berg and given command of the Catholic garrison established there. The town became the principal logistical and political center for Montréal's clientele for his future military operations.[150] The capture of Villeneuve-de-Berg, then, allowed Montréal to expand his military patronage in the Vivarais region.

Montmorency's confidence in Montréal appears to have grown quickly, because he entrusted Montréal with increasingly broad powers.[151] When Montmorency departed to join the king's army at the siege of Montauban, he left Montréal in charge of Bas Languedoc with the regiments de Languedoc, Péraut, Hannibal, and Mazargues under his command, giving him access to new sources of patronage, increased financial support, and wider command authority. Montréal quickly showed that the governor of Languedoc's trust was not misplaced. His small army rushed to relieve the town of Serrières, which had been besieged in September by a Huguenot force under the baron de Brison. Montréal's troops soundly defeated Brison's men, capturing their artillery and forcing them to retreat. Montréal's victory effectively halted Huguenot offensive action in Bas Languedoc, since Brison could not carry out siege operations without artillery.[152]

These new responsibilities were soon confirmed by Montréal's promotion to maréchal de camp.[153] However, his extensive military service and the maintenance of his enlarged clientele increasingly burdened his finances. A later genealogist would describe Montréal as "having almost always made war at his own expense, [and] having greatly upset his fortune. The grade of maréchal de camp only produced occasions to multiply his expenses."[154] Nevertheless, the position of maréchal de camp gave Montréal an enhanced status in Languedoc noble society and increased patronage opportunities. When Montmorency besieged Marsillargues in August 1622, Montréal was on an equal footing with the marquis de Portes, and the two maréchaux de camp acted as Montmorency's main subordinates during the siege.[155]

Montréal, increasingly called "le brave Montréal" by his contemporaries, had gained an enviable military reputation, and it was said that "no one knew the art of war better in the defiles and gorges of Vivarais."[156] According to a church history of the region, Montréal's Catholic soldiers had such confidence in him that "when he was at their head, anything was possible."[157] Such praise reflected Montréal's growing importance as a warrior noble in Vivarais and the significance of his flourishing military clientele.

As a sign of Montréal's increased prominence, Louis XIII directly summoned him to raise troops when civil war again broke out in Vivarais in 1626. Montréal acted as maréchal de camp for a Catholic force that the comte de Tournon was assembling in Vivarais. As maréchal de camp, Montréal used his patronage to organize the newly levied infantry and cavalry, and he took charge of managing the artillery taken from Bagnols. Montréal defended Villeneuve-de-Berg and confronted the Huguenot forces along the Rhône in 1626–1627.[158] By 1628, Montréal commanded a much larger infantry regiment of ten companies, an indication of his regional power and influence.[159] This expansion of his regiment allowed Montréal to build clientage by selecting new clients to serve under him or by appointing existing seigneurial clients as military officers. Montréal's military clients could count on benefiting from a patron who had intimate connections with the most powerful warrior nobles in the province.[160]

A large Huguenot army under the duc de Rohan threatened Vivarais in 1628, giving Montréal another opportunity to exercise broad command and to expand his clientage bonds. The duc de Montmorency and the prince de Condé were leading operations in Haut Languedoc and the duc de Ventadour was dealing with problems in Velay, so Montréal was the senior Catholic commander in Vivarais. The Vivarais Catholics "would have been completely in disorder and confusion without the presence of monsieur de Montréal," according to one account. Montréal gathered forces to defend Vivarais and issued a call for nobles to join him "in the common defense of their belongings, their lives, and their honor."[161] Guillaume de Balazuc de Montréal summoned his military clientele and fixed the rendezvous for his army at his government of Villeneuve-de-Berg. A large number of noble followers served under Montréal's command in bands of volunteers and cavalry companies—a sign of Montréal's prominence in Vivarais noble life. As maréchal de camp, Montréal commanded a number of regiments, but also gained additional direct authority by commanding detachments from other regiments and independently raised companies. In 1628, Montréal commanded at least twenty independent companies of infantry, apart from those in his own regiment, giving him direct connections to a total of thirty noble captains as clients—the equivalent of commanding three regiments.[162] His army now numbered about two thousand infantry and two hundred cavalry. Balazuc de Montréal dispersed some of his troops into garrisons, including at

CLIENTAGE AND FRIENDSHIP 113

least 150 men at Villeneuve-de-Berg under the command of his son, the seigneur de Joanas. Montréal's military clientele displayed its power and its ability to quickly secure central Vivarais against Huguenot offensives. Montréal's army then launched operations around Le Pouzin along the Rhône river and took Mirabel by siege.[163]

In 1629, when civil war flared up again in Vivarais, Richelieu included Montréal's regiment on a list of units that could be quickly raised for service against the Huguenots.[164] Throughout the 1620s, Montréal had fashioned an enviable clientele in Vivarais using his military offices and local connections. Although he initially had little prestige, his growing military reputation garnered him praise and new followers. Montréal gained extensive rewards during his service in Vivarais in the 1620s. His government of Villeneuve-de-Berg, as we have seen, was a direct reward for his service at the siege of the town. He was also granted the château de Vaneilles du Bois, close to Chomérac.[165] After the assassination of a regional Huguenot commander, Montréal received his belongings and possessions as a gift from the king.[166] Montréal, a noble of fairly insignificant rank, was thus able to become important in regional noble society and politics because of his well-developed military clientele.

✝

This chapter has offered new evidence on early seventeenth-century warrior noble clientage, stressing the vital role played by violence and civil conflict in giving shape to clienteles. Southern French warrior nobles organized their participation in civil conflicts during the early seventeenth century through complex clientage relationships among their "friends." Clientage thus formed a compelling bond of nobility, shaping southern French nobles' perceptions of violence and arranging their practices of civil warfare. Warrior nobles formed, maintained, and refashioned their clienteles as they participated in successive civil conflicts between 1598 and 1635. We now turn to consider the role that warrior nobles' officeholding played in early modern political culture.

Louis XIII surrounded by scenes of war that depict warrior nobles in relationship to their king. Engraving by Matthäus Merian, *Portrait de Louis XIII en
médaillon et scènes de guerre*, BNF, Estampes, N-2, 1087. Photo courtesy
Bibliothèque Nationale de France.

CHAPTER FIVE

The Dignity and Authority
of Their Charges

Officeholding and Political Culture

In the midst of an increasingly chaotic and serious civil conflict in southwestern France in 1625, Henri de Lévis duc de Ventadour wrote to his fellow noble officers who were in session at a meeting of the estates of Languedoc:

> to renew the offers of my services and to beg you to continue the favor of your affections, in which I desire to preserve myself, and to increase [them] as much as possible. And for this purpose I shall return to Languedoc in a few days to take up my charge, following the wishes of the king, who commanded me to mobilize my company of gendarmes, which I shall do for the great relief of the region . . . desiring nothing with such passion as to show you all how much I am truly, and shall be all my life, Sirs, your most humble and most affectionate servant.[1]

The duc de Ventadour's pledges of service and his dedication to his charge, or office, reveal the vital links between officeholding, service, and power in early modern noble culture. Officeholding framed the political activities of warrior nobles such as Ventadour, who participated in political culture using the powers and qualities of their offices. Nobles believed that offices held dignity, granting rank and prestige to the officeholder and requiring him to uphold the status of his charge. In 1616, a group of nobles called on the king to "maintain the officers of the crown, the governors of the provinces and of the towns of the kingdom, in the dignity and authority of their charges, without which nobody could intercede to arrange and order those who are responsible for their functions."[2] During a period of near-constant religious and civil conflict in southern France, officeholding and service shaped the ways in which provincial warrior nobles participated in social and political life.

Warrior nobles played vital roles in early modern French provincial politics and administration, operating both inside and outside the state institutions and social hierarchies. Although Jürgen Habermas situates the emergence of a modern "public sphere" in the late seventeenth and early eighteenth centuries, recent studies of print culture during the French Wars of Religion reveal an active "public opinion" operating much earlier.[3] Habermas's emphasis on the essentially "bourgeois" nature of the "public sphere" overlooks the broad dimensions of noble involvement in significant political discussion and debate in early modern France.[4] Early seventeenth-century conceptions of the state were fluid, allowing warrior nobles to comment on early modern French political issues and to participate in state development processes.

This chapter uses a historical concept of political culture to investigate the official bonds that linked warrior nobles to other officers and to the royal state. New analytical methods that employ historicized concepts of political culture to examine state/culture relationships and the processes of state development reveal multiple intersections of public/private power.[5] Recent interpretations of French Revolutionary political culture, in particular, offer useful models for considering political cultures as historically located and specific to distinct social groups.[6] Keith Michael Baker, for example, employs a linguistic approach to political culture, arguing that politics is "about making claims. . . . Political culture is, in this sense, the set of discourses or symbolic practices by which these claims are made."[7] The implication of these studies is that the boundaries of political cultures remain permeable, as individual and collective actors shift. While these works sometimes overemphasize the discursive dimensions of political culture, they do effectively reveal how political practices are continually contested and their logics redefined through historical processes.

These approaches suggest envisioning a particular early seventeenth-century French political culture in which warrior nobles actively participated through their military and officeholding practices. This political culture was strongly shaped by the particular contexts of religious reform, confessional conflict, and civil violence after the Edict of Nantes. The religious divisions, family rivalries, and clientage relations described in previous chapters all influenced this political culture, but the "dignity and authority" of officeholding arguably defined how nobles related to the monarch and to the royal government.

Informal and formal power relations merged in warrior nobles' interactions with the monarchical state in this period. Multiple channels of authority bound nobles to other officeholders and linked them to the monarch. Royal attempts to organize and manage officeholding shaped the composition of the military elites and influenced their practices. Although the monarch established the ideal of royal service and promoted officeholding as a means of implementing the king's will, nobles were able to craft their own officeholding strategies and develop their own rationales for royal service. Even as they accepted the ideal of royal service, nobles also developed ways of exercising office in order to gain status and assert their own interests. Warrior nobles participated in early seventeenth-century French political culture through official bonds that were constructed and maintained using a series of intricate representations and practices of officeholding.

CONSTRUCTING PROVINCIAL POWER

All noble officeholders in France held their positions by the grace of the king and could be considered royal agents, but offices did not confer authority and duties in a clearly defined manner. Offices were not "modern" bureaucratic positions with duties fixed by carefully written legal and institutional guidelines. Instead, officers inherited certain practices and precedents when they acquired a new office, but they also brought their own prestige, experience, and abilities to their offices, allowing them to craft their own interpretations of their offices and official authority. Family possession of offices over generations allowed families to exert influence over the form an office would take and over the parameters of its practical authority. Individual nobles shaped their own offices and constructed their relationships with the state through the authorities granted them directly or indirectly by the monarch.

To successfully exercise provincial power, warrior nobles had to find support for their authority and to enunciate justifications for their actions. Warrior nobles sought to use the royal fount of authority to back up their decisions and confirm their power. Nobles used ordinary authority to build their power relationships and employed extraordinary authority to extend their power. Nobles shaped their power relationships through a series of overlapping authorities in the provinces of southern France.

The Royal Fount of Authority

Early modern French monarchs claimed to delegate authority through a communication of *majesté* and a spatial projection of the royal self to agents who embodied the royal person and enunciated the royal voice at a distance. Renaissance political theories and French juridical treaties promoted new ideologies of *majesté* (*majestas*) that linked royal authority to God's glory and terrestrial harmony. Jean Bodin, Pierre de Belloy, Claude d'Albon, Charles Loyseau, and other theorists debated *majesté* and the related concept of sovereignty intensely during the French Wars of Religion.[8] Royal coronations, baptisms, funerals, city entries, processions, and court ceremonies all portrayed *majesté* through rituals in which nobles participated and acknowledged regal symbols. Artistic programs sponsored by the royal family depicted *majesté* through portraits, paintings, prints, medals, statues, and buildings. Tracing the reception and modifications of royal discourses and representations of *majesté* by provincial nobles can reveal the often unexpected manifestations and transmissions of the king's authority.

According to constitutional theories, all official authority emanated directly from the king as God's representative on earth, but it could be projected and represented through royal subjects and institutions. Despite the divine implications of *majesté*, theorists claimed that fundamental laws, or an *ancien constitution*, tempered and interpreted royal authority through consultation with subjects. A mixed monarchy that included various corporate bodies provided advice to the king, conditioned his exercise of authority, and implemented the royal will. Authority and power were personal possessions of the monarch, who insisted on alluding to "my town," "my province," "my army," or "my regiment" to assert the personal bonds of royal authority.[9] The king freely gave a portion of his authority to an officer by conferring the office upon him. Noble officers did not compel the king to relinquish this authority, instead the king granted authority because it pleased him to do so. Each noble officer, then, held in trust a portion of the king's authority and sovereignty. In the early seventeenth century, Marie de Médicis's regency and influence in the king's councils disturbed the theoretical sharing of authority. The perceived masculine nature of *majesté* and the provisions of the Salic Law questioned a female regent's possibility of wielding power and distributing authority. Civil conflicts further complicated the implementation of the king's authority.

Nobles repeatedly emphasized the theoretical notions of the king's granting of authority. The marquis d'Aubeterre, for example, claims to have "the authority, that it pleased the late king and His Majesty to give me in my charges, where I serve him only for honor." Since an officer's authority constituted a portion of the king's own authority, a noble considered challenges to his official authority as direct challenges to the king. Aubeterre declares that another noble, because of "an excess of ambition," wishes "to attack the authority of my charge." So his reaction is to oppose this noble in "the king's interest" and to maintain "the authority that it pleased His Majesty to give me in my government."[10] From the perspective of noble officers, their personal authority was bound intimately with that of the king. Respect due to nobles was simultaneously respect owed to the king.

The prime duty and responsibility of officeholders was the maintenance of the king's authority. Officeholders were not only bound to obey the king themselves, but also to uphold the king's authority within their jurisdictions. Nobles referred continually to this need as they constructed their power relations. The duc de Montmorency justified to the queen regent his use of a compagnie d'ordonnance in Languedoc by stating that he had used it "in diverse occasions to assert the authority of Your Majesties."[11] An officer had to take preventive measures to make sure that nothing upset the king's authority, and the king frequently reminded his officers of these obligations. In 1614, Louis XIII ordered the governor of Languedoc to "take care that nothing comes to pass that could damage my authority and the good of my service."[12] If the king's authority was not recognized or respected within an officer's jurisdiction, he was duty-bound to remedy the situation. One noble arrived in his government in 1618 to find that a château had been seized and that "those who were within [the château] were men charged with crimes who recognized very little the authority that the king gave me for his service in the province. . . . I prepare to repair this fault."[13] Maintaining the king's authority required an officer's constant vigilance and attention.

To maintain the king's authority and to handle their administrative responsibilities, officers further subdivided royal authority by appointing subordinate officers and delegating authority. The process of subdividing authority created imperfect hierarchies, but authority was always assumed to emanate ultimately from the king. Subordinate nobles reinforced their own authority by citing the sources of their authority from superior officers and from the king. For example, the marquis de Portes issued orders for the defense of the château de Tornel, so that it would be "maintained and conserved for the service of the king and under the authority of my lord the duc de Montmorency and our special [authority]."[14] The king was the fount of authority, no matter what channels were used to funnel that authority to an officer.

Ordinary Authority

Officeholders normally received authorization in the form of ordinary, or regular, authority. Ordinary authority was the official authority granted as part of a noble's appointment to a permanent office. Commissions for administrative offices often explained the choice of the noble filling the office, explaining that he had the "qualities" required for the office, but such commissions rarely explained the exact nature of the officer's authority and duties.[15] A noble taking up an office had to establish his ordinary authority and gain the respect which had presumably been given to his predecessor.

Ordinary authority included extensive power over subordinate appointments. Regimental officers had near-total power over their subordinates and administrative officers had substantial appointment powers. As the provincial governor of Languedoc, Henri II de Montmorency asserted and demanded approval right over appointments within the province, for example. In one instance, Montmorency complains to Paul Phélypeaux de Pontchartrain, who was a secrétaire d'État, that provisions for Languedoc offices must be presented to him.[16] Montmorency's conviction in the power granted by his ordinary authority is clear when he recommends an officer to the estates of Languedoc: "I found that only the sieur Lemusnier, who possessed together all the conditions and qualities required, could best acquit himself of this charge according to my taste and my advice."[17] Ordinary authority, then, provided the basic rationale not only for royal administration, but also for noble officeholding.

Ordinary authority was proclaimed through regular routines and ceremonies. An officer's regular authority had to be acknowledged publicly by other officers. Officers frequently declared their ordinary authority by having their orders and declarations published, posted, and announced. The duc de Montmorency published military regulations for the province of Languedoc and publicized the new directives, "so that no one can plead ignorance" to his orders. Montmorency specified that the regulation would be "sent to all of the *sièges royaux, présidiaux*, to the deputies and syndics of the twenty-two dioceses of this province, and to the consuls of the towns, masters of them, to be published in audience. . . . And to all *huissiers* and sergents to make all the necessary publications, writs, and notifications."[18] Officeholders confirmed each other's authority through their ordinary daily activities as they communicated and circulated each other's orders.

EXTRAORDINARY AUTHORITY

Extraordinary authority gave officers special powers granted by the king for a specific purpose and usually for a temporary period. Monarchs extended extraordinary authority to nobles during emergency situations and periods of civil conflict in an attempt to provide crisis-management. Often nobles were given a new, temporary office with special powers that went beyond their permanent offices. Warrior nobles used extraordinary authority to sustain and extend their provincial power.

When Louis XIII gave Henri II de Montmorency command of an army in Languedoc in 1621, he granted him enormous extraordinary authority. Large numbers of troops of all types were placed under Montmorency's control, with the power to command, supply, and discipline them. The king's orders authorize and validate any acts and ordonnances that Montmorency would issue in the "charge of our lieutenant general in the said army." Montmorency was to have broad authority over "all colonels, maréchaux and mestres de camp, *grand mestre* and lieutenant of our artillery, *chefs* and conductors of our soldiers, whether cavalry or infantry, governors of our towns and [fortified] places, and other officers and subjects." Everyone was to "recognize our said cousin the duc de Montmorency as our personal sword and to listen to him and to obey him without protest."[19]

The broad powers given to Henri II de Bourbon prince de Condé in the 1620s reveal how extraordinary authority operated in the early seventeenth century. Louis XIII appointed the prince de Condé as lieutenant general of a field army to operate in southwestern France in 1622, granting him wide-ranging political and military powers. Condé was to go to Guyenne and to take command of all troops there and to "compose a strong army," handling the supplies and expenses of the army. He was instructed "to suppress those who are stirred up against my authority and the public peace" and was given power to negotiate with Huguenot commanders within certain guidelines.[20]

In 1629, Condé was again given command of an army in southern France, receiving even broader powers. The confirmation of his authority by the parlement de Toulouse shows the extent of his extraordinary authority. Condé was to act as lieutenant general of the king's army with "all power, command, and authority over each and every French and foreign soldier, whether horse or foot" in the army. Louis XIII gave Condé authority to act not only in Languedoc, but in Guyenne, Dauphiné, Lyonnais, Forez, Beaujoulais, and "other places where the good of the service of His Majesty requires it."[21] These sweeping official powers went far beyond the ordinary authority of even the most powerful provincial governors.

Noble officers seem to have felt a need to iterate and reiterate their extraordinary authority during civil conflicts. In commissioning Hughes de Conseil to command a château garrison in 1622, the duc de Vendôme stated that he did so as *duc et pair*, provincial governor of Bretagne, and "lieutenant general for the king in his armies of Guyenne, Haut-Languedoc, and the Comté de Foix," emphasizing that he gave "the said Conseil commission and special mandate in virtue of the power given to me by His Majesty." Everyone, he asserted, should recognize this exceptional power and obey Conseil's orders relating to the garrison.[22] Military elites also used their extraordinary authority to buttress ordinary authority previously granted them. Provincial governors already had broad authority within their provinces, but they were frequently given additional extraordinary powers to deal with civil conflict.

Some officers had extraordinary power to levy taxes and contributions. Noble officers often tolerated excesses of over-levying, looting, pillage, ransoming, extortion, and financial coercion, but they also regularly ordered taxation and contributions as a permitted, and legal, side of resource mobilization. Discussion of a revocation by Henri II de Montmorency of some of his own previous ordonnances makes clear that the governor of Languedoc had been ordering levies of taxes and contributions to pay for his troops. The estates of Languedoc, pleased that Montmorency had revoked the authorizations for contributions, then complained that several nobles "have sent special couriers toward the king to obtain from His Majesty power to execute their ordonnances of contribution in moneys for the subsistence of their troops, despite the said revocation."[23]

Military commanders, and especially army commanders such as a lieutenant general or maréchal de France, had special powers to create new officers as necessary. If a commander needed to create a new subordinate, he could simply appoint one. Military commanders created a new fortress governor each time they seized a town or château. This practice became a factor in nobles' motivation to serve, and nobles came to expect to be appointed governors of châteaux or towns that they personally captured.

Extraordinary authority could also be linked to a noble's existing personal authority. When the prince de Condé wanted to establish a garrison at the château de Grandval in 1628, he merely expanded the powers of Antoine de Labastier seigneur de Grandval, ordering him "to put in this place the number of twenty-five foot soldiers—the most seasoned that he can find—to take up garrison there and to watch meticulously over the guard and preservation of the said place along with him."[24] The seigneur de Grandval's existing local authority was thereby expanded and reinforced among other area nobles. This sort of expansion of seigneurial and local powers appears to have been a routine response to situations of civil conflict.

Transmitting Authority

Southern French warrior noble officers enacted royal decisions and enforced policies by transmitting authority to residents of their jurisdictions. Each royal edict and parlementaire *arrêt* was sent to the sénéchaux, baillis, and governors

throughout France, who were responsible for publicizing new legislative decisions through public readings and civic postings of printed acts.[25] Official royal
communication also flowed through the letters written by the king, his secretaries, and councilors to the noble officers in charge of regional and local administration. Warrior nobles interpreted legislation, directives, and advice in formulating their approaches to enacting royal policies. Warrior nobles represented
important political actors in translating monarchical will into applicable authority among French subjects.

In considering how best to implement policies, warrior nobles accessed dis-
parate channels of political and news information beyond official monarchical
edicts and parlementaire legal opinions. Information circulated through a diz-
zying array of print media in the early seventeenth century. In urban centers,
colporteurs sold books, pamphlets, and prints providing news of court affairs
and military activities.[26] Polemical pieces, satirical works, and *canards* criticized
policies and discussed contemporary political issues. The *Mercure françois*, an
early gazette, collected and reprinted pamphlets and official acts, distributing
information from the French court and beyond.[27]

Despite their distance from the Bourbon court and the city of Paris, southern
French warrior nobles seem to have been well informed of political and social
developments. The print media from this period consisted to a great extent of
"iconotexts," which employed juxtapositions of image and text, integrating oral
and written techniques of communication.[28] Correspondence among nobles,
sometimes accompanied by printed pamphlets and manuscript *mémoires*—
similar to Italian *avvisi*—shared information about the latest events and political
developments at court and throughout French society. Southern French nobles
presumably also received extensive news through oral communication in audiences, interviews, and conversations with other nobles and officials. The circulation of written and oral information thus framed nobles' participation in early
seventeenth-century public opinion and political culture.

Warrior nobles were immersed in the religious discussions and debates of
the French Wars of Religion. They attended and participated in religious services, processions, and ceremonies in which the worldly roles of believers were
contemplated or discussed. Nobles listened to sermons and street preaching by
Catholic and Reformed preachers, who often promoted sharply polemical positions and advocated violence against confessional enemies. Pamphleteers and
engravers produced pious images, devotional texts, and religious polemics,
which many noble readers avidly sought. Street preachers and pamphleteers
stoked religious controversy in early seventeenth-century France.

Warrior nobles were not merely consumers of political and religious communication, but also active producers of information. Officers frequently reported regional news and information to royal family members, secretaries, and other nobles. Their correspondence often mixed oral and written communication, with couriers and printed enclosures supplying additional information to expand on themes presented in written letters. The circulation of information among nobles permitted discussions of policy formation and implementation, as well as criticism of political decisions made by ministers and other noble officers. Nobles actively presented their own political positions through speeches and ceremonies in the urban centers of southern France. Noble officers also sponsored the printing of their own ordonnances and official documents intended both to communicate royal authority and to confirm their own power in local contexts. During civil conflicts, nobles often sponsored or directly published pamphlets and manifestos presenting their political positions and programs.[29] The production and dissemination of such polemical works allowed nobles to engage in policy discussions and shape public opinion both at court and in their own regions.

Overlapping Authorities

The royal practice of partitioning and granting their ordinary authority continually grew as new layers of officials were created by successive monarchs. This partitioning led to overlapping jurisdictions and potentially conflicting authorities. Granting extraordinary authority streamlined and simplified governance in theory, but in practice it often contributed to conflicts over jurisdiction, rank, precedence, and official power. Overlapping and competing authorities were normal aspects of early modern French officeholding.

Numerous layers of overlapping jurisdictions divided each province. A contemporary narrative of the siege of Montauban gives some idea of the potential for confusion and conflict over jurisdictions. This account describes Montauban as the seat of a bishopric under the authority of the archbishop of Toulouse, as well as a community that was simultaneously under the authority of the estates of Quercy, the cour des aides de Montpellier, the généralité de Bordeaux, the parlement de Bordeaux, and the government de Guyenne.[30] The provincial governor, provincial lieutenant general, estates, parlement, and certain other courts all held power over the entire province. A province was subdivided into dioceses, sénéchausées, and *pays* (or regions)—none of which held coterminous boundaries. Municipalities claimed certain privileges and liberties, exercising a certain limited level of autonomy. Town and fortress governors exercised authority within the communities they protected. Huguenot organizations and noble "protectors" had broad local authority in certain areas. Each of these officers represented a distinct "royal" authority center, capable of asserting authority derived from the same ultimate source. In some situations, meaningful numbers of provincial elites managed to work together effectively, and this sort of cooperation was vital for responding to crises.

But overlapping jurisdictions ultimately produced competing authorities. Provincial political struggles typically related to questions of jurisdiction over judicial cases, administrative responsibilities, and military duties. Rivalries between various officers and courts could complicate these disputes over the boundaries of authority. Assemblies, such as the almost yearly meetings of the estates of Languedoc, were sites of political and social competition. Ceremonial parades, entries, greetings, and celebrations led to quarrels over precedence. Competition over the distribution, confirmation, and control of appointments and rewards within the province sparked disagreements and even feuds. The provincial governors, parlements, and other courts all claimed powers of approval over certain appointments within their jurisdictions. The parlements de Toulouse and de Bordeaux asserted the right to verify royal acts. Many issues could thus spur competition between officers, even in peacetime situations.

The simplest form of conflicts merely questioned an officeholder's source of authority and demanded proof of that authority, however asking for verification could lead to serious limits on a noble officer's authority. In a 1615 letter, the marquis d'Aubeterre requested that the secrétaire d'État "send the power and express command of the king to mobilize the five remaining companies to be raised for my regiment. As much as my friends would like to go on campaign, they see only the charge that I [already] have from His Majesty," which specified that he was authorized to raise five companies. Aubeterre thus already had the authority to raise troops, but he needed extraordinary authority to raise the additional companies that he wanted to field. More important, the five companies that he had already raised using his normal authority were of little use without express orders granting extraordinary authority from the king: "I have indeed mobilized the said five hundred men, but the captains do not wish to advance without seeing my power."[31]

Aubeterre complained that the maréchal de Roquelaure, lieutenant general in Guyenne, did not recognize his authority, on the grounds "that my letters of governor, not being verified by parlement, are not considerable." Roquelaure's refusal to recognize his authority, Aubeterre said, amounted to an attack "not only on my particular authority, but on that of all of the provincial governors, lieutenants of the king, and officers of the crown of France." He sought special provisions to verify his status and authority to represent the king in the province in Roquelaure's absence.[32] Conflicts of authority, always present in early modern society, only escalated during civil conflicts.

PROVINCIAL POWER RELATIONS

Early seventeenth-century warrior nobles used their royal offices and authority to construct their provincial power relations and to mobilize political support. Almost all of the warrior nobles in Languedoc and Guyenne could be considered royal officeholders, since these nobles held offices directly conferred or confirmed by the king. Although many scholars stress the relationship between "royal agents" and the monarch as the key dynamic of early modern politics and power, provincial political culture and power relations arguably centered on the interrelations between the various provincial officers who all claimed to act in the name of the king. The contours of provincial officeholding and political power can be analyzed by examining three broad categories of royal officeholders: high command officers, provincial officers, and regimental officers. The high command officers with landholdings in southern France or operating in the region wielded enormous—but sometimes transitory—power and influence in Languedoc and Guyenne. Provincial administrative and military officers dominated regional political culture and organized civil conflict. Regimental officers regularly involved in civil warfare in southern France engaged in regional religious politics, whether or not they were "native" nobles. The political roles played by noble officeholders in each of these categories of will be examined in turn.

The High Command in Southwestern France

Royal high command officers became significantly involved in the civil warfare in southern France during the early seventeenth century. The image of decline so prevalent in studies of high command officers has not taken into account their continuing significance in these civil conflicts. While only a few nobles from southern France held high command, those who did so had enormous influence and power in the region. High command officers who were not native to the area were important actors when royal armies campaigned in southern France. The frequency of military operations in Languedoc and Guyenne encouraged sustained intervention by a range of royal commanders.[33]

The *connétable*, or constable, was the chief military officer of the French monarchy. The secretary of one connétable explained the powers of the office: "the ordonnances of war are made purely the charge of the connétable. He is lieutenant general of all the armies of the king, without having need of other power than that which his provisions give him . . . in the absence of the king, he orders all things."[34] The office of connétable was thus granted extensive powers, including direction of the accounting of the *ordinaire* and *extraordinaire des guerres*, but it lacked continuity and can hardly be considered a bureaucratic institution. Each connétable was appointed for life, but the office was not venal and was not controlled by a lineage.

During the early seventeenth century, the connétable proved useful to the king and significant for conduct of civil conflicts in southwestern France. Henri I de Montmorency served as connétable from 1593 to 1614. After Montmorency's death the office remained vacant, possibly because a connétable would be too powerful during the regency government. However, Charles d'Albret duc de Luynes emerged as Louis XIII's chief advisor after orchestrating the assassination of Marie de Médicis's favorite Concini in 1617. The king rewarded Luynes in 1621 by naming him connétable, allowing him to conduct much of the recruitment and to direct the military campaign in southwestern France that year. After Luynes died in December 1621, the king quickly appointed François de Bonne duc de Lesdiguières—then the most experienced and victorious French military commander—connétable in 1622.[35] Lesdiguières would go on to lead military operations in eastern Languedoc in 1625 and 1626, but after he died in 1626, the king never appointed another connétable.

The *lieutenant-général du roi* rivaled the authority and prestige of the connétable, acting as the royal commander of the main royal field army or of a group of armies and forces in a region. A lieutenant general's field command was a temporary post, not an office held in perpetuity, and typically only one was appointed during a campaigning season.[36] Lieutenant generals commanding armies were almost always named from the highest ranking nobility and from the royal family. The prince de Condé and the duc de Vendôme acted as lieutenant generals of armies in Languedoc and Guyenne during several campaigns in the 1620s. Since the early years of the French Wars of Religion, the appointment of a lieutenant general had granted sweeping powers over the mobilization, command, and financing of a field army and other troops under his given jurisdiction. A lieutenant general acted as the king's direct representative, commanding royal forces as if the monarch "were himself present," holding authority over all other military officers in their jurisdictions, with the power to communicate with them, to order them, and to summon them.[37]

The post of *maréchal de France*, or field marshal, was only slightly less prestigious than the offices of connétable and lieutenant-général du roi. Usually, about a dozen nobles held positions as maréchaux at a time and these posts were much sought after—competitions and lobbying over appointments to maréchal actually led to civil conflict several times in the early seventeenth century. Each maréchal carried a baton, symbolizing his special authority and rank granted directly by the king. The batons also served to reference the batons of Roman commanders and to associate the maréchaux with the historical tradition of Roman victory. The maréchaux de France held major military commands during wartime, commanding field armies or large bodies of troops. If the king was personally commanding a field army, then several maréchaux would advise the king in near-daily war councils.[38]

A number of maréchaux de France held land and offices in Languedoc and Guyenne during the early seventeenth century. Antoine de Roquelaure seigneur de Roquelaure, a powerful noble from Gascogne, became maréchal in 1615. Pons de Lauzières marquis de Thémines, who was named maréchal de France in 1616, held land in both Languedoc and Guyenne and acted as an active army commander throughout the civil wars of the early seventeenth century. Jacques-Nompar de Caumont duc de La Force served as a royal army commander several times after his appointment as maréchal. Jean du Caïla de Saint-Bonnet marquis de Toiras, from an influential family in Bas-Languedoc, was named maréchal de France and took part in several campaigns against the Huguenots in the 1620s. Gaspard III de Coligny seigneur de Châtillon was made maréchal de France in 1622 after he abandoned the Calvinist cause and left his command of Huguenot forces in Bas-Languedoc. Henri II de Montmorency, the provincial governor of Languedoc, received his baton of maréchal de France in 1630.

Other maréchaux de France were important in the southwest because of their frequent presence there as military commanders. Maréchal Jean-François de La Guiche comte de Saint-Géran commanded troops in southern France. François-Annibal d'Estrées duc d'Estrées led forces in southern France in the 1620s, as did Charles de Choiseul marquis de Praslin. Henri de Schömberg campaigned in Guyenne and Languedoc in the 1620s and in 1632 as a maréchal, before being granted the provincial government of Languedoc. François de Bassompierre advised Louis XIII during several campaigns in the southwest.

The *amiral de France, Guyenne et Bretagne* commanded fleets and organized coastal defenses. Henri II de Montmorency was appointed to this admiral's post in 1612. The admiral had the power to name a vice-admiral, and Montmorency named his uncle to this post in 1613.[39] Montmorency commanded a fleet that saw action off La Rochelle in 1625, but his exercise of the office of admiral interfered with his handling of the civil conflict in Languedoc as governor of that province the same year. Louis XIII eliminated the office of admiral in 1626, as part of a reorganization of naval administration by Richelieu.

The high command included several officers who controlled all units of a particular troop type. Henri III had created the office of *colonel général d'infanterie* for one of his favorites, the duc d'Épernon, who held the office until his ultimate disgrace in 1638. The colonel général d'infanterie had the theoretical power to appoint all officers in all French infantry regiments. But, as David Parrott observes, "it seems clear that the vaunted power of appointment never existed in the form that has been assumed, and that it was an incidental prerogative of Épernon's, enjoyed in practice only for the few years between 1584 and 1588." The colonel général was in practice allowed only to nominate candidates, subject to approval by the king.[40] Épernon's nominations were challenged and at times his authority was completely bypassed, as when several infantry offices were "given without his consent" in 1618.[41] The duc d'Épernon also had to contend with periodic attempts by royal ministers to eliminate or suspend his office of colonel général.

The colonel général de l'infanterie did not have jurisdiction over all infantry, though. Separate officers oversaw the recruitment and mobilization of mercenary infantry units outside of France. The *colonel générale des suisses et grisons* commanded Swiss mercenaries. On several occasions, Swiss troops were raised and directed to Languedoc and Guyenne, where they participated in numerous sieges. A *colonel des bandes italiennes* existed, but apparently did not intervene directly in the campaigns in southwestern France. Alphonse d'Ornano acted as *général des bandes et corses au service du roi*, but few details remain on this office and its impact in the civil wars. As *grand maréchal de camp des gens de guerre allemands* or *colonel des reîtres*, Henri de Schömberg almost certainly played the key role in contacting German princes and negotiating contracts for assembling German troops for campaigns in southern France in the 1620s.[42]

Some French infantry units also operated outside the administration of the colonel général de l'infanterie. The *colonel général de gens à pied françois en Hollande* commanded French forces active in the Netherlands. This office, held by the seigneur de Châtillon after Harambure stepped down from this charge, made its holder a key Protestant leader. Since French intervention in the Netherlands was almost always to support Dutch Calvinists against Habsburg Catholics, French Calvinists looked to this officer to support Huguenot causes and to push for French interventionism in the Netherlands. Châtillon was from the staunchly Calvinist Coligny family and grandson of the famous Admiral Coligny, who had led Huguenot military forces during the early stages of the French Wars of Religion. The seigneur de Châtillon held several offices in Languedoc and was also able to use his colonel général position to expand his influence throughout the province.[43]

Several cavalry commanders were considered part of the high command. A *colonel général de la cavalerie légère* commanded all the non-gendarme cavalry, composed of *chevaux-légers* and *arqubusiers-à-cheval*. The duc d'Angoulême acted as colonel général de la cavalerie légère in the 1620s in Languedoc. The comte d'Alès, an important noble from Bas-Languedoc, was colonel général de la cavalerie in 1629.[44]

The *grand maître et surintendant de l'artillerie* supervised all the king's artillery and commanded the artillery train of the main royal army. The grand maître had jurisdiction over the founding, munitions, personnel, and supplies of the artillery located at the king's arsenal in Paris and at fortifications throughout the provinces. Maximilien de Béthune duc de Sully had used this office to reform the royal artillery and the royal arsenal at Paris in the early seventeenth century, but he was disgraced and removed from office in 1610, during the early days of Marie de Médicis's regency. Louis de Pontis praised the grand maître for the conduct of the batteries at the siege of Montauban in 1621. Henri de Schömberg held the office from 1622 to 1632, when the grand maître also played a significant role in southern France through his command of artillery during numerous campaigns in the region, battering numerous "rebel" towns and châteaux into submission.[45]

The *maréchaux de camp*, sometimes referred to as *maréchaux des camps et armées du roi*, were high-ranking military officers with broad powers. Several maréchaux de camp might act as subordinate commanders for a field army, under a connétable or lieutenant general. A maréchal de camp assigned to a field army was to handle the daily routine of ordering marches, rations, and quarters for that army. Maréchaux de camp might be given independent commands too, but perhaps only in exceptional cases.[46] Sometimes a maréchal de camp was named as a *maréchal général de camp*, which seems to have been simply a designation as the senior maréchal de camp. As maréchal général de camp in 1621, the duc de Lesdiguières was responsible for assigning quarters and lodgings, supplying provisions and munitions, and handling the dispositions of the entire royal army and its encampments. The maréchaux de camp also played an important role as mediators between the high command and provincial and regimental officers.[47]

High command officers exerted enormous power on other nobles in southern France, but this power was limited by the extensive demands placed on them. Nobles who possessed high command offices tended to be very mobile, traveling nearly constantly. These nobles were often away from the provinces of Languedoc and Guyenne, handling situations in other provinces and at court. High command officers had broad and multiple responsibilities and had to be concerned with rivalries with other *grands*.

Provincial Officers in Languedoc and Guyenne

A wide range of provincial officers handled administrative and military roles in Languedoc and Guyenne. Provincial government operated through overlapping layers of administration, since court jurisdictions, administrative areas, tax regions, and ecclesiastical divisions crisscrossed each province, and their boundaries rarely coincided. William Beik's model of the 233 individuals who comprised the "truly influential powers" in Languedoc during the late seventeenth century gives an idea of the variety of provincial officers.[48] Provincial elites acted within and between these interlaced official jurisdictions, often building power relations by using multiple offices to extend their influence. These nobles tended to be much more focused on provincial politics than high command officers. Provincial officers generally resided in the provinces where they held office and left only for exceptional campaigns or occasional trips to the royal court and other locations.

The most important provincial officers were the *gouverneurs* of the eleven major provinces, or "major governors" as Robert Harding calls them.[49] Each of these provincial governors' jurisdictions, or *gouvernements*, comprised an entire province. Jean du Tillet, writing in the 1570s, describes the provincial governors as "ordained for force, for the purpose of conserving the provinces committed to them in tranquillity, peace, and repose; defending them from any seditious subjects or from foreign enemies; keeping these provinces and their fortresses well repaired, supplied, and furnished with whatever is necessary for their defense; and aiding justice in the said provinces, with a strong arm when needed."[50] The historian Robert Harding convincingly argues that while many of the provincial governors' duties were military, these officers also had wide-ranging administrative and political roles. From a monarchical perspective, this meant that governors were "all-purpose executors of the royal will."[51]

Provincial governors handled broad aspects of military and provincial administration, always claiming to act in the name of the king. As military administrators, governors commanded troops, appointed officers, supervised garrisons, and managed arsenals and munitions stores within the province. Governors not only supervised ordinary military expenses and troop payments in peacetime, but also organized war finances to defend their provinces during civil wars. Governors routinely presented and implemented royal directives within their provinces, resolved political differences between provincial elites, and guided the meetings of the provincial estates, often urging the members to implement royal requests. They surveyed regional politics and developments, reporting their findings to the monarch and circulating the latest news.

Provincial governors also acted as mediators between the royal court and regional elites. Governors were prominent nobles with vast influence in the provinces they governed. Marriage ties and patron-client relations connected the governors with numerous provincial elites, forging additional channels of mediation and political influence. Provincial governors cultivated their personal authority and produced images of power that enhanced their roles as mediators. The demands on them as mediators required them to divide their time and energies between their provinces and the royal court. While the king desired a royal agent functioning in his province, regional elites frequently requested that governors spend more time at court to request royal favors for them and to protect provincial interests. The governors of Guyenne and Languedoc spent most of their time in their provinces, though, partly due to the numerous civil conflicts there. At least in southern France, the provincial governors acted both as powerful regional elites and vital royal agents in the early seventeenth century.

Three generations of the Montmorency family dominated life in Languedoc during the late sixteenth and early seventeenth centuries as governors of Languedoc. Anne de Montmorency had been governor of Languedoc for over thirty years when the French Wars of Religion broke out in 1562. His son, Henri I de Montmorency, then acted as governor from 1563 until his death in 1614.[52] Henri II de Montmorency succeeded his father in the government and held the post until Louis XIII stripped him of his offices after the 1632 civil war.[53] Montmorency was captured in battle at Castelnaudary against Henri de Schömberg's royalist army and tried by the parlement de Toulouse for the crime of lèse-majesté. Schömberg was rewarded with Montmorency's former government of Languedoc after the latter's execution, but he died later that year and was succeeded by his son, Charles de Schömberg.

The governor of Guyenne was potentially just as powerful as the governor of Languedoc, but limiting factors reduced the influence of this office during much of the early seventeenth century. Henri II de Bourbon prince de Condé was gov-

ernor of Guyenne from 1596 until 1618. Condé's opposition to royal favorites in
several civil wars severely undermined his ability to exercise his provincial authority, and his imprisonment from 1616 to 1619 cut Condé off completely from
his provincial base. The young Henri de Lorraine duc de Mayenne then received
the government of Guyenne in 1618. Mayenne, like Montmorency, seemed to
many nobles to be an ideal young nobleman. Mayenne backed Marie de Médicis
during a royal family dispute in 1620, though, weakening his credibility with
Louis XIII and his chief advisor, the duc de Luynes, and he was trying to regain
favor when he was killed at the siege of Montauban in 1621.[54] Jean-Louis de La
Valette duc d'Épernon was granted the provincial government of Guyenne in
1622. The duc had gained much power at court as one of the *mignons* of Henri
III in the 1580s, but by the 1620s, he had long been marginalized at court. He
had lost further favor by backing Marie de Médicis, like Mayenne. The appointment to the government of Guyenne gave Épernon a real opportunity for regional domination, since he had large landholdings in Guyenne and enormous
influence among the Guyenne nobility. According to one historian of Guyenne,
"Épernon's powers as governor were so vaguely and broadly defined that he
could claim control over almost all public matters in Guyenne." Épernon did
play an active part in civil wars in Guyenne from 1622 to 1629 using his powers
as governor of the province. When offered the position of lieutenant general
under the prince de Condé in 1628, Épernon refused, saying that he could not
submit to subordination and that "besides the sole charge of governor of Guyenne, which authorizes him to make himself obeyed in all that he desired within
his government, he had no need for that of any other nature." Épernon eventually came into conflict with the powerful archbishop of Bordeaux and Richelieu
in the 1630s, and he was removed from the government in 1638.[55]

At least one *lieutenant-général* executed the orders of the governor within each
province and acted as his second-in-command. These officers should not be confused with the lieutenant generals in the high command, discussed above. The
lieutenant generals of provinces worked to administer provinces and were acting
governors when the latter were absent from their provinces. A lieutenant general
of a province needed to have a close relationship with his governor to be effective.[56] Only one provincial lieutenant general served in Languedoc in the early
seventeenth century. Anne de Lévis duc de Ventadour was the provincial lieutenant general from 1593 to 1622. Anne's son, Henri de Lévis duc de Ventadour,
succeeded his father from 1622 until 1632, when Henri exchanged governments
to become governor of Limousin. The Lévis family worked closely with the Montmorency governors and the two families were intermarried. In the aftermath of

the 1632 civil war, three lieutenant generals were appointed to administer the province. Just-Henri de Tournon comte de Tournon, Louis d'Arpajon vicomte d'Arpajon, and Hector de Gélas de Voisins marquis d'Ambres were rewarded with these posts for their loyalty.[57] Antoine de Roquelaure marquis de Roquelaure served as the provincial lieutenant general in Guyenne, but was later replaced by Pons de Lauzières marquis de Thémines and Timoléon d'Espinay marquis de Saint-Luc.[58]

An additional, though less powerful, *lieutenant du roi* or *gouverneur du pays* sometimes controlled a *pays*, or region. The king created a lieutenance du roi in Gévaudan and the Cévennes for Antoine-Hercule de Budos marquis de Portes in 1617. A lieutenant du roi's powers were vague and ill-defined. The governors of *pays* were frequently the sénéchaux, nobles holding the title of *sénéchal et gouverneur du pays*.[59]

A number of *sénéchaux* and *baillis* administered regions of each province. A *sénéchal* was the officer in charge of administering a *sénéchausée* and presiding over its court. While some historians have referred to the sénéchaux as judicial officers, Roland Mousnier is right to insist that "the real functions of the *baillis* and *sénéchaux* were mainly military and political." William Beik also indicates the military and administrative roles of sénéchaux, but argues that they had "only local importance." Nicholas B. Fessenendon has a similar view, calling the sénéchal a "sub-governor," who was "supposed to aid the governor in perform-ing his duties, but usually exercised little power." The sénéchaux oversaw the selection of nobles to serve as representatives for meetings of the Estates Gen-eral, as in 1614. The sénéchaux also had the responsibility of assembling the *ban et arrière-ban*, or feudal levies, if the king convoked them.[60] Within the govern-ment of Languedoc, there were eight sénéchaux governing the sénéchausées of Toulouse, Lauragais (at Castelnaudary), Carcassonne, Béziers, Montpellier, Beaucaire and Nîmes, Le Puy, and Castres. In addition, a bailli de Gévaudan handled local justice and administration in that region, and another bailli served in Vivarais.[61] Five sénéchaux served in Guyenne in the Périgord, Rouergue, Quercy, Bazadais, and Agenais-Condomais regions. Several of these sénéchaux were particularly important in regional politics. François de Noailles, who was sénéchal in Rouergue, handled large recruitment operations and regularly re-ported to the court on regional affairs. The marquis d'Aubeterre, sénéchal in Agenais and Condomais, also handled recruitment and negotiations in south-western France. The marquis de Thémines governed the sénéchausée of Quercy, but he was also a powerful landholder in both Languedoc and Guyenne. He eventually also served as an army commander and maréchal de France.[62]

Gouverneurs particuliers, or fortress governors, commanded the garrisons of towns, citadels, and châteaux. These offices were sometimes known as "captaincies" because their commanders were often given the title of captain. Town and château governors were responsible for the loyalty and defense of the fortifications and towns under their command. Most major cities and towns in Languedoc and Guyenne had garrisons and fortress governors. These governors exercised considerable power in the areas surrounding their towns and châteaux. Fortress governors were frequently *grands* who also held major army commands or provincial offices, thus they acted as distant but vital protectors. Many nobles held more than one government within the same region. For example, the seigneur de Châtillon was governor of both Montpellier and Aimargues in Bas Languedoc.[63] Certain fortress governors seem to have been given added status and authority by the monarch by identifying them as key governors, and in some cases the king funded their garrisons directly. Numerous additional fortress governors commanded Huguenot strongholds, including the fortresses designated with the legal distinction of places de sûreté, or security towns. Since the vast majority of places de sûreté in the kingdom were located in the provinces of Guyenne and Languedoc, prominent local Calvinist nobles had opportunities to command these Huguenot strongholds.

The *intendants* were administrative officers sent on special executive missions to provinces or to armies. Scholarly attention to the intendants as royal officials has made them perhaps the best-known ancien régime administrative officers. Historians have arguably overemphasized the importance of intendants in seventeenth-century administration, partially because of their focus on the personal reign of Louis XIV.[64] The early seventeenth-century intendants were certainly not prominent officers, though, and their identities remain hazy. Raymond de Viçose and Miles Marion were active as intendants in Guyenne and Languedoc during the early seventeenth century, but their administrative roles are unclear.[65] One intendant, Charles Machault, did play an important role in the 1632 civil war, but he was also a *maître des requêtes*. At this point, the intendants were not yet major provincial actors in southern France, and they often seem to have reported directly to the provincial governors.[66]

Some judicial and financial officers participated in civil warfare. The parlement de Toulouse and the parlement de Bordeaux, the main sovereign courts in southwestern France, registered and published royal acts against "rebels." Sylvie Daubresse demonstrates how the predominantly Catholic présidents, or presiding judges, of the parlement de Paris acted to reestablish public order, promote religious unity, suppress heresy, and enforce justice during civil conflicts.[67]

Judges in parlements throughout France supplied food, munitions, and supplies to armies operating within their jurisdictions. Occasionally, parlements would raise their own regiments, officered in part by members of the court. The chambre des comptes de Montpellier and the cour des aides de Montpellier gradually reimbursed individuals for expenditures and losses incurred during the civil wars. These two courts merged into the cour des comptes, aides et finances de Montpellier in 1629. From its seat at Castres, the chambre de l'édit de Languedoc, a *chambre mi-partie* attached to the parlement de Toulouse, adjudicated in cases involving sensitive religious questions, since half of the magistrates were Catholic and half were Calvinist. While few members of these judicial bodies can be considered as members of a warrior noble elite, some magistrates did act as military commanders, or had had significant prior military service. Other magistrates' judicial and financial roles thrust them into military administration roles which required them to coordinate closely with military officers during civil wars.[68]

Each urban community in southwestern France had a committee of *consuls* who governed the municipality. Consuls were magistrates elected by urban elites for one-year terms. Their administrative duties included maintenance of fortifications, financing of garrisons, provisions for passing troops. Consuls were frequently nobles with prior military experience and their roles in crisis management made them key figures in provincial politics. The localized conflicts and the frequency of sieges in southern France prompted the consuls to participate actively in civil warfare.[69]

French archbishops and bishops played very important secular roles in Languedoc and Guyenne, including participation in political and military activities. The bishops were almost always noble and frequently were members of powerful regional families. Many bishops in Languedoc had close political ties to the Montmorency family. In Languedoc, the archbishop of Narbonnne acted as head of the estates of Languedoc when they met. Bishops also played important roles in introducing political, religious, and military initiatives during estates sessions.[70] The bishops were quite involved in military preparations and even recruitment. The archbishop of Narbonne participated in recruitment efforts during the civil wars in southern France. The bishop of Montpellier was involved in supplying and guarding garrisons in his diocese in 1621, while the archbishop of Bordeaux participated in naval building and supply efforts in Guyenne.[71] A number of bishops in southern France came from Franco-Italian families and were closely involved in efforts to promote the Counter-Reformation.

The barons of the estates of Languedoc were important regional elites, each dominating an area within the province of Languedoc. The province of Guyenne had no provincial estates, but in Languedoc twenty-two barons had the right to entry to the estates of Languedoc as delegates of the nobility. Although Languedoc's estates are often seen as an example of representative government and a prime source of opposition to royal "absolutism," the estates cannot realistically be considered representative. William Beik points out that "the bishops did not represent the interests of cathedral chapters, regular clergy, or local priests; the barons stood for their hereditary family rights, not for the body of the nobility; the consuls spoke only for the municipal oligarchies from which they came." Barons sat in the estates not by virtue of an office, but by title. A baron entered the estates by holding a baronnie that had been granted the right of entry to the estates. The barons who attended estates meetings were important provincial elites, and they normally also held military offices.[72]

While the provincial officers were a small group, they dominated the political and social life of Languedoc and Guyenne. Provincial administrative officers acted as intermediaries between the royal court, the provincial nobles, and other inhabitants. The provincial officers also coordinated with high command officers who were in southern France, occasionally even serving as their subordinates. Some of the provincial administrators were either from courtier families or from families newly installed in southern France. But, many of the provincial officers were nobles born in Languedoc and Guyenne who were intimately familiar with regional noble politics. A much larger number of "native" nobles from southern France participated in civil warfare through their regimental offices.

Regimental Officers

Provincial nobles had many opportunities to serve as regimental and company officers during the early seventeenth century. Numerous infantry regiments and cavalry companies were raised in Languedoc and Guyenne to fight in the civil wars, and many nobles were needed to command these units. Moreover, regimental officers from other areas of France served in southern France frequently, and temporarily acted as provincial elites. Some of these remained in garrisons, becoming permanent members of the provincial military elite.

The *mestre de camp* was the commander of an infantry regiment, with a rank that later became known as colonel. The mestre de camp's status was based on the prestige of his regiment, which generally depended on its seniority. The commanders of regiments raised in Languedoc and Guyenne were often closely affiliated to the provincial governors and army commanders. Mestres de camp had enormous patronage powers because of these links and due to their ability to appoint captains in their regiments.[73] Jean de Billon's *Les Principes de l'art militaire*, an important contemporary treatise, provides advice on how a mestre de camp should select his subordinate captains.[74]

A captain was normally the commander of an infantry or cavalry company, the fundamental military organizational units in the late sixteenth and early seventeenth centuries. Captains directed daily military operations of their companies and often commanded operations independently, making them the most important military officers in the armies of the French Wars of Religion, since: "it was at the company level itself that the principal functions of command and administration were provided."[75] Contemporary military treatises emphasized the significance of captains' charges by detailing their diverse military, political, and social roles.[76] A wide range of military officers were actually subsumed under the designation of captain, and manuscript military records demonstrate discrepancies in captains' authorities and wide variations in their company types and strengths, with accompanying distinctions in officers' pay, status, duties, and responsibilities.

An infantry captain's situation and opportunities depended largely on the distinctions between types of infantry regiments, which had differing characteristics depending on their designation as *gardes, vieux, petit-vieux*, foreign, or French. Within each regiment, some companies were considered more prestigious than others. In each infantry regiment, the first company was singled out as the *compagnie colonelle* and could have additional soldiers in it to reflect its higher prestige. The captain of such a company commanded the entire regiment in the absence of the mestre de camp and acted as his second-in-command. In some regiments, the mestre de camp acted as *capitaine colonelle* also, leaving the everyday running of the company to the lieutenant. Although 100 men was the normal size of a company, an infantry captain's commission might assign unit strength at from 50 to 200 men. Recruitment difficulties, fighting, disease, and desertion all reduced companies from their theoretical strengths, creating further disparities in company strength and status. Captains differed in their financial resources and personal ability to handle these problems and recruit replacements successfully.

The military and political roles of cavalry captains were even more varied. The sizes of cavalry companies varied from 30 to 100, reflecting the wealth and prestige of their commanders. During the French Wars of Religion, cavalry officers could command one of several types of cavalry, each with its own charac-

teristics. A captain of a *compagnie d'ordonnance* held a prestigious and politically valuable post, since these companies were composed of heavily armored
gendarmes, most of whom were noble.[77] These companies were expensive to maintain and the price of purchasing the command of a compagnie d'ordonnance
was exorbitant. Compagnies d'ordonnance were typically commanded by great
nobles, who often used them as bodyguards, filling posts with clients. Since
they were not organized into regiments, and their captains were not responsible
to a mestre de camp, these captains had more flexibility and independence than
other captains. The captains of the *chevaux-léger* companies were in charge of
more lightly armored cavalry. The *carabiniers* and *arquebusiers-à-cheval* companies were composed of mounted men who were trained to use firearms. These
companies were numerous and less costly to maintain. Cavalry commanders
tended to have an enormous political and social advantage over their infantry
counterparts, since many of the cavalrymen in their units would be noble.[78]

Other captains had little or no connection to a company establishment. The
title of captain could be given as an honorific to a noble. For example, a high-
ranking noble might claim as one of his titles *capitaine de cent hommes* or *capitaine
de deux cent hommes*, even if the company had been disbanded after a previous
conflict. The rank of captain could also be applied to garrison commanders, ir-
respective of whether infantry or cavalry were posted to the garrison. These
captains ranged from the insignificant to the powerful, since garrisons could
vary from a handful to hundreds of men. The title of captain was frequently
given to officers leading tiny bands of men, especially during recruiting efforts.
Captains could occasionally be non-noble, but most significant captains were
noble.[79]

A captain commanded his company through a small group of subordinate
officers. An infantry company typically had a *lieutenant*, an *enseigne*, and two
sergents. A cavalry company had a *lieutenant*, an *enseigne*, and a *guidon*. These
subordinate officers' status varied according to the prestige of their units and
their captains. Each lieutenant was the assistant to the captain of his company
and acting commander if the captain was absent or incapacitated. Lieutenants
were frequently nobles who had family connections to their captains. Ensigns
were lower-grade infantry officers who might be young noblemen, and a *cornet* was
the equivalent in the cavalry. Sergeants were noncommissioned officers and
were rarely nobles.

A number of key personnel in a company fulfilled specialized roles that gave
them a low-ranking officer status. These posts included drummers, fifers, *fourriers*,

and surgeons in infantry companies, or trumpeters and *maréchal des logis* in cavalry companies. The company *états des troupes*, or muster rolls, often relegated these officers to the end of the document, and frequently without even listing their names. Other états listed all officers first, in descending order of rank from captain to the lowest-ranking officers. It is perhaps indicative of these officers' status that some états des troupes actually designated these personnel as *bas officiers*. While some of these low-ranking officers might be noble youths, the vast majority were probably non-nobles with no prospect of ennoblement or entry into the regimental military elites.

Regimental officers often compelled provincial officers and institutions to give them money, food, and supplies for their troops. The regimental officers aided provincial officers in managing provincial politics. The officers in command of companies and regiments played key roles in conducting military campaigns and in aiding high commanders with political support, recruitment, and money.

PERFORMING ROYAL SERVICE

The king tried to structure power relationships, but as nobles exercised office they not only served the king, they advanced their own interests and attempted to fulfill their own desires. In 1615, a noble from Guyenne wrote to the secrétaire d'État to confirm that he had received his brevet for an office of maréchal de camp. His letter immediately lays out his understanding of the relationship between his military service and the new office: "I received [the letter] that you kindly wrote me on 19 December, together with the brevet of maréchal de camp. I pray that God may give me the grace to be worthy of this charge, bringing to it the affection and sincere wish that I have to use my life faithfully in all that concerns the king's service." He goes on to promise to be "always your servant," and stresses "the affection that I have in serving Your Majesty."[80]

The *service du roi*, the king's service, lay at the heart of the relationship between nobles and their king, yet early seventeenth-century French understandings of royal service were multifaceted, not focused exclusively on the state. While royal attempts to organize officeholding relied fundamentally on the notion of the king's service, noble officeholders developed their own understandings of their service and its role in the political culture. Warrior nobles engaged power through their exercise of office, expressing their power relationships through an exaggerated language of service that was integral to officeholding. Ideals of service structured nobles' offers of service and their obligations to serve. Nobles thus performed royal service not only to fulfill their official duties and personal obligations to the king, but also to participate in political culture.

Exercise of Office

Early seventeenth-century nobles actively engaged in a range of officeholding practices that allowed them to wield power. Warrior nobles expected officers to perform their official capacities in accordance with social norms, not merely to act on the king's whims. Ideally, officeholders would fulfill the functions and roles associated with their offices through their service.[81] Noble officers operated within a service culture in which their peers made qualitative assessments of their abilities to discharge the functions and responsibilities of their offices. However, these assessments of a noble's performance of his office's functions and responsibilities had little to do with any abstract civil standard—instead, an office's functions were fulfilled and assessed based on social and political criteria. Officeholding both displayed and upheld the social distinctions of nobility, while encouraging noble officers to serve.[82]

The distinction between *bons offices* and *mauvais offices,* or good and bad offices, illustrates the personal nature of office and political significance of official acts for nobles. *Office* implied a sense duty or obligation, and *bons offices* indicated that the obligations were being met in terms of providing required services. The concept was active—a noble performed or did *bons offices*. One noble concludes a request hoping that "you will render me all sorts of good offices in this [matter]."[83] The sense of good offices was sometimes extended from instances of service to include a general idea of favor or good wishes. Emmanuel de Crussol duc d'Uzès's offers of service to the secrétaire d'État are accompanied by his hopes for the "continuation of [the secrétaire's] good offices."[84] Another noble makes explicit this connection between good offices and favors: "I know, Sir, that these are the effects of your good offices, which have made up for my want of merit, and that you have multiplied your favors so much toward me that I have no hope of being able to return [them] through my services."[85] Conversely, the idea of *mauvais offices* indicated a disservice, an injustice, or a failure to properly fulfill the functions of an office. Jean-Paul d'Esparbès de Lussan complained of "the displeasure that I received," because "the bad offices that M. de Vic conveyed to Their Majesties have reduced me to despair."[86] Personal disservices were viewed as improper acts and failures to discharge offices, as well as being signs of disfavor or malevolence. Early seventeenth-century nobles saw official acts as reflecting political and social relationships.

Notions of the inherent qualities of office were balanced by a recognition that a noble's personal qualities defined and shaped his office. Rank and status granted by office at best complemented the officer's own prestige, which derived from his character and family. Nobles holding the same grade of office were hardly considered equals. Conflicts over precedence abounded, precisely because noblemen defined their offices even more than their offices defined them.

Nobles' appreciation of the personal nature of office and their distinctions between the proper and improper discharge of functions point to the importance of the person holding office, the *officier*.[87] All those who served or aided the king were considered royal officers, and royal documents sometimes mention the king's *domestiques et officiers*. Royal officers could include persons entrusted with financial, administrative, ecclesiastical, or military duties. A wide range of individuals with differing ranks, responsibilities, and privileges could all be referred to as officers. Each office could involve diverse responsibilities, instead of clearly defined duties. A noble holding the office of sénéchal, for example, had judicial, administrative, and military responsibilities. This ambiguity in the conception of official positions allowed noble officeholders to define their own power relationships through the king's service. Thus, royal service was organized by the king, but frequently used by nobles for their own purposes through their exercise of office.

Absenteeism—officers' absences from their posts and use of replacements—has often been seen as a serious problem, endangering royal service. David A. Parrott criticizes noble officers for their "insubordination" and their absences without *congé*, or leave, calling the situation "the peculiar 'French disease' of officer absenteeism."[88] Officer absenteeism was actually a necessary aspect of the French officeholding practices and key to the exercise of office. Military and administrative officers were frequently absent in order to perform vital military duties elsewhere, such as recruiting, overseeing subordinate officers, gathering supplies, or procuring support from the royal court or from other governmental bodies. A noble officer's absence from his unit was sometimes required in order to manage his personal finances, which were frequently the unit's financial lifeline. Officer absence did not necessarily indicate neglect or incompetence, since nobles normally provided clients to act as their substitutes during their absences. Henri de Budos, a high-ranking noble with significant military experience, commanded his brother's regiment while he was away during the 1621 campaign.[89] Frequent officer absences were not only expected but normally accepted in early seventeenth-century France as a routine part of the exercise of office and the operation of power relationships.

The Exaggerated Language of Service

Warrior nobles who acted as royal officers used an exaggerated affective language of service in discussing power relationships, and their expressions of love for the king's service abound. One noble asserted that he had "no other ambition in the world but to serve Your Majesties and to render proof of my faithfulness and of my most humble obedience."[90] A letter of recommendation for the duc d'Uzès speaks of the "zeal and affection that Monsieur the duc d'Uzès carries in [the king's] service."[91] The duc de Ventadour was pleased in 1618 by "the satisfaction that [His Majesty] appears to have in my faithful services, which I shall continue [to give him] until the last breath of my life," saying that he has "a heart full of affection for Your Majesty's happiness and for the grandeur of his state and crown."[92]

Pledges of self-sacrifice were a central part of this noble language of service. Nobles frequently expressed their willingness to lay down their lives for their king. Promises to serve with each drop of blood or every ounce of strength fill noble correspondence. A noble officer vows that he is "ready to employ all that I have of life and belongings to render to Your Majesty the most humble service, which is your due."[93] The marquis d'Aubeterre similarly pledges that he will never fail, "in all other occasions, as in this one, concerning your service to render all sorts of submissions, respect, and obedience—even my life," and he assures the king that the new governor of Guyenne can testify to his obedience.[94]

Ideals of Service

Service involved not just rhetoric, but a broad, idealized conception of military activity, which nobles expressed in a variety of ways. One noble stated his ideal as "serving the king and Your Majesty [the regent] with dignity . . . for the good of his service and the peace of the province."[95] Nobles associated royal service with the idea of acting as a *serviteur*, or servant, to the king. Service carried the idea of bearing arms, thus a common meaning of *serviteur*, dating from the medieval period, was an esquire, or one who "carries arms after his master."[96] The expression *faire service*, usually meaning to perform service, shows the active nature of the conception of service. For example, a noble pledges to the secrétaire d'État that he "will always be full of affection to perform service for him." Royal service, then, was viewed as an action or performance by a noble for the good of the king.[97]

Conceptions of service assumed that the king would constantly observe, assess, and evaluate nobles' service. Nobles were clearly aware of the king's role as assessor of service, as one noble's comments show: "I shall amass all of the infantry I can and promise to do [this] in such a way that the king will be satisfied with my service." Nobles with whom the king was satisfied could be considered *bons serviteurs*, good servants. The king frequently referred to nobles who implemented his will as his *bons serviteurs*, but nobles used the concept, too. A noble asks the secrétaire d'État to intervene "for my companions and for me . . . [who] are not treated as *bons serviteurs* of the king as they have always shown themselves to be." The opposite concept of *mauvais serviteurs* was also utilized by the king and nobles, and the distinctions between *bon* and *mauvais serviteurs* were closely connected to the monarch's ability to brand nobles as "rebels" guilty of lèse-majesté.[98]

The king's assessment of service points to the importance of serving under his eyes. Joël Cornette finds a key link between nobles' conceptions of service and their physical proximity to the king.[99] Nobles strongly desired, and arguably needed, for the king to observe their service in person. In 1621, for example, the baron de Polignac wrote directly to the king, expressing his desire to serve close to "his person," and to assure him that it was his greatest "ambition" to have the opportunity to "display my most humble and faithful services."[100] Service relationships between nobles and the monarch could not be validated without the king actually witnessing those services. If the king was not present to assess services personally, intermediaries had to report on and assess services for the king—a situation that nobles strongly disliked. Thus, they complained bitterly at not being able to serve personally with the king. The marquis de Thémines's intense desire to serve with the king led him to plead, "Do not, Sire, permit that I spend the rest of my days far from Your Majesty, as I do now, and without means to receive satisfaction for the bloodiest injury ever done to a man of my sort."[101] This emotional appeal certainly fits well with a description of an assault at the siege of Montauban in which a "quantity of nobility" attacked while the king and connétable came "to see this exercise and to be spectators."[102] Louis de Pontis vividly describes marching "in sight of the king and of the army, whose attentive eyes watched me" during an attack at the siege of Montauban.[103]

Service to the king gave warrior nobles opportunities to acquire glory in combat. François de Noailles expressed his lust for glory, saying that "my extreme desire to acquire glory for myself by serving the king faithfully and well is something that I have inherited."[104] Nobles felt that their military service allowed them to share in the glory of the king's arms. "I find myself in such a glorious employment and with so many beautiful occasions . . . to share in the glory that the arms of the king here receive," a noble from Languedoc serving at the siege of La Rochelle wrote.[105] Warrior nobles frequently expressed disappointment at having missed opportunities to gain glory. When they did get to serve gloriously, nobles recognized that all glory ultimately derived from God, who required veneration and service. Inasmuch as the "glory of such praiseworthy actions" proceeded from the Holy Trinity, it was eternal, a Catholic pamphlet proclaimed.[106] Huguenots similarly attributed all glory to God, emphasizing humble service and preparation for martyrdom.[107] The conception of service as a duty and obligation presented great contradictions for warrior nobles during civil conflicts. The king frequently stated his need to maintain "confidence" in nobles' "affection" and the "continuation" of their services.[108] Warrior nobles were to consider serving the king as an obligation, and obedience to the king was considered glorious.[109]

Offers of Service

Southern French nobles expressed their eagerness to participate in early seventeenth-century warfare through written offers of service. In a typical example, a noble rejoices at the outbreak of a war: "the news of this birth of war in Italy is the subject of this dispatch that I am sending to Their Majesties to offer all that I possess of goods and friends to employ them in the current situation, and to show as much passion for the king's service as my unhappiness [which] has kept me far from the occasions to display it."[110] Although this letter refers to a foreign war, there was no lack of offers to serve in civil conflict. During one civil conflict, a noble writes to express, in a very similar fashion, "the affection that I have always had to employ myself in your service, offering myself at this hour to serve the king in such fashion and place as Your Majesty judges most necessary."[111] The duc de Ventadour repeatedly offered his services, asking the king and the estates of Languedoc "to use me and my service freely in all occurrences."[112] Large numbers of nobles offered to serve at the outbreak of each civil war. Some were thrust into conflict by the circumstances of chaotic civil warfare, but most were eager to serve.

Nobles' offers of service display their strong commitment to an idealized conception of royal service, based on a desire to wage war—a noble served because he wanted to do so. Statements of worth stressed the willingness to serve, and requests for appointments to offices were brimming with expressions of desire. A noble claims that the regent will find "no one in the world who wishes to serve as much as I do. I pray to God that I can render to you the proofs according to my desire; I shall search for occasions [to do so] most eagerly."[113]

Religious warfare and civil conflict clearly brought new opportunities for nobles wanting to serve. One noble laments the end of a conflict, which seems likely to deprive him of the opportunity to satisfy "the desire that I have to serve Your Majesty," and thus avoid "the regret of seeing myself . . . less than my predecessors."[114] Offers of service were hardly limited to nobles seeking new offices, though. Noble officeholders saw civil conflicts as opportunities to continue their services, to show their loyalty, and to demonstrate their usefulness. One noble officeholder promises that the king will be able to recognize his "passion" and his "desire in the exercise of this charge and the execution of all [the king's] commands."[115] Nobles' offers to serve often displayed their commitment to political and religious causes. Huguenot nobles were eager to serve against Spanish Catholic troops in Savoy, Valtellina [in Lombardy], and Flanders—or against *malcontent* Catholic nobles in France. Many Catholic nobles displayed excitement over the prospects of fighting Huguenot "rebels" and punishing their "heretical" communities.

Nobles desired not only to serve but to be commanded. Their requests to serve were not mere ploys to obtain new offices: they wanted opportunities for active military service. François de Noailles promises the secrétaire d'État in 1618 that "in all that you do me the favor to counsel or command, I shall willingly arrange myself, desiring nothing in the world other than to render my actions agreeable to you and to be able to bear witness by my obedience that I am, Sir, your most humble and most faithful servant."[116] A recommendation from the same noble shows again a close relationship between command and service. The bearer of the recommendation has shown "the diligence that he rendered [the king] in his service following the command and commission that His Majesty gave him."[117]

Obligations of Service

Nobles' passionate offers of service show their sense of obligation to the king, but their conceptions of service were complicated by an ambiguous relationship to the notion of duties. The royal ideal of service included anything done "for the good of my service," as defined by the king. Nobles' service was intended to promote the common good and to execute the king's wishes. In letter after letter, the king justified his actions through this ideal of service. For example, in 1621,

Louis XIII wrote that "having judged [it] opportune for the good of my service," he was sending several regiments to garrison fortifications in Languedoc. According to the king, French nobles were obligated to provide him military service, if asked.[118]

The monarch might view nobles' service principally as duty, emphasizing responsibilities and obligations, but nobles rejected a simple duty-bound understanding of it. Duty was one aspect of service, but not necessarily the predominant one. Nobles frequently acknowledged duties by admitting that service could be defective—a noble could fail in his service. Henri II de Montmorency, writing to request an appointment for a Languedoc noble, argues that his "affection for king's service would be somehow defective if he failed to recommend to Your Majesty those who serve him with dignity in this province, among which the sieur Galepin is one of the most zealous."[119] Montmorency intends for this phrase to buttress his recommendation, but it also reveals that he realizes that the servants and officers of the king are fallible and that some standards exist for service. The duc d'Uzès also conceives of service as duty: "At the first order that Your Majesty gave me . . . I abandoned all my concerns to come render him the service that I owe him."[120] Jean-François de La Guiche seigneur de Saint-Géran writes glowingly to the secrétaire d'État, "I am so happy, Sir, that you have as much confidence in my service as I have an obligation to merit it."[121]

Nobles' sense of obligation led them to send the king assurances and reassurances of their desire to serve. In 1614, the duc de Montmorency sent Marie de Médicis, "new assurances of my most humble devotion to [Louis XIII's] service," pleading that the king "continue the honor of his good graces, as to someone who will never breathe air other than that of the commands of Your Majesty."[122] Nobles asserted the quality of their service and their obedience by stressing their constancy and their unending faithfulness to the king.

Spilling their blood was an important literal and symbolic obligation for the noble officers. One noble rejoices in the "happy success that the force of [His Majesty's] victorious arms and the grandeur of his royal clemency carries in his affairs for the peace of his people and the affirmation of his authority, for which I desire to contribute my services and my blood."[123] Warrior nobles repeatedly pledged their blood and bodies in the service of their king, seeing the spilling of blood from their wounds as proofs of their faithfulness and obedience to the monarch.

Nobles often saw no contradiction, however, between their obedience and promoting their own interests. Since their authority was granted by the king, they could construe their personal interest as coinciding with the king's interest.

A noble could thus portray actions in his own interest as actions done for the king. There was no need to hide this rationale either. For example, when the duc de Montmorency wrote recommending the duc d'Uzès to the queen regent for his actions taken in Languedoc in 1613, he specifically praised Uzès as "having as much consideration for the service of Your Majesty as for his own interest." Corruption amounted to disobeying the king or abusing the king's service, so conflicts of interest only arose when nobles failed to align their interests with those of the king.[124]

The obligations of service could become the focus of controversy during civil conflicts through argumentation and dispute over the meaning of past examples of service. Jean-Paul d'Esparbès de Lussan, upset at not being awarded the post of maréchal de France, explains to the maréchal Antoine de Roquelaure that he feels slighted, after the "the services that I have given to six kings." Lussan blames enemies who are "envious of my honor," asserting that "my request is just, having spent my blood in all the places that present themselves, for the service of my kings."[125] Roquelaure's reply is interesting. He affirms that he and Lussan are "good friends," and that he has honored Lussan. It is because of this feeling of friendship that he writes, he says. But, Roquelaure's friendly counsel also turns Lussan's record of service into a threat. He warns Lussan that "you who have at all times served the kings of France would not wish, because of some discontentment that you might have had, to lose in a moment what you have acquired over all your life through such hazards and loss of your blood, which I have seen flowing in the past." Roquelaure concludes that Lussan's best course is to beg forgiveness of the king, who "will have his arms open to receive you in his grace and to forget what has happened." Roquelaure closes his letter with yet another reminder of the obligations of service, saying that he is confident that Lussan's intentions will meet with the king's approval, because of their long "friendship."[126]

Warrior nobles felt obliged to continue serving the king, and they took special pains to recount their recent services in their correspondence. Recent services were important reminders for the king, who stressed the importance of continuing service. The emphasis on recent services was only magnified in context of frequent civil conflicts. The latest services gained increased value because of the shifting alliances and loyalties so present during civil warfare. In appointing the duc de Ventadour to a new office, Louis XIII stresses his recent services as lieutenant-général in Languedoc, "where he has always shown his affection and faithfulness, inviolable even in the latest movements in the said province of Languedoc."[127] Nobles attempted to associate their most recent services with their long legacy of service. One noble establishes his history of "all sorts of obedience" and his long service to Henri IV, before reminding Louis XIII of his recent military service in Gascogne "combating the designs of the enemies of the state."[128] The obligations of service served both as incentives to compel nobles to serve and as ways for nobles to relate their service to the king and to society. Warrior nobles continually reasserted their personal value and worth through their service.

✝

This chapter has considered the relationships between early modern French nobles and the royal state through their officeholding and service. Provincial military elites dominated the political and social life of Languedoc and Guyenne during the French Wars of Religion through their constructions of authority and their officeholding practices. These nobles articulated their political positions through the official roles that bound them personally to the king, and the sources of authority defined the parameters of their relationships with the royal state. Southern French nobles held a wide variety of high command, provincial, and regimental offices, and the king attempted to direct officeholding through official appointments, oversight, and inducements. However, the ability of the monarch to organize and direct officeholding remained limited, despite significant royal intervention in the regional politics of southern France. The distribution of royal authority throughout multiple layers of officers with conflicting jurisdictions and competing interests fractured royal authority. The royal ideal of service remained a central concept in early seventeenth-century political culture, but was not exclusively focused on king. Warrior nobles also promoted their own status and burnished their reputations through officeholding, and their flexible conceptions of these offices allowed them to engage in political activities. The bonds of officeholding, as we shall see, were closely related to noble honor culture in early seventeenth-century Languedoc and Guyenne.

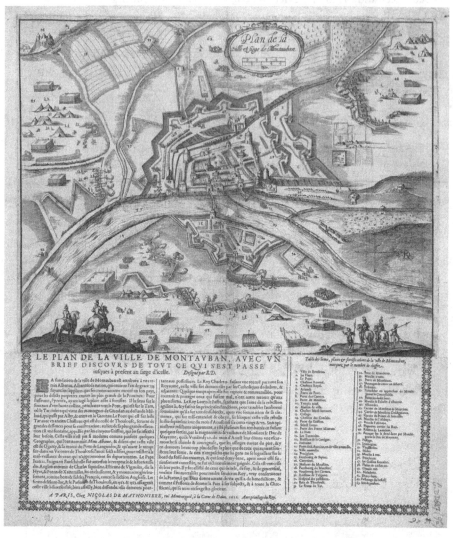

Siege view and description of a siege, an important site for displays of honor and proofs of courage. Engraving by Nicolas de Mathonière, *Plan de la ville et siège de Montauban* *(1621)*, BNF, Cartes et Plans, GE DD 627 (96). Photo courtesy Bibliothèque Nationale de France.

CHAPTER SIX

Actions the Most Perilous Being
the Most Honorable

Honor and Courage

A Catholic noble who fought in Languedoc in the 1620s argued that "honor being the most precious recompense that one could acquire from a good action, and the actions the most perilous being the most honorable, it would be wrong for these troops to remain silent about the glory that they acquire in this process."[1] Early modern French nobles clearly valued honor very highly, and they frequently discussed their personal and family honor in their correspondence. Late sixteenth- and early seventeenth-century moralists and intellectuals debated the nature of honor in treatises and pamphlets that were widely read by French nobles. Such writings clearly influenced elite ideas, but warrior nobles also seem to have to held notions of honor peculiar to their specific culture. By the early seventeenth century, an elaborate honor culture had developed that bound warrior French nobles together through shared values and assumptions that went beyond the limits of their clienteles.

This honor culture emerged in a period of social upheaval and sweeping cultural transformations. Confessional conflict and civil warfare challenged the very notions of honor in French society, particularly reshaping the honor culture of warrior nobles. Political divisions, religious animosities, and civil violence exposed the contradictions and conflicts inherent in warrior noble honor culture. Nobles who held military offices found it extremely difficult to live up to the expectations of the honor culture while fighting in bitter civil warfare. Continued religious renewal and increasing confessionalization in late sixteenth-century France created new identifications that challenged existing honor categories and prompted frequent challenges. Meanwhile, the spread of rapiers and new fencing techniques prompted an expansion of dueling in noble culture. All of these developments produced significant transitions in early seventeenth-century warrior noble honor conceptions and practices that characterized honor bonds.

CONCEPTIONS OF HONOR

Early seventeenth-century French warrior noble honor culture revolved around a series of interrelated concepts of worthiness and nobility. A warrior noble's honor, I argue, was composed of four overlapping conceptions: sanctity, quality, reputation, and precedence. Although each of these facets was an abstract ideal of nobility, they could nonetheless be expressed and displayed in everyday life.[2] Sanctity honor involved a sense of holiness and character, while qualitative honor embodied noble status and degree. Virtue and courage were the basis of a warrior noble's reputation, but prerogatives and privileges defined his precedence honor. Each of these dimensions promoted values of honorable nobility that warrior nobles aspired to uphold.

Early seventeenth-century warrior nobles believed that honor had a source, a spring at which nobles drank. Honor flowed from diverse sources, which bathed and anointed worthy nobles. God was the ultimate giver of all honor, but divine favor and abundant nature were especially associated with the granting of honorable sanctity. Noble birth and inheritance bestowed qualitative honor, although promotion augmented some nobles' quality. Military service and the exercise of office enabled nobles to acquire reputation honor. Official ranks and authorities established honor as precedence for warrior nobles. Honor was viewed as a possession, something that personally belonged to a nobleman once received from one of these sources. Identifying different origins of his personal honor, Henri II de Montmorency distinguished between "the honors that I possess of the liberality of Your Majesty and from the succession of the late monsieur le connétable," referring to his late father.[3] The imagery of a wellspring of honor, which was popular in noble culture, drew on Neoplatonic ideals of virtue. A pamphlet celebrated the maréchal de Schömberg as "a treasure of faithfulness, prudence, and courage to France, and this great person was like a sea where all of the virtues came together." This account invoked ancient models of virtue in praising Schömberg as a worthy noble: "now if all riches yield to virtue according to Plato and there is no treasure more honorable and more durable than this same virtue according to Socrates, then how great is the renown of our Alexander."[4] Honorable warrior nobles believed that they drank at the wellspring of virtue.

Expressions of honor culture represented the internal feelings that nobles developed and enunciated concerning honor. Each conception of honor was experienced in a distinct way, evoking different emotions and sensations. These feelings and emotions are difficult for historians to access, but personal writings of some nobles give us some indications, as do discussions of noble ideals of honor. Warrior nobles expressed the different facets of honor through piety, dignity, pride, and superiority.

Personal performances embodied specific practices through which nobles displayed their honor, some of which were somewhat theatrical and ritualistic, while others were rather unscripted and improvised. Certain personal rituals and individual actions were associated with a specific conception of honor. Communal performances of honor were the group actions and rituals related to a specific honor conception. Group enactments of honor culture were often responses to, or recognitions of, individual nobles' performances. Communal performances might include nobles participating in ritual ceremonies or collective activities relating to honor. Veneration, adoration, accolade, and deference were among the diverse methods of performing honor communally.

Each honor conception depended on a regulator to evaluate nobles and to adjudicate conflicts between them. Clergy and religious authorities could judge nobles' sanctity. Judicial authorities could decide competing claims to qualitative respect. Peer opinion determined many disputes over noble reputation. Military and administrative officers could regulate precedence, but the king could also intervene to enhance or diminish a warrior noble's honor. Regulating groups acted essentially as moderators, promoting ideals and negotiating problems.

Seventeenth-century French nobles' conceptions of honor were related to notions of masculinity. Gender theories argue for differing notions of masculinity within a society, applicable for different social groups, or even constructed personally by individuals. French warrior nobles seem to have employed competing notions of fraternal, paternalistic, exemplary, and aggressive masculinity, which were each related to a specific conception of honor.

Warrior nobles combined these four facets of honor culture in different ways, producing variations between different families, clienteles, and regions. Nobles holding dissimilar ranks or exercising diverse offices might assert different understandings of honor by emphasizing certain aspects of honor culture and deemphasizing others. Religious beliefs, pious practices, and confessional identities all influenced honor conceptions. Civil and religious warfare also shaped this honor culture by influencing nobles' understandings of their relationship to violence in civil warfare.

Honor as Sanctity

French nobles conceived of honor as sanctity, a sense of holiness and character upheld by devotion to God. An early seventeenth-century treatise on nobility argues that "the foundation of all [virtues] is religion, which is, in my opinion, only a pure sentiment that we have of God."[5] A noble's personal conscience and faith established his relationship to God and his place in the world. A Calvinist noble described conscience and arms as the two poles of honor, emphasizing that a noble could be *"homme de bien* for his conscience; one could achieve the glorious praise of a saint without ever serving as captain or soldier, like Saint John the Baptist, Saint Stephen, and others—that is briefly what concerns one's conscience."[6] Catholics similarly viewed conscience as crucial to their conception of honor. During a family dispute over seigneuries, the elderly Henri I de Montmorency opposed a proposed sale of lands, indicating that "my conscience and my honor constrain me to oppose [the plan] as long as it pleases God to leave me in this world."[7] Montmorency expressed concern that his brother and other relatives were buried on the seigneuries to be alienated, implying that the family's sanctity would be harmed by abandoning their deceased kin. During this period of religious revival and confessional conflict, warrior nobles seem to have valued their sense of sanctity very highly, associating honor closely with religiosity.

Warrior nobles thought of sanctity honor as natural and divine in origin—a gift to worthy noble recipients on the part of the Creator. Catholics saw sanctity as an aspect of their faith and free will. Jean Calvin emphasized God's gift of mercy, affirming that "we are indeed sanctified, that is, consecrated to the Lord in complete purity of life, our hearts formed to obedience to the law."[8] Huguenot nobles thus associated sanctity honor with righteousness, believing themselves members of the elect according to the doctrine of predestination.

Devout Christians felt a powerful duty to honor God and to extol his creation, but Protestants and Catholics developed different notions of how best to honor God in the sixteenth century. Calvin taught that "inasmuch as we are God's creatures, we ought to serve his honor and glory, and obey his commandments."[9]

Adherence to the Word of God and obedience to divine law guided the religious behavior of Huguenot nobles. Calvin admonished Reformed elites to remain virtuous and pious, warning against the dangers of pride, greed, and worldly honors. This sentiment was echoed by Huguenot moralists and nobles such as Philippe Du Plessis de Mornay in treatises on nobility and Christian life.[10] Catholic revival leaders also stressed obedience, but exhorted their followers to honor God through spirituality and asceticism.[11] Many early seventeenth-century Catholic nobles embraced similar Catholic revival conceptions of honoring God through spiritual engagement and pious acts.

Nobles expressed sanctity honor through their personal piety, which involved contemplation, prayer, and worship. Calvinist nobles expressed their sanctity honor through personal and family religiosity. Since they regarded the Word of God as guiding every aspect of life, Calvinist elites engaged in daily Bible reading and prayer in their homes.[12] Pious Huguenot nobles attended the Sunday *prêche*, or Calvinist worship service, at their local temple each week. Noblemen presumably listened closely to the ministers' sermons that provided explication of the Word of God, since "the most pious members of the congregation knew they would have to review and discuss the sermon at home afterward."[13]

Calvinist nobles also engaged in public displays of personal piety. Ever since the publication of Clément Marot's psalter in 1539, psalm singing had been a popular and distinctively Calvinist form of piety.[14] Huguenot militants employed psalm singing to disrupt Catholic masses and processions, and successive royal edicts prohibited it during the French Wars of Religion.[15] Calvinist nobles participated in Reformed synods and political assemblies, often in defiance of regional or royal authorities. Calvinists emphasized leading a strict moral life and rejecting idolatry, and Huguenot nobles dressed more austerely than their Catholic counterparts. Huguenot nobles had long acted as pious laypersons by sponsoring Calvinist ministers and providing coreligionists with access to Reformed worship services at their châteaux. In the aftermath of the Edict of Nantes, Huguenot nobles in southern France provided funding for the construction of new Calvinist temples in many communities. Involvement in these temple-building projects was an "act of faith" for the Huguenot nobles who assisted in their construction.[16] Many early seventeenth-century Huguenots stressed their loyalty to the king as piety: "Those of the Reformed religion [have] the great good and singular honor from God to be numbered among the most humble, most obedient, and most faithful servants and subjects of Your Majesty."[17] Some Huguenot nobles therefore used their sanctity honor to identify themselves as loyalists.

As a Languedoc Calvinist elite indicated, "I find myself to be a good servant of the king as well as a man of religion."[18]

Catholics expressed their sanctity honor through very different forms of personal religiosity. Catholic nobles performed penance, gave confession, and attended mass. The extensive use of books of hours, rosaries, crucifixes, and reliquaries by Catholics during the civil wars of the early seventeenth century indicates the importance of personal piety and daily prayer for Catholic nobles.[19] Many Catholic nobles commissioned family chapels in their homes and local churches for their personal devotions. Catholic families maintained close connections with religious orders and relied on family members who had taken vows to confirm the sanctity of their lay relatives.

Southern French nobles who adhered to Roman Catholicism also established their sanctity honor through participation in collective rituals and civic religious activities. Catholic nobles marched in religious processions and attended celebrations of high mass at cathedrals on major holy days. As Catholic revival movements swept through Languedoc and Guyenne in the late sixteenth and early seventeenth centuries, noblemen avidly founded and joined lay confraternities to reassert their sanctity.[20] Catholic nobles participated in popular Forty Hours and Stations of the Cross devotions, which often attracted large crowds of lay activists. Attending public preaching by Capuchin and Jesuit priests underscored the importance of abhorring heresy and striving to convert heretics to Catholic Reformation religiosity.

Warrior nobles of both confessions displayed their sanctity honor through personal participation in defending their faith and fighting for confessional causes. The Huguenot nobles who fought for a small minority of Calvinists in France could not hope to eliminate papalism, but they did see themselves as fighting to defend the true faith. Louis II de Baschi baron d'Aubais "fought for the purity of the service of God" with the Huguenot armies of the duc de Rohan in Languedoc.[21] Many nobles participated in fighting against confessional enemies in Germany and Italy, either by forming armed bands or by traveling individually to join their coreligionists. Some nobles even left France to join crusades against the Ottomans as sanctity performances.[22] All of these personal performances of religious zeal reflected nobles' sanctity honor.

Early seventeenth-century French warrior nobles commemorated their dead, celebrating the sanctity of the fallen and honoring worthy peers, royalty, and God through veneration, a reverential respect or awe rendered out of obligation. Veneration represented a communal performance of sanctity honor, since respect shown through veneration displayed divine order and inspiration. Humans, by extension, were to be venerated based on their God-given worthiness. The most elevated form of veneration in French society was when nobles honored the king, who was due veneration by virtue of his anointed position as God's representative on earth. Veneration was granted to monarchs as a sign of reverential respect, especially at coronation ceremonies and other formal rituals, but it could also be extended to noblemen as a mark of consideration. Veneration was expressed through honorific ceremonies and gestures that celebrated, recognized, and affirmed sanctity honor. Noble attitudes to death displayed the importance of sanctity within their honor culture, so elegies, funeral ceremonies, genealogies, and histories all emphasized honoring the dead through veneration.

Reactions to the deaths of nobles from Languedoc and Guyenne during the 1621 civil war show the close relationship between sanctity honor and veneration. The young Henri de Lorraine duc de Mayenne was killed while reconnoitering at the siege of Montauban in 1621. As governor of Guyenne, he had taken a series of towns in the province earlier in the year and had helped to invest Montauban itself. These services, as well as his leadership and heroism during the siege of Montauban, were stressed by many contemporaries, who confirmed Mayenne's honor by venerating him. His recent participation in civil conflicts and his aid for Marie de Médicis against Luynes's administration and Louis XIII's wishes were conveniently forgotten in an effusion of elegies and veneration.[23] The Lauzières de Thémines family also mourned the deaths of two young men during the same campaign. Antoine de Lauzières marquis de Thémines was killed in an assault on Montauban, and his brother Charles was killed a few months later at the siege of Monheur. Warrior nobles saw the Lauzières family's sacrifice as worthy of veneration. Louis XIII mourned the dead brothers and honored them. A desire to confirm the family's enhanced sanctity may have played a role in the king's later granting of the office of maréchal de France to the head of the Lauzières family.[24]

Religious authorities regulated sanctity honor by approving or rejecting nobles' understandings of the relationships between religion and honor. Both Calvinist ministers and Catholic clergy determined religious policies which defined the acceptable parameters for warrior nobles' sanctity honor. Prominent early seventeenth-century Calvinist ministers such as Daniel Chamier and Pierre Girard influenced Huguenot nobles' behavior by confirming or denying the morality and correctness of their actions. The minister Vignier openly discussed his sense of caring for his flock and ensuring their obedience to the king's laws and to the Word of God.[25] Catholic clergy served as spiritual advisors and confessors to Catholic nobles, providing them with religious counsel on a daily basis. Jesuits seem to have been especially popular as confessors for members of the royal family and many powerful noble families in the early seventeenth century.[26] Nobles who perceived of themselves as particularly pious even engaged in theological debates and pamphleteering over religious ideas and controversies.

A fraternal masculinity of Christian brotherhood undergirded sanctity honor for members of both confessions. Calvinist nobles bonded fraternally with their noble coreligionaries based on their shared sense of sanctity. Calvin's conception of the "communion of the saints" presented the elect as a community of Christ's "brothers and companions," bound together by partaking the body of Christ spiritually.[27] Southern French Calvinist nobles applied the notion of Christian brotherhood to their "union of churches" during early seventeenth-century civil conflicts.

Catholic nobles in southern France promoted Christian brotherhood through participation in lay Catholic organizations and military orders. Late sixteenth-century and early seventeenth-century Catholic revival movements urged lay piety and activism. Many nobles joined informal Catholic lay groups and confraternities to share their spirituality and experience "devotional brotherhood." Confraternities marched collectively in religious processions and civic ceremonies that displayed members' fraternal unity and penitential piety, often including ritualistic self-mortification.[28] A number of warrior nobles from Languedoc and Guyenne were admitted to the prestigious Order of Saint John of Jerusalem, or Knights of Malta, which was seen as highly honorable. Catholic nobles across France aspired to enter the ranks of the Ordre du Saint-Esprit, or Order of the Holy Spirit, as confirmation of their sanctity honor. This military order had been founded by Henri III in 1578 and had become a powerful symbol of militant Catholicism by the early seventeenth century.[29] François d'Escoubleau cardinal de Sourdis recommended a noble to Marie de Médicis who was among the "many knights who aspire to the Order of the Holy Spirit in these quarters," certifying that he "had made all of the preparations to render himself capable of this honor" and emphasizing "the purity of his actions."[30] Additional nobles from Languedoc and Guyenne were invited by the king to join the Order of the Holy Spirit during the promotions of 1619 and 1633. All of these organizations encouraged a sense of fraternity among inductees, who were considered equals in sanctity honor. A poem written by François de Bassompierre to celebrate his induction into the

Order of the Holy Spirit in 1619 reveals this fraternal masculinity by asking: "Superb chevaliers whose splendor is so grand / That for other mortals it offends the eyes / What ardor does command / And makes you aspire to offices in the skies?" Bassompierre describes the fraternity that he feels with the other "superb chevaliers" with whom he shares the honor of membership in the Order of the Holy Spirit. Sanctity honor is shown in his assertion that "Heaven gives its marks / To those whom Earth has given its laurels." To be worthy, he concludes, the Holy Spirit must "gleam in your souls."

Honor as Quality

Honor could be seen as moral worth, a quality possessed by warrior nobles by virtue of their noble status. Qualitative honor was closely related to a noble's precise station or, as one noble put it, being "of my condition and of my quality."[31] Each noble held a unique honorable status that was conferred by seigneurial titles, landholdings, and rights. In an important treatise in 1608 classifying diverse French seigneuries and analyzing a broad spectrum of seigneurial rights, the jurist Charles Loyseau defined seigneurie as *puissance en propriété*, or power in property.[32] Ownership of seigneuries and a feeling of natural superiority thus forged a paternalistic sense of masculinity that sustained qualitative honor.

Qualitative honor was largely defined by warrior nobles' conceptions of nobility as a distinct social order. Loyseau viewed the nobility as more fundamental than offices and inherently distinct from other orders in society. Loyseau also directly linked honor to noble order, arguing that "beyond this external decoration [of badges and insignia], two other prerogatives of honour proceed from orders, namely title and rank."[33] Michel de Montaigne similarly finds the origin of nobility in a qualitative definition of honor: "It is probable that the first of the virtues to appear among men, giving them superiority over others, was the one by which the stronger and the more courageous made themselves masters of the weaker and so acquired individual rank and dignity; or else those nations, being most warlike, gave the prize and the title highest in dignity to the virtue which they were most familiar with."[34]

The concept of *honnête homme*, which could be translated as honorable man or gentleman, provided a powerful expression of honor as a vital quality in early seventeenth-century noble culture. Nicolas Faret's influential treatise on courtly behavior, *L'Honneste-homme ou, l'art de plaire à la court* (1630), presents honor as a quality granted to nobles at birth, but that must be cultivated and allowed to follow its natural inclinations.[35] Ellery Schalk, following Norbert Elias's model of a "civilizing" society, argues that "the ideal of the *honnête homme*—a concept that assumes essentially the new idea of nobility—took shape and developed throughout the seventeenth century."[36] Warrior nobles certainly used the concept, often describing their peers, and especially high-ranking *grands*, as *honnête hommes* in their correspondence and reports.[37] But, contemporary usage of *honnêteté* hardly bears out Schalk's conclusions that nobility and virtue were now considered separately or that an entirely new conception of noble birth suddenly emerged at the royal court.[38] Provincial nobles also used a qualitative notion of honor, as in a Catholic account of civil conflict in Languedoc that relates: "the sieur Chabreilles was accompanied by all the honorable men of his government to the number of eighty cavalry and a hundred infantry."[39] A narrative of the 1622 siege of Montpellier describes a noble who was killed at the siege as a "very honorable and useful man."[40] Nobles acknowledged a peer's *honnêteté*, or honorable quality, in social settings and in writing. A 1629 report noted that a noble being considered for an office was indeed "recognized as an honorable gentleman."[41]

Several related expressions reveal the association of honor with an inherent qualitative status. Nicolas Faret uses the concepts of *homme de bien* and *gentilhomme* almost interchangeably with *honnête homme* to refer to nobles' honorable qualities.[42] The frequent use of the *homme de bien* and *homme d'honneur* in noble correspondence reveals how nobles thought themselves deserving of honor because of their noble quality.[43] An account of an atrocity stresses that "the honorable men of Vivarais will have this satisfaction that these inhumanities and this felony touch them not at all, seeing that they were all committed by brutal peasants or lesser men, where they were not assisted by one single man of condition." The author assures his readers that "these cruelties . . . would not have been suffered by a nobleman [*homme de bien*]."[44] The phrase "persons of honor" was used in the same manner; a description of a siege combat records that the sieurs de Boissy and de Peroles and "other persons of honor from the town" repulsed the attacks of Huguenot troops under Alexandre de Blacons seigneur de Mirabel-Blacons.[45] The use of *homme de condition* emphasized even more overtly the qualitative distinction between nobles and non-nobles. By extension, condition could refer to degrees of nobility also, with "men of condition" indicating high nobility.

Qualitative honor flowed from several sources, but above all from birth. A noble child entered the world qualitatively determined by his family's blood, distinguished from non-nobles and established at a certain degree of noble status.[46]

Both the father's and the mother's degrees of nobility determined the child's quality. Blood imagery cemented the idea of birth as a determinant of quality for early modern nobles.[47] Closely related to a noble's birth, his inheritance also gave him considerable qualitative honor. Warrior nobles normally received seigneuries, titles, and wealth through their inheritance. Typically, a noble received some of his inheritance at birth or as a child, then inherited additional properties and titles at adulthood and finally assumed his full inheritance at the death of his father.

Marriage was another vital source of qualitative honor. Noble parents sought honorable marriages for their children through extensive negotiations of alliance with other noble families. Efforts at arranging marriages were vital for warrior noble families, because marriage provided a potential route to sustaining, or even improving, qualitative honor. Inheritance, seigneuries, and wealth were all linked to marriage, and a family's collective honor was on the line during marriage negotiations. For nobles in southern France, marriage also represented a "fusion of honor," combining the qualities of the two families in marriage. Anne de Lévis duc de Ventadour thus described the duc de Sully's *honnêtes offres* of marriage alliance with his family.[48] Personal qualitative honor was subsumed within family honor, and children were the products of the qualities of their parents. Henri I de Montmorency thanked the queen regent profusely for arranging a marriage for his son that would secure the qualitative honor of his family.[49]

Promotion provided a final source for qualitative honor through noble degrees. The king could promote noblemen to a higher grade of nobility for their services in civil wars. Louis XIII elevated the baronnie de Saint-Remèze to a comté for Antoine du Roure in 1621.[50] Many nobles were promoted in Languedoc and Guyenne during the early seventeenth century. Promotion could also extend to commoners, who were occasionally ennobled for their services to the king. Ennoblement could be linked to civil warfare, since some nobles were ennobled, at least in part, for their loyalty during civil conflicts and for their services against "rebels." Few official ennoblements were registered in Languedoc during this period, but the king did grant nobility to a few military officers.[51] Many early seventeenth-century warrior nobles worried about non-nobles achieving promotion by purchasing seigneuries that held noble title and honorable quality.[52]

Nobles expressed their quality through their feelings of dignity. The personal aspects of qualitative honor engendered a feeling of individual dignity based on one's degree of status. Negotiating during a civil conflict, Jean-Paul d'Esparbès de Lussan wrote, "I am one of the first gentlemen of this kingdom who has rendered [the king] most humble service and obedience, and in this manner I made my most humble supplication to him." Lussan's request thus reflected his personal quality, but also his disappointment that he had not received the appointment he had desired from the king. "I do not know the first [person] who has been frustrated by the fruit of [the king's] promises," he claimed, implying that his dignity had been slighted.[53] Other great nobles in Guyenne and Languedoc, such as the duc de Montmorency and the duc d'Uzès, voiced similar ideas. Anne de Lévis duc de Ventadour complained in 1611 that he was the "only one in France of my quality" not to have had the opportunity to visit court since the death of Henri IV to pay respects to Marie de Médicis.[54]

Personal performances involving qualitative honor included participation in the ceremonies of feudal homage and marriage. While feudal vassalic ties meant little politically or socially for nobles in the early seventeenth century, some nobles still performed ceremonies of homage in fulfillment of their qualitative honor in the late sixteenth and early seventeenth centuries.[55] Marriage ceremonies acted to cement qualitative honor bonds between noble families. Warrior nobles sought alliances that would allow them to participate in elaborate marriage ceremonies celebrating their qualitative honor. For example, the marriage of Jacques II d'Isarn and Marie de La Garde de Chambonnas in 1613 allowed both of their families to confirm their honorable quality as significant Catholic seigneurs in Languedoc.[56] Nobles attached such importance to weddings as revealing quality that marriage contracts would be used by nobles as one of the principal *preuves de noblesse* later in the seventeenth century. Although most noble marriages were carefully arranged alliances, ideals of marital love and companionship promoted an honorable attachment between marriage partners.[57] Some contemporaries portrayed the marriage of Henri II de Montmorency and Maria Felicia Orsini as a model of spousal devotion.[58]

French nobles, their entourages, and broader communities engaged in performances of adoration that confirmed warrior nobles' qualitative honor. Nobles offered dignified praise to their peers and superiors on occasions that celebrated individual nobles' qualities. A poem written on the occasion of an urban entry by Pons de Lauzières marquis de Thémines encouraged him "to admire in yourself your noble quality."[59] Warrior nobles received such admiration during the formal introductions, investments, and promotions that marked their embodiment of titles and their assertions of seigneurial power. When installed as governor of Bordeaux, Henri II de Bourbon prince de Condé was explicitly honored for his quality as prince of the blood.[60] The adoration of certain honored nobles through such formal ceremonies and through spontaneous adulation therefore validated those nobles' sense of difference from others.

Law acted as a regulator of qualitative honor, since natural law was seen as justifying receipt of honor by birth, and inheritance laws governed the distribution of quality through noble lineages. The king's role as dispenser of justice allowed his council and his parlements to adjudicate differences over qualitative honor.[61] Legal disputes frequently erupted between nobles over the inheritance of properties, but also over the related qualitative honor attached to seigneuries. The marriage between Louis d'Arpajon and Gloriande de Thémines produced an inheritance dispute after Gloriande's death in 1635. One party in the ensuing lawsuit claimed that "Jean-Louis d'Arpajon, her only son—in spite of himself—was elected and called to all of the properties of the family," implying a concentration of qualitative honor in this one heir to the exclusion of other claimants.[62] While lawsuits were pending over inheritance disputes, there was always a threat that nobles might resort to violence to assert their quality and position over their rivals. François de Noailles comte d'Ayen thus acted in his government in 1618 to be sure that "no one pursues his rights by force."[63] Serious legal battles arose over titles and properties that were stripped of nobles accused of lèse-majesté and granted to other relatives, and Louis XIII himself had to adjudicate qualitative honor in determining provincial nobles' right of entry to the estates of Languedoc following the 1632 civil war.[64] Warrior nobles thus routinely appealed to judicial authorities to confirm their honorable quality through legal decisions.

Qualitative honor involved a paternalistic masculinity that posited male figures as possessing honor due to their natural position as protectors and caregivers. Paternalistic masculinity was seen as natural, biological, and divinely sanctioned. Elder nobles and nobles who were heads of important families or lineages easily commanded much paternal respect. The duc d'Épernon was initially not accepted by his peers when promoted to the rank of duc et pair under Henri III, but his quality was no longer disputed by Louis XIII's reign. Many nobles used paternalistic symbolism to establish paternal masculinity and to reinforce their sanctity honor. Paternalistic masculinity reinforced honor ideals of protecting the weak, providing for lesser beings, and supplying paternal care. Warrior nobles saw themselves as guardians and protectors of their families and clienteles. The ideas of paternalistic masculinity created a need for nobles to receive paternal respect and to be obeyed.[65]

Honor as Reputation

A noble officer's honor as reputation was defined by his virtue and courage. "True honor," according to one prominent southern French noble, "flows from God to the king."[66] Nobles acquired a reputation through their bellicose deeds and honorable acts done in the name of the king, seen as "the center from which emanates this brilliant character of honor, which distinguishes men one from another."[67] Royal service in the king's armies and provincial governments was thus the main source of reputation honor. Establishing a record of virtuous acts and courageous deeds produced honor, and reputation was an assessment of that record that could be compared with other nobles' honor.

Warrior nobles believed that reputation emanated from their military service and their exercise of office. Their willingness to engage in civil conflict, despite the numerous hardships and dangers involved, is in part explained by the notion that military combat was intrinsically honorable. Nobles regularly emphasized the links between honor and service in their correspondence: "I am too well paid, Sire, for my services—seeing that it has pleased Your Majesty to remember me, which is a grace to me that I hold more dear than all the honors in the world," Jean-François de La Guiche seigneur de Saint-Géran wrote enthusiastically to Louis XIII.[68] Warrior nobles' reputation honor stemmed not only from their bellicose deeds, but also from their wise counsel and advice, especially on military matters. Nicolas Faret stresses the importance of nobles providing the king with advice on maintaining discipline and order in his armies.[69] The duc de Lesdiguières similarly envisions a vital role for warrior nobles as military advisors, insisting that "the sovereign also take the counsel of wise and experienced captains."[70]

Nobles found the sources of reputation in their merits and services. A noble's reputation stemmed from the granting of honors by the king, as Louis XIII himself explained when he rewarded a noble in 1622, saying that he "more willingly gave this recognition of his services [because] the qualities that meet in him render him worthy to possess the same honors as those of his name and *maison*."[71] The monarch played an important role in promoting and defining the conception of honor as reputation, since the king enhanced the reputation of nobles most directly by rewarding them and conferring offices on them. Warrior nobles believed that offices granted honor, and the monarch actively encouraged this conception. A grant of an office might pronounce that "the king has cast a glance at you to give you an honorable employment, since His Majesty gives you the conduct of his regiment and his cornets of cavalry."[72] The most honorable employment was that given directly by the king.

Unlike qualitative honor, honor as reputation could not spring from birth, although men of good birth were considered more likely to attain reputational honor. Loyseau carefully argued that virtue stemmed from the "rational soul of men," which came "immediately from God." A child's education and development, rather than his birth, contributed to virtue, according to Loyseau. Contemporary warrior nobles might not have accepted all of the jurist's musings on the noble order, but they could well agree that virtue was individual, because it was an aspect of reputational honor.[73] Warrior nobles understood reputation to be tied to a nobleman's own actions, not to his family's honor. A pamphlet portraying the glories of Henri II de Montmorency's ancestors in 1612 makes this point forcefully. After noting Montmorency's distinguished genealogy on both his father's and mother's sides, and that "the first prince of the blood [is] his brother-in-law and his very close cousin," it qualifies this by observing that "the nobility and generosity of blood are not recognized so much in public histories, titles of houses, and paintings of dead ancestors, as in the high and magnanimous actions of successors."[74] As this pamphlet shows, honor could be based on a noble's personal actions and behavior, the roots of his reputation, rather than his inherent quality or his natural sanctity. The personal aspects of reputation also allowed nobles to take pride openly in their own accomplishments.

Experiencing combat was an essential personal performance for honor as reputation. Battles and sieges provided nobles with opportunities for proving their valor and distinguishing themselves by their heroic exploits. Nobles avidly sought out combat, believing that their actions on the battlefield or in siege-works might enhance their reputations. A Catholic noble in Languedoc asserted that on the basis of their bravery in a skirmish in Vivarais, he and his comrades should be ranked among "the most honorable . . . in these wars." Five or six hundred men had faced an entire Huguenot army, but had "the effrontery to attack [it] and the power to block it for two hours," until reinforcements arrived.[75] The precious nature of honor spurred warrior nobles into intense indirect competition, and they vied for the opportunities to gain honor through participation in battle.

The noble community responded to reputational honor with accolades and effusive praise. The duc de Lesdiguières emphasized the vital importance of martial reputation, asserting that "everyone will admit and approve that it is more praiseworthy and honorable than anything else for a military leader to fight valiantly and to defeat his enemy."[76] Communal recounting of the honorable deeds and the memories of past heroism sustained noble reputation. Peer opinion confirmed nobles' reputations, judging the heroic or unheroic nature of nobles' actions, behavior, and bearing. In addition to the vital importance of being seen to be heroic by the king, nobles relied on other nobles' witnessing or learning of their service to build their reputations. Peer judgment helps to explain nobles' need to publicize their honorable actions. Reputational honor could only be enhanced if recognized and confirmed by other nobles.

When their honorable service could not be viewed by the king or a considerable number of their peers, nobles solicited literary and artistic work to advertise their services and enhance their reputations. This desire to demonstrate honorable actions means that writings specifically crafted for noble patrons are the best literary sources for gaining an understanding of noble values.[77] Poems praising nobles' honorable reputations were read on ceremonial occasions such as formal entries into towns.[78] Of course, these literary productions cannot be interpreted as representing the ideas of nobles directly, but they certainly indicate discussions of reputation that were acceptable to warrior nobles. Many of these literary works praised nobles for their victories in battles and sieges, as in a poem dedicated to the duc d'Épernon in 1627 that celebrated his numerous victories and his "many beautiful warrior acts."[79]

Publications detailing royal activities and military campaigns recognized the services of nobles in the king's armies, enhancing their notoriety and reputation. A pamphlet reporting the capture of a fortress in Languedoc by the governor of Montpellier explained that he should be commended, because "the happy successes with which the enterprises of His Majesty are favored everywhere, to the disadvantage of his enemies, deserve to be published in order to praise God, who is the author of his holy intentions and the avenger of his rebels, and to give honor to those who acquire it justly by the merit of their services."[80] In this sense, honor is reputation gained through meritorious service to the king, and recognized publicly. The pamphlet continues by proclaiming that "this action acquired for [the governor] honor and praise from the devout, the curious, and even those of so-called reformed religion, who have voluntarily consented."[81] Pamphlets celebrating royal victories, then, may have been intended as royal propaganda, but they simultaneously served as noble propaganda, enhancing the reputations of certain nobles. The duc de Mayenne received accolades for his leadership in the combats leading to the investment of Montauban in 1621. A celebratory pamphlet praised Mayenne's abilities and leadership as the keys to the successful encirclement of the Huguenot fortified city. "Now joyous at this victory that he had won against the rebels from His Majesty," the pamphlet narrates, Mayenne "commanded his cavalry to have courage" and prepared to attack. "Finally courageous, they conveyed themselves promptly to the rebel's [lines] . . . and gave them a shock. Having arrived, he positioned his army across from the château, with two pieces of artillery, which battered it furiously. Now they were quite shocked, whether from their fear or from the defeat of their troops."[82] Here, the duc de Mayenne's personal leadership is presented as the key to the victories and to the successful investment of Montauban. Mayenne's reputation was undoubtedly enhanced by the attention lavished on him in print and by the army, but he did not long enjoy it—he was killed while reconnoitering for an assault later in the siege. Nonetheless, publications praising warrior nobles' bellicose deeds cemented their reputations and enhanced their families' honor.[83]

Reputation honor promoted an exemplary notion of masculinity. Nobles were expected to exhibit masculine courage and virtue through their manliness and honorable acts. Exemplary masculinity had to be shown and displayed, as nobles tried to achieve a masculine ideal of courage and virtue.[84] Warrior nobles valued their ancestors' reputations as honorable precedents and moral exempla. Nobles read histories of their ancestors with interest and seriousness, hoping for inspiration to emulate their heroic deeds. In his youth, Henri II de Montmorency was excited "by the example of his grandfather, whose life he regularly studied."[85] A siege narrative encouraged Alexandre du Puy de Tournon marquis de Saint-André de Montbrun, a Calvinist warrior noble, to remember that "this ancient stem from which you have issued has in the past made foreigners feel its victorious arms and the admirable effects of a martial courage. And you, in imitating the virtues of your ancestors . . . show the enemies of the Reformed religion that you profess the rigor of your arms." Saint-André de Montbrun thus established a reputation that would serve to inspire and educate other Calvinist nobles, who, "instructed by your zeal and courage, would desire to read and meditate on your conquests, so as to be mirrors in imitating your virtues."[86]

Honor as Precedence

Honor as precedence was defined by the privileges and prerogatives associated with office and rank. Conceiving of honor as precedence required quantifying it and establishing degrees of honor, which were displayed through ceremonies and social interactions that involved ordering, ranking, and deference. The historian Kristen B. Neuschel discusses the hierarchical aspects of honor and the importance of "lesser" noblemen associating with nobles who had greater honor. She shows how the "rankings of honor" could be displayed within households and in daily life.[87] A vague hierarchy of honor formed based on noble social rankings, offices, and political positions, but precedence rankings would always remain somewhat ill-defined, changeable, and contestable. The lack of clearly defined hierarchies in early seventeenth-century noble society produced the continual negotiation of rank and competition for precedence, which served as the sources of precedence honor. As we have seen above, multiple authorities and overlapping jurisdictions created ambiguity and confusion, leading to conflicts over precedence and power.[88]

Nobles' honor as precedence originated in their officeholding and official rankings. Commissions usually explicitly gave noble officers a sense of precedence by establishing recognizable powers. A 1621 commission indicated that the noble who received the office was "to enjoy all the rights, honors, and prerogatives dependent on and belonging to the said charge."[89] When the duc de Lesdiguières was given command of troops in 1621, the king acknowledged that this office carried with it the power: "to have, to hold, and from now on to exercise . . . the said charge, with all the honors, authorities, powers, functions, prerogatives, preeminences, and rights that go with it . . . in the same manner as they have been used in the past by those who have previously held [the office], and with the wages, estates, and appointments that will be ordained."[90] All royal offices granted special powers and specific prerogatives to officers that effectively established new precedence relationships between the officeholder and other nobles.

Direct recognition from the king was also a source of precedence honor. Provincial nobles claimed honor from the letters that they received from the king or from the *grands*. Nobles frequently began their letters by thanking the addressee for the honor of his or her recent letter. While this practice might seem at first glance to be a mere formality, it shows an important facet of honor culture. Provincial nobles truly felt honored to receive letters from the king, his ministers, and the *grands*. The nobles of Languedoc and Guyenne were rarely at the royal court, so correspondence with courtiers was their only regular contact with it. Letters from the king and from powerful nobles would be saved and valued by provincial nobles for generations. Later, during the *recherches de noblesse* of Louis XIV, provincial nobles would use letters from court as part of their proofs of nobility.[91] Some noble families from Languedoc claimed that they had been honored with commissions and letters from the king, but that they had been destroyed during the destruction of the earlier civil wars.

Warrior nobles expressed their precedence honor through feelings of superiority to other nobles and commoners. Their self-worth seems to have been expressed through attitudes of dominance. Nobles with greater precedence honor sensed their advantage over others and appreciated their supremacy, enjoying each victory in competitions over precedence. Challenges to precedence honor thus simultaneously disturbed nobles' self-esteem and governing ability. A prominent Guyenne noble asserted defensively in 1621 that "I am a very honorable man and in my vicinity no one could serve the king as usefully or as powerfully as me."[92] Nobles sought to confirm their ascendancy over other nobles through such precedence disputes.

Personal performances of precedence honor involved recognizing the prerogatives of higher-ranking military officers. Warrior nobles were expected to defer to commanders who were clearly their superiors. After giving Antoine-Arnaud de Pardaillan seigneur de Gondrin orders to raise two regiments, Louis XIII asked him "for the good of my affairs to defer to the said sieur maréchal de Thémines, considering his quality of maréchal of France—which concerns you, too, since you have occasion to hope for [this quality] in consideration of your merits and ancient services—[but] it would be reasonable for everyone else [to defer] to your position."[93] Nobles' precedence honor was constantly displayed during military campaigns, since the military units they commanded marched, camped, and fought according to a nominally established order. Frequent precedence competitions occurred when nobles officers disputed their peers' status and their units' positions during military operations. During the 1622 civil war, Louis de Chabans recounts, the regiment de Navarre angered the officers and soldiers of the gardes françaises by attempting to take the lead in a march.[94]

Participation in ceremonies that displayed ranking demonstrated individual nobles' precedence honor. Ritual ceremonies as ordinary as mass or as irregular as entries to assemblies included processions ordered by rankings. Nobles participating in ceremonial entries into towns followed prescribed precedence order. Acknowledgment of a noble's precedence honor involved mutual esteem, respect, and courtesy among peers. To prevent continual disputes over precedence, most organizations had established protocol governing precedence. The estates of Languedoc, for example, developed rules governing precedence at their meetings and ceremonies, but they were subject to challenge and were revised a number of times.[95] These attempts to manage precedence honor merely diffused precedence competition somewhat, though. Many ceremonies still engendered disagreements and even outright fights over precedence.

Dueling is probably the best-known of all personal performances of precedence honor in early modern France. Dueling has often been seen as an ultimate test of honor and the linchpin of the French honor system. François Billacois and Robert Nye, in particular, have interpreted dueling as the sine qua non of early modern honor. Billacois sees dueling as a "total social phenomenon," a sort of "touchstone" explaining seventeenth-century French society as a whole.[96] However, dueling and the conventions that surrounded it remained principally confined to one sphere of honor, that of precedence. Warrior nobles fought duels over various insults, but especially those that directly challenged their precedence honor. Medieval duels had performed a judicial role in settling legal disputes between nobles, but early modern duelists now invoked divine providence to uphold their precedence by validating their just causes in disputing with their rivals.[97] Victory over an opponent in a duel thus vindicated a noble's precedence honor and dismissed his rival's precedence challenge.

Other performances of precedence honor were also important, if less conspicuous. Seeking favors always involved nobles' precedence honor, since they competed directly over the benefits of royal gifts. Nicolas Le Roux describes a "humanist economy of favor" that provided an ideal for the distribution of favors among sixteenth-century court nobles, but that was also disrupted during the French Wars of Religion by opposition to royal favorites—especially Henri III's *mignons*.[98] In the early seventeenth century, warrior nobles' attitudes to royal favor figured in a series of precedence disputes over the selection of maréchaux de France.[99] Honor was bestowed on nobles who could successfully apply for favors from royal family members, but no noble would be able to receive a positive response to every request. Henri I de Montmorency complained directly to Marie de Médicis that: "after all the submissions that a faithful servant must make, I am permitted to present to Your Majesty my just sadness that . . . my demands have found so little favor." Having submitted his requests already several times, Montmorency felt "frustrated with this wait."[100] When nobles' requests were not quickly granted, their precedence honor could be called into question. Ultimately, receiving regular and frequent favors maintained or augmented nobles' precedence honor.

Communal performances of precedence honor were based on deference, since warrior nobles constantly had to take account of the distinctions of rank and hierarchy established by precedence. A noble's precedence could only be confirmed by other nobles acknowledging his rank and acquiescing to their claims to precedence. Gestures, signs, and discourses were all created to demonstrate deference to nobles with superior precedence. William Beik has demonstrated the significance of gestures of personal respect in seventeenth-century French society, revealing the sharp indignation that individuals felt when other people denied them the respectful gestures they felt they were owed.[101] Warrior nobles were especially sensitive to such disrespect precisely because it challenged their precedence honor. A noble's superior precedence could only be displayed or maintained by convincing or forcing inferiors to defer to him.

Civic ceremonies and religious processions confirmed precedence rankings within communities and corporate bodies. Warrior nobles participated in communal rituals in their various roles as seigneurs, town governors, and military officers. Each ceremonial event ordered participants according to rank, creating precedence tensions that nobles had to negotiate. Religious processions also relied on precedence ordering, which was often complicated by nobles' multiple roles in confessional communities. Calvinist nobles might be protectors and sponsors of a temple, as well as member of the congregation. Catholic nobles who joined in religious processions could march as parishioners, donors, and confraternity members. An early seventeenth-century treatise claimed that Catholic nobles disputed "pre-eminence in churches and the honours in them . . . who will be the loftiest in life and death . . . who shall lead processions, and . . . who shall give the blessed bread first."[102] Since "seating arrangements in church were a microcosm of the village hierarchy and to lose one's place was to lose honour and cede power and authority,"[103] sacred spaces became sites of precedence competitions.

Military authorities and their martial culture regulated precedence honor by influencing noble behavior in situations where precedence was challenged. The *salles d'armes* and armies of the religious wars provided warrior nobles with weapons training that emphasized a body mechanics of orchestrated postures, graceful movements, and fluid attacks.[104] The many *maîtres d'armes* forged practical honor conventions as they taught nobles to control their passions and maintain tight discipline over their minds and bodies in their exercise of arms.[105] The teachings of *maîtres d'armes* on honor and arms often clashed with the opinions of moralists who upheld virtues and condemned dueling. Sixteenth- and seventeenth-century treatises on honor and nobility repeatedly warned of the dangers of jealousy and ambition, which often resulted in bloody quarrels.[106] The martial honor conventions were based largely on problem-solving, adjudicating differences between nobles and providing remedies for misconduct and misbehavior. Such notions of honor established principles of fairness in dueling, including the use of seconds and having even numbers in quarrels. The martial culture fostered by military officers and *maîtres d'armes* promoted dueling, even though these officials attempted to deal with the problem of insults and impugning honor—actions upsetting honor as precedence.[107]

Achieving and maintaining precedence honor demanded an aggressive masculinity. Defense of prerogatives and privileges was enacted through assertions of manliness. Warrior nobles were expected not only to react defensively to attacks on their precedence honor, but were to initiate challenges to other nobles' prerogatives to increase their own precedence. Only aggressive behavior in the form of challenges and direct competition could produce situations in which to increase precedence honor.

PRACTICES OF HONOR

Warrior nobles engaged in honor practices, a series of meritorious activities that related simultaneously to several different facets of honor culture. The practices of honor were partially aimed at bringing differing aspects of honor into line with each other, handling differences and deciding conflicts between nobles. A noble with high qualitative honor but lower reputational honor might want opportunities to serve so that he might have a chance at gaining reputation. A noble who had high precedence but low qualitative honor might be challenged by nobles with higher qualitative honor. The military elites of southern France discerned diverse ways, or paths, to acquire and to maintain honor. An account describing the division of spoils taken in combat reveals the idea of diverse methods of gaining honor, suggesting multiple practices of honor that nobles employed. After the money was distributed among the nobles and soldiers, "no one had much, and it was necessary for everyone to take satisfaction in the ways of honor for which each searched."[108] Practices of command, proofs of courage, and admiration provided warrior nobles with important ways of increasing their honor, but they also had to act constantly to preserve their honorable status.

Command

Warrior nobles' conceptions of honor had a strong military cast and they considered command one of the most important honor practices. Early seventeenth-century nobles envisioned military command much as many medieval nobles must have regarded personal combat. Commanding troops in battles and sieges allowed noble officers to gain honor as reputation, to compete for honor as precedence, and to demonstrate honor as quality. Each military commission and administrative appointment created potential conflicts of precedence among provincial nobles. Commanding reflected a noble's honor because the art of war was itself considered an honorable profession. According to one noble fighting in Languedoc, "it is just that the art of war is held as the highest, the most elevated, and the most honorable [art] for all those who practice it, since it is the one where it is appropriate to have higher intellect, better leadership, and more courage than any other."[109]

Early seventeenth-century practices of command provide evidence of the adaptability of the early modern nobility. Historians frequently assume that nobles were traditional and inherently conservative, but French warrior nobles quickly adopted the use of artillery in the sixteenth century. By the early seventeenth century, nobles' writings rarely disparaged artillery or looked down on engineers and artillery commanders; instead, artillery command became highly desired and nobles competed to command batteries at sieges. As Catholic troops prepared to besiege a Huguenot town during the 1622 civil war, "it took a long time before agreeing on the command of the petard and on the [other commands] that everyone desired."[110]

The ideal of command involved both fulfilling a superior's desires and executing his orders. Nobles felt honor at receiving commands from the king or from great nobles, and they strove to meet this ideal of command. The duc de Ventadour reported to the king in 1618 that everything that happened within his command was "following the wishes and intention of Your Majesty." In this instance, "as also in all other occurrences where I shall be honored with his commands," Ventadour pledged, "I shall execute them with the perfect obedience that I am obliged to render you."[111] He seems to have done a remarkably good job at making his actions match his rhetoric on command, even if some other nobles failed to reach the command ideal.

Attaining independent command was considered highly honorable for warrior nobles. As one southern French noble explained it, independent command required "the intellect to form a plan that equals not only those of the experts, but that surpasses the intellect and the thought of others through some new invention." Noble commanders also needed to display "the leadership to execute [their plan] well, using a sound and sure judgment, observing well the ordering of time, place, persons." A noble exercising independent command had to recognize that his plans unfolded in circumstances that were "infinite," requiring him to respond to unforeseen occurrences and "as the proverb rightly says: to wage war with the eye."[112] When the duc de Montmorency was given an independent command by the prince de Condé, Montmorency's secretary emphasized that "the command was honorable, but the means that he gave him to execute it were quite weak."[113]

Warrior nobles competed for the honor of specific commands in siege combats and battles. Nobles sought to have the honor of attacking key points of fortifications, seeing danger and risk as opportunities to win more honor. Audacity and boldness gave nobles an advantage in this competition, many military elites thought. As Catholic troops tightened their siege at Sommières in 1622, their commanders debated how to clear a fortified *faubourg*, or suburb, filled with about 800 Huguenot defenders. "Most of the opinions at the council of war advised dislodging them with canons, which had not yet arrived, when the duc [de Montmorency] promised to oust them that same hour," according to one narrative. "Nobody having disputed this honor, [Montmorency] gave the regiment de Picardie the right, that of Fabregues the left, and put himself at the head of the battalion supporting them. Good luck followed boldness in this combat," and Montmorency's troops seized the *faubourg*.[114] Command was often seen as based on boldness and courage, as in the preceding example, but experience was also an ideal. An account praises a noble commander as a "wise and experienced captain" esteemed for his "honor and courage."[115]

The honor of commanding was in part dependent on the suitability of the charge for the noble officer. An honorable command seems to have been one suited to the officer's precedence and quality honor. When the connétable de Montmorency sought an office for his brother-in-law, Antoine-Hercule de Budos vicomte de Portes, he emphasized that "the [close] affection that I carry for Monsieur the vicomte de Portes joined to his merit make me beseech Your Majesty most humbly to agree to give him some honorable command in the infantry."[116] The command had to be suitable to the noble officer because as one noble put it, "it is very easy for all those who have such spirit to form their good designs; but it is quite difficult for everyone, and impossible for most, to execute them." This noble felt that officers must never take their own initiative "without having received the consent of their superiors, and those who do otherwise are responsible for the death of those whom they expose in contravention of military laws, [and] are consequently subject to exemplary punishment."[117] During the 1621 civil war, a southern French noble sought advice on whether the king would prefer him "to serve His Majesty with honor" by defending his château and town or by arming to join the king's army.[118] Alexandre de Lévis marquis de Mirepoix was serving as a noble volunteer at the siege of Nérac in 1621, when he discovered that his father had begun to assemble a force to fight against Huguenots in the region. Although he believed himself obliged by "my duty and my honor" to join his father, he nonetheless wanted a direct command from the king to do so.[119]

Narrative sources hint at contemporary models of successful military leadership. A noble's account of a combat near Nîmes describes Guillaume de Balazuc de Montréal as an ideal commander, "brave, valiant, and vigilant, and endowed with the perfections that render a captain recommendable." Having heard of the movements of a Huguenot force under Alexandre de Blacons seigneur de Mirabel-Blacons, Montréal quickly led the regiments de Portes and Pérault into action. Having located the Huguenot troops, "he charged the enemy in so lively a way, and with such a generous claim to honor, that he put to flight the said Blacons, killed and ran down four hundred men, captured many prisoners, reached the artillery, looted the munitions, and—preferring victory to plunder—enriched the soldiers with the baggage. The sieur de Montréal lost very few of his soldiers."[120]

Proofs of Courage

Warrior nobles relied on proofs of courage to justify their honorable status and to gain increased honor. Courageous acts provided the substance of reputation honor and the hope of acquiring more precedence and qualitative honor. Louis de Chabans thus described honor as representing "public recompense for glorious or virtuous actions, but principally those of courage."[121] The king cited courageous service as the reason for granting a pensions, offices, promotions, and favors. When Louis XIII granted a pension to Marc-Antoine de Grave sieur de Longues, he noted that Grave had given "signal proofs of his courage and of his valor" in combat.[122] Noble officers considered courage "the most necessary part [of command] . . . to put the rest into action without any trouble or fear of danger."[123]

A number of signs displayed proofs of courage and served as reminders of them. Descriptions of combat specify horses killed under nobles and describe nobles leading attacks with their swords in their hands. Wounds and scars bore witness to the courage of nobles who had been in battle. Based on a remarkable manuscript list of wounds that provides rare evidence of injuries suffered by officers during one siege early in the French Wars of Religion, James B. Wood concludes that warrior nobles established "a community of shared dangers signified by the marks left by the violence of mid-sixteenth-century warfare on the bodies of the men who survived it."[124]

Discussions and tales of combat dispensed honor and adjudicated honor claims. The need for proofs of courage highlighted the importance of storytelling in noble culture. After the battle of Castelnaudary in 1632, the marquis de Brezé and eight cavalry cornets accompanied the captured duc de Montmorency along the route to Toulouse. The captive had ample time to discuss the battle with his captors, who had also been in action at Castelnaudary. In the evening, Montmorency saw, "among the officers of the troops escorting him, Beauregard Champrou, who had his arm in a scarf, from a pistol shot that he had given him on the day of Castelnaudary—this wound was to him all the more honorable since the duc de Montmorency avowed that one of [the wounds] on his face had been inflicted by Beauregard." Montmorency thus not only confirmed Beauregard's honor by acknowledging his claim that he had been shot by Montmorency, but gave further proofs of Beauregard's courage by stipulating that he himself had been wounded by Beauregard. Also present was a distressed noble named Laurière, who believed that he had killed Montmorency's horse. Perhaps to assuage Laurière's remorse, however, the duc refuted this "proof" of courage with details of the combat, indicating that his horse had been killed elsewhere in the fighting.[125]

Courage had to be established and defended in noble honor culture. A memoir extolling the "warlike deeds" performed in the course of the siege of Montauban by the Huguenot Saint-André de Montbrun insists that even though the author who has "drawn up the painting, put there the colors, traced the lines, and finally proposed it in public to be contemplated" himself witnessed "your conquests," it is up to Montbrun to argue his case "against the slander of several tongues that lie impudently."[126] Only when courage was demonstrated clearly was it accepted by noble peers.

Proofs of courage could be used in persuasive rhetoric on political questions. When Gaston d'Orléans summoned the duc de Montmorency to join his forces during the 1632 civil war, his commission lauded his courage: "You—who have given such proofs of your valor and your prudence in all of your battles and memorable combats on sea and on land, where you have been always victorious over the enemies of this state—have placed the reputation of the king's arms in such high relief through all of your glorious success in Italy, which is due only to your courage, which is now formidable to all the princes of Europe."[127] This powerful confirmation of Montmorency's personal courage and military leadership cited the duc's recent victories in Italy and implied that he was solely responsible for the successes of the royal army. The commission then goes on to declare that Montmorency has "the sword of France as a hereditary legacy in your house because of the most grand and signal services that have been rendered to this state by the connétables, your father and grandfather." Montmorency's proofs of courage were thus reinforced by "the memory of the actions" that his predecessors had fought, which were "full of honor and glory."[128]

Admiration

Admiration of nobles was celebrated in military life through ceremonies that recognized their reputation and precedence honor. Although early seventeenth-century military reviews had not yet acquired the formal character that they would later assume, martial ceremonies—such as reviews, artillery salutes, armed processions, and civic entries—not only recognized reputation and precedence honor, but also promoted a more egalitarian notion of qualitative honor among those of noble status. Some nobles staged theatrical tournaments to demonstrate their excellent horsemanship and to receive the admiration of their fellow nobles.[129]

Powerful regional warrior nobles used civic entry ceremonies, which could rival those accorded to the king, to gain attention and build their authority. Toulouse prepared elaborate entertainments for the frequent entries of the ducs de Montmorency and de Ventadour in the 1610s and 1620s, and these nobles reciprocated by sponsoring artistic and theatrical activities during their stays.[130] After his naval victory off La Rochelle in 1625, Montmorency left the royal court to return to Languedoc and hold a meeting of the provincial estates. "He had never received honors equal to those rendered him at his arrival," according to his secretary. "The parlement of Toulouse sent him a distinguished deputation to express the joy that the entire court felt at the glory that he had acquired in naval combat." After the meeting of the estates, "the most apparent of the nobility who had rendered themselves near to him passed the winter there, and the diversions that had been a little withdrawn from his court since the war, came back with the same sweetness as before."[131]

Admiration of nobles during civic entries often involved their qualitative and precedence honor. The duc de Mayenne's entries to Bordeaux were lavish, but not unexpected since he was governor of the province. The residents of Montauban greeted the marquis de Thémines with poetry and ceremonies on the occasion of his entry to the town as the new sénéchal.[132] The duc d'Épernon's frequent entries to towns in Guyenne had more to do with his qualitative honor and his strong political connections in the area, since he received honors there even before he became governor of the province.[133]

Warrior nobles' civic entry ceremonies also had interesting gendered aspects. While the celebration of nobles through entries was ordinarily strongly masculine, admiration could extend to powerful noblewomen as well. Maria Felicia Orsini, the duc de Montmorency's wife, was greeted by the bishop of Lavaur and other deputies sent by the estates of Languedoc when she returned to the province from the royal court in 1617. When she arrived at Toulouse to join her husband in 1619, the duc Montmorency proclaimed "the contentment that I felt at my wife's entry and reception in this city, seeing that she had the most honorable [entry] that one could have, with a very beautiful company of nobility composed of around a thousand gentlemen, whose affection I recognized as bearing entirely on the good of His Majesty's service."[134] The governor clearly regarded the entry ceremony as reflecting on himself and on the king, not just his wife. Admiring noblewomen may have been partially linked to their family's standing and services, but these ceremonies indicate a significant notion of honor for noblewomen that paralleled noblemen's honor as veneration. Noblewomen participated in regional and court politics, and admiration was a way of recognizing their position and honor, as shown by the ceremonies performed by the estates of Languedoc in 1626 to thank madame de Montmorency for her advocacy at court.[135]

Preservation of Honor

Warrior nobles were always preoccupied with preserving their honor. Nobles' impulsive defense of their honor through dueling is perhaps most familiar, but not every possible attack upon honor necessitated such an immediate and violent reaction. Nobles had to leap to the defense of their honor when confronted with a direct threat to it. Refusing to recognize a noble's sanctity during a religious ceremony, for example, could be damaging. Honor as quality could be attacked by challenging an officer's nobility or title. Reputation could be attacked by suggesting that the reputation was undeserved, or that the noble had shown coward-ice or acted improperly in battle. Honor as precedence could be challenged in many ways by refusing to give the deference due to a superior or by challenging rank. Actions prejudicial to honor typically necessitated immediate reaction, or some degree of dishonor would result. William Ian Miller sees this type of re-sponse as a "norm of reciprocity," a response typically used as a defense against insult.[136] Seventeenth-century nobles, though, seem to have reacted with a vari-ety of strategies to "conserve" their honor, as they often put it.

A noble from the Vivarais praised his fellow Catholic nobles in the region for their "common defense of their goods, their lives, and their honor." The com-manding officer in the area had little do to, he declared, "because he had so many honorable persons in this region."[137] Whether or not the Vivarais nobles served as meritoriously as this account suggests, the emphasis on nobles' per-sonal defense of honor corresponds closely to other descriptions of nobles' mo-tivations for participation in civil warfare. Defending honor also served to jus-tify violence committed by nobles. In 1616, the duc d'Épernon hinted in a letter to Louis XIII that he might personally take revenge on a rival for a slight to his honor, which he shrewdly presented as an attack on the king's honor as well. Épernon says that "if I could exercise the right of reprisal against the tenants of the said sieur de Jarnac for the exactions . . . that he has made on [my tenants], I dare to promise that Your Majesty will find nothing objectionable, so as to prevent him in future from indulging in such actions, so prejudicial to his honor."[138]

Denial of admiration and respect could inflict a serious blow to a noble's dignity and precedence honor. Épernon was offended by the parlement de Bor-deaux's initial refusal to accord him full honors as governor of Guyenne. The members of parlement eventually participated in the elaborate ceremonies for the governor's entry to Bordeaux in 1623, but the incident led to a long-standing enmity between Épernon and the parlement's premier président.[139]

Wartime disputes between military elites often involved challenges to a noble's courage and honorable reputation. Two Huguenot commanders, Alex-andre du Puy de Tournon marquis de Saint-André de Montbrun and Jacques de Pons marquis de La Caze, began to quarrel bitterly during the 1625 civil war. Saint André de Montbrun was furious with La Caze for abandoning the de-fense of Montauban and joining the royal army. He accused La Caze of being dishonorable, implying that he was a traitor. La Caze defended himself, saying that "if he would like to say that I have never acted as a good and honorable man, he falsely and meanly lies. To the contrary, I maintain what I said above: that he is a tyrant, and broker, and deserter of our churches, thus he has neither honor, nor virtue, nor probity." La Caze concluded his counterattack on Saint André de Montbrun by calling on "all princes, seigneurs, gentlemen, and others of whatever condition to say on their honor and conscience if—during my stay in Montauban—I treated or negotiated, either directly or indirectly, anything against the service of our churches, [or against] the good and safety of the said city, or that could prejudice the conscience and reputation of a man of honor."[140]

Administrative and military officers attempted to conserve their precedence honor during disputes with other nobles that were engendered by competition, direct challenges to authority, and conflicts of overlapping jurisdictions. In the midst of an ongoing quarrel with the premier président of the parlement de Paris, the duc de Montmorency claimed that his "reputation would be tarnished by the sufferance of such an usurpation." Montmorency asked the king to aid him in "the conservation of this honor, which I would handle carefully in order to employ it for a glorious purpose."[141] Even if nobles were not confronted with such direct attacks on their reputation and precedence, they still needed to act continually to preserve their honor.

A dispute in 1616 provides an interesting case of one noble's strategies for preserving precedence and qualitative honor. The marquis d'Aubeterre complained that a président of parlement had acted "to the prejudice of the authority that it has pleased the late king and His Majesty to give me in my charges, where I serve him only for honor." He accused the président of "an excess of ambition" and of seeking "to assume the authority of my said charge" and, in the "particular quality of président," to take precedence over him even outside parlement. Aubeterre seems to have been particularly affronted by the judge's challenge to his precedence. Based on his rank as marquis d'Aubeterre alone, he asserted, no one from Guyenne—except "monsieur le maréchal de Roquelaure in his capacity as lieutenant general of the king"—could claim precedence over him, and he noted that in his capacity as governor: "I was received, liked, honored, and obeyed by seigneurs, gentlemen, towns, and communities that are in the territory of my charges without any contradiction." He asked that the secrétaire d'État adjudicate the dispute and confirm his honor, writing: "I implore you, monsieur, for [the king's] service, to report what you judge just and reasonable, and to consider that . . . honor . . . is the most valuable thing in the world to me." The king should write as soon as possible to the judge so that everyone would "be retained in their duty."[142]

Preserving honor often entailed resolving honor dilemmas, quandaries that entailed potential loss of honor and that nobles had to negotiate. Honor dilemmas presented ambiguous circumstances where no action could with certainty preserve honor. In such circumstances, warrior nobles had to find acceptable ways of disengaging their honor, sometimes even accepting limited loss of reputation or status in order to maintain their honor. Preserving honor by disengaging was not just a face-saving response to honor dilemmas, but could paradoxically offer positive aspects.

If reputation was primarily won in combat, it may seem paradoxical that warrior nobles could ever accept failure in combat, but they were hardly suicidal. Military officers sought to avoid dishonor in battlefield failures, but they understood well that not all attacks would succeed, and they recognized distinctions between acceptable and unacceptable failure. Warrior nobles could even gain honor in failed ventures in certain cases by conducting an honorable withdrawal during battles and sieges. An account of the siege of Montpellier praises the "honorable retreat" of a Huguenot noble and his troops after an attack.[143] If surrounded during failed military operations, a noble in danger of capture might even honorably surrender in some circumstances.

Nobles defending towns and châteaux could surrender following the conventions of siege warfare. Commanding officers who surrendered a town at the first sight of enemy troops or before formal siegeworks were advanced would be liable to serious condemnation and possible dishonor and death. But once besiegers began an artillery barrage, defending nobles might have several opportunities to surrender honorably. Negotiations accompanied the daily activities of almost all sieges. If the defenders had insufficient artillery or a depleted garrison, one might legitimately seek honorable terms with the besiegers. Once a breach was created in the walls, the defending commander had another chance to surrender with honor. Negotiated capitulations could have various terms, and surrendering noble officers were typically allowed to keep their weapons. In some cases, troops were permitted to keep their weapons and supplies, marching out of their fortified positions with musicians playing and flags waving. Sometimes surrendering officers and troops had to accept neutrality, agreeing not to participate in warfare for a set period of time.[144] The Huguenot troops who were besieged in Réalmont in 1628 attempted to obtain such an "honorable composition" from the Catholic commander, the prince de Condé.[145]

Engaging and disengaging honor from political and religious causes during military campaigns was a vital method for preserving it in a period of rampant civil conflict. Noble officers consciously engaged their honor in circumstances of their choosing. One noble explained that "my honor . . . could only be engaged in serving the king well and with dignity as my care and my actions."[146] Nobles served of their own free will, and by the grace of the king if in royal service. Just as nobles engaged their reputations by entering military service, they could also disengage them by leaving service. Once a noble's honor was engaged in a cause, however, it was difficult—but not impossible—for him to disengage it. Warrior nobles could not always leave military service with honor, but they could do so in some instances. Leaving the king's service with honor involved obtaining *congé*, or leave, approved by the king or one of his agents. Nobles could sometimes preserve their honor by changing their political alignment. The marquis de La Caze left the service of the Huguenot garrison of Montauban, saying that he "could not serve our churches with utility or satisfaction to my honor and besides there were other reasons." He insisted that he wanted his departure to be honorable, but said that his fears for his own safety led him to leave discretely.[147] Even successful disengagement of honor was not always recognized by all nobles, especially when disengagement involved reengagement of honor by changing allegiances.

Warrior nobles could suffer dishonor when they failed to effectively disengage their honor from doomed causes and failed initiatives. Dishonor represented a loss of honor that was temporally located and bounded, and nobles seem to have thought of dishonor as an event, rather than as a state. The failure of an attack or a lack of courage in combat could dishonor a noble by questioning his reputation at a particular moment, forcing him to act to preserve his honor. Repudiations and embarrassments diminished nobles' honor, but never destroyed it completely.

The ways in which honor could be diminished can be seen through discontent, discredit, and disgrace, three forms of disruption of warrior nobles' relationship to the honor culture. Discontented nobles were often dissatisfied with their relationship with the royal government and harbored resentments at checks to their reputation. Nobles who suffered an even more serious dissolution of their honor bonds could be seen as discredited, unable to effectively confirm their dignity, quality, and precedence. Disgrace amounted to a serious rupture of a noble's honor bonds that was confirmed by royal condemnation, which operated through what Nicolas Le Roux calls a "pedagogy of disgrace."[148] Disgraced nobles had to struggle to maintain their waning reputations while working to rebuild their damaged honor bonds, often through lengthy processes of reconciliation.[149]

Religious warfare revealed the cracks and contradictions existing in warrior noble honor culture. The ambiguity of honor culture and the conflicts that it produced meant that the honor culture system was chaotic and contentious. No binary division between honor and dishonor existed. Instead, a range of appraisals of a noble's honor existed between an honor ideal and the ultimate negation of that ideal. During civil conflicts, dishonor was frequently linked to nobles' adherence to and abandonment of political and religious causes. Many Huguenot nobles were disgusted when the duc de Lesdiguières refused to join the Calvinist military movement led by Rohan, then converted to Catholicism. The seigneur de Châtillon first led, then abandoned, the Calvinist militant cause in Languedoc in 1621, losing the support of local Huguenots where he held governorships. Huguenot nobles often retaliated against fellow Calvinists who abandoned the militant Huguenot cause or who converted to Catholicism by burning their châteaux. Similarly, Catholic nobles punished any nobles who were previously designated as "rebels" or who defected to join Huguenot armies by burning their châteaux. The seigneur de Cheylus, who had recently joined the duc de Rohan's Calvinist army, was singled out for retribution in 1628: "To begin the punishment of his rebellion," read one account, "the said château de Mauras had been pillaged, and afterwards burned and ruined, along with other houses that could favor the passage of rebels from Privas to Le Pouzin."[150]

Conflicts between nobles could normally only be resolved through warfare and simultaneous protracted negotiations. When Henri II de Montmorency threw his support to Gaston d'Orléans in 1632, Louis XIII branded Montmorency a "rebel," declaring "the said duc de Montmorency, maréchal de France, governor, and our lieutenant general in Languedoc, guilty of lèse-majesté, stripped of all grades, dignities, and honors; the duchy of Montmorency extinct and reunited to our crown, and each and all of the other lands, seigneuries, and goods, mobile and immobile, to us acquired and confiscated."[151] Such acts did not negate all honor, and disgraced nobles might maintain the respect and allegiance of their followers, even though they might not have full access to their political power and offices. Even the severe disgrace of being branded a rebel was normally temporary, and nobles' status was reinstated upon an agreement and accommodation, whether a formal peace or not. Rituals of reconciliation attempted to restore friendship and reestablish political relationships following "rebellions" or serious disputes between nobles.[152]

Reconciliation rituals could be complex and contradictory, however, especially when a rebel noble was captured before a settlement had been reached.

Punishments of nobles supporting Gaston d'Orléans in the 1632 civil war were exceptionally harsh. The duc de Montmorency, the vicomte de Lestrange, and other nobles were executed when captured. Louis XIII ordered prolonged disgraces for the families of the nobles who had joined the army of Montmorency and d'Orléans during the war.[153]

The contradictions in noble honor culture are well illustrated by the "betrayal" of Henri de Gondi duc de Retz during the 1620 civil war between Louis XIII and Marie de Médicis. As the two armies prepared for combat at Ponts-de-Cé, rumors circulated that the queen mother and the king had reached a settlement. Whether disgusted with Marie de Médicis or fearful of openly opposing the king, the duc de Retz withdrew his 1,500 troops and marched them off the battlefield. When Louis XIII's troops then attacked, Marie's disorganized army was easily defeated. Marie and her son rapidly negotiated a peace agreement, leaving Retz in a difficult situation, despised by Marie de Médicis and derided by Louis XIII for his dishonorable conduct.[154] This "betrayal" reminds us how fragile causes could be during the civil wars of the early seventeenth century, but also how powerful honor was in shaping conflict. The complex and contradictory positions adopted by French nobles such as the duc de Retz suggest the possibilities of developing comprehensive cultural studies of organized violence to better understand early modern French society.

Formal truce negotiations and comprehensive peace agreements provided some nobles with ways out of honor dilemmas. The particular negotiated points of political control, religious accommodation, military demobilization, and financial remuneration were thus crucial to warrior nobles' abilities to preserve their honor. Nobles discussed honorable settlements, just peaces, honorable capitulations, and respectable agreements. The *grands* and other military commanders considered an honorable settlement one that gave them some compensation for their expenses during the course of the civil conflict. The duc de Rohan, for example, discusses the need for "honorable recompensation" in his manifesto of 1627, since honor was considered an essential part of the just dues of any peace.[155]

✝

This chapter has traced the outlines of early seventeenth-century warrior noble honor culture and shown how it was shaped by civil conflict. I have argued that warrior nobles in this period conceived of honor through overlapping conceptions of sanctity, quality, reputation, and precedence. Nobles were thus bound together by complex and often conflicting honor relationships, rather than by the ties of fidelity that some scholars have proposed. Members of the provincial military elite exhibited their honorable nature through a variety of performances, including command, proofs of courage, and admiration. Honor was always highly contested in early seventeenth-century noble culture, forcing warrior nobles to demonstrate their sanctity, ensure their quality, defend their reputation, and maintain their precedence. The next chapter will examine how each of the bonds of nobility operated within the culture of revolt when warrior nobles engaged in civil violence.

PART THREE

The Culture of Revolt

I Picart delineavit et incidit.

Equestrian statue of a warrior noble brandishing his sword, evoking the rituals of arming. Engraving by Jean Picart, *Statue équestre, cavalier en armure*, BNF, Estampes, Ed 56 (C)-Pet fol. Photo courtesy Bibliothèque Nationale de France.

CHAPTER SEVEN

The Call to Arms from All Quarters

Rituals of Arming

R umors of war circulated throughout southern France in 1625, prompting a noble to record that "all of a sudden, we heard armorers everywhere, and the hammering of arms, which everyone amassed; soon afterwards, we saw nothing but the enrollment of soldiers and heard the call to arms from all quarters."[1] At the first hints of disorder, warrior nobles across the extensive provinces of Languedoc and Guyenne rapidly mobilized troops and braced themselves for yet another civil war. As they armed, nobles engaged in rituals of arming that confirmed their status as warrior nobles and simultaneously announced the outbreak of civil violence.

Arlette Jouanna's insightful study of noble violence in early modern France, entitled *Le Devoir de révolte*, proposes that nobles performed "rituals of revolt"— actions and gestures through which they expressed themselves, socialized, and formed groups within the context of revolt. The rituals described by Jouanna include joining political-religious leagues, concluding alliances, and financing revolt.[2] Perhaps the most significant ritual that *Le Devoir de révolte* explores is the *prise d'armes*, or taking up of arms. Jouanna's intriguing interpretation of "rituals of revolt" can be usefully extended and reconceptualized as a series of signs, symbols, images, and gestures that nobles employed ritualistically to represent and express their participation in civil violence. These rituals held special meaning for early modern French warrior nobles, who defined their nobility through deeply held notions of the profession of arms.

Rituals of arming provided warrior nobles with common experiences and understandings of violence, initiating them into the practices of warfare and

uniting them in multiple armed communities. Nicholas B. Dirks's anthropological work on ritualized gestures and symbolic inversions in episodes of collective violence provides useful tools for understanding early modern French
warrior nobles' rituals. Dirks envisions rituals as concerned with "contest and
struggle" just as much as "power and order," developing a simultaneous critique
of Clifford Geertz's essentialized meanings of rituals and of Bourdieu's symbolic interpretations of ritualistic practices. "Ritual," Dirks argues, "now appears
not only as a powerful way to produce the reality effect of the natural, but also as
a way to contest and even appropriate that reality itself."[3] The everyday practices
and rituals of civil violence were rarely as exposed as they were at the outbreak
of early seventeenth-century civil conflicts.[4]

This chapter considers how rituals of arming shaped warrior nobles' preparations for conflict as they instigated violence in early seventeenth-century southern France. Despite their diverse motivations, nobles all justified their entry into
civil violence through representations of defiance, disorder, and royal service.
Provincial military elites participated in a culture of revolt, employing similar
practices to take up arms, assemble their clienteles, and recruit troops. As civil
conflicts rapidly widened, warrior nobles directed military mobilization by managing space and ensuring communications with their armed clienteles and their
allies.

INSTIGATING VIOLENCE

Civil conflicts in early seventeenth-century France rarely broke out with clearly
discernible beginnings. Instead, religious tensions and political differences gradually increased as violent incidents such as urban protests, duels, abductions,
and murders threatened to grow into broader, more extensive civil conflicts.
French people from all social backgrounds disputed political decisions, contested
legal decisions, and challenged authorities. As civil conflicts began to progress
and widen, warrior nobles in southern France dealt with increasingly ambiguous situations, in which the causes, issues, and participants in civil conflict were
difficult to identify. The regional nobles were often unsure whether or not full-
scale civil warfare would actually result and what form it would take. In these
ambiguous contexts, warrior nobles had to assess which actions might be interpreted by the monarch as revolt. Warrior nobles issued challenges and responded
to provocations through ritualized behavior that demarcated revolt and independent initiatives that fashioned their religious and political stances.

Markers of Revolt

Warrior nobles often exchanged provocations, challenges, and insults in a noble culture that was contentious and preoccupied with honor. Provocative gestures and insulting language took on heightened significance as civil conflicts broke out. In theory, the king wielded a brand of revolt, with his ability to declare anyone guilty of lèse-majesté, but in the context of civil disorder in southern France, nobles rarely waited for royal designation of "rebels." Markers of revolt—signs and symbols that demarcated a state of conflict—distinguished behavior and actions as potentially "loyal" or "rebel." Early seventeenth-century French people recognized challenges and provocations that signaled the outbreak of civil conflict. Warrior nobles ritually announced the outbreak of civil violence using markers that ritually proclaimed their grievances and political causes.

Some warrior nobles initiated violence by issuing formal challenges to their opponents, announcing their "quarrels" with them. Nobles could send messengers to issue challenges or post placards in urban centers to call out their enemies.[5] While challenges have been examined as rituals of dueling, they were also utilized more broadly within noble culture.[6] The publication of nobles' letters or manifestos might single out opponents for an audience of noble readers. Ritually challenging a peer often provoked violent responses by honor-bound nobles. As they armed, some nobles even challenged their enemies to meet their cavalry companies in battle, instigating skirmishes.

Verbal insults and indignant gestures could ritually mark civil violence. Warrior nobles often insulted their peers, and early seventeenth-century French nobles described how unrestrained anger and uncontrolled passions produced insults and violence. Historians have often associated insults with dueling and feuding, notably discussing how "giving the lie" and "mad blood" led to violence among early modern nobles.[7] However, the importance of insults in broader civil violence has been overlooked. Noble correspondence, government reports, and court records demonstrate a rich vocabulary of insults employed by nobles to mock their opponents and rivals. After one violent clash, a Languedoc noble claimed that another officer had "proffered all sorts of injuries."[8] In such cases, insults that described a noble as a *coquin* (scoundrel), *lâche* (coward), *coïon* (coward), *villain* (common), a man of base and vile condition, timid, or swineherd challenged his honor and status. Verbal abuse could also associate with malicious or dangerous behavior by calling nobles artificial, false, lying, perfidious, insolent, or *méchant* (wicked). Insults accused nobles of mistreating their peers or performing *mauvais offices*. Nobles used invective to charge "bloody" and "murderous" enemies with the hideous crimes of conspiracy, treason, sedition, mutiny, assassination, murder, rebellion, and tyranny.[9]

Gate-closing rituals openly challenged nobles' authority and provoked violent responses. Warrior nobles' first experience of a revolt often consisted of a curt refusal of entry or a gate firmly shut before them. The complaints of a sénéchal in Guyenne show the frustration such officers experienced as they encountered limits on their authority. He writes that "I would never have thought that my presence was so necessary to the province. All the towns that I passed in my sénéchausée and government of Agenois received me with all the affection and good [cheer] that I could hope for, except at Tonneins where they closed the gates to me and [later] . . . sent three hundred arquebusiers to fight me."[10] Noble officers considered towns and châteaux that refused them entry to be defying royal will, and hence engaging in rebellion. Early seventeenth-century French people recognized the significance of the closing of gates, as contemporary memoirs and letters indicate. André Delort, a Catholic resident of Montpellier, begins his description of the 1621 civil war by stating that "the Huguenots closed all the gates."[11] Similarly, the duc de Rohan found the gates of Figeac closed to him and his Calvinist forces in 1621, challenging Rohan's authority to lead that community in the midst of a widening civil war.[12]

The symbolism of gates in contemporary art, architecture, and literature reveals why the closure of gates represented such a potent provocation to nobles. Despite the new developments of bastioned fortifications in the sixteenth century, many fortifications employed decorated gates that evoked triumphal arches.[13] City gates served as important sites of symbolic greetings for legitimate authorities entering urban spaces, as the extensive literature on royal entry ceremonies has shown.[14] Refusing the king entry constituted a great personal insult as well as an act of lèse-majesté. During his military campaign in southern France in 1622, Louis XIII reported that "last Wednesday I was thinking of coming to stay in Négrepelisse [believing] that they would not refuse me their gates." The king expressed his disbelief that "the inhabitants fired on several of my officers who had advanced, and having summoned them through a trumpeter and an archer of my guards, they persisted in their rebellion and fired once again on the said archer and trumpeter."[15] Nobles recognized the symbolic offense of shutting gates to royal authority. During the siege of Monheur, the marquis de Mirabeau negotiated a capitulation for himself and his followers, begging the king's pardon for having "closed the gates of Monheur against him" and claiming that he had been unaware that the king was in the besieging army.[16]

Provincial governors, administrative officers, town governors, and nobles who owned residences within towns claimed the right of entry to communities and expected to be formally received at the gates. During the early stages of civil conflict in 1621, the Calvinist noble François de Béthune comte d'Orval wanted to cross a river at Lectoure with "a great number of men," but he was denied passage by a Catholic noble who held the passage under the duc de Mayenne's authority. Although the Catholic noble claimed to have used "honorable means" in refusing the comte passage, he reported that Orval "had his heart wounded to the quick."[17]

Incidents of social violence and disorder often contested nobles' authority and marked the beginning of civil violence. In urban communities, religious processions, artisan protests, and civic celebrations could all turn violent, challenging municipal authorities and regional nobles alike.[18] During the late sixteenth and early seventeenth centuries, confessional protests could occasionally provoke iconoclastic attacks, clerical murders, or even religious massacres. Rural protests and disturbances, often labeled by historians as peasant revolts, sometimes merged with broader religious and civil violence. Signs of rural disorder and banditry, including stealing letters, appropriating taxes, vandalizing properties, hostage-taking, and seizing residences, directly challenged local nobles' honor and seigneurial power.[19] Peasants who seized or burned châteaux compelled nobles to respond violently to uphold their authority.[20]

Assembling and refusing to disband also marked the beginning of civil conflict. Administrative officers who discovered unauthorized troops or noble assemblies within their jurisdictions often issued orders for them to disband. A failure to demobilize would normally lead to violence as other warrior nobles began to assemble their personal military forces to defend themselves or take action against the troops already assembled. Nobles developed strategies for dealing with conflict, engaging their personal loyalties and searching for legitimacy. Even if the sides in a civil conflict were not yet clear at the outbreak of conflict, nobles understood that some of the mobilized forces would eventually be considered rebels. Warrior nobles had to define their duty and distinguish which military units would be considered royalist forces, but establishing which nobles and forces were royalist was virtually impossible since almost all warrior nobles were royal officers of some type. Thus, the designations of royal officers or royal agents that are frequently employed by historians are not very helpful in understanding the outbreak of civil conflicts. The challenges and counterchallenges over the legitimacy of nobles' mobilizations instigated violence and provoked retaliation.

Independent Initiative

Widespread local mobilizations occurred at the outbreak of each civil conflict as warrior nobles began organizing military forces. Powerful regional nobles mobilized their compagnies d'ordonnance and raised new infantry regiments, while authorizing specific local nobles to raise regiments or companies, increase garrison sizes, and assert their control over key strategic positions. Local nobles needed no prodding to raise forces on their own authority to protect their own châteaux and governments. Towns could authorize nobles to increase their urban garrisons. Huguenot assemblies empowered nobles to raise forces to protect their places de sûreté. Often warrior nobles mobilized forces at the first hint of civil conflict, only choosing sides later.

The independent initiative displayed by the duc de Mayenne at the outset of the 1621 civil conflict provides fascinating evidence of the choices available to nobles who instigated violence. Henri de Lorraine duc de Mayenne arrived in the province of Guyenne in 1621 as tensions between Catholics and Calvinists there escalated into open civil war. Religious agendas and sectarian politics had fueled growing conflict across southern France, and now a royal army was assembling to enforce Louis XIII's policies concerning spiritual renewal and confessional communities. The young duc de Mayenne had only recently "reentered the good graces of the king" after participating in another recent civil conflict. Mayenne entered Bordeaux with some troops to reinforce his own control over the city in his capacity as provincial governor of Guyenne. He then requisitioned seven artillery pieces from the municipal arsenal and in less than five days recruited a field army of about 3,000 men, most of whom were presumably Catholics. More soldiers assembled around Marmande, a small town located east of Bordeaux, and Mayenne brought his troops from Bordeaux to join them there. He then directed his small army toward the nearby town of Nérac, situated upriver from Marmande and controlled by Huguenots. After a short march, the Catholic troops quickly invested Nérac and began siege operations that would soon force the town to surrender.[21] Mayenne and his troops went on to fight extensively in the civil warfare engulfing the provinces of Guyenne and Languedoc in 1621, and the duc himself was killed at the siege of the Huguenot city of Montauban later that year.

Political pamphlets, memoirs, and poems written in 1621 celebrated Mayenne as a military hero, one calling him a "prince as *généreux* as one could find in Christendom."[22] Assessing his initiative in the civil warfare that raged across southern France in the early seventeenth century is more complicated, however.

Mayenne could be considered a royal agent acting directly on behalf of the king and the royal state. After all, the title page of one pamphlet commemorating the victory at Nérac proclaimed that Mayenne had indeed taken the town, but specified that he was "executing the commands of His Majesty."[23] The duc could instead be viewed as a regional power-broker and clientele leader who was concerned primarily with maintaining his authority within Guyenne. Although Mayenne was a powerful *grand*, he seems to have been immersed in local and regional politics in southwestern France. Or he might be understood as a devout Catholic and lay activist who aimed to avenge Calvinist attacks and to protect his fellow Catholics living in the area. His family had long been associated with militant Catholic politics and Counter-Reformation religious reform in France. His uncle had been the leader of the Catholic League movement until his assassination in 1588, when his father, Charles de Lorraine duc de Mayenne, emerged as the principal Leaguer chief. It is possible that young Henri de Lorraine was continuing his family's agenda of advancing Catholic causes, as suggested by his insistence on installing a Catholic governor and garrison at Nérac.[24] The duc de Mayenne's interests and loyalties remain unclear, especially since royalist pamphlets had demonized him for his participation in civil conflicts in the 1610s and had challenged his support of Marie de Médicis as recently a year before his "heroic" campaign and tragic death.[25]

Provincial warrior nobles across southern France experienced the pervasiveness of civil conflict, the demands of conflicting authorities, and the costs of mobilization. Taking individual initiative involved a personal engagement in violence and a resolution to act. Royal ministers expected noble military and administrative officers to react quickly to any threats in their jurisdictions. As soon as he heard that a Huguenot army had laid siege to Saint-Georges in September 1621, François de Noailles comte d'Ayen "immediately dispatched to all of the nobility and the communities of this region to amass as many men as they could." Noailles projected that "today I shall have more than one hundred gentlemen together, and if these towns do not fail their word, I shall have here more than eight hundred infantry."[26] Henri II de Montmorency often displayed the independent initiative characteristic of provincial governors during civil conflicts. When civil conflict broke out in 1619, Louis XIII sent orders to the duc to raise his compagnie d'ordonnance and to publish an *ordonnance* prohibiting all levies made without the king's permission. Montmorency responded that he had already "had published the said prohibitions in the extent of my government." As for his gendarmes, Montmorency reported that he had already begun preparing his men for a military campaign.[27]

Noble Associations

Warrior nobles confirmed their independent initiatives by seeking political support for them, forming noble associations and groups, and requesting military assistance from their allies and clients. They created associations by engaging their kin, clienteles, and alliances through discussion, correspondence, agreement, and, organization. As Arlette Jouanna points out, contemporaries used a variety of concepts to refer to these noble groupings, including *associations, ligues, unions, partis, factions,* and *cabales.*[28] Often, these terms were used in a pejorative sense by the monarch, or by opposing groups of nobles, to describe enemies. Some leaders of noble leagues tried to build solidarity through ritualized oath-taking ceremonies and symbols of association.

Political causes sometimes motivated groups of nobles, ranging from local associations of nobles to widespread coalitions unified by a specific agenda. Political positions and rivalries created other noble associations, as when nobles assembled to oppose the Spanish Marriages in 1615, when Louis XIII and his sister both married into the Habsburg dynasty. Occasionally, widespread provincial groups could coalesce. The favored position of Concino Concini in the royal government in 1616–1617 produced widespread warrior noble opposition, but Louis XIII's decisive approval of the assassination of Concini in April 1617 quickly defused this issue. The imprisonment of Henri II de Bourbon prince de Condé from 1616 to 1619 led to calls for his release by many great nobles and might have produced a widespread noble grouping, but failed to do so. The imprisonment and exile of Marie de Médicis produced a somewhat widespread noble reaction in 1619–1620, but the refusal of many powerful nobles, including the duc de Montmorency, to join her and the duc d'Épernon limited this noble movement to a few regions.[29] Such grandiose leagues promoted their causes through the publication of political manifestos, which attracted much attention and debate.[30]

Warrior nobles occasionally joined together in broad associations to support certain very specific causes that appealed to the ideals of nobility and noble privilege in general, which usually arose over the imprisonment or trial of nobles accused of participating in revolt. A few such cases involved nobles in Languedoc and Guyenne. The imprisonment of important nobles with clienteles and connections in southern France brought warrior nobles from these provinces together in their defense. Henri I de Montmorency argued on grounds of noble quality for the release of Charles de Valois comte d'Auvergne, who had been imprisoned for conspiracy.[31] When François de Montmorency comte de Bouteville was arrested for dueling and held in the Bastille, noble supplications for his pardon poured into the royal court. Henri II de Montmorency and his clients in particular tried to save Bouteville's life, but failed to win the king's clemency.[32] In 1632, many Languedoc nobles would be pleading for Montmorency's own life following the disastrous battle of Castelnaudary. These exceptional cases involving clemency campaigns tended to unite warrior nobles in broad mutual support for noble privilege, status, and dignity. There were also occasional appeals for regional nobles to band together in mutual defense as when the duc de Ventadour called for "all the nobility of the region" to join together "in the common defense of their belongings, their lives, and their honor."[33]

Warrior noble culture was rarely so united. Religious and political causes were much more prevalent, with nobles joining together to assert specific religious agendas within the political culture. Normally, warrior noble culture coalesced around noble patrons, clienteles, and regional causes. Regional religious associations were never blanket organizations encompassing all of the nobles of one or the other major confessions within France. Instead, specific groups of Catholic or Huguenot nobles coalesced around specific political goals and confessional agendas. Nobles often formed associations based on common religious beliefs and concerns, such as regional Huguenot defensive groups. Henri II de Rohan duc de Rohan, the leading Calvinist military leader in the early seventeenth century, published manifestos that attracted significant Huguenot followings.[34] Militant Catholic associations formed around local confraternities and groups of ex-Leaguer nobles that advanced extremist agendas.[35] More moderate Catholic nobles cooperated in defensive leagues intended to protect cities and towns from Huguenot attacks.

Arming also involved disrupting communications and cutting social ties at the openings of civil conflict. The militarization of noble culture during civil wars disrupted peacetime warrior noble activities, ending their normal gatherings, conversations, and diversions.[36] Nobles' normal greetings and gestures of *amitié* were often unreturned by peers who questioned their actions. Ritual calls for assistance and summons for military support were accepted or rejected by allies and clients. As nobles assembled in groups, they also rebuffed offers of association from other nobles and rejected some of their clientage and alliance connections. Nobles erected barriers to communication that disrupted social contact and interaction. Sometimes, even families were split by civil conflicts as nobles took sides, disturbing the ability of family members to communicate effectively and resolve family problems. The sense of uncertainty and division within noble culture indicated that a conflict was turning into revolt. The outbreak of civil conflict divided warrior nobles from each other and forced them to take positions on religious, political, and local issues in chaotic circumstances.[37]

JUSTIFYING VIOLENCE

Warrior nobles who engaged in civil violence attempted to justify their actions and protect themselves from reprisals. While provincial nobles exercised personal violence, they associated themselves with the king's authority and claimed to be acting to uphold the royal monopoly over legitimate violence. Public and private justifications for violence blurred during civil conflicts, producing confusion over authority claims and legitimate executive power. Commissions shaped the language in which nobles justified their exercise of violence, allowing them to assert and to contest power simultaneously.

Royal Monopoly as Ideal

Early modern French monarchs considered the authorization of military recruitment to be a royal prerogative. In theory the king personally initiated all recruitment of troops within his kingdom, delegating authority to selected royal appointees to execute his orders. Once troops were recruited and assembled into armies, the king took possession of them and selected army commanders to lead them. The monarch further emphasized his royal prerogative to recruit by continually referring to units as "my troops" or "my infantry" or "my army." The king asserted a royal monopoly on the organization of violence—all military forces were theoretically to be created, mobilized, and used at the personal discretion of the monarch.[38] But, as with most forms of early modern authority, the royal authority to recruit was delegated, divided, and partitioned. French monarchs allowed noble officers to select their own subordinates. Military officers were permitted to recruit troops on their own initiative when circumstances made the king's formal authorization impractical. The royal prerogative frequently amounted to a mere subsequent approval of recruitment already undertaken. Examination of mobilization practices during the early seventeenth-century civil conflicts seriously questions the effectiveness of the monarch's personal monopoly on the organization of violence.

French kings clearly regarded their royal prerogative to organize violence as more than a mere theory. Successive monarchs and their ministers had made various attempts to control recruitment and the exercise of violence within the kingdom. The edicts on dueling issued by Henri IV and Louis XIII have often been seen as part of the royal policies to control violence and "domesticate" the nobility, but recent studies dismiss such efforts as hesitant and unsuccessful.[39] In the early seventeenth century, Louis XIII used the judicial system, and particularly the parlements, to assert his prerogatives on recruitment. During each conflict in southwestern France, the parlement de Toulouse registered edicts forbidding recruitment by anyone not directly commissioned by the king.[40] When the king and the parlements branded nobles as rebels, the unauthorized levying of troops and the granting of commissions were the chief accusations made against them.[41] Provincial governors and other administrative officers were asked to enforce the king's edicts and some genuinely tried to prevent violations, but these efforts to curtail unauthorized mobilization were not particularly effective. The contexts of religious conflict and political instability in the early seventeenth century repeatedly prompted southern French nobles to take up arms. Nobles who felt insecure and threatened by enemies felt justified in measures aimed at self-defense. The king's own mobilization and political systems also undermined attempts to curb mobilization that he and his ministers regarded as illegal.

Warrior nobles justified their participation in civil violence using the notion of the royal monopoly of violence. French kings routinely granted provincial governors, military officers, and administrative officials limited powers of recruitment as extensions of their personal monopoly of violence. During civil warfare in 1622, the provincial governor of Languedoc ordered that "no levy shall be made there without His Majesty's commission or mine." Here, the governor essentially associates his authority to recruit with that of the king, an assertion underscored by his declaration that violators of his orders were to be "punished as disturbers of the public peace," rebels against the king.[42] Officers such as this governor were permitted to recruit for the king, acting for the king in absentia with full royal authority. This process of identification allowed provincial governors, and perhaps other regional officers, to act credibly in the name of the king, but often without royal direction.

A competing tradition of self-defense further eroded the royal monopoly over violence. Warrior nobles claimed the right to self-defense. As Antoine de Roquelaure marquis de Roquelaure put it: "the law of nature permits us to defend ourselves when someone wants to draw [their sword] on us."[43] Provinces and localities had long assumed the responsibilities of paying for own defense and handling their own security problems, even revolt and heresy. Town walls and civic militias represented potential threats to royal control of military force, even though the king regarded the towns as "his." Municipal privileges and civic identities dating from the medieval period granted the *bonnes villes* a limited right of self-defense.[44] Dioceses and provinces recruited and maintained military units to defend themselves during conflicts. Diocesan assemblies and provincial estates acted to suppress rebellion and handle disputes for the king, but also in self-defense. Actions taken to protect oneself were widely regarded as legitimate, even if it contradicted the king's personal will and his recruitment prerogative.

Political instability and a lack of trust in times of civil warfare helped routinize mobilization practices. By the early seventeenth century, the taking up of arms had become a normal activity after decades of civil conflict. When the duc d'Épernon was "informed that all of the partisans of the queen [mother] had taken up arms," during the 1620 civil war, "he did as the others and also put troops on foot."[45] Épernon's actions powerfully demonstrate the ineffectiveness of the royal monopoly on violence, since as soon as one warrior noble began to raise troops, others felt compelled to do so also. Nobles armed to compete with rivals, to impress royal family members, to protect their interests, or to support religious causes. Royal ministers realized that the monarchy did not hold an effective monopoly on violence and that it needed extragovernmental recruitment, but in measured amounts, in specific areas and circumstances, and for limited time periods. The king depended on provincial noble officers to recruit troops and to engage in violence that was both private and public.

Private Violence as Public Violence

The ineffectiveness of the royal monopoly of violence ensured that public and private power intertwined and merged around the control and exercise of violence. Each outbreak of civil war led warrior nobles to levy personal military forces, troops raised without the king's permission. Other ostensibly private forces were tolerated by the king, and sometimes even funded by the royal treasury. Although nobles' personal military mobilization had become a routine aspect of civil warfare, many contemporaries saw private violence as a serious public problem. Southern French people frequently complained about the damages and expenses caused by troops raised without royal permission. The provincial estates of Languedoc and the parlement de Toulouse both deplored the destruction caused by troops raised without the permission of the king.[46] Such complaints did reflect very real problems of military discipline and control, and the destruction that troops inflicted on French communities was so pervasive that it has been called a "tax of violence."[47] However, these complaints also reflect one of the most important tropes of justifying violence, claiming that private violence was public violence.

Châteaux garrisons show the ambiguities of private and public duties, obligations, and interests. Nobles had long had the seigneurial right of the *guet et garde,* whereby inhabitants of their seigneurie could be called up for militia duty to guard their châteaux and repair fortifications.[48] Sometimes, nobles were granted additional garrisons of their private possessions. In 1621, the sieur de Montravel and other nobles in Velay "unexpectedly obtained a certain ordonnance from monseigneur de Montmorency ordering the inhabitants of Cardeyrol to guard his château all day and night, and in addition to place there a garrison of fifty men, for whom the inhabitants would provide until further notice."[49] Communities throughout southern France periodically provided financing for garrisons in nobles' residences, especially during civil conflicts.

Private garrisons were publicly sanctioned during the civil wars of the late sixteenth and early seventeenth centuries. Soldiers manning the garrisons of important nobles' châteaux were often paid out of public funds with the blessing of the king. Henri de Lévis duc de Ventadour received three thousand livres in 1628 to cover the costs of maintaining garrisons in his châteaux, "to be divided among his garrisons as he saw fit."[50] Other nobles requested and received commissions to recruit men to garrison their own châteaux.[51] During civil conflicts, provincial governors and army commanders issued numerous commissions and orders for nobles to recruit soldiers to garrison their châteaux and to guard their seigneuries. For example, the duc de Montmorency ordered the baron d'Alès "to attend . . . carefully to the guard and conservation of the places of Salindre and Saint-Privat-des-Vieux," by raising a garrison of twenty-five men. The inhabitants of these two villages were to pay for maintenance of Alès's men, costs eventually to be repaid by the diocese.[52]

The blending of private and public is particularly striking in the case of nobles' bodyguards. Most nobles lived and traveled with large retinues of armed followers, and even regular bodyguards. The royal government not only tolerated such bodyguards, but explicitly ordered the creation of some personal bodyguard units, and even offered to pay for them. Louis XIII wrote to Henri II de Bourbon prince de Condé in 1625 that "having judged that is necessary for the conservation of your person to give you guards. . . . I write you the present [letter] to the end that you raise as promptly as you can a company of forty mounted musketeers, called carabiniers, of the most valiant and hardened soldiers that you can choose to reside next to you and to serve to guard your person; and assure yourself that I shall pay them their wages and appointments."[53] These royal payments to the bodyguards must have made issues of command and loyalty ambiguous. One wonders how secure Condé, who had been imprisoned by Louis XIII from 1616 to 1619, would have felt with these bodyguards.

Personal bodyguards could serve state needs, such as the protection of key officers. Soon after his abandonment of the Huguenot army in Bas Languedoc in 1622, the seigneur de Châtillon received "orders from His Majesty to raise thirty carabiniers or arquebusiers à cheval to serve me as guards, also orders for the augmentation of my garrison."[54] Châtillon's change of allegiance made him a valuable example to other Huguenots, and Louis XIII understandably wanted to protect him. Similarly, the gendarmes in the duc de Montmorency's compagnie d'ordonnance served him as private bodyguards.[55]

The justifications for participating in civil warfare ceaselessly juxtaposed public need with private interest. Warrior nobles readied their bodyguards, expanded their garrisons, and mobilized new military units in the name of the king's service. Nobles frequently discussed the importance of having a legitimate cause for mobilization. Political and religious causes motivated nobles and provided them with a sense of legitimization.[56] For example, the duc d'Épernon was ready to oppose Marie de Médicis's advisor Concino Concini in early 1617, but he hesitated. His secretary recorded that the duc "thus wanted to arm, but he lacked a cause and even a pretext, and one rendered oneself criminal to do so without this." However, Huguenot troops from La Rochelle soon took the field, giving Épernon the excuse for which he had waited.[57]

The military forces formed by noble officers had both public and private aspects. As warrior nobles mobilized their own personal forces, they justified their recruitment campaigns as necessary public acts and excused any ensuing violence as being for the common good. Military officers controlled enormous patronage powers to distribute commands and favors within their infantry regiments and cavalry companies. They often exercised wide latitude in the conduct of operations, allowing them to accomplish private goals and public goals at the same time. Violence represented a very personal part of warrior nobles' everyday lives, yet it was almost always discussed through the language of legitimate public violence.

Commissions as Forms

Commissioning practices formalized the blending of public and private in the organization of violence. French monarchs issued royal letters of commission to officers, providing them with temporary military and administrative powers— especially for military recruitment and command. A commission was an official act by the king to partition royal authority within the body politic. Geoffrey Parker provides an excellent account of how an early modern commission system was envisioned to work in his study of the Spanish Army of Flanders:

> Recruiting by commission was superbly suited to the needs of the early modern state. All power remained in royal hands. . . . The central authority decided who should receive a commission (and issued the patent), scheduled the areas in which recruiting might take place, the number of men to be raised, the time which might be taken and the destination to which the troops were to march. Under the commission system, the principal recruiting officer was always the captain and the principal unit the company. The regimental cadres were fixed arbitrarily by the crown: the king himself named the captains, the colonel and all other staff officers.[58]

However precisely the Spanish military system fit this model, the situation in France was quite different. An altered commissioning process became routinized in France because of the repeated mobilizations during successive civil conflicts. Commissions provided the literary form for recruitment—dictating wording, structuring language, and formalizing roles.

Even this highly structured literary form could be bent, reshaped, and pilfered, however. French kings regularly relinquished control over the commissioning processes to subordinate officers. When Louis XIII left Fontainebleau in April 1621 with a small army, nobles were raising troops in various regions to support the royal force. The duc de Mayenne was in Guyenne "with commissions sufficient to raise troops there and maintain [the king's] service."[59] Without royal oversight and direction, Mayenne was free to implement the king's commissions as he saw fit. Commissions could be printed, with only names changed, in order to speed the commissioning process.[60] Warrior noble officers thus used the commissions system to justify violence and assert authority during the early seventeenth century.

The practice of issuing blank commissions deflated the king's authority that the documents were meant to convey. Commissions would be drawn up with identical wording, leaving space for the names of the officers to be inserted later. Louis XIII routinely issued bundles of blank commissions to selected military officers to carry out their mobilizations, allowing them to name their subordinates using the commissions.[61] Sometimes the number of troops to be raised by the officer was also left blank, giving the noble in charge of mobilization the authority to determine how many men each subordinate officer would be able to raise. Blank commissions gave the nobles in charge of recruitment enormous latitude to influence the mobilization process and exercise patronage. Groups on all sides of civil conflicts employed blank commissions to facilitate their mobilization operations. Marie de Médicis issued numerous blank commissions during the civil wars of 1619–1620.[62] Huguenot military leaders often used blank commissions during early seventeenth-century religious conflicts.[63] Calvinist generals also used blank ordonnances to authorize supplies and payments for their troops, and some of these were even printed.[64]

Noble officers frequently used commissions even more informally, stretching the boundaries of the commission's legitimacy as a royal document. François de Noailles was already recruiting troops in 1615 when he heard from another noble officer that the king had sent him commissions, which he had not yet received.[65] The duc de Montmorency ordered officers to raise troops in 1627, indicating to one captain that he intended "to use the commissions that you previously had under the charge of monsieur the baron de Pérault, meanwhile I shall have them renewed for you."[66] These former commissions should have had no value, because they were ephemeral documents intended to give authority to officers at designated times for specific purposes. Yet, the baron de Pérault recruited his troops and exercised his authority anyway.

Commissioning practices so confused public and private authority that officers bearing royal commissions found the authorities granted them in the commissions insufficient or unrecognized. Henri II de Montmorency felt compelled to issue an ordonnance to reinforce the authority of a commission in 1625, declaring that he has seen the *lettres patentes* issued by the king to commission the marquis d'Ambres to recruit 150 chevaux-légers. The duc de Montmorency orders that everyone in his government is to "recognize, obey, and hear the said sieur d'Ambres."[67] The duc's avowal that he has seen the commission is meant to validate the commission and ensure that Ambres is recognized as a legitimate captain. That Montmorency felt compelled to issue such a proclamation suggests that Ambres's commission alone was not giving him enough authority to operate effectively as captain.

Nobles branded as rebels would not have been recognizable by the forms of their commissions. Practically all nobles taking up arms used commissions as the basis of their authority. When civil war broke out in France in 1615, the English ambassador, Sir John Throckmorton, reported that "betwixt the French king and the prince of Condeye and his party their are 500 newe commissions geven out for the leveing of souldiers."[68] Supposedly rebel nobles appropriated the literary form of the royal commission and used it to legitimize their mobilization efforts. Henri II de Montmorency's commissions issued during the mobilization for his so-called rebellion in 1632 are not distinguishable from his earlier royal commissions. Montmorency commissioned the baron de Sorgues, saying that "the place of Sanssulz is ordained for the levy and assembly of a company of 100 foot of the regiment that we have ordered the sieur baron de Sorgues to put on foot in order to serve the king in the present circumstances."[69] Such commissions allowed nobles to assert that their personal acts of mobilization represented legitimate service to their king.

Huguenot assemblies and army commanders borrowed from the literary form of the royal commission for their own recruiting operations in the southern France. Huguenot commissions included a careful justification of their recruitment powers. A Calvinist commission issued in 1621 partly replicates a royal commission, using standard language and leaving blanks for the names of officers and numbers of men to be inserted later. The commission opens by establishing the authority of "The General Assembly of the Reformed Churches of France and the sovereignty of Béarn" to order recruitment. The assembly declares that it is mobilizing because the Calvinist churches are "persecuted by the enemies of the state and of our religion who abuse the affection and the conscience of the king." The assembly claims to remain loyal and obedient to the king, "we proclaim before God and men to remain firm, recognizing that [the king] has been given to us by God as our sovereign lord." Instead of challenging the king's legitimacy, they claim that "it is entirely necessary for our conservation to draw up just defenses and to oppose [with] legitimate and natural means the violence and oppression to the end of conserving . . . the authority of His Majesty and his edicts, the liberty of our consciences, and the safety of our lives." This argument shows a departure from earlier Huguenot theories of resistance, which at times advocated overthrowing an ungodly king. Having explained the necessity of the levy, the assembly orders that: "in virtue of the power to us given by all of the churches of this kingdom and the sovereignty of Béarn and [having] confidence in your capacity, valor, and experience in feats of arms, we have given [and] give power and commission, under the name and authority of His Majesty for the good of his service, defense and protection of his subjects of the said religion, to raise and put on foot as fast as possible a company of ____ French mounted musketeers." Commissions issued by Reformed assemblies specified that the troops raised would operate under the jurisdiction of the provincial general, who was "by us selected and named as chief and general of the province." Following the royal form of commissions, the assembly decrees that the captain has the power to name his subordinate officers, and that he will be expected to follow "the military ordonnances of this kingdom," as well as the regulations issued by the assembly.[70]

Commissions, then, were legalistic documents that granted the authority for recruitment, but their form was transparent, pliable, and transportable. The very documents meant to ensure the royal monopoly over recruitment prevented any real implementation of that authority. Warrior nobles' appropriations of commissions confirmed the tenuousness of the royal monopoly over legitimate use of force, allowing them to express their personal uses of violence through the language of commissions.

TAKING UP ARMS

Even as they justified their decisions to act, warrior nobles began to take up arms. Once civil conflicts broke out, nobles acted quickly to organize violence and direct warfare. The provincial warrior nobles took the lead in mobilizing and planning warfare in Languedoc and Guyenne. Using their châteaux as bases, they attempted to manage regional conflicts while contributing to large-scale military campaigns. Warrior nobles handled recruitment, assembled troops, and financed war efforts during civil conflicts.

Châteaux as Operational Bases

Southern French nobles used their châteaux as bases for controlling space and organizing mobilization. The châteaux of Languedoc and Guyenne were constructed in a broad range of architectural styles, often exhibiting an asymmetrical aspect due to many successive alterations and expansions over decades, if not centuries.[71] The widespread destruction of châteaux during the French Wars of Religion gave many nobles opportunities to rebuild their châteaux in newer Renaissance or neoclassical styles. Renaissance architectural and design treatises were circulating in early seventeenth-century France, and they certainly influenced some château-rebuilding efforts in southern France.[72] The Hautefort family added a Renaissance triumphal arch to their château de Boulogne in Vivarais, and Henri de Narbonne-Caylus built an entirely new château at Lunas after his family's medieval château was dismantled in 1630.[73]

The military roles of early modern French châteaux have been largely ignored by historians and art historians. Sixteenth- and seventeenth-century châteaux are commonly assumed to have been country mansions or palaces, filled with art but not with arms. Many of the châteaux that were built or rebuilt in Languedoc and Guyenne during the early seventeenth century had significant defensive elements, however. Sections of older medieval architecture were often retained;

thus, in most châteaux, "certain heavy fortifications were almost always bound to remain: a tower or two, perhaps flanking a highly defensible older portion of the château; a moat; a fortified gate or a drawbridge surmounted by a guard tower."[74] The château de Belvézet, apparently built around 1609, had a strong defensive design, with two round towers and a rectangular walled structure.[75] The château de Restinclières, near Montpellier, was rebuilt with square defensive towers during this period. Early seventeenth-century French nobles could turn to new treatises on military engineering and fortifications for technical information and fortification designs as they rebuilt their châteaux.[76]

Defensive architectural features further demonstrate the military significance of early seventeenth-century châteaux. Many southern French châteaux were built on defensive sites such as hilltops, or were located at strategic points on key roads, overlooking villages, or guarding river crossings. Some châteaux, such as Villevielle, were completely surrounded by walls. The Montmorency family's château Le Parc was enclosed by tall fortified walls.[77] Many nobles left medieval structures in place as they restored their residences, and the château de Margon retained much of its thirteenth-century defensive architecture, for example. New defensive modifications and additions during the sixteenth century prepared châteaux for effective firearms defense. Barbicans and gun loops were constructed along the rooftop of the château de Sorbs. Another noble residence in Languedoc, the château d'Arboras, had gun loops in each tower.[78]

Many châteaux were surrounded by outlying buildings—mills, chapels, monasteries, stables—that could be used defensively.[79] Pigeonniers, stone-roofed pigeon houses, could also be used defensively. Some château designs clearly incorporated pigeonniers into the defensive architecture. At the château Le Peyrat, for example, a pigeonnier perches high above the gateway leading to the court, ready to act as a gatehouse if necessary.[80] Châteaux situated adjacent to village or town fortifications could benefit from the surrounding defensive works as long as the inhabitants could be kept under control. The château de Villevieille practically adjoined the town of Sommières, effectively extending its fortifications.[81]

The châteaux of prominent nobles served as magazines, essential sites for localized recruitment. Nobles assembled large armories of muskets, pikes, swords, and assorted weapons. Corselets, helmets, pieces of armor, and protective gear would be stacked high, while full and partial suits of armor would stand on racks, ready to wear. Nobles stockpiled gunpowder, cords, musket balls, artillery shot, and other vital munitions in their châteaux. Wagons and containers would have to be ready to transport and distribute munitions. Equipment for the maintenance and repair of weapons and armor would be on hand. While

Armaments in the Château de Rieux in Languedoc in 1632

Weapons	Armor	Artillery and Munitions
Firearms:	150 pikeman's	4 small guns, *petites pièces*
111 muskets	corselets with	*de campaigne de fonte*
	hausse-col	*verte*
13 *gros mousquets de forte*	1 *pair d'armes d'orées*	1 medium gun, *aveq les*
à croq	*aveq le pot*	*armes de Rieux*
2 *gros mousquets à croq*	2 helmets	50 small shot, *comme*
de fer		*d'oranges*
20 *arquebusiers à mache*	1 mail coat	
10 carbines	*les [brassards] et [tassets]*	
	de deux pairs d'armes	
4 wheelock arquebuses		
4 pistols (2 with holsters)		
Polearms:		*Equipment:*
10 pikes of Biscay		3 drums
1 pike of *canne d'inde*		8 *bouchiers ou pavois a*
ferrées		*l'antique*
4 halberds		1 camp bed
2 shortened pikes		1 war tent
16 military forks		
32 *ordres*		
Other:		
7 crossbows		

Source: Archives Départementales de l'Aude, 2 E 17, f° 12.

châteaux were not the only magazines in southern France, their armories were vital for noble recruiting efforts and even for many towns' defensive measures. So, when Huguenots from Nîmes sacked the nearby château de Cabrières in 1621, they took weapons and "all of the munitions like balls, cords, and powder."[82] Some nobles maintained artillery as private assets, and their châteaux arsenals might include several pieces of artillery and stockpiles of munitions. The duc de Bouillon, for example, controlled his own artillery in Guyenne.[83] Noble military officers and town governors sometimes requisitioned artillery pieces from municipalities under their control and transferred guns to their châteaux for use in their own personal artillery forces.

The contents of one noble's château allows some idea of the scale of the arsenals in regional châteaux. After the death of François de la Jugie comte de Rieux in battle at Castelnaudary in 1632, a royal notary inventoried the contents of his château in Languedoc in great detail (see table), giving us a sense of such a warrior noble's personal accoutrements and implements of command. Rieux had kept his personal arms in the "highest [room] in the home, called the watchtower [*galetas*]." His boots, his swords, a scimitar, and several hats were found in a small study adorned with a map of France, which presumably could have been used for conducting operations, along with his great seal and two small seals bearing his coat of arms, used for sealing letters and documents. The study also contained other precious belongings, such as letters from the king and valuable books, including several military treatises. Several harnesses for the comte's horses hung in the room, ready for use.[84]

Châteaux like Rieux's also served as major supply centers for troop mobilization and military operations. Nobles stockpiled food, grain, wine, fodder, horses, wagons, and equipment. Like large grain silos, châteaux held huge reserves of grains, which could provide the basic ration for seventeenth-century troops, bread. Within the walls of the château de Rieux, 150 *cestiers* (approximately 281 bushels) of wheat were stored in one building and 378 *cestiers* (708 bushels) in another.[85] The château had nine warhorses, a hackney, a nag, and seven mules within its walls, and other horses could be quickly gathered from the seigneurie. The nearby barn had two wagons and two hay wagons, which could be used to transport provisions. The comte's seigneurie could provide provisions for troops from its vineyards, wheat, sheep, steers, and goats.[86] When the duc de Rohan captured the château de Theyrargues in 1628, he reportedly took enough wheat to supply his army during its next siege.[87]

A well-prepared château posed a formidable challenge to enemies and projected a defensive ideal. A Vivarais noble evokes this notion of defense in praising the fortifications of the château de Salavas: "in this lower court was a ravelin of great length, where one had to pass four doors to arrive at the drawbridge, and from there to a small lower court that separated a new dwelling from the old; in this last [court] there was a rock [outcropping] named Baldacet, which formed a keep above all the rest, where there was a cistern, oven, wood, flour, two good *fauconneaux* [small cannon], grenades, *petards* [explosive devices used in sieges], rations and munitions, earth [for constructing earthworks] . . . , and a place for sheltering more than two hundred men from cannon [fire]."[88] Fortified châteaux served as places of refuge and defense for coreligionaries. The château de Chambonas, for example, often sheltered Catholic refugees during civil wars under the protection of Catholic noble Henri de La Garde.[89] A well-provisioned, well-armed château gave a noble a base to project his symbolic power as well as military force. Noble households supplied the personnel needed to organize mobilization efforts. The number of servants, workers, and officers serving a noble varied widely, with great nobles often having a hundred or more household personnel. The carpenters, armorers, blacksmiths, lackeys, bakers, and other specialized personnel could easily find suitable roles within a noble's military entourage, if necessary.

Nobles clearly recognized the importance of châteaux as centers of mobilization and bases of operation. They acknowledged the symbolic power of châteaux and respected them as military threats. Norbert Elias rightly emphasizes the importance of the relationship between château architecture and noble rank, as shown by nobles' conspicuous consumption in building and furnishing their châteaux.[90] But this display was only part of nobles' programs of projecting and representing power, reflecting much more than spending competitions. The importance of châteaux as sites of power is shown by nobles' frequent attacks on their enemies' residences and bases of operation. The patterns of seventeenth-century civil warfare revolved around the spatial relationships between châteaux.

Filling the Ranks

At the outbreak of civil conflict, noble officers all confronted the problem of finding men to fill the ranks of their units. Recruitment was frequently carried out in contested areas where several different officers were competing for recruits. John A. Lynn categorizes seventeenth-century methods of obtaining recruits into three broad groupings: regular, mercenary, and compulsory recruitment.[91] During the early seventeenth century, the vast majority of troops were enrolled using regular recruitment. Mercenary recruitment was usually done by foreign military officers operating beyond France's borders, but French nobles may occasionally have been able to hire troops in Germany or Italy themselves.[92] Some foreign-born soldiers who had settled in France as military migrants probably served in some companies, and James B. Wood has unearthed some evidence of the widespread origins of soldiers in certain companies during the French Wars of Religion.[93] The only significant form of compulsory recruitment available to nobles was the *ban et arrière-ban*, often known as the feudal levy.

The *ban et arrière ban* was a medieval form of compulsory short-term military service by nobles based on their status as vassals or sub-vassals. Only the king had the authority to call on his nobles to take up arms, and he could summon the nobles of a specific province, of several provinces, or of the entire kingdom to do so. The bailli and sénéchaux organized the nobles with fiefs within their jurisdictions, ordering nobles to assemble at the seat of their bailliage or sénéchausée. They were expected to serve for a set time, usually fixed at three months within the kingdom and up to forty days beyond its frontiers. Nobles served in the king's feudal levy under medieval systems of feudal obligations. A royal fiefholder, and by extension his subordinate fiefholders, owed service to the king in exchange for the grant of the fief. A noble was expected to serve personally in the levy of the bailliage or sénéchausée where his principal fief was located. He could send another "experienced" noble in his place if he was unable to answer the summons. Each noble was to contribute a monetary payment for each of his fiefs in other bailliages or sénéchausées. Nobles who served in the levy were to be armed as chevaux-légers.[94]

The *ban et arrière-ban* was still used during the early modern period, but only occasionally and usually in response to a major crisis. During the French Wars of Religion, monarchs summoned feudal levies only in 1589. In the context of civil conflict, using a feudal levy rarely made sense, since its rationale of compulsory service by all nobles within an area clashed with the monarch's prerogative of controlling recruitment. The king usually opted for an attempt to maintain limits on which nobles mobilized and participated in civil warfare. Calling a *ban et arrière-ban* potentially undermined these efforts at limiting recruitment and threatened to give disloyal nobles a justification for mobilizing. Louis XIII summoned his nobles for "feudal" service only once, in 1635, at the outbreak of war with Spain.[95]

Noble cavalry were recruited through an unofficial *ban et arrière-ban*, however, since provincial governors could compel nobles to volunteer for service. The duc de Montmorency issued orders in 1622 that "all gentlemen of our government shall be at the same time obliged to have arms and a horse [ready] to bring themselves close to us when we enter the dioceses of their residence, or to hold themselves ready to serve the king at the first command, on the pain of being stripped and deprived of the privilege of nobility, their fiefs and courts seized and put in the hands of His Majesty."[96] This unofficial levy only affected nobles, though, so the vast majority of recruits entered the ranks through forms of regular recruitment.

Regular cavalry recruitment seems to have drawn heavily on noble officers' kinship and clientele relations. Many nobles served as rank-and-file members of cavalry units, completely filling some cavalry units with noble recruits. Sometimes whole companies of cavalry were made up of a noble officer's extended family members. Captains occasionally experienced difficulties in finding enough recruits or mounts for their cavalry companies. One noble complained that although he would raise his company of gendarmes as quickly as he could, "the incommodity of the nobility and the intrigues and levies that one has made in this region . . . prevent me from rendering [the company] as promptly complete and as strong as I would desire."[97] Potential noble recruits also had options of serving as noble volunteers, aides to generals, or officers.

French commoners became infantry soldiers in regular recruitment in the early seventeenth century by voluntarily accepting a bounty. Noble officers acted as military entrepreneurs when they accepted commissions for recruitment, investing their own money and status in their soldiers by paying these bounties for recruits and covering other costs of raising their regiments or companies.[98] Bounty costs fluctuated as part of a market of recruits. Officers competed for infantry recruits, and bidding wars could occur, driving the costs of bounties high. While competition over recruits gave potential recruits some leverage against officers, they also suffered from this "voluntary" recruiting process. Men could be pressed into service, cajoled or coerced into taking a bounty against their wishes. This sort of abuse of the "voluntary" recruitment system was known as *racolage* and it was probably predominant.[99]

Warrior noble captains recruited peasants living on their seigneuries into their infantry companies. Seigneurial recruitment was certainly a prevalent method of recruiting men, especially for newly created infantry units. When Alexandre de Castelnau offered his services to raise troops against a possible English landing to aid French Huguenots in 1627, he claimed that he could raise 100 gentlemen from among his friends and 2,000 infantrymen from among the inhabitants of his lands.[100] Trace evidence in a number of documents suggests that seigneurial recruitment was prevalent in southern France, but insufficient sources remain to determine the extent of this type of recruitment.

Noble officers also recruited city and town dwellers and visitors as soldiers. James B. Wood argues that infantry units relied heavily on urban residents as recruits, finding that over half of the soldiers in the infantry companies he sampled had been born in sizeable towns and cities.[101] Army commanders often ordered municipal leaders to raise troops within their communities, as in a 1628 ordonnance issued by the duc de Rohan.[102] The duc de Montmorency called on all the communities in his province "to place the [muster] roll of those who could serve on campaign promptly in the hands of the syndic or the consuls of the principal cities of each diocese."[103] He specified that "from among the said men shall be made selection of a number of them who, without risking the security of the said places, could serve on campaign at the first command under the charge of the said commander, and at the expense of the said cities, towns, and parishes."[104] The provincial governor could then indicate towns to be used by recruiting officers to fill the ranks of their infantry units.

Huguenot and Catholic recruitment techniques were very similar. The Calvinist baron de Ganges claimed to have spent 1,500 livres in raising an infantry regiment in 1621, a cost in line with contemporary Catholic recruitment costs.[105] Huguenot nobles could sometimes obtain financial support from uniquely Calvinist institutions when conducting recruitment. The Calvinist provincial assembly of Languedoc authorized payments to the seigneur de Pillon to assist him in recruiting an infantry regiment in August 1621, providing 3,000 livres up front and promising another 1,000 livres once the troops were ready to march.[106] Despite the assistance granted by such provincial assemblies, Huguenot captains seem to have relied much more on informal clientele and financial networks to fill the ranks of their companies. Conversions and political divisions eroded Huguenot noble leadership in the early seventeenth century, however, making it increasingly difficult for them to assemble their troops effectively.

Assembling Troops

Once individual recruits were found, they had to be assembled into military units. A company might be completely recruited in one town, but other companies were filled with soldiers from towns and villages spread across an entire diocese. Recruits had to be led to a common location and organized into distinct military units. These military units then had to be assembled, often in areas where enemy units were already in the field. During periods of civil warfare, even the assembly of a company could be difficult to accomplish. Conducting recruitment operations could be a difficult and dangerous activity, so officers who assembled troops had to deal with the operational aspects of mobilization.

For the assembly of their troops, officers fixed rendezvous—frequently secure châteaux or towns that could be used as operational bases both during recruitment and subsequent military campaigns. New recruits often had to be armed, clothed, and trained, and the encampments and communities where they assembled had to provide food and shelter to growing numbers of soldiers. Urban centers often served as rendezvous for any large gatherings of troops, and especially for entire field armies. Townspeople might display a sense of civic pride by recruiting, arming, and supplying military units. The Catholic city of Toulouse raised several regiments in 1621 to contribute to the royal siege of Montauban.[107] The Huguenot cities of Montauban and Montpellier both raised their own Calvinist infantry regiments during several civil conflicts. The Montauban regiments seem to have been recruited by quarter, indicating the municipal politics and local pride potentially involved in raising troops.[108]

The duc de Montmorency demanded rapid action by townspeople in Languedoc at the outbreak of civil warfare, ordering municipal leaders to hold reviews of the men capable of bearing arms. "And if they have never been armed before, they shall be instructed to equip themselves in a week's time—counting from the day of publication of the present regulation—with a musket, fork, and bandolier, or with a pike, burgonet, and corselet, depending on which armament is considered most appropriate."[109] Montmorency also expected towns to provide gunpowder, munitions, and other supplies for his assembling troops. Noble officers had to inspect the troops arriving at a rendezvous and ensure that they were effectively equipped and prepared for military campaigns. Urban elites, often from old noble families, played important roles in supplying and preparing troops arriving in their towns for a military rendezvous.

Noble officers and army commanders selected assembly points according to various operational and strategic concerns. Sometimes, a rendezvous was held as close as possible to enemy strongholds, to threaten them immediately. This was the case with the prince de Condé's army that assembled in Foix in order to strike the town of Pamiers in 1628.[110] In other situations, the place was chosen with the aim of cutting the enemy's supply lines or threatening enemy communications. When Guillaume de Balazuc de Montréal mobilized in Vivarais in 1628, "the general rendezvous was given at Villeneuve-de-Berg—being the place the most convenient to the passage of enemies, and in the heart of the region—from which part of the troops were dispersed in the places where there was the most to fear, like Aubenas, Vogué, Rouons, Balazuc, St-Jean, Lavilledieu, and Saint-Germain, and the rest remained at Villeneuve for the safety of this place, [which was] extremely desired, as well as to aid others who might be attacked."[111]

Nobles sometimes mobilized troops specifically to block enemy recruitment efforts or to prevent the relief of siege operations. In 1621, the maréchal de Roquelaure protected the duc de Mayenne's forces besieging Nérac by operating along a river "with 300 gentlemen that he had brought, and four separate companies raised in the region, which served only to guard and cut off several paths from which aid could come. He was very useful there, and he served there with care and pain, for he remained on horseback day and night for fifteen days."[112]

Officers also acted against those who impeded their own mobilization operations. The duc de Montmorency prescribed punishments for anyone who tried to disrupt authorized recruitment in Languedoc.[113] Catholic nobles used localized recruitment to attempt to block the duc de Rohan's reinforcement of the defenses of Montauban during the siege of the city in 1621. According to one account, "the maréchal de Thémines and the sieur de Cornusson have raised some fiery soldiers either to oppose themselves to the troops that the duc de Rohan has in the province, or to destroy the wheat of the inhabitants of Montauban, or to assist the duc de Mayenne at the siege of Nérac."[114] Merely assembling troops at a military rendezvous could be a serious challenge during civil wars.

MANAGING SPACE

When civil warfare broke out, warrior nobles recruited troops across extensive areas and had to contend with the difficulties of distance in assembling their personal armies and forces. Officers managed the spatial aspects of mobilization by situating their recruitment efforts in relation to strategic sites, geographic features, and enemy strongholds. Armed forces assembled around nobles' châteaux and governments, which served as centers of broad recruitment areas. Nobles ritually defined political and social space as they mobilized during civil conflicts.

Distance and Communication

Warrior nobles in Guyenne and Languedoc were often isolated, separated by considerable distances from their patrons, clients, and allies. As nobles prepared to respond to the instigation of civil violence, they had to secure their châteaux and fortifications, while sending couriers out to summon their subordinates and clients to assemble their forces. Mountainous and hilly regions, poor roads, fortifications, and the mixed-confessional religious geography of southern France all slowed troop movements, forcing nobles to take the initiative in independent action at the outbreak of civil conflicts.

Warrior nobles had to respond to these problems of communication and distance by using a flexible style of warfare. When fighting broke out, a multitude of localized military conflicts occurred as nobles launched small-scale offensives. At the local level, warrior nobles attempted to establish zones of control around their châteaux and town governments, resulting in skirmishes and small battles. Cooperation or intimidation of consuls, civic elites, and municipal garrisons was essential for maintaining control of towns. Eliminating rivals' châteaux and forts that controlled routes and threatened security was indispensable during civil conflicts, leading to attacks and attempts to subvert fortification defenses. Intense fighting and waves of destruction often accompanied the initial outbreak of civil warfare as warrior nobles conducted these localized offensives.

Field armies recruited by powerful nobles carried out regional offensives as civil conflicts expanded. Warrior nobles with regional offices and followings such as the ducs de Montmorency, de Ventadour, de Rohan, and d'Épernon could carry out significant independent military offensives that spanned broader geographic areas. Regional armies were capable of conducting skirmishes, sieges, assaults, and field battles. Prominent warrior nobles operating in their own regions could act using a high degree of independence and flexibility, even opening multiple avenues of operations and shifting fronts during a campaign. The duc de Rohan often campaigned across Haut Languedoc, Bas Languedoc, the Cévennes, and Vivarais in the same year. Maréchal de Thémines campaigned both in Haut Languedoc and in Foix during 1625. The duc de Montmorency frequently shifted his areas of operation across the different regions of the immense province of Languedoc.

During widespread civil wars, major armies could be formed to overcome the constraints of local and regional conflicts. Large Catholic and Huguenot armies occasionally conducted major offensives across multiple provinces. The size of the armies involved and the infusion of extraprovincial forces distinguished these major offensives from regional ones. The arrival of royal *vieux régiments* could bolster regional forces, forming a major royalist army. Supplementing regional armies with regiments raised in other regions or foreign mercenaries could produce concentrations of military force sufficient to attempt major offensive actions. When these large armies formed in southern France, warrior nobles struggled to coordinate their forces, and supply problems compounded the problems of distance and communications.

As military operations escalated, warrior nobles worked actively to disrupt their enemies' communications. Noble officers could forbid their clients and subordinates to communicate with enemy nobles and military forces. Even conventional courtesies to enemy commanders broke down frequently in civil warfare. Communications through official connections and hierarchies were broken off as nobles chose differing sides in civil conflicts. Army commanders and provincial officers banned all commerce and communication with people they considered rebels, and rewarded those who acted to disrupt their opponents' correspondence. Two Catholic soldiers in Lodève received rewards for arresting a man "charged with letters and packets from monsieur de Rohan."[115] Nobles and communities were often ordered to refrain from trading even basic food products, such as wheat and wine, with rebels. Supplying rebels or providing lodgings for them was considered illegal. During one civil war, the duc de Montmorency issued "prohibitions to all the subjects of the king, whether of this province or the neighboring ones, to converse or commerce either by sea or land, . . . with the said rebels, to take them wheat, to let them mill it or cook it." Montmorency also called on provincial nobles in Languedoc to block rebels' use of mountain passes, roads, boats, towns, and rivers to cut off their supplies, food, and communications, ordering punishments to enforce these restrictions. Violators would be arrested and their belongings confiscated. Other interdictions of communications with rebels threatened death to offenders. Such prohibitions allowed little room for neutrality during civil conflicts and also made even basic movement and communication difficult for the people of southern France.[116]

Recruitment Areas

Recruitment areas could be specified by the royal government, but determining them was frequently left to the judgment of provincial nobles. Of course, the central government's selection of which officers to commission gave some indication of which areas would probably be used. Nobles recruited in regions where they had political connections, seigneuries, châteaux, and official power. So, the duc de Mayenne and the duc d'Épernon recruited in Guyenne, the seigneur de Châtillon in Bas Languedoc, and the marquis de Portes in Gévaudan. Assigning recruitment areas was an important way to manage space and assert control.

The deliberations of the estates of Languedoc give some indication of the practices of using recruitment areas. For example, in October 1621, the king ordered the marquis d'Annonay to raise a regiment of 1,000 men. The estates members were informed that "Montmorency had assigned him the towns of La Grasse, Fanjaux, Limoux, and St-Papoul in the dioceses of Narbonne, Mirepoix, Alet, and the said St-Papoul for the levy." The estates recommended that the deputies of these towns and dioceses work together to avoid problems in supplying or controlling the troops.[117]

Officers assigned recruitment areas to their subordinates and attempted to manage the mobilization process. Specifying areas for nobles to use in recruiting helped avoid overburdening an area and prevented officers from directly competing with their fellow officers for recruits. When the provincial governor of Languedoc assigned recruitment areas to his followers in 1632, he sent word to Gabriel de Boyer baron de Sorgues to recruit an infantry company, instructing him which town to use as an assembly point. The community was instructed to "receive them and furnish them the accustomed money and lodgments during fifteen days."[118] Effective management of recruitment areas was vital for a successful levy. Army commanders sometimes took a very personal role in managing recruitment areas. The duc de Vendôme personally raised 150 men in the diocese of Castres as part of a recruitment effort aimed at raising 2,000 men for his army in 1622.[119]

Henri II de Montmorency's choices of recruitment areas in 1621 show the flexibility and adaptability of provincial military systems during civil wars. Montmorency raised three separate field armies within his government to respond to different threats during that year. Each army mobilized and campaigned in a different part of Languedoc. The governor first raised an army around Pont-Saint-Esprit to counter Huguenot forces in Vivarais in February 1621. This army was composed of 3,000–4,000 infantry of the regiments de Languedoc, de Pérault, de Hannibal, d'Ornano, and de Montréal. His 500 cavalry was made up of his own company of gendarmes, along with Ventadour's and Portes's companies. All these troops were recruited in Bas Languedoc and Vivarais. Montmorency also took several cannon from Pont-St-Esprit. The marquis de Portes reinforced the army with troops levied in Gévaudan. Montmorency's army campaigned against the seigneur de Châtillon's army and conducted sieges at Vals and Vallon-Pont-d'Arc. Around June, Montmorency disbanded this army, placing some troops in garrisons and dismissing others.[120]

By the first of July, Montmorency had formed a new field army at Comps, a village just north of Beaucaire on the Rhône. Montmorency had recruited troops in parts of the dioceses of Uzès, Nîmes, and Montpellier for this force of 3,500 infantry and 400 cavalry. This army included seven infantry regiments, part of Montmorency's gendarmes, the chevaux-légers de Cauvisson, and the chevaux-légers de Pérault. Montmorency left Beaucaire in early July, taking several artillery pieces and "necessary munitions" with him to attack Marguerittes, a town near Nîmes, but this army only briefly conducted operations.[121]

After participating in the meeting of the estates of Languedoc in mid-September 1621, Montmorency assembled a third field army. This time, he chose to recruit in Haut Languedoc, assembling his force at Rabastans for a march to reinforce the king's siege of Montauban. His army was composed of about 3,000 infantry, including the regiments de Languedoc, de Rieux, de Moussoulens, de La Roquette, de Réaux, and de Fabrègues. Montmorency's 400–500 cavalry included 100 noble volunteers. The duc led his force into the siegeworks at Montauban on 28 September. These soldiers would remain at the siege until it was lifted. Montmorency had created three different field armies in widely separated parts of the province of Languedoc, all in less than a year. These forces had performed completely distinct missions in differing circumstances. Montmorency's flexible use of recruitment areas shows the effectiveness of localized recruitment in civil warfare.[122]

A royal attempt to manage mobilization can be seen in Louis XIII's efforts to organize his supporters' recruitment efforts in southwestern France in 1620 to oppose Marie de Médicis's growing numbers of followers. The king, who was "resolved to put forces on foot to maintain my authority and punish those who would like to separate," asked Antoine-Arnaud de Pardaillan seigneur de Gondrin, the provincial lieutenant general of Guyenne, to raise two regiments of infantry and some cavalry "in the extent of your charge." The king notified Gondrin that he had "sent him commissions and orders for the provision of his troops." Gondrin was expected to "amass together the troops" and to "make a battalion [*gros*] of the said troops together with my good servants who would like to join you." Gondrin was authorized to lead his troops "to the places you judge necessary within your charge, whether to comfort and assist my good servants and the towns and places which have need, or to strike those who rise up against my authority and rip [them] into pieces." He was asked to "do what you judge to be the most advantageous for the good of my service and the maintenance of my authority." The king also informed Gondrin that he had "given commission to my cousins the prince de Joinville and maréchal de Thémines to assemble the troops that I have ordered to be levied in Auvergne, Limosin, and Guyenne, to draw up an army there and thus to exploit whatever they judge to be for the good of my service." Gondrin was instructed to coordinate with Joinville and Thémines.[123]

The supposedly rebel nobles who opposed royal ministers and advisers similarly selected recruiting areas carefully. Marie de Médicis and her supporters formed several armies in 1620, but she also requested nobles to recruit to handle local problems. She wrote to the marquis de La Valette, "My cousin, I am sending you my commissions to put on foot the troops that I judge necessary in your quarters to oppose the malicious designs of those who think to find their advantage in my ruin and in the loss of the true servants of the king and the state."[124] As the son of the powerful duc d'Épernon, who was already raising an army to aid Marie de Médicis, La Valette needed little prodding.

Since Calvinists constituted a relatively small religious minority in France, Huguenot nobles had to select recruitment areas that boasted a significant Calvinist population, therefore much of the Huguenot recruitment occurred in the hilly and mountainous regions of Calvinist strength in Guyenne and Languedoc. Huguenot towns and places de sûreté provided logistical bases for their recruiting efforts.[125] Huguenot field armies may have relied more heavily on urban recruitment and town garrisons in assembling their armies than did royal or Catholic armies. Huguenot communities threatened by siege formed militia units for their own defense, as when the city of Montauban raised thirty infantry companies to defend itself in 1621.[126]

Rapidity of Mobilization

Managing space involved dealing with distance and coordinating the timing of actions. The time necessary to recruit individual soldiers, to prepare equipment, and to move to a military rendezvous all affected the assembly of an army. During civil warfare, the rapidity of mobilization was vital, not only for the conduct of operations, but to secure loyalties and to establish negotiating strength. Slow recruitment could seriously compromise a military campaign even before formal operations commenced.

Army commanders normally expected extraordinarily rapid recruitment efforts by their officers. A couple of weeks, or even mere days, might be all the time that a noble had to recruit companies or regiments. The Huguenot duc de Rohan certainly expected a lightening response when, on 28 May 1628, he ordered the consuls of Alès "to form 100 soldiers conducted by a captain and other officers, to go to the province of Vivarais and bring the said soldiers, arms and munitions to Barjac on the third of June precisely."[127] After the consuls received the orders, to meet the Rohan's schedule, the town would have to raise, equip, and march the company twenty-one miles in less than six days.

The duc de Montmorency hurried to recruit an army in Bas Languedoc in 1627, saying "at my return from Haut Languedoc, having found the rebels armed and in the country, I resolved to oppose myself to them promptly." The duc summoned officers to raise troops, asking him to "put your company back on foot and to take up positions where the said sieur de Pérault orders you, so that it shall be ready to march in eight days."[128] A week was apparently considered a reasonable length of time for raising a company, since other commissions specified similar periods.

Nobles' recruiting operations frequently proceeded ahead of their deadlines and outpaced those of their rivals. At the king's request, the marquis de Portes raised his regiment of Languedoc, 200 cavalry, and 200 carabins in 1615 and headed north, leaving the province. The king specified that he wanted the units to be assembled in three weeks. But, "in a few days 200 gentlemen came to fall into ranks under the happy ensigns . . . because of which, Aumale surrendered on discretion, without waiting for proof of the vigor of his forces. . . . He took the town and château de Chaumont in less than eight days, for which Paris gives particular thanks." On another occasion, the marquis de Portes prepared to attack the château de Péronne. He had 50 "gentlemen volunteers," but only twenty-four hours later, this number had grown to 120.[129]

While Languedoc and Guyenne lay at the peripheries of the French monarchy, the rapidity of mobilization in those provinces seems comparable with the situation in other provinces. When François de La Rochfoucauld mobilized near Poitiers in 1619, he claimed that "two days ago, at one o'clock, I received the letter that the king wrote me on the first of this month, and as I was already prepared to obey, I wrote to all my friends, who are so dispersed that it will take at least four days to assemble them together . . . eight days' time might have rendered me strong if I had been notified earlier."[130] The same year, Henri de Schömberg, who had 500 gendarmes already under arms with him, reported to the king that he hoped to raise several hundred more in four to five days.[131]

At the outbreak of civil warfare, nobles raced to assure the control of nearby urban centers. Any large-scale recruitment operations relied on using towns and cities as supply centers, since a substantial population base was necessary to provide for the material needs of a field army. Urban areas also provided administrative personnel to mobilize and manage goods for the soldiers. Municipalities had important religious centers that could serve as focal points for loyalties, so they frequently served as secure operational bases. Toulouse was a major operational center for Catholic nobles in Languedoc, while Montauban, Montpellier, and Nîmes served as important Huguenot bases.[132]

Many noble officers in Languedoc and Guyenne employed their personal influence in urban centers to ensure bases of operation. Town and château governors were considered responsible for guaranteeing the loyalties of their governments to the king. Urban hôtels served as secondary bases for warrior nobles who aimed to influence municipal politics and control urban populations. Nobles who could successfully place their allies, clients, or supporters in consul posts during annual elections would have improved chances of influencing municipal religious and political affiliations during civil conflicts. Urban spaces were highly contested during civil conflicts, and the consuls and town governors controlled access through the city walls, gates, and fortifications. The nobles who were quickest to arm and to establish control in urban areas could arbitrate in conflicts, delineate the provisions of religious settlements for the community, and set the terms of coexistence within mixed-confessional communities. The speed of mobilization could easily determine the fate of whole communities during civil conflicts.

✝

Rituals of arming thus prepared early seventeenth-century French nobles for engaging in civil violence and influenced the development of conflicts. The gestures and language of the culture of revolt expressed the ways in which warrior nobles instigated and justified their participation in violence. Ritualistic behavior affected nobles' practices of taking up arms as they recruited troops and organized for warfare. Nobles also employed rituals in managing space as they readied themselves, their clients, and their troops to face the chaos and disorder of civil warfare. Having considered the call to arms, we shall now examine the organization of personal armies and the maintenance of military forces on campaign in the next chapter.

An early seventeenth-century army on the march. Drawing in Benedit de Vassallieu, "Discours sur la conduite et l'emploi de l'artillerie," BNF, Mss. fr. 388, detail of f° 82v–83. Photo courtesy Bibliothèque Nationale de France.

CHAPTER EIGHT

A Great Multitude of Soldiers

Personal Armies

A s political contention and confessional hostility mounted in Guyenne late in the summer of 1613, one of the prominent nobles of Périgord reportedly worked "to raise a great multitude of soldiers," assembling his own field army of 2,000–3,000 infantry before "leading them to besiege a town in peacetime."[1] While this account expresses shocked indignation at this sudden mobilization, the military elites of Guyenne and Languedoc often managed to assemble impressive personal military forces during early seventeenth-century civil conflicts. Some provincial warrior nobles were even able to field armies capable of conducting independent campaigns and siege operations.

This chapter considers how warrior nobles fielded and funded personal military forces, assembled around military commanders through complex processes of accretion that drew in various armed components. Once organized, such an army had to be supplied and sustained through improvised measures. Early seventeenth-century observers of civil warfare often described field armies as organisms that fed continually on blood. Contemporaries discussed the difficulties of satisfying armies' appetites, and the cardinal de Richelieu offered a "remedy" for the subsistence of armies.[2] Early seventeenth-century military thinkers and reformers were deeply concerned with using military drill to establish discipline and, ideally, to form military units into articulated single bodies whose each and every movement was orchestrated by their commanders.[3] Corporeal metaphors referred not only to the state as a body politic, but also to a field army as a corpulent giant, resembling François Rabelais's Gargantua.[4] Provincial warrior nobles played central roles in organizing civil warfare by constructing, maintaining, and financing their personal armies.

CONSTRUCTING ARMIES

In the early seventeenth-century, French field armies were formed in ways which were quite distinct from the contemporary Spanish or Swedish armies that are more frequently studied. Charles Tilly calls the predominant system of warmaking during the fifteenth to seventeenth centuries "brokerage," a system based on "mercenary forces recruited by contractors," and state reliance on "independent capitalists" for loans, enterprise, and taxation.[5] Applying John A. Lynn's suggestive model of army style, one could characterize the French field armies of the early seventeenth-century civil wars as "aggregate-contract" armies that already incorporated some elements of the "state-commission" army style. This seems to support his theory, since he posits the late sixteenth and early seventeenth centuries as the point of transition from the aggregate-contract to state-commission army style.[6] The French king and his nobles constructed field armies using techniques similar to those used by other contemporary states, but adapted to French society and to the circumstances of religious and civil warfare.

Nucleus of an Army

Early modern French field armies normally formed around a nucleus, or core, of military units. Scholars have frequently pointed to a small standing army as a nucleus for royal armies, and contemporaries certainly contemplated this idea. Richelieu recommended in 1627 that

> the king must always have a corps of 10,000 infantry and 1,500 cavalry [ready] to go at a moment's notice, with His Majesty at their head. The corps must be kept in a place where the king sees it frequently so as to keep it whole, otherwise the dispersed troops will always be in the pay of their leaders and the king poorly served. Only a few troops are needed in Poitou, the Cévennes, and Languedoc, with men who would be notified of the routes by which they are to march and who would furnish them with food, hay, and oats at a certain price, with most of the costs to be settled in council and paid by the king, for which a specific levy would be made afterwards in the places where the troops had passed.[7]

But Richelieu's recommendations were an impractical fantasy in the circumstances that prevailed. Such a force would have been ill suited both for internal civil conflicts in southern France and for external threats from Spain or Savoy. The French monarch did maintain a few units on a permanent basis in the early seventeenth century, but these royal standing forces were divided into garrisons, the largest concentrations normally being around Paris and the northeastern border facing the Habsburg Netherlands. Such a force could not react quickly to threats posed by "rebel" nobles and Huguenots in southern France. Standing forces had to unite with other standing forces and newly raised troops to form field army organizations capable of conducting operations. The king's standing forces did not amount to a standing army in the sense of the corps that Richelieu had envisaged.

Significant distinctions differentiated peacetime and wartime armed forces in early seventeenth-century France. Peacetime royal armed forces in the early seventeenth century essentially consisted of royal garrisons located throughout the kingdom. Royal garrisons could be drawn from the so-called *vieux* and *pétits-vieux régiments* (senior infantry regiments that were permanently established), parceled out into company-strength garrisons. Many garrisons seem to have been composed of locally raised forces, however. The designation as a "royal" garrison had more to do with the source of payments for the troops than with anything else. There seems to have been no centralized record-keeping of garrison sites and sizes, however. Individual *commissaires des guerres,* royal officers who managed regular war finance, and other financial administrators kept track of garrison payments and lists of the garrisons for which they were responsible. A list of payments by Jean Fabry, a commissaire des guerres, to garrisons gives some idea of the royal garrisons in Bas Languedoc, but it shows only the garrisons that Fabry paid himself.[8] Other royal garrisons existed in Bas Languedoc and many more in Haut Languedoc.

None of the field armies that fought in the civil wars in early seventeenth-century France were composed exclusively of standing armed forces. A royal field army led personally by the king might form around his household troops and *vieux régiments,* but the insufficiency of royal standing forces alone for any active campaigning is shown by Paul Phélypeaux de Pontchartrain's assessment of Louis XIII's nuclear army in 1620. He recounts that, "the king resolved to leave Paris, having with him at the moment only the regiments of his gardes françaises and [gardes] suisses on foot, his company of gendarmes, his chevaux-légers, very poorly armed and incomplete, and his officers and domestics, and bodyguard—of the seigneurs and the nobility, there were very few there."[9] This force of royal household troops may have numbered several thousand men, but it was incapable of any serious operations without significant reinforcements.

The king could not consistently rely on his other standing forces, the *vieux régi-ments* and compagnies d'ordonnance, as a nucleus for a field army. Companies of a *vieux régiment* were frequently dispersed into garrisons all across France. Other *vieux régiments* remained together, but posted in their home provinces and unable to quickly join the royal household troops at court. The compagnies d'ordonnance were likewise spread out and their loyalties to their captains made them of questionable use during periods of civil warfare. Thus, standing regular forces contributed to many operations, but only occasionally formed the organizational basis for field armies.

Armies led by provincial governors or lieutenant generals tended to coalesce around the noble officer's own household troops and compagnies d'ordonnance. For Huguenot armies, the nucleus would be Calvinist nobles' household troops and town garrisons. Huguenot armies were constructed to deal with the defensive needs of the local Huguenot assemblies, so the places de sûreté provided troops and recruiting bases to form the nucleus of a Huguenot field army. The main Huguenot garrisons in Guyenne were used to form Calvinist armies in that province.[10]

The Huguenots in the province of Languedoc could also draw upon large numbers of garrisons to form their army nuclei. The official places de sûreté provided the principal Calvinist garrisons in Languedoc.[11] But other garrisons were located in Huguenot nobles' châteaux and governments, as well as in towns with a Calvinist-dominated population. Only the places de sûreté had official legal standing and received royal funds to pay for their garrisons, but many Huguenot nobles and communities were willing to pay to maintain garrisons where places de sûreté were lacking. During civil wars, these garrisons provided the core of troops around which Huguenot armies were created.

Each field army was a unique creation, assembled for distinct purposes within specific political and military contexts. James B. Wood notes the wide discrepancies in the proportion of infantry to cavalry in the royal field armies of the 1560s and 1570s.[12] Army size and composition varied widely during the French Wars of Religion, depending especially on the commander and his clients, but some basic elements can be discerned.

Army Elements

A variety of military units were needed to form a field army, and each had a specialized role within the organization. Tactical, strategic, social, and political imperatives shaped the functions and operations of each unit type. Although contemporaries often discussed differences in troop types based on regional or "national" characteristics, Wood convincingly demonstrates several reasons for unit specialization within French armies.[13] Army commanders thus had to assemble various army elements to form effective field armies.

Royal household cavalry would normally accompany a field army commanded personally by the king. The king's household cavalry might also accompany important field armies led by the king's favorites. Several royal family members also had household cavalry units, and field armies of great nobles and royal family members often relied on these forces for their shock troops.

The *compagnies d'ordonnance*, established by Charles VII in 1455, provided the bulk of the gendarmes during the French Wars of Religion. Each company was commanded by a prominent noble and was in theory a standing unit held in garrison and paid by the royal treasury. But the compagnies d'ordonnance can hardly be considered part of a standing permanent army during periods of civil warfare in France. Not all companies were kept under arms, and those that were followed their captains, since the companies were recruited through clientage ties. The gendarmes were considered shock troops, to be used in battle as the major offensive punch of an army. They were mobile, but expensive.[14] Other gendarmes served as bodyguards in the households of significant nobles, especially the *grands*. These personal guard units were almost identical to the compagnies d'ordonnance, except that they normally received no pay from the king. The clientele recruitment so prevalent in all gendarme units was even more essential in guard units.

Noble volunteers served as cavalry, buttressing the numbers of gendarmes in field armies. Many nobles served voluntarily in the armies fighting in southern France, especially in large-scale operations like the siege of Montauban in 1621, where many Calvinist nobles and their entourages aided the defenders.[15] During sieges, noble volunteers frequently fought as infantry. At the siege of Nérac in 1621, Catholic noble volunteers "mingled with the regiments and one saw with each mestre de camp 150 gentlemen, pike in hand, with as much obedience as the disciplined soldiers,[which] is not ordinary."[16]

The royal household cavalry and gendarmes were supported by other cavalry units, especially the *chevaux-légers*, which are frequently misconstrued as light cavalry. These units were normally medium cavalry, armored nearly as well as the gendarmes but probably mounted on smaller horses. The chevaux-légers were armed with swords instead of the lances carried by the gendarmes they supported. The chevaux-légers were not quite as expensive as the gendarmes to maintain.[17]

Support cavalry also consisted of *arquebusiers à cheval, carabiniers,* and *reiters.* Arquebusiers à cheval and carabins seem to have been essentially identical, cavalry mounted on small horses armed with pistols and arquebus. These troops may have acted at times as mobile infantry, fighting dismounted. The German *reiters,* who had played such a vital role in the wars of the 1560s and 1570s, rarely participated in the early seventeenth-century French civil wars, largely due to the onset of the Thirty Years' War in Germany. When they did appear in French armies, reiters were armed with pistols and swords, acting as medium cavalry or mounted infantry.[18] All of these support cavalry were expected to aid the heavy cavalry on the battlefield. They provided mobility for the army by scouting, mounting siege relief efforts, and preventing enemy attempts to relieve sieges. These were vital roles for a style of warfare which relied heavily on siege warfare and raiding.

The royal household infantry served as the personal bodyguard for the king and as an elite infantry force in many royal field armies. An army commanded by the king in person would have elements of the bodyguards with him. The *gardes françaises* was immense, composed of twenty companies of 120 men each. The *gardes suisses* was made up of two companies, each of 300 men. These companies were parceled out to different garrison, bodyguard, and operational forces. Companies of the gardes françaises served in a number of armies in Languedoc and Guyenne during the early seventeenth century.[19]

Infantry regiments composed of French subjects formed the backbone of all field armies fighting in the civil wars, since they were far more numerous than the cavalry or artillery. Infantry were organized into five-, ten-, or twenty-company regiments, with varying company sizes. French regimental organization had gradually developed in the late sixteenth century and was not standardized. The six *vieux régiments* held seniority within the French regular infantry and were large semi-permanent organizations, with twenty companies each. The *petits-vieux régiments,* each composed of ten companies, were developing into regular standing forces in the early seventeenth century.[20] An infantry company was normally composed of 100 men, although some companies might number as many as 150 or 200 men. During campaigns, attrition would reduce companies' effectives to far below their assigned strengths. A muster roll from 1616 gives us a glimpse at a typical infantry company of 100 men. It was composed of a captain, a lieutenant, an ensign, two sergeants, two corporals, a drummer, a fifer, 30 musketeers, 30 pikemen, and 31 arquebusiers.[21] On the battlefield the infantry ideally provided endurance and a stable line of battle. An infantry regiment might conduct operations as a unit, but regiments were frequently divided, with various

companies performing differing duties in diverse locations. All of the companies of a regiment that were present at a combat would fight together in a *gros
d'infanterie*, or battalion. A *gros* might also be a larger formation of infantry composed of numerous companies from several regiments.[22]

Foreign infantry played important specialist roles in many French armies.
Swiss infantry served in royal armies and in personal armies led by "rebel" nobles. A *colonel général des suisses* handled royal recruitment of Swiss infantry by
negotiating with Swiss cantons and individual Swiss captains. The Swiss units
were armed almost exclusively with pikes and were valued for their battlefield
prowess as shock troops. Their usefulness in sieges, garrison duty, and other
operations was limited, though. German *Landsknecht* infantry were considered
more versatile, having a balance of pike and musket-armed troops. German
princes negotiated with Louis XIII or with French nobles for terms of recruitment, which might specify a force raised and equipped by the German prince or
provide for French officers to enter a prince's territory to recruit their own units.
Lorraine soldiers, including the Phalsbourg regiment, campaigned with royal
armies in Languedoc in the 1620s. Italian infantry played a small role in the
early seventeenth-century civil wars, primarily due to frequent wars in northern Italy and increasing Spanish Habsburg involvement in the Thirty Years'
War. Corsican infantry also appear to have served in southern France in small
numbers.[23]

Since sieges characterized much of the warfare in Languedoc and Guyenne,
artillery provided major offensive power for a field army, allowing it to force
a decision more quickly in small sieges and to commit to sieges of large, well-
defended towns. But artillery pieces were not absolutely necessary for campaigning. Many armies had limited artillery forces, and significant artillery trains
were often procured only when a lengthy siege seemed imminent. Most field
armies took small towns and châteaux by assault, since defenders in many towns
in southern France often had little or no effective artillery. Moreover, many
towns were located on hilltops or in mountainous regions, where transporting
artillery to the site and employing artillery effectively was extremely difficult.

Artillery was classified into two broad categories, siege artillery and lightweight artillery. Siege artillery pieces had to be powerful enough to blast apart
fortifications and produce breaches. Four main types of siege guns were used:
cannon, grand culverin, bastarde, and *moyenne.* All of these guns were heavy and
difficult to transport. Lightweight artillery consisted of artillery pieces that were
deemed too light for use against fortifications, but could be effective against
enemy personnel. Two major types of lightweight artillery existed, the *faucon*

and *fauconneau*. Artillery pieces were produced by craftsmen using artisanal practices, giving an individual character to each piece. The lack of standardization in artillery caliber and the wide variety of artillery pieces meant that separate shot had to be procured and transported for each type of artillery, and potentially for each individual gun.[24]

Field armies operating in southern France needed pioneers and engineers to maneuver in difficult terrain and to conduct sieges. Some Huguenot and Catholic armies hired professional specialists to improve fortifications and conduct sieges. Italian and French military engineers both worked to improve the defenses of Huguenot cities in southern France and served in the armies besieging them.[25] Pioneers performed dangerous, vital work on trenches and fortifications during siege operations. Field armies needed engineers and pioneers for crossing rivers, improving roads, and maneuvering artillery, especially in the mountainous Cévennes and Vivarais.

Supply trains and support personnel were essential to the very existence of field armies. A very small force might be able to perform a *chevauchée*, raiding while living off the land, but an army of any consequence depended on a logistical tail of wagons, wagoneers, munitions, and supplies. A supply base would be used as a depot for rations, fodder, equipment, shot, arms, and gunpowder. Field armies on the march could use the established *étapes* system at times, but in other situations, rations would be purchased or requisitioned. No field armies had regular supply services or professional logistical personnel, so civilian merchants and entrepreneurs provided supplies and rations to troops for a cost.

Naval forces could also play a role in military operations in Languedoc and Guyenne. Operations conducted along the Rhône, Tarn, Gard, and Garonne river valleys were aided by riverine naval support, primarily in a supply and transport capacity. Riverine transport of artillery and munitions was especially important.[26] Vessels were also used to patrol hostile areas and observe enemy strongholds, as when Catholic nobles outfitted several boats to watch over the Huguenot-controlled town of Le Pouzin on the Rhône in 1628. Mediterranean galleys seem not to have had much of a role in the warfare in Languedoc, but naval vessels off the Atlantic coast did play a limited role supporting operations on land in Guyenne, especially around the mouth of the Garonne river. Dutch ships tried to transport arms to Calvinist militants in southern France, rounding Gibraltar and landing along the Languedoc coast. But naval participation in the Languedoc and Guyenne conflicts remained limited, unlike the substantial naval component to the operations at the siege of La Rochelle further up the

Atlantic coast. The only major naval operation involving Languedoc seems to have been preparations by the duc de Montmorency, admiral of France, to lead a flotilla to the siege of La Rochelle.[27]

Army Styles

Commanders assembled army elements in different combinations around army nuclei to produce effective field armies. While each field army was thus a unique creation, some patterns may be discerned. Royal field armies under the direct command of the king were normally large armies, sometimes over 20,000 men strong. The king assembled armies using his household troops, *vieux régiments*, and locally raised forces. Field armies led by high command or provincial officers were generally smaller, often composed of 3,000–6,000 men. A relatively representative example is the army that Pons de Lauzières marquis de Thémines assembled to campaign in Haut Languedoc and Foix in 1625. This force of about 5,500 infantry and 600 cavalry consisted of five infantry regiments and seven companies of cavalry—which were all from Languedoc, where Thémines had estates, apart from the regiment de Normandie. When the army headed to Foix, Thémines recruited several additional regiments in that region.[28]

The field armies commanded by "rebel" nobles were similar to the royalist armies led by nobles such as Thémines. Usually, no *vieux régiments* would bolster the strengths of "rebel" forces, though. The field army that the duc d'Épernon raised to support Marie de Médicis in 1617 was a fairly typical "rebel" army. He led four regiments of infantry and 500–600 noble cavalry recruited from among his relatives and clients. Épernon's bodyguards, 120 men wearing his livery, completed his army of about 4,500 infantry and 700 cavalry. After launching his campaign, Épernon recruited more troops, and his army may have risen to 9,000.[29]

Huguenot army style varied from other army styles somewhat, yet Calvinist armies had needs similar to royal armies or Catholic "rebels." Huguenot field armies were normally equipped to take châteaux and towns by siege or assault, and they might have to fight battles against small and moderate-sized enemy armies. Most important, Huguenot armies had to be able to relieve sieges of Calvinist-controlled towns. In the sixteenth century, Huguenot armies had frequently contained large numbers of German mercenaries and allies, but in the early seventeenth, French Calvinists could count on little foreign manpower. English and Dutch aid to Huguenots in this period was largely in the form of supplies, arms, money, and providing refuge. The one major foreign intervention in this period was the duke of Buckingham's attempt to aid the Huguenot defense of La Rochelle. Jean de Pablo argues that German reiters "constituted the essential element of the Huguenot cavalry" in the late sixteenth century,[30] and lack of them may therefore have seriously hampered the Huguenot armies in the early seventeenth century. Steven Lowenstein finds many similarities between the royal military system and the Huguenot armed forces, asserting that the Huguenot provincial units were "organized almost exactly like the royal army."[31] Lowenstein suggests that the Huguenot armies were more modern than their Catholic counterparts, arguing that "the companies of the Protestant army tended to be the same size or perhaps slightly smaller than the analogous units in the royal army. This represented the modernizing tendency of armies of the period, away from large unwieldy units towards smaller ones, easier to maneuver in an age of firepower."[32] Manuscript muster rolls and account books indicate no consistent difference between the size of companies based on confession, and I would argue that no basis exists for attributing modernity to the Calvinist forces. Huguenot armies did exhibit a few special characteristics, though, since Reformed circles and assemblies structured Huguenot army style somewhat differently, and the Huguenot high command relied heavily on a small group of noble protectors as commanders.[33]

MAINTAINING ARMIES

While the royal treasury provided warrior nobles with some financial aid for recruiting troops, maintaining troops in the field was left largely to their officers. David Parrott finds that "far more than the system for the initial recruitment of the troops, the mechanism by which they were paid once *sur pied* would appear to have been devised with the express purpose of spreading the financial burden across from the crown to its officers."[34] Army commanders and regimental officers had to provide for the needs of their troops on campaign or personally arrange for others to take care of those needs.

The Costs of Mobilization

The costs of the initial recruitment of troops could be staggering. Officers had to find and summon recruits, outfit them, equip them, and arm them. Certain troops would bring their own equipment and arms, particularly noble volunteers and gendarmes. Officers might provide troops with some articles of clothing, but no standard uniforms existed. Some nobles dressed their units, especially gendarmes or bodyguards, in their livery. Initial recruitment costs seem to have varied widely by troop type and situation, and cavalry units were certainly much more expensive to raise than infantry. Parrott provides some evidence suggesting that a company of gendarmes would cost a minimum of 2,000 écus (equivalent to 6,000 livres) to raise, and he estimates the cost of raising an infantry company in the 1630s as 3,000 livres.[35] Yet mobilization costs seem to have varied widely during the civil conflicts of the early seventeenth century. The costs of raising some companies reached the levels cited above, but the seigneur de Châtillon allowed only 300 livres for the sieur de Pesat to raise his infantry company in 1621.[36]

The dramatic army growth of the late sixteenth and early seventeenth centuries greatly expanded mobilization costs.[37] Although the French royal state had to meet some military expenditures in peacetime, massive military mobilizations during wartime severely burdened royal financial systems. Wood stresses that royal military budgets in France reflected costs that were "overwhelmingly labor-intensive."[38] Entirely new regiments and companies were formed during each civil conflict in this period, and these new military units were mobilized at the expense of their officers.[39]

The costs of raising a five-company infantry regiment illustrate the difficulties of assessing the expenses of mobilization. Regiments with five companies and a nominal strength of about 500 men were commonly raised in southern France, allowing some basis for comparative analysis of mobilization costs. In March 1621, the Estates of Languedoc approved payments of 200 écus (or 600 livres) to each captain in the five Catholic regiments, each with a strength of five companies, being raised by the duc de Montmorency.[40] The baron de Ganges, commander of a Huguenot regiment in 1621, received 1,500 livres "for the expenses that are advisable to make in the raising of a regiment of five companies of 100 infantry each that we have ordered him to put on foot."[41] Just over a month later, Huguenot mestre de camp du Pillon received 4,500 livres in two payments for raising an identical regiment.[42] The syndic of Vivarais paid the Catholic baron de Pérault 1,500 livres in 1628 "to pay for half of the costs of the levy of 500 men of the said regiment." The other half of the total 3,000 livres estimated as the cost of raising Pérault's regiment was presumably paid by the baron himself.[43] So the compensation paid to nobles for their expenses in raising infantry regiments, which were—at least on paper—identical, could actually vary enormously.

It is unclear how significantly the actual costs of raising troops varied, since nobles had to deal with local economic situations. Officers seem to have had their own personal recruitment practices and procedures. The duc de Rohan, for example, ordered the southern French Reformed communities that raised companies to provide the troops with four days of rations when they left to join other Huguenot forces.[44] Some variations in mobilization costs may be explained by difficulties in finding recruits or by rising wages, but varying amounts of payments to nobles could also reflect individual political circumstances. Attempts to attract preferred noble officers may have raised mobilization costs. Certain differences in recruitment costs may also reflect the status and rank of the nobles conducting the mobilization.

Warrior nobles employed a semi-entrepreneurial approach to the enormous initial costs of mobilizing military forces. Officers frequently appealed for direct state aid to finance recruitment. The marquis d'Aubeterre requested money to recruit troops and to pay his soldiers already under arms in 1615, protesting that he lacked both funds and support in the region, "where the soldiers slip away to enjoy the license that they find among the enemy troops."[45] Claude d'Hautefort similarly complained of the extraordinary expenses he incurred in mobilizing for civil war.[46]

Contributions from the royal government and local communities provided seed-money to assist warrior nobles in covering the initial costs of mobilization. Army commanders and mestres de camp sometimes offered financial incentives to motivate other nobles to serve with them. The duc de Lesdiguières was given charge of recruitment efforts in 1619. He wrote to a noble that

> having been commanded by the king to raise a regiment of foot for his service, I thought it possible that you would do me the favor of taking a company. I have always hoped to receive proofs of your friendship on such occasions, and as none could be more important, I believe also that you will accept an offer that gives you the means to serve His Majesty usefully, even as you assist me. They promise me 400 écus per company and I shall likewise give you as much as I can. I await your response.[47]

Officers frequently used both state funds and their own fortunes to pay for recruitment and for their subordinates. Thus, in seeking additional resources from the royal government, nobles could cite the great expenses they had already incurred.[48]

Mobilization went on continuously during civil conflicts. Early seventeenth-century nobles never considered recruitment complete, and they frequently discussed "refreshing" their companies and regiments.[49] Mobilization costs thus represented continuous expenditures, as noble officers searched for new recruits to replace casualties. Officers sometimes split the costs of renewing units with the central government or with other regional elites. Noting that he had "received orders from monseigneur le prince to hold [the baron de Pérault's] regiment together, and from monsieur de Montmorency to bring it up to the number of 1,000 infantry," the duc de Ventadour ordered the syndic and deputies of Vivarais, "to pay the sieur de Pérault the sum of 1,500 livres to pay half of his expenses for the levy of 500 men for his said regiment, which the said syndic and deputies shall be constrained [to do], as for the personal affairs of His Majesty."[50] Noble military officers probably bore most of the costs of recruiting replacements, as well as of maintaining their troops in the field.

Bread, Wine, and Meat

During the French civil wars of the early seventeenth century, officers' and soldiers' staple food was the *pain de munition*, or bread ration, and the symbolic value of bread was probably as great for early modern soldiers as it was for contemporary peasants and artisans.[51] Field army commanders specified the quality and amount of rations to be issued. The duc de Montmorency specified that in his army, "the bread must be 18 ounces in dough and . . . 16 ounces baked." The wine ration for his troops was to be a *quarton* per soldier, presumably using the local liquid measures, which varied. Meat would be given out when it was available.[52] Lynn finds that "although the system of providing rations changed, the amount of food, particularly bread, prescribed for men on campaign remained essentially constant." Royal regulations issued in 1629 and 1636 set soldiers' daily ration at 24 ounces of bread, one pint of wine, and one pound of meat.[53] During early seventeenth-century civil conflicts, however, ration amounts seem to have been more variable.

Feeding an army involved distributing huge amounts of bread, wine, and meat to soldiers according to their unit type and rank. Graduated amounts of rations were given out to soldiers in different cavalry and infantry companies, and the compagnies d'ordonnance were especially favored due to their units' higher status and to the large number of nobles serving in their ranks. Each gendarme received 6 loaves of bread, while each cavalry trooper in the chevaux-légers and arquebusiers à cheval companies got 4 loaves. Soldiers in infantry companies and artillery crews received 3 loaves daily.[54] While the individual infantry soldiers received less rations than cavalrymen, there were usually far more infantry units than cavalry units in an army, and the infantry companies were often larger than cavalry companies. The companies of chevaux-légers in the duc de Montmorency's army in 1621 each received 200 loaves of bread daily.[55]

Other receipts show variances in the rations distributed to chevaux-légers. Keeping an army in the field also required supplying garrisons and prisoners with food. Documents concerning the feeding of prisoners are very rare, but records of the seigneur de Châtillon's Huguenot army in 1621 specify payments for bread rations for Catholic prisoners held at Lunel.[56]

Officers were given rations not only for themselves, but for their servants and followers. Contemporary logistical and war finance documents show the rations given out to a field army's officers.[57] The descending scale of the amount of rations reflects the varying scale of the noble officers' followings as well as their status. High-ranking commanders had extensive numbers of household members, clients, and subordinates to feed daily, and these followers, who were mostly nobles, expected to be fed well. Soldiers in cavalry units received more rations than their infantry counterparts. This situation may have been due to the additional servants and lackeys that cavalrymen normally had with them. Feeding warrior noble officers and their entourages was a significant financial and supply challenge.

Royal ordonnances and military treatises often stipulated that soldiers were to purchase their rations daily from local communities, but financial shortfalls and payment delays frequently made this impossible. Wood explains that:

> the bread ration, even though the center of the soldiers' diet, was not enough in and of itself to nourish the army, and when pay failed, and loans from their officers dried up, or even when there was pay but local conditions of shortage greatly inflated prices, troops were unable to obtain the portions of meat, wine, legumes, and other fresh products which they desperately needed, and thought they were entitled to, without extorting it from their civilian hosts, the localities they were staying in, or the areas they were passing through.[58]

Because of these logistical problems, most armies fed their soldiers through complex contributions systems that required urban communities and dioceses to provide rations for the troops operating in their areas. A field army's provosts and archers negotiated prices with merchants and consuls.[59] Consuls kept records of the number of troops who lodged within their walls, and for how many days. Dioceses were to prepare supplies in advance in case of passage of troops. Montmorency indicated that in each diocese in Languedoc, "there shall likewise be a small store of munitions and wheat to have recourse to if the need arises there. To these ends, [the dioceses] are given power, following [the orders] that we have here from His Majesty, to impose in the accustomed manner the sum that they judge necessary for this effect."[60] The costs of supplying troops would later be claimed by towns and dioceses against the next taxation levied on them.

Noble military officers negotiated contracts with merchants to supply their military forces, which often represented armed communities as large as the most populous cities in southern France.[61] The civilian merchants who provided the *pain de munition*, wine, and other food that constituted the soldiers' rations became known as *munitionnaires*.[62] During long sieges, huge contracts could be awarded to munitionnaires to supply daily rations. The royal army camped outside La Rochelle in 1572 contracted with merchants from Niort "to furnish *every day*, for a period of six months, 30,000 12-ounce loaves of bread, 10,800 *pintes* of wine, and 20,000 *livres* of beef."[63] A merchant in Bourg-Saint-Andéol contracted to provide an extraordinary 39,966 loaves of bread to five Catholic regiments marching to join the siege of Privas in 1629.[64]

Rations and supplies seem to have been distributed in an improvised manner. The fragmented accounting documents for field armies operating in southern France in the early seventeenth century suggest that military officers issued separate orders to supply their units and detachments. The muster rolls and account books, which recorded the payments and supplies distributed to troops, often include entries for detachments as small as fifteen men. Numerous receipts survive showing rations given to small bands of soldiers and artillery as they moved about Languedoc and Guyenne, sometimes covering only a few days' supplies.[65] Military officers seem to have used multiple financial officers, merchant contractors, and artisans to feed their troops. Bakers, butchers, and small merchants often traveled with armies, providing additional food to troops.[66]

Warrior nobles were also closely involved in the actual distribution of rations to their troops. Noble captains, lieutenants, and ensigns often signed receipts for their units' rations in their own hands. In other cases, nobles' clients and household members who were not company or regimental officers handled the daily rations. Some of the rations provided to Guillaume de Balazuc de Montréal's forces in 1622 were received by two of his *hommes de chambre*.[67] Captains and mestres de camp often paid out of their own pockets for soldiers' rations during campaigns. Claude de Calvière baron de Saint-Côme claimed that he had provided the wine ration for his entire regiment "out of his own purse" during 1621.[68]

Wages, Lodging, and Supplies

Maintaining troops on campaign also involved organizing supplies, lodging, and wages for the soldiers, as well as paying for those services. Paying soldiers' wages was a vital aspect of maintaining troops in the field and holding an army together. Wood finds that around 90 percent of royal military budgets in the 1560s and 1570s went to pay soldiers' salaries rather than for military supplies and equipment.[69] The budgets of French monarchs throughout the late sixteenth and early seventeenth centuries similarly allocated vast sums for soldiers' pay.

Even with royal attention to wages, paying soldiers' salaries was complex and costly. Soldiers' wages varied by rank and by unit type, and cavalrymen were paid much more than infantrymen. The ordonnances issued by the king, army commanders, or military officers fixed pay scales, sometimes calculating wages based on monthly rates, although a "month" normally represented an arbitrary number of days of service, often fixed at 36 days. Many military officers adopted more flexible pay scales based on a daily rate, which could be applied to payments when funds were available. André Corvisier cites a 1629 daily pay scale of 6 sous for common soldiers and 12 for veterans.[70] A pay scale issued by the duc de Montmorency attempted to provide a standard daily wage of 7 sous for all the infantry units under his command in 1622.[71] Cavalry troopers received much higher wages: a carabinier might be paid upwards of 20 sous and a gendarme 27 sous. The monthly wages for the seventy-four officers and men in the duc de Rohan's company of gendarmes in 1622 totaled a staggering 7,300 livres.[72] Wages for companies varied widely based on the reputation of their unit and the status of their captain, even within the same class of military unit. The arquebusiers à cheval in the marquis de Portes's company received 27 livres monthly, while the chevaux-légers in Disimieu's similar company earned 40 livres per month. Gendarmes serving in the duc de Montmorency's company received 180 livres per month, twice as much as those in Rohan's company.[73]

Whatever their stipulated wages, soldiers routinely went unpaid for long periods of time. Pay was regularly months in arrears, sometimes wages lagged more than a year behind. Lack of payment of soldiers' wages was at least in part due to noble officers' inability or unwillingness to pay them. Warrior nobles often asked the monarch for money to pay their troops, as Antoine Jaubert de Barrault comte de Blaignac did in 1616.[74] Another military officer who was on campaign that year complained of having no way to pay his troops in the field. When he found out that his troops were not to be paid through the accounts of the maréchal de Roquelaure, he pleaded with the king: "I have withdrawn, waiting to know what moneys it pleases Your Majesty to arrange for me for the maintenance of my soldiers."[75] However, claims of monetary exhaustion must be interpreted cautiously, acknowledging that warrior nobles often employed such rhetorical language in order to seek additional funds.

Army commanders and military officers arranged lodging and supplies for their troops on campaign. A complex system of *routes et étapes* had been developed by the sixteenth century for moving troops along predetermined military routes within the kingdom.[76] This system had been devised to facilitate troop movements within the kingdom during peacetime or during foreign wars. A series of commissaires de guerres administered the *étapes* system and coordinated billeting practices for field armies within France.[77] During the early seventeenth century, a variety of commissaires and other local officials managed the payments and logistical arrangements for lodging.[78]

Noble officers made use of the *étapes* system, yet its regularized logistical practices could hardly function normally during civil wars. The duc de Montmorency tried to organize the quartering of his troops through general regulations for the entire province of Languedoc. The syndics, commissaires, and other officers in charge of quartering troops were to specify "the number of days that the said soldiers will have to remain there, the nights or dinners of their passage, and the number of men of which the companies are composed, which could equally be verified by the consuls of the said places."[79] Montmorency issued extraordinarily detailed orders regarding the movements of troops as he assembled a field army in Languedoc in 1622:

> When marching, the infantry should make three leagues a day, and the cavalry four, without turning to the right or to the left, and should lodge where their orders send them and not elsewhere. If they are paid, they must be content to have fire, bed, light, and other necessities. And if they are not, they are to have bread, wine, meat, oats, and fodder up to the limit of their pay. . . . Otherwise, everyone would be permitted to demand other things from the said quarters, from other parishes, or from their hosts.[80]

The thousands of payment orders, receipts, account books, and complaints conserved in archives across southern France demonstrate the diversity of local responses to such directives.

In addition to coordinating the *étapes* system, nobles arranged necessary supplies and transportation through forced contributions and requisitioning. Horses had to be provided with large amounts of oats and fodder daily. In Montmorency's army, four *picotins* (approximately eight liters) of oats were to be given to each horse.[81] Military officers organized forage parties to gather fodder for their forces' horses, since "an army simply had to harvest its own fodder most of the time, and the task of reaping it was great."[82] Boats sometimes were requisitioned and used for riverine transport of supplies, especially on the Garonne and the Rhône.

Garrisons proliferated throughout Languedoc and Guyenne during civil wars, creating logistical difficulties for the army commanders and officers who managed their supplies. The pay of wartime garrisons was similar to that of infantrymen with field armies; indeed, many of the soldiers in such garrisons were detached from armies.[83] Regional military and administrative officers handled most southern French garrisons, but the royal government sometimes issued orders for the payment of certain garrisons, as shown in an *état* for Languedoc in 1615.[84] Expenditures for garrisons seem normally to have been handled on an ad hoc basis. The *trésorier général de l'extraordinaire des guerres* in Bas Languedoc composed an *état* of the payments to specific garrisons that were intended to disrupt Huguenot communications between Nîmes and the Cévennes in 1621.[85]

The cost-sharing arrangements used so often in war financing led to disputes over paying for garrisons. When Montmorency permitted some Velay nobles to create garrisons for their châteaux in 1621, he allowed them to charge the cost to town consuls, which would eventually be repaid by the syndics of the dioceses. However, this angered the consuls and the syndics, who opposed Montmorency's policy at the meeting of the estates of Languedoc later in the year. They first complained that the garrisons were actually unnecessary, charging that in one case "the said château is not considerable and there are no enemies of the king within six leagues." The consuls requested that a list be drawn up of "the unnecessary garrisons newly established in their dioceses." They felt that Montmorency was unaware of the burdens the dioceses were already bearing, and they requested that he "avoid seeking to ordain garrisons in the future or assigning payment to the towns and dioceses with first having heard the consuls and syndics on the necessity of the said garrisons."[86]

FINANCING ARMIES

"Too often taxation has been conceptualized as extraction," William Beik argues in a critique of the historians of early modern French finances and taxation, "What was really at stake, however, was distribution."[87] Indeed, the historiography of war finance has unfortunately focused on central governmental administration, seeing war finance as a problem of government effectiveness at resource mobilization.[88] According to state-centered theories of early modern finance, sinews of war carried vital resources through the body politic under the direction of the king. From this perspective, money represented the essential element necessary for waging warfare. The monarchical perspective of much war finance and taxation historiography becomes clear in discussions of the inefficiencies, corruption, and wastage that disrupted the flow of money to the king. Such studies use statist language to blame "corrupt" officers, "financier cartels," and "predator" contractors for frustrating royal ministers' policies. Analyses of war finance thus tend to privilege a bureaucratic vision of early modern governments and concentrate on the duties of various financial officers and their institutions.[89]

Historians attempting to reconstruct patterns of war finance during the civil conflicts of the late sixteenth and early seventeenth centuries face serious difficulties. The funding of civil warfare produced voluminous stacks of ordonnances, receipts, muster rolls, accounting books, and other financial documents. But these documents are parceled out to various archives and no coherent series of sources exists. Financial documents were usually only preserved in order for the holder of the documents to gain compensation for his expenditures. So the selection of remaining documents may not be representative, and they are often grouped together in ways convenient to individual financial officials, not to historians. Few local and regional administrations kept comprehensive budgets, further complicating the analysis of war finance. Finally, many documents were destroyed through the violence of civil warfare or by officers fearful of being branded as rebels.[90] Research on war finance must consider the complex shuffling of funds between a multitude of nobles, officials, and institutions involved in early modern finance. Following the entire paper trail of money during periods of civil war could threaten to consume a researcher's lifetime, but we can attempt a foray into the fragmentary sources, realizing at the outset that a full picture of early seventeenth-century war finance can probably never be adequately drawn.

This section examines how nobles financed civil warfare by tracing expenditures, allowing us to understand the everyday financing of civil warfare in the early seventeenth century. Beik's detailed analysis of "tax flows" in the province of Languedoc during Louis XIV's reign offers an intriguing model for interpreting expenditures on military forces and supply.[91] During the civil conflicts of the early seventeenth century, warrior noble officers played a key role in funding warfare, arranging credit, coordinating war finance, and authorizing military spending.

Accessing Financial Systems

Le nerf de la guerre, or the sinews of war, emerges as an important concept for war finance in contemporary discussions of army mobilization. This metaphor may have originated in descriptions of Roman catapults, but classical authors such as Tacitus, Cicero, and Vegetius had each offered definitions of the sinews of war in financial terms.[92] Fifteenth- and sixteenth-century humanist scholars and writers had debated this notion, and Niccolò Machiavelli expanded the concept, arguing that "Men, arms, money, and provisions are the sinews of war, but of these four, the first two are the most necessary; for men and arms will always find money and provisions, but money and provisions cannot always raise men and arms."[93] French humanists and military intellectuals added to the Renaissance Italian discourses on war finance, and François Rabelais had one of the characters in his popular satire *Gargantua* remark that "les nerfz des batailles sont les pecunes."[94] Armand de Gontaut baron de Biron explained that "the most important and chief point is finances, because without these, everything is stayed and nothing can be executed, it being the sinews of war."[95] Richelieu famously remarked that: "on a toujours dit que les finances sont les nerfs de l'Estat," reformulating the concept of sinews of war in a way that would become increasingly popular for seventeenth-century theories of mercantilism.[96]

The extension of money along the stretching tendons of the body politic provided a powerful metaphor for the process of financing warfare. The possession of piles or stacks of coins signified financial power through the ability to pay for officers' and soldiers' wages, food, supplies, weapons, and equipment. The continuous and unimpeded distribution of money indicated effective war finance and reflected the monarch's financial power, yet discussions of the channeling and circulation of money also suggest ways in which nobles accessed financial flows within France.

The accessibility of money was crucial to the waging of warfare, according to contemporary notions of the sinews of war. Money shortages and excessive debt were assumed to halt conflict, since they restricted monetary flow. Modern historians often follow this assumption, stressing the scarcity of gold and silver coins in early seventeenth-century France.[97] Certainly, the availability of coins presented problems for war finance, but Wood argues that during the early stages of the French Wars of Religion, "though a lack of money may have helped to bring each individual civil war to a halt. . . . it never prevented them from almost immediately breaking out again and becoming a chronic and almost continuous phenomenon."[98] Early seventeenth-century war finance was not as dependent on coins as the repeated evocations of the sinews of war might have us believe. Warrior noble officers found ample opportunities to utilize private and public monetary flows to finance civil warfare. Pension payments, official stipends, loans, gifts, and donations all fed money to military officers.

Attempts to manage currencies and prices during the sixteenth-century religious wars had produced increased flexibility in French finances. The so-called Price Revolution of the 1520s–1590s had produced massive inflation, with shipments of silver and gold from the Americas upsetting the stability of bimetallic currencies throughout Europe. Skyrocketing prices for staple crops and other goods, coupled with population growth and religious conflict, produced more frequent famines and complicated war finance.[99] Successive French royal governments attempted to deal with inflationary pressures, improve monetary flows, and restrict counterfeiting. Henri III had made the gold écu the standard monetary unit in accounting in 1577, but Henri IV changed monetary policy and restored the livre tournois as the money of account in 1602.[100] While monetary theorists continued to debate the ideal configuration of the monetary system during Louis XIII's reign, the livre as a money-of-account allowed more flexibility for both the king's financiers and the noble officers who were financing civil warfare in the early seventeenth century.

The sinews of war that fed early seventeenth-century civil warfare represented much more than monetary flows. Researchers exploring the concept of a General Crisis of the Seventeenth Century rightly highlight the extensive nonbudgetary and nonmonetary aspects of early modern states' financial systems.[101] In addition to utilizing currency, warrior nobles accessed diverse credit flows as they organized war finance. A wide range of credit mechanisms were available to noble military and administrative officers. Recent evidence on the ways in which nobles provided credit to finance Louis XIV's wars provocatively suggests possible avenues of noble financing of warfare earlier in the seventeenth century.[102] Noble officers could obtain credit by distributing favors, extending military protection, and promising future appointments to their clients and supporters.

The key relationships between captains and their infantry or cavalry companies were at the heart of the war financing system. Noble captains provided the key steady funding to their companies during civil warfare, supplemented by maintenance payments made by town consuls. Each captain received his funding through various direct payments made by a wide network of financial supporters. The king, corporate bodies, and individual warrior noble officers acquired funds through taxation, loans, and tax seizures, then made direct and indirect payments to officers to finance their war-making efforts. Reimbursements allowed financiers and noble officers to recoup at least part of their expenditures in civil war.

Redirecting Financial Flows

Taxation mobilized vast funds that were intended to fill the king's coffers and finance royal government, yet even in peacetime taxation served multiple purposes. Beik shows that less than half of the tax revenues from the province of Languedoc went directly to the king in the late seventeenth century due to the "sharing-out" of revenues with provincial nobles.[103] During the early seventeenth-century, even less tax funds seem to have reached the monarch because of the chaos of civil conflict and local demands for expenditures on warfare. The *recettes* of each tax *généralité* in the kingdom were used to finance civil warfare, but in war-torn regions, few of the *recettes* were ever paid to the royal government during civil conflicts.[104]

Warrior nobles implemented tax policies and facilitated tax collection during civil wars in southern France. Even during peacetime, tax collection procedures were incredibly complex, as Beik has aptly demonstrated for late-seventeenth-century Languedoc.[105] Numerous variations in tax laws and customs across regions of southern France created complications for tax collectors. The comté de Foix, for example, claimed specific tax privileges for the region, including a special contribution to the comte de Foix and local nobles.[106] These sorts of complications and variations were only magnified during civil conflicts. Henri II de Montmorency had to order the financial officials in the diocese de Montauban to proceed with collecting the *taille* in 1616, specifying that the funds would go to the *trésorier de l'extraordinaire des guerres* in order to pay the garrison at Ville-mur.[107] The redirecting of *taille* revenues to support local military activity seems to have been normal during the late sixteenth and early seventeenth centuries. James Collins argues that "a very significant part of the war budget was paid at the regional and local levels," pointing especially to the *taillon* and the *crue des prévôts des maréchaussées* taxes. Parrott supports Collins's analysis, emphasizing the "instability of this revenue system."[108]

Noble officers decided how tax collection should be administered within their jurisdictions during civil wars. The *taille* and *taillon* taxes were used heavily to pay for localized warfare. The provincial officers who issued the commissions for assessing the *taille* were the same officers who issued commissions for recruitment, allowing them to easily coordinate the use of both.[109] Nobles collaborated with numerous *trésoriers de France* on the raising and redirection of tax revenues, including the *trésoriers de la gendarmerie de France*, who raised taxes that went directly to pay noble officers.[110] The various *comptes* of the *trésoriers de l'extraordinaires des guerres*, such as Jean Fabry, demonstrate close coordination with provincial administrative officers in Languedoc.[111] Henri I de Montmorency gave explicit orders for the *trésoriers de France* in Bas Languedoc to divert taxes for military expenses during a period of civil unrest in 1613, even if full-scale civil war never broke out.[112] The duc d'Épernon raised an army in 1617 to oppose Huguenot armed aggression around La Rochelle, funding it with confiscated tax money and his own personal wealth.[113]

Provincial governors and lieutenant generals often instructed the *receveurs des tailles* and *receveurs généraux du taillon* within their provinces as to how to impose taxes. Article 74 of the Edict of Nantes stated that "those of the said religion may not in the future be surcharged and burdened more than the Catholics with any ordinary or extraordinary charges, according to their goods and faculties."[114] Nonetheless, Catholic army commanders and noble military officers operating in southern France seem to have singled out Huguenot towns and Calvinist residents of mixed-confessional communities to contribute taxes in order to pay Catholic soldiers' wages.[115] Conversely, Huguenot army commanders such as the duc de Rohan and the seigneur de Châtillon were often accused of taxing Catholic inhabitants of towns under their control.

Financial officials often found it impossible to raise taxes in war-torn areas, leading noble officers to intervene in tax collection more directly. Each diocese would normally send taxes collected to the bureaus of the *receveurs généraux,* but during civil wars the transportation of large amounts of coins proved very difficult. Military officers had to provide armed escorts to facilitate the transportation of any taxes that were collected. In Languedoc, the *receveurs généraux* gathered tax revenues at their offices in Toulouse and Montpellier when possible, but the office in the mixed-confessional city of Montpellier had to be transferred to Béziers in the early seventeenth century because of difficulties in transporting taxes.

When civil warfare prevented taxes from being raised in Gévaudan in 1622, Henri II de Montmorency ordered the marquis de Portes, his uncle, to raise troops that would allow the financial officers in the diocese to impose taxes amounting to 45,500 livres. The taxes raised would then go directly to the *commissaire de l'extraordinaire des guerres,* who would pay Portes and his 700 soldiers.[116] This sort of symbiotic relationship between tax collection and war finance seems to have been prevalent in this period. Military forces often actively collected taxes to finance their own campaigns, or they simply confiscated taxes that had already been collected.[117] Some military units stole taxes outright from their opponents during civil conflicts. A Huguenot raiding party operating in Rouergue in July 1621 reportedly seized the *taille* revenues and confiscated Catholics' belongings.[118] Later that year, Calvinist "rebels" seized taxes that had already been collected by the Catholic *receveur particulier* in Figeac, leading the parlement de Toulouse to transfer the *receveur's* office to the more secure Catholic town of Cahors.[119]

The estates of Languedoc coordinated war finances within the province, meeting during almost every civil conflict in the early seventeenth century. Noble members of the estates made contingency plans in December 1620 for the possibility of the outbreak of civil warfare in the province. The royal campaign in Béarn in fall 1620 had caused alarm in Calvinist communities throughout France and the transfer of the governorship of Privas had led to fighting in Vivarais between Huguenots and Catholics. In case of civil war, the estates of Languedoc and the sénéchausées would be assembled "to make the necessary advances by loan." The estates would also "give power to order the imposition to the said Pennautier, *trésorier de la Bourse*, up to the sum of 10,000 écus to provide for the advance which must be made for the levy of soldiers, which shall be distributed by the ordonnances of My Lord the duc de Montmorency governor of the province." If disorder and civil war intensified, the governor was to summon the estates to authorize more expenditures.[120] The provincial estates of Languedoc sometimes authorized individual payments for specific garrisons, as when the estates approved funds for the garrison of Grèze during their 1620 meeting.[121]

Nobles frequently redirected diocesan finances, ordering the *assiettes*, or diocesan assemblies, to issue payments to garrisons and captains in their own dioceses, or even neighboring ones. Dioceses sometimes complained about the onerous nature of such payments, as when the sieur de Rochepierre, syndic of Vivarais, claimed that the diocese was "greatly pressed on the payment of notable sums ordered either for diverse captains established in garrison in the said diocese or for the recompense of captains for claimed services made with their companies during these movements."[122] Each diocese in Languedoc and Guyenne could complain of similar financial burdens. The diocese of Albi provided for the wages and costs of supplying the bishop of Albi's regiment and the baron de Lescure's gendarmes in 1621, using loans to contribute 39,560 livres to cover the expenses of these units for four months. The diocese was to pay the interest on the loans taken out, but it was promised that it would later be compensated on the next imposition of the *taille*.[123] Dioceses often advanced future tax revenues or simply rerouted taxes already collected in order to finance military units and supplies.

Each diocese had some degree of latitude over its participation in war finance. Dioceses were expected to contribute for the recruitment and maintenance of military units, but they had near complete discretion over how to raise the necessary funds. Sometimes diocesan assiettes even determined the amount they would grant. Montmorency ordered the twenty-two dioceses in his government to prepare supplies and munitions to support the Catholic war effort in 1622, but he only called on each diocese to "impose in the accustomed manner the sum that they judge necessary to this end."[124] Military officers and nobles within the assiette assemblies thus coordinated regional war finances.

Consuls regularly paid for the wages, rations, and lodging of the troops that passed through their communities. Municipal leaders kept accounts of their expenses in hope of being compensated through reimbursements or credit against future taxation. A regulation issued by the governor of Languedoc insisted that "all the said costs shall be advanced, if possible, by the hosts or by the most neighboring of the said towns and parishes, then liquidated and imposed." But the consuls were to keep track of "the damages and interests that the said communities may have suffered."[125] Army commanders ordered communities to pay for their troops, but had to work with local magistrates to facilitate payments. The duc de Vendôme ordered "the consuls and inhabitants of the towns of Lautres, Graulhet, and other Catholics of the diocese of Castres to deliver . . . the sum of 2,200 livres to employ for the payment of the monthly wages of the 150 men, which the said diocese must furnish for its part, and a portion of the 2,000 men ordained by His Majesty to be levied and maintained during three months by several dioceses of this region and destined to serve in this army." Vendôme instructed the inhabitants to "borrow or impose on the diocese the necessary money" to pay for the troops that he had raised himself.[126]

A number of commissaires distributed money and managed the transactions within the financial system in conjunction with noble officers. The commissaires acted as inspectors and overseers, distributing payments only after verifying numbers of troops. Louis XIII sent the sieur de Rozeaux "among the troops of my army" to enforce his regulations and to oversee the payment of his troops.[127] However much commissaires may have wished to act as direct agents of the king, they were dependent on their ability to coordinate with powerful local noble officers who frequently gave their own orders. Adrian de Monluc, who was governor of Foix, thus ordered the regional *receveur des dîmes* to pay 600 livres for repairs of the château de Montault and the payment of its garrison.[128]

Constructing Alternative Economies

Historians of early modern war finance often assume that "military expenses could be met only with specie," but a whole series of alternative payment methods were available to the warrior nobles who managed everyday war expenditures in early seventeenth-century France.[129] The conditions of civil warfare encouraged the development of unofficial economic relations, illegal commerce, and alternative exchanges in southern France.[130] Noble military officers drew extensively on alternative financing during early seventeenth-century civil conflicts. Regardless of their religious and political affiliations, nobles employed multiple monetary and credit sources to finance civil war. Even royal armies required alternative financing, as demonstrated by a rare document that identifies twenty-four separate funding sources for the payment of a single month's costs of the maréchal de Cossé's royalist army in 1570.[131]

The financing of "rebel" Catholic and Huguenot forces differed little from the war finance practices used to fund the king's army. Nobles acting against royal ministers seized royal taxes, but also took control of the royal financial administration when possible. Royal financial and administrative officers ended up on all sides of each civil conflict. Other financiers remained neutral, financing their noble colleagues whatever their loyalties. Warrior nobles could always appropriate sections of the royal financial system and use them to finance their mobilization efforts.

The Huguenot war finance apparatus largely mirrored financial systems improvised by other unauthorized noble officers, but it seems to have had some unique features. Although many historians have portrayed Calvinist political assemblies, coin minting, and military organizations as evidence of a Huguenot "state within a state," the improvisations that Huguenots used to finance warfare locally seem to have been remarkably similar to those used by southern French Catholic nobles.[132] Steven Lowenstein argues that although the Huguenot and royal financial administrations differed in scale and complexity, they "differed little in methods or basic outlook."[133] Calvinist financiers, like their Catholic counterparts, collected money through direct taxation, indirect taxation, seizures of church property, and plunder. Direct taxation may have been the most important method of Huguenot war finance, since Reformed financiers obtained loans from individuals and towns against promises from future taxes. Calvinists did at times use informal networks and temple collections to collect money for military defenses or to send to their spiritual center in Geneva.[134] The overall effectiveness of the Calvinist financiers and their ability to procure needed funds for the Huguenot war effort in the 1620s remains unclear.

Huguenot military officers coordinated the financing of the Calvinist war effort in southern France. The Reformed general assemblies could not micromanage the financing of the entire war. The important Huguenot political and financial center of La Rochelle was far from Languedoc and frequently fairly inaccessible. According to Lowenstein, there were three interests involved in Huguenot provincial finances: the provincial assembly, the diocesan assiettes, and the army commanders.[135] Much of the financing was managed by army commanders, who could order payments whether there was money to cover the payment or not. Arrears could always be paid later. The seigneur de Châtillon, a

Huguenot military leader in Bas Languedoc in 1621, called for a *receveur general des finances* to pay the baron de Ganges 1,500 livres to raise an infantry regiment as quickly as possible.[136] Huguenot military commanders had to cooperate with Reformed assemblies for the system to work.

Huguenots engaged their own financial officers, such as commissaires des guerres, to oversee payments to cover mobilization costs and local defenses. Because of their vulnerability, Huguenot commissaires seem to have been more careful than their Catholic counterparts to ensure the accountability of the officers in charge of recruitment. So, although the Huguenot mestre de camp du Pillon was paid 3,500 livres in advance to recruit a regiment of five companies, he was to receive an additional 1,000 livres only "after the said companies are on foot [and] they are on the point of leaving the province."[137] Commissaires were to keep account books and to report back to the assemblies. Huguenot army commanders had to keep Reformed assemblies contented. This is probably why Châtillon ordered Pierre Peronneuse, a Huguenot commissaire, to pay 3,000 livres to reimburse the Huguenot assembly of the Cévennes and Gévaudan for some of its expenses.[138]

Even more prevalent were the alternative financial techniques employed by both Calvinist and Catholic noble officers. Warrior nobles of every religious and political affiliation authorized extraordinary taxes and alternative financial measures to raise funds during civil wars. Anne de Lévis duc de Ventadour imposed special tariffs on commerce during the 1621 civil war, noting that "it will be impossible to continue the raising of money in the form of the *taille* as has been done up to now for the payment of garrisons."[139] The Calvinist-dominated town of Alès levied a special tax on Catholic residents to pay for their "protection."[140]

Alternative financing relied heavily on hastily negotiated wartime loans. Warrior nobles borrowed money extensively during civil warfare to pay for the mobilization and support of troops. Nobles used jewelry and other assets to secure loans and alternative credit during civil conflicts.[141] The royal family provided a model for nobles by seeking loans of their own during civil conflicts, and Marie de Médicis allegedly used some of her diamond jewelry to obtain a loan in 1619 when she desperately sought troops.[142] Henri II de Montmorency reportedly secured a loan of 200,000 écus in Lyon using some of his wife's jewelry in order to pay for raising troops in Languedoc in 1621.[143] Wartime loans seem to have often relied on extremely high interest rates.[144]

Other means of alternative finance included confiscating tariffs and tolls, or levying new ones. Various annuity, pension, and rentes payments could be seized. In Languedoc, extensive and valuable salt deposits along the Mediterranean coast could be used to help finance warfare.[145] In 1622, a Huguenot commander in Bas Languedoc proposed to attack the Tour Charbonnière "in order to take salt, and by this means money to cover the costs of war."[146] Nobles authorized the minting of new coins and promoted fraudulent credit in order to pay for their military forces. Officers could also exchange goods and services for nonmonetary assistance, such as food, supplies, lodging through alternative economic exchanges.[147]

Pillage and seizure of goods provided further funds for noble military officers through a second-hand market that was probably quite extensive. Nobles regularly seized properties and belongings as part of their mobilization efforts. The king and his ministers sometimes allowed selected noble officers to draw on royal properties such as forests and crops for the alternative financing of their military activities. Inevitably, other nobles copied this practice of pillaging royal belongings and did so without the king's blessing. The parlement de Toulouse was also involved in coordinating aspects of war finance during civil wars, and at times provided legal support for pillaging. The premier président of that court, boasted during mobilizations for civil conflict in 1627 that "I employed the king's moneys very usefully through advances."[148] The court seized residences, seigneuries, belongings, and money of prominent rebels, reallocating these properties to loyal noble officers and thus extending them credit.

While the alternative economies constructed during civil wars in southern France were ephemeral, the financial improvisations resorted to must have had long-term social and economic effects. The royal government engaged in massive deficit spending during civil conflicts, and nobles and communities also incurred enormous costs during civil wars and were often left with crushing debts afterwards.[149] Repayment of wartime loans could take years, and merely paying the debt service was often difficult. City and town consuls hoped to be reimbursed for the gifts and loans that they provided during conflicts, but they frequently had to wait months or years for repayment.[150] After each civil conflict, peace agreements allowed most nobles to seek reimbursement for their military expenditures, even if they had been branded "rebels." The chambre des comptes and cour des aides in Montpellier handled many such requests, subject to verification through états, controlles des troupes, and quittances.[151]

†

This chapter has explored the ways in which southern French warrior nobles organized, supplied, and financed personal armies between 1598 and 1635. Provincial nobles were the key organizers of civil warfare in early modern France. Royal control over recruitment was minimal and the king actually relied heavily on extralegal recruitment. The majority of recruitment during the civil wars was localized, even when it was done for royal armies. The royal state did assert some influence over army mobilization, but it was always mediated by the provincial nobles who conducted recruitment operations. Noble officers found recruits and assembled them into effective units, despite chaotic conditions in war-torn Languedoc and Guyenne. And the regional nobility played an important role in forming, paying, and leading the armies that fought there. The organization of violence depended heavily on provincial nobles' abilities in managing war finances. Historians' perception of war finances as a problem of resource mobilization has downplayed the importance of regional nobles and overemphasized the financiers and direct taxation. Too often historians studying early modern French finances look ahead to the crown's late eighteenth-century financial problems and to the question of whether or not the financial crisis that led to the French Revolution could have been avoided.[152] Parrott rightly argues that "a proportion of army expenses would be shouldered by provincial governors and other *grands* whose personal relationship with the king had traditionally been defined through military service."[153] Nobles from Languedoc and Guyenne collaborated with a variety of royal officials and administrators in financing and waging warfare, but regional initiatives were vital to the success of any military campaign. The final chapter examines how warrior nobles performed violence within the culture of revolt in early seventeenth-century France.

A siege assault, one of the key violent performances for warrior nobles. Engraving in Jean Errard, *La Fortification démonstrée et réduicte en art. Par feu J. Errard* (Paris: n.p., 1622), f° 60. Photo courtesy Bibliothèque Nationale de France.

CHAPTER NINE

The Zeal of This Nobility

Violent Performances

Warrior nobles enthusiastically immersed themselves in violence during the fractious conflicts that divided southern France. A Languedoc noble praised "the zeal . . . of this nobility for the king's service," demonstrating provincial warrior nobles' passionate commitment to royal service and to the profession of arms.[1] Early seventeenth-century military elites often described their ardent desire for war and impatience to engage in combat in passionate terms. The culture of revolt cultivated intimate experiences of violence in nobles' daily lives, offering them opportunities to present armed acts before an audience of their noble peers. Warrior nobles engaged in a variety of violent performances during civil conflicts, demonstrating their noble status and giving meaning to their bellicose activities.

Eager for opportunities to organize and direct warfare, noble officers enthusiastically adopted an emerging "culture of command."[2] Southern French nobles and their troops waged war through overlapping forms of civil violence, the most important of which were raiding, sieges, and battles. Confessional strife, shifting political alignments, and changing royal administration influenced the organization and direction of civil warfare in early seventeenth-century France. French warrior nobles' practices of command in civil conflicts differed markedly from their experiences of external warfare in Italy, the Netherlands, or Germany in this period. The exercise of command represented a vital performance for warrior nobles operating in the culture of revolt.

The close camaraderie and intense emotions of armed service created a violent community of warrior nobles. Civil conflict became a routine aspect of early seventeenth-century French society and a common shared experience for warrior nobles. The provincial military elites observed the horror, death, and destruction of civil warfare differently from other members of French society. Warrior nobles faced civil warfare through similar everyday activities and combat experiences, which provided expression for the close personal bonds of nobility between them. Shared experiences in civil conflict seem to have forged a sort of group cohesion among military officers.

Fervent religious motivations fueled many nobles' involvement in early seventeenth-century civil conflict. Henri II de Bourbon prince de Condé, a newly converted Catholic, displayed a "holy zeal and an incomparable courage against the enemies of the king," especially targeting Huguenots during the civil wars of the 1620s.[3] Calvinist nobles were equally enthusiastic in their military engagement, as exemplified by a Reformed assembly that praised the Calvinists of Montauban and Castres for "your zeal for the glory of God."[4] Warrior nobles presented their religiosity through their personal participation in confessional politics and religious violence.

Orchestrating warfare, participating in armed communities, and promoting religious causes gave conflicts a larger meaning for nobles. Personal displays of violence confirmed the broader pursuits through which warrior nobles engaged in civil conflict. Southern French warrior nobles embraced violence zealously during civil wars as an exciting fulfillment of their noble aspirations and their bonds of nobility. Warrior nobles' personal performances of violence ultimately reshaped noble culture and influenced the dynamics of civil conflict.

THE ORCHESTRATION OF CIVIL WARFARE

Warrior nobles enthusiastically directed military operations during civil wars, displaying a strong desire to command and a determination to wage war. Nobles' expressions of their passion for violence has often obscured their elaborate orchestration of warfare, leading historians to dismiss early modern nobles' war-making activities as devoid of strategic conceptions. The civil wars in early seventeenth-century France have often been portrayed as positional, with campaigns carried out by centralized royal armies against static rebel forces that remained purely defensive. Historians often merely follow the route of the king's personal field army and gaze simply from the monarchic perspective on civil conflict, so that local or "rebel" forces appear only when encountered in sieges, negotiations, or battles involving the king's army. A. Lloyd Moote argues, for example, that the 1621–1622 campaigns of Louis XIII utilized "no complicated military strategy.

Any Protestant walled town in his path was asked to surrender; if it refused, the town was taken by siege."[5] Examining the local and regional civil conflicts in Languedoc and Guyenne more closely demonstrates that provincial warrior nobles actually organized warfare using complex military and political strategies. While one dimension of these civil conflicts was indeed positional, other aspects of early seventeenth-century civil violence were very mobile and active. Warrior nobles fought in battles, sieges, relief attempts, raids, ambushes, and assassinations across southern France in warfare that was widespread and dynamic.

During the civil wars of the early seventeenth century, organized violence was characterized by a close interplay between three major forms of warfare—raiding, siege, and battle. Although each of these forms of warfare would have been recognized by contemporary nobles as distinct, they also seem to have understood the commonalities and interconnections between them. Provincial warrior nobles were the key orchestrators of violence in the civil wars in Languedoc and Guyenne, organizing warfare that was dynamic, mobile, and highly destructive.

Coordinating Raiding Warfare

Raiding warfare proliferated during civil conflicts in early modern France. The concept of raiding warfare has been developed theoretically in a body of anthropological and historical literature stemming from Harry Holbert Turney-High's influential work on "primitive war," which conceived of raiding warfare as divided by a "military horizon" from "true war," and thus suggested that "a raid is hardly more of a war than is a modern burglary."[6] The practices of raiding warfare in premodern France complicate Turney-High's dichotomy of primitive/modern warfare, however. Medieval "private war" and *chevauchées,* military campaigns of deliberate devastation carried out by cavalry, were complex forms of raiding, coercion, and resource extraction.[7] Localized raiding warfare continued to play a significant role in early modern wars involving large-scale urbanized societies. Raiding parties operated from bastioned fortifications to obtain resources and control territories, a practice referred to by contemporaries as *petite guerre* (small war).[8] In early modern civil conflicts, raiding acquired heightened significance, becoming an absolutely vital—if not the principal—form of conflict.

Warrior nobles coordinated innumerable raiding parties to accomplish diverse purposes and goals. During campaigns, foraging for food and fodder gave armies a daily impetus to raid the surrounding countryside. Raiding parties performed reconnaissance missions for field armies, gathering military intelligence and probing for enemy forces.[9] Warrior nobles enacted reprisals and conducted vendettas through raids on their personal enemies. Local political and religious struggles were often accompanied by episodes of raiding. Personal economic gain, political advancement, and religious fulfillment all provided strong motivations for warrior nobles to participate in raiding operations in southern France.

Whatever the initial motivations for nobles to launch raiding campaigns, economic factors played a major role in raiding warfare. The pillaging and extortion that normally accompanied raiding operations could produce large-scale economic gain for warrior nobles and soldiers. Suppressing enemy raiding groups and bandits to protect artisanal industries and commercial goods was vital to local economies. A force from the Catholic garrison of Aubenas tried to keep access open to the weekly market held in the town on Saturdays, which had frequently been interrupted by raiding Huguenots forces.[10] If raiding parties were able to operate freely, they could easily destroy key aspects of local economic frameworks, as when Catholic troops burned the windmills of Nîmes, which were located on a hill outside the city walls.[11] The capacity of troops to destroy crops, trees, vineyards, and agricultural products could be devastating, as when the prince de Condé's troops destroyed vineyards around the town of Roque-courbe in the diocese of Castres in 1628.[12] The destruction or seizing of livestock was often a main rationale for raids. Particularly in the Cévennes mountains, where sheep and cattle were a major part of the economy, raiding could wreck local economies. A group of Catholic nobles planned to launch a raid in the Alès region in 1621 with at least two hundred infantry and a hundred cavalry drawn from their châteaux and governments in the area, targeting livestock especially. Assembling at dawn near Alès on the chosen day, this force followed the Gard river, "ravaging the entire plain" and stealing "a great many animals." When the Huguenot garrison of Alès sent troops out to disperse the raiding Catholics, they were routed, allowing the Catholics to continue their foray.[13]

Sometimes small to medium-sized armies carried out campaigns of widespread economic destruction that were reminiscent of medieval *chevauchées*. Henri II de Montmorency directed a systematic destruction of crops in areas of Bas Languedoc in 1628, targeting the countryside around Nîmes, which was "entirely in rebel hands, and furnished not only provisions to Nîmes and to the Cévennes . . . but also served to refresh the army of monsieur de Rohan, who drew on large quantities of money there for his soldiers' pay."[14] In July, Montmorency organized a base of operations at the village of Marguerittes, with rations and supplies for six days. His soldiers then "burned the wheat, and desolated all the countryside that furnished food or contributions to the enemy." The duc's troops bypassed Nîmes and proceeded northwest to La Calmette, "from which he torched everything within three leagues." Sources suggest that Montmorency's troops carried out a thorough raiding campaign and give hints at the techniques of destruction they employed. The soldiers "burned large numbers of villages, to constrain the inhabitants to withdraw into the towns, so as to starve them." Montmorency's raiding troops deliberately destroyed "all of the barrels, cookware, and presses to make oil, so that they would lose their harvests of wine and [olive] oil." Montmorency extended his destructive raiding campaign into the nearby valleys, "which is the nursery for soldiers and the best land for the rebels."[15] An encounter battle erupted near Clarensac when Huguenot troops apparently tried to curtail the raids by Montmorency's troops. This attempt failed, and Montmorency's army continued its devastating march, with the cavalry burning crops around Uzès and Alès, forcing the nearby villagers to take refuge within the walls of these towns. After further skirmishing, Montmorency halted his raiding campaign and led his army back to the shelter of Beaucaire. His raid had

> caused the burning of fifty entire villages or parishes. He placed in hunger not only Nîmes, but also Uzès, Alès, Anduze, and all of the Cévennes. He constrained the residents of all those areas to withdraw into the towns, which can nourish them for a very short time. He deprived monsieur de Rohan of the power to draw on the money and provisions of these towns, making him unable to supply his army—except if he found himself strong enough to maintain [the army] in Catholic lands—and really discredited him among those of his party.[16]

Large-scale raiding campaigns like Montmorency's demonstrated the effectiveness of raiding warfare, but they required extensive preparation and supplies, which limited the ability of warrior nobles to launch such sustained raiding forays.

Far more common were the pervasive small-scale raids that characterized the civil wars of the early seventeenth century. Warrior nobles almost constantly engaged in localized attacks and raiding expeditions in the vicinity of their châteaux and governments. During the siege of Montpellier in 1622, intense raiding criss-crossed the Vivarais region, as Huguenot garrisons ventured forth to skirmish with Catholic raiding parties. Calvinist troops from Mirabel clashed regularly with Catholic soldiers from Villeneuve-de-Berg, and, according to a Catholic source, there were "continually skirmishes between them, in which the Catholics had gained such a great advantage that they ordinarily beat the rebels, but not without losing a good number of brave men on both sides."[17] Winter usually meant the end of the campaigning season for major field armies, but not the end of raiding. When troops that had been recruited in Vivarais were "constrained, by the rigor of winter, to leave the countryside of Bas Languedoc and take up quarters in Vivarais," these soldiers were carefully "lodged in the places most suitable to prevent the raids and ravages of the enemies." The Catholic troops were hardly dormant during the winter. The seigneur de La Baume and his infantry worked diligently to keep the road from central Vivarais to Bas Languedoc clear of Huguenot raiding parties.[18]

Raiding parties constantly had to be aware of the dangers of enemy forces concentrating to disrupt their activities, though. When Catholic forces raided areas surrounding Calvinist-controlled towns in Bas Languedoc 1622, they encountered little opposition at first. "Finally," according to a Calvinist source, "after having ruined the countryside of the surrounding villages and exercised a thousand cruelties and villainies in raping wives and daughters everywhere, the dread of monsieur de Rohan's gathering troops constrained them to retire to join the king's troops who were already advancing into Bas Languedoc."[19] As a raid on Ruoms shows, raiding warfare could be dangerous and was not always profitable. The seigneurs de Guy and Peschaire organized "two or three ambushes with a number of men to seize the peasants' harvest and their livestock," near Ruoms. Instead, their raiding parties were detected by Ruoms's sentinels, allowing some villagers to surprise the raiding force and kill two of its leaders.[20]

Raiding warfare was also intimately connected with fortifications and positional warfare during the early seventeenth-century civil conflicts. Positional warfare encouraged raiding because of the foraging, blockading duties, economic destruction, and relief attempts so vital to siege operations. During prolonged sieges, parties raided the surrounding areas, seizing food, pillaging belongings, and destroying crops. The location of fortifications played a vital role in raiding warfare, since raiding was often conducted by small bands of infantry and cavalry that needed to be able to find refuge quickly if a large enemy force appeared. Control of fortifications along key roads and rivers could severely disrupt communications, because of the ability of raiding forces to shelter within their walls. For example, when Calvinists seized Vals-les-Bains in central Vivarais in 1621, the Catholics immediately realized its significance for raiding operations. According to one Catholic noble, "this loss was very important for Vivarais, being in the middle of the Catholics on the road from Velay and from Auvergne, where all commerce was interrupted, and the liberty of raids and ravages was introduced in this region, which suffered much from this loss."[21] In mountainous regions that had only a few roads following streams and rivers, raiding parties operating from fortifications could easily choke off all communications up the valleys.

Conducting Siege Warfare

Warrior nobles directed hundreds of sieges in southern France during the civil wars of the early seventeenth century. A survey of the major sieges conducted in this period shows both the difficulties and the possibilities of major siege operations. The royal army carried out a methodical and efficient siege of Saint-Jean-d'Angély in western France in 1621, but the siege of Montauban later that year dragged on for months before Louis XIII abandoned it. Montpellier survived a long siege in 1622, submitting to the besieging royal army only once a general peace agreement had been hammered out. La Rochelle suffered a debilitating siege in 1627–1628 and finally surrendered after starvation and disease had taken a major toll. Privas fell to Catholic besiegers after a short siege in 1629, its small garrison seemingly confused and overwhelmed by the large royal army besieging it. A more careful investigation of sieges in Languedoc and Guyenne reveals that siege warfare was hardly slow-paced and conservative.

Siege warfare was significant because of the importance of political affiliations and confessional identities in determining communities' loyalties and controlling populations during civil conflicts. From the monarch's perspective, subduing "rebel" cities and towns was a top priority, but many methods were acceptable in gaining at least an acknowledgment of authority. For regional nobles, assuring the safety of their clients and promoting the exercise of their religion was key. Ruses and negotiations were often used to win over, question, or subvert the loyalties of garrison officers and town governors. Sometimes ruses succeeded in capturing towns bloodlessly, as when Calvinist troops seized the town of Vals-les-Bains by surprising the garrison during a feast in 1621.[22]

The pace of siege warfare was in part determined by the defensive schemes used in the early seventeenth-century, which were characterized by intensive defensive artillery and musketry fire from bastioned fortifications. Besiegers used trenches to approach fortifications, establish batteries, and batter chosen bastions, which would then be assaulted. Mining concentrated huge gunpowder deposits under sections of enemy positions before exploding them. This concentration of firepower and explosives made the trenches a killing zone that attackers could ultimately escape only through siege assault or flight. Army commanders in southern France launched assaults quickly and often during siege operations. Many of the sieges were completed successfully by assaults that carried the defenses or that forced the defenders to capitulate. But conducting quick-paced siege operations entailed risks, and failed assaults could be very costly. A large-scale assault by Catholic troops at the siege of Montauban in 1621 illustrates the bloodiness of warfare in the siege trenches. When the attackers were repulsed, "those who were in the trenches . . . spied a means to save themselves, but in vain because there was not one single one of them . . . who was not killed or wounded."[23] While bastioned fortifications in southern France may have slowed formal siege operations, the possibility of relief may have forced commanders to resort to assaults as soon as the artillery had breached the defenses. Instead of making sieges slower, bastioned systems in this context may in some cases have actually sped up their operations.

Frequent sorties by defenders also made siege warfare active. Especially during the many sieges fought in the Cévennes mountains, sorties were potentially damaging to the besiegers' operations, because if defenders broke through the encircling blockade, they might easily bring in supplies or escape into the cover of the woods and mountains. Sorties often became part of the nightly routine of siege warfare. A major sortie from Montpellier shows how bloody this type of combat could be. When some five hundred Huguenot troops sortied from Montpellier to seize boats and supplies along a nearby river, they were detected and charged by Catholic cavalry, who cut them down as they fled back to the besieged town. After this sortie, the defenders "did not dare to defend the wheat, which was [then] burned right up to the river banks." This Catholic source claimed that almost four hundred of the sortie force were killed.[24]

While descriptions of early modern warfare often stress the indecisiveness of positional warfare, siege warfare in southern France could be quite decisive during this period. Time and again, sieges forced the issue of loyalty that was so vital in civil conflicts. Siege warfare was potentially decisive because it forced Calvinist nobles to agree to individual peaces and submit to Catholic forces and to religious occupation. Many other Huguenot nobles were killed in siege warfare or executed in the aftermath of sieges. Siege warfare was also significant because Calvinist towns that surrendered to Catholic forces were forced to accept Counter-Reformation Catholicism. The practice of Reformed Christianity was increasingly threatened, and previously secure Calvinists were subjected to daily doubts, competition, or even reconversion attempts by Catholics.

Aspects of siege warfare might appear to have been purely positional, but siege relief attempts made this type of warfare both mobile and dynamic during the French Wars of Religion. The possibility of relieving a siege was much easier in the context of civil war than it was in international war. Besieging armies had to worry about enemy forces coming from any direction and about the potential of enemy nobles and towns raising new troops in the immediate vicinity of the siege operations. Besieging forces had to remain highly mobile, blockading the besieged town or château, but also covering all roads, guarding bridges, and observing nearby enemy-held châteaux. The duc de Rohan mustered several attempts to relieve the siege of Montauban in 1621, and despite several failures, he was finally successful in getting a relief force into the beleaguered city. The arrival of these reinforcements, coupled with the heavy Catholic losses from assaults and disease, prompted Louis XIII to abandon the siege.[25] Relief forces merely threatening battle could be enough to disrupt a siege. For example, as the duc de Montmorency was besieging the small town of Marguerittes in 1621, a Huguenot force of 1,800 infantry and 300 cavalry from nearby Nîmes approached through the olive groves "almost to musket range" of the Catholic besiegers. Montmorency's army continued with its siege for several days, but "as he saw that it was not a place that he could guard, he abandoned [the siege] and returned to Beaucaire."[26] The innumerable skirmishes to contest blockades, prevent envelopment, or turn back relief forces sometimes escalated, and developed into full-fledged battles.

Directing Battle

Although siege warfare was certainly important throughout the civil wars of the early seventeenth century, armies still engaged in formal battles. Some historians of sixteenth- and seventeenth-century warfare suggest that battles became infrequent if not insignificant in this period. Wood argues that battles were simply too risky and costly, and hence to be avoided by commanders. During the French Wars of Religion, he contends, "for the crown and its principal military leaders the narrow margin of victory [at the battle of Dreux] . . . merely strengthened the appreciation of the high and uncontrollable risks involved in committing the main defensive instrument of the realm to the chance and chaos of a pitched battle." Wood insists that "it was the loss of so many great nobles and hundreds of gentlemen members of the gendarmerie [in battle] that was shocking" to early modern army commanders.[27] While most of the battles fought in Languedoc and Guyenne during between 1598 and 1635 were small clashes involving regional forces, battle was nonetheless a vital part of civil warfare in the early seventeenth century. Noble army commanders engaged in battle when they found opportunities for formal battlefield combat. Catholic armies frequently sought battle in southern France, and Huguenots armies were willing to give battle when they were not heavily outnumbered. Some major battles, and many small ones, were fought during the civil wars of the early seventeenth century. Interpreting the patterns of battle in these provinces is difficult because the local nature of the cases of battle and the thin documentation. Thus, it is difficult to fully assess battlefield practices of the civil wars in early seventeenth-century France and compare them with contemporaneous battles in other regions. However, the sources do allow us to glimpse some of the characteristics of battles in this period and examine their dynamics.

The warrior nobles fighting in Languedoc and Guyenne in the early seventeenth century were no novices at battle. Nobles from those provinces had had plenty of opportunities to gain experience with battle, both in civil wars within France and in foreign wars. Many nobles could remember the fighting during the wars of the Catholic League in the 1580s and 1590s. Calvinist nobles from Languedoc and Dauphiné served in Savoy and Italy in the 1610s, fighting several battles. Other Huguenots served in the Netherlands before the 1608 truce and after the resumption of war in 1621. Some Guyenne nobles served at the battle of Ponts-de-Cé, fought between Louis XIII's army and a force loyal to Marie de Médicis in Anjou in 1620. Many Catholic nobles from Languedoc participated in the battle of Susa pass in Savoy in 1629 and in the subsequent campaign in Italy. When given command of the French army in Italy in 1630, Henri II de Montmorency gained a major battlefield victory at the battle of Carignan.[28]

Army commanders during this period showed little reluctance to engage in battle, and warrior nobles often expressed a strong desire for battle. According to one of his secretaries, the duc de Montmorency was burning with a desire for battle against the duc de Rohan in 1627. Montmorency's army marched into sight of the city of Nîmes and stopped for two hours, waiting for a Huguenot force to come out from the town to do battle: "he desired with such passion to encounter the duc de Rohan, in a place where he could force him to combat." Ironically, when Montmorency linked up with the Catholic forces under the duc de Ventadour and Guillaume de Balazuc de Montréal, he found that Rohan's army had passed by earlier in the day. Montmorency was "very sensibly touched to have missed by two hours the occasion that he so ardently desired."[29] While army commanders did not lack a willingness to engage in battle, they wanted to do so by bring opposing armies to battle in circumstances favorable to their own forces. This notion emerges from a pamphlet narrating the prince de Condé's campaign in the Cévennes mountains in 1628. "It is notable," the author remarks, "that one of the principal causes that drove monsieur le prince to the mountains of Castres [in the Cévennes] is the plan to close the passage from Languedoc and the comté de Foix to monsieur de Rohan, to force him to battle or to retire shamefully into Nîmes . . . by this means, the rebel places of the comté [de Foix] and Haut Languedoc would remain without hope of aid."[30] Battle could destroy an enemy army if it could be brought into combat in the proper conditions.

Armies normally marched in compact columns that could relatively quickly be readied to fight. When armies arrived within sight of each other, they usually maneuvered to face each other, rearranging all of their units and forming up *en bataille*, or in battle order. Infantry companies would be grouped together to form a number of battalions or even larger bodies, called *gros*, positioned in a linear or checkerboard arrangement. The infantry units would also send out men, called *enfants perdus*, or "lost children," to skirmish with enemy troops and reconnoiter. Cavalry companies would form up on the wings of the armies or in gaps left between the infantry units. If the armies had mobile artillery trains, batteries would be sited to bombard enemy troops.[31]

The battle of Souilles, fought in Haut Languedoc in November 1627, shows some of the methods that generals employed to try to bring their opponents to battle. The duc de Rohan's Huguenot army of between 4,000 and 6,000 infantry and perhaps 1,500 cavalry was encamped around Revel, when a Catholic army under the duc de Montmorency assembled nearby at Saint-Félix-Lauragais and Roumens. Montmorency had 1,500 infantry, and his "particular friends had come to find him with a large number of nobles, who joined with his company, Ventadour's, and Lignères's, rendering him a bit stronger in cavalry than the enemy." Montmorency's troops captured several prisoners, who gave details of Rohan's forces, which were now heading south from Revel toward Foix. Montmorency set out with his army out to pursue the Huguenot army and force them to battle. Rain slowed the advance, and Rohan's troops had passed the village of La Pomarède before the Catholic army caught up with them. Montmorency's troops seized a bridge to try to block Rohan's army, but the Calvinist troops found a ford near château Dejean and crossed the river, maneuvering within sight of the Catholic forces to seize the château. Meanwhile, Montmorency reconnoitered from a nearby hill and put his army *en bataille*. Rohan arranged his troops to face Montmorency's army. Using what was probably a fairly typical maneuver formation, the Calvinist forces formed four battalions of infantry, which Rohan arranged in diamonds, leaving great spaces in between them for his cavalry. The Huguenots positioned their baggage train between the infantry battalions and formed the cavalry up facing the Catholic army. Rohan later commented that this formation was effective because he could change his line of advance easily, while maintaining "good order." Rohan later claimed that he was resolved either to pass the Catholic forces and resume his march to Foix, or to fight. Montmorency was also wanted to fight, but Moussoulens and La Courtete, two older noble advisors, advised him not to attack, stressing the "poor state and weakness of his infantry." Montmorency reportedly replied, "I shall attack them in a place where pistols and swords are more useful than muskets." Montmorency thus decided to let Rohan's army march on; he would wait to attack at Castelnaudary, where the countryside was more favorable for cavalry. But, at this moment, a skirmish broke out, and the battle Montmorency so desired began without coordination or direction.[32]

What followed was a brisk, but limited battle that displayed the importance of cavalry in early seventeenth-century battle. Montmorency and his followers were able to see from their hilltop vantage point that the Catholic advance guard had gotten isolated and entangled in combat with some of the Huguenot units. The advance guard was in an increasingly precarious situation after some of the Catholic cavalry were forced to retire in disorder. The infantry of the advance guard was too far advanced to be supported, and when its attack was repulsed, two Calvinist battalions pursued the Catholic infantry, charging with "pikes lowered," right at them. Reacting quickly, Montmorency ordered his gendarmes to charge to halt the Huguenot advance. When the gendarmes charged, "all the first rank" were killed or wounded, but this charge halted the Huguenot attack and allowed the Catholic cavalry to rally and the infantry "to regain courage." Everyone was "animated by the presence of their general," according to a Catholic source. Rohan called off the Calvinist attack at this point, refusing to let his troops pursue the Catholics across the river. Montmorency had rallied his advance guard, but fighting trailed off as night fell. The Huguenot army resumed its march toward Mazères and Montmorency led his men to Castelnaudary. While many infantry were undoubtedly killed in this battle, sources mention only that some nobles were wounded and about forty-five of their best horses were killed.[33] Although the opposing armies did not fully engage each other during the day's fighting, the battle of Souilles suggests the capabilities of cavalry to change the momentum of battle and dictate how armies fought.

Another minor battle fought in 1622 at Lavérune, just west of Montpellier, between the armies of the duc de Rohan and the seigneur de Châtillon demonstrates how encounter battles developed. The battle at Lavérune was part of the preliminary fighting leading up to siege of Montpellier. Rohan's Calvinist army had just received the capitulation of the Catholic garrison at Saint-George-d'Orques when a largely Catholic force under the seigneur de Châtillon, who had recently deserted the Huguenot cause, and Henri II de Montmorency approached, and a skirmish developed between Lavérune and Saint-Jean-de-Védas. Châtillon's advance guard took up positions along the Mosson river, building a hasty half-moon (a semi-circular redoubt) at the bridge over the river and occupying a mill. They sent out skirmishers to prevent being surprised by enemies.

Rohan's Huguenot army accepted the challenge, and the steadily increasing musketry fire became "first a small skirmish, [and] finally brought about a great combat." As the skirmishing grew heavier, both armies deployed into battle formations and maneuvered to support the troops already engaged. Rohan sent two regiments and five hundred volunteer cavalry to join the skirmish, supported by his entire army, which "already marched in battle order with the cavalry in the aisles and cannon in appropriate places." Châtillon's troops repulsed the initial Calvinist attacks around the bridge, killing the Huguenot commander La Blaquière and several of his officers, disordering the Calvinist troops. Rohan broke off the attack after this initial failure, and the Catholic troops were apparently reluctant to follow up on their success, because the Huguenot cavalry heavily outnumbered the Catholics.[34]

Battles were fought using a variety of different troop types, each of which performed a different role in combat. Cavalry, as Wood has argued, remained decisive on the battlefield, playing the key attack role for an army and potentially able to destroy an enemy force.[35] Mixed-weapon infantry formations ideally gave an army a certain solidity and cohesiveness and sheltered the cavalry when it fell back. Infantry units also attacked enemy infantry, charging with their pikes. The *enfants perdus* harassed the enemy with sporadic arquebus and musket fire. Artillery pieces were large and heavy, making them difficult to maneuver into position, and they could not be repositioned in battle, because their civilian laborers and pioneers would not handle them in combat. Artillery fire could prepare the way for advances and blunt attacks by enemy units, but significant use of battlefield artillery seems to have been rare during the fighting in early seventeenth-century France.[36]

The extensiveness of battle in civil warfare can be seen in the 1621 campaign in Languedoc and Guyenne. A series of small battles were fought in Haut Languedoc during the siege of Montauban and its aftermath. Henri de Bourbon marquis de Malauze, a Calvinist commander who was supposed to aid in Montauban's defense, led his troops against a Catholic force near Fauch in September 1621, but the Huguenots lost the battle and were forced to retire into the town, where they were soon compelled to capitulate. The duc de Rohan assembled a relief force that fought its way into Montauban in late September.[37] After the siege of Montauban was lifted, the opposing armies partially demobilized, leaving some troops in the region. A small Catholic army fought a Huguenot force from Montauban toward the end of January in a battle near Lavaur.[38] Far away from Montauban, other small battles erupted. In Foix, the comte de Carmaing and his small Catholic army defeated Huguenots under the baron de Léran near Varilhes on 15 November 1621.[39] Small battles also occurred in Vivarais and Bas Languedoc that year. When the Huguenot commander Alexandre de Bla-cons seigneur de Mirabel-Blacons led an expedition from Nîmes to besiege a nearby château in August 1621, a Catholic force under Guillaume de Balazuc de Montréal met them in battle on 15 August near Nîmes, routing Blacons's force, killing or capturing around four hundred Huguenot troops, and seizing their artillery and munitions.[40]

Battles fought in other regions of France during the 1620s had a great impact on the warfare in Languedoc and Guyenne. The duc de Rohan's brother, Benja-min de Rohan seigneur de Soubise commanded an army of 5,000 infantry, 500 gendarmes, and 300 mousquetaires à cheval in the vicinity of La Rochelle in 1622. But, when Louis XIII's army, composed of about 7,000 men, managed to launch a surprise attack on Soubise's army at the Ile-de-Riez early on the morn-ing of 16 April 1622, his Huguenot army crumbled. Soubise and some of his troops escaped to La Rochelle, but many prisoners were taken and the Huguenot artillery, baggage, and many standards were taken.[41] The collapse of this force allowed La Rochelle to be blockaded and allowed Louis XIII to send large num-bers of Catholic forces to Guyenne and Languedoc, putting increased strategic pressure on the Calvinists in those provinces. Huguenots had similar high hopes for Soubise's project to threaten Catholic forces by landing a small Calvin-ist army on the Ile-de-Ré near La Rochelle in September 1625. But a Catholic army of 3,000 infantry and 150 chevaux-légers under Jean du Caïla de Saint-Bonnet marquis de Toiras and François de La Rochefoucauld attacked Soubise's army on 14 September 1625. The Catholic advance guard, composed of chevaux-légers, *enfants perdus*, two companies of the regiment de Champagne, led the attack, followed by the main body of the army, formed by four infantry battal-ions, and a rear guard. The Catholic troops' disciplined attack routed the Hugue-not army, and Soubise had to take flight by boat to the Ile-d'Oléron, then to En-gland. The marquis de Toiras, a Catholic noble from Languedoc, not only won his reputation as a commander at this victory, but was named governor of Ile-de-Ré by a grateful Louis XIII. Toiras built a citadel at Saint-Martin and a fort at La Prée to consolidate his victory.[42] Soubise's failure to effectively harass the Catholic forces in western France increasingly forced Calvinists in Guyenne and Languedoc on the defensive.

Early seventeenth-century Huguenot armies were still able to attempt battle at times and several small battles were fought in Haut Languedoc and Bas Languedoc in 1625. The duc de Rohan engaged Catholic forces in battle around

Pierre-Segade and the château de Viane in 1625, inducing the Catholic commander, the marquis de Thémines, to withdraw his army and head for Foix,
leaving the Rohan's army free to harass the Catholic communities in Haut
Languedoc. Calvinist forces under Lusignan meanwhile fought a small battle at
Teillet, and another small battle was fought at Bellegarde in Bas Languedoc
under the Huguenot commander Claude de Calvière baron de Saint-Côme and
his troops from Nîmes.[43]

Many small battles were closely related to sieges and blockades. Battles could
be desperate and costly for besieged and blockaded towns. For example, a June
1629 battle outside Nîmes greatly affected that city. François-Annibal d'Estrées's
army was blockading Nîmes when a group of reportedly 4,000 infantry came
out from the city walls to meet the Catholics in battle. A brief battle was fought,
with about three hundred soldiers killed. A Catholic source claimed that "twenty
of the children of the best townspeople were taken prisoner."[44] The residents of
Nîmes not only failed to disrupt the blockade of their city, but suffered a local
political setback.

The battle of Castelnaudary, fought in Languedoc during the 1632 civil war,
presents a perplexing case for historical interpretation. The army of maréchal de
Schömberg, operating under direct royal authority and advancing through Haut
Languedoc, seems to have caught the duc de Montmorency's army somewhat by
surprise. When Schömberg's troops began advancing unexpectedly across a
stream toward Montmorency's army near Castelnaudary, Montmorency and a
group of nobles rode out from their main battle lines to reconnoiter. Although
some historians have speculated that Montmorency was on a suicide mission,
his group probably blundered into Schömberg's advancing forces and came
under fire from the gardes françaises. Some sort of skirmish arose, in which
Montmorency's reconnaissance party was engaged by the gardes françaises and
two cavalry companies. Montmorency was seriously wounded—some accounts
say that he received as many as seventeen wounds—and a number of his companions were killed. Montmorency's secretary insists that those who blamed
Montmorency for going "headlong into danger" did so unfairly, because expos-
ing oneself to danger was "a fault that nearly all the great captains are guilty of,
and that one could reproach him of with the same injustice as the former king
of Sweden [Gustav II Adolf], who was taken leading the scouts of his army, and
who until his death had always been the first to come to blows [with the enemy]."
After the capture of Montmorency by the enemy, his army retired before the opposing armies could become completely engaged.[45]

THE FABRICATION OF ARMED COMMUNITIES

The culture of revolt forged sociability in warrior noble culture through nobles' participation in civil conflict in early seventeenth-century France, creating a culture distinct from that of commoners and other nobles who were not engaged in war-making. The religious reform movements and the religious wars of the sixteenth century had already severely disrupted earlier conceptions of noble community in southern France during the late sixteenth century, dividing nobles along confessional lines. The fresh memories of previous civil conflicts helped to harden the divisions between many noble families. Active participation in civil conflict in the early seventeenth-century civil wars further disrupted the notions of noble community in southern France.

Although civil conflict tended to break down social bonding and disrupt noble culture, it could also build it up. Civil warfare actually bound many warrior noble families, their allies, and their clients closer together during times of crisis. Warrior nobles faced possible injury, imprisonment, punishment, and death when they participated in the culture of revolt. Their families often had to deal with the uncertainties, attacks, reprisals, and ransom demands that accompanied civil warfare. Many noble families and their communities donned somber black shades in mourning in the aftermath of combat. Warrior noble clienteles had to respond with empathy, solidarity, and support during crises that affected their members. Civil warfare both disrupted social connections and established new bonds of nobility through shared experiences of civil conflict.

Military campaigns and combat forged armed noble communities through the common understandings and emotional attachments that formed during civil conflicts. Camp socializing celebrated the military elite's social distinctiveness as members of violent communities. Collective performances of combat forced nobles to confront their fears of death, establishing a shared appreciation of risk and bravery. Warrior nobles enthusiastically participated in civil warfare in part because it gave them a strong sense of community.

Socializing on Campaign

During periods of civil warfare, armed clienteles and military units became the key sites of warrior noble bonding and social interaction. Nobles built camaraderie through their everyday shared activities of dining, conversation, and prayer, even as they marched and fought together. Warrior nobles cherished weapons and celebrated violence in the context of the daily practices of raiding and siege

warfare. Their common experiences of life on the march and in army encampments strengthened their relationships and provided sustaining motivation for
their ongoing participation in civil warfare.

The attire that warrior nobles wore on military campaigns identified them as
members of distinct armed communities. While clothing always served as a sign
of nobility in the early seventeenth century, distinguishing nobles from other social groups, warrior nobles' military attire and accoutrements set them even further apart from non-nobles during civil conflicts. Warrior nobles gathered in
armed groups, enclosed in partial armor and carrying swords—an important
symbolic distinction of nobility that was employed much more regularly during
civil warfare than at other times.[46] But campaigning in civil conflict also reinforced
notions of noble lineage and group identities through military units', clienteles',
and households' use of similar dress, comprised of donning liveries, wearing colored sashes, and bearing coats of arms. Dress fueled jealousies and rivalries, with
noble patrons and their clienteles competing in ostentatious displays.[47] In civil
conflicts, these distinctions of dress became means of identifying friends and
foes, as well as focusing loyalties and hatreds. Henri II de Montmorency's gendarmes and bodyguards wore a livery of blue cassocks immediately recognizable
to his noble allies and enemies throughout the province of Languedoc.[48]

Martial friendship reinforced bonds between nobles serving together in civil
wars in early seventeenth-century France. As we have seen, when warrior nobles
referred to friendship, amitié, in their correspondence, they frequently associated it with armed collaboration in civil warfare. Friendship was also intertwined
with notions of military clientage, as when Montmorency wrote that he was
pleased by the "friendship that you have for me" when a noble agreed to raise an
infantry company for him.[49] During military campaigns, patrons surrounded
themselves with "friends," who seemed to include all of their clients.[50] Civil
wars allowed noble patrons to assemble their clienteles and cultivate their relationships with armed companions on campaign and in combat.

Warrior noble patrons and their clients often lodged together while conducting military operations, taking up common quarters in encampments and
towns. Nobles with châteaux near the area of fighting hosted their clients and
provincial noble allies, providing them with lodging, food, and entertainment.
Nobles frequently occupied châteaux during military campaigns, often lodging
in the homes of their personal enemies. During sieges, the commanders and
nobles of the investing army would take up residence in the nearby châteaux and
monasteries, living at the expense of their hosts, who could usually only hope to
eventually recover their expenses.

Warrior nobles on campaign forged bonds *à table*, dining together and conversing about the conflicts that they were engaged in. Clientage activities often originated at the table, and a client was frequently thought of as a noble who "ordinarily eats at [his patron's] table."[51] This notion may have created tensions when powerful noble patrons sat at the tables of other patrons, as happened when the duc de Montmorency and other prominent regional nobles ate at the duc d'Épernon's table.[52] Siege warfare provided abundant opportunities for noble bonding during dinners. Attacking forces would divide their forces into quarters or sectors ringing the besieged town, each commanded by a noble or group of nobles. Most evenings, the overall army commander or one of the sector commanders would host the senior officers of the besieging army for dinner.

These dinners could be leisurely suppers or formal councils of war, during which nobles discussed military operations and strategy. Warrior nobles acted as military advisors at such councils, proposing specific plans to army commanders. During sieges, nobles offered nightly assessments of the progress of siegeworks and proposed new attacks, vying to have their advice adopted. Competition between nobles seems to have extended to hosting dinners during sieges, and nobles noted when a dinner was extraordinary. François de Bassompierre seemed impressed when "monsieur the maréchal de Roquelaure held a magnificent feast for the principals of the army in the evening," describing a war council dinner at the siege of Montauban in 1621 in detail. Bassompierre himself hosted a spectacular dinner at Lunel during the 1622 campaign for a stunning array of nobles, including the maréchal de Crequy, Henri de Schömberg, Claude de Bullion, the duc de Montmorency, and the comte d'Alès.[53]

Warrior nobles also bonded through the hardships that they endured in civil warfare. While nobles certainly fared much better than common soldiers, they did share in many of the harsh conditions of military campaigns. Their lavish dinners could be curtailed or cut out altogether by shortages of supplies or lack of time to dine. Many a noble dinner during sieges was interrupted by unexpected assaults or sorties. Even noble cavalry sometimes ran short of food, as shown by an urgent message to a commissaire in 1621. "If you do not give us orders for bread and wine for the gendarmes of the company of monsieur, for the carabiniers, and . . . in brief for all those who are here," wrote Raimond de Thézan baron de Poujol, "I do not see the means of their subsistence, as they have eaten so little."[54]

The shared experience of the dangers of combat built a comradeship in arms among groups of warrior nobles. Nobles who fought as volunteers often served together in improvised units, fighting alongside common infantry units. At the siege of Montauban, for example, Catholic nobles fired muskets along with the other besiegers.[55] Contemporary descriptions of combats and siege frequently refer to noble commanders leading attacks "accompanied by a great number of nobles."[56] A sense of adventure and risk may have thus contributed to some nobles' sense of camaraderie.

Engaging in Combat

Warrior nobles formed common perceptions of warfare based on their shared experiences of combat. Nobles used similar organizational methods, tactical formations, and weaponry techniques in raids, sieges, and battles. Warrior nobles often confronted combat situations with recognizably similar approaches, making references to the same warrior practices, such as entering combat *en bataille*, in all the styles of warfare. Warrior nobles from Languedoc and Guyenne and their contemporaries celebrated combat in each of its forms by stressing their similarities.[57]

Early seventeenth-century combats often began with a series of preliminary activities and rituals that nobles and soldiers performed before engaging their enemies. Noble commanders seem to have assembled councils of war consisting of their subordinates and advisors to discuss tactics, as Henri II de Montmorency did before the battle of Castelnaudary.[58] Prayers and sometimes entire religious services were held as part of the lead-up to fighting. The contrasts between priests celebrating mass just across from Reformed ministers giving sermons must have been jarring—as well as compelling—to the men waiting to enter combat. Army commanders frequently made speeches to their men before combat, as when the duc de Rohan "exhorted his troops into combat."[59]

The tactical organizations and small unit tactics used by troops seem to have been fairly similar in all types of combat, even if there were variations and special techniques employed in certain situations. In combat, infantry were normally organized into units that combined pikemen, musketeers, and arquebusiers. Infantry formations were usually arranged in groups, so that the different units could support one another, but leaving room for cavalry to maneuver around them. The dispositions of regiment de Phalsbourg as it advanced to seize Privas in 1629 provide a glimpse at the supportive tactics used by infantry units. The regiment had five companies positioned in the most advanced trenches. Fifty men were chosen from among these companies to lead the advance. A lieutenant would command this advance guard, using ten musketeers and two sergeants as scouts. This advance guard would be followed by two companies, supported by three more companies fifty paces behind them. A larger attack wave of five additional companies would follow "in a single body, at a hundred paces distance," sustained by ten more companies in two battalions. The troops would take precautions, upsetting the barricades in front of their trenches only across their own frontage, in case they had to withdraw.[60]

Cavalry fought in relatively small formations, using swords and pistols when they encountered enemy forces. Little evidence emerges about whether or not early seventeenth-century French cavalry actually used the much-discussed caracole tactics, a wheeling technique that allowed mounted pistoleers to produce rolling fire against their enemies. A skirmish fought on 18 June 1625 offers some ideas on how nobles experienced cavalry combat. Catholic gendarmes in the companies of Ambres and Saint-Jean-de-Lerm, which were "well mounted," encountered about two hundred Huguenot cavalry that were "rather poorly equipped and amassed from diverse places." The cavalry skirmished for a while in a "grim and furious" combat until the Calvinists finally "took flight," losing about fifty of their number killed or taken prisoner.[61]

Warrior nobles experienced intense artillery fire in siege combats and in some battles. Besieging armies' batteries were used to bombard fortifications and create breaches in the walls. Artillery fire would typically be concentrated in sieges to batter down one or two bastions in preparation for infantry assaults led by noble officers. Fortifications' concentrated defensive artillery fire would have been terrifying for nobles engaging in siege approaches and assaults. Artillery seems to have played a more limited role in field battles, with batteries of smaller guns firing from a distance at enemy lines. Field artillery could be very effective if attacked directly, however, as batteries blasted away at tightly packed infantry and cavalry formations.

A skirmish fought near Alès reveals the flexibility in the formations and tactics employed by warrior nobles and their military units in early seventeenth-century combat. Fighting ensued when the Huguenot garrison of Alès tried to drive off a Catholic raiding group of two hundred infantry and more than one hundred cavalry led by the seigneur de Vinezac and several other Catholic nobles. One hundred Calvinist infantry and twenty-five gendarmes took up defensive positions around a farm, with a strong reserve of three hundred infantry supporting them. The Catholics formed two small battalions of infantry to oppose the Calvinists and threw out sixty men as *enfants perdus*. When some of the Huguenots charged and disordered the Catholic screen, the seigneur de Vinezac divided one of his battalions in two, ordering a sergeant to counterattack with half of a battalion while Vinezac led the other half to surround the farm. Vinezac's quick reorganization of his troops allowed the Catholics to trap the Huguenot soldiers at the farm, where they were unable to retire into the farmhouse because "a young noble lady and several women had barricaded themselves inside." The main body of Calvinist infantry were positioned too far away to assist their comrades, so the advanced Huguenot troops were routed, losing thirty or forty killed.[62]

Combat subjected warrior nobles to the brutality of musket balls and artillery shot that crushed bones and maimed limbs. Nobles and soldiers alike fought through withering arquebus and musket fire during intense combats, leaving many horribly wounded and disfigured. Gunshot wounds often became infected, forcing surgeons to amputate limbs. Cavalry combats produced up-close pistol wounds, as well as slashing and piercing sword wounds.[63] While nobles were exposed to many of the same dangers of injury and death that common soldiers faced, the care of wounded nobles and the treatment of their dead bodies set them apart from commoners. Warrior nobles who survived combat discussed their wounds and preserved their memories of their violent performances as signs of their valorous military service.

THE PROMOTION OF RELIGIOUS CAUSES

Warrior nobles experienced civil violence as an expression of religious activism. Religious reform movements and confessional passions encouraged a renewed attention to personal religiosity and piety during the civil wars of the late sixteenth and early seventeenth centuries. Many warrior nobles in Languedoc and Guyenne practiced their religion regularly, praying daily and attending religious services frequently, even during military campaigns. Nobles displayed their piety through Bible reading and devotional activity in army encampments. Early seventeenth-century noble correspondence is filled with biblical allusions and references to pious behavior in battles and sieges. For warrior nobles, intense personal belief was dedicated to promoting religious causes through confessional activism.

Lay activism and passionate belief were powerful motives for violence in early seventeenth-century France. While clergy, organized churches, and institutions directed widespread reform movements, much of the local religious activity in Languedoc and Guyenne was led by the laypeople in congregations. Robert A. Schneider notes that even in the staunchly Catholic city of Toulouse, where one might expect religious activity to have been structured and directed by episcopal authorities, "it was not the archbishop but primarily the new and reformed religious orders that first stimulated the Counter-Reformation in the city."[64] Activism was not confined merely to large cities like Toulouse, but could be a powerful force in all types of communities, even in the armed communities in which warrior nobles thrived. Counter-Reformation Catholic piety stressed personal activism through confraternities, civic rituals, and charity—often directed toward militant causes and missionary work. Many Calvinist nobles were inspired to display their piety through aggressive defense of their temples and communities.[65] Nobles' lay activism brought energy and intensity to militant reform movements, strengthening religious causes and simultaneously deepening confessional conflicts. Warrior nobles often incorporated their religiosity into their performances of violence, displaying their confessional allegiances and testifying to their fervent beliefs.

Taking up the Cross

Gaspard-Armand de Polignac vicomte de Polignac took up a cross during a Catholic procession in Le Puy-en-Velay in 1609, helping to bear it in celebration of the founding of a Capuchin church that was intended to support missionary work to convert Calvinists in the surrounding region.[66] Early modern French nobles, such as Polignac, felt that they had a personal role to play in the divine plan, and they each regarded their confession as having the only correct way of worshipping God. Serving God meant implementing a politicized and confessionalized religious agenda, using violent means if necessary. Warrior nobles fought for God, participating personally in religious warfare to occupy sacred space and to assert confessional dominance in southern France.

Taking up the cross was an important metaphor for warrior nobles, who expressed their piety actively by sponsoring proselytization and promoting their confessions. Both Calvinist and Catholic religiosity involved personal charity and service to their churches and clergy. Catholic nobles believed that supporting religious institutions, personnel, and causes amounted to performing personal service to God. The theology of the cross advanced by both Luther and Calvin influenced Huguenot nobles' notions of taking up the cross. Calvin understood personal charity to play a key role in an individual's religion, and his followers believed in a direct involvement in religion through morality and community.[67] Calvinist nobles in southern France were especially concerned with establishing a godly community in a Catholic-dominated kingdom.

Early seventeenth-century French nobles promoted piety and morality in their armed clienteles and military units. Nobles of both confessions believed that their clients should express their piety outwardly through moral behavior and actions on campaign. Warrior noble patrons asserted control over their families' and clients' religious practices, regarding collective piety as vitally important.[68] A noble officer's reputation for piety was continually evaluated and assessed in army encampments. Warrior nobles who served as army commanders and regimental officers seem to have been expected to display pious behavior. The piety shown by leaders could inspire their clienteles and troops through their role in promoting faith, saying prayers, and attending religious services in camps. In both battles and sieges, nobles' participation in combat was a bond of faith and piety between coreligionaries, perhaps similar to the bonding experienced by pilgrims traveling together. Piety thus provided crucial sustaining motivation to keep warrior nobles and their troops actively involved in military campaigns.[69]

Warrior nobles' religious militancy also fueled religious confrontations in southern France. Warrior nobles engaged in struggles over municipal *consulats* emphasizing the piety of elite candidates and promoting confessionalized programs of religious renewal. Following one *consulat* election, a Catholic noble rejoiced that "we have elected in this place strongly Catholic consuls, great servants of the king, persons who have much to lose and [who are] very agreeable to the good people."[70] The emphasis on religious reputation and confessional identification shown in this commentary suggests the significance of pious behavior in local political struggles. Warrior nobles competed to control municipal governments throughout Languedoc and Guyenne, in part to allow members of their confession access to sacred spaces and to promote confessional allegiances in communities. Religious activism shaped civil violence and influenced broader dimensions of political culture. For example, a letter by Henri II de Montmorency recommending a Languedoc noble commended not only the latter's service but his zeal for "the progress and advancement of the Apostolic and Roman religion."[71] Through confessional militancy, nobles established personal connections to their sacred communities and to their clienteles.

Religious activism and militancy contributed to warrior nobles' combat motivation, inspiring them in battle. Calvinist and Catholic nobles described combat in the language of ordeals and trials of faith during the French Wars of Religion, and the beliefs of many nobles were severely tested during the civil conflicts of the early seventeenth century. Catholic nobles in southern France believed that heresy threatened them constantly. Beleaguered Huguenot nobles besieged by Catholic armies felt that their faith was being tested during sieges. Pious nobles of both confessions were expected to deal with such suffering and trials without wavering in their faith. Taking up the cross thus went beyond maintaining a reputation for piety, prompting nobles to engage in militant action to defend their faith.

Submitting to God's Will: Catholic Militancy

Many Catholic nobles from Languedoc and Guyenne participated in civil warfare as zealous advocates of reestablishing Catholic practice in southern France.[72] Restoring the church in war-torn France required the submission of all "true" believers to God's will. Late sixteenth- and early seventeenth-century French Catholics believed that relating to God involved fully accepting divine direction. Conforming to the will of God was a central concern of early seventeenth-century Catholic devotional writers such as Benoît de Canfield and François de Sales.[73] Fervent Catholics' spirituality was shaped by an emotional release experienced through what they saw as complete obedience to divine guidance. Barbara Diefendorf argues that for devout Catholics, "the aim of all good spiritual direction was not to create dependence on another but to tame—ideally, to destroy—the penitent's self-will, so as to leave her [or him] dependent on, and totally submissive to, the will of God."[74]

The act of surrendering oneself to God transpired through personal devotion and lay religiosity. French Catholic nobles engaged in hours of prayer, often while secluded in private chapels. Private devotions employed simple implements such as crucifixes, prayer beads, images of saints, and books of hours to facilitate contemplation of God. Many Catholics cultivated an interior spirituality that sometimes included trances, visions, and other forms of mysticism. Spiritual guidance was available through Ignatius of Loyola's *Spiritual Exercises* (1548), François de Sales's *Introduction à la vie dévote* (1608), and other spiritual writings. Devout Catholics absorbed themselves in singing during their personal devotions and domestic observances.[75]

French Catholics embraced God through various forms of asceticism in the early seventeenth century, and warrior nobles could view their military campaigns as temporary ascetic experiences, analogous to the hermitical retreats, pilgrimages, and solitary contemplation performed by other *dévots*.[76] During civil conflicts, militant Catholic nobles founded convents and monasteries in captured towns, following ascetic devotional models that were popular in this period.[77] Southern French Catholic noblemen enthusiastically promoted the spread of the Feuillants, Capuchins, Jesuits, Ursulines, Visitandines, and other religious orders dedicated to restoring Catholicism throughout France. Hundreds of new monasteries and convents were founded in the early seventeenth century, with forty-eight new women's convents founded between 1604 and 1650 in Paris alone.[78] Many warrior noble families were simultaneously involved in supporting Catholic religious reform and Catholic political causes in this period through their military activities.

Catholic warrior nobles participated in devotional practices even when they were conducting military operations. Catholics sought closeness to God through outward devotional acts, often intended to fulfill personal vows. Lay religiosity involved daily participation in collective rituals and religious activities outside of the context of the mass. French Catholics gathered in chapels, homes, and streets to pray, sing, and listen to preaching.[79] Lay Catholics, including warrior nobles, participated in an intense revival of Marian devotion at shrines and chapels across France, especially at ones that were restored to Catholics through the fighting in Languedoc and Guyenne.[80] The Catholic faithful in religiously mixed southern France cultivated their relationship to God through their collective militant and devotional activities.

Catholic nobles throughout France were inspired by Marie de Médicis's displays of piety and support for Catholic reform. The queen mother's own devotional activities demonstrate how devout Catholics could combine various aspects of religiosity in their personal piety. Marie de Médicis went on a number of pilgrimages to the shrine of the *vierge noire*, at Nôtre Dame de Liesse, near Laon, in the early seventeenth century.[81] The queen mother provided financial patronage and political backing for the Feuillants and their missionary work in France.[82] Following Henri IV's reinstatement of the Jesuits within France in 1603, Marie de Médicis assisted in the expansion of the Society of Jesus in the kingdom, selecting the Jesuit Jean Suffren as her confessor in 1615.[83] The queen mother actively supported the publication of religious texts, including a new Bible printed in Paris.[84] Marie de Médicis's well-publicized devotional activities and religious patronage provided examples for devout Catholic nobles in southern France who wanted forceful action to reopen pilgrimage sites and churches controlled by Huguenots.

A *dévot*'s submission to God was signified through pain and self-mortification. Bodily suffering and flagellation played important roles in Catholic lay piety in the late sixteenth and early seventeenth centuries.[85] Brad S. Gregory demonstrates Post-Tridentine Catholics' "impulse to imitate Christ through the patient suffering of adversity."[86] Henri III and his noble entourage had set a moving royal example of piety and suffering in collective penitence ceremonies during the 1580s. Catholic Leaguers had adopted many of these same devotional practices, despite their growing suspicions that their "blasphemous" king was promoting penitence as a duplicitous show.[87] Leaguers had doubted the sincerity of Henri de Navarre's conversion to Catholicism in 1593 in part because they felt that he had failed to perform appropriate penitential acts.[88] The *dévots* of the early seventeenth century focused on a more personal approach to penance and suffering, which was "intended to destroy self-will so as to allow the mortified subject to be infused with the will of God," according to Barbara B. Diefendorf. Many warrior nobles became dedicated *dévots*, employing hair-shirts, whips, and thorns in ritualistic self-mortification. "Ascetic self-discipline," Diefendorf argues, "produced individuals who were humble and yet confident in their intimate knowledge of the will of God."[89] Self-mortification and personal suffering became important aspects of Catholic militancy for warrior nobles in southern France.

Early seventeenth-century devout Catholic nobles resigned themselves to the possibility of meeting violent death as they risked their lives in the service of God. Submission to divine will demonstrated Catholics' determination and resolve in their efforts to restore the church, even if they faced martyrdom. Brad Gregory defines a Counter-Reformation "ethos of martyrdom" that inspired Catholics to resist "heretical seduction" and to suffer persecution, interrogation, torture, and death. Catholic writers of martyrologies and hagiographical collections glorified and exalted martyrdom, portraying Christ as "the king of martyrs." Lay Catholics, he suggests, viewed martyrdom as "the highest form of the imitation of Christ."[90] Failing to appreciate the broader dimensions of Catholic martyrdom in the European Wars of Religion, Gregory's analysis of it concentrates overly on English Henrician and Dutch Catholic martyrs.[91] Allan A. Tulchin reminds us that French Calvinists massacred hundreds of Catholics in Nîmes and La Rochelle in the 1560s, when the conditions were ripe for mass murder.[92] In taking into account only the victims of judicial violence and massacre, historians often seriously underestimate the magnitude of Catholic martyrdom during the French Wars of Religion. Lay Catholic nobles, priests, and missionaries killed in religious conflict and siege warfare during the civil wars of the late sixteenth and early seventeenth centuries were often celebrated as martyrs by their contemporaries, both through direct references and through religious art such as paintings of massacres and martyrdom by Nicolas Poussin.[93]

The beliefs and practices of Counter-Reformation Catholicism reinforced French Catholic nobles' determination to oppose Calvinist heresy within the kingdom and to demonstrate their obedience to God. Episcopal leadership in French dioceses and clerical debate in a series of assemblies of the clergy stressed the importance of Catholic believers' submission to God.[94] Many southern

French Catholic nobles and civic elites were swept up in the religious renewal of the Counter-Reformation movement, believing that they were performing their divinely ordained duty in combating "heretical" Calvinists. "Our interests consist only in the service of God, the maintenance of the king's authority, the peace of his subjects, [and] the execution of his sovereign justice," members of the parlement de Toulouse asserted in a letter to the duc de Montmorency.[95] Living in a region filled with so many "heretics" required Toulousains to demonstrate patience by submitting to the will of God and waiting for divine action to restore the true Church.

Defending the Faith: Calvinist Militancy

Militant Calvinist nobles promoted the notion of defending their churches through union and common action, claiming to act in "a just and legitimate defense" of their churches. Huguenot deputies signed unions joining Reformed churches across the kingdom in common action against the "pernicious designs" of the Catholics, who wanted to "exterminate" them. Denouncing the "passion and rage of our enemies," and their "barbarous cruelties," Calvinists deplored the demolition of their temples and the "interdictions of all exercise of religion in several churches." The Huguenot defense of Reformed religion within France emphasized attacks and massacres perpetrated by Catholics, often claiming that "persecution is overt." However, although Calvinists objected to religious persecution in the early seventeenth century, they no longer challenged the king's right to rule as the *prince légitime et naturel*.[96]

Huguenot militancy centered on religiously motivated Calvinist nobles who were willing and able to mobilize forces to defend their churches and protect the Huguenot faithful. Throughout the religious wars of the late sixteenth and early seventeenth centuries, Huguenot nobles acted as protectors of Calvinist-dominated communities and places de sûreté. Henri de La Tour vicomte de Turenne had been a powerful protector of Montauban as early as the 1570s, and Huguenot nobles such as Claude de La Trémouille duc de Thouars had played an important role in negotiating the Edict of Nantes.[97] François de Bonne duc de Lesdiguières and the duc de Bouillon continued to provide protection for Huguenot places de sûreté following the 1598 peace. Alan James correctly argues that early seventeenth-century Calvinist military activity represented "a militancy that permeated beyond the confines of the assembly."[98] A commission issued by the Huguenot political assembly at La Rochelle to Calvinist nobles stressed the "piety, virtue, sufficiency, capacity, valor, and experience in arms" of the chosen officers, who had an "entire fidelity and singular affection for the advancement of God's glory and the conservation of the said churches."[99]

Pious Calvinist nobles were active participants in worship services and in the lives of their local congregations. Calvinist temples provided a focal point for religiosity and militancy in Huguenot communities. The context of expanding civil conflict in Languedoc in 1621 gave the temple of Nîmes a heightened importance in the annual ceremonies of installing new consuls, who led the inhabitants "to the temple to hear the word of God."[100] Temples provided sites for expressions of communal unity and obedience, as when the Huguenot defenders gathered in the temple of Montauban to take an oath during siege of Montauban in 1621.[101] The duc de Rohan reminded a wavering Huguenot community of "the power of the general union so solemnly sworn in our churches to never abandon this common vessel in which we have all embarked."[102] The limited protections of the Edict of Nantes prompted many Huguenot communities to build new temples or improve existing ones in the early seventeenth century, and nobles were involved in funding their construction. These building projects provoked Catholic hostility, however, and "the number of potential targets increased in the wake of the Edict of Nantes and some temples were the objects of repeated attacks."[103] Calvinist nobles sought to protect their temples as part of their militant defense of their faith and the "true" church of God.

For Calvinist nobles, defending the church also meant actively participating in and relating to the Reformed religious and political assemblies. Many Calvinist nobles played important roles in Huguenot political assemblies, despite their differences and rivalries.[104] In defense of their churches, Huguenots complained of the "ordinary contraventions committed against the edicts of His Majesty to the prejudice of the good of our churches in the regions of Gévaudan in the Cévennes." Catholic nobles, many Huguenots claimed, were oppressing their Calvinist subjects or allowing them to be persecuted. Huguenots cited the "justice" of their "cause," arguing that the king would not permit such an "oppression" of his subjects.[105] Huguenot nobles who were unable to attend meetings of Reformed assemblies often coordinated their political and military activities with their deputies.

Martyr stories encouraged Huguenot nobles to embrace Calvinist activism and militancy. Huguenot nobles could be inspired to emulate the deaths of Calvinist martyrs who had been persecuted during the reign of Henri II or killed during the religious conflicts of the late sixteenth century. Luc Racaut argues that Jean Crespin's *Histoire des Martyrs* (1554) was "perhaps the single most important text for the elaboration of a distinct Huguenot identity."[106] Calvinist martyr stories emphasized the power of personal religious conviction and taught that "God did not allow useless suffering."[107] Apocalyptic belief helped fuel Calvinist militancy, especially in the mixed-confessional and war-torn areas of southern France.

Huguenot nobles in southern France tried to defend their churches and communities against Catholic encroachment. Catholic missionary conversion campaigns by the Jesuits, Capuchins, and other religious orders particularly threatened Huguenot churches. Calvinists in Languedoc used all methods to defend their confession, even appealing to the Catholic provincial governor, the duc de Montmorency, to prevent the introduction of Jesuits in the province.[108] Huguenot nobles coordinated with civic leaders and ministers to preserve Calvinist practice and to insulate their communities against Catholic proselytizing. Calvinist nobles worked with municipal consistories to maintain community discipline. Nobles often provided shelter, food, assistance, and protection to Reformed ministers traveling in southern France, including itinerate ministers. Calvinist leaders during the religious wars increasingly defended their faith by stressing "the conservative and conformist nature of their movement."[109] Many early seventeenth-century Huguenots adopted defensive attitudes that aimed at conserving their communities and preserving Calvinist practice wherever possible.

Although Calvinist militancy attracted many early seventeenth-century Huguenot nobles, not all Calvinists joined in militant Huguenot causes, seeing piety in their neutrality or loyalism during civil conflicts. The Huguenots of Bordeaux wrote to Henri IV in 1603, "in this holy and firm intention, placing our souls before God in our prayers, whether public or private, that He grant to Your Majesty a long and happy life, a firm and assured house, a tranquil and peaceful reign."[110] Calvinist nobles such as Sully and Du Plessis Mornay used similar arguments in avoiding engagement in Calvinist militancy.[111] Militant Huguenot nobles and their supporters reacted angrily against Calvinist moderates, whom they regarded as traitors. A Huguenot commission in 1622 called for all nobles in the Albigeois and Rouergue to follow Henri de Bourbon marquis de Malauze or be treated as "deserters of the common defense and union of the churches."[112]

Opposing Heresies

The obligations that warrior nobles felt toward their confessions went well beyond submitting to God or defending their churches. Both Calvinist and Catholic nobles felt that they needed to take assertive stances against heresy in their own communities and regions. Religious activism encouraged warrior nobles to confront members of an opposing confession directly and openly. Early seventeenth-century French people often acknowledged the king's special duty to suppress heresy within his kingdom, and warrior nobles may have seen their opposition to heresy as according well with the king's will.

Religious activism dictated that nobles engage in personal attempts to oppose heresy within their own communities, seigneuries, and governments. The warrior nobles' role in administering seigneurial justice may have given them a sense of duty in providing protection to their confession and also in opposing heresy in their seigneuries. Opposition to heresy by local nobles was important, because the prosecution of heresy by church and civil courts was mired by jurisdiction disputes and conflicting interests.

Catholic nobles seem to have taken considerable pride in their personal actions opposing heresy. Jean-Baptiste d'Ornano, a prominent Catholic noble in Vivarais, opposed the opening of a Calvinist collège or any other Protestant educational institution in his town of Aubenas to prevent any further spreading of heresy in his mixed-confessional region.[113] The parlement de Toulouse proudly claimed that their town was free of the "infection" of heresy in the 1620s. The members of parlement and other residents referred to Toulouse as a "Catholic city."[114] The exclusion of the unfaithful and the overt opposition to heresy were vital to conceptions of civic pride and piety in predominantly Catholic cities such as Toulouse or Paris.[115] When the seigneur de Mirepoix relieved the beleaguered Catholic town of Pamiers in 1621, he was praised as "the liberator and savior of this miserable land . . . , having always shown himself passionate and zealous in the service of God and of his king."[116]

Confraternities provided sites for militant Catholic nobles to participate in devotional activities and organize religious violence. Robert Harding demonstrates the links between confraternities and militant religious activism, particularly during the 1570s.[117] Catholic nobles continued to join confraternities in the early seventeenth century, acting to fulfill their religious duty to oppose heresy. Andrew E. Barnes portrays confraternities' chapels as both devotional and ritual centers that served as "headquarters of anti-Protestant forces."[118] Violence and piety blurred in confraternities' devotional and militant activities.[119]

Many Huguenots continued to regard Catholics as unrepentant and ignorant, misled by the pope and his supposedly malicious clergy. Calvinists feared Catholic missionary activity in southern France and were outraged at what they saw as Catholic pollution within their godly communities. Calvinist militants repeatedly attempted to block the entry of Catholic clergy into their communities, preventing Catholic minorities from performing rituals and processions openly in Huguenot-dominated towns.

Opposition to heresy often employed a language of confessional rights and privileges, echoing established religious and political positions. France lay under the legal regime of the Edict of Nantes, which all reform groups used to justify their defensive religious claims.[120] Calvinists cited specific guarantees for their confession, while the parlement of Toulouse repeatedly cited the Edict of Nantes as ordaining incremental changes favorable to Catholics.[121] Some recent studies have found evidence of confessional coexistence, and Keith Luria argues that "despite the religious tensions, Catholic and Huguenot neighbors found grounds on which to cooperate and negotiate local reconciliation."[122] Although certain forms of limited coexistence can be discerned in early seventeenth-century France, opposition to heresy ensured that religious contestation and conflict dominated life in the mixed-confessional provinces of Languedoc and Guyenne in this period. Thus, for example, Catholics in the mixed-confession city of Montpellier long bitterly remembered the "rebellion of the heretics" of 1621–1622 that had driven them from their homes and sacked their churches.[123]

✝

Early seventeenth-century warrior nobles were eager to taste combat and immerse themselves in violence. They devised elaborate performances of violence as they commanded troops, bonded with peers, and advanced their confessional programs. Warrior nobles' direction of military campaigns determined the forms of violence that were unleashed on French society. The common experiences of combat and military socialization may at times have bridged divisions among nobles, but distinct armed communities also forged solidarity in violence. Strong religious zeal motivated many nobles' participation in civil violence in this period, reinforcing the profound confessional divisions within French culture. Violent performances sustained warrior nobles' participation in the culture of revolt.

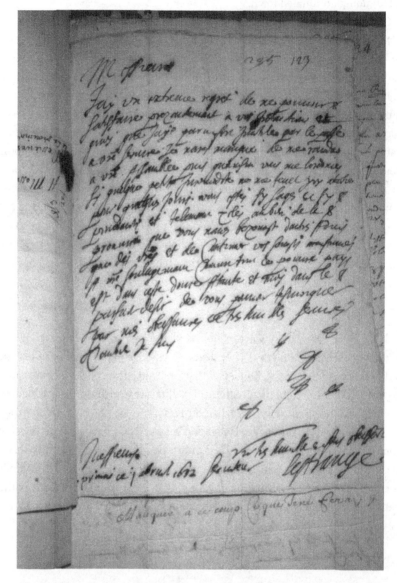

Claude d'Hautefort vicomte de Lestrange, letter to the estates of Languedoc dated 1 April 1632, a few months before his execution during that year's civil war. AD Hérault, A 44, f° 123. Photographed by the author.

Conclusion

V iolence permeated the daily lives of provincial nobles in southern France in the early seventeenth century. Personal participation in civil warfare defined the warrior nobility and shaped their political culture in this period. Provincial military elites participated in religious violence and civil conflict through bellicose activities that ordered their the social and cultural practices. In sharp contrast to previous historical arguments that the very conceptions of nobility were becoming less focused on military roles in the late sixteenth and early seventeenth centuries, the experiences of the warrior nobles in Languedoc and Guyenne examined in this study reveal that violence continued to be a way of life for many nobles.[1] Armed provincial nobles embraced warrior pursuits as an appropriate way to assert their political and religious aims through civil warfare.

Contemporary notions of the profession of arms envisioned martial practices as integral aspects of nobility. Early modern understandings of arms, *métier*, and violence—rather than chivalric legacies—promoted the profession of arms as the proper sphere of noble activity. The exercise of arms defined warrior nobles as members of a provincial military elite and established their identity as a social group distinct from the rest of French society. The ideal of the profession of arms encouraged provincial nobles to engage in incessant civil violence in Languedoc and Guyenne. When religious tensions threatened to produce confessional violence in Languedoc in 1603, Calvinists armed "as though at war," and Catholic nobles were ready to "mount their horses at the first command" to attack their Huguenot neighbors.[2] This account of localized mobilization suggests how fully the values of the profession of arms were ingrained in southern French warrior noble culture. During a period of pervasive religious and civil conflict, warrior noble household organizations and kinship practices became intimately associated with the profession of arms. Martial education, training, and experience prepared noblemen for the political, social, and military roles they would exercise in civil warfare. The ways in which provincial nobles employed wealth and *crédit* served their participation in civil warfare.

The bonds of nobility became closely linked to military practices that were attuned to waging localized civil conflicts during the early seventeenth century. Warrior noble culture remained resilient during this period of intense civil conflict, as nobles adapted their personal clientage relationships to participate more effectively in violence and provincial politics. François de Noailles comte d'Ayen claimed that he had been asked "to assemble my friends" to block Huguenot forces in Rouergue during the 1621 civil war. Describing clientage bonds as an expression of noble friendship, Noailles wrote of "his happiness that in no time I found many nobles resolved to assist me."[3] His understanding of clientage demonstrates the important role that clientage relations played in nobles' military activities. Southern French nobles' modes of assembling their "friends" partly confirm Kristen B. Neuschel's conclusion that clientage relations were not "strictly hierarchical or exclusive relationships," because the clientage bonds that provincial nobles constructed were loose, flexible, and multiple.[4] Officeholding enmeshed nobles in complex webs of authority, and they had to negotiate the multiple loyalties and overlapping jurisdictions of provincial politics carefully. The blurring of private and public through simultaneous uses of official and personal relationships located warrior nobles both inside and outside the royal state, according to contemporary conceptions of politics. Overlapping jurisdictions and unclear official designations produced a highly complex framework of authority in Languedoc and Guyenne, prompting honor disputes and precedence conflicts among provincial elites. An elaborate honor culture promoted martial values and guided warrior nobles' personal and collective performances of violence.

A culture of revolt became firmly ensconced in warrior noble culture in southern France by the end of the sixteenth century. Provincial military elites instigated violence through rituals of arming that justified their participation in civil violence and influenced the patterns of civil conflicts. Despite the king's ability to label nobles with the brand of revolt, warrior nobles established their own justifications for violence that guided their participation in civil warfare. Each warrior noble's *prise d'armes* was a crucial political act and an assertion of authority. As civil conflict escalated in Quercy in 1604, with reports of widespread "troubles" and "assemblies," the marquis de Thémines "left his house . . . accompanied by more than one hundred gentlemen of his friends."[5] Thémines's taking up of arms shows how rapidly warrior nobles could mobilize their own military forces and prepare to engage in civil violence. Provincial military elites organized their own personal armies, since the royal state lacked an effective monopoly over violence and the already tenuous networks of authority in southern France became even more problematic during civil conflicts. Prominent regional nobles constructed and maintained aggregate-contract field armies through complex processes of recruitment, mobilization, and war finance. These noblemen represented the key organizers of civil warfare in the early seventeenth century, orchestrating all aspects of the conduct of civil warfare—from recruitment to combat—according to their own understandings of the culture of revolt. Warrior nobles' ability to command troops and direct military operations allowed them to assert their political and religious agendas through their confessional activism. Warrior communities grew up during military campaigns, as nobles shared their experiences of violence and discussed their perceptions of civil conflict.

Examining provincial noble culture in the context of civil conflict reveals the significance of these warrior pursuits in early modern French history. The research strategies and interpretive methodologies employed in this study suggest ways of investigating political culture and civil violence that may be useful for research on conflicts in diverse regions during the European Wars of Religion or on civil wars in other historical periods. Exploiting diverse archival military records, noble correspondence, and administrative documents in conjunction with printed pamphlets and treatises permits this study to articulate new perspectives on the characteristics of noble culture and practices of civil warfare. The concept of warrior pursuits demonstrates the interpretive power of combining methods from the disciplines of cultural history and military history, offering a new model for investigating the cultural history of warfare.

Much more research is needed to understand the complex intersections of religion, violence, and political culture in early modern France. Historians of early modern warfare should incorporate cultural history more fully into their research and should consider the religious dimensions of conflicts in greater detail. Cultural historians of early modern France need to address warfare more directly—contemplating the production of violence and its impact on society, as well as studying the representations of war.

Struggles over provincial power, confessional agendas, and noble politics between 1598 and 1635 in Guyenne and Languedoc led to widespread civil warfare, promoted and perpetuated by a culture of revolt. These wars were connected to broader civil and confessional conflicts in this period in other regions of the kingdom, including Poitou, Aunis, Saintonge, Béarn, Dauphiné, and Provence. The most sustained conflict occurred in Languedoc and Guyenne, however, principally because of the large concentration of Huguenots in these confessionally mixed provinces. Catholic provincial nobles, sometimes assisted by royal armies, won a series of victories in these regional civil wars that altered the political situation in southern France, determining the religious fate of France and weakening this culture of revolt in the 1630s.

A gradual decline of religious militancy in French political culture accompanied the waning of the culture of revolt, as the profession of arms became less associated with confessional identities. Catholic religious politics increasingly focused on eliminating Huguenots' privileges and diminishing their legal status within the kingdom. Many Calvinist nobles converted to Catholicism or emigrated in this period, leaving the surviving isolated Reformed communities struggling to preserve their sacred boundaries and confessional identities.[6] Catholic and Calvinist militancy continued to flare up occasionally in localized areas—particularly in the Cévennes mountains—throughout the seventeenth century, yet the passions of the late sixteenth- and early seventeenth-century religious revivals gradually faded as the basic religious tensions were resolved to the detriment of Huguenot communities. While religious belief continued to play a significant role in French politics and culture throughout the seventeenth century, confessional militancy diminished beginning in the 1630s.

Major shifts in the provincial military elite in southern France disrupted regional bonds of nobility, altering political patterns and lessening the potential for civil warfare in the 1630s. Many of the prominent warrior nobles in southern France had been killed or executed during the conflicts of the early seventeenth century. Notably, the powerful Montmorency family's three-generation position of dominance in Languedoc was shattered by the disastrous 1632 civil war. A contemporary pamphlet described the nobles of Languedoc as kneeling before their new governor, the maréchal de Schömberg:

> Great duc, soul and spirit of the province, since you are the governor, the hope of the people of Languedoc in its desolation, the object of joy of the afflicted, and the assurance of us all; since your arrival is happy for the province, which—exhausted from miseries, all ruined, bled, and liquidated—awaits with impatience the happy day of your coming, as one who will make the goodness, favors, and graces of the

king flow from the heavens, which the poor people of Languedoc and those here among us, innocent and guilty, have so much need.[7]

Schömberg successfully installed himself as provincial governor of Languedoc after his 1632 victory, but his sudden death and his successor's relative detachment from regional affairs meant that the Schömberg family never dominated the province as the Montmorencys had. Louis XIII divided the office of lieutenant general of Languedoc into three separate lieutenancies in 1633, and the Lévis-Ventadour family gave up its lieutenancy, shifting its administrative focus to the province of Limousin. An influx of nobles from other provinces had taken up offices and landholdings in Guyenne and Languedoc in the aftermath of each successive civil conflict, shifting clientage bonds in southern France. Henri II de Bourbon prince de Condé's influence in Languedoc and Guyenne had grown throughout the 1620s and 1630s due to his military commands in the provinces and his inheritance of Montmorency's landholdings, but Condé was rarely present in southern France in the 1630s, since he was increasingly involved in court politics and had a new position as governor of Burgundy. In Guyenne, rivalries and court politics undermined the duc d'Épernon's influence and he was ultimately disgraced in 1638. The instability of warrior noble clientage and the fragility of the provincial administrative and military positions seem to have made southern French nobles less prepared to instigate civil conflicts as the seventeenth century progressed.[8]

Royal family members' diminishing ability to organize and promote civil conflicts undermined the legitimacy of the culture of revolt. Louis XIII's control over the composition of the royal council and ministries was confirmed by the Day of Dupes in November 1630, which prompted Marie de Médicis to flee from the kingdom into exile and fueled the subsequent civil warfare in 1631 and 1632 between the king and his brother, Gaston de Bourbon duc d'Orléans. The animosities between Louis XIII and Gaston d'Orléans moderated slightly after the latter returned to France and accepted a diminished role in the state, and Gaston's potential to foment civil conflict was neutralized. As Marie de Médicis's sojourn in the Spanish Netherlands lengthened, her status as a permanent exile was gradually accepted. The prince de Condé had become a strong ally of the king by the 1630s, strengthening Louis XIII's position as head of the royal family. The problem of an unclear royal succession remained until 1638, when the future Louis XIV was finally born. While the disputes between royal family members were never fully resolved, the clarified succession and the submission of Gaston d'Orléans somewhat diffused tensions within the Bourbon dynasty. The decreased role of the royal family in governance and the gradual dissipation of the royal family crisis in the 1630s removed a vital means for warrior nobles to justify their *prise d'armes* and to legitimize their participation in civil warfare.[9]

After France entered the Thirty Years' War in 1635, prolonged foreign warfare and sweeping military changes accelerated the decline of the culture of revolt, and new conceptions of warrior pursuits emerged. The expanded scale of warfare and the sustained rise in French wartime army sizes in the 1630s and 1640s increased the number of military offices available to warrior nobles.[10] Local recruitment, mobilization, and logistics could now be separated from military operations and coordinated with provincial administrative officers and royal officials as a state-commission army style emerged. Although the personal military forces of warrior nobles continued to play a significant role in the armies fighting against the Spanish in the 1630s, the warrior nobles of Languedoc and Guyenne were increasingly linked to a military system that relied more heavily on the direction of the monarch and his ministers in organizing warfare. Warrior nobles and their military offices thus became more firmly connected to a growing royal military system by the mid-seventeenth century. Their political culture increasingly centered on new conceptions of the profession of arms that linked military officeholding to royal service in foreign warfare.

Changing patterns of civil warfare also prompted significant changes in warrior nobles' bellicose practices. The civil warfare of the early seventeenth century could be considered as a sort of "Fronde before the Fronde," since warrior nobles again participated heavily in civil conflict between 1648 and 1652. Warrior nobles from southern France organized and led military forces in widespread civil conflict much as they had done in the 1610s and 1620s, but the Fronde exhibited very different dynamics from these earlier civil wars. The parlements and the emerging new nobility played a more substantial role in the Fronde than they had earlier in the century. Urban conflicts and potentially revolutionary politics were more extensive and sustained during the Fronde, especially in Paris and Bordeaux. Significant foreign intervention by mercenary forces, especially supporting the cardinal de Mazarin, influenced the course of the conflict. Unlike the civil warfare of the early period, the Fronde included little religious conflict, and much of the fighting was centered around Paris and other major urban centers that housed parlements and predominantly Catholic populations, rather than in the remaining Calvinist communities and rural areas in Languedoc and Guyenne.[11]

The diminishing influence of the culture of revolt created a separation between warrior noble culture and civil warfare that would have lasting conse-
quences for the Bourbon royal state and French society. The transitions in the
patterns of civil warfare and in the style of military systems also signaled new
directions in French state development. Rather than implementing the crucial
phase of absolutism, as A. D. Lublinskaya argues, the civil warfare in early
seventeenth-century Languedoc and Guyenne determined the shape of the confessional settlement and resolved the religious divisions within the nobility,
forging a new basis of cooperation between regional nobles and the monarch.[12]
Some of the same provincial warrior nobles who had participated in these civil
conflicts ultimately dismantled the culture of revolt and adapted their warrior
pursuits to the changing military contexts. Although regional nobles were not
given a great role in the royal council and ministries, their status within the
expanding military system and the provincial military administration was significant. State development in the early seventeenth century involved improvised responses to the pressures of religious turmoil and civil warfare, instead
of the implementation of absolutist designs or conscious state-building projects
devised by Louis XIII and Richelieu. The state development patterns emerging in
the early seventeenth century began to refocus the royal state on healing the wounds
of religious and civil warfare, allowing Catholic warrior nobles and the king to
begin to negotiate ways of collaborating more effectively.

The transformations that progressively weakened the culture of revolt in the
1630s created new priorities in warrior noble culture. Military practices and the
profession of arms became dissociated from civil warfare, allowing the bonds of
nobility to operate more widely, as nobles socialized while participating together
in military campaigns beyond France's borders. The changes in military systems, civil conflict, and state development played a significant role in altering
royal service culture during the *Grand Siècle*. Warrior noble political culture
remained centered on clientage, but military officers could now draw on their
multiple patrons and diverse connections without having to make stark choices
between them in a context of civil warfare—where personal protection, confessional agendas, and localized politics had dominated their concerns.

Warrior noble culture was ultimately transformed in the mid-seventeenth
century, not by the disappearance of perceptions of a duty to revolt, but rather
by the disruption of the culture of revolt, the reorientation of the profession of
arms, and the adaptation of the bonds of nobility. The particular confessional
agendas and political aims that the warrior nobles of Languedoc and Guyenne
had advanced during the early seventeenth-century civil wars gradually shifted,

along with their warrior pursuits. As long as the profession of arms and the bonds of nobility were inextricably linked to the culture of revolt, the "warlike deeds" that provincial nobles performed could be seen as "heroic gestures," enacted through their "beautiful warrior acts."[13]

Abbreviations

AAE	Archives de la Ministère des Affaires Étrangères, Paris
AC	Archives Communales
ACL	François de Bonne duc de Lesdiguières, *Actes et correspondance du connétable de Lesdiguières,* edited by Louis-Archambaud Douglas and Joseph Roman, 3 vols. (Grenoble: E. Allier, 1878–1884)
AD	Archives Départementales
AG	Archives de Guerre, Château de Vincennes
AM	Archives Municipales
AN	Archives Nationales, Paris
Annales ESC	*Annales: Économies, Sociétés, Civilisations*
Annales HSS	*Annales: Histoire, Sciences Sociales*
ASF	Archivio di Stato di Firenze, Florence
BM	Bibliotheque Municipale
BNF	Bibliothèque Nationale de France, Paris
BSHPF	*Bulletin de la Société d'Histoire du Protestantisme Française*
CSV	*Les Commentaires du soldat du Vivarais. Ou se voit l'origine de la rébellion de la France et toutes les guerres que, durant icelle, le pays du Vivarais a souffertes, divisés en trois livres, selon le temps que lesdites guerres sont arrivées. Suivis du Voyage du duc de Rohan en Vivarais, l'en 1628; de la Relation de la révolte de Roure en 1670; Et d'une Anecdote extraite du journal manuscrit de J. de Banne, chanoine de Viviers* (1908; reprint, Valence: La Bouquinerie, 1991)
Du Cros	Simon Du Cros, *Histoire de la vie de Henry dernier duc de Montmorency, contenant tout ce qu'il a fait de plus remarquable depuis sa naissance jusques à sa mort* (Paris: Antoine Sommaville & Augustin Courbé, 1643)
Girard	Guillaume Girard, *Histoire de la vie du duc d'Espernon* (1655; reprint, Paris: Montalant, 1730)
Haag	Eugène Haag and Émile Haag, *La France protestante ou vies des protestants français qui se sont fait un nom dans l'histoire depuis les premiers temps de la réformation jusqu'à la reconnaissance du principe de la liberté des cultes par l'assemblée nationale,* 10 vols. (1847–1860; reprint, Geneva: Slatkine, 1966)

HGL	Claude de Vic and Joseph Vaissete, *Histoire générale de Languedoc*, 15 vols. (1730–1745; reprint, Toulouse: Privat, 1872–1892)
HRHRC	Harry Ransom Humanities Research Center, Austin, Texas
La Roque M	Louis de La Roque, *Armorial de la noblesse de Languedoc. Généralité de Montpellier*, 2 vols. (1860; reprint, Montpellier: Le Clerc, 1995)
La Roque T	Louis de La Roque, *Armorial de la noblesse de Languedoc. Généralité de Toulouse* (1863; reprint, Marseille: Laffitte, 1980)
LCR	*Lettres, instructions diplomatiques et papiers d'état du cardinal de Richelieu*, edited by Georges d'Avenel. 8 vols. (Paris: Imprimérie Impérial [puis Nationale], 1853–1877)
MdP	Mediceo del Principato collection, ASF
Mss. fr.	Manuscrits français series in the Département des Manuscrits, BNF
NAF	Nouvelles acquisitions français series in the Département des Manuscrits, BNF
NCL	Louis-Fermin-Herve Bouchitté, ed., *Négociations, lettres et pièces relatives à la conférence de Loudun* (Paris: Imprimérie Impériale, 1862)
NCM	*Nouvelle collection des mémoires pour servir a l'histoire de France depuis le XIIIᵉ siècle jusqu'à la fin du XVIIIᵉ*, edited by Joseph-François Michaud and Jean-Joseph-François Poujoulat, 32 vols. (Paris: L'Éditeur du Commentaire Analytique du Code Civil, 1836–1839)
PFHF	*Pièces fugitives pour servir a l'histoire de France avec des notes historiques & géographiques*, edited by Charles de Bachi marquis d'Aubais, 2 vols. (Paris: Hugues-Daniel Chaubert & Claude Herissant, 1759)
SHAT	Service Historique de l'Armée de Terre, Château de Vincennes

Notes

INTRODUCTION

1. Adémar de Monteil comte de Grignan to [?], 1 November 1614, BNF, Clairambault 1131, f° 252–253.

2. Pierre II Fabry de Roqueyrolz, "Mémoire concernant les Rlg^res de la province de Languedoc," AN, TT 430, f° 34.

3. Gaches, *Suite des mémoires*, 17.

4. Jouanna, *L'Idée de race en France*, 1: 326–332.

5. Laval, *Desseins de professions nobles et publiques*, 19–20, 25–37.

6. Billon, *Les Principes de l'art militaire*; Drévillon, *L'Impôt du sang*, 275–296, 321–351.

7. François de Bonne duc de Lesdiguières, "Discours de l'art militaire," in *ACL*, 2: 542–543.

8. Souhait, *Le Parfaict gentil-homme*; Pelletier, *La Nourriture de la noblesse*; Loyseau, *Traité des seigneuries*; Faret, *L'Honneste-homme*. And see analysis of such treatises in Dewald, *Aristocratic Experience and the Origins of Modern Culture*, 45–68, 104–145.

9. Arnauld, *Presentation de Monsieur de Montmorency en l'office d'Admiral de France*.

10. Anne de Lévis duc de Ventadour to M. Castillon, Paris, August 1608, BNF, Mss. fr. 3602, f° 48.

11. Nicot, *Thresor de la Langue Francoyse*, 165.

12. Henri I de Montmorency duc de Montmorency to Marie de Médicis, La Grange, 20 March 1614, BNF, Clairambault 1131, f° 188.

13. Nicholas B. Dirks, Geoff Eley, and Sherry B. Ortner, "Introduction," and Sherry B. Ortner, "Theory in Anthropology since the Sixties," in *Culture/Power/History*, ed. Dirks et al., 3–6, 372–411; Certeau, *L'Invention du quotidian*.

14. BNF, Dupuy 100, f° 109.

15. Jouanna, "Des réseaux d'amitié aux clientèles centralisées," 21–38.

16. *Recit tres-veritable*.

17. AN, TT 430, f° 22.

18. *CSV*, 172; François I Esparbès de Lussan marquis d'Aubeterre to Paul Phélypeaux seigneur de Pontchartrain, Agen, 12 November 1615, BNF, Clairambault 366, f° 24–25.

19. *Harangue faicte au Roy, par messieurs de Montpellier*.

20. *Reglement pour les gens de guerre*.

21. Du Cros, 16–17.

22. *Discours de la Confidence.*

23. "Abbregé des exploitz de guerre de deffunct monseigneur le mar^al de Praslin faict par luy mesme," BNF, Mss. fr. 15616; *Immortalité du carrousel de Monseigneur d'Espernon.*

24. *La Prise et reduction de la ville et chasteau de Nerac.*

25. Jouanna, *Le Devoir de révolte,* 384–388.

26. Nicolas de Verdun, premier président du parlement de Toulouse, to Henri IV, Toulouse, 14 September 1604, BNF, Mss. fr. 23198, f° 183–186.

27. Jouanna, *Le Devoir de révolte,* 368–390.

28. Sandberg, "'Se couvrant toujours . . . du nom du roi,'" 423–440.

29. Biron, *Letters and Documents,* 1: 59–64.

30. Lynn, "Evolution of Army Style," 505–545.

31. François Duval, *Mémoires,* 169.

32. Dewald, *Aristocratic Experience and the Origins of Modern Culture*; Neuschel, *Word of Honor*; Schalk, *From Valor to Pedigree*; Constant, *La Noblesse française aux XVIe et XVIIe siècles.*

33. Le Person, *"Practiques" et "Practiqueurs"*; Le Roux, *La Faveur du roi*; Jouanna, *Le Devoir de révolte*; Kettering, *Patrons, Brokers, and Clients in Seventeenth-Century France.*

34. Carroll, *Blood and Violence in Early Modern France*; Brioist et al., *Croiser le fer*; Billacois, *Le Duel.*

35. Elias, *Civilizing Process* and *Court Society.*

36. Carroll, *Blood and Violence in Early Modern France.*

37. Schalk, "The Court as 'Civilizer' of the Nobility."

38. Asch, *Nobilities in Transition*; Lukowski, *European Nobility in the Eighteenth Century*; Dewald, *European Nobility*; Scott, ed., *European Nobilities in the Seventeenth and Eighteenth Centuries.*

39. Lublinskaya, *French Absolutism,* 1–3. David Parker, *Making of French Absolutism,* 59–60, concurs, calling the 1620s "perhaps the most crucial phase in the enormously protracted but progressive extension of royal authority."

40. Nicholas B. Dirks, "Ritual and Resistance: Subversion as a Social Fact," in *Culture/Power/History,* ed. Dirks et al., 483–503; Ortner, "Theory in Anthropology," ibid., 388–403.

41. Michel de Certeau uses the concept of *la perruque,* "the wig," to explain a myriad of techniques that subjects can use to divert, reroute, and misappropriate—especially referring to "the worker's own work disguised as work for his employer." This translation comes from Certeau, *The Practices of Everyday Life,* trans. Steven Rendall, 25. On the concept of *la perruque,* see Certeau, *L'Invention du quotidian,* xxxv–liii, 43–49, 239–255.

42. Beik, "Absolutism of Louis XIV," 195–224; Henshall, *Myth of Absolutism*; Mettam, *Power and Faction*; Bonney, "Absolutism," 93–117.

43. Veena Das and Arthur Kleinman, "Introduction," in *Violence and Subjectivity,* ed. Das et al., 1–18.

44. D'Cruze and Rao, eds., *Violence, Vulnerability and Embodiment*; Juergensmeyer, *Terror in the Mind of God,* 122–126; *Violence and Subjectivity,* ed. Das et al.; Scarry, *Body in Pain,* 60–157.

45. Das, *Life and Words*, 1–17; Das and Kleinman, "Introduction," in *Violence and Subjectivity*, ed. Das et al., 16.

46. Kalyvas, *Logic of Violence in Civil War*; and see also Levi, *The Drowned and the Saved*.

47. Sandberg, "'To Deliver a Greatly Persecuted Church,'" 33–64; Grandjean and Roussel, eds., *Coexister dans l'intolérance*.

48. Diefendorf, *From Penitence to Charity*; Sorrel and Meyer, eds., *Les Missions intérieurs*.

49. Lynn, "Evolution of Army Style," 505–545; Geoffrey Parker, *Military Revolution*; Rogers, ed., *Military Revolution Debate*.

50. See, e.g., Hickey, *Coming of French Absolutism*; Beik, *Absolutism and Society in Seventeenth-Century France*.

PROLOGUE

1. *Reduction de la ville de Privaz.*

2. Du Cros.

3. AD Hérault, C 7059, f° 102–105; AD Hérault, 1 E 239, f° 14; BNF, Cinq Cens de Colbert, f° 393–394.

4. *Premiere lettre de Monsieur le duc d'Espernon.*

5. Louis XIII to Bernard Nogaret de La Valette marquis de La Valette, Tours, 10 May 1621, BNF, Nouv. Acq. Fr. 5246, f° 19.

6. Girard.

7. Ambeville to Louis XIII, Cognac, 23 May 1621, BNF, Clairambault 377, f° 699; *La prise des advenues et passages de La Rochelle*; *La Deffaicte de Quatre Cens Hommes sortis de la Rochelle*.

8. *Declaration des eglises reformees de France et souveraineté de Bearn.*

9. See Châtillon's correspondence and ordonnances in AD Hérault, B 22590 and AD Hérault, B 22603; Aigrefeuille, *Histoire de la ville de Montpellier*, 2: 46.

10. Deliberations of the estates of Languedoc held at Beziers and Carcassonne, October–November 1621, AD Hérault, C 7059, f° 76–78; *La Deffaicte de quatre cents hommes par le sieur de Mont-Real*.

11. *Les Actes de l'assemblée nouvellement tenue à Nismes par les députés des Églises réformées du Languedoc*; *Manifeste de M. de Chastillon*; Aigrefeuille, *Histoire de la ville de Montpellier*, 2: 51–57.

12. Souriac, "Les Places de sûreté protestantes."

13. In addition to Alexandre Dumas's *Les Trois Mousquetaires* (1844) and Edmond Rostand's *Cyrano de Bergerac* (1897), see the artwork of Eugene Delacroix, Paul Delaroche, Jean-Louis-Ernest Meissonier, and Henri Motte.

14. Brioist et al., *Croiser le fer*, 44–63.

15. Loyseau, *Treatise of Orders*, 103.

16. Ford, *Robe and Sword*.

17. Bohanan, *Old and New Nobility in Aix-en-Provence*; Descimon, "Birth of the Nobility of the Robe."

18. Van Orden, *Music, Discipline, and Arms*.

19. Nicot, *Thresor de la Langue Francoyse*, 43.

20. *Le Mars resussité de la Gendarmerie; Reglement qve le Roy vevt & entend estre dores-nauant obserué par les gens de Guerre*.

21. *La Deffaicte de Quatre Cens Hommes sortis de la Rochelle*.

22. *Signalee deffaite de la garnison de Nismes par monsieur le mareschal dEstree*.

23. "Memoire ou journal du siege de Montpellier," BNF, Mss. fr. 23339, f° 170–171; Nicot, *Thresor de la Langue Francoyse*, 668–669.

24. The terms "warrior nobles" and *"noblesse guerrière"* are often used, but without clear definitions: Neuschel, *Word of Honor*, 1–5; Béchu, "Noblesse d'épée et tradition militaire."

25. Alfonse d'Ornano to Henri I de Montmorency duc de Montmorency, Bordeaux, February 1607, BNF, Mss. fr. 3592, f° 90.

26. Faret, *L'Honneste-homme*, 95.

CHAPTER 1: SOUTHERN FRANCE AND ITS WARRIOR ELITE

1. *HGL*, 11: 917–920; "Cahier présenté par Messieurs les députés de la noblesse de Languedoc à l'assemblé des états généraux tenue en la ville de Paris en l'année 1614," *HGL*, 12: 1638–1648; Hayden, *France and the Estates General of 1614*.

2. "Reglement faict par monseigneur le duc de Montmorancy & de Dampville pair & admiral de France de Guienne & de Bretaigne gouverneur & lieutenant general pour le Roy en Lang.oc sur ce que Monsieur de St. Geniers gouverneur de Narbonn en labsence de mond. seigneur aura a faire pour ce que est cy appres a prinne," AD Hérault, G 1835; *HGL*, 11: 917–923.

3. *Le Roi d'armes du Languedoc*.

4. Chabans, *Histoire de la guerre des Huguenots*, 558.

5. Faret, *L'Honneste-homme*, 15–17, trans. in Dewald, *Aristocratic Experience and the Origins of Modern Culture*, 45.

6. For recent attempts to analyze the profession of arms, see Chagniot, *Guerre et so-ciété à l'époque moderne*, 131–140; Dewald, *Aristocratic Experience and the Origins of Modern Culture*, 45–68; Constant, *La Noblesse française aux XVIe et XVIIe siècles*, 11–31; Schalk, *From Valor to Pedigree*, 3–20.

7. Neuschel, *Word of Honor*, 64–65; Jouanna, *Le Devoir de révolte*, 384–388.

8. Dewald, *Aristocratic Experience and the Origins of Modern Culture*, 45–68.

9. *Dictionnaire historique de la langue française*, ed. Rey et al., 1235–1236, 1641–1642.

10. *Officier* could still refer to judicial and administrative officials, but "the dominant usage" of *officier* in early modern French "concerned the hierarchies of the police and mili-tary" (ibid., 1360). Jean Chagniot argues that the term *officier* only began to be used for military commanders around 1635, in Chagniot, "La Lente maturation de l'armée perma-nente," in *L'Officier français*, ed. Crubois, 11–12. However, late sixteenth-century and early seventeenth-century documents demonstrate that *officier* was already being used fre-quently to refer to military officers.

11. Sandberg, "'Generous Amazons Came to the Breach,'" 654–688; Lynn, *Women, Armies, and Warfare*.

12. Connell, "Big Picture," 601 (italics in original); and see also id., *Masculinities*, 3–44.

13. Specific studies of French masculinity include Nye, *Masculinity and Male Codes of Honor in Modern France*; Reddy, *Invisible Code*.

14. La Roque de La Lontière, *Traité de la noblesse*, n.p.

15. Loyseau, *Treatise of Orders*, 16–17.

16. *CSV*, 212.

17. Nassiet, *Parenté, noblesse et états dynastiques*, 20–23. Another estimate, in Orléa, *La Noblesse aux États généraux*, 56, cited in Jouanna, *Le Devoir de révolte*, 16–18, finds 20,000 to 30,000 noble families, or 100,000 to 150,000 nobles, out of a population of 15 million. The proportion of nobles to the overall population gradually declined to about 0.52 percent of the population by 1789, according to Dewald, *European Nobility*, 22–27.

18. Blaufarb, *French Army, 1750–1820*, 48–49, estimates that 60 percent of adult male nobles in late eighteenth-century France were active or retired military officers.

19. Le Roy Ladurie, *Peasants of Languedoc*, 51.

20. For a discussion of *preuves de noblesse*, see Jouanna, "Mémoire nobiliaire," 197–206.

21. Blanchard, "Une Approche de la noblesse languedocienne," in *Sociétés et idéologies*, ed. Fouilleron et al., 1: 15–35; on earlier *enquêtes*, see Nassiet, *Parenté, noblesse et états dynastiques*, 21.

22. Beik, *Absolutism and Society in Seventeenth-Century France*, 42–43.

23. Blanchard, "Une Approche de la noblesse languedocienne," in *Sociétés et idéologies*, ed. Fouilleron et al., 1: 23.

24. "Lettres de Noblesse registres en la Chambre des Comptes de Montpellier," BNF, Mss. fr. 22253, f° 2–4.

25. "Genealogie de la noble famille des Auzolles en Auvergne faicte lan 1620," BNF, Cabinet d'Hozier 22, f° 489.

26. *L'Antiquité de Bourdeaus* (1565) describes "ceste grande Guiene d'Auguste," which was later divided.

27. The six sénéchausées of Périgord, Rouergue, Quercy, Bazadais, Agenais and Condomais, and Bordeaux were particularly important administrative divisions. See Fessenden, "Épernon and Guyenne," 7–41.

28. Major, *From Renaissance Monarchy to Absolute Monarchy*, 155–158; Monlezun, *Histoire de la Gascogne*, 5: 481–482.

29. "Traité des princes, conseillers et autres ministres de l'estat de France," in *Foreign Intelligence and Information in Elizabethan England*, ed. David Potter, 77.

30. Pontchartrain, *Mémoires concernant les affaires de France sous la régence de Marie de Médicis*, in *NCM*, 5: 353.

31. "Ce qu'on dit icy des affaires de la court," BNF, Mss. fr. 15582, f° 270–271.

32. The cour des aides en Guyenne was founded only in 1629, so documents dealing with Guyenne nobles in the early seventeenth century are dispersed throughout different

archival holdings. See Bège-Seurin, "Droit et identité nobiliaire," 166–179; Cocula, "La fin du parti protestant en Guyenne," 73–90.

33. Benedict, "Huguenot Population of France, 1600–85," 77–78.

34. *L'Hevrevse arrivee dv roy dans Bourdeaus.*

35. Beik, *Urban Protest in Seventeenth-Century France,* 16–18, 133–143; Boutruche, *Bordeaux de 1453 à 1715.*

36. Fessenden, "Épernon and Guyenne," 7–41.

37. Gaufreteau, *Chronique Bordeloise,* 2: 22.

38. "Estat des places tant villes que chãux que ceux de la religion reformée en France ont du roy pour leur seureté ou ils tiennent gens de guerre pour le payement desquels sa ma^té delivre certaine sõe a quatre tresoriers quilz eslisent en leurs assemblées generalles de trois ans en trois ans," BNF, Mss. fr. 7605, f° 85–89.

39. For an introduction to the Gascogne region, see Bordes, "La Gascogne" in *Régions et régionalisme en France,* ed. Gras and Livet, 139–154.

40. Ian Roy, "Introduction," in Monluc, *Habsburg-Valois Wars,* 1.

41. Monluc, *Habsburg-Valois Wars,* 217. The translation here is Ian Roy's.

42. "Traité des princes, conseillers et autres ministres de l'estat de France," in *Foreign Intelligence and Information in Elizabethan England,* ed. David Potter, 76.

43. *La Revolte du pays de Gascogne.*

44. Pierre Duval, *Description de la France,* 167.

45. Monlezun, *Histoire de la Gascogne,* 5: 473–475.

46. Brunet, "Anatomie des réseaux ligueurs," 167–171.

47. Solon, "Le rôle des forces armées en Comminges avant les guerres de religion," 19–40; Brunet, "L'Évêque ligueur Urbain de Saint-Gelais," 151–176.

48. Antoine II de Cous évêque de Condom to Paul Phélypeaux seigneur de Pontchartrain, Condom, 8 June 1621, BNF, Clairambault 377, f° 723–725; Nérac had an annual average of 408 Calvinist baptisms in the early seventeenth century, according to Benedict, "Huguenot Population of France, 1600–85," 77.

49. Benedict, "French Cities from the Sixteenth Century to the Revolution," 9.

50. Mateu, "Un siècle paradoxal (XVIIe siècle)," 129–172; Garrison, *Protestants du Midi,* 66; Messines, "Contre-Réforme et Réforme catholique en Agenais," 193–201; Beik, *Urban Protest in Seventeenth-Century France,* 76–78.

51. Hanlon, *Confession and Community,* 22–23, 37.

52. Garrison, *Protestants du Midi,* 23–25.

53. "Estat des places . . . ," BNF, Mss. fr. 7605, f° 85–89; "Plans de Places Fortes," BNF, Mss. fr. 15380, f° 15; Garrison, *Protestants du Midi,* 23, 66.

54. "Plans de Places Fortes," BNF, Mss. fr. 15380, f° 61; "Articles presentez au Roy par les depputez des communaultez de ceux de la Religion et les responces Aoust 1625 en juillet 1625," BNF, Mss. fr. 4102, f° 150–152.

55. "Plans de Places Fortes," BNF, Mss. fr. 15380, f° 45; "Memoire ou journal du siege de Montpellier," BNF, Mss. fr. 23339, f° 171–172.

56. Benedict, "French Cities from the Sixteenth Century to the Revolution," 9.

57. Fessenden, "Épernon and Guyenne," 27.

58. "Estat des places . . . ," BNF, Mss. fr. 7605, f° 85–89.

59. Cassagnes-Brouquet, *Vierges noires*, 185–188.

60. Fessenden, "Épernon and Guyenne," 27.

61. BNF, Mss. fr. 15381, f° 156–159.

62. Rome, *Les Bourgeois protestants de Montauban au XVIIe siècle*, 13; Le Bret, *Histoire de Montauban.*

63. Montauban had an average 673 Protestant baptisms per year in the first years of the seventeenth century. Benedict, "Huguenot Population of France, 1600–85," 75–79; Conner, *Huguenot Heartland*, 16, 151.

64. Guicharnaud, *Montauban au XVIIe*, 25–41.

65. Le Bret, *Histoire de Montauban*, 2: 99–105.

66. Maag, "Huguenot Academies," 139–156.

67. For François de Noailles's view of Rouergue, see correspondence in BNF, Clairambault 364, 366, 377, 378; Fessenden, "Épernon and Guyenne," 27; Kalas, "Marriage, Clientage, Office Holding."

68. Mouysset, "La place du pouvoir consulaire à Rodez."

69. Lançon, "Les confréries du Rosaire en Rouergue."

70. Benedict, "Huguenot Population of France, 1600–85," 83.

71. François de Noailles comte d'Ayen to Louis XIII, L'Arche, 3 May 1621, BNF, Clairambaut 377, f° 643–645; Jean II de La Valette baron de Cornusson to Louis XIII, Toulouse, 28 April 1621, BNF, Clairambault 377, f° 625–626.

72. "Memoire des villes et bourgs des tenues par ceux de la relligion tant au bas Languedoc que Hault Lang^oc Sevenes et Rouergue," BNF, Mss. fr. 15828, f° 5; Garrison, *Protestants du Midi*, 182–183.

73. *La Prise remarquable de Marguerites.*

74. "Rolle des principales & plus ancieñes maizons du Languedoc dont j'ay peu avoir memoire," BNF, Mss. fr. 20235, f° 300–310.

75. Catel, *Memoires de l'histoire du Languedoc*, 42–43, 49. On pastel cultivation, dye production, and commerce, see Schneider, "Crown and Capitoulat," 201; Lacombe-Saboly, "Le compte de voyage de Dominque Guaches."

76. Bennessar, "Des années de la Ligue aux jours de Fronde," 271–291; Beik, *Absolutism and Society*, 61–64.

77. Schneider, *Public Life in Toulouse*, 12–42, 136–155.

78. Davis, *Return of Martin Guerre*, 73–74; Catel, *Memoires de l'histoire du Languedoc*, 48; Bourdieu-Weiss, "Un architecte toulousain du XVIIe siècle," 157–170; Tollon, "L'emploi de la brique," 85–104.

79. Schneider, *Public Life in Toulouse*, 90–131; id., "Crown and Capitoulat," 202–203; Greengrass, "*Sainte Union* in the Provinces," 469–496; Davies, "Persecution and Protestantism," 31–51; Brenac, "Toulouse, centre de lutte contre le protestantisme," 31–45.

80. Bennessar, "Des années de la Ligue aux jours de Fronde," 276–280.

81. Benedict, "Saint Bartholomew's Day Massacre in the Provinces," 205–225.

82. Graule, *Histoire de Lescure.*

83. Conner, *Huguenot Heartland*, 93, 100–101.

84. Eurich, "'Speaking the King's Language,'" 175–192; Benedict, "Huguenot Population of France, 1600–85," 77.

85. Artigaut, *Les Protestants de Castres*, 8–12; Capot, *Justice et religion en Languedoc*, 41–77.

86. Eurich, "'Speaking the King's Language,'" 120.

87. Mentzer, *Blood and Belief*, 6–7.

88. Beik, *Absolutism and Society in Seventeenth-Century France*, 121.

89. *HGL*, 12: 1638–1648; AD Aude, 2 E 17; BNF, Clairambault 366.

90. Guilaine and Fabre, eds., *Histoire de Carcassonne*, 109–129.

91. Fauré, *La Noblesse dans le diocese de Carcassonne*; Mahul, *Cartulaire et archives des communes . . . de Carcassonne*.

92. Harding, *Anatomy of a Power Elite*, 149–154.

93. "Recit veritable de la prise de la ville de Pamiers Capitale du Pays de Foix . . . ," BNF, Dupuy 100, f° 298–301; Joseph d'Esparbès de Lussan, évêque de Pamiers, to Paul Phélypeaux seigneur de Pontchartrain, Toulouse, 10 June 1621, BNF, Clairambault 377, f° 717.

94. Davis, *Return of Martin Guerre*, 8–14.

95. Larguier, "Narbonne et la voie méditerranéenne du pastel," 149–167.

96. BNF, Languedoc-Bénédictins 105, f°62–83; La Roque M, 1: 239–241.

97. AD Hérault, B 22739; AD Hérault, B 22617; La Roque M, 1: 493–495.

98. Beik, *Absolutism and Society in Seventeenth-Century France*, 236, 241–242; Dubost, *La France italienne*, 178, 184, 191, 201, 254–255, 265, 287.

99. Jouanna, "De la ville marchande à la capitale administrative," in *Histoire de Montpellier*, ed. Cholvy, 152–155; Lafage, "Montpellier et le siège de 1622," 58–59; Baumel, *Montpellier au cours des XVIᵉ et XVIIᵉ siècles*, 142–162; Aigrefeuille, *Histoire de Montpellier*.

100. Montpellier had an annual average of 366 baptisms per year in the first decade of the seventeenth century, according to Benedict, "Huguenot Population of France, 1600-85," 75–79.

101. Benedict, "Confessionalization in France?" in *Society and Culture in the Huguenot World, 1559–1685*, ed. Mentzer and Spicer, 53–54.

102. Irvine, "From Renaissance City to Ancien Régime Capital: Montpellier, c. 1500–c. 1600," 107–109.

103. Benedict, "Huguenot Population of France, 1600–85," 83.

104. Jouanna, *La France du XVIᵉ siècle*, 8–10.

105. Michel, "Nîmes et son histoire."

106. Benedict, "Huguenot Population of France, 1600–85," 75–79; Tulchin, "Michelade in Nîmes, 1567."

107. Pugh, "Social Welfare and the Edict of Nantes," 349–376; id., "Catholics, Protestants, and Testament Charity," 479–504; Mentzer, "Morals and Moral Regulation in Protestant France."

108. AD Lozère, C 1804; Rémy Chastel, "Les Luttes des Mendois," 65–82; Beik, *Absolutism and Society in Seventeenth-Century France*, 236.

109. Burel, *Mémoires*, 173–174, 365; Mours, *Le Protestantisme en Vivarais et en Velay*.

110. The *vierge noire* of Le Puy-en-Velay is celebrated in Gissey, *Discours historiques de la très ancienne dévotion de nostres Dame du Puy*; Cassagnes-Brouquet, *Vierges noires*, 158–159, 166–170.

111. Burel, *Mémoires*, 483–484.

112. Ibid., 470–471, 493–494, 508–509.

113. Besset, "Essai sur la noblesse Vivaroise"; Chareton, *La Réforme et les guerres civiles en Vivarais*; Entrevaux, *Armorial du Vivarais*; Banne, *Mémoires*.

114. Denis and Foray, *Le Siege de Privas en 1629*, 1–14; Mours, *Le Protestantisme en Vivarais et en Velay*, 161–164.

115. Burel, *Mémoires*, 470; Carlat, "La Renaissance au château de Tournon."

CHAPTER 2: NOBLE HOUSEHOLDS AND KINSHIP

1. Phélypeaux de Pontchartrain, *Mémoires concernant les affaires de France sous la régence de Marie de Médicis*, in NCM, 5: 326–331.

2. Du Cros, 11–16; a series of letters dating from the period of the transition of Languedoc's provincial government from Henri I de Montmorency to his son can be found in BNF, Clairambault 1131; for a recent overview of the Montmorency family, see Kermina, *Les Montmorency*.

3. Neuschel, *Word of Honor*, 78–93.

4. See, e.g., Henri I de Montmorency duc de Montmorency to Marie de Médicis, La Grange, 25 August 1613, BNF, Clairambault 1131, f° 180. Auvergne, Montmorency's son-in-law, had been imprisoned in 1605 for his involvement in a plot; for details see Duccini, *Concini*, 221–222.

5. Henri II de Montmorency duc de Montmorency to Marie de Médicis, Pézenas, 20 December 1614, BNF, Clairambault 1131, f° 281. Henri II de Montmorency was Charles de Valois's brother-in-law by his marriage to Henri's half-sister Charlotte.

6. La Rochefoucauld, quoted in Moote, *Louis XIII*, 249–250. The remark has been cited by Georges d'Avenel, Yves-Marie Bercé, Sharon Kettering, and David Parrott, among others. The translation is Moote's.

7. Bourdieu, *Outline of a Theory of Practice*, 33–38; id., *Logic of Practice*, 160–161.

8. Fontaine, "Rôle économique de la parenté," 5–16.

9. For discussions of "family strategy" methodologies, see Fontaine and Schlumbohm, "Household Strategies," 1–17; Moen and Wethington, "Concept of Family Adaptive Strategies." Hareven notes criticisms of "family strategies" but defends the concept in "What Difference Does It Make?" 317–344.

10. Rosental, "Les Liens familiaux?" 69.

11. Motley, *Becoming a French Aristocrat*, 71–79; Greenblatt, *Renaissance Self-Fashioning*, 109–110.

12. Crouzet, "Les fondements idéologiques de la royauté d'Henri IV," 165–194; Farr, *Authority and Sexuality*, 19–21.

13. Richelet, *L'Hymne des peres de famille*.

14. Serres, *Théâtre de l'agriculture*; Cornette, "Crise des Valeurs."

15. "In reality the consensus of Protestant and Catholic reformations converged, not upon the instructional role of parents, but on the catechising duties of the clergy," Bossy, *Christianity in the West*, 118–119, argues.

16. Watt, "Impact of the Reformation and Counter-Reformation," 125–154.

17. Burguière, "L'État monarchique et la famille," 330–331.

18. Richelet, *L'Hymne des peres de famille*. On Ronsard's poetry as a polemical response to the diffusion of the Reformation in France, see *Histoire et dictionnaire des guerres de religion*, ed. Jouanna et al., 44–45, 114–117.

19. Sales, *Introduction à la vie dévote*.

20. AD Hérault, 1 E 1421, f° 125.

21. Benedict, *Christ's Churches Purely Reformed*, 509–513.

22. Nicholls, "Theatre of Martyrdom," 49–73.

23. Huguenot family strategies for survival hint at the ideal of suffering, which was an important component of Huguenot confessional identities. Mentzer, *Blood and Belief*, 12–26.

24. "Voyage de M. le duc de Rohan en Vivarais," in *CSV*, 244.

25. Alexandre de Lévis marquis de Mirepoix to Paul Phélypeaux seigneur de Pontchartrain, Terride, 2 July 1621, BNF, Clairambault 377, f° 799–800.

26. Delumeau and Roche, eds., *Histoire des pères et de la paternité*.

27. Hardwick, *Practice of Patriarchy*, ix.

28. Mentzer, *Blood and Belief*, 142.

29. Chabans, *Histoire de la guerre des Huguenots*, 596–597.

30. Davis, "Women on Top," 124–151.

31. On ideals of marital love, see Dewald, *Aristocratic Experience and the Origins of Modern Culture*, 121–131.

32. On the emotionless family, see Ariès, *L'Enfant et la vie familiale sous l'Ancien Régime*.

33. Vallambert, *Cinq livres de la maniere de nourrir et gouverner les enfans*.

34. Héroard, *Journal*.

35. Motley, *Becoming a French Aristocrat*, 54.

36. Gutton, *Domestiques et serviteurs*.

37. Elzière, *Histoire des Budos*, 127–145.

38. Freedman, "Philosophical Writings on the Family," 292–342.

39. Audisio, "Famille et religion."

40. Henri d'Albert to Charles de Choiseul marquis de Praslin, Paris, 5 September 1625, HRHRC, Mss. 121, on the behalf of the father, a certain monsieur Perraut, perhaps a member of the extended Fain family.

41. Rosental, "Les Liens familiaux?" 69–70.

42. Marie de Médicis, was certainly acutely aware of her husband's adultery, but also had seen how her father Francesco I de' Medici's marriage to his mistress Bianca Cappello created sensation and scandal in Florentine society.

43. Loyseau, *Treatise of Orders*, 98–101; La Roque de La Lontière, *Traité de la noblesse*, 137–144, 405–417.

44. Deyron, *De la genealogie de monsieur le baron d'Aubais*.

45. Jouanna, *L'Idée de race en France*, 1: 243–255.

46. Loyseau discusses the right to use coats of arms in his *Treatise of Orders*, 85–87.

47. Le Moyne, *De l'art des devises*.

48. Du Cros, 9.

49. Deyron, *De la genealogie de monsieur le baron d'Aubais.*

50. Charles de Choiseul marquis de Praslin, "Abbregé des exploitz de guerre de deffunct monseigneur le maréchal de Praslin faict par luy mesme," BNF, Mss. fr. 15616, f° 20–27.

51. Compte de Pierre Deffos, 1626, AD Tarn, C 888; see also Smith, *Culture of Merit,* 65–78.

52. AD Hérault, 1 E 227.

53. For an example, see Antoine de Roquelaure marquis de Roquelaure to Louis XIII, n.p., 2 June 1618, BNF, Clairambault 374, f° 104–105.

54. M. de Berton to Paul Phélypeaux seigneur de Pontchartrain, Avignon, 27 November 1615, BNF, Clairambault 366, f° 74–75.

55. A history of the military service of the Joirac family that seems to have been written in the eighteenth century pays particular attention to the participation of the family in the civil wars in Languedoc, and at the siege of Privas in particular. This history was intended to serve as justification for a young Joirac male's appointment to a military office. "Mémoire," BNF, Languedoc-Bénédictins 105, f° 275–279.

56. "Genealogie de la noble famille des Auzolles en Auvergne faicte lan 1620," BNF, Cabinet d'Hozier 22, f° 489.

57. On the practice of changing names, see: La Roque de La Lontière, *Traité de la noblesse,* 280–281.

58. This comment refers specifically to the case of Alexandre de Lévis seigneur de Mirepoix, in Nassiet, "Réseaux de parenté et types d'alliance dans la noblesse (XVe–XVIIe siècles)," 106.

59. Constant, *La Noblesse française aux XVIe et XVIIe siècles,* 93–116; 167–175; id., *Nobles et paysans en Beauce*; Jouanna, *L'Idée de race en France,* 1: 153–186.

60. For a detailed analysis of marriage alliances in sixteenth-century Paris, see Diefendorf, *Paris City Councillors,* 155–251.

61. Brunelle, "Dangerous Liaisons," 75–103.

62. Le Roy Ladurie and Fitou, "Mariages saint-simoniens," 361–380, finds that *grands* meticulously avoided marrying low-ranking nobles or non-nobles.

63. In the case of Huguenot nobles, Protestant policies of eliminating clerical celibacy raised the possibility of noble kinship with ministers, but I have discovered no evidence of ministers marrying into Huguenot noble families.

64. Nassiet, *Parenté, noblesse et états dynastiques.*

65. Charles d'Arpajon baron de Broquier entered a marriage with his first cousin Rose d'Arpajon, see: BNF, Pièces Originales 104, f° 95.

66. An example of such a marriage between Louis de Bourbon prince de Condé and Eléonore de Roye, contracted in 1551, is provided in Neuschel, *Word of Honor,* 141–143.

67. Sperling, "Marriage at the Time of the Council of Trent," 67–108.

68. Neuschel, *Word of Honor,* 78–79.

69. Henri II de Montmorency and his father both thanked the queen mother for arranging his marriage: Henri II de Montmorency to Marie de Médicis, Pézenas, 20 December 1612, BNF, Clairambault 1131, f° 170; Henri I de Montmorency duc de Montmorency to Marie de Médicis, Avignon, 13 June 1613, BNF, Clairambault 1131, f° 173.

70. Henri I de Montmorency duc de Montmorency to Marie de Médicis, Beaucaire, 30 June 1613, BNF, Clairambault 1131, f° 177–178.

71. Dubost, *La France italienne*, 282–283.

72. *Memoire concernant la cassation des testament & codicilles de feu monsieur le duc d'Arpajon* (n.p., 1658), BNF, Pièces Originales 104.

73. La Roque de La Lontière, *Traité de la noblesse*, 281.

74. For contemporary examples of marriage ceremonies and alliances in Languedoc, see: AD Hérault, A 48, f° 112; AD Hérault, 1 E 938. I hope to delve into marriage registers and develop data on marriage ceremonies in the future.

75. Benedict, "Confessionalization in France?" 53–61.

76. Schneider, *Public Life in Toulouse*, 240–252.

77. Heuraire [?] to Nicolas IV de Neufville seigneur de Villeroy, Aix-en-Provence, 20 December 1615, BNF, Mss. fr. 15582, f° 75–76.

78. AD Hérault, 1 E 1372.

CHAPTER 3: *CRÉDIT* AND NOBLE FINANCES

1. Girard, 280–281.

2. Dewald, *European Nobility*, 60–107.

3. Huppert, *Les bourgeois gentilhommes*, 120.

4. Major, "Noble Income, Inflation, and the Wars of Religion in France," 21–48.

5. Weary, "House of La Tremoille," D1001–D1038.

6. For some examples of documents discussing sales, purchases, and improvements of seigneuries, see AD Gard, 1 E 2428.

7. Eurich, *Economics of Power*, 1–43; Harding, *Anatomy of a Power Elite*, 135–159, 228–230; Boltanski, *Les Ducs de Nevers*, 148–150.

8. Nassiet, *Parenté, noblesse et états dynastiques*, 118–125.

9. Fessenden, "Épernon and Guyenne," 213–219.

10. Baumgartner, *Change and Continuity in the French Episcopate*, 56–57.

11. Dewald, *Aristocratic Experience and the Origins of Modern Culture*, 146–173.

12. Kalas, "Marriage, Clientage, Office Holding," 365–383.

13. For example, quittances show that the Polignac family provided a daughter's dowry in at least five installments over more than ten years. BNF, Pièces Originales 2319, f° 299–300.

14. Harding, *Anatomy of a Power Elite*, 149–154.

15. Eurich, "'Speaking the King's Language,'" 117–138, provides data on Protestant and Catholic dowries, both noble and non-noble, in Béarn.

16. Boltanski, *Les Ducs de Nevers*, 150–154.

17. Parsons, "Money and Sovereignty in Early Modern France," 59–79.

18. Major, "Noble Income, Inflation, and the Wars of Religion in France," 46–48.

19. Mentzer, *Blood and Belief*, 31–32, 48–49, 58–60.

20. For key studies of *rentes* in sixteenth- and seventeenth-century Europe, see Tracy, *Financial Revolution in the Habsburg Netherlands*; Huppert, *Les Bourgeois gentilhommes*, 120–144.

NOTES TO PAGES 58–67   307

21. Mentzer, *Blood and Belief,* 58–60.

22. Harding, *Anatomy of a Power Elite,* 141–142.

23. Bayard, *Le Monde des financiers,* 364–365.

24. AD Hérault, 1 E 1483.

25. See the negotiations concerning pensions at the conference of Loudun in 1616 in *NCL;* BNF, Mss. fr. 15582.

26. Mousnier, *La Vénalité des offices;* Doyle, *Venality.*

27. For a discussion of the problems of the purchase system for military offices, see Lynn, *Giant of the* Grand Siècle, 228–231.

28. Mousnier, *La Vénalité des offices,* 342–343.

29. BNF, Mss. fr. 23246, f° 3–4.

30. BNF, Mélanges de Colbert 322, f° 5–6.

31. Fessenden, "Épernon and Guyenne," 201–202.

32. BNF, Mélanges de Colbert 322, f° 7–8.

33. Mousnier, *La Venalité des offices,* 356–364.

34. BNF, Mélanges de Colbert 322, f° 5–6.

35. Deliberations of the estates of Languedoc held at Carcassonne, 1 January 1622, AD Hérault, C 7059, f° 124.

36. Elzière, *Histoire des Budos,* 127–145.

37. See numerous examples in the AD Hérault, B series.

38. Henri II de Montmorency duc de Montmorency to Marie de Médicis, Beaucaire, 26 July 1614, BNF, Clairambault 1131, f° 205–206.

39. Pontis, *Mémoires,* 192–193.

40. Eurich, *Economics of Power,* 173–174.

41. Alberti, *L'Architecture;* Androuet du Cerceau, *Livre d'architecture;* Roche, *History of Everyday Things,* 99–100.

42. Touzery-Salager, *Les Châteaux du bas-Languedoc.*

43. AD Aude, 2 E 17, f° 12.

44. Dewald, *Aristocratic Experience and the Origins of Modern Culture,* 157–158.

45. Mark Potter, "Good Offices," 599–626.

46. Shepard, "Manhood, Credit and Patriarchy in Early Modern England," 75–106.

47. Jouanna, *Le Devoir de révolte,* 65–66.

48. Kettering, *Patrons, Brokers, and Clients in Seventeenth-Century France,* 43–44.

49. Henri I de Montmorency duc de Montmorency to Marie de Médicis, La Grange, 20 March 1614, BNF, Clairambault 1131, f° 188.

50. Kettering, *Patrons, Brokers, and Clients in Seventeenth-Century France,* 43–44.

51. Commission of Henri II de Montmorency duc de Montmorency, Pézenas, 17 May 1622, AD Tarn, C 1167, f° 227.

52. Motley, *Becoming a French Aristocrat,* 92–95.

53. Inventaire, AD Aude, 2 E 17, f° 12.

54. Harding, *Anatomy of a Power Elite,* 174; Dewald, *European Nobility,* 151–157.

55. Pluvinel, *Instruction du roy;* Motley, *Becoming a French Aristocrat,* 98–153. On fencing's role in educational ideals, see Brioist et al., *Croiser le fer,* 134–137.

56. Maag, "Huguenot Academies," 139–156.

57. Nelson, *Jesuits and the Monarchy*, 110–126.

58. Motley, *Becoming a French Aristocrat*, 169–185.

59. Kettering, "Household Service of Early Modern French Noblewomen," 55–85.

60. McGowan, *Vision of Rome in Late Renaissance France*, 4.

61. Motley, *Becoming a French Aristocrat*, 187–191.

62. Matteo Bartolini to Cosimo II de' Medici, Paris, 27 February 1620, ASF, 4635, n.f.; *Voyage de Monsieur le prince de Condé. . . . en Italie.*

63. "Pour me servir de mémoire des chozes les plus remarquables que j'ey veues a mon voiage d'Italie, que je coumence le dernier jour de l'an mil six cens neuf, pour accomplir le veu que j'aves a Notre-Dame de Lorrette," AD Ardèche, 1 Mi 35.

64. Henri de Schömberg comte de Nanteuil to Cosimo II de' Medici, Lyon, 19 July 1617, ASF, 4759, n.f.

65. Roberts, "Military Revolution, 1560–1660," 13–36; Geoffrey Parker, *Military Revolution*, 19–21.

66. Allen, *Philip III and the Pax Hispanica*.

67. Henri de Nogaret de La Valette comte de Candalle to Belisario di Francesco Vinta, Civitavecchia, 18 June 1613, ASF, MdP 4759, n.f.

68. Joachim Ernst Markgraf von Brandenburg-Anspach to Louis XIII, Anspach, 27 February 1616, BNF, Clairambault 366, f° 403–404.

69. Hale, *War and Society in Renaissance Europe*, 137–140; Constant, *La Noblesse française aux XVIe et XVIIe siècles*, 167–175; Chagniot, *Guerre et société à l'époque moderne*, 24.

70. Alexandre de Lévis vicomte de Mirepoix, speech at the estates of Languedoc held at Béziers, 23 September 1621, AD Hérault, C 7059, f° 12.

71. Harding, *Anatomy of a Power Elite*, 177.

72. Hardwick, *Practice of Patriarchy*, 17–49.

73. Mentzer, *Blood and Belief*, 104–109.

74. For an example, see: "Testament de Louis de Pluviers," AD Hérault, 1 E 1421, f° 125; Pugh, "Catholics, Protestants, and Testamentary Charity," 479–504.

75. Henri II de Montmorency duc de Montmorency to Marie de Médicis, Beaucaire, 1 July 1614, BNF, Clairambault 1131, f° 207–211.

76. BNF, Mss. fr. 23246, f° 3–4.

77. Daubresse, *Le Parlement de Paris*, 313–353. On the Estates General of 1614 and the *paulette*, see Moote, *Louis XIII*, 64, 72–73; Chaussinand-Nogaret, *Histoire des élites en France du XVIe au XXe siècle*, 148–152; Hayden, *France and the Estates General of 1614*, 116–122.

78. Doyle, *Venality*, 10–11.

79. Henri II de Montmorency duc de Montmorency to Louis XIII, Pézenas, 22 December 1614, BNF, Clairambault 1131, f° 282.

80. François d'Estrades to Paul Phélypeaux seigneur de Pontchartrain, Agen, 31 September 1619, BNF, Clairambault 375, f° 311–312.

81. Henri II de Montmorency duc de Montmorency to Marie de Médicis, Beaucaire, 26 July 1614, BNF, Clairambault 1131, f° 205–206.

82. Henri II de Montmorency duc de Montmorency to Louis XIII, Pézenas, 19 December 1614, BNF, Clairambault 1131, f° 243.

83. Gurson de Foy to Louis XIII, Gurson, 17 November 1615, BNF, Clairambault 366, f° 46–47.

84. Harding, *Anatomy of a Power Elite*, 157–158.

85. Loyseau, *Treatise of Orders*, 66–81.

86. Jouanna, *Le Devoir de révolte*, 281–312.

87. Henry I de Montmorency duc de Montmorency to Marie de Médicis, La Grange, 14 January 1614, BNF, Clairambault 1131, f° 187.

88. Baumgartner, *Change and Continuity in the French Episcopate*, 55–83.

89. For an overview of legal institutions in seventeenth-century Languedoc, see Beik, *Absolutism and Society in Seventeenth-Century France*, 77–97.

90. For an example of a 1620 case involving noble Guy de Bonnail, see AD Hérault, 1 E 851. On the *chambre de l'Édit*, see Mentzer, *Blood and Belief*, 62–64; Capot, *Justice et religion en Languedoc*.

91. Harding, *Anatomy of a Power Elite*, 153, 177.

CHAPTER 4: CLIENTAGE AND FRIENDSHIP

1. François d'Esparbès de Lussan marquis d'Aubeterre to Paul Phélypeaux seigneur de Pontchartrain, Condom, 8 June 1621, BNF, Clairambault 377, f° 731–733.

2. Anne de Lévis duc de Ventadour to Henri I de Montmorency duc de Montmorency, n.d. [1598?], BNF, Mss. fr. 3586, f° 74.

3. Pontis, *Mémoires*, 108.

4. Desaiques to Paul Phélypeaux seigneur de Pontchartrain, Bordeaux, 30 March 1613, BNF, Clairambault 362, f° 275.

5. Jouanna, *Le Devoir de révolte*, 384–388.

6. Le Roux, *La Faveur du roi*, 247–254.

7. Fessenden, "Épernon and Guyenne."

8. Girard, 378–380.

9. Du Cros, 42–43; Quittance, 26 November 1627, AD Hérault, B 22739; *HGL*, 11: 1058–1059, 1079.

10. *La Prise et reduction de la ville et chasteau de Nerac.*

11. BNF, Mss. fr. 15584, f° 115–116.

12. *Relation envoyée au roy par monsieur le mareschal de Schomberg; HGL*, 11: 1119–1123.

13. AD Hérault, B 22659; "Declaration de Monsieur le duc de Rohan Pair de France, etc., Contenant la Justice des raisons de motifz qui l'ont obligé a Implorer l'assistance du Roy de la grande Bretagne et prendre les armes pour la deffence des Eglises reformées de ce Royaume," BNF, Dupuy 100, f° 174–184; Deyon and Dcyon, *Henri de Rohan*, 71–91.

14. Ordonnance du maréchal de Thémines, AD Hérault, C 8406; *Defaicte furieuse de deux cens maistres, sortis de Castres, Puilaurens, & autres villes rebelles.*

15. Alfonse d'Ornano to Henri IV, Bordeaux, 26 August 1602, BNF, Mss. fr. 23197, f° 54; Alfonse d'Ornano to Henri IV, Bordeaux, 13 September 1602, BNF, Mss. fr. 23197, f° 107.

16. BNF, Mss. fr. 23246; AD Haute-Garonne, B 1913, f° 353–357.

17. *La Prise des villes de la Caune et Sainct Sever en la comté de Castres par Monseigneur le Prince.*

18. Rohan, *Mémoires,* 212–213.

19. *Le Voyage de M. le duc de Rohan en Vivarais,* in *CSV,* 242–243; AD Hérault, B 36, f° 252.

20. *CSV,* 3–7, 18; Mours, *Le Protestantisme en Vivarais et en Velay,* 158–167.

21. BNF, Languedoc-Bénédictins 100, f° 292; Richelieu, *Papiers de Richelieu,* ed. Grillon, 1: 213; 2: 313.

22. *Recit tres-veritable de ce qui s'est passé le mercredy 19. janvier 1628; La prise du fort de Corconne, en Languedoc;* Louis XIII to Gabriel de La Vallée des Fossées marquis d'Everly, Suippe la Longue, 14 June 1632, AD Hérault, A 44, f° 117.

23. BNF, Languedoc-Bénédictins 71; Richelieu, *Papiers de Richelieu,* ed. Grillon, 1: 505.

24. Burel, *Mémoires,* 443–445; La Roque M, 1: 36–37.

25. Burel, *Mémoires,* 508–511.

26. Beik, *Urban Protest in Seventeenth-Century France,* 73–94.

27. Alexandre de Lévis marquis de Mirepoix to Paul Phélypeaux seigneur de Pontchartrain, Terride, 2 July 1621, BNF, Clairambault 377, f° 799–800; Deliberations of the estates of Languedoc held at Béziers and Carcassonne, 23 September 1621, AD Hérault, C 7059, f° 12.

28. BNF, Pièces Originales 359, f° 51; BNF, Languedoc-Bénédictins 71, f° 375–385.

29. Ordonnance, 4 January 1616, BNF, Clairambault 366, f° 319.

30. Harding, *Anatomy of a Power Elite,* 149–154.

31. François de Noailles comte d'Ayen to Paul Phélypeaux seigneur de Poncharrain, L'Arche, 24 May 1618, BNF, Clairambault 374, f° 102–103.

32. François de Noailles comte d'Ayen to Louis XIII, L'Arche, 10 August 1620, BNF, Clairambault 377, f° 235.

33. "Procès-verbal du comte d'Ayen," BNF, Clairambault 362, f° 170–172.

34. Lettres patentes, BNF, Clairambault 957, f° 315–322; BNF, Mss. fr. 3589.

35. Desaiques to Paul Phélypeaux seigneur de Pontchartrain, Bordeaux, 30 March 1613, BNF, Clairambault 362, f° 275.

36. François I d'Esparbès de Lussan marquis d'Aubeterre to Paul Phélypeaux seigneur de Pontchartrain, Agen, 9 January 1616, BNF, Clairambault 366, f° 327–328.

37. "Lettre de l'Assemblée du bas Languedoc a lassemblée generalle pour ladvertir de la nommination quilz ont faitte du duc de Rohan pour leur general," BNF, Mss. fr. 4102, f° 49; "Acte de lassemblee provinciale du haut Languedoc et haute Guyenne . . . ," BNF, Mss. fr. 4102, f° 145; *Departement des provinces dv royavme de France.*

38. Lowenstein, "Resistance to Absolutism," 78–78a.

39. AD Hérault, B 22664; AD Hérault, B 22796; *HGL,* 11: 998–999; Lowenstein, "Resistance to Absolutism," 97–114.

40. Rohan, *Mémoires,* 406–407.

41. Baumel, *Montpellier au cours des XVIᵉ et XVIIᵉ siècles,* 207–208.

42. *HGL,* 11: 1049; Sauzet, *Contre-réforme et réforme catholique en bas Languedoc,* 275–276.

43. AD Hérault, B 22615.

44. AM Toulouse, EE 5; "Rolle des principales & plus anciēnes maisons de Languedoc donc j'ay peu avoir memoire," BNF, Mss. fr. 20235, f° 300–310.

45. AD Haute-Garonne, C 708; Deliberations of the estates of Languedoc held at Toulouse in 1621, AD Hérault, C 7059, f° 94; AD Haute-Garonne, B 413, f° 230; Charles de Valois duc d'Angoulême to Louis XIII, 4 September 1621, BNF, Clairambault 378, f° 37–38; "Tableau du siege de Montaulban 1622," BNF, Mss. fr. 18756; Deliberations of the estates of Languedoc held at Béziers, 29 October 1621, AD Hérault, C 7059, f° 70–72.

46. AD Tarn, C 890; BNF, Languedoc-Bénédictins 107, f° 53–60.

47. Richelieu to Marie de Médicis, Suze, 29 April 1629, in *LCR*, 291–294.

48. *Arrest de la cour de parlement contre les rebelles.*

49. Gilles Le Masuyer to Armand-Jean du Plessis cardinal de Richelieu, Toulouse, 22 April 1628, in Richelieu, *Papiers de Richelieu*, ed. Grillon, 3: 214–215; Ordonnance du prince de Condé, Villemur, 5 July 1629, AM Toulouse, A 22, f° 153.

50. François I d'Esparbès de Lussan marquis d'Aubeterre to Paul Phélypeaux seigneur de Pontchartrain, Agen, 12 November 1615, BNF, Clairambault 366, f° 24–25, 25–26.

51. Ibid.

52. Loyseau, *Traité des seigneuries.*

53. Major, "'Bastard Feudalism' and the Kiss," 509–535.

54. Henri I de Montmorency duc de Montmorency to Laboureur, lieutenant au baillage de Montmorency, Chantilly, 27 November 1608, BNF, Mss. fr. 20609, f° 247; Henry II de Montmorency duc de Montmorency to Louis XIII, Montpellier, 28 October 1614, BNF, Clairambault 1131, f° 247–249.

55. Major, "'Bastard Feudalism' and the Kiss," 523.

56. For a 1603 seigneurial purchase, see BNF, Pièces Originales 1492, f° 16–20.

57. For examples of sales of seigneuries in early seventeenth-century Languedoc, see AD Hérault, B 34, f° 7; AD Hérault, 1 E 1430–1431; AD Hérault, 1 E 938; AD Gard, 1 E 406; AD Gard, 1 E 2428; AD Haute-Garonne, B 467, f° 683.

58. AD Hérault, 2 57/57, f° 12–13.

59. AD Hérault, B 36, f° 188.

60. Henri I de Montmorency duc de Montmorency to Laboureur, lieutenant au baillage de Montmorency, Paris, 6 March 1611, BNF, Mss. fr. 20609, f° 249.

61. For an assertion of seigneurial justice, see Supplication, Mss. fr. 18085, f° 5–6.

62. Henri I de Montmorency duc de Montmorency to Laboureur, lieutenant au baillage de Montmorency, Ecouen, 15 August 1608, BNF, Mss. fr. 20609, f° 250.

63. For a 1614 lease, see BNF, Pièces Originales 1693, f° 62.

64. On Roure family seigneuries, see BNF, Languedoc-Bénédictins 105, f° 107–113.

65. See various estate management documents in BNF, Mss. fr. 20609.

66. "Acte de declaration & donnation faicte par m.re Fran. dAmboise comte dAubejoux de la terre & baronnie de Castelnau de Levy a m.re Fran. Jacq. dAmboise son fils," AD Hérault, A 48, f° 112.

67. See AD Hérault, A 48, f° 112, for an example.

68. Durand-Tullou, *Le Loup du Causse*, 79–80.

69. AD Gard, 1 E 406.

70. Elias, *Civilizing Process*, 68–105.

71. Gourgues to Paul Phélypeaux seigneur de Pontchartrain, Bordeaux, 21 August 1611, BNF, Clairambault 362, f° 55–56.

72. Lynn, ed., *Feeding Mars.*

73. Quittance, 18 November 1627, AD Hérault, B 22744.

74. "Tableau du siege de Montaulban 1622," BNF, Mss. fr. 18756, f° 63.

75. Lynn *Giant of the* Grand Siècle, 239–241, suggests the financial problems of providing for followers in his discussion of "the added burden of officer extravagance."

76. AD Hérault, A 47, f° 122–123.

77. Ordonnance de Henri de Rohan, 24 August 1628, AD Hérault, B 22758.

78. Deliberations of the estates of Languedoc held at Béziers and Carcassone, 29 December 1621, AD Hérault, C 7059, f° 119.

79. For an example, see "Inventaire sommairement faict de tout ce que cest treuue dans le chasteau & mairie seigneuriale de Masargues . . . ," BNF, Mss. fr. 12068, f° 81–106.

80. Quittances, 1627, AD Hérault, B 22739.

81. Ordonnance de Henri II de Montmorency duc de Montmorency, Baignolz, 20 June 1628, AD Lozère, C 1791.

82. Ordonnance de Henri II de Rohan duc de Rohan, 25 August 1628, AD Hérault, B 22758.

83. Cunningham and Grell, *Four Horsemen of the Apocalypse,* 124–137.

84. Lynn, *Women, Armies, and Warfare,* 33–50.

85. Pontis, *Mémoires,* 98–99.

86. "Ordre fait par Mr. le duc de Montmorenci quil veut etre observé pour la delivrance des prisoniers de guerre et entretenement des gardes d'iceux," BNF, Languedoc-Bénédictins 94, f° 114; comte de Lauzun to Louis XIII, Lauzun, 30 January 1616, BNF, Clairambault 366, f° 363–364.

87. Briet to Paul Phélypeaux seigneur de Pontchartrain, Caulmont, 29 September 1613, BNF, Clairambault 363, f° 125–126.

88. Souriac, "Les Places de sûreté protestantes."

89. AD Haute-Garonne, B 1913, f° 366–368.

90. *Declaration du roy, par laquelle les princes, ducs, & seigneurs y denommez, sont declarez criminels de leze Majesté; L'Arrivee de monsieur le duc d'Espernon.*

91. "La Suitte du tableau du siege de Montauban . . . ," BNF, Mss. fr. 18756, f° 75; "Mémoires de Vignolles," in *PFHF.*

92. "Memoires envoiéz au Roy par le duc de Rohan touchant les affaires du bas Languedoc, le 6 janvier 1623," BNF, Mss. fr. 4102, f° 76–77.

93. AD Haute-Garonne, B 1913, f° 353–357.

94. AD Haute-Garonne, B 1913, f° 353–357.

95. AD Hérault, A 47, f° 122–123.

96. "Rolle de la compagnie dordonnance de Monseigneur le duc de Ventadour logee au pñt lieu de Rochemaure . . . ," AD Hérault, B 22607.

97. François d'Escoubleau cardinal de Sourdis to Marie de Médicis, Bordeaux, 3 July 1611, BNF, Clairambault 362, f° 39–41.

98. "Le Discours de l'entree de messeigneurs le duc d'Espernon et marquis de La Vallette en la ville de Metz auec les pourtraits des arcs triomphaux," BNF, Mss. fr. 24103.

99. AD Haute-Garonne, B 347, f° 295, 304; B 350, f° 470; B 1879, f° 92.

100. See, e.g., "Arrest de la cour de parlem^t portant deffences a monsieur le prince de Condé & aues q^e l'assistent de continuer leurs assemblees," BNF, Brienne 200 (NAF 7171), f° 87–90.

101. "Relation des charges resulants du proces de Campredon, 6 avril 1626," BNF, Dupuy 93, f° 105–108.

102. Labatut, *Les Ducs et pairs de la France,* 92; *HGL,* 11: 719, 806, 854; AD Hérault, B 36, f° 467–469; AD Hérault, A 48, f° 45–46; AD Lozère, C 1792; AD Tarn, C 890; AD Tarn, C 900; BNF, Languedoc-Bénédictins 71, f° 46–47; BNF, Cabinet d'Hozier 14; Balteau, 3: 1056–1060; Richelieu, *Papiers de Richelieu,* ed. Grillon, 3: 307–312.

103. François de Noailles comte d'Ayen to Paul Phélypeaux seigneur de Pontchartrain, La Faye, 8 December 1615, BNF, Clairambault, 366 f° 102–103. François de Noailles comte d'Ayen to Paul Phélypeaux seigneur de Pontchartrain, Malemort, 10 September 1616, BNF, Clairambault 368, f° 214–215.

104. Bassompierre, *Journal,* 3: 68, 78–79. *HGL,* 11: 971, 973. "Tableau du siege de Montaulban 1622," BNF, Mss. fr. 18756, f° 49.

105. The Clermont de Lodève family is listed in the "Rolle des principales & plus ancieñes maisons de Languedoc donc j'ay peu avoir memoire," BNF, Mss. fr. 20235, f° 300–310.

106. Bassompierre, *Journal,* 3: 68n.

107. *HGL,* 11: 1009.

108. Gilles Le Masuyer, premier président du parlement de Toulouse, to Armand-Jean du Plessis cardinal de Richelieu, Toulouse, 29 September 1627, BNF, Mss. fr. 15583, f° 224–225.

109. Deliberations of the estates of Languedoc held at Pézenas, 18 May 1629, AD Hérault, C 7070, f° 31–32.

110. Louis d'Arpajon vicomte d'Arpajon to Armand-Jean du Plessis cardinal de Richelieu, May 1628 and 24 December 1628 in Richelieu, *Papiers de Richelieu,* ed. Grillon, 3: 307–312 and 584–585; *HGL,* 12: 1762; AD Tarn, C 900.

111. Ordonnance of Louis d'Arpajon vicomte d'Arpajon, 1 April 1629, AD Tarn, C 900.

112. Deliberations of the estates of Languedoc held at Pézenas, 21 May 1629, AD Hérault, C 7070, f° 33–34.

113. Deliberations of the estates of Languedoc held at Pézenas, 30 May 1629, AD Hérault, C 7070, f° 43–44.

114. *HGL,* 11: 1047–1048.

115. "Advis donné au roy depuis les lettres de Lorraine surprises par Vaubecour," in *LCR,* 4: 269–273.

116. Graule, *Histoire de Lescure;* BNF, Languedoc-Bénédictins 106, f° 83–112.

117. AD Tarn, C 870. The company of chevaux-légers is listed in another document as a company of *maîtres,* or gendarmes.

118. AD Tarn, C 870.

119. AD Tarn, C 870; AD Tarn, C 871; BNF, Clairambault 1131, f° 174; BNF, Clairambault 1131, f° 191–192; BNF, Clairambault 1131, f° 226–229.

120. AD Tarn, C 872.

121. AD Tarn, C 871.

122. AD Tarn, C 872.

123. État des troupes, 29 June 1621, AD Tarn, C 873.

124. Gaspard de Seguy to the consuls and syndic of Albi, camp at Lombers, 1 September 1621, AD Tarn, C 874.

125. AD Tarn, C 873.

126. *HGL*, 11: 947; AD Hérault, B 22722; AD Tarn, C 872. On Vendôme see: BNF, Clairambault 1131; AD Tarn, C 1167. On Malauze, see BNF, Languedoc-Bénédictins 94, f° 116–117; *Relation veritable et journaliere de tout ce qui s'est passé en France & Pays Estrangers*; BNF, Clairambault 378, f° 150–169.

127. *HGL*, 11: 996. On Teillet, see Mayzou, *Réalmont*, 151–152.

128. AD Tarn, C 889; AD Tarn, C 891; *LCR*, 215–219.

129. AD Tarn, C 892; AM Albi, EE 61.

130. Ordonnance du duc de Montmorency, AD Tarn, C 890.

131. AD Tarn, C 891; Condé to Richelieu, June 1628, in Richelieu, *Papiers de Richelieu*, ed. Grillon, 3: 350–354.

132. AD Hérault, A 44, f° 107.

133. AD Hérault, 1 E 1372.

134. AD Hérault, 1 E 1372; AD Hérault, 1 E 939; *HGL*, 11: 920.

135. BNF, Languedoc Bénédictins 100, f° 316.

136. Ordonnance de Châtillon, Montpellier, 19 August 1621, AD Hérault, B 22796.

137. AD Hérault, B 22796; BNF, Cabinet d'Hozier 22, f° 502; La Roque M, 1: 40–42; Durand-Tullou, *Le Loup du Causse*, 156.

138. "Discours tendant à voir si, ayant la guerre avec l'Espagne en Italie, il faut aussy au-dedans du royaulme. 25 November 1625," Richelieu, *Papiers de Richelieu*, ed. Grillon, 1: 226–233; Rohan, *Mémoires*, 276.

139. Rohan, *Mémoires*, 318.

140. AD Hérault, B 22790, f° 89–90.

141. Rohan, *Mémoires*, 350–352.

142. Ibid., 360, 367–369; *HGL*, 11: 1020–1023.

143. Ibid., 369, 373, 378.

144. Ibid., 412, 415.

145. Ibid., 421–422, 424.

146. BNF, Cabinet d'Hozier 22, f° 502; "De la genealogie de monsieur le baron d'Aubais," BNF, Cabinet d'Hozier, 22, f° 506.

147. La Roque M, 1: 45–46; Vedel, *Balazuc et Pons de Balazuc*.

148. AD Hérault, B 22587; Elzière, *Histoire des Budos*, 110, 130, 244.

149. *CSV*, 21–22.

150. *HGL*, 11: 940.

151. Quittances, 1621, AD Hérault, B 22606.

152. *CSV*, 37–38.

153. Montréal was actually granted the office of maréchal de camp in January 1622, according to BNF, Languedoc-Bénédictins 103, f° 92.

154. BNF, Languedoc-Bénédictins 103, f° 92–99.

155. Bassompierre, *Journal*, 3: 95–96.

156. Abbé Soulavie, quoted in Vedel, *Balazuc et Pons de Balazuc*, 53.

157. "Histoire du diocèse de Viviers," quoted in Vedel, *Balazuc et Pons de Balazuc*, 53–54.

158. Louis XIII to Guillaume Balazuc de Montréal, Paris, 8 January 1626, copy, BNF, Languedoc-Bénédictins 103, f° 92.

159. Quittances, 1628, AD Hérault, B 22770.

160. *CSV*, 139.

161. *CSV*, 117–118, 127–128; AD Hérault, B 22768; Ordonnance du duc de Ventadour, Le Puy-en-Velay, 18 March 1628, AD Hérault, B 22746, f° 1.

162. AD Hérault, B 22746, f° 29–41, 47–56.

163. *CSV*, 117–118, 127–128; AD Hérault, B 22765; AD Hérault, B 22768.

164. Armand-Jean du Plessis cardinal de Richelieu to Marie de Médicis, Suze, 29 April 1629, in *LCR*, 291–294.

165. *CSV*, 157.

166. Vedel, *Balazuc et Pons de Balazuc*, 54.

CHAPTER 5: OFFICEHOLDING AND POLITICAL CULTURE

1. Henri de Lévis duc de Ventadour to the estates of Languedoc, 15 March 1625, AD Hérault, A 44, f° 101.

2. Minute, BNF, Mss. fr. 15582, f° 204–205.

3. Habermas, *Structural Transformation of the Public Sphere*, 14–26. On "public opinion" during in late sixteenth and early seventeenth-century France, see Duccini, *Faire voir, faire croire*; Racaut, *Hatred in Print*; Vittu, "Instruments of Political Information," 160–174; Te Brake, *Shaping History*, 63–108; Sawyer, *Printed Poison*.

4. The notion of a "bourgeois" public sphere has been criticized from a number of angles, most comprehensively in Fraser, "Rethinking the Public Sphere," 109–142.

5. Formisano, "Concept of Political Culture" 393–426; Steinmetz, ed., *State/Culture*.

6. K. M. Baker, ed., *The French Revolution and the Creation of Modern Political Culture*; Hunt, *Politics, Culture, and Class*.

7. K. M. Baker, *Inventing the French Revolution*, 4–5.

8. Le Roux, *La faveur du roi*, 162–165, 207–209; Bakos, *Images of Kingship*, 93–121.

9. BNF, Mss. fr. 15616, f° 142–143.

10. François I d'Esparbès de Lussan marquis d'Aubeterre to Paul Phélypeaux seigneur de Pontchartrain, Agen, 9 January 1616, BNF, Clairambault 366, f° 327–328.

11. Henri II de Montmorency duc de Montmorency to Marie de Médicis, Pézenas, 22 August 1614, BNF, Clairambault 1131, f° 226–229.

12. Louis XIII to Henri II de Montmorency duc de Montmorency, 26 November 1614, BNF, Clairambault 1131, f° 270–271.

13. François de Noailles comte d'Ayen to Paul Phélypeaux seigneur de Ponchartrain, L'Arche, 24 May 1618, BNF, Clairambault 374, f° 102–103.

14. Mandement de Henri de Budos marquis de Portes, AD Hérault, B 15804.

15. For an example of a governor's commission, see AG, A1 14, f° 59.

16. Henri II de Montmorency duc de Montmorency to the consuls of Narbonne, 5 August 1620, AD Aude, C 1266.

17. Henri II de Montmorency duc de Montmorency to the estates of Languedoc, Beaucaire, 22 April 1629, AD Hérault, A 44, f° 109.

18. *Reglement pour les gens de guerre.*

19. "Lettres par lesquelles le roi donne la conduite de l'armée qu'il veult laisser en Languedoc au seigneur duc de Monmoranci pair & admiral de France, gouverneur et lieutenant de sa Ma^té aud. pais de Languedoc," AD Haute-Garonne, B 1913, f° 293.

20. Louis XIII to Henri II de Bourbon prince de Condé, camp at Saugeon, 5 May 1622, AN, K 113A, f° 3; "Pouvoir à M. le Prince pour commander l'armée de Languedoc. 1627," AN, K 113A, f° 29.

21. Enregistrement of lettre patentes for Henri II de Bourbon prince de Condé, AD Haute-Garonne, B 480, f° 59.

22. Vendôme, commission for captain Conseil, camp at Loubeux, 22 September 1622, AD Tarn, C 1167, f° 283.

23. Deliberations of the estates of Languedoc held at Pezenas, 30 May 1629, AD Hérault, C 7070, f° (3) 43-44.

24. Ordonnance de Henri II de Bourbon prince de Condé, Toulouse, 24 February 1628, AD Tarn, C 891.

25. Daubresse, *Le Parlement de Paris*, 13-43.

26. Fontaine, *History of Pedlars in Europe.*

27. *Le Mercure François*; Vittu, "Instruments of Political Information," 160-174; Chartier, "Pamphlets et gazettes," 501-526.

28. Wagner, *Reading Iconotexts*; Montandon, ed., *Iconotextes.*

29. Jouanna, *Le Devoir de révolte*, 368-377.

30. "Tableau du siege de Montaulban 1622," BNF, Mss. fr. 18756, f° 3-7.

31. François I d'Esparbès de Lussan marquis d'Aubeterre to Paul Phélypeaux seigneur de Pontchartrain, Agen, 12 November 1615, BNF, Clairambault 366, f° 26-27.

32. François I d'Esparbès de Lussan marquis d'Aubeterre to Paul Phélypeaux seigneur de Pontchartrain, Agen, 9 January 1616, BNF, Clairambault 366, f° 327-328.

33. On high command offices in the sixteenth and seventeenth centuries, see Parrott, *Richelieu's Army*, 463-504; Lynn, *Giant of the Grand Siècle*, 282-318; Wood, *King's Army*, 73-80; Hélène Michaud, "Les Institutions militaires," 29-43.

34. Videl, *Histoire du connestable de Lesdiguières*, 764-766.

35. Louis XIII had offered the office of connétable to Lesdiguières in 1621, but Lesdiguières, a Calvinist, refused it, since the king insisted on a conversion. In 1622, Lesdiguières changed his mind and converted when he was given a second chance at the office.

36. Wood, *King's Army*, 73-80.

37. Ibid., 74-75.

38. Parrott, "Richelieu, the *Grands*, and the French Army," 147-148.

39. Elzière, *Histoire des Budos*, 128-129, 242.

40. Girard, 211-212; Fessenden, "Épernon and Guyenne," 10, 18, 200-201; Parrott, "Administration of the French Army," 314-321; Lynn, *Giant of the Grand Siècle*, 100-102.

41. Girard, 287.

42. BNF, Mélanges de Colbert 322, f° 21–24; BNF, Languedoc Bénédictins 71, f° 15–18; Lynn, *Giant of the* Grand Siècle, 103.

43. BNF, Languedoc Bénédictins 71, f° 357–367.

44. Wood, *King's Army*, 130–131; Lynn, *Giant of the* Grand Siècle, 102–103; AG, A1 13, f° 116.

45. BNF, Mss. fr. 4561, f° 98–108; Pontis, *Mémoires*, 165; Wood, *King's Army*, 155–156.

46. Wood, *King's Army*, 77, 78; Lynn, *Giant of the* Grand Siècle, 289–290.

47. "Provisions de la charge de maréchal général des camps et armées pour M. de Lesdiguières, 30 March 1621," SHAT, *Ordonnances Militaires*, vol. 13, f° 75; AD Hérault, B 22706.

48. Beik, *Absolutism and Society in Seventeenth-Century France*, 44.

49. Harding, *Anatomy of a Power Elite*, 5–17.

50. Jean du Tillet quoted in Babeau, *La province sous l'ancien régime*, 1: 256–257.

51. Harding, *Anatomy of a Power Elite*, 14.

52. On Henri I de Montmorency, see Davies, "Duc de Montmorency, Philip II and the House of Savoy," 870–892; id., "Neither Politique nor Patriot?" 539–566; Greengrass, "Noble Affinities in Early Modern France," 275–311.

53. On Henri II de Montmorency, see Du Cros; Du Chesne-Tourangeau, *Histoire genealogique de la maison de Montmorency et de Laval*; Hepp, "Considérations morales et politiques autour d'Henri de Montmorency," 83–91.

54. AG, A1 12, f° 57; *Mercure françois*, 5: 262–266; Fontenay-Mareuil, *Mémoires*, 169.

55. Girard, 426; Fessenden, "Épernon and Guyenne," 42–43.

56. Babeau, *La Province sous l'ancien régime*, 1: 312–325.

57. AG, A1 14, f° 59; Mousnier, *Institutions of France under the Absolute Monarchy*, 2: 475–476.

58. Fessenden, "Épernon and Guyenne," 27.

59. Elzière, *Histoire des Budos*, 131.

60. Mousnier, *Institutions of France under the Absolute Monarchy*, 2: 266–268; Beik, *Absolutism and Society Seventeenth-Century France*, 47, 49; Fessenden, "Épernon and Guyenne," 27–28; *HGL*, 11: 918; Baldwin, *Government of Philip Augustus*, 220, 233–239.

61. *HGL*, 11: 195, 285; Beik, *Absolutism and Society in Seventeenth-Century France*, 47, 49.

62. The number of offices could fluctuate, and one document lists nine sénéchaux in Guyenne: Albret, Armaignac, Commignes, Périgord, Bigore, Marsan, Tartas, Lannes, and Rouergue. BNF, Dupuy 100, f° 134–138; Fessenden, "Épernon and Guyenne," 27–28.

63. AD Tarn, C 871; BNF, Dupuy 127, f° 120–143.

64. Beik, *Absolutism and Society in Seventeenth-Century France*, 49, 98–116;

65. Buisseret, "Stage in the Development of the French Intendants," 27–38.

66. Baxter, *Servants of the Sword*; Bonney, *Political Change in France under Richelieu and Mazarin*; Dubost, "Absolutisme et centralisation en Languedoc," 376–377.

67. Daubresse, *Le Parlement de Paris*, 71–120.

68. Beik, *Absolutism and Society in Seventeenth-Century France*, 77–97; Capot, "Les Magistrats de la chambre de l'édit," 63–88.

69. Beik, *Urban Protest in Seventeenth-Century France*, 73–79.

70. Beik, *Absolutism and Society in Seventeenth-Century France*, 51–53, 121–125.

71. AD Hérault, C 7059 (82–83); Mandement de Henri II de Montmorency duc de Montmorenc, Carcassonne, 28 December 1621, copy, AD Hérault, B 6337; Fessenden, "Épernon and Guyenne," 89.

72. Beik, *Absolutism and Society in Seventeenth-Century France*, 117–146; Mousnier, *Institutions of France under the Absolute Monarchy*, 1: 612–627.

73. Documents refer variously to *colonels*, *colonels des legionnaires*, and *mestres de camp*. BNF, Clairambault 1131, f° 188. Mss fr. 15616, f° 83–84. Mss. fr. 18756, f° 47–48.

74. Billon, *Les Principes de l'art militaire*.

75. Wood, *King's Army*, 79–80. On the company as the "basic organizational unit" of the seventeenth-century French army, see Parrott, *Richelieu's Army*, 48–50.

76. Billon, *Les Principes de l'art militaire*.

77. Boltanski, *Les Ducs de Nevers et l'état royal*, 102–106.

78. Lynn, *Giant of the Grand Siècle*, 489–500; Wood, *King's Army*, chap. 5; Love, "'All the King's Horsemen,'" 511–533.

79. Desachy-Delclos, "Les Élites militaires en Rouergue au XVIe siècle," 9–11.

80. Adrien de Monluc comte de Carmaing to Paul Phélypeaux seigneur de Ponchartrain, Montesquieu, 17 January 1615, BNF, Clairambault 365, f° 11.

81. Contemporary usages of *office* suggest that nobles held a very broad conception of officeholding. The expression *faire office de* shows the linkage of the idea of an office to specific functions or specific instances of service. *Dictionnaire historique de la langue française*, ed. Rey et al., 1359. For an example of the use of *faire office de*, see Louis XIII to Henri II de Montmorency duc de Montmorency, 26 November 1614, BNF, Clairambault 1131, f° 270–271.

82. AD Hérault, 1 E 183.

83. François de Noailles comte d'Ayen to Paul Phélypeaux seigneur de Pontchartrain, La Fage, 28 February 1616, BNF, Clairambault 366, f° 405–406.

84. Emmanuel de Crussol duc d'Uzès to Paul Phélypeaux seigneur de Pontchartrain, Assier, 17 June 1613, BNF, Clairambault 1131, f° 357; Emmanuel de Crussol duc d'Uzès to Paul Phélypeaux seigneur de Pontchartrain, Assier, 17 March 1613, BNF, Clairambault 1131, f° 352–353.

85. Adrien de Monluc comte de Carmaing to Paul Phélypeaux seigneur de Pontchartrain, Montesquieu, 17 January 1615, BNF, Clairambault 365, f° 11.

86. Jean-Paul d'Esparbès de Lussan to Antoine de Roquelaure marquis de Roquelaure, Blaye, 21 October 1616, BNF, Clairambault 369, f° 136–137.

87. The term *officier* was used to designate "one who holds an office, a charge," according to *Dictionnaire historique de la langue française*, ed. Rey et al., 1359.

88. Parrott, "Administration of the French Army," 147–150.

89. Deliberations on troops at the estates of Languedoc held at Beziers, 17 December 1621, AD Hérault 7059, f° 103.

90. Antoine Jaubert de Barrault comte de Blaignac to Marie de Médicis, Barrault, 29 January 1616, BNF, Clairambault 366, f° 359–360.

91. Henri I de Montmorency duc de Montmorency to Marie de Médicis, La Grange-des-Prés, 12 December 1613, BNF, Clairambault 1131, f° 185.

92. Anne de Lévis duc de Ventadour to Louis XIII, La Voulte, 7 January 1618, BNF, Clairambault 374, f° 6. See also BNF, Clairambault 374, f° 12.

93. Alexandre de Lévis marquis de Mirepoix to Louis XIII, Mirepoix, 15 March 1618, BNF, Clairambault 374, f° 54–55.

94. François I d'Esparbès de Lussan marquis d'Aubeterre to Louis XIII, Blaye, 24 August 1618, BNF, Clairambault 374, f° 257–258.

95. François I d'Esparbès de Lussan marquis d'Aubeterre to Marie de Médicis, Villeneuve d'Agenois, 14 November 1615, BNF, Clairambault 366, f° 30–31.

96. Nicot, *Thresor de la Langue Francoyse.*

97. Antoine-Arnauld de Pardaillan seigneur de Gondrin to Paul Phélypeaux seigneur de Pontchartrain, Gondrin, 17 October 1616, BNF, Clairambault 369, f° 113–114.

98. François de Noailles comte d'Ayen to Paul Phélypeaux seigneur de Pontchartrain, Villefranche-en-Rouergue, 31 August 1621, BNF, Clairambault 378, f° 35–36; François d'Estrades to Paul Phélypeaux seigneur de Pontchartrain, Agen, 20 February 1616, BNF, Clairambault 366, f° 387–388. For examples of the king's use of *bons serviteurs*, see BNF, Clairambault 1132, f° 286; BNF, Clairambault 1132, f° 286–287; BNF, Clairambault 378, f° 20–21.

99. Cornette, *Roi de guerre.*

100. Pons de Lauzières marquis de Thémines to Louis XIII, Thémines, 6 October 1619, BNF, Clairambault 375, f° 314–317; BNF, Clairambault 378, f° 44–45; BNF, Clairambault 378, f° 46–47.

101. Pons de Lauzières marquis de Thémines to Louis XIII, Thémines, 6 October 1619, BNF, Clairambault 375, f° 314–317.

102. "Tableau du siege de Montaulban 1622," BNF, Mss. fr. 18756, f° 54–56.

103. Pontis, *Mémoires,* 164–167.

104. François de Noailles comte d'Ayen to Paul Phélypeaux seigneur de Pontchartrain, La Farge, 8 January 1613, BNF, Clairambault 362, f° 213–214.

105. Pons de Lauzières marquis de Thémines to Antoine-Hercule de Budos marquis de Portes, camp at La Rochelle, 9 January 1626, BNF, Dupuy 93, f° 73.

106. "Le Psaultier des rebelles de ce temps," BNF, Mss. fr. 23060, f° 169–172.

107. James, "Huguenot Militancy and the Seventeenth-Century Wars of Religion," 209–223.

108. Louis XIII to François de Bonne duc de Lesdiguières, n.d., copy, BNF, Mss. fr. 3722, f° 160.

109. Henri II de Montmorency duc de Montmorency to Louis XIII, Pont-St-Esprit, 1 May 1621, BNF, Clairambault 1131, f° 302–303.

110. Emmanuel de Crussol duc d'Uzès to Paul Phélypeaux seigneur de Pontchartrain, Assier, 17 June 1613, BNF, Clairambault 1131, f° 357.

111. Comte de Louvenstein-Rochefort [?] to Marie de Médicis, Rochefort, 12 September 1616, BNF, Clairambault 368, f° 197–198.

112. AD Hérault, A 44, f° 101, 90.

113. François I d'Esparbès de Lussan marquis d'Aubeterre to Marie de Médicis, Aubeterre, 21 January 1616, BNF, Clairambault 366, f° 356–357.

114. Emmanuel de Crussol duc d'Uzès to Paul Phélypeaux seigneur de Pontchartrain, Assier, 25 December 1612, BNF, Clairambault 1131, f° 349.

115. François de Noailles comte d'Ayen to Louis XIII, Malemort, 10 September 1616, BNF, Clairambault 368, f° 216–217.

116. François de Noailles comte d'Ayen to Paul Phélypeaux seigneur de Pontchartrain, 14 January 1618, BNF, Clairambault 374, f° 27.

117. François de Noailles comte d'Ayen to Paul Phélypeaux seigneur de Pontchartrain, [?], 27 November 1615, BNF, Clairambault 366, f° 73.

118. AD Gard, 1 E 264; Louis XIII to Charles de Machault, Lyon, 11 September 1630, AN, K 113B, f° 536.

119. Henri II de Montmorency duc de Montmorency to Marie de Médicis, Pézenas, 1 October 1614, BNF, Clairambault 1131, f° 236.

120. Emmanuel de Crussol duc d'Uzès to Louis XIII, Paris, 1 October 1620, BNF, Clairambault 1131, f° 364.

121. Jean-François de La Guiche seigneur de Saint-Géran to Paul Phélypeaux seigneur de Pontchartrain, Molins, 28 August 1619, BNF, Clairambault 375, f° 296–297.

122. Henri II de Montmorency duc de Montmorency to Marie de Médicis, Pézenas, 17 December 1614, BNF, Clairambault 1131, f° 275.

123. François I d'Esparbès de Lussan marquis d'Aubeterre to Louis XIII, Blaye, 17 August 1621, BNF, Clairambault 378, f° 29–30.

124. Henri I de Montmorency duc de Montmorency to Marie de Médicis, La Grange-des-Prés, 12 December 1613, BNF, Clairambault 1131, f° 185.

125. Jean-Paul d'Esparbès de Lussan to Antoine de Roquelaure seigneur de Roquelaure, Blaye, 21 October 1616, BNF, Clairambault 369, f° 136–137.

126. Antoine de Roquelaure marquis de Roquelaure to Jean-Paul d'Esparbès de Lussan, n.d., BNF, Clairambautlt 369, f° 138.

127. AG, A1 14, f° 59.

128. Jacques d'Escars marquis de Merville [?] to Louis XIII, Bordeaux, 15 March 1618, BNF, Clairambault 374, f° 56–57.

CHAPTER 6: HONOR AND COURAGE

1. *CSV*, 146–147.

2. For etymologies of words related to the concept of honor, see entries for *honnête, honneur, honorer, honte,* and *réputater* in *Dictionnaire de la langue française*, ed. Rey et al., 970–972, 1777–1778.

3. Henri II de Montmorency duc de Montmorency to Marie de Médicis, Pézenas, 19 June 1614, BNF, Clairambault 1131, f° 198–199.

4. *Manifeste des bons françois, sur la mort desplorable de monseigneur le mareschal de Schombert.*

5. Faret, *L'Honneste-homme*, 66–68.

6. Jacques de Pons marquis de La Caze, "Verbal de Monsr le marquis de La Case sur les affaires de Montauban et mouvemens de 1625," BNF, Mss. fr. 15823.

7. Henry I de Montmorency to Marie de Médicis, La Grange, 14 January 1614, BNF, Clairambaul 1131, f° 187.

8. Calvin, *Institutes,* trans. Battles, 34–35.

9. Ibid., 16.

10. Du Plessis de Mornay, *De la verité de la religion Chrestienne*; Bouwsma, *John Calvin,* 195.

11. Diefendorf, *From Penitence to Charity,* 49–76.

12. Mentzer, *Blood and Belief,* 163.

13. Benedict, *Christ's Churches Purely Reformed,* 496–497.

14. Editions of Marot's psalter continued to be popular among Huguenots well into the seventeenth century. Marot, *Les Pseaumes de David.*

15. Diefendorf, *Beneath the Cross,* 136–144.

16. Spicer, "'Qui est de Dieu oit la parole de Dieu,'" 181–183.

17. Vosgrand [?] to Henri IV, Clairac, 15 September 1601, BNF, Mss. fr. 23196, f° 323.

18. M. Danchies to M. Gargouliau, Montpellier, 12 September 1628, BNF, Mss. fr. 18972, f° 2–4.

19. For examples of the use of reliquaries and crucifixes, see *Histoire veritable de tovt ce qvi s'est faict & passé dans la ville de Thoulouse, en la mort de Monsieur de Montmorancy*; Armand-Jean du Plessis cardinal de Richelieu to Marie de Médicis, Pézenas, 5 August 1629, in *LCR,* 3: 402.

20. Schneider, *Public Life in Toulouse,* 167–187, 221–240.

21. Deyron, *De la genealogie de monsieur le baron d'Aubais.*

22. Sauzet, *Au Grand Siècle des âmes,* 13–27, 45–55.

23. "Discours funebre sur la mort de Henry de Lorraine duc de Mayenne et d'Aiguillon, pair et grand chambellan de France, gouverneur et lieutenant general pour le roy au gouvernement de Guyenne," BNF, Mss. fr. 23060, f° 49–64; "Quatrain sur la mort du mesme duc de Mayenne," BNF, Mss. fr. 23060, f° 69–71. Pontis praises the duc de Mayenne and regrets his loss in his *Mémoires,* 148–151.

24. Fontenay-Mareuil blames the duc de Mayenne for Lauzières's death, since Mayenne ordered him on the fatal assault which was "repoussé avec perte d'une infinté de gens," in François Duval, *Mémoires,* 162–163; La Roque M, 1: 325.

25. Vignier to Auguste Galland, Roquecourbe, 3 November 1627, BNF, Mss. fr. 15828, f° 84; Greengrass, "Informal Networks in Sixteenth-Century French Protestantism," 91–92; Conner, *Huguenot Heartland,* 206–207.

26. Bireley, *Jesuits and the Thirty Years War,* 1–32, 44–56, 63–72.

27. Calvin, *Institutes,* trans. Battles, 60–63, 109–110; Bossy, *Christianity in the West,* 140.

28. Schneider, *Public Life in Toulouse,* 221–240.

29. Greengrass, *Governing Passions,* 64–65; Boucher, "L'Ordre du Saint-Esprit dans la pensée politique et religieuse d'Henri III," 129–142.

30. François d'Escoubleau cardinal de Sourdis to Marie de Médicis, Bordeaux, 1 February 1613, BNF, Clairambaut 362, f° 221.

31. Gurson de Foy to Louis XIII, Gurson, 17 November 1615, BNF, Clairambault 366, f° 46–47.

32. Loyseau, *Traité des seigneuries*, 6–7.

33. Loyseau, *Treatise of Orders*, 13.

34. Montaigne, "On Rewards for Honour," 2.7, in *Complete Essays*, trans. Screech, 431.

35. Faret, *L'Honneste-homme*, 7–19, 40–65, 174–176.

36. Schalk, *From Valor to Pedigree*, 131–132.

37. Rambures to Paul Phélypeaux seigneur de Pontchartrain, Bergerac, 15 August 1621, BNF, Clairambault 378, f° 48–50.

38. Schalk, *From Valor to Pedigree*, 139–140, 202–206.

39. *CSV*, 124–125.

40. "Memoire ou journal du siege de Montpellier," BNF, Mss. fr. 23339, f° 187–188.

41. Mémoire, 29 June 1629, BNF, Mss. fr. 3829, f° 79.

42. Faret, *L'Honneste-homme*, 15–17.

43. Pons de Lauzières marquis de Thémines to Paul Phélypeaux seigneur de Pontchartrain, Roquelaure en Rouergue, 1612, BNF, Clairambault 362, f° 168–169; Antoine III de Gramont comte de Gramont to Paul Phélypeaux seigneur de Pontchartrain, Bidache, 9 Janaury 1621, BNF, Clairambault 377, f° 519.

44. *CSV*, 52.

45. *CSV*, 58.

46. Jouanna, *L'Idée de race en France*, 1: 28–35.

47. Loyseau, *Treatise of Orders*, 98–100, 107–108.

48. Anne de Lévis duc de Ventadour to Henri I de Montmorency duc de Montmorency, Paris, 9 August 1608, BNF, Mss. fr. 3602, f° 46.

49. Henri I de Montmorency duc de Montmorency to Marie de Médicis, Beaucaire, 30 June 1613, BNF, Clairambault 1131, f° 177–178.

50. AD Haute-Garonne, B 1913, f° 309–311.

51. AD Hérault, B 36, f° 6–8.

52. The legality of sales of "moyennes seigneuries" is discussed in Loyseau, *Traité des seigneuries*, 125–126. On the sale of the seigneurie of Montlaur in Languedoc, see "Rolle des principales & plus anciefies maisons de Languedoc donc j'ay peu avoir memoire," BNF, Mss. fr. 20235, f° 300–310.

53. Jean-Paul d'Esparbès de Lussan [?] to Marie de Médicis, Aubeterre, 14 November 1616, BNF, Clairambault 369, f° 327–328.

54. Anne de Lévis duc de Ventadour to Marie de Médicis, La Voulte, 24 October 1611, BNF, Clairambault 362, f° 79.

55. BNF, Mss. fr. 5481, f° 513–515; BNF, Mss. fr. 18833, f° 89–107; BNF, Mss. fr. 18085, f° 2–4; BNF, Languedoc-Bénédictins 105, f° 107–113.

56. La Roque M, 1: 265–267; BNF, Languedoc-Bénédictins 105, f° 292.

57. Dewald, *Aristocratic Experience and the Origins of Modern Culture*, 120–129.

58. Du Cros, 269–300; *Histoire veritable de tovt ce qvi s'est faict & passé dans la ville de Thoulouse, en la mort de Monsieur de Montmorancy.*

59. Tissandier, *Paranymphe du devoir*.

60. François d'Escoubleau cardinal de Sourdis to Marie de Médicis, Bordeaux, 3 July 1611, BNF, Clairambault 362, f° 39–41.

61. Daubresse, *Le Parlement de Paris*, 247–311.

62. *Memoire concernant la cassation des testament & codicilles de feu monsieur le duc d'Arpajon.*

63. François de Noailles comte d'Ayen to Paul Phélypeaux seigneur de Ponchartrain, L'Arche, 24 May 1618, BNF, Clairambault 374, f° 102–103.

64. *Declaration du roy en faveur du sieur de Latude pour avoir entree aux Estats de Languedoc a cause de la Baronie de Gange.* The families of nobles who were denied entry to the estates of Languedoc were eventually reinstated.

65. Nye, *Masculinity and Male Codes of Honor in Modern France*, 3–14.

66. Jean de Monluc-Balagny, quoted in Harding, *Anatomy of a Power Elite*, 68.

67. Caux, *Catalogue general des gentils-hommes de la province de Languedoc.*

68. Jean-François de La Guiche seigneur de Saint-Géran to Louis XIII, Molins, 28 August 1619, BNF, Clairambault 375, f° 288–289.

69. Faret, *L'Honneste-homme*, 114–115.

70. François de Bonne duc de Lesdiguières, "Discours de l'art militaire," in *ACL*, 2: 541–578.

71. Louis XIII to Louis de Bourbon comte de Soissons, camp at Montpellier, 2 October 1622, BNF, Mss. fr. 3722, f° 70–71.

72. Armand-Jean du Plessis cardinal de Richelieu to François d'Escoubleau cardinal de Sourdis, Mourvaux, 20 July 1632, BNF, Mss. fr. 6385, f° 21.

73. Loyseau, *Treatise of Orders*, 66–67.

74. Arnauld, *Presentation de Monsieur de Montmorency en l'office d'Admiral de France.*

75. *CSV*, 146–147.

76. François de Bonne duc de Lesdiguières, "Discours de l'art militaire," in *ACL*, 2:541–578.

77. Examples include: *Ode pour monseigneur le duc de Bellegarde*; "Sonnet," BNF, Mss. fr. 4102, f° 202.

78. Tissandier, *Paranymphe du devoir.*

79. *Immortalité du carrousel de Monseigneur d'Espernon.*

80. *La prise du fort de Corconne.*

81. Ibid.

82. *Assaut donné contre la ville de Montauban.*

83. Praise of the Lauzières family's services in the early seventeenth century later produced further accolades: *Mémoire a consulter et consultation pour messires Jean-Joseph & Marc-Antoine de Lauziers de Themines frères.*

84. Connell, *Masculinities*, 30, 185–186, 214–215.

85. Du Cros, 9.

86. "La Suitte du tableau du siege de Montauban . . . ," BNF, Mss. fr. 18756, f° 70.

87. Neuschel, *Word of Honor*, 93–95, 168–173. On honorific privileges, see Bitton, *French Nobility in Crisis*; Bush, *Noble Privilege.*

88. Carroll, *Blood and Violence in Early Modern France*, 49.

89. Commission, copy, AD Hérault, 1 E 239, f° 13.

90. *Provisions de la charge de marechal general des camps et armées pour Mr. de Lesdiguieres.*

91. See various documents relating to nobles' *prevues de noblesse* in the Hozier, Pièces Originales, and Languedoc-Bénédictins collections at the BNF.

92. Antoine III de Gramont comte de Gramont to Paul Phélypeaux seigneur de Pontchartrain, Bidache, 9 Janaury 1621, BNF, Clairambault 377, f° 519.

93. Louis XIII to Antoine-Arnaud de Pardaillan seigneur de Gondrin, Paris 6 July 1620, BNF, Clairambault 1132, f° 286–287.

94. Chabans, *Histoire de la guerre des Huguenots*, 123–124.

95. AD Hérault, C 7746.

96. Billacois, *Le Duel*, 7–10.

97. Brioist et al., *Croiser le fer*, 247–255.

98. Le Roux, *La Faveur du roi*, 20–48, 717–721.

99. See, e.g., Méry de Vic [?] to Louis XIII, Bordeaux, 14 October 1616, BNF, Clairambault 369, f° 92–94.

100. Henry I de Montmorency duc de Montmorency to Marie de Médicis, La Grange-des-Prés, 29 December 1613, BNF, Clairambault 1131, f° 186.

101. Beik, *Urban Protest in Seventeenth-Century France*, 28–30.

102. Paul de Montbourcher, quoted in Carroll, *Blood and Violence in Early Modern France*, 65.

103. Ibid., 73, 81.

104. On the bodily geometry of arms, see Van Orden, *Music, Discipline, and Arms in Early Modern France*, 186–234; Brioist et al., *Croiser le fer*, 133–197.

105. On *maîtres d'armes*, see Brioist et al., *Croiser le fer*, 71–128.

106. Faret, *L'Honneste-homme*, 21.

107. Stewart sees this aspect of honor as reciprocal, proposing the idea of "reflexive honor," when honor codes demand a "counterattack" by the wronged party, in his *Honor*, 64–65.

108. *CSV*, 86–87.

109. *CSV*, 79–80.

110. Du Cros, 43–46.

111. Anne de Lévis duc de Ventadour to Louis XIII, La Voulte, 7 January 1618, BNF, Clairambault 374, f° 6.

112. *CSV*, 79–80.

113. Du Cros, 149–151.

114. Du Cros, 63–64.

115. *CSV*, 66–69.

116. Henri I de Montmorency duc de Montmorency to Marie de Médicis, Bains de Balarue, 10 May 1613, BNF, Clairambault 1131, f° 175.

117. *CSV*, 79–80.

118. Fiesc [?] to Paul Phélypeaux seigneur de Pontchartrain, Bressuire, 10 May 1621, BNF, Clairmabult 377, f° 655.

119. Alexandre de Lévis marquis de Mirepoix to Paul Phélypeaux seigneur de Pontchartrain, Terride, 2 July 1621, BNF, Clairambault 377, f° 799–800.

120. *La Deffaicte de quatre cents hommes par le sieur de Mont-Real.*

121. Louis de Chabans, quoted in Carroll, *Blood and Violence in Early Modern France*, 60.

122. Lettres patentes, AD Hérault, 1 E 1483.

123. *CSV*, 79–80.

124. Wood, *King's Army*, 114–118.

125. Du Cros, 278–279.

126. "La Suitte du tableau du siege de Montauban . . . ," BNF, Mss. fr. 18756, f° 70.

127. Commission, AD Hérault, A 53, f° 120–122.

128. Ibid.

129. See, e.g., *Immortalité du carrousel de Monseigneur d'Espernon.*

130. Schneider, *Public Life in Toulouse*, 140–141.

131. Du Cros, 134–136.

132. Tissandier, *Paranymphe du devoir.*

133. Girard, 402; Fessenden, "Épernon and Guyenne," 44–48.

134. Henri II de Montmorency duc de Montmorency to Paul Phélypeaux seigneur de Pontchartrain, Toulouse, 20 January 1619, BNF, Clairambault 1131, f° 301.

135. *HGL*, 11: 929, 1004.

136. Miller, *Humiliation*, 6–7.

137. *CSV*, 117–118.

138. Jean-Louis de La Valette duc d'Épernon to Louis XIII, Bordeaux, 23 August 1616, BNF, Clairambault 368, f° 93–95.

139. Fessenden, "Épernon and Guyenne," 44–48.

140. Jacques de Pons marquis de La Caze, "Verbal de Monsr le marquis de La Case sur les affaires de Montauban et mouvemens de 1625," BNF, Mss. Fr. 15823.

141. Henri II de Montmorency duc de Montmorency to Marie de Médicis, Pézenas, 28 June 1614, BNF, Clairambault 1131, f° 200–201.

142. This entire paragraph is drawn from François I d'Esparbès de Lussan marquis d'Aubeterre to Paul Phélypeaux seigneur de Pontchartrain, Agen, 9 January 1616, BNF, Clairambault 366, f° 327–328.

143. "Memoire ou journal du siege de Montpellier," BNF, Mss. fr. 23339, f° 170–171.

144. *CSV.*

145. Chabans, *Histoire de la guerre des Huguenots*, 580–581.

146. François I d'Esparbès de Lussan marquis d'Aubeterre to Paul Phélypeaux seigneur de Pontchartrain, Agen, 20 November 1615, BNF, Clairambault 366, f° 60–61.

147. Jacques de Pons marquis de La Caze, "Verbal de Monsr le marquis de La Case sur les affaires de Montauban et mouvemens de 1625," BNF, Mss. fr. 15823.

148. Le Roux, *Le Faveur du roi*, 417–456.

149. For a fascinating analysis of Louis de Gonzague duc de Nevers's "labyrinth of justification" following his disgrace in 1585, see Le Person, *"Practiques" et "Practiqueurs,"* 271–373.

150. *La Prise de la ville de Chaumerac en Vivarests.*

151. *Declaration du roy, contre le duc de Montmorancy.*

152. Xavier Le Person argues that Henri III prolonged the duc de Nevers's status of disgrace when the duc sought to reenter the king's graces without admitting fault, in his *"Practiques" et "Practiqueurs,"* 271–373.

153. "Declaration du Roy pour priver de lentrée des Estatz de Languedoc les barons prevenus du crime de rebellion," AD Hérault, A 48, f° 1.

154. ASF, MdP 4635; Major, "The Revolt of 1620," 404–405.

155. "Declaration de Monsieur le duc de Rohan Pair de France, etc., Contenant la Justice des raisons de motifz qui l'ont obligé a Implorer l'assistance du Roy de la grande Bretagne et prendre les armes pour la deffence des Eglises reformées de ce Royaume," BNF, Dupuy 100, f° 174–184.

CHAPTER 7: RITUALS OF ARMING

1. *CSV*, 73–74.

2. Jouanna, *Le Devoir de révolte*, 368–390.

3. Nicholas B. Dirks, "Ritual and Resistance: Subversion as a Social Fact," in *Culture/ Power/History*, ed. Dirks et al., 483–503.

4. Dirks's methodological approaches to ritual share much with Michel de Certeau's techniques of analyzing the practices of everyday life in Certeau, *L'Invention du quotidien*.

5. BNF, Clairambault 362, f° 105–108; BNF, Dupuy 93, f° 105–108; Anne de Lévis duc de Ventadour to Henri I de Montmorency duc de Montmorency, Montpellier, 18 February 1598 [?], BNF, Mss. fr. 3586, f° 50–51; Gentil [?] to Henri IV, Agen, 30 May 1603, BNF, Mss. fr. 23197, f° 330–331.

6. Carroll, *Blood and Violence in Early Modern France*, 36.

7. Ibid., 83–92; Taylor, "Credit, Debt, and Honor in Castile," 8–27; Muir, *Mad Blood Stirring*.

8. AD Haute-Garonne, B 1913, f° 366–368.

9. Stuart Carroll finds more cases of vulgar language and curse words in his sources, perhaps because he employs judicial records extensively, in his *Blood and Violence in Early Modern France*, 89–91.

10. François d'Esparbès de Lussan marquis d'Aubeterre to Paul Phélypeaux seigneur de Ponchartrain, Agen, 4 November 1615, BNF, Clairambault 366, f° 5.

11. Delort, *Mémoires inédits d'André Delort sur la ville de Montpellier*, 1.

12. François de Noailles comte d'Ayen to Paul Phélypeaux seigneur de Pontchartrain, Rodez, 21 June 1621, BNF, Clairambault 377, f° 771–773.

13. Pollak, "Representations of the City in Siege Views," 605–646.

14. On civic entries in early modern France, see *Les Entrées royales*, ed. Vaillancourt and Wagner; Boureau, "Les Cérémonies royales françaises," 1253–1264; Bryant, *King and the City in the Parisian Royal Entry Ceremony*.

15. *Lettre du roy, envoyee a Monseigneur le mareschal de Souvré*.

16. Chabans, *Histoire de la guerre des Huguenots*, 193–195.

17. Blainville to Paul Phélypeaux seigneur de Pontchartrain, 14 [?] June 1621, BNF, Clairambault 377, f° 735–737.

18. Beik, *Urban Protest in Seventeenth-Century France*.

19. On the taking of prisoners at the outbreak of civil conflict, see *Mercure françois*, 11: 739–740.

20. Bercé, *History of Peasant Revolts*.

21. Tanneguy de Verigniez seigneur de Blainville to Paul Phélypeaux seigneur de Pontchartrain, 14 [?] June 1621, BNF, Clairambault 377, f° 735–737; *La Prise et reduction de la ville et chasteau de Nerac*; "Mémoires de Vignolles," in *PFHF*.

22. *La Prise et reduction de la ville et chasteau de Nerac*. See also *Recit veritable de la reduction du Mas-de-Verdun*; "Le Tombeau de monseigneur le duc de Mayenne. Ou le temple de la magnanimité. À l'ame de monseigneur le duc de Mayenne," BNF, Mss. fr. 23060.

23. *La Prise et reduction de la ville et chasteau de Nerac*, BNF, 8° Lb³⁶ 1695.

24. Pierre d'Escodéca seigneur de Boisse-Pardaillan to Paul Phélypeaux seigneur de Pontchartrain, n.d., BNF, Clairambault 377, f° 789–792.

25. *Assemblee generale des messieurs les princes en la vile de Poictiers*; *Coppie de la lettre du Roy escrite à monseigneur le duc de Mayenne*; *Declaration du Roy, pour la reunion à son domaine et confiscation des biens des ducs de Nevers, de Vendosme, de Mayenne, mareschal de Buillon, marquis de Coeuvre, et president le Jay*; *Declaration du roy contre les ducs de Vendosme, de Mayenne, mareschal de Buillon, marquis de Cœuvre, le president le Jay*.

26. François de Noailles comte d'Ayen to Paul Phélypeaux seigneur de Pontchartrain, Rodez, 5 September 1621, BNF, Clairambault 378, f° 40–41.

27. Henri II de Montmorency duc de Montmorency to Louis XIII, Narbonne, 26 March 1619, BNF, Cinq Cens de Colbert 97, f° 51.

28. Jouanna, *Le Devoir de révolte*, 368–384.

29. Henri II de Montmorency duc de Montmorency to Marie de Médicis, Toulouse, 10 mars 1619, BNF, Cinq Cens de Colbert 97, f° 130.

30. *Declaration de Monseigneur le Prince contre les ennemis du roy*; *Premiere lettre de Monsieur le duc d'Espernon*; *Declaration de Messieurs les princes au roy*; Jouanna, *Le Devoir de révote*, 147–179.

31. Henri I de Montmorency duc de Montmorency to Marie de Médicis, La Grange, 25 August 1613, BNF, Clairambault 1131, f° 180.

32. Du Cros, 134–136.

33. *CSV*, 117–118.

34. *Manifeste de Monsieur de Rohan*; *Declaration de Monsieur le duc de Rohan*.

35. On ex-Leaguer nobles, see Descimon and Ruiz Ibáñez, *Les Ligueurs de l'exil*.

36. *CSV*, 73–74.

37. BNF, Clairambault 366, f° 16–29.

38. Lynn, *Giant of the Grand Siècle*, 347–348; Parrott, *Richelieu's Army*, 287–292.

39. Carroll, *Blood and Violence in Early Modern France*, 5–10; Brioist et al., *Croiser le fer*; Billacois, *Le Duel*.

40. "Defences de faire aucunes levées de gens de guerre sans expresse permission du roi signé par un des secretaires d'estat, et seelées du grand seau," AD Haute-Garonne, B 1914, f° 91.

41. BNF, F 46974 (7); BNF, F 46974 (11).

42. *Reglement pour les gens de guerre*.

43. Antoine de Roquelaure marquis de Roquelaure to Marie de Médicis, Auch [?], 19 September 1611, BNF, Clairambault 362, f° 65.

44. Wolfe, "Walled Towns during the French Wars of Religion," 317–348; Bernard Chevalier, *Les Bonnes villes de France*.

45. Girard, 345.

46. Gilles Le Masuyer, premier président of the parlement de Toulouse, to the estates of Languedoc, read at the estates of Languedoc held at Béziers and Carcassonne, 30 September 1621, AD Hérault C 7059, f° 24.

47. Lynn, "How War Fed War," 286–310.

48. On the right of *guet et garde* and its changing applications on seigneuries, see Salmon, *Society in Crisis* 39–40; Root, *Peasants and King in Burgundy*, 159–164.

49. Deliberations of the estates of Languedoc held at Béziers and Carcassonne, 28 September 1621, AD Hérault, C 7059, f° 22–23.

50. "Estat du payement que sera faict aux gens de guerre a pied françois par nous restablis en garnisons pour le service du Roy en aulcunes villes & places du pays de Viverois pour leur solde & entretennement durant trois mois de la presente annee a commancer du premier de septembre 1628," AD Hérault, B 22765.

51. Jean-Louis Nogaret de La Valette duc d'Épernon to Louis XIII, Bordeaux, 23 August 1616, BNF, Clairambault 368, f° 93–95.

52. Ordonnance de Henri II de Montmorency duc de Montmorency, 13 July 1621, AD Hérault, B 22603.

53. AN, K 113A, f° 18.

54. Journal of Gaspard III de Coligny seigneur de Châtillon, BNF, Mss. fr. 23246, f° 5–8.

55. AD Hérault, B 22735.

56. Jouanna, *Le Devoir de révolte*, 341–367.

57. Girard, 280–281.

58. Geoffrey Parker, *Army of Flanders and the Spanish Road*, 35.

59. Gaubertin, *Histoire des guerres du roy Louys XIII*.

60. "Commission à Mons' de Bioule pour la levée d'un regiment d'infanterie, 1628," SHAT, Bibliothèque, Collection des ordonnances militaires, vol. 13: 1612–1629: Louis XIII, f° 126.

61. AD Hérault, C 7059, f° (94).

62. BNF, Cinq Cens de Colbert 2, f° 68–69; *Coppie des lettres de commission de la Royne mere. Pour la leuee de ses gens de guerre* (n.p.: n.p., n.d. [1620]), BNF, 8° Lb[36] 1379.

63. Commissions, BNF, Dupuy 100, f° 70, 87.

64. Ordonnance de Henri II de Rohan duc de Rohan, 12 January 1622, AD Hérault, B 22590.

65. François de Noailles comte d'Ayen to Louis XIII, La Faye, 8 December 1615, BNF, Clairambault 366, f° 100–101.

66. Henri II de Montmorency duc de Montmorency to seigneur de Laudun, Lunel, 3 October 1627, AD Gard, 1 E 521.

67. Ordonnance of Henri II de Montmorency duc de Montmorency, Béziers, 16 April 1625, AD Tarn, C 883.

68. Sir John Throckmorton to vicomte de l'Isle, 1615, in *Report on the Manuscripts of . . . Viscount de l'Isle*, 5: 306–307.

69. "Mandement de Mr. de Montmorenci au Baron de Sorgues," copy, BNF, Languedoc-Bénédictins 94, f° 272.

70. Commission, La Rochelle, 9 August 1621, BNF, Dupuy 100, f° 70.

71. Touzery-Salager, *Les Châteaux du Bas-Languedoc*, 13–34.

72. Vitruvius, *Architecture*; Androuet du Cerceau, *Livre d'architecture*; Alberti, *L'Architecture*.

73. Riou, *Ardèche*, 38–49; Touzery-Salager, *Les Châteaux du Bas-Languedoc*, 319.

74. Neuschel, "Noble Households in the Sixteenth Century," 600.

75. Soutou, "Une Maison-forte du XVIIᵉ siècle," 353–361.

76. Errard de Bar-le-Duc, *La Fortification*.

77. Touzery-Salager, *Les Châteaux du Bas-Languedoc*, 320.

78. Ibid., 29, 92.

79. *CSV*, 65–66; Touzery-Salager, *Les Châteaux du Bas-Languedoc*, 182, 321.

80. Touzery-Salager, *Les Châteaux du Bas-Languedoc*, 29.

81. BNF, Mss. fr. 15380, f° 109; Touzery-Salager, *Les Châteaux du Bas-Languedoc*, 205–214.

82. Rolle, AD Gard, 1 E 374, f° 67.

83. BNF, Clairambault 373, f° 65.

84. Inventaire, AD Aude, 2 E 17, f° 12. Presumably, the château would have had even more arms and supplies before the civil war in which the comte de Rieux lost his life.

85. A *cestier* was a measure used in Languedoc for wheat and other dry goods, a counterpart to the *setier* or *sestier* in some other regions of France. The *cestier* varied by town in Languedoc, but was generally smaller than the *setier* of Paris, although both measures fluctuated. See Usher, *History of the Grain Trade*, 365–368. The *cestier* of Béziers amounted to approximately 66 litres, according to Le Roy Ladurie, *Paysans de Languedoc*, 2: 820.

86. Inventaire, AD Aude, 2 E 17, f° 12.

87. *CSV*, 119.

88. *CSV*, 119–120.

89. "Genealogie de la maison de La Garde de Chambonas faite à l'instance de messire Henry Joseph de La Garde . . . ," BNF, Languedoc-Bénédictins 103, f° 264–266; Riou, *Ardèche*, 64–73.

90. Elias, *Court Society*, 54–65.

91. Lynn, *Giant of the* Grand Siècle, 347–396.

92. On foreign troops in seventeenth-century French armies, see Parrott, *Richelieu's Army*, 292–312.

93. Wood, *King's Army*, 86–97.

94. *Reglemens du feu roy Louis XIII sur la convocation du ban et arriere-ban*; AD Gard, 1 E 521.

95. Louis XIV would call up the *ban et arrière ban* in 1674 and in 1689.

96. *Reglement pour les gens de guerre*.

97. M. de Montmart [?] to Louis XIII, n.d., BNF, Clairambault 366, f° 1–2.

98. Parrott, *Richelieu's Army*, 277–365; Lynn, *Giant of the* Grand Siècle, 284–286.

99. Lynn, *Giant of the* Grand Siècle, 347–396; Rowlands, *Dynastic State*, 204–206.

100. Alexandre de Castelnau baron de Clermont-Lodève to Armand-Jean du Plessis cardinal de Richelieu, Castelnau-en-Quercy, 24 June 1627, AAE, France 785, f° 171; this document is analyzed in Richelieu, *Papiers de Richelieu*, ed. Grillon, 2: 246–247.

101. Wood, *King's Army*, 91.

102. Ordonnance de Henri II de Rohan duc de Rohan, 28 May 1628, copy, AD Hérault, B 22758.

103. *Reglement pour les gens de guerre*.

104. Ibid.

105. Ordonnance de seigneur de Châtillon, Montpellier, 2 July 1621, AD Hérault, B 22603.

106. Ordonnance de l'assemblée de la province de Cévennes et Gévaudan, Saint-Hippolyte, 13 August 1621, AD Hérault, B 22603.

107. Deliberations of the estates of Languedoc held at Toulouse, 1 July 1621, AD Hérault, C 7059, f° 88–90.

108. "Tableau du siege de Montaulban 1622," BNF, Mss. fr. 18756, f° 11–12.

109. *Reglement pour les gens de guerre*.

110. "Recit veritable de la prise de la ville de Pamiers Capitale du Pays de Foix . . . ," BNF, Dupuy 100, f° 298–301.

111. *CSV*, 117–118.

112. "Mémoires de Vignolles," in *PFHF*.

113. *Reglement pour les gens de guerre*.

114. "Tableau du siege de Montaulban 1622," BNF, Mss. fr. 18756, f° 12–14.

115. Deliberations of the estates of Languedoc held at Pézenas, 30 May 1629, C 7070, f° 45.

116. *Reglement pour les gens de guerre*; AD Haute-Garonne, C 2128; Delort, *Mémoires inédits d'André Delort sur la ville de Montpellier*, 14–15, 37.

117. Deliberations of the estates of Languedoc held at Béziers and Carcassonne, 4 October 1621, AD Hérault, C 7059, f° 28–29.

118. "Mandement de Mr de Montmorenci au Baron de Sorgues," copy, BNF, Languedoc-Bénédictins 94, f° 272.

119. Ordonnance du duc de Vendôme, 22 August 1622, AD Hérault, C 8406.

120. Henri II de Montmorency to Louis XIII, Pont-Saint-Esprit, 1 May 1621, BNF, Clairambault 1131, f° 302–303; Du Cros, 28–31; *HGL*, 11: 940.

121. Deliberations of the estates of Languedoc held at Beaucaire, 7 March 1621, AD Hérault C 7059, f° 102–104; *La Prise remarquable de Marguerites*; *HGL*, 11: 944–945.

122. Bassompierre, *Journal*, 2: 349n1; *HGL*, 11: 948; Du Cros, 41.

123. Louis XIII to Gondrin, Paris, 6 July 1620, BNF, Clairambault 1132, f° 286–287.

124. Marie de Médicis to marquis de La Valette, Angers, 17 July 1620, BNF, NAF 5245, f° 141.

125. James, "Huguenot Militancy and the Seventeenth-Century Wars of Religion," 209–223; Souriac, "Les Places de sûreté protestantes."

126. Mss. fr. 18756, f° 7–9, 11–12.

127. Ordonnance de Henri II de Rohan duc de Rohan, Meyrueis, 28 May 1628, AD Hérault, B 22758.

128. Henri II de Montmorency duc de Montmorency to seigneur de Laudun, Lunel, 3 October 1627, AD Gard, 1 E 521.

129. Malherbe, quoted in Elzière, *Histoire des Budos*, 130.

130. François V de La Rochefoucuald comte de La Rochefoucauld to Paul Phélypeaux seigneur de Pontchartrain, Poitiers, 9 April 1619, BNF, Cinq Cens de Colbert 97, f° 72.

131. Henri de Schömberg comte de Nanteuil to Louis XIII, Ebvrion, 10 April 1619, BNF, Cinq Cens de Colbert 97, f° 208–209.

132. Brenac, "Toulouse, centre de lutte contre le protestantisme," 31–45.

CHAPTER 8: PERSONAL ARMIES

1. François d'Escoubleau cardinal de Sourdis to Marie de Médicis, Bordeaux, 8 September 1613, BNF, Clairambault 363, f° 89–90.

2. Richelieu, *Testament politique*, ed. Hildesheimer, 309.

3. Van Orden, *Music, Discipline, and Arms in Early Modern France*, 187–234; McNeill, *Keeping Together in Time*; Geoffrey Parker, *Military Revolution*, 6–24.

4. This image of the French army of seventeenth century as a giant appears in Lynn, *Giant of the Grand Siècle*, ix: "I keep safe the memory of an invisible giant. The son of kings, this armed colossus once towered above his foes to bestride a continent."

5. Tilly, *Coercion, Capital, and European States*, 28–30.

6. Lynn, "Evolution of Army Style in the Modern West," 505–545. I served as research assistant for this project.

7. Richelieu, *Mémoires*, in *NCM*, 1: 440.

8. "Estat de la depece que le roy veut et ordonne estre faicte par son con^er et tres^er general de lextraordinaire de ses guerres M. Jean Fabry tant pour les solde & entrettenement des gens de guerre a pied françois estans et qui tiendront garnison pour le service de sa Ma^té es villes & places fortes du gouvernement de Languedoc," AD Hérault, C 8400.

9. Pontchartrain, *Mémoires concernant les affaires de France sous la régence de Marie de Médicis*, in *NCM*, 5: 415.

10. Pierre Boyer, "Les Lauriers Triomphans du grand Alcide Gaulois, Louys XIIIe roy de France & de Navarre," BNF, Mss. fr. 15381, f° 156–159; "Mémoire des villes de sûrété," BNF, Languedoc-Bénédictins 94, f° 57–58.

11. "Mémoire des villes de sûrété," BNF, Languedoc-Bénédictins 94, f° 57–58.

12. Wood, *King's Army*, 73.

13. Ibid., 80, 110–113, 123–124, 133–140.

14. Ibid., 119–152; Harding, *Anatomy of a Power Elite*, 21–26.

15. BNF, Mss. fr. 18756, f° 7–9.

16. "Mémoires de Vignolles," in *PFHF*.

17. Wood, *King's Army*, 129–131.

18. On *reiter* organization, see ibid., 137.

19. On the origins of the gardes françaises, see ibid., 107–109; Belhomme, *Histoire de l'infanterie en France*, 1: 318–319; Susane, *Histoire de l'infanterie française*.

20. For regimental histories of the *vieux* and *pétit-vieux* régiments, see Susane, *Histoire de l'infanterie française*.

21. États des troupes, AD Tarn, C 870.

22. For descriptions of *gros d'infanterie* in combat, see *CSV*, 55–58; Wood, *King's Army*, 106–110.

23. On Phalsbourg's regiment, see BNF, Mss. fr. 25849, f° 506–510; Wood, *King's Army*, 110–113.

24. Wood, *King's Army*, 157–158.

25. Buisseret, *Ingénieurs et fortifications avant Vauban*, 89–91, 113–115.

26. Concerning riverine transport in the early French Wars of Religion, see Wood, *King's Army*, 171–172.

27. AD Hérault, B 22608; AD Hérault, C 7059, f° 38; AD Hérault, B 22771; BNF, Clairambault 366; BNF, Clairambault 369.

28. *HGL*, 11: 992–993; Rohan, *Mémoires*, 257.

29. Girard, 280–281.

30. Pablo, "L'Armée Huguenote," 208.

31. Lowenstein, "Resistance to Absolutism," 207.

32. Ibid., 208.

33. BNF, Languedoc-Bénédictins 94, f° 116–117.

34. Parrott, "Administration of the French Army," 202.

35. Ibid., 198–199.

36. Ordonnance de seigneur de Châtillon, Lunel, 21 July 1621, AD Hérault 22603.

37. Geoffrey Parker, *Military Revolution*, 45–81; Lynn, *Giant of the* Grand Siècle, 32–64; id., "Pattern of Army Growth" 1–27.

38. Wood, *King's Army*, 283.

39. Lynn, *Giant of the* Grand Siècle, 233–234.

40. Deliberations of the estates of Languedoc held at Carcassonne, 16 March 1621, AD Hérault, C 7059, f° 79–80.

41. Ordonnance de Châtillon, Montpellier, 2 July 1621, AD Hérault 22603.

42. Ordonnance, Saint-Hippolite, 13 August 1621, AD Hérault, B 22603.

43. Ordonnance de Henri de Lévis duc de Ventadour, Bourg-Saint-Andéol, 15 April 1628, AD Gard, 1 E 521.

44. "Establissement de la milice fait par monseigneur le duc de Rohan pair de France prince de Leon & chef & general des eglises reformées de ce royaume ez provinces du Languedoc & Guienne, Sevenes, Gevaudan & Vivarez, et son conseil pour estre garde et obserué de point en point selon sa forme et teneur," BNF, 8670, f° 93.

45. François I d'Esparbès de Lussan marquis d'Aubeterre to Paul Phélypeaux seigneur de Pontchartrain, Agen, 4 and 9 November 1615, BNF, Clairambault 366, f° 5 and 14–15.

46. Claude d'Hautefort vicomte de Lestrange to Paul Phélypeaux seigneur de Pontchartrain, Privas, 5 May 1620, BNF, Clairambault 377, f° 171–172.

47. François de Bonne duc de Lesdiguières to Tanneguy de Verigniez seigneur de Blainville [?], Grenoble, 15 July 1619, in *ACL*, 2: 246.

48. Antoine-Arnauld de Pardaillan seigneur de Gondrin [?] to Paul Phélypeaux seigneur de Pontchartrain, Cauze, 16 June 1621, BNF, Clairambault 377, f° 745–747.

49. Richelieu argued: "il faut souvent rafraischir les armées par nouvelles levées, sans lesquelles, bien qu'elles soient fortes pour leurs contrôles, elles seront très foibles en effet" in his *Testament politique*, ed. Hildesheimer, 316.

50. Ordonnance de Henri de Lévis duc de Ventadour, Bourg-Saint-Andéol, 15 April 1628, AD Gard, 1 E 521.

51. Camporesi, *Bread of Dreams*.

52. "Estat des vivres qui seront distribués par chuung jour aux gens de guerre tant de cheval que de pied de larmee du Roy commandee en Lang^oc par Monseigneur le duc de Montmorency et de Dampville pair & admiral de France gouverneur & lieut gñal po^r sa Ma^te aud^t Lang^oc &c.," AD Hérault, B 22690.

53. Lynn, *Giant of the* Grand Siècle, 113–114; Corvisier, "La Paix nécessaire mais incertaine," in *Histoire Militaire de la France*, ed. Contamine, 1: 343–346.

54. "Estat des vivres . . . ," AD Hérault, B 22690.

55. Ordonnance de Henri II de Montmorency duc de Montmorency, 20 June 1621, AD Hérault, B 22706.

56. AD Hérault, B 22598.

57. "Estat des vivres . . . ," AD Hérault, B 22690.

58. Wood, *King's Army*, 244.

59. Provosts and archers were given authority to set prices in Champagne in 1616. Louis XIII to Charles de Choiseul marquis de Praslin, Blois, 6 May 1616, BNF, Mss. fr. 15616, f° 86.

60. *Reglement pour les gens de guerre*.

61. On military communities see Sandberg, "'The Magazine of All Their Pillaging,'" 76–96.

62. Lynn, *Giant of the* Grand Siècle, 108–109.

63. BNF, Mss. fr. 4554, f° 102–104, cited in Wood, *King's Army*, 243n13.

64. "Estat au vray de la despence faicte par Jaques Seruier bourgeois de la ville du Bourg Sainct Anduol a cause du fournissement par luy fait . . . ," AD Hérault, B 22789.

65. See, e.g., "Rolle de la despance que este faicte pour conduire le canon a Lunel le mercredy xvie mars g viC xxii," AD Hérault, B 22590.

66. For sources on bakers and butchers with armies, see AD Hérault, B 22606; AD Hérault, B 22744; AN, E 68B, f° 1.

67. Quittances, AD Hérault, B 22707.

68. AD Hérault, B 22596.

69. Wood, *King's Army*, 282.

70. Corvisier, "La Paix nécessaire mais incertaine," 343–346.

71. *Reglement pour les gens de guerre*.

72. "Rolle de la monstre & reveue faicte en armes au devant la porte de l'attes de ville de Monp.r a soixante quatorze hommes darmes de la compagnie dordonnan. soubz la charge de Monseigneur le duc de Rohan chefz et general des eglises refformes de ce royaulme et provinces de Languedoc et Haulte Guienne pour le mois davril dernier," AD Hérault, B 22659.

73. "Rolle . . . ," AD Hérault, B 22739; "Rolle de la monstre & reveue . . . ," AD Hérault, B 22659; "Rolle . . . ," AD Hérault, B 22772; "Rolle . . . ," AD Hérault, B 22772.

74. Antoine Jaubert de Barrault comte de Blaignac to Louis XIII, Barrault, 29 January 1616, BNF, Clairambault 366, f° 361–362.

75. Antoine Jaubert de Barrault comte de Blaignac to Louis XIII, Barrault, 25 January 1616, BNF, Clairambault 366, f° 361–362.

76. Lynn, *Giant of the* Grand Siècle, 132–140; Corvisier, "La Paix nécessaire mais incertaine," 343–346; Sturgill, "Changing Garrisons," 193–201.

77. Wood, *King's Army*, 243–244.

78. Lynn, *Giant of the* Grand Siècle, 88–92.

79. *Reglement pour les gens de guerre.*

80. Ibid.

81. "Estat des vivres . . . ," AD Hérault, B 22690.

82. Lynn, *Giant of the* Grand Siècle, 129.

83. "Estat de la depece que le roy veut et ordonne estre faicte par son con^{er} et tres^{er} general de lextraordinaire de ses guerres M. Jean Fabry tant pour les solde & entrettenement des gens de guerre a pied françois estans et qui tiendront garnison pour le service de sa Ma^{té} es villes & places fortes du gouvernement de Languedoc." AD Hérault, C 8400.

84. "Estat de la despence que le roy veult ordonne estre faicte par son con^{er} et tresorier general de lextraord^{re} de ses guerres m^{e} Simon Collon . . . ," AD Hérault, A 46, f° 360.

85. "Estat du payement que sera faict par Monsieur le tresorier general de lextraordinaire des guerres Mr. Simon Coffon con^{er} du Roy ou Mr. Pierre Pourtales trezorier principal dudit extraordinaire des guerres en Languedoc aux gens de guerre a pied françois," AD Hérault, G 1591.

86. Deliberations of the estates of Languedoc held at Béziers and Carcassonne, 28 September 1621, AD Hérault, C 7059, f° 22–23.

87. Beik, *Absolutism and Society in Seventeenth-Century France*, 245. Rowlands echoes Beik's criticism, observing that the emphasis "has been on the raising and mobilising of resources, and much less on the deployment and spending of money." Rowlands, *Dynastic State*, 109.

88. For a critical examination of the historiography of logistics, see Lynn, "History of Logistics," 9–27.

89. Parrott, *Richelieu's Army*, 225–276, 373–396.

90. Bonney, "What's New about the New French Fiscal History?" 639–667; Eurich, *Economics of Power.*

91. Beik, *Absolutism and Society in Seventeenth-Century France*, 245–278.

92. Tacitus *Histories* 2.24; Cicero *Philippicae* 5.12.32; Cuomo, "Sinews of War."

93. Machiavelli, *Art of War*, trans. Farneworth, 204.

94. Rabelais, *Gargantua*, ed. Calder, 261.

95. Biron quoted in Wood, *King's Army*, 279.

96. Richelieu, *Testament politique*, ed. Hildesheimer, 343.

97. Parrott, *Richelieu's Army*, 241–246.

98. Wood, *King's Army*, 279.

99. On the Price Revolution, see Cunningham and Grell, *Four Horsemen of the Apocalypse*, 200–246; Goldstone, "Monetary versus Velocity Interpretations of the 'Price Revolution,'" 176–181; Fisher, "Price Revolution," 883–902.

100. Parsons, "Money and Sovereignty in Early Modern France," 59–79.

101. Steensgaard, "Seventeenth-Century Crisis," 32–56; Dewald et al., "Forum: The General Crisis of the Seventeenth Century Revisited," 1029–1099.

102. Potter, "Good Offices."

103. Beik, *Absolutism and Society in Seventeenth-Century France,* 245–278.

104. Wood, *King's Army,* 287–290.

105. Beik, *Absolutism and Society in Seventeenth-Century France,* 245–278.

106. BNF, Mss. fr. 18085, f° 7.

107. Ordonnance de Henri II de Montmorency duc de Montmorency, Toulouse, 3 May 1616, AD Hérault, C 8405.

108. Collins, *Fiscal Limits of Absolutism,* 112–113; Parrott, *Richelieu's Army,* 230–232.

109. Jean-Paul d'Esparbès de Lussan to Louis XIII, Blaye, 12 February 1616, BNF, Clairambault 366, f° 383–384; François de Noailles comte d'Ayen to Louis XIII, Malemort, 10 September 1616, BNF, Clairambault 368, f° 216–217.

110. Louis de Cardaillac comte de Bioule received a payment from the *trésorier de la gendarmerie de France* in 1636, according to BNF, Pièces Originales 595, f° 60.

111. "Estat de la dep^ce que le roy veut et ordonne estre faicte par son con^er et tres^er general de lextraordinaire de ses guerres m^e Jean Fabry . . . ," AD Hérault, C 8400; "Estat de la recepte et despence faicte par deffunct Mr Jehan Fabry vivant con^er du Roy et tres^r gñal de lex^re des guerres . . . ," BNF, Mss. fr. 16718.

112. Henry I de Montmorency duc de Montmorency to Marie de Médicis, La Grange-des-Prés, 5 September 1613, BNF, Clairambault 1131, f° 182–183.

113. Girard, 280–281.

114. "Edict of Nantes," trans. Parsons, in *Edict of Nantes,* ed. Goodbar, 54.

115. See, e.g., "Memoire po^r les villes de Viguieres, d'Anduze, Alés, le Vignan, & Ambroix pour les logemens . . . ," AD Hérault, G 1836.

116. Ordonnance de Henri II de Montmorency duc de Montmorency, Béziers, 16 March 1622, AD Hérault, B 22661; "Estat au vray des recept et despence faict par Mr. Jean Roux receveur particulier des tailles au dioce. de Mande de lImpon. de la somme de quarante sept mil cinq cens livres faict sur ledit diocese en l'annee mil six cens vingt deux . . . ," AD Hérault, B 22661.

117. Collins, *Fiscal Limits of Absolutism,* 101–103.

118. François de Noailles comte d'Ayen to Paul Phélypeaux seigneur de Pontchartrain, Villefranche-en-Rouergue, 10 July 1621, BNF, Clairambault 377, f° 815–818.

119. Arrêt du parlement de Toulouse, 18 November 1621, AD Haute-Garonne, B 413, f° 44.

120. Deliberations of the estates of Languedoc held at Pézenas, 20 December 1620, AD Hérault, C 7059, f° 49.

121. Deliberations of the estates of Languedoc held at Béziers, 10 June 1620, AD Hérault, C 7059, f° 31.

122. Deliberations of the estates of Languedoc held at Béziers, 28 September 1621, AD Hérault, C 7059, f° 23.

123. Supplement du syndic d'Albi, AD Tarn, C 875.

124. *Reglement pour les gens de guerre.*

125. Ibid.

126. Ordonnance of César de Bourbon duc de Vendôme, Briatexte [?], 22 August 1622, copy, AD Hérault, C 8406.

127. Louis XIII to Charles de Choiseul marquis de Praslin, Béziers, 24 and 25 July 1622, BNF, Mss. fr. 15616, f° 143 and 143–144.

128. Ordonnance d'Adrien de Monluc comte de Caramaing, Toulouse, 4 January 1616, BNF, Clairambault 366, f° 319.

129. Parrott, *Richelieu's Army*, 241.

130. On alternative exchanges and unofficial economies, see Fontaine, ed., *Alternative Exchanges.*

131. Wood, *King's Army*, 290–292.

132. Conner, *Huguenot Heartland*, 167–189.

133. Lowenstein, "Resistance to Absolutism," 149–150, 157–167, 184.

134. Greengrass, "Informal Networks in Sixteenth-Century French Protestantism," 78–97.

135. Lowenstein, "Resistance to Absolutism," 151–154.

136. Ordonnance de Gaspard III de Coligny seigneur de Châtillon, Montpellier, 2 July 1621, AD Hérault, B 22603.

137. Ordonnance, Saint-Hippolite, 13 August 1621, AD Hérault, B 22603.

138. Ordonnance de Gaspard III de Coligny seigneur de Châtillon, Montpellier, 1 July 1621, AD Hérault, B 22603.

139. Anne de Lévis duc de Ventadour to the estates of Vivarais, Baignolx, 23 October 1621, AD Ardèche, C 1048, f° 50.

140. "Compte que Jean Valmalette comme exateur des des impozes pour la garde personnelle sur ceux faizans profession de la religion romaine en la pñt ville dAllez remet a vous messieurs les consulz & con^el de lad^t ville," AD Hérault, B 22757; "Compte de Firmin Lapize exateur des deniers de la garde personnelle des catholiques dAllez. 1628," AD Hérault, B 22757.

141. See, e.g., AD Ardèche, E Depot 83 BB2, f° 5.

142. Charles d'Albert duc de Luynes to Béthune, Paris, 25 March 1619, BNF, Cinq Cens de Colbert 97, f° 121.

143. *HGL*, 11: 940.

144. Wood, *King's Army*, 285.

145. Deliberations of the estates of Languedoc held at Pézenas, 23 December 1620, AD Hérault, C 7059, f° 57.

146. Rohan, *Mémoires*, 205–206.

147. Fontaine, *Alternative Exchanges.*

148. Gilles Le Masuyer to Armand Jean du Plessis cardinal de Richelieu, Toulouse, 29 September 1627, BNF, Mss. fr. 15583, f° 224–225.

149. Wood, *King's Army*, 295–300.

150. AD Ardèche, E Depot 83 BB2, f° 18.

151. See, e.g., AD Hérault B, 22590, 22603, 22609, 22659, 22712, 22746.

152. For an overview of recent scholarship on French early modern finances, see Bonney, "What's New about the New French Fiscal History?" 639–667.

153. Parrott, *Richelieu's Army*, 229.

CHAPTER 9: VIOLENT PERFORMANCES

1. *CSV*, 178–179.

2. Lynn, *Giant of the* Grand Siècle, 248–281.

3. *La Prise et reduction de la ville et chasteau de Sully.*

4. "Lettre envoiee par ceux de la Rochelle aux consuls & habitans des villes de Montauban et Castres," BNF, Dupuy 100, f° 221.

5. Moote, *Louis XIII*, 24–125.

6. The classic, but much-contested, work on raiding warfare is Turney-High, *Primitive War.*

7. Rogers, *War Cruel and Sharp.*

8. Satterfield, *Princes, Posts, and Partisans*; Lynn, *Giant of the* Grand Siècle, 538–546.

9. For a discussion of the connections between raiding and military intelligence, see Lynn, *Giant of the* Grand Siècle, 316–318.

10. *CSV*, 148–149.

11. Du Cros, 183–185.

12. *HGL*, 11: 1027.

13. *CSV*, 56–57.

14. *Récit véritable de ce qui s'est passé au degast es environs de Nismes.*

15. Du Cros, 166–168.

16. *Récit véritable de ce qui s'est passé au degast es environs de Nismes.*

17. *CSV*, 66–69.

18. *CSV*, 186.

19. "Memoire ou journal du siege de Montpellier," BNF, Mss. fr. 23339, f° 164–165.

20. *CSV*, 64–65.

21. *CSV*, 97–98.

22. *CSV*, 100–101.

23. "Tableau du siege de Montaulban," BNF, Mss. fr. 18756, f° 31–32.

24. Du Cros, 57–60.

25. *HGL*, 11: 943–951.

26. Du Cros, 39.

27. Wood, *King's Army*, 203.

28. On the battle of Carignan, see Armand-Jean du Plessis cardinal de Richelieu to Marie de Médicis, Saint-Jean de Muriane, 12 July 1630, BNF, Mss. fr. 3829, f° 28.

29. Du Cros, 149–154.

30. *La Prise des villes de la Caune et Sainct Sever.*

31. François de Bonne duc de Lesdiguières, "Discours de l'art militaire," in *ACL*, 2: 541–578.

32. Du Cros, 141–147; Rohan, *Mémoires*, 322–326.

33. Du Cros, 141–147; Rohan, *Mémoires*, 322–326.

34. Du Cros, 51–56. Rohan, *Mémoires*, 207–209.

35. Wood, *King's Army*, 204. On cavalry tactics and its battlefield role, see Love, "'All the King's Horsemen,'" 511–533.

36. On field artillery and its use in battle, see Wood, *King's Army*, 153–162, 184–197; Lynn, *Giant of the* Grand Siècle, 500–512.

37. *HGL*, 11: 950–951.

38. Ibid., 960–961.

39. Ibid., 954–955.

40. *La Deffaicte de quatre cents hommes par le sieur de Mont-Real.*

41. Louis XIII to Antoine-Arnaud de Pardaillan seigneur de Gondin, Aspremont, 17 April 1622, BNF, Clairambault, 1132, f° 288–289; Hardÿ de Périni, *Batailles françaises*, 3: 18–19.

42. BNF, Mss. fr. 15616, f° 20–27; Hardÿ de Périni, *Batailles françaises*, 3: 52–55.

43. *HGL*, 11: 994–995.

44. Armand-Jean du Plessis cardinal de Richelieu to Marie de Médicis, camp at Alès, 10 June 1629, in *LCR*, 339–340.

45. Du Cros, 262–265; *Relation envoyée au roy par monsieur le mareschal de Schomberg.*

46. *CSV*, 73–74.

47. For an example of the calculated decisions of noble dress, including golden trim and a colored scarf, see Jacques de Pons marquis de La Caze, "Verbal de Monsr le marquis de La Case sur les affaires de Montauban et mouvemens de 1625," BNF, Mss. fr. 15823.

48. *CSV*, 143–144.

49. Henri II de Montmorency duc de Montmorency to Montbrun, n.p., n.d. [1632], copy, BNF, Languedoc-Bénédictins 94, f° 272.

50. Girard, 282, 285–286, 290.

51. On the significance and meaning of noble dining practices, see Neuschel, *Word of Honor*, 160–173; Elias, *Civilizing Process*, 68–104; BNF, Dupuy 100, f° 211.

52. Girard, 289.

53. Bassompierre, *Journal*, 2: 336–340, 381; 3: 105.

54. Raimond de Thézan baron de Pujol to M. du Faur, La Bastide, 8 September 1621, AD Hérault, B 22617.

55. "Tableau du siege de Montaulban 1622," BNF, Mss. fr. 18756, f° 38–39.

56. See, e.g., "Tableau du siege de Montaulban," BNF, Mss. fr. 18756, f° 61.

57. Valdor, *Les Triomphes de Louis le Juste.*

58. Du Cros, 262–265.

59. Du Cros, 51–56.

60. *CSV*, 216–219.

61. *Defaicte furieuse de deux cens maistres, sortis de Castres, Puilaurens, & autres villes rebelles.*

62. *CSV*, 56–57.

63. Carroll, *Blood and Violence in Early Modern France*, 135–140; Cunningham and Grell, *Four Horsemen of the Apocalypse*, 124–137.

64. Schneider, *Public Life in Toulouse*, 167–174.

65. James, "Huguenot Militancy and the Seventeenth-Century Wars of Religion," 209–223.

66. Burel, *Mémoires*, 499–500.

67. Pelikan, *History of the Development of Doctrine*, 4: 127–244; Selinger, *Calvin Against Himself*, 60.

68. Dewald, *European Nobility*, 176–178.

69. The concept of "sustaining motivation" comes from Lynn, *Bayonets of the Republic*, 21–40.

70. François d'Estrades to Paul Phélypeaux seigneur de Pontchartrain, n.d. [1618], BNF, Clairambault 374, f° 10.

71. Henri II de Montmorency duc de Montmorency to Marie de Médicis, Pézenas, 1 October 1614, BNF, Clairambault 1131, f° 236.

72. This section is adapted from Sandberg, " 'Re-establishing the True Worship of God,' " 139–182.

73. Le Brun, "Théologie et spiritualité," in *Le XVIIe siècle*, ed. Truchet, 218–19.

74. Diefendorf, *From Penitence to Charity*, 70–71.

75. Packer, "Collections of Chaste Chansons for the Devout Home," 175–216.

76. Diefendorf, *From Penitence to Charity*, 49–76. For a description of women's ascetic devotional activities in Toulouse, see Charlotte de Saint-Claire to Cristina di Lorena, Toulouse, 10 July 1635, ASF, 5950, f° 569.

77. Joanne Baker, "Female Monasticism and Family Strategy," 1091–1108.

78. Diefendorf, *From Penitence to Charity*, 135–138.

79. Fehleison, "Appealing to the Senses."

80. On the revival of Marian devotion in Guyenne, see Hanlon, *Confession and Community*, 156–161, and id., "Piété populaire," 115–127.

81. Marie de Médicis to Ferdinando I de' Medici, Saint-Germain-en-Laye, 13 August 1603, ASF, MdP 4729, f° 81.

82. Marie de Médicis to Cristina di Lorena, Paris, 30 July 1615, ASF, MdP 4729A, f° 360.

83. Nelson, *Jesuits and the Monarchy*; Bireley, *Jesuits and the Thirty Years War*, 77–78.

84. Marie de Médicis to Ferdinando II de' Medici, Paris, 26 April 1628, ASF, MdP 4729A, f° 529.

85. Silverman, *Tortured Subjects*, 111–130.

86. Gregory, *Salvation at Stake*, 276.

87. Le Roux, *La Faveur du roi*, 593–602. For other evidence of self-mortification in the 1570s and 1580s, see: Schneider, *Public Life in Toulouse* 90–131.

88. Wolfe, *Conversion of Henri IV*, 159–163.

89. Diefendorf, *From Penitence to Charity*, 75–76.

90. Gregory, *Salvation at Stake*, 277–80, 292–94.

91. Wandel, "Review of Brad S. Gregory, *Salvation at Stake*," 1169–72, discusses Gregory's problematic focus on the Henrician martrys.

92. Tulchin, "Michelade in Nîmes, 1567," 1–35.

93. Nicolas Poussin, *The Martyrdom of Saint Erasmus* (1628), Pinacoteca, The Vatican, Rome; Chastel, *French Art*, 142–149.

94. Parsons, *Church in the Republic*, 227–73.

95. Parlement de Toulouse to Henri II de Montmorency duc de Montmorency, Toulouse, 20 February 1624, BNF, Clairambault 378, f° 466.

96. "Acte de ceux de la religion pretendue refformée assemblez a Anduze par lequel ilz promettent de vouloir demeurer fermes en leur union et en la jonction de leurs armes avec celle du roy d'Ang^{re} & des s^{rs} de Rohan & de Soubize," BNF, Dupuy 100, f° 296–297.

97. Conner, *Huguenot Heartland*, 172–175; Garrison, "Les Grands du parti protestant et l'édit de Nantes."

98. James, "Huguenot Militancy," 217–218.

99. "Copie de l'une d'environ quarante commissions de la Rochelle dont le s^r de Mont Chrestien estoit saisy po^r les distribuer par les provinces . . . ," BNF, Dupuy 100, f° 87.

100. "Reg^{re} des desliberaõns politiques de la maison consulaire de Nymes 1621," BNF, Languedoc-Doat 258, f° 1.

101. "La Suitte du tableau du siege de Montauban . . . ," BNF, Mss. fr. 18756, f° 76.

102. Henri II de Rohan duc de Rohan to the consuls de Réalmont, Brassac, 20 October 1627, BNF, Mss. fr. 15828, f° 108.

103. Spicer, " 'Qui est de Dieu oit la parole de Dieu,' " 175–192.

104. Wada, "La Représentation des régions."

105. Huguenot deputies of the Assembly of Anduze to Paul Phélypeaux seigneur de Pontchartrain, Anduze, 20 April 1618, BNF, Clairambault 374, f° 83.

106. Racaut, *Hatred in Print*, 63–64.

107. Greengrass, "Informal Networks in Sixteenth-Century French Protestantism," 82–84.

108. "Les demandes qu'on faict messieurs de la Religion a monsieur de Monmorcy," AN, TT 430, f° 30.

109. Watson, "Preaching, Printing, Psalm-Singing," 19–20.

110. Huguenots de Bordeaux to Henri IV, Bordeaux, 25 December 1603, BNF, Mss. fr. 23197, f° 552.

111. Barbiche and Dainville-Barbiche, *Sully*, 337–404; Fornerod, "L'Édit de Nantes et le problème de la coexistence confessionnelle," 225–252.

112. "Commission a mr. le marquis de Malause pour commander aux quatre colloques du haut Languedoc," BNF, Languedoc-Bénédictins 94, f° 116–117.

113. Canault, *Vie du maréchal J.-B. d'Ornano*, 313.

114. Parlement de Toulouse to Henri II de Montmorency duc de Montmorency, Toulouse, 20 September 1624, BNF, Clairambault 378, f° 467–468.

115. Diefendorf, *Beneath the Cross*, 28–48; Brenac, "Toulouse, centre de lutte contre le protestantisme," 31–45.

116. Henri d'Esparbès de Lussan de Pamiers to Paul Phélypeaux seigneur de Pontchartrain, Toulouse, 13 July 1621, BNF, Clairambault 377, f° 829–830.

117. Harding, *Anatomy of a Power Elite*, 61–67.

118. Barnes, "Religious Anxiety and Devotional Change," 389–406.

119. Hoffman, *Church and Community*, 35–42.

120. Françoise Chevalier, "Les Difficultés d'application de l'édit de Nantes," 303–320.

121. Parlement de Toulouse to Henri II de Montmorency duc de Montmorency, Toulouse, 20 September 1624, BNF, Clairambault 378, f° 467–468.

122. Luria, *Sacred Boundaries*, xvii.

123. AD Hérault, G 2002.

CONCLUSION

1. Schalk, *From Valor to Pedigree*; Elias, *Civilizing Process*; Elias, *Court Society*.

2. François de Clary to Henri IV, Toulouse, 6 January 1603, BNF, Mss. fr. 23197, f° 346–347.

3. François de Noailles comte d'Ayen to Paul Phélypeaux seigneur de Pontchartrain, Villefranche-de-Rouergue, 10 July 1621, BNF, Clairambault 377, f° 815–818.

4. Neuschel, *Word of Honor*, 17.

5. Nicolas de Verdun, premier président du parlement de Toulouse, to Henri IV, Toulouse, 14 September 1604, BNF, Mss. fr. 23198, f° 183–186.

6. Luria, *Sacred Boundaries*.

7. *La Noblesse de Languedoc aux pieds du roy*.

8. BNF, Languedoc-Bénédictins 71; Béguin, *Les Princes de Condé*; Beik, *Absolutism and Society in Seventeenth-Century France*, 234–244.

9. Bercé, "Les Coups de majesté des rois de France," 491–505.

10. Parrott, *Richelieu's Army*, 64–222; Lynn, *Giant of the* Grand Siècle, 32–64.

11. Ranum, *The Fronde*.

12. Lublinskaya, *French Absolutism*.

13. *Immortalité du carrousel de Monseigneur d'Espernon*. On "warlike deeds" and "heroic gestures," see "La Suitte du tableau du siege de Montauban . . . ," BNF, Mss. fr. 18756, f° 70; Arnauld, *Presentation de monsieur de Montmorancy en l'office d'admiral de France*.

Bibliography

ARCHIVAL SOURCES

Archives Nationales

E 68, 1684
H1 748, 866, 1013–1015
K 110–113, 199, 691, 697, 907, 1173, 1176
M 522–523, 638–661, 858
MM 931, 952, 979
O1 3–8
T 1251, 158, 192
TT 234, 252, 259, 273, 275, 430, 432, 437
U 799
8 AP
111 AP
273 AP
306 AP

Bibliothèque Nationale de France, Département des Manuscrits

Armorial General d'Hozier 2058
Baluze 95, 146, 244, 259, 322–323
Blondeau 124, 153, 169, 179
Cabinet d'Hozier 14–16, 18, 22, 29, 33, 211–212, 245, 246, 292, 318, 334
Cabinet des Titres 651
Cinq Cents de Colbert 2, 4, 12, 43, 54, 91, 97, 98, 136–138, 163, 209, 289
Clairambault 172, 207, 362–381, 506, 728, 957, 1124–1125, 1128, 1130–1133, 1137
Dupuy 26, 27, 46, 81, 92–94, 100, 127–128, 201, 240, 343, 370, 380–381, 487, 495, 850
Languedoc (Bénédictin) 71, 94, 100–108
Languedoc (Doat) 35, 94, 258
Manuscrits Français 3234, 3559, 3566, 3568, 3569, 3589, 3602, 3672, 3674–3675, 3712,
    3715, 3722, 3802, 3807, 3809–3813, 3829, 3832, 3840, 3846, 4014, 4020, 4102, 4561,
    4705, 4754, 4765, 4779, 4805, 4808, 4811, 4823, 5481, 6385–6386, 6644, 6556, 7605,
    8574, 8653, 8670, 10946, 12068, 14503, 14506, 15380–15381, 15581–15585, 15587, 15616,
    15621, 15817, 15823–15824, 15827–15828, 15831, 15899, 16182, 16184, 16536, 16697, 17501,

17539, 17544, 17831, 18085, 18088, 18424, 18430, 18457, 18756, 18833, 18972, 20161, 20235, 20473, 20477, 21719, 22253, 23042, 23060, 23154, 23196–23198, 23246, 23339, 23344, 24103, 24092, 24262, 25843–25849, 26406, 32292, 32296–32297, 32401, 32520, 32796, 32924, 32924, 32982

Mélanges de Colbert 322

Nouvelles Acquisitions Français 5245–5246, 7182

Pièces Originales 104, 175, 246–247, 569, 574, 595, 1097, 1492, 1693, 2028, 2319

Bibliothèque Nationale de France, Département des Cartes et Plans

Ge.AF.Pf 28 (13), (43)

Ge.B.563

Ge.C.21592

Ge.CC.715 (10), (11)

Ge.D.10165

Ge.D.17159

Ge.DD.584

Ge.DD.1146

Ge.DD.2633

Ge.DD.2987 (372), (388) B, (656) B, (702), (1444) B, (1447), (1448), (1466) B, (1480)

Ge.DD.4121 (136), (137), (143), (145), (155), (156), (161), (162)

Ge.FF.4476 bis

Ge.FF.7307

Ge.FF.13419

Archives de Guerre, Château de Vincennes

A1 11–14, 18–23, 41

MR 61, 62

Bibliothèque, SHAT

A1 b 1175: Collection des ordonnances militaires, vol. 13–14

Archives Diplomatiques, Ministère des Affaires Étrangères

Fonds Languedoc 1627, 1628

Mémoires et documents 781, 782, 789, 790

Archives Départementales de l'Ardèche

B 70–71

C 341–343, 534, 939, 1048–1055, 1474

1 Mi 739

1 Mi 293 R8–11

E Depot 75 FF 1

E Depot 81 CC 24

E Depot 83 BB 2

E Depot 83 DD 2

E Depot 83 EE 1
1 J 772
39 J 12

Archives Départementales de l'Aude

B 32, 1965, 1988, 2082
13 C 72
23 C 40–41
33 C 3
53 C 2
62 C 25
C 1259, 1262, 1266, 1271, 1273–1275
2 E 13, 17, 102
3 J 203
5 J 27
7 J 23

Archives Départementales du Gard

C 852–859, 1213–1217
1 E 53, 264, 959–960, 2455, 2483–2484, 2562, 2648
2 E 1/365–366
G 446–447

Archives Départementales de l'Hérault

B 22587–22600, 22603, 22605, 22608, 22609, 22618, 22632, 22659, 22661, 22664, 22690, 22693, 22698, 22699, 22706, 22744–22746, 22750, 22758, 22783–22784, 22790, 22796
C 7053, 7058–7060, 7076, 7746, 8400, 8405–8406, 8410, 8634, 8655, 8670–8672
1 E 229, 239
3 F 2
G 1418, 1835, 2181, 4143

Archives Départementales de la Haute-Garonne

B 409, 413, 419, 455, 461
C 706–713, 815–817, 846, 952–958, 972–974, 2126–2130

Archives Départementales de Lozère

C 820, 1790–1794, 1804–1805
E 168
G 973–975
15 J 41
45 J 13
47 J 48

Archives Départementales du Tarn

B 94
C 58, 207, 265, 278, 869–879, 883–894, 900, 1167–1170
E 64

Archives Municipales de Montpellier

EE 910–916, 926–947, 956–958
Clavaire CC 683–810
Talamus Historique 11

Archives Municipales de Toulouse

AA 16, 21–23, 48
EE 5–6

Archives Communales d'Albi

EE 61, 63, 64
II 21

Archives Communales de Béziers

BB 2–3
CC 104–105, 109
EE 3, 5, 11
GG 203

Archives Communales de Castres

BB 35

Archives Communales de Montauban

21 DD 2
22 DD 1, 22 DD 2, 22 DD 3
1 EE 1, 1 EE 2, 1 EE 3
3 EE 1, 3 EE 2
17 GG 2
19 GG 1
21 GG 1

Bibliothèque Municipale de Montpellier

Rare books and manuscripts collections

Bibliothèque Municipale de Toulouse

Rare books and manuscripts collections

Newberry Library, Chicago

Rare books and pamphlets collections

Rare Book Room, University of Illinois at Urbana-Champaign

Rare books and microfilms collections

Harry Ransom Center Rare Book Room, University of Texas at Austin

Rare books, pamphlets, and manuscripts collections

Bibliothèque Nationale de France, Cabinet des Estampes

Collection Hennin, Tômes 19–28
Qb1 series

PUBLISHED PRIMARY SOURCES

Les Actes de l'assemblée nouvellement tenue à Nismes par les députés des Églises réformées du Languedoc . . . contre M. de Chastillon. . . . N.p.: n.p., 1622.

Alberti, Leon Battista. *L'Architecture et art de bien bastir du seigneur Leon Baptiste Albert, Gentilhomme Florentin, divisée en dix livres.* Paris: Jaques Kerver, 1553.

Androuet du Cerceau, Jacques. *Livre d'architecture de Jacques Androuet, du Cerceau. . . .* Paris, 1559, 1615.

L'Antiquité de Bourdeaus. Presentée au Roy le treziesme jour d'Avril, l'an mille cinq cens soixante cinq. Poitiers: Enguilbert de Marnef, 1565.

Antoine Arnauld, *Presentation de Monsieur de Montmorency en l'office d'Admiral de France. 1612.* Paris: Denis du Val, 1612. BNF, 8° Ln²⁷ 14695.

Arrest de la cour de parlement contre les rebelles. Toulouse: Raymond Colomiez, 1628. AD Tarn, C 207.

L'Arrivee de monsieur le duc d'Espernon, vers sa majesté. . . . Lyon: Claude Armand dit Alphonce, 1620.

Assaut donné contre la ville de Montauban, Avec la défaite des troupes des sieurs de la Rochelle, & de Thurlinol, par Monsieur le duc de Mayenne, le 26 de Juillet 1621. Lyon: Guillaume Marniolles, 1621. BNF, 8° Lb³⁶ 1716.

Assemblee generale des messieurs les princes en la vile de Poictiers. Ensemble leur declaration faicte au Roy, avec l'arivee de monsieur le duc du Mayne vers sa majesté en ladicte ville le 9. de septembre. Lyon: François Yvrad, n.d.

Banne, Jacques de. *Mémoires de Jacques de Banne, chanoine de Viviers.* Edited by Auguste Le Sourd. Aubenas: Habauzit, 1917.

Bassompierre, François de. *Journal de ma vie. Mémoires du maréchal de Bassompierre.* 4 vols. Paris: Société de l'Histoire de France, 1870–1877.

Billon, Jean de. *Les Principes de l'art militaire.* Lyon: Barthelemy Ancelin, 1615.

Biron, Armand de Gontaut, baron de. *The Letters and Documents of Armand de Gontaut, Baron de Biron, Marshal of France (1524–1592).* Collected by Sidney Hellman Ehrman. Edited by James Westfall Thompson. Berkeley: University of California Press, 1936.

Bouchitté, Louis-Fermin-Herve, ed. *Négociations, lettres et pièces relatives a la conférence de Loudun.* Paris: Imprimerie Impériale, 1862.

Bouffard-Madiane, Jean de. *Mémoires de J. de Bouffard-Madiane sur les guerres civiles du duc de Rohan, 1610–1629.* Edited by Charles Pradel. Paris: Picard, 1897.

Burel, Jean. *Mémoires de Jean Burel. Journal d'un bourgeois du Puy à l'époque des Guerres de religion.* Saint-Vidal: Centre d'Étude de la Vallée de la Borne, 1983.

Calvin, John. *Institutes of the Christian Religion.* Translated by Ford Lewis Battles. Grand Rapids, MI: William B. Eerdmans, 1975.

Canault, Jean. *Vie du maréchal J.-B. d'Ornano, baron d'Aubenas-en-Vivarais, gouverneur du frère de Louis XIII (1581–1626).* Edited by Jean Charay. Grenoble: Quatre Seigneurs, 1971.

Catel, Guillaume de. *Histoire des contes de Toulouse.* Toulouse: Pierre Bosc, 1633.

———. *Mémoires de l'histoire du Languedoc.* . . . Toulouse: Pierre Bosc, 1633.

Caux, Henry de. *Catalogue general des gentils-hommes de la province de Languedoc.* Pézenas: Jean Martel, 1676.

Chabans, Louis de, seigneur du Maine. *Histoire de la guerre des Huguenots faicte en France sous le regne du roy Louys XIII avec les plans des sieges des villes en taille douce. Par monsieur le baron de Chabans, gentil'homme ordinaire de la chamber du roy, gouverneur de Saincte Foy, & general de l'artillerie de la serenissime republique de Venise.* Paris: Toussaint du Bray, 1634.

Les Commentaires du soldat du Vivarais. Ou se voit l'origine de la rébellion de la France et toutes les guerres que, durant icelle, le pays du Vivarais a souffertes, divisés en trois livres, selon le temps que lesdites guerres sont arrivées. Suivis du Voyage du duc de Rohan en Vivarais, l'en 1628; de la Relation de la révolte de Roure en 1670; Et d'une Anecdote extraite du journal manuscrit de J. de Banne, chanoine de Viviers. 1908. Reprint, Valence: La Bouquinerie, 1991.

Coppie de la lettre du roy escrite à monseigneur le duc de Mayenne le avril. Coppie de la lettre de monsieur de Pont-Chartrain à monseigneur le duc de Mayenne le 3 avril 1620. N.p., 1620.

Declaration de messieurs les princes au roy. Paris: Isaac Mesnier, 1619. BNF, 8° Lb[36] 1276.

Declaration de monseigneur le Prince contre les ennemis du roy, & de l'Estat. N.p.: n.p., 1615. BNF, 8° Lb[36] 597.

Declaration de monsieur le duc de Rohan pair de France, &c. N.p.: n.p., 1627. BNF, 8° Lb[36] 2516.

Declaration des eglises reformees de France et souveraineté de Bearn, de l'injuste persecution qui leur est faict par les ennemis de l'Estat & de leur religion. Et de leur legitime & necessaire defense. La Rochelle: Guillaume Delachaulx and Marin Canoel, 1621.

Declaration du roy contre les ducs de Vendosme, de Mayenne, mareschal de Buillon, marquis de Cœuvre, le president le Jay, & tous ceux qui les assistent. Verifiee en parlement le treiziesme fevrier 1617. Paris: F. Morel and P. Mettayer, 1617.

Declaration du roy en faveur du sieur de Latude pour avoir entree aux Estats de Languedoc a cause de la Baronie de Gange. N.p., n.d. AD Hérault, A 48, f° 5.

Declaration du roy, contre le duc de Montmorancy, verifiée, & registrée en la cour de parlement de Tolose le premier jour de septembre mil six cens trente-deux. Lyon: Jean Jullieron, 1632. BNF, F 46974 (11).

Declaration du roy, par laquelle les princes, ducs, & seigneurs y denommez, sont declarez criminels de leze Majesté. . . . Lyon: Nicolas Jullieron, 1620.

Declaration du roy, pour la reunion à son domaine et confiscation des biens des ducs de Nevers, de Vendosme, de Mayenne, mareschal de Buillon, marquis de Coeuvre, et president le Jay. Paris, 10 mars 1617. Paris: F. Morel and P. Mettayer, 1617.

Defaicte furieuse de deux cens maistres, sortis de Castres, Puilaurens, & autres villes rebelles. Par monsieur d'Ambres, & monsieur S.Jean du Lerm. . . . Paris: Adrian Bacot, 1625. BNF, 8° Lb³⁶ 2335.

La Deffaicte de quatre cents hommes par le sieur de Mont-Real, aupres de Nismes en Languedoc. Ensemble la victoire obtenuë par monseigneur de Montmorancy sur les troupes du sieur de Chastillon. Paris: Joseph Guerreau, n.d. BNF, 8° Lb³⁶ 2032.

La Deffaicte de quatre cens hommes sortis de la Rochelle. Tant habitans que trouppes estrangeres mis en desroute. Par monsieur le duc d'Espernon. Rouen: Jacques Besonge, 1621. BNF, 8° Lb³⁶ 1737.

Delort, André. *Mémoires inédits d'André Delort sur la ville de Montpellier au XVIIᵉ siècle (1621–1693).* 1876. Reprint, Marseille: Laffitte, 1980.

Departement des provinces dv royavme de France, que l'assemblee tenuë à la Rochelle a faict à chacun des princes & seigneurs de la Religion, à sa volonté. Aix: Jean Tholozan, 1621.

Deyron. *De la genealogie de monsieur le baron d'Aubais.* N.p., 1646. BNF, Cabinet d'Hozier 22, f° 506.

Discours de la Confidence. Au Roy. N.p., n.d. BNF, Clairambault 366, f° 219–230.

Du Chesne-Tourangeau, André. *Histoire genealogique de la maison de Montmorency et de Laval justifiee par chartes, tiltres, arrests, & autres bonnes & sertaines preuves.* Paris: Sabastien Cramoisy, 1624.

Du Cros, Simon. *Histoire de la vie de Henry dernier duc de Montmorency. Contenant tout ce qu'il a fait de plus remarquable depuis sa naissance jusques à sa mort.* Paris: Antoine Sommaville & Augustin Courbé, 1643.

Du Plessis de Mornay, Philippe. *De la verité de la religion Chrestienne.* Paris: Claude Micard, 1585.

Duval, François, marquis de Fontenay-Mareuil. *Mémoires de Messire François Duval, marquis de Fontenay-Mareuil, maréchal des camps et armées du roy, conseiller d'état, nommé à l'ordre du Saint-Esprit, ambassadeur en Angleterre en 1626, et deux fois a Rome et 1641 et 1647.* In *Nouvelle Collection des Mémoires pour servir a l'histoire de France depuis le XIIIᵉ siècle jusqu'à la fin du XVIIIᵉ,* edited by Joseph-François Michaud and Jean-Joseph-François Poujoulat [cited as *NCM*]. Vol. 5. Paris: Firmin Didot, 1837.

Duval, Pierre. *Description de la France et de ses provinces, où il est traitté de leurs noms anciens et nouveaux, degrés, estendüe, figure, voisinage, division, etc.* . . . Paris: J. Du Puis, 1663.

"The Edict of Nantes with Its Secret Articles and Brevets." Translated by Jotham Parsons. In *The Edict of Nantes: Five Essays and a New Translation,* edited by Richard L. Goodbar, 41–68. Bloomington, MN: National Huguenot Society, 1998.

Errard de Bar-le-Duc, Jean. *La Fortification demonstree et reduicte en art par feu J. Errard de Bar le Duc.* Paris: n.p., 1620.

Faret, Nicolas. *L'Honneste-homme ou, l'art de plaire a la court.* Paris: Toussaincts du Bray, 1630.

Freton, Louis. "Commentaires de Louis Freton, seigneur de Servas." In *Pièces fugitives pour servir a l'histoire de France avec des notes historiques & géographiques,* edited by Charles de Bachi marquis d'Aubais [cited as *PFHF*]. Paris: Hugues-Daniel Chaubert & Claude Herissant, 1759.

Gaches, Jacques. *Suite des mémoires de J. Gaches (1610–1620)*. Edited by Charles Pradel. Albi: Imprimerie G.-M. Nouguiès, 1894.

Gariel, Pierre. *Les Gouverneurs anciens & modernes de la Gaule Narbonnoise, ou de la province du Languedoc*. Montpellier: Daniel Pech, 1669. Reprinted in *Collection des cent-quinze de la société des bibliophiles languedociens*. Montpellier: C. Coulet, 1873.

———. *Idée de la ville de Montpellier recherchée et présentée aux honnêtes gens*. Paris: Pech, 1665.

Gaubertin, Pierre Boistel de. *Histoire des guerres du Roy Louys XIII, depuis son advenement à la couronne jusqu'en l'an 1622*. Rouen: Jacques Besonge, 1622.

Gaufreteau, Jean de. *Chronique Bordeloise*. 2 vols. Bordeaux: Charles Lefebvre, 1878.

Girard, Guillaume. *Histoire de la vie du duc d'Espernon*. 1655. Reprint, Paris: Montalant, 1730.

Gissey, Odo de. *Discours historiques de la très ancienne dévotion de nostres Dame du Puy, ou du Puy nostre Dame. Ensemble plusieurs belles remarques, tant des evesques du Velay, que d'autres choses ecclesiastiques & seculieres*. 2nd ed. Toulouse, 1627.

Harangue faicte au Roy, par messieurs de Montpellier. N.p., 1622. BM Montpellier, 30239.

Héroard, Jean. *Journal de Jean Héroard*. Edited by Madeleine Foisil. 2 vols. Paris: Fayard, 1989.

L'Hevrevse arrivee dv roy dans Bourdeaus, et ce qui s'y est passé despuis. Avec les ceremonies, qui furent faictes aux espousailles de Madame sœur aisnée de sa Majesté, iusques à son despart vers l'Espagne. Lyon: Nicolas Jullieron, 1615.

Histoire veritable de tovt ce qvi s'est faict & passé dans la ville de Thoulouse, en la mort de Monsieur de Montmorancy. Ensemble les interrogations qui luy ont esté faictes & les responces à icelles. N.p., 1633. BNF, 8° Lb³⁶ 2908.

Immortalité du carrousel de Monseigneur d'Espernon, duc et pair de France, colonel de l'infanterie françoise, gouverneur & lieutenãt general pour le roy en Guyenne. Avec le trophée de ses victoires. Paris: Carroy, 1627. BNF, Ye 16473.

La Roque de La Lontière, Gilles-André de. *Traité de la noblesse, de ses différentes espèces*. Paris: Estienne Michallet, 1678.

Laval, Antoine de. *Desseins de professions nobles et publiques*. Paris: Abel l'Angelier, 1613.

Le Bret, Henry. *Histoire de Montauban*. 1668. Reprint, Marseille: Laffitte, 1976.

Le Moyne, Pierre. *De l'art des devises*. Paris: Sebastien Cramoisy and Sebastien Mabre Cramoisy, 1666.

Le Roi d'armes du Languedoc, ou essais héraldiques, généalogiques et historiques de la noblesse de cette province. Paris: Imprimerie de Monsieur, 1784.

Lesdiguières, François de Bonne, duc de. *Actes et correspondance du connétable de Lesdiguières*. Edited by Louis-Archambaud Douglas and Joseph Roman. 3 vols. Grenoble: E. Allier, 1878–1884.

Lettre du roy, envoyee a monseigneur le mareschal de Souvré. Sur le sujet de la prise de Negrepelisse prise par force par l'armee de sa Majesté. Ensemble le preparatif du siege de Sainct Anthonin par monseigneur le duc de Vendosme. Tours: Jean Oudot, 1622. BNF, 8° Lb³⁶ 1982.

Louvet de Beauvais, Pierre. *Remarques sur l'Histoire de Languedoc. Des Princes qui y ont commandé sous la seconde & troisiéme lignée de nos Roys jusques à son entiere reünion à la*

Couronne: des Estats Generaux de la Province, & des Particuliers de chaque Diocese. Toulouse: Fr. Boude, 1657.

Loyseau, Charles. *Traité des seigneuries.* Paris: A. L'Angelier, 1608.

———. *A Treatise of Orders and Plain Dignities.* Translated by Howell A. Lloyd. Cambridge: Cambridge University Press, 1994.

Machiavelli, Niccolò. *The Art of War.* Translated by Ellis Farneworth. Rev. ed. New York: Da Capo Press, 1965.

Manifeste de M. de Chastillon contre les calomnies des rebelles et ennemis du roi. . . . Paris: P. Rocolet, 1622.

Manifeste de monsieur de Rohan, pour ce qui s'est passé à S. Jehan d'Angely, avec la prosopopee dediee à madame Henriette de Rohan. La Rochelle: n.p., 1613. BNF, 8° Lb^{36} 189.

Manifeste des bons françois, sur la mort desplorable de monseigneur le mareschal de Schombert. Dedié a madame la mareschalle de Schombert. Paris: Jean Brunet, 1632. BNF, Clairambault 1132, f° 327–334.

Marot, Clément. *Les Pseaumes de David, mis en rime Françoise par Clement Marot & Thodore de Beze.* Geneva: Jean de Tournes, 1611.

Le Mars resussité de la Gendarmerie. N.p., 1615. BNF, 8° Lf^{51} 12.

Mémoire a consulter et consultation pour messires Jean-Joseph & Marc-Antoine de Lauziers de Themines frères. Toulouse: J. Rayet, 1774 [?]. AD Hérault, 1 E 227.

Memoire concernant la cassation des testament & codicilles de feu monsieur le duc d'Arpajon. N.p., 1658. BNF, Pièces Originales 104.

Le Mercure François ou, Suitte de l'Histoire de Notre Temps . . . 18 vols. Paris: Estienne Richer, 1611–1643.

Mervault, Peter. *The Last Famous Siege of the City of Rochel together with the Edict of Nantes.* London: John Wickins, 1680.

Monluc, Blaise de. *The Habsburg-Valois Wars and the French Wars of Religion.* Edited by Ian Roy. London: Longman, 1971.

Montaigne, Michel de. *The Complete Essays.* Translated by M. A. Screech. London: Penguin Books, 1987.

Nicot, Jean. *Thresor de la Langue Francoyse, tant ancienne que moderne.* Paris: David Douceur, 1606.

La Noblesse de Languedoc aux pieds du roy. . . . Paris: P. Mettayer, A. Estienne, and C. Prevost. BNF, 8° Lb^{36} 2948.

Ode pour monseigneur le duc de Bellegarde, pair et grand escuyer de France. Paris: n.p., 1621. BNF, Clairambault 378, f° 57–60.

Pelletier, Thomas. *La Nourriture de la noblesse, où sont représentées, comme un tableau, toutes les plus belles vertus, qui peuvent accomplir un jeune gentilhomme.* Paris: Veuve de M. Patisson, 1604.

Phélypeaux, Paul, seigneur de Pontchartrain. *Mémoires Concernant les affaires de France sous la Régence de Marie de Medicis.* In Vol. 5 of *Nouvelle Collection des Mémoires relatifs a l'Histoire de France,* edited by Joseph-François Michaud and Jean-Joseph-François Poujoulat [cited as *NCM*]. Paris: Didier, 1837.

Pluvinel, Antoine de. *Instruction du roy, en l'exercice de monter à cheval.* 1625. Reprint, Amsterdam: Jean Schipper, 1666.

Pontis, Louis de. *Mémoires (1676)*. Edited by Andrée Villard. Paris: Honoré Champion, 2000.

Potter, David, ed. *Foreign Intelligence and Information in Elizabethan England: Two English Treatises on the State of France, 1580–1584*. Cambridge: Cambridge University Press and Royal Historical Society, 2004.

———. *The French Wars of Religion: Selected Documents*. New York: St. Martin's Press, 1997.

Premiere lettre de Monsieur le duc d'Espernon. Envoyee au roy le dixseptiesme janvier 1619. Metz: n.p., 1619. BNF, 8° Lb^{36} 1164.

La Prise de la ville de Chaumerac en Vivarests. Par monseigneur le duc de Montmorency. Avec l'execution de six vingts des rebelles qui ont esté penduz à la veuë du Pousin. Et le pillage & bruslement du chasteau de Mauras, & autres maisons qui pouvoient favoriser le passage des rebelles de Privas audit Pousin. Paris: Jean Barbote, 1628. BNF, 8° Lb^{36} 2634.

La Prise des advenues et passages de La Rochelle. Pour le bloquement d'icelle. Par monsieur le duc d'Espernon. Suyvant le commandement du roy. Lyon: Claude Armand: 1621.

La Prise des villes de la Caune et Sainct Sever en la comté de Castres par Monseigneur le Prince. . . . Paris: Jean Barbotte, 1628. Copy, BM Montpellier, 30017.

La Prise du fort de Corconne, en Languedoc. Par monsieur le marquis de Fossez, gouverneur de la ville & citadelle de Montpellier. . . . Paris: Jean Barbotte, 1628. BNF, 8° Lb^{36} 2589.

La Prise et reduction de la ville et chasteau de Nerac, au service du Roy. Par monsieur le Duc de Mayenne, suivant l'execution des commandemens de sa Majesté. Paris: Isaac Mesnier, 1621. BNF, 8° Lb^{36} 1695.

La Prise et reduction de la ville et chasteau de Sully par monsieur le Prince de Condé, le 20. Juillet, 1621. Paris: Joseph Guerreau, 1621. BNF, 8° Lb^{36} 1713.

La Prise remarquable de Marguerites en Languedoc prés de Nismes, faicte par monseigneur le Duc de Montmorency, Admiral de France, Gouverneur & Lieutenant General pour le Roy, audit pays de Languedoc. Ensemble les noms et qualitez des morts, prisonniers & blessez en nombre de plus de quatre cents. Paris: Abraham Saugrain, 1621. BNF, 8° Lb^{36} 1691.

Provisions de la charge de marechal general des camps et armées pour Mr. de Lesdiguieres, pair et marechal de France. Du 30 mars 1621, N.p., 1621. SHAT, A1b 1175, f° 75.

Rabelais, François. *Gargantua*. Edited by Ruth Calder. Geneva: Droz, 1970.

Recit tres-veritable de ce qui s'est passé le mercredy 19. janvier 1628. en l'entreprise faicte par monsieur le duc de Rohan sur la ville & citadelle de Montpellier (Montpellier: Jean Pech, 1628), BNF, 8° Lb^{36} 2598.

Récit véritable de ce qui s'est passé au degast es environs de Nismes, Uzes, Anduze et Alez, en la préseance du duc de Rohan et de son armée, avec la deffaite de son avant-garde, et le nombre des blessez et pris prisonniers. Par monseigneur de Montmorency, duc et pair de France, gouverneur pour le roy au païs de Languedoc. Paris: Jean Barbotte, 1628. BNF, 8° Lb^{36} 2640.

Recit veritable de la reduction du Mas-de-Verdun, de l'Isle en Jourdain, & de Mauvoizin au service du Roy. Par messieurs le duc de Mayenne, et mareschal de Themines. Le 27. & 28. Juillet dernier. Paris: Abraham Saugrain, 1621. BNF, 8° Lb^{36} 1718.

Reduction de la ville de Privaz a l'obeissance dv roy, par monseigevr de Montmorancy grand admiral de France. Contre les rebelles dudict lieu. . . . Lyon: n.p., 1620.

Reglemens du feu roy Louis XIII sur la convocation du ban et arriere-ban, ordonnez estre fait és années 1635 & 1639. Versailles: François Muguet, 1689. BNF, Mss. fr. 21719, f° 22–27.

Reglement pour les gens de guerre. Fait par monseigneur le duc de Montmorency & d'Amville, gouverneur & lieutenant general pour le roy au pays de Languedoc. Toulouse: Jean Boude, 1622. AD Tarn, C 207.

Reglement qve le Roy vevt & entend estre doresnauant obserué par les gens de Guerre, tant de cheual que de pied, & par les Habitans des lieux par où les Trouppes passeront & logeront pour la fourniture des Estapes. Paris: Pierre Mettayer, A Estiene, and C. Prevost, 1630. BNF, F 46966 (18).

Relation envoyée au roy par monsieur le mareschal de Schomberg. Du combat fait entre les armes qu'il commande & l'armee de monsieur pres de Castelnaudarri le premier de septembre 1632. . . . Paris: Bureau d'Adresse, 1632. BNF, 8° Lb³⁶ 2891.

Relation veritable et journaliere de tout ce qui s'est passé en France & pays estrangers. Depuis le depart du roy de sa ville capitale de Paris, jusqu'à present. Paris: Joseph Bouillerot, 1622. BNF, Clairambault 378, f° 150–169.

La Revolte du pays de Gascogne, contre le duc de Rohan & ses alliez. Extraict d'un lettre escrite le sixiesme de decembre, par un gentil homme de Pamiers, à un sien amy dans Paris. Paris: Anthoine de Brueil, 1615.

Richelet, Nicolas. *L'Hymne des peres de famille a S. Blaise, de P. de Ronsard, commenté par Nicolas Richelet, Parisien.* Paris: Nicolas Buon, 1618.

Richelieu, Armand Jean du Plessis, duc de. *Les Papiers de Richelieu: Section politique intérieure, correspondance et papiers d'état.* Edited by Pierre Grillon. Vols. 1–3. Paris: A. Pedone, 1975–1979.

———. *Letters of the Cardinal Duke of Richelieu: Great Minister of State to Lewis XIII of France.* London: A. Roper, A. Bosvile, and T. Leigh, 1698.

———. *Lettres, instructions diplomatiques et papiers d'état du cardinal de Richelieu.* Edited by Georges d'Avenel. 8 vols. Paris: Imprimerie Impériale [puis Nationale], 1853–1877.

———. *Mémoires du Cardinal de Richelieu: Sur le règne de Louis XIII, depuis 1610 jusqu'à 1638.* 3 vols. Edited by Joseph-François Michaud and Jean-Joseph-François Poujoulat. Paris: Éd. du commentaire analytique du Code civil, 1837–1838.

———. *Testament politique de Richelieu.* Edited by Françoise Hildesheimer. Paris: Société de l'Histoire de France, 1995.

Rohan, Henri I de. *Mémoires du duc de Rohan.* Vol. 18 in *Collection des mémoires relatifs a l'histoire de France,* ed. Claude-Bernard Petitot. Paris: Foucault, 1822.

Saint-Blancard, Jacques. *Journal du siège du Mas-d'Azil en 1625 écrit par J. de Saint-Blancard, défenseur de la place, contré le maréchal de Thémines.* Edited by C. Barrière-Flavy. Foix: Veuve Pomiès, 1894. First published in *Bulletin de la Société Ariégeoise des Sciences, Lettres et Arts* 4 (1894).

Sales, François de. *Introduction à la vie dévote.* Rouen: R. Lallement, 1608.

Serres, Olivier de. *Théâtre de l'agriculture et mesnage des champs.* Paris: J. Métayer, 1600.

Shaw, William, and Geraint Dyfnallt Owen, eds. *Report on the Manuscripts of the Right Honourable Viscount de l'Isle.* Vol. 5: *Sidney Papers, 1611–1626.* London: Her Majesty's Stationery Office, 1962.

Signalee deffaite de la garnison de Nismes par monsieur le mareschal dEstree. Avec la perte de six cens hommes taillez en pieces, quantité de blessez & prisonniers. Paris: Jean Martin, 1629. BM Montpellier, V. 5581.

Souhait, François du. *Le Parfaict gentil-homme.* Paris: Gilles Robinot, 1600.

Tissier, Jean, ed. *Documents inédits pour servir a l'histoire de la province de Languedoc et de la ville de Narbonne en particulier, 1596–1632.* Narbonne: F. Caillard, 1903.

Valdor, Jean. *Les Triomphes de Louis le Juste XIII du nom, roy de France et de Navarre.* Paris: Antoine Estiene, 1649.

Vallambert, Simon de. *Cinq livres de la maniere de nourrir et gouverner les enfans de leur naissance.* Poitiers: Mamez & Bouchetz, 1565.

Videl, Louis. *Histoire du connestable de Lesdiguières. Contenant toute sa vie, avec plusieurs choses memorables, servant à l'histoire générale.* Grenoble: Jean Nicolas, 1649.

Vignolles. "Mémoires de Vignolles: Affaires de Guienne." In *Pièces fugitives pour servir a l'histoire de France avec des notes historiques & géographiques,* edited by Charles de Bachi marquis d'Aubais [cited as *PFHF*]. Paris: Hugues-Daniel Chaubert & Claude Herissant, 1759.

Vitruvius. *Architecture, ou art de bien bastir.* Translated by Jean Martin. Cologny: Jean de Tournes, 1618.

Voyage de Monsieur le prince de Condé en Italie depuis son partement du Camp de Montpellier, jusques à son retour en sa maison de Mouron, ensemble les remarques des choses les plus notables qu'il a veuës en sondit voyage. Paris: Toussianct Quinet, 1634.

Wilkinson, Maurice, ed. "Documents Illustrating the History of the Wars of Religion in the Perigord (1588–1592)." *English Historical Review* 23 (April 1908): 292–317.

SECONDARY SOURCES

Aigrefeuille, Charles d'. *Histoire de la ville de Montpellier depuis son origine jusqu'à notre temps.* 4 vols. 1875–1882. Reprint. Marseille: Laffitte, 1976.

Alcouffe, Daniel, Emmanuel Coquery, Gérard Mabille, and Marie-Laure de Rochebrune, eds. *Un Temps d'exubérance. Les Arts décoratifs sous Louis XIII et Anne d'Autriche.* Paris: Réunion des Musées Nationaux, 2002.

Allen, Paul C. *Philip III and the Pax Hispanica, 1598–1621: The Failure of Grand Strategy.* New Haven, CT: Yale University Press, 2000.

Ariès, Philippe. *L'Enfant et la vie familiale sous l'Ancien Régime.* Paris: Librairie Plon, 1960.

Armstrong, Megan. "Spiritual Reform, Mendicant Autonomy, and State Formation: French Franciscan Disputes before the Parlement of Paris, 1500–1600." *French Historical Studies* 25 (Summer 2002): 505–530.

Arnold, Thomas. *The Renaissance at War.* London: Cassell, 2001.

Artigaut, René. *Les Protestants de Castres et l'Édit de Nantes, 1598–1685.* Castres: Société Culturelle du Pays Castrais, 1985.

Asch, Ronald G. *Nobilities in Transition, 1550–1700: Courtiers and Rebels in Britain and Europe.* London: Arnold, 2003.

Aubresse, Sylvie. *Le Parlement de Paris ou la voix de la raison (1559–1589).* Geneva: Librairie Droz, 2005.

Audisio, Gabriel. "Famille et religion. Les Vicissitudes testamentaires d'un noble proven-çal (1555–1569)." In *Le Second Ordre, L'idéal nobiliaire. Hommage à Ellery Schalk,* edited by Chantal Grell and Arnaud Ramière de Fortanier, 31–42. Paris: Presses de l'Université de Paris Sorbonne, 1999.

Babeau, Albert. *La Province sous l'ancien régime.* 3 vols. Paris: Firmin-Didot, 1894.

Baker, Joanne. "Female Monasticism and Family Strategy: The Guises and Saint Pierre de Reims." *Sixteenth Century Journal* 28 (Winter 1997): 1091–1108.

Baker, Keith Michael. *Inventing the French Revolution: Essays on French Political Culture in the Eighteenth Century.* Cambridge: Cambridge University Press, 1990.

———, ed. *The French Revolution and the Creation of Modern Political Culture.* Oxford: Oxford University Press, 1987–1989.

Bakos, Adrianna E. *Images of Kingship in Early Modern France.* London: Routledge, 1997.

Baldwin, John W. *The Government of Philip Augustus: Foundations of French Royal Power in the Middle Ages.* Berkeley: University of California Press, 1986.

Barbiche, Bernard, and Ségolène de Dainville-Barbiche. *Sully. L'Homme et ses fidèles.* Paris: Fayard, 1997.

Barnes, Andrew E. "Religious Anxiety and Devotional Change in Sixteenth Century French Penitential Confraternities." *Sixteenth Century Journal* 19 (Autumn 1988): 389–406.

Barnes, Robin. "Varieties of Apocalyptic Experience in Reformation Europe." *Journal of Interdisciplinary History* 103 (Autumn 2002): 261–274.

Baumel, Jean. *Montpellier au cours des XVIᵉ et XVIIᵉ siècles. Les guerres de religion (1510–1685).* Montpellier: Causse, 1976.

Baumgartner, Frederic J. *Change and Continuity in the French Episcopate: The Bishops and the Wars of Religion, 1647–1610.* Durham, NC: Duke University Press, 1986.

Baxter, Douglas Clark. *Servants of the Sword: French Intendants of the Army, 1630–70.* Urbana: University of Illinois Press, 1976.

Bayard, Françoise. "Entre clientèles ancienne et nouvelle: les financiers français du XVIIᵉ siècle." In *Patronages et clientélismes, 1550–1750 (France, Angleterre, Espagne, Italie),* edited by Charles Giry-Deloison and Roger Mettam, 85–99. Lille: Université Charles de Gaulle (Lille III) and Institut Français du Royaume-Uni, 1995.

———. *Le Monde des financiers au XVIIᵉ siècle.* Paris: Flammarion, 1988.

Beaumont, Stéphane, ed. *Histoire d'Agen.* Toulouse: Privat, 1991.

Béchu, Philippe. "Noblesse d'épée et tradition militaire au XVIIIᵉᵐᵉ siècle." *Histoire, Économie et Société* 2 (1983): 507–548.

Bège-Seurin, Denise. "Droit et identité nobiliaire. La Jurisprudence de la Cour des Aides de Guyenne au XVIIᵉ siècle d'après le recueil de Fontainemarie." In *L'Identité nobiliaire. Dix siècles de métamorphoses (IXᵉ–XIXᵉ siècles),* edited by Jean-Marie Constant, 166–179. Beaufay: Brunet, 1997.

Béguin, Katia. *Les Princes de Condé. Rebelles, courtisans et mécènes dans la France du Grand Siècle.* Seyssel: Champ Vallon, 1999.

Beik, William. *Absolutism and Society in Seventeenth-Century France: State Power and Provincial Aristocracy in Languedoc.* Cambridge: Cambridge University Press, 1985.

———. "The Absolutism of Louis XIV as Social Collaboration." *Past and Present* 188 (August 2005): 195–224.

———. "The Parlement of Toulouse and the Fronde." In *Society and Institutions in Early Modern France,* edited by Mack P. Holt, 132–152. Athens: University of Georgia Press, 1991.

———. *Urban Protest in Seventeenth-Century France: The Culture of Retribution.* Cambridge: Cambridge University Press, 1997.

Belhomme, Victor. *Histoire de l'infanterie en France.* 2 vols. Paris: Henri Charles-Lavauzelle, 1893–1902.

Benedict, Philip. "Between Whig Traditions and New Histories: American Historical Writing About Reformation and Early Modern Europe." In *Imagined Histories: American Historians Interpret the Past,* edited by Anthony Molho and Gordon S. Wood, 295–323. Princeton, NJ: Princeton University Press, 1998.

———. *Christ's Churches Purely Reformed: A Social History of Calvinism.* New Haven, CT: Yale University Press, 2002.

———. "Confessionalization in France? Critical Reflections and New Evidence." In *Society and Culture in the Huguenot World, 1559–1685,* edited by Raymond A. Mentzer and Andrew Spicer, 44–61. Cambridge: Cambridge University Press, 2002.

———. *The Faith and Fortunes of France's Huguenots, 1600–85.* Aldershot, UK: Ashgate, 2001.

———. "Faith, Fortune and Social Structure in Seventeenth-Century Montpellier." *Past & Present* 152 (1996): 46–78.

———. "French Cities from the Sixteenth Century to the Revolution." In *Cities and Social Change in Early Modern France,* edited by Philip Benedict, 6–66. London: Unwin Hyman, 1989.

———. "The Huguenot Population of France, 1600–85." In *Faith and Fortunes of France's Huguenots, 1600–85,* 34–120. Aldershot, UK: Ashgate, 2001. Originally published as Philip Benedict, *The Huguenot Population of France, 1600–1685: Demographic Fate and Customs of a Religious Minority,* in *Transactions of the American Philosophical Society* 81, part 5 (1991).

———. "The Saint Bartholomew's Day Massacre in the Provinces." *Historical Journal* 21 (1978): 205–225.

———. "Settlements: France." In *Visions, Programs, and Outcomes,* vol. 2 of *Handbook of European History, 1400–1600: Late Middle Ages, Renaissance, and Reformation,* edited by Thomas A. Brady Jr., Heiko A. Oberman, and James D. Tracy, 417–454. Grand Rapids: William B. Eerdmans, 1995.

———, ed. *Cities and Social Change in Early Modern France.* London: Unwin Hyman, 1989.

Benedict, Philip, Guido Marnef, Henk van Nierop, and Marc Venard, eds. *Reformation, Revolt and Civil War in France and the Netherlands, 1555–1585.* Amsterdam: Royal Netherlands Academy of Arts and Sciences, 1999.

Bennessar, B. "Des années de la Ligue aux jours de Fronde (vers 1560–vers 1630)." In *Histoire de Toulouse,* edited by Philippe Wolff, 271–291. Toulouse: Privat, 1973.

Bercé, Yves-Marie. "Les Coups de majesté des rois de France, 1588, 1617, 1661." In *Complots et conjurations dans l'Europe moderne,* edited by Yves-Marie Bercé and Elena Fasano Guarini, 491–505. Rome: École française de Rome, 1996.

————. "De la criminalité aux troubles sociaux. La Noblesse rurale du Sud-Ouest de la France sous Louis XIII." *Annales du Midi* 76 (1964): 41–59.

————. *History of Peasant Revolts: The Social Origins of Rebellion in Early Modern France.* Ithaca, NY: Cornell University Press, 1990.

————. *Révoltes et révolutions dans l'Europe moderne, XVIᵉ–XVIIIᵉ siècles.* Paris: Presses Universitaires de France, 1980.

Berenger, Jean. "Les Armées françaises et les guerres de religion." *Revue internationale d'histoire militaire* 55 (1983): 11–28.

Besset, Charles. "Essai sur la noblesse Vivaroise." *Revue du Vivarais* (1912): 217–232, 264–281, 306–319, 346–358, 413–430, 436–448.

Bien, David D. "Manufacturing Nobles: The Chancelleries in France to 1789." *Journal of Modern History* 61 (September 1989): 445–486.

Billacois, François. *Le Duel dans la société française des XVIᵉ–XVIIᵉ siècles. Essai de psychosociologie historique.* Paris: École des Hautes Études en Sciences Sociales, 1986.

Bireley, Robert. *The Jesuits and the Thirty Years War: Kings, Courts, and Confessors.* Cambridge: Cambridge University Press, 2003.

Bitton, Davis. *The French Nobility in Crisis, 1560–1640.* Stanford, CA: Stanford University Press, 1969.

Blanchard, Anne. "Une Approche de la noblesse languedocienne. La maintenue de 1668–1672." In *Sociétés et idéologies des temps modernes. Hommage à Arlette Jouanna,* edited by Joël Fouilleron, Guy Le Thiec, and Henri Michel, 1: 15–35. Montpellier: Université de Montpellier III-Paul-Valéry, 1996.

————. "La Prise d'armes des protestants en Languedoc (1621–1622)." *Académie des sciences et lettres de Montpellier,* n.s., 18 (1987): 89–93.

————. "Vers la ceinture de fer. Milieu du XVIᵉ–début du XVIIIᵉ siècle." In *Histoire militaire de la France,* vol. 1: *Des origines à 1715,* edited by Philippe Contamine, 449–483. Paris: Presses Universitaires de France, 1992.

Blanchard, Joël. "Le Spectacle du rite. Les entrées royales." *Revue Historique* 305, 3 (July 2003): 475–519.

Blaufarb, Rafe. *The French Army, 1750–1820: Careers, Talent, Merit.* Manchester: University of Manchester Press, 2002.

Bloch, Marc. *French Rural History: An Essay on Its Basic Characteristics.* Translated by Janet Sondheimer. Berkeley: University of California Press, 1966.

Bohanan, Donna. *Old and New Nobility in Aix-en-Provence, 1600–1695: Portrait of an Urban Elite.* Baton Rouge: Louisiana State University Press, 1992.

Boltanski, Ariane. *Les Ducs de Nevers et l'état royal. Genèse d'un compromis (ca 1550–ca 1600).* Geneva: Librairie Droz, 2006.

Bonney, Richard. "Absolutism: What's in a Name?" *French History* 1 (1987): 93–117.

————. *The King's Debts: Finance and Politics in France, 1589–1661.* Oxford: Clarendon Press, 1981.

————. *Political Change in France under Richelieu and Mazarin, 1624–1661.* Oxford: Oxford University Press, 1978.

————. "What's New about the New French Fiscal History?" *Journal of Modern History* 70 (September 1998): 639–667.

Bordes, Maurice. "La Gascogne à la fin de l'ancien régime. Une province?" In *Régions et régionalisme en France du XVIIIe siècle à nos jours*, edited by Christian Gras and Georges Livet, 139–154. Paris: Presses Universitaires de France, 1977.

———. *Histoire de la Gascogne des origines à nos jours*. Roanne: Horvath, 1977.

———, ed. *Histoire d'Auch et du pays d'Auch*. Roanne: Horvath, 1980.

Bossy, John. *Christianity in the West, 1400–1700*. Oxford: Oxford University Press, 1985.

Boucher, Jacqueline. "L'Ordre du Saint-Esprit dans la pensée politique et religieuse d'Henri III." *Cahiers d'histoire* 18 (1973): 129–142.

Bourdieu, Pierre. *Logic of Practice*. Translated by Richard Nice. Stanford, CA: Stanford University Press, 1990.

———. *Outline of a Theory of Practice*. Translated by Richard Nice. Cambridge: Cambridge University Press, 1977.

Bourdieu-Weiss, Catherine. "Un Architecte Toulousain du XVIIe siècle. Claude Pacot." *Annales du Midi* 113 (April–June 2001): 157–170.

Boureau, Alain. "Les Cérémonies royales françaises entre performance juridique et compétence liturgique." *Annales ESC* 46 (1991): 1253–1264.

———. "Pierre Affre, sculpteur toulousain du XVIIe siècle. Aspects méconnus de sa vie." *XVIIe siècle* 211 (April–June 2001): 215–231.

Bourquin, Laurent. *Noblesse seconde et pouvoir en Champagne aux XVIe et XVIIe siècles*. Paris: Sorbonne, 1994.

Boutruche, Robert, ed. *Bordeaux de 1453 à 1715*. Vol. 4 of *Histoire de Bordeaux*, edited by Charles Higounet. Bordeaux: Fédération historique du Sud-Ouest, 1966.

Bouwsma, William J. *John Calvin: A Sixteenth-Century Portrait*. Oxford: Oxford University Press, 1988.

Brenac, Madelaine. "Toulouse, centre de lutte contre le protestantisme au XVIIe siècle." *Annales du Midi* 77 (1965): 31–45.

Brioist, Pascal, Hervé Drévillon, and Pierre Serna. *Croisser le fer. Violence et culture de l'épée dans la France moderne (XVIe–XVIIIe siècle)*. Seyssel: Champ Vallon, 2002.

Brunelle, Gayle K. "Dangerous Liaisons: *Mésalliance* and Early Modern French Noblewomen." *French Historical Studies* 19 (Spring 1995): 75–103.

Brunet, Serge. "Anatomie des réseaux ligueurs dans le sud-ouest de la France (vers 1562–vers 1610)." In *Religion et politique dans les sociétés du Midi*, edited by Nicole Lemaitre, 153–191. Paris: CTHS, 2002.

———. "L'Évêque ligueur Urbain de Saint-Gelais (1570–1613). Du Comminges à Toulouse, ou la voie espagnole." In *Paix des armes, paix des âmes*, edited by Paul Mironneau and Isabelle Pébay-Clottes, 151–176. Paris: Société Henri IV and Imprimerie Nationale Éditions, 2000.

Bryant, Lawrence M. *The King and the City in the Parisian Royal Entry Ceremony: Politics, Ritual, and Art in the Renaissance*. Geneva: Droz, 1986.

Buisseret, David. *Ingénieurs et fortifications avant Vauban. L'Organisation d'un service royal aux XVIe–XVIIe siècles*. Paris: CTHS, 2002.

———. "Monarchs, Ministers, and Maps in France before the Accession of Louis XIV." In *Monarchs, Ministers, and Maps: The Emergence of Cartography as a Tool of Govern-*

ment in Early Modern Europe, edited by David Buisseret, 99–123. Chicago: University of Chicago Press, 1992.

———. "A Stage in the Development of the French Intendants: The Reign of Henri IV." *Historical Journal* 9 (1966): 27–38.

Burguière, André. "L'État monarchique et la famille (XVIe–XVIIIe siècle)." *Annales HSS* (March–April 2001): 330–331.

Camporesi, Piero. *Bread of Dreams: Food and Fantasy in Early Modern Europe.* Translated by David Gentilcore. Oxford: Polity Press, 1989.

Capot, Stéphane. *Justice et religion en Languedoc au temps de l'édit de Nantes. La chambre de l'édit de Castres (1579–1679.* Paris: École de Chartes, 1998.

———. "Les Magistrats de la chambre de l'édit de Languedoc (1579–1679)." *Annales du Midi* 108 (January–March 1996): 63–88.

Carabin, Denise. "Deux institutions de gentilshommes sous Louis XIII: *Le Gentilhomme de Pasquier* et *L'Instruction du Roy* de Pluvinel." *XVIIe siècle* 218 (January–March 2003): 27–38.

Carlat, Michel. "La Renaissance au château de Tournon sous Claude de La Tour-Turenne (1535–1591)." *Revue du Vivarais* 107 (January–March 2003): 123–142.

Carmona, Michel. *Marie de Médicis.* Paris: Fayard, 1981.

Carroll, Stuart. *Blood and Violence in Early Modern France.* Oxford: Oxford University Press, 2006.

Cassagnes-Brouquet, Sophie. *Vierges noires.* Rodez: Rouergue, 2000.

Cassan, Michel. "Les Multiples Visages des confréries de dévotion. L'Exemple de Limoges au XVIe siècle." *Annales du Midi* 99 (January–March 1987): 35–52.

———. "Pour une enquête sur les officiers 'moyens' de la France moderne." *Annales du Midi* 108 (January–March 1996): 89–112.

———. "Seigneurs et communautés villageoises au temps des guerres de Religion." *Revue historique* 618 (2001): 433–449.

———. *Le Temps des guerres de religion. Le cas du Limousin (vers 1530–vers 1630).* Paris: Publisud, 1996.

———, ed. "Élites militaires et élites judiciaires aux XVIe et XVIIe siècles." Special issue, *Annales du Midi* 108 (January–March 1996).

Certeau, Michel de. *L'Invention du quotidien. 1. Arts de faire.* 1980. Reprint. Paris: Gallimard, 1990.

———. *The Practices of Everyday Life.* Translated by Steven Rendall. Berkeley: University of California Press, 1988.

Chaboche, Robert. "Les Soldats français de la guerre de Trente Ans. Une Tentative d'approche." *Revue d'Histoire Moderne et Contemporaine* 20 (January–March 1973): 10–24.

Chagniot, Jean. *Guerre et société à l'époque moderne.* Paris: Presses Universitaires de France, 2001.

———. "Guerre et société au XVIIe siècle." *XVIIe siècle* 148 (1985): 249–256.

———. "La Lente Maturation de l'armée permanente." In *L'Officier français des origines à nos jours,* edited by Claude Croubois, 11–14. Saint-Jean-d'Angély: Bordessoules, 1987.

Chantrel, Laure. "Les Notions de richesse et de travail dans la pensée économique française de la seconde moitié du XVIe et au début du XVIIe siècle." *Journal of Medieval and Renaissance Studies* 25 (Winter 1995): 129–158.

Chareton, Victor. *La Réforme et les guerres civiles en Vivarais, particulièrement dans la région de Privas (Valentinois), 1544–1632.* Paris: Documents d'Histoire, 1913.

Chartier, Roger. *Cultural History: Between Practices and Representations.* Translated by Lydia G. Cochrane. Ithaca, NY: Cornell University Press, 1988.

———. *The Cultural Origins of the French Revolution.* Translated by Lydia G. Cochrane. Durham, NC: Duke University Press, 1991.

———. "Le Monde comme représentation." *Annales ESC* 44 (1989): 1505–1520.

———. "Pamphlets et gazettes." In *Histoire de l'édition française*, vol. 1: *Le Livre conquérant: Du Moyen Age au milieu du XVIIe siècle*, edited by Roger Chartier and Henri-Jean Martin, 501–526. Paris: Fayard and Cercle de la Librairie, 1989.

Chastel, André. *French Art: The Ancien Régime, 1620–1775.* Translated by Deke Dusinberre. Paris: Flammarion, 1996.

Chastel, Rémy. "Les Luttes des Mendois pour la conquête du pouvoir municipal sous l'Ancien Régime." *Revue du Gévaudan, des Causes et des Cévennes* 2 (1996): 65–82.

Châtellier, Louis. "Les Jésuites et l'ordre social." In *Les Jésuites à l'âge baroque (1540–1640)*, edited by Luce Giard and Louis de Vaucelles, 143–154. Grenoble: Jérôme Millon, 1996.

Chaussiand-Nogaret, Guy. *Histoire des élites en France du XVIe au XXe siècle. L'Honneur, le mérite, l'argent.* Paris: Tallandier, 1991.

Chevalier, Bernard. *Les Bonnes Villes de France du XIVe au XVIe siècles.* Paris: Aubier, 1982.

Chevalier, Françoise. "Les Difficultés d'application de l'édit de Nantes d'après les cahiers des plaintes (1599–1660)." In *Coexister dans l'intolerance. L'édit de Nantes (1598)*, ed. Michel Grandjean and Bernard Roussel, 303–320. Geneva: Labor et Fides, 1998.

Chevallier, Pierre. *Louis XIII.* Paris: Fayard, 1979.

Cholvy, Gérard, ed. *Histoire de Montpellier.* 2nd ed. Toulouse: Privat, 2001.

Christin, Olivier. *La Paix de religion. L'autonomisation de la raison politique au XVIe siècle.* Paris: Seuil, 1997.

Church, William F. *Richelieu and Reason of State.* Princeton, NJ: Princeton University Press, 1972.

Clarke, Jack Alden. *Huguenot Warrior: The Life and Times of Henri de Rohan, 1579–1638.* The Hague, 1966.

Clarke de Dromantin, Patrick and Gaston de Lestang. "Les Qualifications nobles sous l'Ancien Régime. Définition et utilisation." In *L'Identité nobiliaire. Dix siècles de métamorphoses (IXe–XIXe siècles)*, edited by Jean-Marie Constant, 180–188. Beaufay: Brunet, 1997.

Cocula, Anne-Marie. "La Fin du parti protestant en Guyenne." In *Adhésion et résistances à l'État en France et en Espagne, 1600–1660*, edited by Anne-Marie Cocula and Marie Boisson-Gabarron, 73–90. Pessac: Presses Universitaires de Bordeaux, 2001.

Collins, James B. *Fiscal Limits of Absolutism: Direct Taxation in Early Seventeenth-Century France.* Berkeley: University of California Press, 1988.

Connell, R.W. "The Big Picture: Masculinities in Recent World History." *Theory and Society* 22 (October 1993): 597–623.

———. *Masculinities.* Cambridge: Polity, 1995.

Conner, Philip. *Huguenot Heartland: Montauban and Southern French Calvinism during the Wars of Religion.* Aldershot, UK: Ashgate, 2002.

Constant, Jean-Marie. *Nobles et paysans en Beauce aux XVIème et XVIIIème siècles.* Lille: Université de Lille III, 1981.

———. "Noblesse et élite au XVIe siècle. Les problèmes de l'identité noble." In *L'Identité nobiliaire. Dix siècles de métamorphoses (IXe–XIXe siècles),* edited by Jean-Marie Constant, 45–61. Beaufay: Brunet, 1997.

———. *La Noblesse française aux XVIe et XVIIe siècles.* Paris: Hachette, 1985.

———, ed. *L'Identité nobiliaire. Dix siècles de métamorphoses (IXe–XIXe siècles).* Beaufay: Brunet, 1997.

Contamine, Philippe, ed. *Histoire militaire de la France.* Vol. 1. *Des origines à 1715.* Paris: Presses Universitaires de France, 1992.

Cornette, Joël. "Crise des valeurs et recomposition sociale au temps d'Henri IV. Olivier de Serres ou le modèle du parfait gentilhomme des champs." In *Le Second Ordre. L'idéal nobiliaire. Hommage à Ellery Schalk,* edited by Chantal Grell and Arnaud Ramière de Fortanier, 275–289. Paris: Presses de l'Université de Paris-Sorbonne, 1999.

———. "La Révolution militaire et l'état moderne." *Revue d'histoire moderne et contemporaine* 41 (1994): 696–709.

———. *Le Roi de guerre. Essai sur la souveraineté dans la France du Grand Siècle.* Paris: Payot & Rivages, 1993.

Corvisier, André. *Armies and Societies in Europe, 1494–1789.* Translated by Abigail T. Siddall. Bloomington: Indiana University Press, 1979.

———. "Clientèles et fidélités dans l'armée française aux XVIIe et XVIIIe siècles." In *Hommage à Roland Mousnier. Clientèles et fidélités en Europe à l'époque moderne,* 213–236. Paris: Presses Universitaires de France, 1981.

———. "Guerre et mentalités au XVIIe siècle." *XVIIe siècle* 148 (1985): 219–232.

———. "La Paix nécessaire mais incertaine, 1598–1635." In *Histoire Militaire de la France,* vol. 1: *Des origins à 1715,* edited by Philippe Contamine, 331–351. Paris: Presses Universitaires de France, 1992.

Croubois, Claude, ed. *L'Officier français des origines à nos jours.* Saint-Jean-d'Angély: Bordessoules, 1987.

Crouzet, Denis. "Les Fondements idéologiques de la royauté d'Henri IV." In *Avènement d'Henry IV, quatrième centenaire. Provinces et pays du Midi au temps d'Henri de Navarre: 1555–1589.* Pau: Association Henri IV, 1989, 1990.

———. *Les Guerriers de Dieu. La violence au temps des troubles de religion, vers 1525–vers 1610.* 2 vols. Seyssel: Champ Vallon, 1990.

Cunningham, Andrew, and Ole Peter Grell. *The Four Horsemen of the Apocalypse: Religion, War, Famine, and Death in Reformation Europe.* Cambridge: Cambridge University Press, 2000.

Cuomo, Serafina. "The Sinews of War: Ancient Catapults." *Science* 303 (February 2004): 771–773.

Das, Veena. *Life and Words: Violence and the Descent into the Ordinary.* Berkeley: University of California Press, 2007.

Das, Veena, Arthur Kleinman, Margaret Lock, Mamphela Ramphele, and Pamela Reynolds, eds. *Remaking a World: Violence, Social Suffering, and Recovery*. Berkeley: University of California Press, 2001.

Das, Veena, Arthur Kleinman, Mamphela Ramphele, and Pamela Reynolds, eds. *Violence and Subjectivity*. Berkeley: University of California Press, 2000.

Daubresse, Sylvie. *Le Parlement de Paris ou la voix de la raison (1559–1589)*. Geneva: Droz, 2005.

Davies, Joan. "The Duc de Montmorency, Philip II and the House of Savoy: A Neglected Aspect of the Sixteenth-Century French Civil Wars." *English Historical Review* (1990): 870–892.

———. "Neither Politique nor Patriot? Henri, Duc de Montmorency and Philip II, 1582–1589." *Historical Journal* 34 (1991): 539–566.

———. "Persecution and Protestantism: Toulouse, 1562–1575." *Historical Journal* 22 (March 1979): 31–51.

Davis, Natalie Zemon. *The Return of Martin Guerre*. Cambridge, MA: Harvard University Press, 1983.

———. "Rites of Violence." In *Society and Culture in Early Modern France*, 152–187. Stanford, CA: Stanford University Press, 1975.

———. "Women on Top." In *Society and Culture in Early Modern France*, 124–151. Stanford, CA: Stanford University Press, 1975.

D'Cruze, Shani, and Anupama Rao, eds. *Violence, Vulnerability and Embodiment: Gender and History*. Oxford: Blackwell, 2005.

Delumeau, Jean, and Daniel Roche, eds. *Histoire des pères et de la paternité*. Paris: Larousse, 1990.

Denis, Lucien, and Simone Foray. *Le Siege de Privas en 1629*. Privas: Société d'Histoire et d'Archéologie de Privas, 1994.

Dent, Julien. *Crisis in Finance: Crown, Financiers, and Society in Seventeenth-Century France*. London: David and Charles, 1973.

Desachy-Delclos, Sylvie. "Les Élites militaires en Rouergue au XVIe siècle." *Annales du Midi* 108 (January–March 1996): 9–27.

Descimon, Robert. "The Birth of the Nobility of the Robe: Dignity versus Privilege in the Parlement of Paris, 1500–1700." Translated by Orest Ranum. In *Changing Identities in Early Modern France*, edited by Michael Wolfe, 95–123. Durham, NC: Duke University Press, 1997.

Descimon, Robert, and José Javier Ruiz Ibáñez. *Les Ligueurs de l'exil. Le refuge catholique français après 1594*. Seyssel: Champ Vallon, 2005.

Dewald, Jonathan. *Aristocratic Experience and the Origins of Modern Culture: France, 1570–1715*. Berkeley: University of California Press, 1993.

———. *The European Nobility, 1400–1800*. Cambridge: Cambridge University Press, 1996.

Dewald, Jonathan, Geoffrey Parker, Michael Marmé, and J. B. Shank. "Forum: The General Crisis of the Seventeenth Century Revisited." *American Historical Review* 113 (October 2008): 1029–1099.

Deyon, Pierre, and Solange Deyon. *Henri de Rohan. Huguenot de plume et d'épée, 1579–1638*. Paris: Perrin, 2000.

Dictionnaire historique de la langue française. Edited by Alain Rey et al. Paris: Dictionnaires Le Robert, 1992.

Diefendorf, Barbara B. *Beneath the Cross: Catholics and Huguenots in Sixteenth-Century Paris.* Oxford: Oxford University Press, 1991.

———. *From Penitence to Charity: Pious Women and the Catholic Reformation in Paris.* Oxford: Oxford University Press, 2004.

———. "The Huguenot Psalter and the Faith of French Protestants in the Sixteenth Century." In *Culture and Identity in Early Modern Europe (1500–1800): Essays in Honor of Natalie Zemon Davis,* edited by Barbara B. Diefendorf and Carla Hesse, 41–63. Ann Arbor: University of Michigan Press, 1993.

———. *Paris City Councillors in the Sixteenth Century: The Politics of Patrimony.* Princeton, NJ: Princeton University Press, 1983.

Dirks, Nicholas B., Geoff Eley, and Sherry B. Ortner, eds. *Culture/Power/History: A Reader in Contemporary Social Theory.* Princeton, NJ: Princeton University Press, 1994.

Downing, Brian M. *The Military Revolution and Political Change: Origins of Democracy and Autocracy in Early Modern Europe.* Princeton, NJ: Princeton University Press, 1992.

Doyle, William. *Venality: The Sale of Offices in Eighteenth-Century France.* Oxford: Oxford University Press, 1996.

Drévillon, Hervé. *L'Impôt du sang. Le métier des armes sous Louis XIV.* Paris: Tallandier, 2005.

Dubled, Henri. "Le Duc Henri de Rohan et la révolte des protestants du Midi jusqu'à la paix d'Alès (1617–1629)." *Annales du Midi* 99 (January–March 1987): 53–78.

Dubost, Jean-François. "Absolutisme et centralisation en Languedoc au XVIIe siècle (1620–1690)." *Revue d'histoire moderne et contemporaine* 37 (1990): 369–397.

———. *La France italienne, XVIe–XVIIe siècle.* Paris: Aubier, 1997.

Dubourg, Jaques. *Les Guerres de religion dans le Sud-Ouest.* Bordeaux: Sud-Ouest, 1992.

Duby, Georges, ed. *Histoire de la France urbaine.* Vol. 3. *La Ville classique de la Renaissance aux Révolutions,* edited by Emmanuel Le Roy Ladurie. Paris: Seuil, 1981.

Duccini, Hélène. *Concini. Grandeur et misère du favori de Marie de Médicis.* Paris: Albin Michel, 1991.

———. *Faire voir, faire croire. L'opinion publique sous Louis XIII.* Seyssel: Champ Vallon, 2003.

Dupâquier, Jacques, et al. *Histoire de la population française.* Vol. 2, *De la Renaissance à 1789.* Paris: Presses Universitaires de France, 1988.

Durand-Tullou, Adrienne. *Le Loup du Causse. La légende d'un compagnon de Rohan (1594–1638).* Paris: Payot & Rivages, 1994.

Elias, Norbert. *The Civilizing Process.* Translated by Edmund Jephcott. Oxford: Blackwell, 1994. Originally published as *Über den Prozess der Zivilisation,* 2 vols. (Basel: Haus zum Falker, 1939).

———. *The Court Society.* Translated by Edmund Jephcott. New York: Pantheon Books, 1983. Originally published as *Die höfische Gesellschaft* (Darmstadt: Hermann Luchterhand Verlag, 1969).

Elliott, J. H. *Richelieu and Olivares.* Cambridge: Cambridge University Press, 1984.

Elzière, Jean-Bernard. *Histoire des Budos. Seigneurs de Budos en Guyenne et de Portes-Bertrand en Languedoc.* Nîmes: Renaissance du château de Portes, 1978.

Entrevaux, Benoit d'. *Armorial du Vivarais*. 1908. Reprint. Marseille: Laffitte, 1973.

Estebe, Janine. "The Rites of Violence: Religious Riot in Sixteenth-Century France: A Comment." *Past and Present* 67 (May 1975): 127–130.

Eurich, S. Amanda. *The Economics of Power: The Private Finances of the House of Foix-Navarre-Albret during the Religious Wars*. Kirksville, MO: Sixteenth Century Journal, 1994.

———. "'Speaking the King's Language': The Huguenot Magistrates of Castres and Pau." In *Society and Culture in the Huguenot World, 1559–1685*, edited by Raymond A. Mentzer and Andrew Spicer, 175–192. Cambridge: Cambridge University Press, 2002.

Fabre, Chislaine, and Thierry Lochard. "Montpellier: Une Création urbaine." *Monuments historiques* 187 (May–June 1993): 23–28.

Farr, James Richard. *Authority and Sexuality in Early Modern Burgundy (1550–1730)*. New York: Oxford University Press, 1995.

Fauré, Hélène. "La Noblesse dans le diocese de Carcassonne du XVIème siècle a la révolution." 2 vols. Thesis, École Nationale des Chartes, 1990.

Favre, Jean. *Histoire militaire vivaroise. Le Brave Brison, 1619–1628*. Marseille: Leconte, 1961.

Fehleison, Jill R. "Appealing to the Senses: The Forty Hours Celebrations in the Duchy of Chablais, 1597–98." *Sixteenth Century Journal* 36 (Summer 2005): 375–396.

Fessenden, Nicholas Buck. "Épernon and Guyenne: Provincial Politics under Louis XIII." Ph.D. diss., Columbia University, 1972.

Fevre, Lucien. *Life in Renaissance France*. Translated by Marian Rothstein. Cambridge, MA: Harvard University Press, 1977.

Fisher, Douglas. "The Price Revolution: A Monetary Interpretation." *Journal of Economic History* 49 (December 1989): 883–902.

Foa, Jérémie. "Making Peace: The Commissions for Enforcing the Pacification Edicts in the Reign of Charles IX (1560–1574)." *French History* 18, 3 (2004): 256–274.

Fontaine, Laurence. *History of Pedlars in Europe*. Translated by Vicki Whittaker. Durham, NC: Duke University Press, 1996.

———. "Rôle économique de la parenté." *Annales de Démographie Historique* (1995): 5–16.

———, ed. *Alternative Exchanges: Second-Hand Circulations from the Sixteenth Century to the Present*. New York: Berghahn Books, 2007.

Fontaine, Laurence, and Jürgen Schlumbohm. "Household Strategies: An Introduction." In *Household Strategies for Survival, 1600–2000: Fission, Faction and Cooperation*, edited by Laurence Fontaine and Jürgen Schlumbohm, 1–17. *International Review of Social History*, suppl. 8. Cambridge: Cambridge University Press, 2000.

Ford, Franklin L. *Robe and Sword: The Regrouping of the French Aristocracy after Louis XIV*. 1953. Rev. ed. Cambridge, MA: Harvard University Press, 1962.

Formisano, Ronald P. "The Concept of Political Culture." *Journal of Interdisciplinary History* 31 (Winter 2001): 393–426.

Fornerod, Nicolas. "L'Édit de Nantes et le problème de la coexistence confessionnelle dans la pensée de Phlippe Duplessis-Mornay." In *Coexister dans l'intolérance. L'édit de Nantes (1598)*, edited by Michel Grandjean and Bernard Roussel, 225–252. Geneva: Labor et Fides, 1998.

Fraser, Nancy. "Rethinking the Public Sphere: A Contribution to the Critique of Actually Existing Democracy." In *Habermas and the Public Sphere*, edited by Craig Calhoun, 109–142. Cambridge, MA: MIT Press, 1992.

Freedman, Joseph F. "Philosophical Writings on the Family in Sixteenth- and Seventeenth-Century Europe." *Journal of Family History* 27 (July 2002): 292–342.

Garrison, Janine. "Les Grands du parti protestant et l'édit de Nantes." In *Coexister dans l'intolérance. L'édit de Nantes (1598)*, edited by Michel Grandjean and Bernard Roussel, 175–186. Geneva: Labor et Fides, 1998.

———. *Protestants du Midi (1559–1598)*. Toulouse: Privat, 1980.

Goldstone, Jack A. "Monetary versus Velocity Interpretations of the 'Price Revolution': A Comment." *Journal of Economic History* 51 (March 1991): 176–181.

———. *Revolution and Rebellion in the Early Modern World*. Berkeley: University of California Press, 1991.

Goodbar, Richard L., ed. *The Edict of Nantes: Five Essays and a New Translation*. Bloomington: National Huguenot Society, 1998.

Goody, Jack. "Inheritance, Property and Women: Some Comparative Considerations." In *Family and Inheritance: Rural Society in Western Europe, 1200–1800*, edited by Jack Goody, Joan Thirsk, and E. P. Thompson, 10–36. Cambridge: Cambridge University Press, 1976.

Goubert, Pierre. *The French Peasantry in the Seventeenth Century*. Translated by Ian Patterson. Cambridge: Cambridge University Press, 1986.

Gouron, André. "Le Ban et l'arrière-ban d'après les sources languedociennes." In *Fédération historique du Languedoc méditerranéen et du Roussillon. XXVIIme et XXVIIIme congrès, Perpignan-Saint-Gilles (1953–1953)*, 87–100. Montpellier: Paul Déhan, 1956.

Grandjean, Michel, and Bernard Roussel, eds. *Coexister dans l'intolérance. L'édit de Nantes (1598)*. Geneva: Labor et Fides, 1998.

Graule, Henri. *Histoire de Lescure, ancien fief immédiat du Saint-Siège et de ses seigneurs*. Paris: Victor Palmé, 1885.

Greenblatt, Stephen. *Renaissance Self-Fashioning from More to Shakespeare*. Chicago: University of Chicago Press, 1980.

Greengrass, Mark. *France in the Age of Henri IV: The Struggle for Stability*. 1984. Reprint, New York: Longman, 1995.

———. "Functions and Limits of Political Clientelism in France before Cardinal Richelieu." In *L'État ou le roi. Les fondations de la modernité monarchique en France (XVIe–XVIIe siècles)*, 69–82. Paris: Maison des sciences de l'homme, 1996.

———. *Governing Passions: Peace and Reform in the French Kingdom, 1576–1585*. Oxford: Oxford University Press, 2007.

———. "Informal Networks in Sixteenth-Century French Protestantism." In *Society and Culture in the Huguenot World, 1559–1685*, edited by Raymond A. Mentzer and Andrew Spicer, 78–97. Cambridge: Cambridge University Press, 2002.

———. "The Later Wars of Religion in the French Midi." In *The European Crisis of the 1590s: Essays in Comparative History*, edited by Peter Clark. London: George Allen and Unwin, 1985.

————. "Noble Affinities in Early Modern France: The Case of Henri I de Montmorency, Constable of France." *European History Quarterly* 16 (1986): 275–311.

————. "Property and Politics in Sixteenth-Century France: The Landed Fortune of Constable Anne de Montmorency." *French History* 2 (1988): 371–398.

————. "The *Sainte Union* in the Provinces: The Case of Toulouse." *Sixteenth Century Journal* 14 (1983): 469–496.

Greenshields, Malcolm. *An Economy of Violence in Early Modern France: Crime and Justice in the Haute Auvergne, 1587–1664*. University Park: Pennsylvania State University Press, 1994.

Gregory, Brad S. *Salvation at Stake: Christian Martyrdom in Early Modern Europe*. Cambridge, MA: Harvard University Press, 1999.

Grell, Chantal, and Arnaud Ramière de Fortanier. *Le Second Ordre: L'idéal nobiliaire. Hommage à Ellery Schalk*. Paris: Presses de l'Université de Paris-Sorbonne, 1999.

Grell, Ole Peter, and Bob Scribner, eds. *Tolerance and Intolerance in the European Reformation*. Cambridge: Cambridge University Press, 1996.

Grunwald Center for the Graphic Arts. *La Gravure française à la Renaissance à la Bibliothèque Nationale de France*. Los Angeles: Grunwald Center for the Graphic Arts, 1994.

Guggenheim, Ann H. "The Calvinist Notables of Nimes during the Era of the Religious Wars." *Sixteenth Century Journal* 3 (April 1972): 80–96.

Guicharnaud, Hélène. *Montauban au XVIIᵉ, 1560–1685. Urbanisme et architecture*. Paris: Picard, 1991.

Guilaine, Jean, and Daniel Fabre, eds. *Histoire de Carcassonne*. Toulouse: Privas, 1984.

Gutton, J. P. *Domestiques et serviteurs dans la France de l'Ancien Régime*. Paris: Aubier Montaigne, 1981.

Haag, Eugène, and Émile Haag. *La France protestante ou vies des protestants français qui se sont fait un nom dans l'histoire depuis les premiers temps de la réformation jusqu'à la reconnaissance du principe de la liberté des cultes par l'assemblée nationale*. 10 vols. 1847–1860. Reprint, Geneva: Slatkine, 1966.

Habermas, Jürgen. *The Structural Transformation of the Public Sphere: An Inquiry into a Category of Bourgeois Society*, translated by Thomas Burger and Frederick Lawrence. Cambridge, MA: MIT Press, 1989.

Hale, J. R. *War and Society in Renaissance Europe, 1450–1620*. Baltimore: Johns Hopkins University Press, 1985.

Hall, Bert S. *Weapons and Warfare in Renaissance Europe: Gunpowder, Technology, and Tactics*. Baltimore: Johns Hopkins University Press, 1997.

Hamscher, Albert N. *The Parlement of Paris after the Fronde, 1653–1673*. Pittsburgh: University of Pittsburgh Press, 1976.

Hanley, Sarah. *The Lit de justice of the Kings of France: Constitutional Ideology in Legend, Ritual, and Discourse*. Princeton, NJ: Princeton University Press, 1983.

Hanlon, Gregory. *Confession and Community in Seventeenth-Century France: Catholic and Protestant Coexistence in Aquitaine*. Philadelphia: University of Pennsylvania Press, 1993.

———. "Piété populaire et intervention des moines dans les miracles et les sanctuaires miraculeux en Agenais-Condomois au XVIIᵉ siècle." *Annales du Midi* 97 (1985): 115–127.

Harding, Robert R. *Anatomy of a Power Elite: The Provincial Governors of Early Modern France*. New Haven, CT: Yale University Press, 1978.

Hardwick, Juile. *The Practice of Patriarchy: Gender and the Politics of Household Authority in Early Modern France*. University Park: Pennsylvania State University Press, 1998.

Hardÿ de Périni, Édouard. *Batailles françaises*. Vol. 3. *Louis XIII et Richelieu*. Châteauroux: A. Majesté & L. Bouchardeau; Paris: E. Flammarion, 1894–1906.

Hareven, Tamara K. "What Difference Does It Make?" *Social Science History* 20 (Autumn 1996): 317–344.

Harris, Robin. *Valois Guyenne: A Study of Politics, Government and Society in Late Medieval France*. Woodbridge, Suffolk, UK: Boydell Press, 1994.

Hayden, J. Michael. *France and the Estates General of 1614*. New York: Cambridge University Press, 1974.

Hénault, Anne. *Le Pouvoir comme passion*. Paris: Presses Universitaires de France, 1994.

Henshall, Nicholas. *The Myth of Absolutism: Change and Continuity in Early Modern Monarchy*. London: Longman, 1992.

Hepp, Noemi. "Considérations morales et politiques autour d'Henri de Montmorency. Une Polyphonie discordante." In *Ethics and Politics in Seventeenth-Century France: Essays in Honour of Derek A. Watts*, edited by Keith Cameron and Elizabeth Woodrough, 83–91. Exeter, UK: University of Exeter Press, 1996.

Herman, Arthur, Jr. "The Huguenot Republic and Antirepublicanism in Seventeenth-Century France." *Journal of the History of Ideas* 53 (April–June 1992): 249–269.

———. "The Language of Fidelity in Early Modern France." *Journal of Modern History* 67 (1995): 1–24.

Herzfeld, Michael. *Cultural Intimacy: Social Poetics in the Nation-State*. New York: Routledge, 1997.

Hickey, Daniel. *The Coming of French Absolutism: The Struggle for Tax Reform in the Province of Dauphiné, 1540–1640*. Toronto: Toronto University Press, 1986.

———. "Le Rôle de l'État dans la Réforme catholique. Une inspection du diocèse de Poitiers lors des Grands Jours de 1634." *Revue historique* 307 (2003): 939–961.

Hoffman, Philip T. *Church and Community in the Diocese of Lyon, 1500–1789*. New Haven, CT: Yale University Press, 1984.

Hohendahl, Peter U. "Critical Theory, Public Sphere and Culture: Jürgen Habermas and His Critics." *New German Critique* 16 (1979): 89–118.

Holt, Mack P. *The French Wars of Religion, 1562–1629*. Cambridge: Cambridge University Press, 1995.

Hunt, Lynn. *The Family Romance of the French Revolution*. Berkeley: University of California Press, 1992.

———. *Politics, Culture, and Class in the French Revolution*. Berkeley: University of California Press, 1984.

Huppert, George. *Les Bourgeois gentilhommes: An Essay on the Definition of Elites in Renaissance France.* Chicago: University of Chicago Press, 1977.

Irvine, Frederick M. "From Renaissance City to Ancien Régime Capital: Montpellier, c. 1500–c. 1600." In *Cities and Social Change in Early Modern France,* edited by Philip Benedict, 107–109. London: Unwin Hyman, 1989.

Jackson, Richard A. *Vive le Roi! A History of the French Coronation from Charles V to Charles X.* Chapel Hill: University of North Carolina Press, 1984.

James, Alan. "Huguenot Militancy and the Seventeenth-Century Wars of Religion." In *Society and Culture in the Huguenot World, 1559–1685,* edited by Raymond A. Mentzer and Andrew Spicer, 209–223. Cambridge: Cambridge University Press, 2002.

Jones, Colin. "The Military Revolution and the Professionalisation of the French Army under the Ancien Regime." In *The Military Revolution Debate: Readings on the Military Transformation of Early Modern Europe,* edited by Clifford J. Rogers, 149–168. Boulder, CO: Westview Press, 1995.

Jordan, Terry G. *The European Culture Area: A Systematic Geography.* 2nd ed. New York: Harper & Row, 1988.

Jouanna, Arlette. "De la ville marchande à la capitale administrative (XVIe siècle)." In *Histoire de Montpellier,* edited by Gérard Cholvy, 152–155. 2nd ed. Toulouse: Privat, 2001.

———. "Des réseaux d'amitié aux clientèles centralisées. Les provinces et la cour (France XVIe–XVIIe siècle)." In *Patronages et clientélismes, 1550–1750 (France, Angleterre, Espagne, Italie),* edited by Charles Giry-Deloison and Roger Mettam, 21–38. Lille: Université Charles de Gaulle (Lille III) and Institut Français du Royaume-Uni, 1995.

———. *Le Devoir de révolte. La noblesse française et la gestation de l'État moderne, 1559–1661.* Paris: Fayard, 1989.

———. *La France du XVIe siècle, 1483–1598.* Paris: Presses Universitaires de France, 1996.

———. *L'Idée de race en France au XVIe siècle et au début du XVIIe.* Rev. ed. 2 vols. Montpellier: Presses de l'Imprimerie de Recherche-Université Paul Valéry (Montpellier III), 1981.

———. "Mémoire nobiliaire. Le Rôle de la réputation dans les preuves de noblesse. L'Exemple des barons des États de Languedoc." In *Le Second Ordre: L'idéal nobiliaire. Hommage à Ellery Schalk,* edited by Chantal Grell and Arnaud Ramière de Fortanier, 197–206. Paris: Presses de l'Université de Paris-Sorbonne, 1999.

———. "Perception et appreciation de l'anoblissement dans la France du XVIe siècle et du debut du XVIIe siècle." In *L'Anoblissement en France, XVème–XVIIIème siècles. Théories et réalités.* Bordeaux: Université de Bordeaux III, 1985.

———. "Protection des fidèles et fidélités au roi. L'exemple de Henri Ier de Montmorency-Damville." In *Hommage à Roland Mousnier. Clientèles et fidélités en Europe à l'époque moderne,* 279–296. Paris: Presses Universitaires de France, 1981.

———. "Réflexions sur les relations internobiliaires en France aux XVIe et XVIIe siècles." *French Historical Studies* 17 (1992): 872–881.

Jouanna, Arlette, Jacqueline Boucher, Dominique Biloghi, and Guy Le Thiec, eds. *Histoire et dictionnaire des guerres de religion.* Paris: Robert Laffont, 1998.

Jouhaud, Christian. "Imprimer l'événement. La Rochelle à Paris." In *Les usages de l'imprimé (XVᵉ–XIXᵉ siècle)*, edited by Roger Chartier, 381–438. Paris: Fayard and Centre National des Lettres, 1987.

———. "Lisibilité et persuasion. Les placards politiques." In *Les Usages de l'imprimé (XVᵉ–XIXᵉ siècle)*, edited by Roger Chartier, 309–342. Paris: Fayard and Centre National des Lettres, 1987.

Juergensmeyer, Mark. *Terror in the Mind of God: The Global Rise of Religious Violence.* Rev. ed. Berkeley: University of California Press, 2001.

———, ed. *Violence and the Sacred in the Modern World.* London: Frank Cass, 1992.

Kalas, Robert J. "Marriage, Clientage, Office Holding, and the Advancement of the Early Modern French Nobility: The Noailles Family of Limousin." *Sixteenth Century Journal* 27 (Summer 1996): 365–383.

———. "The Noble Widow's Place in the Patriarchal Household: The Life and Career of Jeanne de Gontault." *Sixteenth Century Journal* 24 (Autumn 1993): 519–539.

Kalyvas, Stathis N. *The Logic of Violence in Civil War.* Cambridge: Cambridge University Press, 2006.

Kelley, Donald R. *The Beginning of Ideology: Consciousness and Society in the French Reformation.* Cambridge: Cambridge University Press, 1981.

Kermina, Françoise. *Les Montmorency. Grandeur et déclin.* Paris: Perrin, 2002.

Kettering, Sharon. "Clientage during the French Wars of Religion." *Sixteenth Century Journal* 20 (Summer 1989): 221–239.

———. "Friendship and Clientage in Early Modern France." *French History* 6 (June 1992): 139–158.

———. "Gift-Giving and Patronage in Early Modern France." *French History* 2 (June 1988): 131–151.

———. "The Historical Development of Political Clientelism." *Journal of Interdisciplinary History* 18 (Winter 1988): 419–447.

———. "The Household Service of Early Modern French Noblewomen," *French Historical Studies* 20 (Winter 1997): 55–85.

———. *Judicial Politics and Urban Revolt in Seventeenth-Century France: The Parliament of Aix, 1629–1659.* Princeton, NJ: Princeton University Press, 1978.

———. "Patronage in Early Modern France." *French Historical Studies* 17 (Autumn 1992): 839–862.

———. *Patrons, Brokers, and Clients in Seventeenth-Century France.* New York: Oxford University Press, 1986.

———. "State Control and Municipal Authority in France." In *Edo and Paris: Urban Life and the State in the Early Modern Era,* edited by James L. McClain, John H. Merriman, and Ugawa Kaoru, 86–101. Ithaca, NY: Cornell University Press, 1994.

Kleinman, Arthur, Veena Das, and Margaret Lock, eds. *Social Suffering.* Berkeley: University of California Press, 1997.

Labatut, Jean-Pierre. *Les Ducs et pairs de la France au XVIIᵉ siècle. Étude sociale.* Paris: Presses Universitaires de France, 1972.

Lacombe-Saboly, Michèle, "Le Compte de voyage de Dominique Guaches, facteur d'un pastelier toulousain au XVIᵉ siècle." *Annales du Midi* 110 (April–June 1998): 169–184.

Lafage, Valérie. "Montpellier et le siège de 1622." In *Adhésion et résistances à l'État en France et en Espagne, 1600–1660,* edited by Anne-Marie Cocula and Marie Boisson-Gabarron, 57–72. Pessac: Presses Universitaires de Bordeaux, 2001.

Lamoignon de Basville, Nicolas. *Mémoires pour servir à l'histoire de Languedoc.* Amsterdam: Pierre Boyer, 1734.

Lançon, Pierre, "Les Confréries du Rosaire en Rouergue aux XVIe et XVIIe siècles." *Annales du Midi* 96 (1984): 121–133.

Langer, Herbert. *The Thirty Years' War.* Translated by C. S. V. Salt. 1978. Reprint. New York: Dorset Press, 1990.

Larcade, Véronique. "La Clientèle du duc d'Épernon dans le Sud-Ouest du royaume." *Annales du Midi* 108 (January–March 1996): 29–38.

———. "La Rébellion des Grands en France (1620–1660): 'le passé d'une illusion'?" In *Adhésion et résistances à l'État en France et en Espagne, 1600–1660,* edited by Anne-Marie Cocula and Marie Boisson-Gabarron, 39–56. Pessac: Presses Universitaires de Bordeaux, 2001.

Larguier, Gilbert. "Narbonne et la voie méditerranéenne du pastel (XVe–XVIe siècles)." *Annales du Midi* 110 (April–June 1998): 149–167.

La Roque, Louis de. *Armorial de la noblesse de Languedoc. Généralité de Montpellier.* 2 vols. 1860. Reprint. Montpellier: Le Clerc, 1995.

———. *Armorial de la noblesse de Languedoc. Généralité de Toulouse.* 1863. Reprint. Marseille: Laffitte, 1980.

Le Brun, Jacques. "Théologie et spiritualité." In *Le XVIIe siècle. Diversité et cohérence,* edited by Jacques Truchet, 218–219. Paris: Berger-Levrault, 1992.

Le Person, Xavier. *"Practiques" et "Practiqueurs". La vie politique à la fin du règne de Henri III (1584–1589).* Geneva: Librairie Droz, 2002.

Le Roux, Nicolas. *La Faveur du roi. Mignons et courtisans au temps des derniers Valois (vers 1547–vers 1589).* Seyssel: Champ Vallon, 2000.

Le Roy Ladurie, Emmanuel. "Family Structures and Inheritance Customs in Sixteenth-Century France." In *Family and Inheritance: Rural Society in Western Europe, 1200–1800,* edited by Jack Goody, Joan Thirsk, and E. P. Thompson, 37–70. Cambridge: Cambridge University Press, 1976.

———. *Les Paysans de Languedoc.* 1969. 2nd ed. 2 vols. Paris: École des Hautes Études en Sciences Sociales, 1985.

———. *The Peasants of Languedoc.* Translated by John Day. Chicago: University of Chicago Press, 1974.

Le Roy Ladurie, Emmanuel, and Jean-François Fitou. "Mariages saint-simoniens et hypergamie féminine." In *Mesurer et comprendre. Mélanges offerts à Jacques Dupaquier,* edited by Jean-Pierre Bardet, François Lebrun, and René Le Mée, 361–380. Paris: Presses Universitaires de France, 1993.

Levi, Primo. *The Drowned and the Saved.* New York: Vintage Books, 1989.

Lignereux, Yann. "Les 'trois corps du roi'. Les entrées d'Henri IV à Lyon, 1594–1596." *XVIIe siècle* 212 (July–September 2001): 405–415.

Liotard, Charles. "Episodes des premiers temps de la réforme a Nismes (1560–1651)." *Mémoires de l'académie de Nîmes* ser. 7, 7 (1884): 319–362.

Lot, Ferdinand. "Les Armées en présence à la bataille de Dreux." *Revue historique des armées* 152 (1983): 40–45.

———. *Recherches sur les effectifs des armées françaises. Des guerres d'Italie aux guerres de religion, 1494–1562.* Paris: SEVPEN, 1962.

Love, Ronald S. "'All the King's Horsemen': The Equestrian Army of Henri IV, 1585–1598." *Sixteenth Century Journal* 22 (1991): 511–533.

———. "Henri IV et Ivry, le monarque chef de guerre." *Revue historique des armées* 182 (1991): 11–20.

Lowenstein, Steven Mark. "Resistance to Absolutism: Huguenot Organization in Languedoc, 1621–1622." Ph.D. diss. Princeton University, 1972.

Lublinskaya, A. D. *French Absolutism: The Crucial Phase, 1620–1629.* Translated by Brian Pearce. Cambridge: Cambridge University Press, 1968.

Luciani, Isabelle. "Les Jeux floraux de Toulouse au XVIIᵉ siècle. Pratiques poétiques, identité urbaine, intégration monarchique." *Annales du Midi* 114 (April–June 2002): 201–223.

Lukowski, Jerzy. *The European Nobility in the Eighteenth Century.* Basingstoke, UK: Palgrave Macmillan, 2003.

Luria, Keith. *Sacred Boundaries: Religious Coexistence and Conflict in Early-Modern France.* Washington, DC: Catholic University of America Press, 2005.

———. "Separated by Death? Burials, Cemeteries, and Confessional Boundaries in Seventeenth-Century France." *French Historical Studies* 24 (Spring 2001): 185–222.

Lux-Sterritt, Laurence. "Between the Cloister and the World: The Successful Compromise of the Ursulines of Toulouse, 1604–1616." *French History* 16 (September 2002): 247–268.

Lynn, John A. *Bayonets of the Republic: Motivation and Tactics in the Army of Revolutionary France, 1791–94.* Urbana: University of Illinois Press, 1984.

———. "Clio in Arms: The Role of the Military Variable in Shaping History." *Journal of Military History* 55 (January 1991): 83–95.

———. "The Evolution of Army Style in the Modern West, 800–2000." *International History Review* 18 (August 1996): 505–545.

———. *Giant of the Grand Siècle: The French Army, 1610–1715.* Cambridge: Cambridge University Press, 1997.

———. "The History of Logistics and Supplying War." In *Feeding Mars: Logistics in Western Warfare from the Middle Ages to the Present,* edited by John A. Lynn, 9–27. Boulder, CO: Westview Press, 1993.

———. "How War Fed War: The Tax of Violence and Contributions during the Grand Siècle." *Journal of Modern History* 65 (June 1993): 286–310.

———. "The Pattern of Army Growth, 1445–1945." In *Tools of War: Instruments, Ideas, and Institutions of Warfare, 1445–1871,* edited by John A. Lynn, 1–27. Urbana: University of Illinois Press, 1990.

———. *Women, Armies, and Warfare in Early Modern Europe.* Cambridge: Cambridge University Press, 2008.

———, ed. *Feeding Mars: Logistics in Western Warfare from the Middle Ages to the Present.* Boulder, CO: Westview Press, 1993.

Maag, Karin, "The Huguenot Academies: Preparing for an Uncertain Future," In *Society and Culture in the Huguenot World, 1559–1685*, edited by Raymond A. Mentzer and Andrew Spicer, 139–156. Cambridge: Cambridge University Press, 2002.

Maës, Bruno. "Missions et grands sanctuaires de pèlerinage dans les controverses religieuses des XVIIᵉ et XVIIIᵉ siècles." In *Les Missions intérieurs en France et en Italie du XVIᵉ au XXᵉ siècle*, edited by Christian Sorrel and Frédéric Meyer, 177–186. Chambéry: Institut d'études savoisiennes, 2001.

Mahul, M. *Cartulaire et archives des communes de l'ancien diocèse et de l'arrondissement administratif de Carcassonne*. 6 vols. Paris: Didron, 1857.

Major, J. Russell. "'Bastard Feudalism' and the Kiss: Changing Social Mores in Late Medieval and Early Modern France." *Journal of Interdisciplinary History* 17 (Winter 1987): 509–535.

———. *From Renaissance Monarchy to Absolute Monarchy: French Kings, Nobles and Estates*. Baltimore: Johns Hopkins University Press, 1994.

———. "Noble Income, Inflation, and the Wars of Religion in France." *American Historical Review* 86 (February 1981): 21–48.

———. "The Revolt of 1620: A Study of Ties of Fidelity." *French Historical Studies* 14 (Spring 1986): 391–408.

Malettke, Klaus. "The Crown, Ministériat, and Nobility at the Court of Louis XIII." In *Princes, Patronage, and the Nobility: The Court at the Beginning of the Modern Age, c. 1450–1650*, edited by Ronald G. Asch and Adolf M. Birke, 415–440. London: Oxford University Press, 1991.

Mallett, Michael. *Mercenaries and Their Masters: Warfare in Renaissance Italy*. London: Bodley Head, 1974.

Margolf, Diane C. *Religion and Royal Justice in Early Modern France: The Paris Chambre de l'Edit, 1598–1665*. Kirksville, MO: Truman State University Press, 2003.

Martin, Henri-Jean. *The French Book: Religion, Absolutism, and Readership, 1585–1715*. Translated by Paul Saenger and Nadine Saenger. Baltimore: Johns Hopkins University Press, 1996.

Mayzou, Louis. *Réalmont, bastide du XIIIᵉ. Miroir d'un village d'oc, de son canton*. Réalmont: L. Mayzou, 1984.

McCaffrey, Emily. "Memory and Collective Identity in Occitanie: The Cathars in History and Popular Culture." *History and Memory* 13 (Spring–Summer 2001): 114–138.

McCorquodale, Wilmer Hunt. "The Court of Louis XIII: The French Court in an Age of Turmoil, 1610–1643." Ph.D. diss.: University of Texas at Austin, 1994.

McGowan, Margaret M. *The Vision of Rome in Late Renaissance France*. New Haven, CT: Yale University Press, 2000.

McNeill, William H. *Keeping Together in Time: Dance and Drill in Human History*. Cambridge, MA: Harvard University Press, 1995.

Mégret-Lacan, Marie-Christine. "Naissance de l'art équestre." *XVIIᵉ siècle* 204 (July–September 1999): 523–548.

Ménard, Léon. *Histoire civile, ecclésiastique et littéraire de la ville de Nîmes*. Vol. 5. 1873. Reprint. Nîmes: C. Lacour, 1989.

Mentzer, Raymond A., Jr. *Blood and Belief: Family Survival and Confessional Identity among the Provincial Huguenot Nobility*. West Lafayette, IN: Purdue University Press, 1994.

———. "Disciplina nervus ecclesiae: The Calvinist Reform of Morals at Nimes." *Sixteenth Century Journal* 18 (Spring 1987): 89–116.

———. "The Legal Response to Heresy in Languedoc, 1500–1560." *Sixteenth Century Journal* 4 (April 1973): 19–30.

———. "Morals and Moral Regulation in Protestant France." *Journal of Interdisciplinary History* 30 (Summer 2000): 1–20.

Mentzer, Raymond A. and Andrew Spicer, eds. *Society and Culture in the Huguenot World, 1559–1685*. Cambridge: Cambridge University Press, 2002.

Messines, Sandrine. "Contre-Réforme et Réforme catholique en Agenais, à travers les visites pastorales de Nicolas de Villars (1592–1607)." In *Religion et politique dans les sociétés du Midi*, edited by Nicole Lemaitre, 193–201. Paris: CTHS, 2002.

Mettam, Roger. *Power and Faction in Louis XIV's France*. Oxford: Blackwell, 1988.

Meyer, Judith Pugh. "La Rochelle and the Failure of the French Reformation." *Sixteenth Century Journal* 15 (Summer 1984): 169–183.

Michaud, Hélène. "Les Institutions militaires des guerres d'Italie aux guerres de religion." *Revue historique* 258 (1977): 29–43.

Michaud, Jacques, and André Cabanis. *Histoire de Narbonne*. Toulouse: Privat, 1981.

Michel, Henri. "Nîmes et son histoire à l'époque moderne." *Annales du Midi* 110 (January–March 1998): 41–56.

Millen, Ronald Forsyth, and Robert Erich Wolf. *Heroic Deeds and Mystic Figures: A New Reading of Rubens' Life of Maria de' Medici*. Princeton, NJ: Princeton University Press, 1989.

Miller, William Ian. *Humiliation and Other Essays on Honor, Social Discomfort, and Violence*. Ithaca, NY: Cornell University Press, 1993.

Mironneau, Paul and Isabelle Pébay-Clottes, eds. *Paix des armes, paix des âmes. Actes du colloque international tenu au Musée national du château de Pau et à l'Université de Pau et des Pays de l'Adour*. Paris: Imprimerie National Éditions, 2000.

Moen, Phyllis, and Elaine Wethington. "The Concept of Family Adaptive Strategies." *Annual Review of Sociology* 18 (August 1992): 233–251.

Monlezun, J.-J. *Histoire de la Gascogne depuis les temps les plus reculés jusqu'à nos jours*. Vol. 5 and suppl. Auch: Brun, 1850.

Montandon, Alain, ed. *Iconotextes*. Paris: CRCD-Ophrys, 1990.

Moote, A. Lloyd. *Louis XIII, The Just*. Berkeley: University of California Press, 1989.

Motley, Mark. *Becoming a French Aristocrat: The Education of the Court Nobility, 1580–1715*. Princeton, NJ: Princeton University Press, 1990.

Mours, Samuel. "Essai sommaire de géographie du protestantisme réformé français au XVIIᵉ siècle." Parts 1 and 2. *BSHPF* 111 (1965): 303–321; 112 (1966): 19–36.

———. *Le Protestantisme en Vivarais et en Velay des origines à nos jours*. Valence: Imprimeries Réunies, 1949.

Mousnier, Roland. *La Vénalité des offices sous Henri IV et Louis XIII*. Paris: Presses Universitaires de France, 1971.

———. "Les Concepts d'"ordres', d'"états', de 'fidélité' et de 'monarchie absolue' en France de la fin du XVIᵉ siècle à la fin du XVIIIᵉ." *Revue historique* 247 (1972): 289–312.

———. *Les Institutions de la France sous la monarchie absolue: 1598–1789.* 2 vols. Paris: Presses Universitaires de France, 1974–1980. Translated by Brian Pearce as *The Institutions of France under the Absolute Monarchy, 1598–1789* (2 vols., Chicago: University of Chicago Press, 1979–1984).

Mouysset, Sylvie. "Du père en fils. Livre de raison et transmission de la mémoire familiale (France du Sud, XVᵉ–XVIIIᵉ siècle)." In *Religion et politique dans les sociétés du Midi,* edited by Nicole Lemaitre, 139–151. Paris: CTHS, 2002.

Muchembled, Robert. *Popular Culture and Elite Culture in France, 1400–1750.* Translated by Lydia Cochrane. Baton Rouge: Louisiana State University Press, 1985.

Muir, Edward. *Mad Blood Stirring: Vendetta and Factions in Friuli during the Renaissance.* Baltimore: Johns Hopkins University Press, 1993.

Nassiet, Michel. *Parenté, noblesse, et états dynastiques, XVᵉ–XVIᵉ siècles.* Paris: Éditions de l'École des Hautes Études en Sciences Sociales, 2000.

———. "Réseaux de parenté et types d'alliance dans la noblesse (XVᵉ–XVIIᵉ siècles)." *Annales de démographie historique* 90 (1995): 105–123.

Nelson, Eric. *The Jesuits and the Monarchy: Catholic Reform and Political Authority in France (1590–1615).* Aldershot, UK: Ashgate, 2005.

Neuschel, Kristen B. "Noble Households in the Sixteenth Century: Material Settings and Human Communities." *French Historical Studies* 15 (Autumn 1988): 595–622.

———. "Noblewomen and War in Sixteenth-Century France." In *Changing Identities in Early Modern France,* edited by Michael Wolfe, 124–144. Durham, NC: Duke University Press, 1997.

———. *Word of Honor: Interpreting Noble Culture in Sixteenth-Century France.* Ithaca, NY: Cornell University Press, 1989.

Nicholls, David. "The Theatre of Martyrdom in the French Reformation." *Past and Present* 121 (1988): 49–73.

Nicod, E. "Les Troubles du Cheylard (1621–1629)." *Revue du Vivarais* (1912): 201–216, 253–263, 289–299.

Nougaret, Jean, and Olivier Poisson. "Les Villes et leur cathédrale. L'emblématique des quatorze évêchés." *Monuments historiques* 187 (May–June 1993): 29–35.

Nye, Robert A. *Masculinity and Male Codes of Honor in Modern France.* New York: Oxford University Press, 1993.

Olive, Joseph-Laurent. *Mirepoix en Languedoc et sa seigneurie du moyen âge à la veille de la Révolution.* Saverdun: Imprimerie du Champ du Mars, 1979.

Orléa, Manfred. *La Noblesse aux États généraux de 1576 et de 1588. Étude politique et sociale.* Paris: Presses Universitaires de France, 1980.

Pablo, Jean de. "L'Armée Huguenote entre 1562 et 1573." *Archiv für Reformationsgeschichte* 48, 2 (1957): 192–215.

Packer, Dorothy S. "Collections of Chaste Chansons for the Devout Home (1613–1633)." *Acta Musicologica* 61 (May–August 1989): 175–216.

Papaix, J. "Toulouse sous Louis XIII. La Révolte de Montmorency." In *Études régionales pour l'enseignement. II. Aspects Historiques et géographiques du sud-ouest,* 122–126. Toulouse: Privat, 1941.

Parker, Charles H. "French Calvinists as the Children of Israel: An Old Testament Self-Consciousness in Jean Crespin's *Histoire des Martyrs* before the Wars of Religion. *Sixteenth Century Journal* 24 (Summer 1993): 227–248.

Parker, David. *Class and State in Ancien Régime France: The Road to Modernity?* New York: Routledge, 1996.

———. *La Rochelle and the French Monarchy: Conflict and Order in Seventeenth-Century France.* London: Royal Historical Society, 1980.

———. *The Making of French Absolutism.* New York: St. Martin's Press, 1983.

Parker, Geoffrey. *The Army of Flanders and the Spanish Road, 1567–1659: The Logistics of Spanish Victory and Defeat in the Low Countries War.* Cambridge: Cambridge University Press, 1972.

———. "The 'Military Revolution' 1560–1660–A Myth?" *Journal of Modern History* 48 (June 1976): 195–214.

———. *The Military Revolution: Military Innovation and the Rise of the West, 1500–1800.* 2nd ed. Cambridge: Cambridge University Press, 1996.

Parker, Geoffrey and Lesley M. Smith, eds. *The General Crisis of the Seventeenth Century.* 2nd ed. New York: Routledge, 1997.

Parrott, David A. "The Administration of the French Army during the Ministry of Cardinal Richelieu." Ph.D. diss., Wolfson College, Oxford University, 1985.

———. "Power and Patronage in the French Army, 1620–1659." In *Patronages et clientélismes, 1550–1750 (France, Angleterre, Espagne, Italie),* edited by Charles Giry-Deloison and Roger Mettam, 229–241. Lille: Université Charles de Gaulle (Lille III) and Institut Français du Royaume-Uni, 1995.

———. "Richelieu, the *Grands,* and the French Army." In *Richelieu and His Age,* edited by Joseph Bergin and Laurence Brockliss, 135–173. Oxford: Oxford University Press, 1992.

———. *Richelieu's Army: War, Government and Society in France, 1624–1642.* Cambridge: Cambridge University Press, 2001.

Parsons, Jotham. *The Church in the Republic: Gallicanism and Political Ideology in Renaissance France.* Washington, DC: Catholic University of America Press, 2004.

———. "Money and Sovereignty in Early Modern France." *Journal of the History of Ideas* 62 (January 2001): 59–79.

Pelikan, Jaroslav. *A History of the Development of Doctrine.* Vol. 4. *Reformation of Church and Dogma (1300–1700).* Chicago: University of Chicago Press, 1984.

Pettegree, Andrew. "Recent Writings on the French Wars of Religion." *Reformation* 4 (1999): 231–250.

Pithon, Rémy. "La Suisse, théâtre de la guerre froide entre la France et l'Espagne pendant la crise de Valteline (1621–1626)." *Schweizerische Zeitschrift für Geschichte* 13, 1 (1963): 33–53.

Pollak, Martha D. "Representations of the City in Siege Views of the Seventeenth Century: The War of Military Images and their Production." In *City Walls: The Urban*

Enceinte in Global Perspective, edited by James D. Tracy, 605–646. Cambridge: Cambridge University Press, 2000.

———. *Turin, 1564–1680: Urban Design, Military Culture, and the Creation of the Absolutist Capital.* Chicago: University of Chicago Press, 1991.

Potter, Mark. "Good Offices: Intermediation by Corporate Bodies in Early Modern French Public Finance." *Journal of Economic History* 60 (September 2000): 599–626.

Pugh, Wilma J. "Catholics, Protestants, and Testament Charity in Seventeenth-Century Lyon and Nimes." *French Historical Studies* 11 (Autumn 1980): 479–504.

———. "Social Welfare and the Edict of Nantes: Lyon and Nimes." *French Historical Studies* 8 (Spring 1974): 349–376.

Racaut, Luc. *Hatred in Print: Catholic Propaganda and Protestant Identity during the French Wars of Religion.* Aldershot, UK: Ashgate, 2002.

———. "The Polemical Use of the Albigensian Crusade during the French Wars of Religion." *French History* 13 (September 1999): 261–279.

Ranum, Orest. "Courtesy, Absolutism and the Rise of the French State," *Journal of Modern History* 52 (September 1980): 426–451.

———. *The Fronde: A French Revolution.* New York: Norton, 1993.

———. *Richelieu and the Councilors of Louis XIII: A Study of the Secretaries of State and Superintendants of Finance in the Ministry of Richelieu, 1635–1642.* Oxford: Oxford University Press, 1963.

Reddy, William M. *The Invisible Code: Honor and Sentiment in Postrevolutionary France, 1814–1848.* Berkeley: University of California Press, 1997.

Redlich, Fritz. *De Praeda Militari: Looting and Booty 1500–1815.* Vierteljahrschrift für Sozial- und Wirtschaftsgeschichte, suppl. 39. Wiesbaden: F. Steiner, 1956.

———. *The German Military Enterpriser and His Work Force: A Study in European Economic and Social History.* 2 vols. Vierteljahrschrift für Sozial- und Wirtschaftsgeschichte, suppl. 48. Wiesbaden: F. Steiner, 1964–1965.

Riou, Michel. *Ardèche, terre de châteaux.* Montmélian: La Fontaine de Siloé, 2002.

Roberts, Michael. "The Military Revolution, 1560–1660." In *The Military Revolution Debate: Readings on the Military Transformation of Early Modern Europe,* edited by Clifford J. Rogers, 13–36. Boulder, CO: Westview Press, 1995. Lecture delivered in Belfast, 1956, and first published in this form in Michael Roberts, *Essays in Swedish History* (Minneapolis: University of Minnesota Press, 1967).

Roberts, Penny. *A City in Conflict: Troyes during the French Wars of Religion.* Manchester: Manchester University Press, 1996.

———. "Contesting Sacred Space: Burial Disputes in Sixteenth-Century France." In *The Place of the Dead: Death and Remembrance in Late Medieval and Early Modern Europe,* edited by Bruce Gordon and Peter Marshall, 131–148. Cambridge: Cambridge University Press, 2000.

———. "The Most Crucial Battle of the Wars of Religion? The Conflict over Sites for Reformed Worship in Sixteenth-Century France." *Archiv für Reformationsgeschichte* 89 (1998): 247–267.

Roche, Daniel. *A History of Everyday Things: The Birth of Consumption in France, 1600–1800.* Cambridge: Cambridge University Press, 2000.

Rogers, Clifford J. "The Military Revolution in History and Historiography." In *The Military Revolution Debate: Readings on the Military Transformation of Early Modern Europe*, edited by Clifford J. Rogers, 1–10. Boulder, CO: Westview Press, 1995.

———. "The Military Revolutions of the Hundred Years' War." *Journal of Military History* 57 (April 1993): 241–278.

———. *War Cruel and Sharp: English Strategy under Edward III, 1327–1360*. Woodbridge, Suffolk, UK: Boydell & Brewer, 2000.

———, ed. *The Military Revolution Debate: Readings on the Military Transformation of Early Modern Europe*. Boulder, CO: Westview Press, 1995.

Rome, Catherine. *Les Bourgeois protestants de Montauban au XVIIe siècle. Une élite urbaine face à une monarchie autoritaire*. Paris: Honoré Champion, 2002.

Root, Hilton L. *Peasants and King in Burgundy: Agrarian Foundations of French Absolutism*. Berkeley: University of California Press, 1987.

Rosental, Paul-André. "Les Liens familiaux, forme historique?" *Annales de démographie historique* 100 (2000): 49–81.

Rothrock, G. A. *The Huguenots: A Biography of a Minority*. Chicago: Nelson-Hall, 1979.

Rowen, Herbert H. *The King's State: Proprietary Dynasticism in Early Modern France*. New Brunswick, NJ: Rutgers University Press, 1980.

Rowlands, Guy. *The Dynastic State and the Army under Louis XIV: Royal Service and Private Interest, 1661–1701*. Cambridge: Cambridge University Press, 2002.

Sahlins, Peter. "Natural Frontiers Revisited: France's Boundaries since the Seventeenth Century." *American Historical Review* 90 (December 1990): 1423–1451.

Salmon, J. H. M. "A Second Look at the Noblesse Seconde: The Key to Noble Clientage and Power in Early Modern France?" *French Historical Studies* 25 (Fall 2002): 575–593.

———. *Society in Crisis: France in the Sixteenth Century*. London: Methuen, 1975.

Sandberg, Brian. "Financing the Counterreformation: Noble Credit and Construction Projects in Southern France during the Early Seventeenth Century." In *L'edilizia prima della rivoluzione industriale secc. XIII-XVIII: Atti della "Trentaseiesima Settimana di studi", 26–30 aprile 2004*, edited by Simonetta Cavaciocchi. Prato, Italy: Le Monnier, 2004.

———. " 'Generous Amazons Came to the Breach': Besieged Women in the French Wars of Religion." *Gender and History* 16 (November 2004): 654–688.

———. "The Infection of Heresy: Religious Conquest and Confessional Violence in Early Modern France." In *(Re)Constructing Cultures of Violence and Peace*, edited by Richard Jackson, 17–30. Amsterdam: Rodopi, 2004.

———. " 'The Magazine of All Their Pillaging': Armies as Sites of Second-Hand Exchanges during the French Wars of Religion." In *Alternative Exchanges: Second-Hand Circulations from the Sixteenth Century to the Present*, edited by Laurence Fontaine, 76–96. New York: Berghahn Books, 2008.

———. " 'Re-establishing the True Worship of God': Divinity and Religious Violence in France after the Edict of Nantes." *Renaissance & Reformation / Renaissance et Réforme* 29 (2005): 139–182.

———. " 'Se couvrant toujours . . . du nom du roi.' Perceptions nobiliaires de la révolte dans le sud-ouest de la France, 1610–1635." *Histoire, Économie et Société* 17 (1998): 423–440.

———. "'To Deliver a Greatly Persecuted Church': Resituating the Edict of Nantes within the History of Laïcité." *Storica* 38 (2007): 33–64.

Satterfield, George D. *Princes, Posts, and Partisans: The Army of Louis XIV and Partisan Warfare in the Netherlands (1673–1678).* Leiden: Brill, 2003.

Sauzet, Robert. *Au Grand Siècle des âmes. Guerre sainte et paix et chrétienne en France au XVIIᵉ siècle.* Paris: Perrin, 2007.

———. *Les Cévennes catholiques. Histoire d'une fidélité, XVIᵉ–XXᵉ siècle.* Paris: Perrin, 2002.

———. "Les Confréries du diocèse de Nîmes à la fin du XVIIᵉ et au début du XVIIIᵉ siècle." In *Les Confréries, l'Église et la cité. Cartographie des confréries du Sud-Est,* edited by Marie-Hélène Froeschlé-Chopard and Roger Devos. Documents d'ethnologie régionale 10. Grenoble: Centre alpin et rhodanien d'ethnologie, 1988.

———. *Contre-réforme et réforme catholique en bas-Languedoc. Le diocèse de Nîmes au XVIIᵉ siècle.* Louvain: Nauwelaerts, 1979.

Sawyer, Jeffrey K. *Printed Poison: Pamphlet Propaganda, Faction Politics, and the Public Sphere in Early Seventeenth-Century France.* Berkeley: University of California Press, 1990.

Scarry, Elaine. *The Body in Pain: The Making and Unmaking of the World.* Oxford: Oxford University Press, 1985.

———. "Injury and the Structure of War." *Representations* 10 (Spring 1985): 1–51.

Schalk, Ellery. "The Appearance and Reality of Nobility in France during the Wars of Religion: An Example of How Collective Attitudes Can Change." *Journal of Modern History* 48 (March 1976): 19–31.

———. "The Court as 'Civilizer' of the Nobility: Noble Attitudes and the Court in France in the Late Sixteenth and Early Seventeenth Centuries." In *Princes, Patronage, and the Nobility: The Court at the Beginning of the Modern Age, c. 1450–1650,* edited by Ronald G. Asch and Adolf M. Birke, 245–263. Oxford: German Historical Institute London and Oxford University Press, 1991.

———. *From Valor to Pedigree: Ideas of Nobility in France in the Sixteenth and Seventeenth Centuries.* Princeton, NJ: Princeton University Press, 1986.

Schneider, Robert A. "Crown and Capitoulat: Municipal Government in Toulouse, 1500–1789." In *Cities and Social Change in Early Modern France,* edited by Philip Benedict, 191–216. London: Unwin Hyman, 1989.

———. *Public Life in Toulouse, 1463–1789: From Municipal Republic to Cosmopolitan City.* Ithaca, NY: Cornell University Press, 1989.

Schybergson, G. "Le Duc de Rohan et la bourgeoisie protestante de 1622 à 1625." *BSHPF* 29 (1880): 97–115.

———. "Le Duc de Rohan et le parti réformé de 1610 à 1622." *BSHPF* 29 (1880): 49–64.

Scott, H. M. ed. *The European Nobilities in the Seventeenth and Eighteenth Centuries.* 2 vols. London: Longman, 1995.

Selinger, Suzanne. *Calvin against Himself: An Inquiry in Intellectual History.* Hamden, CT: Archon Books, 1984.

Shepard, Alexandra. "Manhood, Credit and Patriarchy in Early Modern England c. 1580–1640." *Past and Present* 167 (May 2000): 75–106.

Shy, John. "The Cultural Approach to the History of War." *Journal of Military History* 57 (October 1993): 13–26.

Silverman, Lisa. *Tortured Subjects: Pain, Truth, and the Body in Early Modern France.* Chicago: University of Chicago Press, 2001.

Smith, Jay M. *The Culture of Merit: Nobility, Royal Service, and the Making of Absolute Monarchy in France, 1600–1789.* Ann Arbor: University of Michgan Press, 1996.

———. "No More Language Games: Words, Beliefs, and the Political Culture of Early Modern France." *American Historical Review* 102 (December 1997): 1413–1440.

———. "Our Sovereign's Gaze: Kings, Nobles, and State Formation in Seventeenth-Century France." *French Historical Studies* 18 (Autumn 1993): 396–415.

Solon, Paul. "Le Rôle des forces armées en Comminges avant les guerres de religion (1502–1562)." *Annales du Midi* 103 (October–December 1991): 19–40.

Sorrel, Christian, and Frédéric Meyer, eds. *Les Missions intérieurs en France et en Italie du XVIᵉ au XXᵉ siècle.* Chambéry: Institut d'études savoisiennes, 2001.

Souriac, Pierre-Jean. "Les Places de sûreté protestantes. Reconnaissance et déclin de la puissance politique et militaire du parti protestant (1570–1629)." Mémoire de Maîtrise d'histoire, Université de Toulouse II (Le Mirail), 1997.

Soutou, André. "Une Maison-forte du XVIIᵉ siècle. Belvézet, commune de La Couvertoirade (Aveyron)." *Annales du Midi* 89 (1977): 353–361.

Sperling, Jutta. "Marriage at the Time of the Council of Trent (1560–1570): Clandestine Marriages, Kinship Prohibitions, and Dowry Exchange in European Comparison." *Journal of Early Modern History* 8 (May 2004): 67–108.

Spicer, Andrew. "'Qui est de Dieu oit la parole de Dieu': The Huguenots and Their Temples." In *Society and Culture in the Huguenot World, 1559–1685*, edited by Raymond A. Mentzer and Andrew Spicer, 175–192. Cambridge: Cambridge University Press, 2002.

———. "'Rest of Their Bones': Fear of Death and Reformed Burial Practices." In *Fear in Early Modern Society*, edited by William G. Naphy and Penny Roberts, 167–183. Manchester: Manchester University Press, 1997.

Steensgaard, Niels. "The Seventeenth-Century Crisis." In *The General Crisis of the Seventeenth Century*, edited by Geoffrey Parker and Lesley M. Smith, 32–56. 2nd ed. London: Routledge, 1997.

Steinmetz, David C. "Calvin and the Absolute Power of God." *Journal of Medieval and Renaissance Studies* 18 (Spring 1988): 65–79.

Steinmetz, George, ed. *State/Culture: State-Formation after the Cultural Turn.* Ithaca, NY: Cornell University Press, 1999.

Stewart, Frank Henderson. *Honor.* Chicago: University of Chicago Press, 1994.

Sturgill, Claude C. "Changing Garrisons: The French System of Étapes." *Canadian Journal of History* 20 (1985): 193–201.

Susane, Louis. *Histoire de l'infanterie française.* 5 vols. Paris: Dumaine, 1876.

Sutherland, N. M. *The Huguenot Struggle for Recognition.* New Haven, CT: Yale University Press, 1972.

Taylor, Scott. "Credit, Debt, and Honor in Castile, 1600–1650." *Journal of Early Modern History* 7 (2003): 8–27.

Te Brake, Wayne. *Shaping History: Ordinary People in European Politics, 1500–1700.* Berkeley: University of California Press, 1998.

Thompson, Janice E. *Mercenaries, Pirates, and Sovereigns: State-Building and Extraterritorial Violence in Early Modern Europe.* Princeton, NJ: Princeton University Press, 1994.

Tilly, Charles. *Coercion, Capital, and European States, AD 990–1992.* Oxford: Blackwell, 1992.

———. *The Contentious French: Four Centuries of Popular Struggle.* Cambridge, MA: Harvard University Press, 1986.

———. "War Making and State Making as Organized Crime." In *Bringing the State Back In,* edited by Peter B. Evans, Dietrich Reuschemeyer, and Theda Skocpol, 169–191. Cambridge: Cambridge University Press, 1985.

Tollon, Bruno. "L'Emploi de la brique. L'originalité toulousaine." In *Les Chantiers de la Renaissance,* edited by André Chastel and Jean Guillaume, 85–104. Paris: Picard, 1991.

Touzery-Salager, Anne. *Les Châteaux du bas-Languedoc. Architecture et décor de la Renaissance à la Révolution.* Montpellier: Espace Sud, 1996.

Tracy, James D. *A Financial Revolution in the Habsburg Netherlands: Renten and Renteniers in the County of Holland, 1515–1565.* Berkeley: University of California Press, 1985.

Tulchin, Allan A. "The Michelade in Nîmes, 1567." *French Historical Studies* 29 (Winter 2006): 1–35.

Turchetti, Mario. "Religious Concord and Political Tolerance in Sixteenth- and Seventeenth-Century France." *Sixteenth Century Journal* 22 (Spring 1991): 15–25.

Turney-High, Harry Holbert. *Primitive War: Its Practice and Concepts.* Columbia: University of South Carolina Press, 1949.

Usher, Abbott Payson. *The History of the Grain Trade in France, 1400–1700.* Cambridge, MA: Harvard University Press, 1913.

Vaillancourt, Daniel, and Marie-France Wagner, eds. "Les Entrées royales." Special issue, *XVIIe siècle* 212 (July–September 2001).

Van Orden, Kate. *Music, Discipline, and Arms in Early Modern France.* Chicago: University of Chicago Press, 2005.

Vedel, Léon. *Balazuc et Pons de Balazuc.* Aubenas: Société d'Exploitation de l'Imprimerie, 1976.

Venard, Marc. "Un Édit bien enregistré. Le quatrième centenaire de l'édit de Nantes." *Revue d'histoire de l'Église de France* 87 (January–June 2001): 27–45.

Vic, Claude de, and Joseph Vaissete. *Histoire générale de Languedoc.* Vols. 11–12. 1730–1745. Reprint, Toulouse: Privat, 1872–1905.

Vittu, Jean-Pierre. "Instruments of Political Information in France." In *The Politics of Information in Early Modern Europe,* edited by Brendan Dooley and Sabrina A. Baron, 160–174. New York: Routledge, 2001.

Wada, Mitsuji. "La Représentation des régions à l'assemblée générale protestante au 16e siècle. Le cas de la province Saintonge-Aunis-Angoumois." In *Coexister dans l'intolérance. L'édit de Nantes (1598),* edited by Michel Grandjean and Bernard Roussel, 186–206. Geneva: Labor et Fides, 1998.

Wagner, Peter. *Reading Iconotexts: From Swift to the French Revolution.* London: Reaktion Books, 1995.

Wandel, Lee Palmer. "Review of Brad S. Gregory, *Salvation at Stake: Christian Martyrdom in Early Modern Europe.*" *Sixteenth Century Journal* 31 (Winter 2000): 1169–72.

Watanabe-O'Kelly, Helen. "Tournaments and Their Relevance for Warfare in the Early Modern Period." *European History Quarterly* 20 (October 1990): 451–464.

Watson, Timothy. "Preaching, Printing, Psalm-Singing: The Making and Unmaking of the Reformed Church in Lyon, 1550–1572." In *Society and Culture in the Huguenot World, 1559–1685*, edited by Raymond A. Mentzer and Andrew Spicer, 10–28. Cambridge, MA: Cambridge University Press, 2002.

Watt, Jeffrey R. "The Impact of the Reformation and Counter-Reformation." In *Family Life in Early Modern Times, 1500–1789*, vol. 1 of *The History of the European Family*, edited by David I. Kertzer and Mario Barbagli, 125–154. New Haven, CT: Yale University Press, 2001).

Weary, William A. "The House of La Tremoille, Fifteenth through Eighteenth Centuries: Change and Adaptation in a French Noble Family." *Journal of Modern History* 49, suppl. (March 1977): D1001–D1038.

Weber, Max. "Politics as a Vocation." In *From Max Weber: Essays in Sociology*, translated and edited by H. H. Gerth and C. Wright Mills. New York: Oxford University Press, 1946.

Wolfe, Michael. *The Conversion of Henri IV: Politics, Power, and Religious Belief in Early Modern France*. Cambridge, MA: Harvard University Press, 1993.

———. "Walled Towns during the French Wars of Religion (1560–1630)." In *City Walls: The Urban Enceinte in Global Perspective*, edited by James D. Tracy, 317–348. Cambridge: Cambridge University Press, 2000.

———. "Writing the City under Attack during the French Wars of Religion." In *Situazioni d'assedio / Cities under Siege / États de Siège*, edited by Lucia Carle and Antoinette Fauve-Chamoux, 197–203. Montalcino: Clio-Polis, 2002.

Wolff, Philippe. *Histoire du Languedoc*. Toulouse: Privat, 1967.

———, ed. *Histoire de Toulouse*. Toulouse: Privat, 1974.

Wood, James B. "The Impact of the Wars of Religion: A View of France in 1581." *Sixteenth Century Journal* 15 (Summer 1984): 131–168.

———. *The King's Army: Warfare, Soldiers, and Society during the Wars of Religion in France, 1562–1576*. Cambridge: Cambridge University Press, 1996.

———. "The Royal Army during the Early Wars of Religion, 1559–1576." In *Society and Institutions in Early Modern France*, edited by Mack P. Holt, 1–35. Athens: University of Georgia Press, 1991.

Zagorin, Perez. *Rebels and Rulers, 1500–1660*. 2 vols. Cambridge: Cambridge University Press, 1982.

Index

absolutism, xxv–xxvi, 137, 291
admiral of France, 60–61, 83, 128–129, 130, 231
Agen, 22, 88, 91–92, 134, 192
Aigues-Mortes, 4, 29, 60, 62, 100
Albert, Charles d', duc de Luynes, 30, 127, 133, 157
Albi, 25, 26, 56, 105, 106–108, 246, 281
Alès, 29, 97, 98, 110, 220, 249, 256–257, 272. *See also under* peaces
amitié: as armed companionship, xix, xxii, 78, 79, 98, 105, 109, 125, 145, 212, 220–221, 263, 269, 286–287; bonds of, 79–80, 101, 113, 148, 183, 197; ideals of, xix, 79–80; kinship and, 49–51, 79, 101; proofs of friendship, 234; *réseaux d'amitié,* xix, 80
armed forces: compared to a giant, 223, 224–232; standing, xxv, 224–226, 227, 228, 290
armies, field: assembly of, 213–214; Catholic, 231, 247–248; elements of, 226–231; Huguenot, 219, 226, 231–232, 248–249; maintenance of, 232–240; maneuvering of, 262–263; nuclei of, 224–226; as organisms, 223–224; organization of, 98, 215–216; personal, xxi–xxiii, 217–218, 223–224, 286–287; royal, 198–199, 218–219, 224–226
armor, 6, 7, 12, 39, 63, 73, 102, 139, 207, 208, 227, 269
army style, xxii, xxvi, 224, 231–232, 287, 290
Arpajon, Louis d', marquis de Séverac et victome d'Arpajon, 49, 103–105, 134, 163
arquebusiers à cheval, 139, 202, 228, 235, 238
arsenals: château, 13, 63, 207–209; municipal, 13, 132, 194; royal, 130
artillerists, 228, 235

artillery: in bastioned fortifications, 259–260, 272, 273; batteries of, 167, 181, 259–260, 263, 265, 272, 273; capture of, 111, 175, 266; lightweight artillery, 208, 209, 228, 229–230, 263, 265; nobles' use of, 99, 121, 130, 173, 177, 208; requisition of, 112, 194, 218; siege, 107, 111, 181, 229, 259
art of war, xvii, xviii, 111, 173–174. *See also* profession of arms
assemblies: *assemblées en armes,* xv, xviii, xxii, 16, 102, 193, 286–287; *assiettes,* 106, 200, 246; civic assemblies, 75, 169; of clienteles, 81, 90–91, 102, 190, 197, 269; Huguenot political assemblies, 4, 24, 83, 88, 155, 194, 205, 212–213, 248–249, 254, 279–280; Reformed synods, 155, 280. *See also* estates; Estates General of France
associations: clienteles and, xvii, xix, 79, 95, 181–182, 196–198; political causes and, xxiii, 80–81, 146, 184, 191, 196–198, 202
Aubenas, 110, 214, 256, 282
authority: appropriation of, xxi, 203–206; challenges to, xx, 3, 87, 91–92, 105, 129; competing authorities, 102, 124–126; concepts of, 35, 65–66, 116–117, 119, 128, 147; extraordinary, 120–122; ordinary, 119–120; partitioning of, 93, 124–125, 147–148, 198, 202–203; royal, xx, 83, 100, 105, 109, 117–119, 149; seigneurial, 46, 93

baillis, 87, 90, 122, 134, 210–211
Balazuc de Montréal, Guillaume de, seigneur de Montréal, 103, 110–113, 175, 214, 237, 262, 266, 314n153
Baschi, Louis II de, baron d'Aubais, 51, 100, 103, 108–110, 156

Bas Languedoc: garrisons in, 225; nobles of, 27–31, 40, 83, 86, 108–109, 128, 130, 135

Bassompierre, François de, 105, 128, 158–159, 270

bastions, 23, 192, 255, 259, 260, 272

battle: desire for, 165, 174, 261, 262; *en bataille*, 263, 271; experience of, 261–267, 271–273

Béarn, 4, 81, 100, 205, 246, 288

Beaucaire, 29, 90, 100, 134, 218

Beaumont, Joachim de, baron de Beaumont-Brison, xxiii, 85, 111

Béthune, Maximilien de, duc de Sully, xxv, 130, 161, 281

Béziers, 28, 87, 134, 245, 329n85

Blacons, Alexandre de, seigneur de Mirabel-Blacons, 160, 175, 266

blood: imagery of, 143, 144, 147, 148, 161, 191–192, 223; kinship and, 34, 43, 46; noble quality and, xviii, 43, 160–161, 162, 165

bodyguards: noble, 15, 39, 57, 63, 82, 85, 97, 99, 101, 139, 201–202, 227, 231, 233, 269; royal, 67, 201–202, 225, 228

body politic, xxi, 35, 203, 223–224, 240, 242

bonds of nobility, xvii, xix–xxi, xxiv, xxvi, xxvii. *See also* clientage; honor; officeholding

Bonne, François de, duc de Lesdiguières, xvii, xx, 104, 127, 130, 164, 165, 168, 183, 234, 279

Bordeaux: as administrative center, 20, 124, 178, 299n27; as Catholic center, 20, 133, 136, 178, 179, 194; parlement de, 74, 124, 125, 135, 179; population of, 20, 88, 281

Bourbon, César de, duc de Vendôme, 42, 104, 107–108, 121–122, 127, 217, 247

Bourbon, Gaston de, duc d'Orléans: as brother of Louis XIII, 42; clientele of, 67, 82; as rebel, xxx, 86, 105, 176–177, 183–184, 289–290; royal family and, 38, 289–290

Bourbon, Henri de, marquis de Malauze, 26, 107, 265, 281

Bourbon, Henri II de, prince de Condé: Catholicism of, 67, 254; clientele of, 25, 91–92, 201–202; as lieutenant general, 121, 122, 127; military leadership of, 112, 174, 181, 204, 214, 256, 262; as provincial governor of Guyenne, 20, 132–133, 162; royal family and, 96, 133, 196, 289

Bourbon family: disputes within, 42, 133, 200, 289–290; nobles and, 34, 48, 57, 58, 66, 67, 96, 118, 124, 127, 158, 170, 227, 249

Bourdieu, Pierre, 34–35, 190

Budos, Antoine-Hercule de, marquis de Portes: family of, 29, 30, 40, 142–143; military leadership of, 110, 111, 119, 142–143, 217, 218, 220, 245; offices of, 11, 61, 134, 174; relations with Montmorencys, 40, 110, 111, 134, 174

Cahors, 23, 56, 245

Caïla de Saint-Bonnet, Jean de, marquis de Toiras, 29, 41, 85–86, 128, 266

Calvière, Claude de, baron de Saint-Côme, 51, 89, 109, 237, 267

Calvin, Jean, 36, 37, 154–155

Calvinism: Bible reading, 36–37, 155, 273; godly community, 36, 64, 154, 155, 158, 274, 282; international movement of, 68, 129, 231, 248; *prêche*, 22, 36–37, 155–156, 280; psalm-singing, 36–37, 155; temples, 29, 155, 171, 248, 274, 279, 280

capitulations, 3, 106, 111, 181, 184, 192, 194, 220, 259, 260, 264

captains: activities of, 14, 16, 211–212, 237, 243; cavalry, 138–139; infantry, 138; types of, 137–139

carabiniers, 139, 201, 202, 228, 238

Carcassonne, 27, 87, 134

Castelnaudary, 82, 105, 132, 134, 176, 197, 208, 264, 267, 271

Castres, 25, 26, 74, 88, 102–103, 107, 108, 110, 134, 136, 254

Catholicism: asceticism, 155, 276–277, 278; Catholic Reformation, 156, 303n15; Council of Trent, 277; devotional practices, 64, 156, 276; mass, 37, 111, 155, 156, 169, 271, 277; processions, 118, 156, 171, 193, 274, 277–278, 283

Catholic League, xxi, 22, 24, 26, 87, 195, 197, 262, 277–278

Catholics: causes of, 146, 156, 195, 197, 273–274, 277–279, 282; crusading by, 29, 68, 74, 156; militancy of, 276–279; religious activism of, 158, 273–276

Caumont, Jacques-Nompar de, duc de La Force, 22, 23, 47, 81, 100, 128 cavalry: maintenance of, 235–236, 238; organization of, 227–228, 233; recruitment of, 210–211; tactics of, 263–265, 272; types of, 138–139. *See also specific types*

Cévennes Mountains: garrisons in, 224; Huguenots in, 85, 240, 249, 280, 288; nobles in, 29–30, 83, 134

châteaux: architecture of, 39, 52, 206–207; armories in, 14, 63, 207–209; as Calvinist centers, 99, 155; construction and repairs of, 20, 55, 64, 95, 201, 247; defense of, 99, 102, 119, 175, 194, 209, 229; destruction of, 87, 183, 193; fortifications of, 13, 39, 63, 206–207; as operational bases, 206–210, 213, 215; as residences, 4, 39–40, 49, 52, 64, 66–67, 89, 94, 96, 106, 269; transfers of, 17, 56

chevaux-légers, 130, 139, 211, 227, 235–236

children: childbirth, 38, 50, 70; family honor and, 39, 42, 50–51, 118, 161; family strategies and, 35, 38, 41, 42, 43, 50, 70, 71

Choiseul, Charles de, marquis de Praslin, 45, 128

civilizing process, xxiv, 96, 160

civil warfare: concepts of, xxi–xxiii, xxvi; descriptions of, xv–xvi, 3–5, 45; orchestration of, 254–267, 287

clergy: archbishops, 20, 21, 28, 56, 105, 124, 133, 136, 273; bishops, xv, 36, 56, 74, 136, 137; confessors, 158, 277; priests, 137, 156, 271, 278; Reformed ministers, 100, 155, 157–158, 271, 281, 305n63. *See also* religious orders

clientage: administrative, 86–88; *créatures*, xx, 91–92; military, 84–86; mixed forms of, 81, 103–110; prestige, 81–83; seigneurial, 92–95; urban, 88–92

clienteles: as armed communities, 268–273; contention within, 102–103; formation of, 80–81; management of, 95–103; reciprocity in, 65, 95–96; refashioning, 103–113

coats of arms, 44, 102, 269, 304n46

coercion, xxvi, 84, 95, 96, 101–103, 122, 255, 266

Coligny, Gaspard III, seigneur de Châtillon: clientele of, 4–5, 71, 83, 100, 109, 202; as Huguenot army commander, 4–5, 109, 183, 217, 218, 233, 236, 245, 248–249; offices of, 4, 29, 60–61, 128, 129–130, 135, 183; as royal army commander, 264–265

colonel généraux, 60, 129–130

combat: camaraderie in, 85, 165–166, 270–271; experiences of, xvi, 5, 14, 165, 174, 176, 181, 259–267, 271–273

command: culture of, 253; exercise of, xxi, xxiii; practices of, 84, 173–175, 208, 254–267

commissaires des guerres, 225, 239, 245, 247, 249, 270

commissions: blank, 203–204; literary form of, 119–120, 168, 176–177, 198, 202–206, 220; powers granted by, 138, 168, 173, 176–177

commoners: as administrators, 94, 98–99; *mésalliance*, 47, 66; nobles and, 6, 15, 160–161, 169, 268, 269, 273, 305n62, 306n15; as officers, 139–140, 161; as soldiers, 95, 98–99, 100, 211–212

common good, xix, 146–147, 200–202

compagnies d'ordonnance: logistical demands of, 97, 101, 233, 235, 238; loyalties of, 226; mobilization of, 194, 195, 226; nobles serving in, 7, 15, 71, 97, 101, 107, 202, 261; organization of, 7, 139, 227; prestige of, 139, 235

companies: as basic organizational units, xxii, 138; organization of, 138–140, 210–213, 226–229

Concini, Concino, 66, 127, 196, 202

Condé. *See* Bourbon, Henri II de

confraternities, 25–26, 156, 158, 171, 197, 274, 282

connétable, xx–xxi, 72, 127, 130, 144, 174, 177, 316n35

conspiracy, 82, 83, 91, 92, 192, 196

consuls: authority of, 89–90, 120, 212, 215, 221, 220; *consulat*, 89–90, 95, 136, 137, 221, 275, 280; urban clienteles and, 89, 91–92, 100

contributions, 105, 122, 234, 236, 239, 256

conversions, 23, 50, 183, 213, 254, 278, 288, 316n35

Counter-Reformation: missionaries, xxvi, 26, 36; opposition to heresy, 278–279; promotion of, 21, 22, 25–26, 36, 95, 136, 195, 274; reestablishment of the mass, 260

courage: courageous acts, 68, 164, 254; proofs of, xxi, 150, 175–177; reputation and, 164–167, 182 court, royal: courtiers, xviii, xxiii, 82, 96, 104, 118, 168, 170, 196–197, 289; courtly behavior, xviii, xx, 8, 13, 60, 118, 159–160, 164; provincial nobles and, xvi, 4, 42, 65, 123, 131, 132–133, 137, 162, 168, 177, 178

crédit: concept of, xviii–xix, 4, 53, 64–66, 286; debts, 55, 56–57, 59, 65, 69–70, 73, 74, 242, 250; experience and, 66–69; jewelry, 58, 249; loans, 58–59, 66, 70, 74, 98, 243, 247–250; patrimony and, 69–73; privileges and, 73–75

Crussol, Emmanuel de, duc d'Uzès, 61, 141, 143, 147, 148, 162

culture of revolt: concept of, xvii, xxi–xxiii, xxvii, 286–292; personal armies and, 223–224; rituals of arming and, 189–190; violent performances and, 253–254, 268

defense: mutual, xvii, xix, 95, 112, 196–198; self-defense, 199–200

demobilizations, 84, 91, 98, 107, 184, 193, 265

dignity, 15, 115–117, 143, 147, 153, 159–163, 179, 182, 197

dioceses: *assiettes* of, 106, 200, 246, 248; defense of, xx, 56, 105, 120, 124, 200, 236

discipline: military, 21, 101, 121, 164, 171, 200, 223, 227; moral, xviii, 29, 36–37, 43, 49, 281; self-discipline, 35, 278

dishonor: concept of, 179–180, 182–183, 184; discontent, 19, 148, 182; discredit, 182, 257; disgrace, 72, 82, 129, 130, 182, 183–184, 289

dueling: precedence disputes and, 16, 65, 75, 103, 170, 171–172, 178, 191; prevalence of, xxiv, 5, 6, 151–152, 171–172, 196–197; royal edicts against, 196–197, 198–199

Edict of Nantes. *See under* peaces

Elias, Norbert, xxiv, 96, 160, 210

engineers, military, 173, 207, 230

ennoblement, 6, 15, 17, 18, 46, 66, 88, 140, 161

entourages: clienteles and, 82, 84, 85, 87, 98, 162, 209; coercion by, 101, 103; as violent communities, xxiii, 7, 13, 63, 201, 227, 236

Escoubleau de Sourdis, François d', 20, 133, 136, 158

Esparbès de Lussan, François I d', marquis d'Aubeterre, 22, 79, 91–92, 118–119, 125–126, 134, 143, 180

Esparbès de Lussan, Jean-Paul d', 141, 148, 161–162

estates: of Languedoc, 11–12, 31, 125, 136–137, 169–170; of Quercy, 124; of Rouergue, 104; of Velay, 30; of Vivarais, 31

Estates General of France, 11–12, 71, 134

Estrées, François-Annibal d', duc d'Estrées, 128, 267

étapes system, 230, 238–239

Fain, Henri de, baron de Pérault, 90, 204, 220, 233, 235

families: branches of, 20, 27, 43, 44, 46, 48, 95; "imperfect families," 40–41, 50

family strategies: concept of, 33, 34–35; education and, 66–69; financial strategies, 54, 57; lineages and, 44–45; marriage strategies, 46–50

Faret, Nicolas, 8, 13, 159–160, 164

favorites, 4, 66, 82, 127, 129, 133, 170, 196, 227

Foix, 27, 28, 102–103, 121, 244, 247

foreign troops, 129, 210, 212, 225, 228, 229, 231–232

fortifications: bastions, 13, 23, 150, 192, 252, 255, 259–260, 272; citadels, 13, 86, 135, 266; gates, 13, 87, 102, 192–193, 221; outworks, 174, 264; town walls, 22–23, 27, 100, 108, 181, 199, 221, 272; treatises on, 207

France: kingdom of, xv–xvi, xxi, 11, 19, 45, 238–239, 288, 290–291; maps of, x, 208–209; political instability in, xvi, 199, 200; population of, 16–17, 299n17

French Wars of Religion (1562–1629), xv–xvi, xxii, xxvi, 25, 123, 261

Garonne River, 19, 20, 22, 25, 26, 27, 230, 239

garrisons: of châteaux, 3, 14, 95, 107–108, 121, 122, 201, 226, 240, 256; maintenance of, 57, 86–87, 135, 136, 225, 226, 239–240, 242, 246, 247, 249; royal, 135, 224–226; of towns, 135, 226

Gascogne: military operations in, 149; nobles of, xvi, xviii, 19, 20–21, 128

Gélas de Voisins, Hector de, marquis d'Ambres, 84, 134, 204

gendarmes, 7, 15, 139, 227, 233. *See also* compagnies d'ordonnance

gender: authority and, 118; family identities
and, 37–38; honor and, 178; theories of, xxvi,
14–15, 153
genealogies, xviii, 18–19, 43, 44, 45–46, 111, 157,
165
gestures, xvi, xix, xxiii, xxiv, 157, 171, 189–190,
191, 197, 221, 292
Gévaudan, 40, 110, 134, 217, 218, 245, 249, 280
Gondi, Henri de, duc de Retz, 184
Gontaut, Armand de, baron de Biron, xxii, 242
Gontaut, Charles de, duc de Biron, 83
governors: provincial governors, xxix, 67,
87–88, 122, 131–133, 137, 193, 195, 199, 201,
211, 226, 245; town or fortress governors, xx,
xxix, 13, 68, 86–87, 135, 259
Gramont, Antoine III de, marquis de
Gramont, 21, 81
grand maître et surintendant de l'artillerie,
130
Guyenne: civil conflict in, xv–xvi, 91–92, 99,
104, 121; confessional divisions in, xviii,
5, 20–24, 223; governor of, 60, 81–82,
132–133, 143, 157, 178, 179, 194–195, 203,
289; lieutenant general of, 87–88, 125–126,
134, 218–219; nobles of, xviii–xix, 4, 19–20,
20–24, 83, 100, 134, 140, 169, 180, 192,
299n32. See also specific regions

Hautefort, Claude d', vicomte de Cheylane
then vicomte de Lestrange, 87, 184, 234
Hautefort, René d', vicomte de Lestrange,
86–87
Haut Languedoc: garrisons in, 225; nobles of,
25–27, 83, 104–105, 106–108; recruitment
in, xxiii, 218
Henri III (de Valois), 4, 66, 82, 133, 158, 163,
170, 277–278
Henri IV (de Bourbon): ascension of, 19;
assassination of, xvi, 162; conversion of,
278; illegitimate children of, 42; nobles
and, xvii, xxv, 149; policies of, xxv, 19, 67,
198–199, 243, 277, 281
heresy: abhorrence of, 95, 156, 175, 283;
executions for, 37; king's duty to combat,
282; opposition to, xxiii, 146, 278, 279,
281–283; pollution of, xvi, 278, 279;
suppression of, 26, 56, 135, 199
honnête hommes, 7, 154, 159–160

honor: conceptions of, 151–154; engaging,
181–182; family honor, xxi, 151, 161; heroic
deeds, xxi–xxii, 164–167, 176, 292;
performances of, 153, 156–157, 162–163,
165–166; personal honor, xxi, 75, 151,
152–153; preservation of, 178–184; sources
of, 152–153, 154, 159, 164–165, 168–169
horsemanship: demonstrations of, 177;
horse-riding, 14, 67, 101, 214; training in, 14
horses: nobles' use of, 7, 63, 101–102, 175–176,
209, 211, 227–228, 264, 285; provisions for,
97, 239
hôtels particuliers: architecture of, 13, 25,
28, 64, 88; clienteles and, 102, 221;
possession of, 22, 25, 27, 28, 40; refuge
in, 88, 99; transfers of, 17; urban culture
and, 13, 25
households: of nobles, xviii, xx, xxiii, 14,
34–43, 47, 51, 63, 67, 168, 209, 236–237,
286; personal secretaries, 33, 39, 53, 127,
174, 177, 202, 267; personnel in, 39, 44,
62, 67, 97, 99, 209, 236; royal household,
123, 124
household troops, royal: cheveaux-légers du
roi, 225; gardes françaises, 85, 138, 169, 225,
228, 267; gardes suisses, 138, 225, 228;
gendarmes du roi, 225
Huguenots: causes of, 21, 42, 85, 89, 100, 109,
128, 129–130, 156, 183, 279–281; identities
of, 280–281, 288, 304n23; military
organizations of, 212–213, 216, 219, 221,
231–232, 266–267; protectors of, 4–5,
22–23, 83, 85, 99–100, 124–125, 135, 156, 171,
205, 213, 232, 279; Reformed ministers,
100, 155, 157–158, 271, 281, 305n63; religious
militancy of, 279–281, 282–283; "state
within a state," 248; war finance of,
248–249

infantry: gros d'infanterie, 219, 229, 263;
maintenance of, 235–240; organization of,
228–229; recruitment of, 211–213, 233–234;
types of, 138, 228–229

Joyeuse, Henri de, duc de Joyeuse, 87
justice: divine, 279; just causes, 280; local and
regional, 131, 134, 135; royal, 72, 131, 135, 163;
seigneurial, 93, 282, 311n61

kinship: concepts of, xviii, 34–37; cousin relationships, 34, 37, 48, 70, 165; household and, 37–43; lineage and, 43–46; marriage and, 46–51; uncles, 34, 37, 40, 46, 72

La Croix, Jean de, baron de Castries, 90

La Guiche, Jean-François de, comte de Saint-Géran, 128, 147, 164

La Jugie, François de, comte de Rieux, 11, 27, 66, 208

Languedoc: administration of, 131–137; governor of, 3–4, 87–88, 122, 131–132; map of, x; nobles of, 3–6, 11–12, 17–18, 24–31

La Rochefoucauld, François V de, comte de La Rochefoucauld, 34, 266

La Rochelle: defense of, 231–232; as Huguenot center, 53, 83, 88, 202, 248, 279; massacre in, 278; military operations around, 85, 202, 237, 244, 266; naval combats off, 129, 177, 230–231; siege of (1627–1628), 34, 145, 230–231, 259. See also under peaces

La Tour, Henri de, vicomte de Turenne, 279

La Tour d'Auvergne, Henri de, duc de Bouillon, 208, 279

La Trémouille, Claude de, duc de Thouars, 279

Lauzières, Pons de, marquis de Thémines: clientele of, 83, 162, 286–287; family of, 23, 49, 104, 163, 157; military leadership of, xxii, 108, 128, 144, 214, 216, 219, 231, 267; offices of, 23, 128, 134, 157, 169, 178

La Valette, Jean de, baron de Cornusson, 90–91, 214

La Vallée des Fossées, Gabriel de, marquis d'Everly, 86

Lavaur, 26, 66, 178, 265

law: ancien constitution, xxi–xxii, 118; divine, 154–155, 158; natural, 36, 163, 199; Salic, 118; tax, 244

lawsuits, 49, 69, 74, 100, 163

Le Pouzin, 109, 113, 183, 230

Le Puy-en-Velay, 30, 86–87, 134, 274

Lescure, Louis I de, baron de Lescure, 103, 106–108, 246

lèse-majesté: charges of, xxi, 99, 144, 183, 191, 192; trials for, 132, 196–197

Lévis, Alexandre de, marquis de Mirepoix, 27, 87, 175

Lévis, Anne de, duc de Ventadour: clientele of, 79, 95, 101; honor of, 143, 161, 162; as lieutenant general of Languedoc, 25, 61, 87–88, 133, 143, 173, 177; marriage of, 47; military leadership of, xxiii, 215, 249; relations with Montmorencys, xviii, 47, 133

Lévis, Antoine-Guillaume de, vicomte de Mirepoix, 69

Lévis, Henri de, comte de La Voulte, then duc de Ventadour: as lieutenant general of Languedoc, 61, 88, 115, 133, 148, 197, 289; services of, 145, 148

Lévis-Léran, Gabriel de, baron de Léran, 27, 102–103

lieutenant generals of provinces, 87–88, 105, 124, 125–126, 133–134, 245, 289

lieutenants du roi, 87, 134

lieutenants-général du roi, 121–122, 127–128, 226

lineages: concept of, xviii, 33, 43–46, 51; creation of, 6, 18; disappearance of, 6, 18, 46; qualities of, 18, 44, 47, 83, 163

lodging, 91, 96–98, 130, 216, 238–240, 247, 250, 269

Lorraine, Henri de, duc de Mayenne: death of, 82, 133, 167, 194; loyalties of, 133, 194–195; military leadership of, 166–167, 194, 203; as provincial governor of Guyenne, 82, 87, 133, 157, 178, 193

Louis XIII (de Bourbon): authority of, 117–122; military leadership of, xxiii, 107, 128, 192, 203, 218–219, 225–226, 254–255, 262, 266; policies of, 194, 195, 198–199; provincial nobles and, xxv, 4–5, 19, 34, 93, 100, 110, 112, 114, 132, 146–147, 163, 164–165, 183–184, 289; royal family and, xvi, 38, 127, 196

Louis XIV (de Bourbon), 17, 45, 135, 168, 241, 243, 289, 329n95

loyalties: civic, 89, 199–200, 213, 221, 259, 282; clienteles and, 80–81, 95–96, 98, 193, 220, 226, 269; conflicting, 80–81, 95, 148, 195, 248, 286; oaths, 34, 196, 280

Loyseau, Charles, 6, 15, 118, 159, 165, 304n46

Lusignan, François de, marquis de Lusignan, 108, 267

Luxembourg, Henri de, comte de Saint-Pol, 27, 99

Lyon, 29, 121, 249

maréchaux de camp: appointments of, 85, 111, 130, 140, 314n153; authority of, 121, 130; clienteles of, 85, 101, 111–113; military leadership of, 104, 111, 134

maréchaux de France: appointments of, 41, 128, 148, 157, 170; authority of, 122, 125–126, 128, 169, 180, 183; clienteles of, 82, 83, 270; military leadership of, 45, 82, 105, 108, 214, 216, 219, 267; war finance and, 238, 248

marriage: mixed-confession, 50; remarriage, 34, 42, 106; reproduction, 34–35, 38–39, 50–51, 66; strategies, 46–49, 54, 56, 57, 70, 162

masculinity: aggressive, 153, 172; concept of, 14–15, 153; exemplary, 153, 167; expressions of, 5, 37, 43, 44, 65, 70, 79, 178; fraternal, 153, 158–159; paternalistic, 153, 159, 163

Médicis, Marie de: exile of, 196, 289; favorites of, 66, 127, 202; household of, 41, 67; marriage of, 162, 304n42; marriage brokering of, 48–49, 161, 305n69; as queen mother, 38, 158; religiosity of, 277

Mediterranean Sea, 27–28, 29, 68, 230, 249–250

mercenaries. *See* foreign troops

mestres de camp, 60, 85, 121, 137–138, 227, 234, 237, 318n73

military leadership, 69, 82, 85, 157, 166–167, 173–175, 177

military orders, 6, 15, 68, 158–159

Military Revolution, xxii–xxiii, xxvi–xxvii, 223, 233, 290

mobilization: continuous nature of, 138, 234–235; costs of, 232–235; practices of, 213–214, 217–219; rapidity of, 219–221

monarchy: concepts of, xxv, xxvi, 73, 117–119, 286, 291; king's council, 73, 118; *majesté*, 117–119; mixed monarchy, xxii, 73, 118; *res publica*, 73; royal agents, 117, 126, 193, 247; royal domains, 250; royal edicts, 123, 155, 198–199; royal ministers, xix, xxiii, 48, 100, 124, 129, 168, 195, 198, 199, 200, 219, 241, 248, 250, 290; royal prerogatives, xxii, 72, 168, 198–200, 202, 211; sovereignty, 117–120

money: circulation of, xxix–xxx, 57, 65, 74, 240, 241–242, 243–247, 249, 250; monetary wealth, 56–59; money-of-account, 57, 243

Monluc, Adrien de, comte de Carmaing, 57, 87, 247

Monluc, Blaise de, xvi, 21, 66, 87

Montauban: garrison of, 182, 213, 219; as Huguenot center, 5, 23–24, 26, 67, 179–180, 214, 221, 254, 279, 280; siege of (1621), 144, 150, 157, 176, 214, 218, 227, 259–260, 261, 265; surrender of, vi, 105

Montmorency, Anne de, duc de Montmorency, 3, 44, 132, 167

Montmorency, Henri I de, duc de Montmorency: clientele of, xviii, xviii–xix, xx–xxi, 47, 170, 174, 196; as connétable, 127, 174, 177; death of, xx–xxi, 11–12, 33; honor of, 152, 154, 162; kinship of, 48–49, 74, 161; as provincial governor of Languedoc, xv, 3, 132

Montmorency, Henri II de, duc de Montmorency: authority of, 3–4, 8, 119, 120, 122; clientele of, 16, 82, 87, 98, 202, 269, 271; honor of, 25, 147, 152, 176–177, 178, 180; kinship of, 33, 37, 40, 44, 65, 72, 110, 165, 167, 196–197; marriage of, 33, 48–49, 162; patronage of, 34, 51, 62, 65, 72, 147, 148, 196–197, 270, 275, 281; as provincial governor of Languedoc, xx–xxi, 3–5, 11–12, 66, 71, 87, 105, 106–108, 111, 132, 196, 201, 211–212, 213–214, 239, 240, 279, 288; as rebel, 82, 132, 183–184, 197, 204–205, 267, 288–289

Montpellier: courts in, 18, 61, 74, 124, 136, 250; Huguenot control of, 192, 213, 221; as mixed-confessional city, 5, 28–29, 50, 67, 86, 100, 192, 245, 283; siege of (1622), xxiii, 7, 23, 160, 181, 257, 259, 260; urban clienteles in, 88, 90, 100, 109. *See also under* peaces

motivation: combat, 271–273, 275; initial, xxii, 44, 145–146, 190, 254; sustaining, 122, 179, 254, 256, 269, 275, 339n69

munitions: capture of, 175, 266; provision of, 99, 107, 136, 214, 218, 230, 246; stockpiling of, 16, 39, 63, 130, 132, 207–209, 230

Narbonne, 28, 136

Négrepelisse, 5, 192

Nérac, 5, 22, 175, 194–195, 214, 227

Nîmes: as Huguenot center, 4, 29, 67, 100, 134, 221, 240, 278, 280; urban clienteles in, 88, 89–90, 108–110

Noailles, François de, comte d'Ayen, 87, 134, 144–145, 146, 163, 195, 204, 286, 301n67

nobility: concept of, 6–7; dimensions of, 16–19; distinctions of, 6, 15, 160–161, 169, 268, 269, 273; noble birth, 152, 160; promotion within, 6, 18, 30, 46, 161–162, 163, 175; *race*, 21, 43; as second order, 11–12, 73, 159; species of, 15–16, 31; treatises on, xviii, xxiii, 8, 13, 15, 154, 155, 159–160, 164; usurpation of, 46, 180

noblesse: d'épée, 6; *de robe*, 6, 135–136; *guerrière*, 2, 6–7, 13–16, 285–286, 298n24; *volontaires*, 7, 15, 85, 211, 227, 270–271

noblewomen: civil conflict and, 14, 34, 35, 37, 272–273; convents and, 276–277; honor of, 42, 50, 178; widows, 41, 47

Nogaret de La Valette, Bernard de, marquis de La Valette then duc de La Valette, 41, 42, 71, 219

Nogaret de La Valette, Henri de, comte de Candalle, 41, 68, 71

Nogaret de La Valette, Jean-Louis de, duc d'Épernon: clientele of, 81–82, 87, 96, 99, 231, 270; *crédit* of, 4, 53, 129, 133, 163, 289; honor of, 163, 178, 179; loyalties of, 4, 5, 133, 196; offices of, 8, 60, 129, 133; as patriarch, 20, 41–42, 71; *prise d'armes* by, 4, 196, 200, 202, 219, 231, 244; as provincial governor of Guyenne, 20, 60, 82, 133, 179; wealth of, 55, 60

Nogaret de La Valette, Louis de, 11, 41, 71

officeholding: appointments, xx, 44–45, 59, 82, 119–120, 125, 146–149; *congé*, 37, 65, 142–143, 182; family organization of, 41, 44–45, 66–75; multiple, xx, 131, 171; official bonds, xx, 115–149; official wealth, 59–62; *paulette*, 71–72; pensions, 60–61, 62, 69, 73, 175, 242, 249; replacements, 70–71; *résignation*, 41, 60, 71; *survivance*, 41, 60, 72

officers: *bas officiers*, 140; financial, 240, 244–246, 249; high command, 126–131; military, xxiii, 7, 15–16, 80; *officier*, 14, 318n87; provincial administrative, 15,

131–137; regimental, 137–140; royal, 117–119, 124–126

offices: concept of, xvii, xix, 75, 115–117, 141–142, 318n81; exercise of, 68–69, 141–143; investments in, 53, 60–61, 71–72; multiplication of, 71–72, 129; transfer of, 17, 44, 47, 59–60, 71–72; venality, 59–60, 71–72

Ornano, Alfonse d', 7, 129

Ornano, Jean-Baptiste d', 282

Orsini, Maria Felicia, duchesse de Montmorency, 33, 48–49, 162, 178

Pamiers, 27, 214, 282

Pardaillan, Antoine-Arnaud de, seigneur de Gondrin, 19, 21, 169, 218

pardons, 4, 34, 42, 192, 196–197

parents: family conflict and, 41–42, 43; family honor and, 38–39, 161; godparents, 50–51; guidance by, 39, 66; parental duties, 37, 38–39

Paris: arsenal in, 130; as Catholic center, 25, 220, 276–277, 282; hôtels in, 40, 87; military forces around, 225–226; parlement de, 71, 135, 180; as printing center, 123, 277; travel to, 11, 40, 123

parlements: chambres de l'édit, 74, 136; premier présidents of, 91, 104, 179, 180, 250; présidents of, 25, 49, 74, 93, 135–136

patriarchy: fatherhood and, 33–34, 37, 38, 79, 161; households and, xviii, 33, 35, 37–43, 63; lineage and, 43–46, 87; marriage and, 47, 48, 57; *pater familias*, 38; patriarchal authority, 36–37, 42, 47, 48, 51, 65, 73–74; patrimony, 46, 47, 54, 69–73

patronage: advocacy, 87, 96, 103, 178; patrons, xix–xx, 7, 49, 51, 57, 58, 62, 79–103, 197, 269–270, 275, 291; protection, 23, 63, 88, 99–100; provision, 96–99

peaces: of Alès (1629), xix, xxix, 100, 105, 108, 110; of Angers (1620), 184; Edict of Nantes (1598), xvi, xvii, xxvi, xxix, 5, 23–24, 74, 116, 155, 245, 279, 280, 283; of La Rochelle (1626), 100, 109; of Loudun (1616), xvi, xix, 59, 307n25; of Montpellier (1622), xix, xxix, 59, 90, 100, 259

peasants: raiding warfare and, 255–258; revolts by, 193; as soldiers, 160, 212, 213; as tenant farmers, 55, 94, 95

Périgord, 22–23, 134, 223, 299n27

Pézenas, 12, 28, 33, 88

Phélypeaux, Paul, seigneur de Pontchartrain, 19, 45, 72, 92, 120, 125, 140, 141, 143–144, 146, 225

piety: displays of, 36, 273, 274–276, 277, 281, 282; family reputation for, 39, 83, 276; ideals of, xviii, 273, 274; impiety, xv–xvi; sanctity, honor, and, 153, 154–159, 279–280

pillage, xv, 59, 107–108, 122, 183, 250, 256, 258

places de sûreté, 5, 20, 22, 23, 28, 29, 30, 99, 135, 194, 219, 226, 279

Polignac, Gaspard-Armand de, vicomte de Polignac, 144, 274

political culture: concept of, 115–117, 287; officeholding and, xx, 140–149, 290; role of violence in, xvii, 101–103, 275, 285, 288; warrior nobles and, xxv–xxvi, 6, 116–117, 123, 126, 197, 291

Pons, Jacques de, marquis de La Caze, 179–180, 182

Pontis, Louis de, 79, 99, 130, 144

precedence: deference and, 153, 167–168, 171, 179; honor as, 167–172; maintaining, 73–75, 178–181; in processions, 118, 156, 171, 193, 274, 277–278, 283

preuves de noblesse, 17–18, 45, 162, 168–169, 299n20

preuves d'honneur, xxi, 146, 147, 150

prises d'armes, xxii, 81, 189–206, 286, 290

prisoners: hostages, 41, 87, 99, 193, 267, 268; political, 34; taking of, 175, 236, 263, 266, 267, 272

Privas: as Huguenot center, 3–4, 30–31, 85, 183, 246; siege of (1629), 85, 108, 237, 259, 271–272, 305n55

profession of arms: crédit and, 53, 73; kinship and, 33, 41, 51; métier des armes, xvii–xix, xxvii, 13–15, 31; new conceptions of, 288, 290, 291–292; nobles' engagement in, 79, 189, 253, 285–286

proof of courage, 150, 175–177, 185

public opinion, 116, 123, 124, 315n3

public sphere, 116, 315n4

Puy de Tournon, Alexandre du, marquis de Saint-André de Montbrun, 167, 179

Puy de Tournon, Charles-René du, marquis de Montbrun, 47

quality, 18–19, 152, 153, 159–163, 173, 174, 178–179, 182, 184–185

Quercy, 23–24, 124, 134, 286, 299n27

raiding warfare: concepts of, 230, 255–256; coordination of, 255–258; economic impact of, 256–257; pervasiveness of, xxvi, 228, 253–254; raiding parties and, xxv, 230, 239, 245, 250, 255, 258; targets of xxvi, 16, 102, 256, 280

ransom, 34, 99, 122, 268

rations: amounts of, 96–97, 234, 235; depots for, 230; provision of, 209, 235–237, 239, 247, 270

Réalmont, 26, 181, 280, 340n102

recherches de noblesse, 17–18, 45–46, 168–169

recruitment: areas of, xxii, 217–219; costs of, 232–235; management of, 99, 106–107, 127, 129–130, 202–206, 215–217; rapidity of, 219–221; rendezvous, 112, 213–214, 219; of replacements, 138, 234–235; royal monopoly on, 198–200, 202; types of, 210–213

refuge, 22–23, 88, 96, 99, 100, 209, 231, 257, 258

regiments: gardes, 85, 138, 169, 225, 228, 267, 331; muster rolls of, 140, 212, 228, 232, 237, 241; organization of, 138, 228–229; petits-vieux, 138, 225, 228; precedence among, 169; types of, 138, 225–226, 228–229; vieux, 138, 216, 225–226, 228, 231

religious orders: Capuchins, 156, 274, 276, 281; Feuillants, 276, 277; Jesuits, 20, 67, 156, 158, 276, 277, 281; missionary activity of, xxvi, 274, 277, 278, 281, 282; patronage of, 274, 276–277; Ursulines, 276; Visitandines, 276

reputation: crédit and, xviii–xix, 65; of families, 18, 24, 41, 44, 46, 83; honor as, xx, 152, 164–167, 173, 175, 177, 178, 179–180, 181–182; peer opinion and, xxi, 43, 61, 62, 96, 141, 153, 166, 169; personal, 46, 53, 85, 87, 110, 111–112, 113, 149, 266

revolt: brand of, xxi, 93, 144, 183, 191, 199, 204, 241, 250, 286; concepts of, xv–xvi, xxi–xxii; duty to, xxi–xxii, 291; markers of, 191–193; rituals of, xxii, 189

Rhône River, 27, 29, 30, 31, 112, 230

Richelieu, Armand-Jean du Plessis, cardinal de, xxv, 82, 91, 104, 113, 129, 133, 223, 224–225, 242, 291

Rohan, Benjamin de, seigneur de Soubise, 83, 266

Rohan, Henri II de, duc de Rohan: clientele of, 83, 84, 88, 90, 97–98, 102–103; as Huguenot commander, 5, 26, 67, 86, 192, 197, 220, 262–267

Roquelaure, Antoine de, marquis de Roquelaure, 19, 21, 88, 125–126, 128, 134, 148, 180, 199, 214, 270

Rouergue, 24, 40, 87, 103–104, 105, 134, 245, 281, 286, 299n27, 317n62

Roux, Jacques du, seigneur du Pillon, 213, 233, 249

Saint Bartholomew's Day Massacre (1572), 25, 83

Saint-Étienne, Balteras de, baron de Ganges, 212, 233, 249

Saint-Jean, François de, seigneurs de Moussoulens, 218, 263

sanctity, xx, 152, 154–159, 163, 165, 178, 184–185

Schömberg, Charles de, duc d'Haluin, 67, 82–83, 132

Schömberg, Henri de, comte de Nanteuil: clientele of, 67, 82–83; honor of, 152–153; military leadership of, 105, 128, 132, 221, 267, 270; offices of, 82, 128, 129, 130, 132, 288–289

seigneurial rights: definitions of, 15, 55, 73, 92–94, 159; guet et garde, 95, 201; seigneurial justice, 93–94, 282, 311n61

seigneuries: co-seigneuries, 93, 95; improvements to, 55, 63–64; management of, 36, 94; multiple, 40, 41–42, 92; seigneurial clientage, 92–95; seigneurial wealth, 52, 53, 55–56, 70; titled, 15, 74, 159, 161, 162; transfers of, 47, 49, 55–56, 70, 88, 93, 163

sénéchaux: authority of, 87, 122–123, 124, 134, 142, 192, 210–211, 299n27, 317n62; clienteles of, 86, 87, 90–91; courts of, 74, 87

service: concepts of, 140–141, 143–145; as duty, 141, 145, 147; ideals of, 143–145; obligations of, 146–149; offers of, 145–146; recounting of, 44–45, 148–149, 166, 176

siege warfare: assaults, 144, 157, 229, 231, 252, 259–260, 261, 270, 271–272; batteries, 107, 111, 181, 229, 259, 272; blockades, 111, 260, 261, 266, 267; breaches, 181, 229, 260, 272; relief attempts, 99, 110, 214, 228, 255, 258, 260–261, 265; sorties, 107, 260, 270; trenches, 107, 230, 259–260, 271–272

sinews of war, 240, 241–243

Sommières, 5, 174, 207

state development: processes of, xv, xvi–xvii, xxiv, 116–117, 291; theories of, xxv, xxvii, 291

strategy, military: concept of, 254–255, 266; formulation of, 95, 193, 214, 270; positional warfare, 254–255, 259–261; strategic points, 13, 29, 30, 194, 207, 215

swords: in combat, 176, 263–264, 272, 273; épées, xxi, 2, 6–7, 63, 73, 188, 199, 207–208, 227, 228, 269; fencing, 67, 151–152, 307n55; identification with, 121, 177; rapiers, 6–7, 12, 151–152

tactics: artillery, 229–230, 272; cavalry, 226, 227–228, 263–265, 266, 272–273; drill and, 223; experience and, 68; infantry, 226, 228–229, 263–265, 266, 271–273

Thirty Years' War (1618–1648), 156, 211, 228, 229, 253, 290

Tonneins, 22, 104, 192

Toulouse: as Catholic center, 25–26, 56, 124, 221, 273–274, 282; parlement de, 25, 74, 82, 102, 104, 105, 121, 125, 132, 135, 136, 176, 177, 199, 200, 245, 250, 279, 282, 283; population of, 25–26; sénéchal de, 26, 90–91, 134, 213; urban clienteles in, 26, 88, 90–91, 177, 178; war finance and, 245, 250

Tournon, Just-Henri de, comte de Tournon, 97, 112, 134

towns: elites of, 90, 215, 279, 281; entries to, 75, 78, 101–102, 118, 125, 162, 166, 169, 177–178, 179, 192–193; faubourgs, 111, 174; identities of, 199–200, 213, 282; militias of, 90, 199–200, 219; as operational bases, 86, 112, 213–214, 215, 219, 221, 226; urban violence, 25, 83, 193, 278, 279

trésoriers, 240, 244, 246, 335n110

Uzès, 11, 29, 218, 257

Valois, Charles de, comte d'Auvergne et duc d'Angoulême, 34, 91, 130, 196, 303n4
Velay, 30, 86–87, 93, 112, 201, 240
Villeneuve-de-Berg, 111, 112–113, 214, 257
violence: civil, 189–190, 193, 253–255, 273, 285–286; confessional, xvii, 8, 25, 83, 102, 116, 151, 156, 193, 253–254, 273–283; instigation of, 190–198, 215; justifications for, xviii, xxi–xxii, 123, 179, 190, 199–206, 221, 280, 283; performative, xxv–xxvi, 175–177, 189–190, 206–221, 253–273, 291–292; public/private, xx, 116, 198, 200–202; royal monopoly of, xxii, 198–200, 202; tax of, 200; urban violence, 25, 83, 193, 278
virtues: expression of, xxi, 171–172, 279–280; honor and, 15, 152, 154, 159, 160, 164–165, 167, 180; imitation of, 44, 167; Neoplatonic ideals of, 35, 152–153
Vivarais: bailli de, 134; civil warfare in, 3, 12, 37, 111–113, 257–258; estates of, 31; nobles of, 30–31, 87, 97, 110–113, 179, 206, 209, 282; population of, 30–31; war finance in, 233, 235, 246

war councils, 128, 174, 270, 271
war finance: alternative financing, 247–250; *extraordinaires des guerres*, 127, 240, 244–245; Huguenot systems of, 248–250; maintenance costs, 235–240; mobilization costs, 232–235; *ordinaires des guerres*, 127; organization of, 240–247
warrior nobles: armed communities of, 85, 253–254, 268–273; definition of, xviii, 2, 6–7, 13–16; as military elites, 2, 6–7, 13–16, 285–286, 298n24
warrior pursuits: definition of, xvi, 7–8; new conceptions of, 290–291; practices of, xxiii–xxvii, 67–69, 285–287
Wars of Mother and Son (1618–1620), 4, 42, 99–100, 133, 157, 184, 195, 196, 200, 204, 218–219, 231, 249, 262
wealth: display of, 62–63, 64, 70, 210; monetary wealth, 56–59; official wealth, 59–62; profession of arms and, xviii, 15–16, 53–54; seigneurial wealth, 55–56; status wealth, 62–64
weapons: identification with, 6–7, 13, 268–269; symbolism of, 6–7, 207–208; training with, 14, 171–172